# Multimedia Transcoding in Mobile and Wireless Networks

Ashraf M.A. Ahmad
*Princess Sumya University of Technology, Jordan*

Ismail Khalil Ibrahim
*Johannes Kepler University Linz, Austria*

**Information Science REFERENCE**

**INFORMATION SCIENCE REFERENCE**

Hershey · New York

| | |
|---|---|
| Director of Editorial Content: | Kristin Klinger |
| Senior Managing Editor: | Jennifer Neidig |
| Managing Editor: | Jamie Snavely |
| Assistant Managing Editor: | Carole Coulson |
| Typesetter: | Chris Hrobak |
| Cover Design: | Lisa Tosheff |
| Printed at: | Yurchak Printing Inc. |

Published in the United States of America by
Information Science Reference (an imprint of IGI Global)
701 E. Chocolate Avenue, Suite 200
Hershey PA 17033
Tel: 717-533-8845
Fax: 717-533-8661
E-mail: cust@igi-global.com
Web site: http://www.igi-global.com

and in the United Kingdom by
Information Science Reference (an imprint of IGI Global)
3 Henrietta Street
Covent Garden
London WC2E 8LU
Tel: 44 20 7240 0856
Fax: 44 20 7379 0609
Web site: http://www.eurospanbookstore.com

Library of Congress Cataloging-in-Publication Data

Multimedia transcoding in mobile and wireless networks / Ashraf M.A. Ahmad and Ismail Khalil Ibrahim, editors.

  p. cm.

  Includes bibliographical references and index.

  Summary: "This book is designed to provide readers with relevant theoretical frameworks and latest technical and institutional solutions for transcoding multimedia in mobile and wireless networks"--Provided by publisher.

  ISBN 978-1-59904-984-7 (hardcover) -- ISBN 978-1-59904-985-4 (ebook)

  1. Multimedia communications. 2. Mobile communication systems. 3. Wireless Internet. 4. Mobile computing. 5. Coding theory. I. Ahmad, Ashraf M. A. II. Ibrahim, Ismail Khalil.

  TK5105.15.M96 2008

  006.7--dc22

British Cataloguing in Publication Data
A Cataloguing in Publication record for this book is available from the British Library.

All work contributed to this book set is original material. The views expressed in this book are those of the authors, but not necessarily of the publisher.

# Table of Contents

**Section I**
**Introduction to Multimedia, Wireless Networks, and Transcoding Essentials,**
**Challenges and Approaches**

## Section II
## Frameworks and Algorithms for Multimedia Transcoding
## in Mobile and Wireless Network

## Section III
## Applications for using Multimedia Transcoding

# Detailed Table of Contents

**Section I**
**Introduction to Multimedia, Wireless Networks, and Transcoding Essentials,**
**Challenges and Approaches**

**Chapter I**

*Baha A. Khasawneh, Princess Sumaya University for Technology, Jordan*

This chapter introduces multimedia and multimedia elements and technology. It presents all the elements of multimedia with an emphasis on the basic building block of each element. This chapter also presents the close relationship between the advancements in multimedia technology and the immense use of the Internet. In addition, various popular image, audio, and video standards are presented with more emphasis on compression standards. Finally, the chapter includes some of the future challenges and issues facing the research community for the advancement of multimedia uses.

**Chapter II**

*Bashar Ahmad, Johannes Kepler University of Linz, Austria*
*Gabriele Kotsis, Johannes Kepler University of Linz, Austria*

This chapter studies and analyzes QoS support for wireless network and the target application that will be a real-time multimedia application. First, they discuss QoS support for multimedia application. Second, a framework for classifying the QoS enhancements has been proposed. Then they study QoS support in IEEE 802.11 and the new QoS extension IEEE 802.11e. Finally, they study and classify the proposed QoS enhancement schemes according to the proposed framework.

## Chapter III

*Hendrik Knoche, University of College London, UK*
*M. Angela Sasse, University of College London, UK*

This chapter provides an overview of the key factors that influence the quality of experience (QoE) of mobile TV services. It compiles the current knowledge from empirical studies and recommendations on four key requirements for the uptake of mobile TV services: (1) handset usability and its acceptance by the user, (2) the technical performance and reliability of the service, (3) the usability of the mobile TV service (depending on the delivery of content), and (4) the satisfaction with the content. It illustrates a number of factors that contribute to these requirements ranging from the context of use to the size of the display and the displayed content. The chapter highlights the interdependencies between these factors during the delivery of content in mobile TV services to a heterogeneous set of low resolution devices.

## Chapter IV

*João Magalhães, Imperial College London, UK*
*Stefan Rüger, Imperial College London, UK*

Most of the research in multimedia retrieval applications has focused on retrieval by content or retrieval by example. Since the classical review by Smeulders, Worring, Santini, Gupta, and Jain (2000), a new interest has grown immensely in the multimedia information retrieval community: retrieval by semantics. This exciting new research area arises as a combination of multimedia understanding, information extraction, information retrieval, and digital libraries. This chapter presents a comprehensive review of analysis algorithms in order to extract semantic information from multimedia content. We discuss statistical approaches to analyze images and video content and conclude with a discussion regarding the described methods.

## Chapter V

*Truong Cong Thang, Information and Communications University, Korea*
*Yong Man Ro, Information and Communications University, Korea*

This chapter studies modality conversion as an important adaptation method. The authors point out two main challenging issues of the problem of modality conversion: (1) the quantification of the content value (quality) when contents are drastically scaled and/or converted to other modalities and (2) the method to accurately decide the modality and the content value for each object given that quantification. The chapter presents detailed solutions as well as open questions to these two issues. Moreover, the chapter discusses the benefits and obstacles, as well as the future trends of modality conversion in realizing the goal of universal multimedia access.

## Section II
## Frameworks and Algorithms for Multimedia Transcoding
## in Mobile and Wireless Network

In the video communication world, the video is encoded once for all, but different users can access different instances of it according to their specific requirements, capabilities, and compatibilities. The aim of this chapter is to highlight the pros and cons of both techniques, presenting solutions based on layered coding and multiple descriptions coding as a valuable alternative to transcoding, especially in those cases where network losses are not negligible.

This chapter provides a comprehensive awareness and understanding of research efforts in the field of extreme rate distributed video transcoding. The basic concepts and theories of rate control are introduced. The authors identify each rate control scheme's strengths and weaknesses and provide a distributed video transcoding system architecture that uses multiple transcoding techniques in the creation of an extreme rate video. Their experimental results show that the appropriate use of multiple transcoding schemes retains a better quality video in an extreme rate control.

This chapter presents several efficient mechanisms for improving the quality of service (QoS) delivered to the client by deploying content-based transcoding schemes. The proposed approaches are performing the required transcoding based on the video content. Some approaches study the texture and temporal features. Other approaches perform object detection in order to determine the important objects to achieve semantic transcoding. Extensive experiments have been conducted, and the results of various video clips with different bit rate and frame rate have been provided.

**Chapter IX**

*Panagiotis Germanakos, National & Kapodistrian University of Athens, Greece*
*Constantinos Mourlas, National & Kapodistrian University of Athens, Greece*

A traditional multimedia system presents the same static content and suggests the same next page to all users, even though they might have widely differing knowledge of the subject. Such a system suffers from an inability to be all things to all people, especially when the user population is relatively diverse. The rapid growth of mobile and wireless communication allowed service providers to develop new ways of interactions, enabling users to become accustomed to new means of multimedia-based service consumption in an anytime, anywhere, and anyhow manner. This chapter investigates the new multi-channel constraints and opportunities emerged by these technologies, as well as the new user-demanding requirements that arise. It further examines the relationship between the adaptation and personalization research considerations, and proposes a three-layer architecture for adaptation and personalization of Web-based multimedia content based on the "new" user profile, with visual, emotional, and cognitive processing parameters incorporated.

**Chapter X**

*Florence Agboma, University of Essex, UK*
*Anotonio Liotta, University of Essex, UK*

This chapter discusses the various issues that surround the development stage of mobile TV services. It highlights the importance of Quality of Experience (QoE), which is a shift in paradigm away from the widely studied Quality of Service. The authors discuss the factors affecting QoE and the types of assessment methods used to evaluate QoE. A QoE-layered model is presented with the aim of ensuring end-to-end user satisfaction. The authors argue that gaining an understanding of users' perceptions and their service quality expectations may assist in the development of QoE models that are user-centric.

**Chapter XI**
HSM:

*Annanda Thavymony Rath, Institute of Technology of Cambodia, Cambodia*
*Saraswathi Krithivasan, India Institute of Technology, Bombay*
*Sridhar Iyer, India Institute of Technology, Bombay*

This chapter deals with enhancing performance of networks through a Hybrid Streaming Mechanism (HSM). In HSM, a client's request triggers the selection of an intermediate node as a streaming point to which multimedia contents are dynamically transferred from the proxy/source; this streaming point streams the contents to the client. Transferred contents are temporarily cached at the streaming point to service future requests for the same content. HSM helps a Content Service Provider's objective of satisfying as many client requests as possible and providing enhanced quality to clients given their delay tolerance. Simulation results demonstrate that by leveraging the delay tolerance of clients and by combining the dynamic download and streaming mechanisms, HSM performs better than directly streaming from edge servers.

**Chapter XII**

This chapter presents the possibility of detecting errors in H.264/AVC encoded video streams. Standard methods usually discard the damaged received packet. Since they can still contain valid information, the localization of the corrupted information elements prevents discarding of the error-free data. The proposed error detection method exploits the set of entropy coded words as well as range and significance of the H.264/AVC information elements. The performance evaluation of the presented technique is performed for different bit error probabilities. The results are compared to the typical packet discard approach. Particular focus is given on low-rate video sequences.

**Section III**
**Applications for using Multimedia Transcoding**

**Chapter XIII**

This chapter provides an overview of second language learning and an approach to how wireless collaborative virtual reality can contribute to resolving important pedagogical challenges. Second language learning provides an exceptional opportunity to employ mobility and multimedia in the context of just-in-time-learning in formal learning situations, or ubiquitous and lifelong learning in more informal settings. The authors hypothesize that virtual reality is a tool that can help teach languages in a collaborative manner in that it permits students to use visual, auditory, and kinesthetic stimuli to provide a more "real-life" context, based in large part on Computer-Supported Collaborative Learning.

**Chapter XIV**

Secure multimedia transcoding is a challenge that operates the encrypted multimedia content directly. In this chapter, the secure transcoding scheme for scalable video coding is proposed and analyzed, together with the introduction to scalable video coding and multimedia encryption, the overview of existing secure transcoding schemes, and some open issues in this field. The chapter is expected to provide researchers or engineers valuable information on secure multimedia transcoding and communication.

**Chapter XV**
Multimedia Transcoding in Wireless and Mobile Networks: Keyless Self-Encrypting/Decrypting
Scheme for Multimedia Transporting Systems............................................................................. 278
*Shadi R. Masadeh, The Arab Academy for Banking and Financial Sciences, Jordan*
*Walid A. Salameh, Princess Sumayya University for Technology, Jordan*

This chapter presents a keyless self-encrypting/decrypting system to be used in various communications systems. Many encryption systems have been devised for the video transmission purpose, but most of them are built around Public Key Infrastructure (PKI). All of the commonly used encryption systems exchange keys that need to be generated using complex mathematical operations that take noticeable time, which is sometimes done once, and exchanged openly over unsecured medium. The authors of this chapter propose an expandable keyless self-encrypting/decrypting system that does not require the use of keys in order o minimize the chances of breaching data exchange security and enhance the data security of everyday communications devices, which are otherwise unsecured.

**Chapter XVI**
DSP Techniques for Sound Enhancement of Old Recordings............................................................. 304
*Paulo A. A. Esquef, Nokia Institute of Technology, Brazil*
*Luiz W.P. Biscainho, Federal University of Rio de Janeiro, Brazil*

This chapter addresses digital signal processing techniques for sound restoration and enhancement. The most common sound degradations found in audio recordings, such as thumps, pops, clicks, and hiss are characterized. Moreover, the most popular solutions for sound restoration are described, with emphasis on their practical applicability. Finally, critical views on the performance of currently available restoration algorithms are provided, along with discussions on new tendencies observed in the field.

**Chapter XVII**
Digital Watermarking for Multimedia Transaction Tracking ............................................................. 339
*Dan Yu, Nanyang Technological University, Singapore*
*Farook Sattar, Nanyang Technological University, Singapore*

This chapter focuses on the issue of transaction tracking in multimedia distribution applications through digital watermarking terminology. The existing watermarking schemes are summarized and their assumptions as well as the limitations for tracking are analyzed. In particular, an Independent Component Analysis (ICA)-based watermarking scheme is proposed, which can overcome the problems of the existing watermarking schemes. Multiple watermarking technique is exploited—one watermark to identify the rightful owner of the work and the other one to identify the legal user of a copy of the work. In the absence of original data, watermark, embedding locations and strengths, the ICA-based watermarking scheme is introduced for efficient watermark extraction with some side information. The robustness of the proposed scheme against some common signal-processing attacks as well as the related future work are also presented. Finally, some challenging issues in multimedia transaction tracking through digital watermarking are discussed.

**Chapter XVIII**

This chapter describes three DWT-based digital image watermarking algorithms. The first algorithm watermarks a given image in the DWT domain, while the second and third algorithms improve the basic algorithm by combining DWT with two powerful transforms. The second algorithm is a hybrid algorithm in which DWT and the discrete cosine transform (DCT) are combined. The third algorithm is also a hybrid algorithm in which DWT and the singular value decomposition transform (SVD) are combined. Performance evaluation results show that combining DWT with DCT or SVD improved the imperceptibility and robustness performance of the basic DWT-based digital watermarking algorithm.

# Foreword

In recent years, there has been a rapidly increasing demand for the development of advanced interactive multimedia applications such as video telephony, video games, and TV broadcasting, which have resulted in spectacular strides in the progress of wireless communication systems. However, these applications are always stringently constrained by current wireless system architectures due to the request for high data rate for video transmission. To better serve this need, 4G broadband mobile systems are being developed and are expected to increase the mobile data transmission rates and bring higher spectral efficiency, lower cost per transmitted bit, and increased flexibility of mobile terminals and networks. The new technology strives to eliminate the distinction between video over wireless and video over wireline networks. In the meantime, great opportunities are provided for proposing novel wireless video protocols and applications, and for developing advanced video coding and communications systems and algorithms for the next-generation video applications that can take maximum advantage of the 4G wireless systems. New video applications over 4G wireless systems is a challenge for multimedia and wireless communication researchers.

There are few problems of mobile and wireless network design and analysis that are as challenging as multimedia security and wireless technology in a virtual reality environment. In mobile ad hoc networks, specific intrusion detection systems are needed to safeguard them, since traditional intrusion prevention techniques are not sufficient in the protection of mobile ad hoc networks. Therefore, an intrusion detection system is another challenge and a fruitful area in which networking can play crucial roles in resolving problems and providing solutions to intrusion detection systems and authenticating the maps produced by the application of the intelligent techniques using watermarking and cryptology technologies.

In short, the book is an indispensable reference and very beneficial to both researchers and developers in the fields of multimedia and wireless technology; in addition, it will be of great use for many youngsters who are new to the field of multimedia in mobile and wireless networks. In addition, this book presents to the multimedia and wireless network communities the state of the art in multimedia transcoding in mobile and wireless networks and will inspire further research and development on new applications and new concepts in new trendsetting directions and in exploiting the multimedia in wireless technology.

Finally, I am pleased and honored to have been asked to write the foreword for this book. The authors, all active researchers in the area of multimedia in wireless networks, should be congratulated for providing this valuable reference book for the research community.

*Professor AboulElla Hassanien*
*Faculty of Computer and Information*
*Cairo University*

# Foreword

Mobile/cellular phones are now being used not only for verbal communications but also for other forms of communication involving multimedia data. The video phone (i.e., video mobile phone) is taking off. Being able to see a person on the other side of the phone line is, to some degree, exciting, which has moved us to a new era of telephone communication. People experience a sense of connection more than ever before. This becomes possible due only to the availability of multimedia features in communication technology, especially in wireless technology.

Watching news on a mobile phone is also becoming increasingly popular. Almost all major TV news networks now offer news on mobile devices. One of the major news networks has a slogan that says, "If you can't move with the news, the news will move with you." This statement truly reflects how the news moves with people through their mobile phones. Latest news, weather forecasts, financial reports, or even interactive road maps are a fingertip away, readily available anytime, anywhere on mobile phones. This kind of multimedia information on mobile devices provides society with a new level of information services.

In addition to communication and information services, there are other forms of mobile multimedia, including interactive and collaborative mobile games, interactive road maps, and mobile mashup, to name just a few. If collaborative games or network games were popular among games addicts in the past, it will not be too far in the future that people will play collaborative games on mobile phones. Interactive road maps are very useful since they offer a "one touch and you will be there" promise, as advertised by one of the major interactive road directory products. Mobile mashup collaborating with the new Web generation has lately been attracting researchers and developers as well as the general public.

All of these exciting mobile multimedia applications would have not been possible without extensive research in this field. Multimedia on the one hand is hungry for resources, while wireless and mobile devices on the other hand face many inherent constraints and limitations. Coupling these two certainly requires unique strategies in order to produce those demanding applications. Independent researches in wireless network and multimedia have to be brought together to identify how to address specific needs imposed by mobile multimedia applications.

This book contains some of the leading works in mobile multimedia. It addresses important issues for the success of adoption of mobile multimedia, including background knowledge in multimedia and wireless networking, current work in mobile multimedia, and some interesting applications. This book will certainly be useful for researchers and research students working in various aspects of mobile multimedia.

*David Taniar, Monash University, Australia*
*Editor-in-Chief Mobile Information Systems (IOS Press)*
*E-mail: dtaniar@gmail.com*

# Foreword

The vital role of multimedia applications in various daily life activities is noticed and appreciated. These applications have been developed through various means such as mobile phones and wireless networks. These instruments became one of the nonluxurious tools that help human beings, particularly in the commercial, scientific, banking, and other sectors, to announce and promote their services using these tools and their associated technologies.

To understand the tremendous usage of these tools, we should first know their functionalities and capabilities. Among the major tasks of these applications are keeping the human being updated on the news all around them by sending news in many multimedia formats.

This book highlights the issues that are related to many applications that the mobile phone can address and handle, from a conventional one that handles conventional communication services to interactive mobile multimedia that handles various types of applications such as gaming, road maps, weather forecasting, and so forth.

This book also includes topics that discuss cellular/mobile phone applications theoretically and experimentally, and it contains valuable information for every researcher, developer, and academic person. The wide spectrum of topics shows the value of this book.

*Walid A. Salameh*
*Dean, King Hussein School for Information Technology*
*Princess Summaya University for Technology*
*Amman-Jordan*
*walid@psut.edu.jo*

# Preface

The great proliferation and enhancements in wireless networking, specifically the development of the wireless Ethernet protocols and the quick deployment and growth of mobile communication protocols and technologies such as 2.5G, 3G, DVBH, and so forth, have enabled a broad spectrum of new applications and systems. The "anytime, anywhere, anyhow" principle of communicating data, emergence of network content providers, and the growing attractiveness of handheld devices are among the factors that have formed the field of multimedia communication in wireless and mobile video. Recently, this field brought about a very sophisticated computing paradigm, the multimedia transcoding in mobile and wireless networks. This paradigm is usually focused on filling the gap between the high resources requirements of multimedia applications and the limited bandwidth and capabilities offered by networking protocols and technologies and handheld devices. In addition, the advance of multimedia systems has had a major influence in the area of image and video coding. The problems of interactivity and integration of video data with computer, cellular, and television systems are relatively new and subject to a great deal of research worldwide. Since the number of networks, types of devices, and content representation formats has increased, interoperability between different systems and different networks is becoming more important. Therefore, multimedia transcoding in wireless and mobile networks must be developed to provide a seamless interaction between content creation and usage.

This book is designed to provide researchers and practitioners with relevant theoretical frameworks and latest technical and institutional solutions for transcoding multimedia in mobile and wireless networks, as well as providing an insight into the field of multimedia and its associated technologies and communication protocols. Moreover, this book establishes the background for understanding those emerging applications and systems that deploy multimedia transcoding and present a standpoint in the future of transcoding wireless and mobile multimedia and its applications. From a technical point of view, the book intends to embody state-of-the-art knowledge of transcoding multimedia for mobile and wireless networks as it is practiced today and as it is embedded in the pioneering technologies and leading research proposals.

The book is intended for people interested in wireless and mobile multimedia transcoding at all levels. The primary audience of this book includes students, researchers, developers, engineers, innovators, and research strategists who are seeking a general overview of how to realize, develop, and integrate multimedia transcoding systems in mobile and wireless environments. While the book can be used as a textbook by students, engineers, and researchers, it can also be used as a reference book.

This book comprises three sections. Section I is an introduction to Multimedia, Wireless Networks, and Transcoding Essentials, Challenges and Approaches. This section is composed of six chapters. Chapter I introduces multimedia and multimedia elements and technology that are influencing and will continue to influence much of the exchanged data over the Internet today. While chapter II presents the importance and applications of wireless communication, such as IEEE 802.11 WLAN, Bluetooth, or Inferred port. IEEE 802.11, it also proposes some enhancement schemes, most of them focusing on enhancing a particular part or mode of the standard by first discussing QoS support for multimedia application and then proposing a framework for classifying the QoS enhancements.

Chapter III provides an overview of the key factors that influence the quality of experience (QoE) of mobile TV services. It compiles the current knowledge from empirical studies and recommendations four key requirements for the uptake of mobile TV services. The next chapter is a comprehensive review of analysis algorithms to extract semantic information from multimedia content, as well as discuss statistical approaches to analyze images and video. The last chapter of Section 1 sheds light on modality conversion as an important adaptation method. The authors of this chapter point out two main challenging issues of the problem of modality conversion: (1) the quantification of the content value (quality) when contents are drastically scaled and/or converted to other modalities and (2) the method to accurately decide the modality and the content value for each object given that quantification.

In Section II, many frameworks and algorithms for multimedia transcoding in mobile and wireless networks are proposed. The first chapter of this section, which happens to be chapter VI of this book, highlights the pros and cons of transcoding and scalable coding techniques, presenting solutions based on layered coding, and multiple descriptions coding as a valuable alternative to transcoding, especially in those cases where network losses are not negligible. Chapter VII outlines comprehensive awareness and understanding of research efforts in the field of extreme rate-distributed video transcoding. The basic concepts and theories of rate control methods, such as a requantization, a temporal resolution reduction, a spatial resolution reduction, and an object-based transcoding, are introduced.

Several efficient mechanisms for improving the QoS delivered to the client by deploying content-based transcoding schemes are introduced in chapter VIII. The proposed approaches are performing the required transcoding based on the video content. Some approaches study the texture and temporal features. Other approaches perform object detection in order to determine the important objects to achieve semantic transcoding. Chapter IX investigates the new multichannel constraints and opportunities of the new means of multimedia-based service, as well as the new user-demanding requirements that arise. It further examines the relationship between the adaptation and personalization research considerations, and proposes three-layer architecture for adaptation and personalization of Web multimedia content based on the "new" user profile, with visual, emotional, and cognitive processing parameters incorporated. Informative discussion on the various issues that surround the development stage of mobile TV services is presented in chapter X. This chapter highlights the importance of QoE, and discusses the factors affecting QoE and the types of assessment methods used to evaluate QoE. It also presents a QoE layered model with the aim of ensuring end-to-end user satisfaction.

Chapter XI presents and elaborates an effective enhancement to the operation of Content Delivery Networks (CDNs) through Hybrid Streaming Mechanism (HSM), whereby an average of more than 40% of client requests are served. Section two ends with chapter XII, which introduces a novel error detection algorithm for H.264/AVC video transmission. In this chapter, the authors present the possibility of detecting errors in H.264/AVC encoded video streams through a proposed error detection method that exploits the set of entropy coded words as well as range and significance of the H.264/AVC information elements.

Section III, the last section of this book, introduces the applications and systems that can benefit from either deploying multimedia transcoding or the transcoding itself. Chapter XIII, the first chapter of section three, provides an overview of second language learning and an approach to how wireless collaborative virtual reality can contribute to resolving important pedagogical challenges. The next two chapters, chapter XIV and chapter XV, discuss security issues in multimedia transcoding. Chapter XIV proposes and analyzes a transcoding scheme for scalable video coding, in conjunction with the introduction to scalable video coding and multimedia encryption, an overview of existing secure transcoding schemes, and some open issues in this field. On the other hand, chapter XV presents an expandable keyless self-encrypting/decrypting system to be used in various communications systems, by which the information is transmitted securely over the medium from the sender to the intended receiver who is supposed to get it in the first place and deter others from getting the information sent.

Chapter XVI addresses digital signal processing techniques for sound restoration and enhancement. The most common sound degradations found in audio recordings, such as thumps, pops, clicks, and hiss are characterized. Moreover, the most popular solutions for sound restoration are described, with emphasis on their practical applicability. Finally, critical views on the performance of currently available restoration algorithms are provided, along with discussions on new tendencies observed in the field.

The last two chapters of this section address the digital watermarking for multimedia to be deployed in transcoding systems. Chapter XVII deals with the issue of transaction tracking in multimedia distribution applications through digital watermarking terminology and proposes an Independent Component Analysis- (ICA-) based watermarking scheme that can overcome the problems of the existing watermarking schemes. Chapter XVIII describes three discrete wavelet transform- (DWT-) based digital image watermarking algorithms in terms of basis of operation, composition, and performance analysis. The ideas described in the chapter can be easily extended to watermarking multimedia objects that include audio and video data contents.

This is a new reference and textbook for multimedia transcoding in wireless and mobile networking. This book sets a solid foundation for the paradigm of multimedia transcoding in wireless networking, as this field has recently emerged, and only a few papers related to it have been published. Many researchers and developers need such a reference to guide them through their work in realizing multimedia transcoding in wireless and mobile environment. This book is the first attempt to introduce the field of multimedia transcoding from all perspectives, and there is no other book that addresses the field thoroughly. This book is expected to be a reference in many future publications or researches in the field of multimedia transcoding in wireless and mobile environment.

# Acknowledgment

We would like to express our deepest feelings of gratitude and thankfulness to those who have helped us in realizing this work, especially the team of reviewers, editorial assistants from IGI Global and chapter contributors.

This work could not have been accomplished without the endless support we have received from our family members especially our parents who have encouraged us from the beginning.

Special thanks go to Bashar Ahmad (Johannes Kepler University of Linz), Mustafa Flaifel (Royal Scientific Society), Walid K.Salameh (Princess Sumya University for Technology), Baha A. Khasawneh (Princess Sumya University for Technology), and any other person we might have forgotten to mention.

# Section I
# Introduction to Multimedia, Wireless Networks, and Transcoding Essentials, Challenges and Approaches

# Chapter I
# Multimedia Essentials and Challenges

**Baha A. Khasawneh**
*Princess Sumaya University for Technology, Jordan*

## ABSTRACT

*This chapter introduces multimedia and multimedia elements and technology that are influencing and will continue to influence much of the exchanged data over the Internet today. It presents all the elements of multimedia with an emphasis on the basic building block of each element and how it integrates with the other elements to achieve a better multimedia content. This chapter also presents the close relation between advancements in multimedia technology and the immense use of the Internet. In addition, various popular image, audio, and video standards are presented with more emphasis on compression standards that are influencing multimedia use. Furthermore, we hope the inclusion of a section dealing with copyrights, ownership, and cross-platform issues will shed light on the challenges facing multimedia producers and owners alike. Finally, the chapter includes some of the future challenges and issues facing the research community for the advancement of multimedia uses.*

## INTRODUCTION

The term *multimedia* or *multimedia technology* is an overloaded term that has diverse meaning to different people, depending on their use of the various multimedia elements. For some, it means the deployment of computers to deliver information in various forms such as text, video, or audio. For others, it is the capacity to manipulate and distribute content via a communication apparatus that includes audio, video, or presentational forms. Nevertheless, multimedia technology is all of that and more; by definition, multimedia is the design, implementation, manipulation, storing, and proper delivery of various types of media to interested users. From this characterization and in order to make this process efficiently effective, a team of specialized individuals and capable machines are essential to ensure that the integrated elements are well designed for the appropriate use, as well as stored and transmitted within the limitation of storage capabilities and the transmission constraints (Vaughan, 2004; Lewis & Luciana, 2005).

Multimedia is divided into three major types: interactive multimedia where users control the delivery of the integrated elements, hypermedia where users are presented with navigational capabilities, and liner multimedia such as TV or radio where users have no control over the flow of information and have no interaction.

In this chapter, we will look at the various types of multimedia elements and their design, usage, integration, storage, and transmission. We will also present the techniques and standards used for compression and delivery of the various multimedia content. Multimedia library techniques and usage are also discussed and presented to highlight the overwhelming use of such media in all aspects of life.

## Multimedia and the Internet

The World Wide Web is the largest collection of networks that shares information on every subject and is considered the largest hypermedia application. Its importance is most visible in the universal and equal access to disperse resources and the diversity of information available to everyone everywhere.

*Figure 1. Popular Web2.0 home pages (Youtube.com and Napster.com)*

In the last decade, most of the information transmitted over the Internet has been of the multimedia nature, including images, music, and video movies. This is evident in the numerous Web pages available to users with all types of interest. As an example, most if not all newspapers have an electronic edition of their newspaper on the Internet, which contains all the printed news in addition to extra up-to-date news, images of current events, forums of discussions, advertisements, and an archive for older editions. Other examples include businesses that sell music of the latest CDs, such as Napster or a business that sells all consumer commodities online.

The Internet started for the exchange of information in its textual form. This was possible with the implementation of the File transmission Protocol (FTP) and the adoption of a new markup language, Hyper Text Markup Language (HTML), that enabled the implementation of Web browsers to include both text and images and to provide links to other resources with ease.

However, with the adaptation of more sophisticated Web languages, a person now can view a movie, launch a music application to listen to music, or play chess with multiple opponents who reside thousands of miles away or even in another country. Web browsers installed in any platform make navigating a Web page as easy as clicking a link to read a newspaper, purchasing a pair of jeans, or viewing a movie trailer form the latest animated movie.

The influence of the Internet on multimedia is evident as it is becoming the most important multimedia delivery vehicle. With the new Web (Web2.0) and its new principles and practices, more multimedia applications, content, and services are bound to be the most predominant issues. As users control their own data, the Web will become a platform that will be influenced by the participant's architecture that enables data to be remixed and transformed, which implies that the Web trusts users and software as more people use the service and participate in its creation. Wikipedia, Yahoo, Napster, and Google sites (see Figure 1) are some of the first examples of Web2.0 where the emphasis is not on applications, but rather on the services and the participation of users and data generators and not data owners. For more information, we advise you to read O'Reilly's important article on Web2.0 (O'Reilly, 2005).

## MULTIMEDIA ELEMENTS

In this section, we introduce the basic elements of multimedia and detail their uses in all aspects of life and the integration of these elements.

### Text

Text is made up of letters, words, sentences, and paragraphs to tell a story, state a fact, report an event, or convey an idea or a belief. It is the most widely used form of communication and is considered a basic element of visual multimedia. In addition to the set of characters that makes a certain language, text also includes numbers, punctuation, symbols, and special characters.

This set of characters appears in every form of multimedia presentation you may come across. Any page title, page content, or picture label includes informative text that gives details to users on the intended information of such content. Text is still the dominant form for explaining what the application is for and how to use it. In addition, text use is more evident in the design of the GUI of applications, including menus that include short meaningful words and symbols, the help menu, how-to help tips, thesauruses, hyperlinks in Web pages, and error reporting.

The power of text or words should not be taken lightly; that is why designers of multimedia projects have to carefully choose the words that convey the idea in a few meaningful words, in addition to other properties of text such as size, color, and effects that grab the reader's attention (Vaughan, 2004; Li & Drew, 2004).

Text technology is concerned with the design of text for multimedia and computer use, which includes the way characters are viewed on a computer monitor or in print. This includes the design of families of characters or what is known as typeface. A typeface includes fonts of different sizes and styles such as **Bold**, *Italic*, and <u>Underline</u>. The size of a font is measured in points; each point is 0.0138 inch. Other attributes of a font design include the vertical space between lines of text (leading), the space between characters pairs (kerning), and others. These properties are important and have proved essential for easy viewing, comfortable reading, and precise printing.

Fonts are divided into two types: serif and sans serif. Serif, the most widely used type in printed text (e.g., Times New Roman), includes strokes or decorations at the edges of letters to guide the reader's eye along a line so it becomes easier to read. On the other hand, sans serif, which has no strokes, is used in computer monitors because of the contrast it has with the screens.

## Graphics and Image Data Types

Still images or graphics are an important multimedia element, and when included in a document, they add flavor and substance. Images have different definition from different perspectives. In mathematical terms, "the image of an element x in a set X under the function f::X→Y, denoted by f(x), is the unique y in Y that is associated with x" (Vaughan, 2004). Commonly, an image is an artifact that reproduces the likeness of some physical or imaginary object. However, from a multimedia perspective, a still image stored and displayed on a computer screen is made up of a number of picture elements called *pixels* with brightness and color. As a matter of fact, we can define an image as a collection of dots with colors, each with a value, and when placed next to each other, they form the entire image. These dots can be black and white or colored.

Digital images can be drawn on paper and stored on a computer in a digital form after being scanned or captured using a digital camera or even drawn directly using image editing software. Images are

*Table 1. List of popular image formats*

| File Format | |
|---|---|
| **Gif87a/Gif89a** | Graphical Interchange Format |
| **JPEG** | Joint Photographic Expert Group |
| **PNG** | Portable Network Graphics |
| **TIFF** | Tagged Image File Format |
| **EXIF** | Exchange\Image File Format |
| **PS/PDF** | Postscript/Portable Document Format |
| **WMF** | Windows Meta File |
| **BMP** | BitMap |
| **PAINT/PICT** | MacPaint and MacDraw |
| **PPM** | X Windows Portable PixMap |

stored and exchanged in many standard formats such as the 8-bit GIF format (Graphics Interchange Format) and JPEG format (Joint Photographic Experts Group), which are considered the most commonly used formats in Web browsers. These two standard formats (image compression formats) are platform-independent and popular due to the small file size that is mostly suitable for exchange over slow network channels. However, other less common formats are used in multimedia such as BMP, PICT, PNG, and TIFF (see Table 1).

Digital images are divided into two types: Bitmap images and Vector images. In the next sections, we discuss these two types and emphasize tier differences (Gonzales & Woods, 2002; Li & Drew, 2004).

## Bitmap Images

Bitmap images (Raster images) are represented as a two-dimensional matrix of pixels where each pixel has a different representation (pixel depth), depending on the image type.

## Binary Images

Binary images or 1-bit monochrome images where each pixel is represented by a single bit and a value (0 or 1) displayed with the colors white or black. These images are most popular for illustrations and simple images due to their small size and low viewing quality. As an example, a binary image with a resolution (i.e., number of pixels per inch) of 600 x 800 has a file size of 60KB, and as seen in Figure 2(a), the quality is poor and contrast is poor because such files comprise only two valued colors: black and white.

## Gray-Level Images

The second image type is gray-level, or 8-bit images. In this representation, each pixel is stored as a single byte and has a value between 0 and 255 of gray colors or shades. As an example, a 0-value pixel is completely black, and a 200-valued pixel is a bright color or close to white. The size of a 600 x 800 8-bit image file with the same resolution would occupy 480KB of storage. Figure 2(b) shows a gray-level image; it is evident that these images have improved viewing quality since each pixel has more contrast.

*Figure 2. (a) monochrome image; (b) gray-level image; (c) colored image*

## 8-Bit Color Images

The first two bit-image types have limited colors, either black and white or shadings of the two colors. The third type of image is a colored image where each pixel is also represented by 8-bit value with colors ranging from 0 to 255. These colors are a combination of the three basic colors: red, green, and blue (RGB color space). However, the main difference with the gray-level image is that the pixel value is not a color; rather, it is an address to an index of colors that is stored in the machine displaying the image. This index of colors is called a look-up table (LUT), which contains all the colors that exist in an image; but due to the fact that if we need to represent each pixel with the value for each color component, we need 24 bits for each pixel. These types of image are discussed in the next section. Furthermore, the LUT is machine-dependent, which means when an image is viewed in a different platform, the colors tend to be different since the LUT is not included within the image file. Although the size of such an image is the same as in gray-level, the viewing quality of an 8-bit color image is more exciting because of the presence of colors. Figure 2(c) shows the same image in 8-bit color representation.

## 24-Bit Color Images

The most popular image type is a rich color image where each pixel is stored as three bytes of color yielding large combinations of colors (16,777,216). Each image is represented as three two-dimensional arrays, one array for each of the three color components (red, green, and blue); in many instances, they are called RGB images. Also, the size of a 24-bit image is large due to this fact, so the same image 600 x 600 in a 24-bit representation would have a resolution of 1.08MB. Figure 3 shows an RGB image and the three separate components displayed as gray-level images.

*Figure 3. Original image and the RGB components*

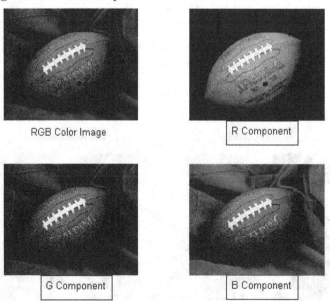

RGB Color Image    R Component

G Component    B Component

*Figure 4. Vector images*

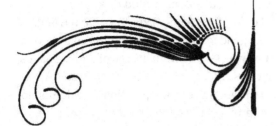  

## Vector Images

A vector image is an image that is made up of one or more objects defined and stored as mathematical equations and not by pixels. These equations specify a point of reference of a line, including direction and endpoint. It is similar to drawing a rectangle on a page (Figure 4 shows a rectangle and a color-filled circle). These shapes or objects have attributes such as fill, color, and outline, which can be edited or changed without affecting the object itself. Also, these objects can be resized, moved, placed over other objects, and mainly animated. However, the main advantages of vector images are the small file size, which makes them easy to store, transmit, and display quickly on computer monitors.

## Audio

Audio or sound, as we know it, is a powerful multimedia element that inspires diverse emotions and senses in humans and animals alike. It is perceived in the form of spoken language, vibrations of musical instruments, or even sounds of animals in joy or stress.

The use of sound is evident in every multimedia product that exists in our daily lives. Can you imagine a computer game with no sound or sound effects? Or have you felt the effects of a surround audio system in a movie theater? Or what is the value of a videoconference or an e-learning project with no sound? Many questions underline the significance of audio in our lives.

Sound is generated as differences in pressure that produce waves that travel in all directions. Depending on its pressure level and frequency, if it reaches the ears of a human being, it is experienced as sound. Some sounds are comfortable to hear, some are very noisy and cause stress, while others are not heard by humans or animals. The science of acoustics studies sound, its measurement and uses, and details its effects. We are interested in the use of sound in multimedia, where is it used, how to generate it, and how to incorporate sound in a multimedia projects. (Pohlmann, 2000)

Many computer applications and Internet Web pages incorporate digital sound with functions such as alerts in case of errors or warnings or at the start or end of a task, and so forth. These sounds, in many instances, are stored on the computer as digital data generated either by a digital musical instrument (*MIDI*) or digitized from existing recordings.

Digitizing is a process of converting a sound from the continuous form (analog) into digital (*discrete form*) by taking a sample of the sound at a given time interval and storing it as an 8-bit or 16-bit sample of data. The frequency of taking samples (sampling rate) of the continuous waves affects the quality of the digitized. The higher the sampling rate, the greater the quality but the larger the file size.

In digital multimedia, audio is sampled at three common frequencies: 11.025kHz, 22.05kHz, and 44.1kHz, and stored as mono or stereo sound either on a CD or on a computer hard disk.

Sound files exist in many formats such as MIDI, MP3 Audio, WAV audio, Windows Media, MPEG audio stream, and so forth. These formats are platform-independent and require the installation of a media player that is capable of recognizing such formats. However, the main advantage of digital sounds is the ability to edit such files using digital audio editors such as Audacity, Adobe Audition, and Apple Quick Time Player, to name a few. These editors provide basic sound editing operations in addition to other advanced operations. For example, many of these tools provide users with the ability to edit, view, combine, and add effects to multiple tracks. Other operations include format conversion, resampling, fade-in and fade-out, trimming, splicing, and reversing.

These editors are built with multilevel capabilities that are of assistance to regular computer users as well as to the advanced audio composer to create exciting sounds and recordings. It also allows various audio formats to be easily integrated into any multimedia product such as games, Web pages, presentations, and educational materials.

## Digital Video

Video is defined as a series of images (*frames*) put together and displayed on a screen one after the other to create the illusion of motion and interactivity. The illusion of motion is created by displaying a number of frames per second where each frame contains a slight difference from the previous one, utilizing the characteristics of the human eye (*vision persistence*) and a psychological phenomenon (*phi*), thus creating the feeling that the object in the series of images is actually moving. Video is the most demanding multimedia elements in terms of storage requirements and transmission cost because of the large size of such files and the fact that it might be broadcast live to a television set, a videoconference, or even a mobile phone (Bovik, 2000; Sayood, 2000).

*Figure 5. Sample of interlaced movie clips (courtesy of plasma.com)*

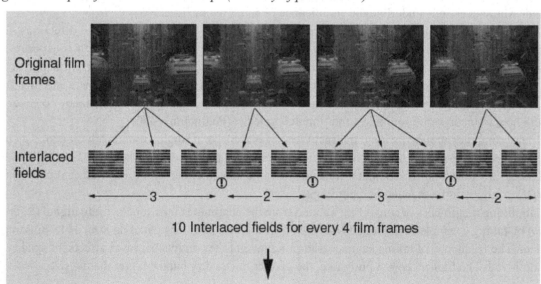

Videos transmitted to most TV sets are analog signals in which they are traced in two popular methods and display 25 to 30 frames per second, depending on the standard used. The first is Progressive Scanning, where a complete picture or an entire frame is traced row-by-row in each time interval; and the second is Interlaced Scanning, where odd-numbered rows are traced first and then even-numbered ones. Figure 5 shows sample interlaced fields for four film frames.

Some of the most popular video standards include (1) National Television Standards Committee (NTSC) used in Japan and the United States, (2) Phase Alternate Line (PAL) used in the UK, Europe, and the Middle East, and (3) Sequential Color and Memory (SECAM) used in France and Eastern Europe.

With tremendous advancements in video use in computers, mobile phones, and the Internet, digital video is enjoying unprecedented popularity. It has many advantages over analog video, including:

- Direct access
- Storage on different digital memory (reusable), which makes it easier to be processed (edited) and integrated into multimedia applications
- More tolerant to channel noise

In many countries around the world, High Definition TV (HDTV) is making its way to be the new standard for TV broadcasting, in which wider screen TVs would give viewers an enhanced sense of vision and a better viewing pleasure. Other standards such as Standard Definition TV (SDTV) and Enhanced Definition TV (EDTV) are to replace all analog broadcast in the United States.

## MULTIMEDIA DELIVERY

Multimedia products can be delivered using several types of portable devices such as compact disks (CDs) or Digital Versatile Disks (DVDs), or online using communication networks and the Internet. However, CDs are the most popular means of delivering and playing music, and are now used to distribute all types of multimedia products, including applications, games, and data storage. This popularity is due to their storage capacity, low price, and transfer rates. A typical CD can hold 500 to 900MB of data, up to 90 minutes of recorded music, and 74 minutes of CD quality movies, and can have a transfer rate up to 7.2Mbps.

DVDs normally can hold up to 7GB of data and twice that in high-quality movies, and is the standard delivery method for almost all 3D games and movies (Lewis & Luciana, 2005; Vaughan, 2004).

The next generation of optical disks that will revolutionize the multimedia industry is the Blu-ray optical disks (see Figure 6), which were developed by a group of leading multimedia and personal computer manufacturers including Dell, Apple, HP, JVC, and TDK. The name Blu-ray comes from blue-violet laser utilized to write and read data on disks, which proved to be superior to ordinary laser.

Blu-ray optical disks will permit a user to record, replay, and rewrite high-definition video (HDV), including MPEG-2 and MPEG-4 formats, in addition to the storage of large amounts of data. A typical Blu-ray 50GB disk can hold up to nine hours of HDV or 23 hours of standard-definition (SD) video at a rate of 36Mbps. For further information on specifications and a future look at Blu-ray, refer to www. blu-ray.com.

*Figure 6. Blu-ray disks by various manufacturers*

## Compression and Multimedia

One of the major challenges of multimedia is how to deliver large amounts of data either synchronously or asynchronously within the limitations of existing networks and storage capabilities. A natural solution to this challenge is compression, which is a process of deriving a smaller representation that provides a significant reduction in data size to reduce both storage requirements and bandwidth limitations. Compression strategies are based on reducing redundancies that normally exit in all multimedia data and on exploiting the characteristics of the human visual and hearing system. Compression techniques have two constraints: either the reconstruction of compressed data is perfect or near perfect. Lossless compression (*reconstructed data after decompression is the same as the data before compression*) and lossy (*reconstructed data is not equal to the original data*) compression techniques are widely used to achieve the goals of compression, and as mentioned before, most of the popular formats for the exchange of multimedia elements are compression formats (Sayood, 2000; Taubman & Marcellin, 2002).

Redundancy reduction is the most popular strategy for compression in which one of four types of redundancies can be exploited to achieve better representation that can benefit from compression. These types include *symbol-level redundancy* and *block-level redundancy*, which are popular for text lossless compression with different compression algorithms (e.g., Huffman coding, RLE, LZ, Arithmetic Coding). The other types, *inter-pixel spatial redundancy* and *inter-pixel temporal redundancies*, are types of lossy compression that are popular in image and video compression techniques.

We chose not to detail the concept of compression in multimedia, despite its importance in the overall delivery of multimedia products and applications, but rather to raise readers' interests and the importance of the topic. However, some of the popular compression standards are also listed in Table 1, and we advise readers to refer to other books that provide detailed descriptions and explanations of the various compression standards for the different multimedia elements. However, we emphasize the effects of compression on the delivery of the various elements and the need for transcoding when dealing with mobile transmission and the challenges it represents.

## ISSUES IN MULTIMEDIA DELIVERY

This section introduces some of the issues that relate to multimedia, such as copyright, ownership, cross platform, and heterogeneity of multimedia elements. The importance of these issues affects the delivery and compatibility of multimedia elements across heterogeneous platforms, particularly in the mobile environment, since it is the currently dominant issue.

### Copyright and Ownership

Copyright and ownership of multimedia productions are still underdeveloped issues in many countries around the world and lack the legal laws to protect such products despite their importance.

Many multimedia products are developed to include either original or nonoriginal text, photos, music, or other artists' work, and might also be produced by many people who cooperated to generate such work. In all cases, ownership and copyright issues include:

- The ownership of the intellectual property rights in the products and a clear definition of a public domain product either as a whole or as separate components.
- The liability of the developer(s) by a faulty product and the developer's right to gain from the product or its future use and reproduction.
- Variations of the original products and how it is treated and how to obtain third parties' permission to use copyrighted works and remuneration.
- How to prove ownership in case of unauthorized use (partial or full).
- The lack of international means of protection from piracy and illegal use or reproduction of multimedia products across international borders.

### Cross Platform

Taking multimedia across platforms includes many issues, such as dealing with text, graphics, video, audio, and programming. These issues include multimedia bandwidth requirements and digital media file sizes.

While text issues include character translation, fonts, styles, and size of displayed text, graphics issues on some platforms such as Mac displays larger than UNIX and PC.

Video issues include display gamma that affect how dark or light an image is displayed, as well as compression and compatible applications that recognize image types and color representations.

Audio issues are simpler, and you would only be concerned with file formats and the search for suitable playing utilities. However, down sampling and sampling of audio, as well as the quality of sound and synchronization between video and audio are also points that characterize the quality of an integrated multimedia product.

## FUTURE DIRECTIONS IN MULTIMEDIA

Despite the challenges facing multimedia, mainly network bandwidth and content limitations, multimedia will continue to dominate most of the exchanged data over the Internet and other public networks.

However, multimedia research, which is multidisciplinary in nature, is advancing toward solving some of the major challenges identified by some of the Interest groups of multimedia such as ACM SIGMM, and IEEE International Symposium on Multimedia, which has been a strong force in advancing the research community and directing the efforts of researchers to tackle multimedia challenges and also "identify deliver applications that impacts users in the real-world."

In 2003, ACM SIGMM suggested that the research community must focus on solving three major challenges. The first challenge is to "make authoring complex multimedia titles as easy as using a word processor or drawing program. The second challenge is to make interactions with remote people and environments nearly the same as interacting with local people and environments. The third challenge is to make capturing, storing, finding, and using digital media an everyday occurrence in our computing environment."

While some advancement has been achieved, other issues have been identified at ISM'06, including issues in the area of:

1.  Mobile multimedia (i.e., resource-awareness and portable development, modeling of multimedia, smart-phones common platform)
2.  Internet/Web/home multimedia (i.e., low effort, high reusability of metadata, intelligent content repurposing, multimodal interfaces)
3.  Gigapixel multimedia (i.e., scalability, hardware configuration, interaction design, etc.)

While the multimedia research community addresses and comes across practical solutions for such challenges, we believe that more sophisticated challenges will surface, and multimedia will continue to progress and influence our lives.

## REFERENCES

Bovik, A. (Ed.). (2000). *Handbook of image and video processing.* San Diego: Academic Press.

Gonzalez, R.C., & Woods, R.E. (2002). *Digital image processing* (2nd ed.). Upper Saddle River, NJ: Prentice Hall.

Lewis, R., & Luciana, J. (2005). *Digital media: An Introduction.* Pearson Prentice Hall.

Li, Z.-N., & Drew, M.S. (2004). *Fundamentals of multimedia.* Pearson Prentice Hall.

O'Reilly, T. (2005). What is Web2.0: Design patterns and business models for the next generation of software. Retrieved from http://www.oreillynet.com/pub/a/oreilly/tim/news/2005/09/30/what-is-web-20.html

Pohlmann, K.C. (2000). *Principles of digital audio* (4th Ed.). New York: McGraw-Hill.

Sayood, K. (2000). *Introduction to data compression* (2nd Ed.). San Francisco: Morgan Kaufmann.

Taubman, D.S., & Marcellin, M.W. (2002). *JPEG2000: Image compression fundamentals, standards and practices.* Norwell, MA: Kluwer Academic Publishers.

Vaughan, T. (2004). *Multimedia: Making it work* (6th Ed.). McGraw Hill.

Vetter, R., Ward, C., & Shapiro, S. (1995). Using color and text in multimedia projections. *IEEE Multimedia, 2*(4), 46–54.

## FURTHER READING IN MULTIMEDIA

Blattner, M.M. (1996). Multimedia interface: Designing for diversity. *Multimedia Tools and Application, 3*, 87–122.

Castelli, V., & Bergman, L.D. (Ed.). ( 2002). *Image databases: Searches and retrieval of digital imagery.* New York: Wiley.

ISO/IEC 21000. (2003). *Information technology—Multimedia framework.* International Standard, Parts 1–7.

Jeffay, K., & Zhang H. (2002), *Readings in multimedia computing and networking.* San Francisco: Morgan Kaufman.

Lowe, D., & Hall, W. (1999). *Hypermedia and the Web: An engineering approach.* New York: Wiley.

Miano, J. (1999). *Compressed image file formats: JPEG, PNG, GIF, XBM, BMP.* Reading, MA: Addison-Wesley.

Nielsen, J. (1995). *Multimedia and hypertext: The Internet and beyond.* San Diego: AP Professional.

Shapiro, L.G., & Stockman, G.C. (2001). *Computer vision.* Upper Saddle River, NJ: Prentice Hall.

Stamou, G., & Kollias, S. (Ed.). (2005). *Multimedia content and the semantic Web, methods, standards, and tools.* John Wiley & Sons, Ltd.

Steinmetz, R., & Nahhrsteddt, K. (1995). *Multimedi: Computing, communications & applications.* Upper Saddle River, NJ: Prentice Hall PTR.

Taubman, D.S., & Marcellin, M.W. (2002). JPEG2000: *Image compression fundamentals, standards, and practice.* Norwell, MA: Kluwer Academics Publisher.

Wang, Y., Ostermann, J., & Zhang, Y.Q. (2002). *Video processing and communication.* Upper Saddle River, NJ: Prentice Hall.

# Chapter II
# QoS Support in Wireless Networks

**Bashar Ahmad**
*Johannes Kepler University Linz, Austria*

**Gabriele Kotsis**
*Johannes Kepler University Linz, Austria*

## ABSTRACT

*Wireless communication has gained a great deal of attention in the last few years from both industry and academia. Nowadays, most computerized devices are equipped with wireless ports such as IEEE 802.11 WLAN, Bluetooth, or Inferred port. IEEE 802.11 WLAN device, in particular, is an ideal wireless communication tool for any mobile-based computer such as a notebook or PDA because of their low cost and high bandwidth. The wireless environment has some characteristics that make supporting QoS a very challenging task. These characteristics are bandwidth scarce, radio channel conditions that vary over the time, and highly packet loss. Legacy IEEE 802.11 standards such 802.11a, b, or g originally do not support QoS, thus many QoS enhancement schemes have been proposed; most of them focus on enhancing a particular part or mode of the standard. QoS support in any system is an accumulative task, as it needs to be maintained throughout all layers. The wireless multimedia application is the best example for proving the accumulative property for its QoS as the user is the final judge about whether the provided quality is satisfactory or not. In this chapter, we will study and analyze QoS support for wireless network and the target application, which will be a real-time multimedia application. First, we discuss QoS support for multimedia application. Second, a framework for classifying the QoS enhancements will be proposed. Next we will study QoS support in IEEE 802.11 and the new QoS extension IEEE 802.11e, and then we will study and classify the proposed QoS enhancement schemes according to the proposed framework. Finally, we will discuss mobility as an important issue for QoS support in wireless environment.*

## INTRODUCTION

Wireless network technology has given the ability to communicate anytime, anywhere; such a feature creates a great market opportunity in terms of business, healthcare, education, and entertainment. However, original WLAN (IEEE 802.11) standard was designed to serve on the best-effort basis, which was fine in order to provide connectivity to non-real-time applications. Nowadays, with the high increases of the data rate capability of IEEE 802.11 (11mbps for 802.11b, and 54mbps for 802.11g), it becomes possible for real-time applications such as multimedia application to be served over a wireless network; in addition, the low cost for this technology increases user demand for such types of services.

Categorizing applications based on their sensitivity to time will yield two types: real-time applications (i.e., a task has to be completed during a specific period of time; otherwise, the output or the result will not be effected), and non-real-time applications (i.e., a task does not have a deadline to be completed). An example of real-time applications is multimedia applications. To ensure synchronization for multimedia application, some requirements (e.g., bandwidth, delay, jitter, percentage of packets loss, etc.) need to be guaranteed. Such requirements are referred to as Quality of Service (QoS). Different multimedia applications require different QoS support; QoS is not a fixed value but varies from one application to another. Each application will have a range of QoS bounded by preferred QoS and acceptable QoS. The preferred QoS corresponds to ideal conditions under which the application would like to run. The acceptable QoS corresponds to the minimum acceptable situation, below which does not make sense for the application. Negotiation takes place between the application and the network service provider to decide the guaranteed QoS (Raghavan & Tripathi, 1998). Parameters such as communication delay, synchronization, and available bandwidth are very critical for a multimedia application. For instance, data transfer applications such as the video-on-demand application can tolerate some end-to-end delay, but it requires a high bandwidth and low bit-error rate. On the other hand, Internet telephony application such as VoIP requires a very low end-to-end delay but smaller bandwidth and slightly higher bit-error rate than VoD application would be acceptable (Jha & Hassan, 2002).The QoS parameters resides in three layers: user layer, application layer, and system layer (see Figure 1). Furthermore, the system layer can be divided into two sublayers: network-and-operating-system layer and device layer. Table 1 shows various QoS parameters in different layers (Bhargava, 2002; Jha & Hassan, 2002).

The developments of the modern computing environment have proposed new concepts such as mobility, heterogeneously, and perceptual QoS to provide the environment elements ability to be connected anywhere anytime. To support such a feature, a mobility function needs to be adopted. IEEE 802.11 standard supports mobility. However, the mobility function in IEEE 802.11 suffers from a high delay

*Figure 1. QoS layers*

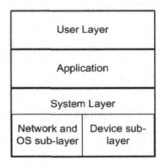

*Table 1. QoS parameters in different layers*

| QoS Layer | QoS Parameters |
|-----------|----------------|
| User | Accuracy, perception ,timeliness, price, and convenience |
| Application | Frame rate, frame size, response time, throughput, and security |
| System | **Operating System:** Buffer size, process priority, scheduling policy, cashing policy, time quantum.<br>**Network:** Bandwidth, throughput, bit-error rate, end-to-end delay, delay jitter, and peak duration |

due to many factors. In order to support better QoS, a robust mobility function needs to be provided. Heterogeneous networks are another important concept in modern computing systems. The network integrating different types of WLAN systems has a mobility limitation, and the network integrating 2.5G and 3G cellular networks has a bandwidth limitation and high investment cost The interaction among the various mobile access networks poses several challenges. One of the important challenges for a heterogeneous network is to ensure QoS; each kind of network supports different service quality to a user. Therefore, a scheme must be developed with which the heterogeneous network can manage these QoS changes with minimum effects, while a mobile STA roams across the different access networks. The QoS term has been used primarily in the networking community to define a set of network performance characteristics such as delay, jitter, bit error rate, packet loss and more. In modern systems, the concept of QoS involves not only network but rather the whole system, including end system.

## QOS SUPPORT CHALLENGES AND LIMITATIONS

There are several ways to characterize QoS in WLAN, such as parameterized or prioritized QoS. Parameterized QoS is a strict QoS requirement that is expressed in terms of quantitative values such as data rate, delay bound, and jitter bound. In a Traffic Specification (TSPEC), these values are expected to be met within the MAC data service in the transfer of data frames between peer stations (STAs). Prioritized QoS is expressed in terms of relative delivery priority, which is to be used within the MAC data service in the transfer of data frames between peer STAs. In a prioritized QoS scheme, the values of QoS parameters such as data rate, delay bound, and jitter bound may vary in the transfer of data frames without the need to reserve the required resources by negotiating the TSPEC between the STA and the AP (Ni, Romdhani & Turletti, 2004).

Wireless environment has some characteristics that make it difficult to support QoS with the already developed QoS techniques. These limitations are:

1. Radio link nature
2. Mobility
3. Mobile or portable device capabilities

In the following, we will describe these limitations and their effects on QoS support.

## Radio Link Limitation

Wireless link compared to wired counterparts has two main disadvantages. The first one is that the radio channel has poor quality and high noise ration, which yields higher bit error rate (BER), and higher BER means high packet loss. Thus, a new challenge is added to the QoS mechanism that is used for wireless environment. The second problem is that radio link quality varies over time. It can vary due to many reasons, such as weather, interference with other mobile users, or some home devices such as microwaves. In addition, barriers such as buildings and bridges can degrade the quality of the wireless link temporarily. The main problem is with variations that happen quite randomly and are usually unpredictable (Jha & Hassan, 2002). WLANs suffer from bandwidth limitations, and radio channels are error prone, affected by multipath shadowing interference.

## Mobility

Since the main advantage of wireless link is flexibility for a mobile device to move inside or outside the base station area, it is also a great challenge for QoS mechanism and network designers. This challenge can be characterized as follows:

- The network route form source to distention is likely to change during the communication session, since the network resources along the route must be reserved in advance to support the desired QoS. The resource reservation task becomes extremely complicated.
- Handoff procedure getting more complicated. For traditional voice calls in circuit-switched cellular network, such handoff is rather easy, as there is no consideration of relocating processing, data, and other contexts. However, handoff for real-time multimedia application in packet-switching wireless networks is more problematic, as a few seconds of disruption can have a detrimental effect on the QoS of the ongoing session.
- Mobility of users may cause the end-to-end path to change when users are roaming. Users expect to receive the same QoS once changing their point of attachment. Problems may arise when the new path cannot support such requirements (Ni et al., 2004).

## Mobile Device

Mobile handsets such as phones or personal digital assistants (PDAs) have some limitation in terms of power, CPU, memory, and interface. Therefore, even when the network has excellent QoS support, the result may still be unacceptable if the mobile device cannot cope with the QoS requirements of the user communication. Hence, QoS management schemes must take into consideration mobile device capabilities.

## FRAMEWORK FOR QOS SUPPORT

Providing QoS gurantee for real-time or multimedia applications (e.g., VoIP or audio/video streaming) is very crucial; such applications demand a specific bandwidth, delay, and packet loss requirements. QoS support in WLAN is a critical and very challenging task since WLAN has some restrictive environment limitations such as bandwidth limitation, noisy nature of radio channel, and contention over the link. In order to provide a full QoS guarantee in a real-time system, we need to maintain QoS in three layers for a real-time system. These layers are user, application, and system layers as shown in Figure 1. Display and synchronization are examples of user level QoS parameters that need to be maintained; these parameters and some others need to be translated to the next layer. In the application layer, there are parameters such as security, other application-dependent parameters, and parameters translated from user layers need to be maintained; afterward they will be passed into the system layer. System layer handles two sublayer QoSs: the network and operating system sublayer and the device sublayer, which does concern timing and throughput requirements, as shown in Table 1.

From the user point of view, perceived QoS encompasses a number of objective and subjective measures of service as one trace through the sequence of events from the setup until the completion of service (Doshi, Eggenschwiler, Rao, Samadi, Wang & Wolfson, 2007). All of the above-mentioned layers need to work together to guarantee QoS support in the whole system.

**User level QoS** specifies the user perception of the media; the user's perspective concerning the presentation quality is very important since the user is the ultimate decision-maker on what is perceived as good quality. For example in lip synchronization, if data are out of synchronization, human perception tends to identify the presentation as artificial or annoying. In user perspective, QoS mechanism in both how a multimedia presentation is understood by the user and the user's level of satisfaction have to be considered. User-perception parameters need to be mapped into lower level technology-based parameters (Gulliver & Ghinea, 2006; Jha & Hassan, 2002).

**Application level QoS** parameters describe the requirements for application services; they are specified in terms of media quality and media relation, in addition to parameters derived from the user level. Media quality includes source/destination characteristics such as media data unit rate and transmission characteristics such as response time and end-to-end delay requirements. Media relations specify relationships among media, such as media conversation, interstream synchronization, and intrastream synchronization. Application level QoS needs to be mapped to system level QoS (Jha & Hassan, 2002).

**System level QoS** parameters describe communication and operating system requirements that are needed by application QoS; parameters include buffer size, process priority, scheduling policy, cashing policy, and time quantum. System-level parameters can be specified in quantitative and qualitative terms. Quantitative criteria are those that can be evaluated in terms of concrete measures, such as bits per second, number of errors, task processing time, and data unit size. Qualitative criteria specify expected services such as interstream synchronization, ordered delivery of data, error recovery mechanisms, and scheduling/caching mechanisms (Abraham, Feder, Recchione & Zhang, 2007). In addition, system-level QoS includes device level QoS, which specifies timing and throughput requirements (Jha & Hassan, 2002).

**Network level QoS** is specified in terms of network load (i.e., ongoing traffic requirements) and network performance (i.e., requirements that must be guaranteed). Network level QoS has parameters for timeliness, bandwidth, and reliability parameters. Timeliness parameters are delay, response time, and jitter. Bandwidth parameters are system level data rate (i.e., system data unit such as bits or bytes per second), application-level data rate (i.e., media data unit such as frame per second), and transaction rate (i.e., number of operations requested per second). Reliability parameters are mean time to failure, mean time to repair, mean time between failures, percentage of time available, packet loss rate, and bit error rate.

## RELATED WORK

Several techniques have been proposed to support QoS in wireless network for multimedia. At the application layer, adaptive real-time applications can adapt changes in network conditions. At the transport layer, resource allocation can be made during connection setup to maintain end-to-end QoS support. At the network layer, techniques to provide mobility management and seamless connectivity can be used. Routing mechanism need to be QoS-aware and handle mobility. At the MAC layer, modifications need to be made so that reservations are respected and QoS guarantees can be supported. Adaptive power control techniques can be used to manage mobility and maintain active links. Error control techniques can be used to protect data signals against error rates.

In this section, we will go through the major techniques that have been proposed to support QoS in wireless environment. To narrow our working domain, we will only investigate those methods and techniques that are based on IEEE 802.11 standard series. A classification method has been used based on the general QoS framework discussion.

### QoS Supports in Standards Work

The IEEE 802.11 WLAN standard covers the MAC sublayer and the physical (PHY) layer of the open system interconnection (OSI) network reference model (LAN MAN Standards Committee of the IEEE Computer Society, 1999). Logical link control (LLC) sublayer is specified in the IEEE 802.2 standard. This architecture provides a transparent interface to the higher-layer users: STAs may move, roam through an 802.11 WLAN, and still appear as stationary to 802.2 LLC sublayer and above. This allows existing TCP/IP protocols to run over IEEE 802.11 WLAN just like wired Ethernet deployed.

IEEE 802.11 standard (LAN MAN Standards Committee of the IEEE Computer Society, 1999), one of the most important standards in emerging wireless LANs , contains two operation functions: distributed coordination function (DCF) and point coordination function (PCF). DCF is used in the contention period (CP) and employs carrier sense multiple access with collision avoidance (CSMA/CA) strategy to provide asynchronous data service on a best-effort basis. PCF is used in the contention-free period (CFP), providing the polling strategy to support time-bounded service. PCF uses a point coordinator (PC), which will operate at the access point (AP), to determine which station on a polling list currently has the right to access a wireless medium.

IEEE 802.11 standard during the design phase was not expected to be deployed very soon; thus, it has some problems in supporting QoS. These problems are summarized as follows. First, any station intending to receive contention-free service shall first send the (re)association frame to the AP during the CP time. Since DCF is governed by a contention-based protocol, the (re)association frames need to compete with all other stations, resulting in an unbounded (re)association delay (Choi & Shin, 2000). Second, IEEE 802.11 does not specify how the operation works under different user priorities. All traffic flows have the same priority to access the wireless medium such that there is no easy way to support the differentiation services for QoS-demanded applications (Choi & Shin, 2000). Third, in PCF, the medium occupancy time or the transmission time of polled station is unspecified. Any polled station is allowed to send arbitrary length frames. This may affect the time guarantee for frames of the other stations on the polling list (Wu, Fan-Jiang & Chou, 2006). Fourth, if pollable stations desiring to leave the polling list, they shall reassociate with the AP via DCF. The station without additional buffered data but having no chance to get off the polling list will respond by a Null frame when polled by the AP. The Null frame is simply wastage of bandwidth (Wu et al., 2006).

*Figure 2. IEEE 802.11e periodic superframe structure*

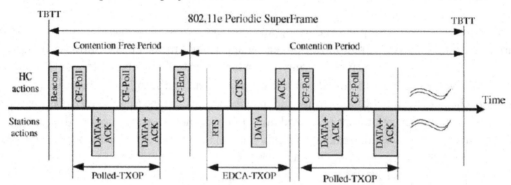

To meet the QoS requirements, the IEEE 802.11 task group E is developing an extension to the 802.11 standard, named 802.11e. In 802.11e draft (LAN MAN Standards Committee of the IEEE Computer Society, 2003), a new access scheme called hybrid coordination function (HCF) is proposed. HCF uses a contention-based channel access method named enhanced distributed channel access (EDCA) mechanism to support prioritized QoS service. In HCF, there is a controlling channel access named HCF Controlled Channel Access (HCCA) mechanism to support parameterized QoS service. A new idea, Transmission Opportunity (TXOP), is proposed as a transmission period that a station has a right to access the wireless medium and not extend beyond the TXOP. The TXOP is used for both the EDCF and HCCA and can obtain both when the medium is free under the EDCF access rules, called EDCF-TXOP, and when the station receives a poll, called polled-TXOP. Figure 2 shows the periodic superframe structure used in 802.11e. The superframe is divided into two periods: Contention Free Period (CFP), which is governed by HCCA; and Contention Period (CP), which is controlled by both EDCF and HCCA.

## QoS Support in MAC Layer

As explained earlier, IEEE 802.11 is a MAC-based protocol. Two main approaches were used to provide QoS for MAC layer: reactive and proactive mechanisms. Reactive mechanism monitors the congestions of resource, and when congestion detected, it will react and take the necessary procedure. Proactive mechanism demands prior information about the request such as possible delay, type of data, bandwidth, and so forth (i.e., service QoS requirements). Admission or denial of service decision will be taken based on the resources and QoS requirements (Doshi et al., 2007).

Based on these two approaches, three methodologies have been found in the literature. The first methodology is actually based on modifying the medium access function inside the MAC in order to utilize the link usage. For DCF-based schemes, many backoff procedures have been proposed; these methods tend to find the optimal backoff time in a way that maximizes the link usage and minimizes the waiting time. For PCF, the basic idea was to enhance pulling function by giving the medium to the STAs, which actually have something to transmit; a priority was also introduced. The second methodology is by introducing the call admission control (CAC) function, mainly for VoIP application; the purpose is to manage the available resource. The last methodology was applied by introducing a service differentiation scheme to the MAC layer. By distinguishing between traffic the higher priority will be fevered over the ordinary ones. However, in the literature, most papers will combine more than methodology to achieve better performance.

For the MAC layer, the main metrics measure the enhancements through the throughput, delay, and packet loss. All proposed methods aim to improve the value of those parameters; nevertheless, other factors will appear, such as cost and complexity of the proposed method. In the remainder of this section, we will report some related work found in the literature that emphasizes these methodologies.

## Medium Access Function Enhancement

QMAC quality of service MAC protocol is proposed in Wu, et al. (2006). QMAC proposes a new function called Quality-of-service Point Coordination Function (Q-PCF), which can coexist with DCF in a manner that permits both to operate concurrently within the same cell. In a cell, the PC takes charge of bandwidth allocation and makes these two coordination functions alternative, with a CFP (during which Q-PCF is active) followed by a CP (during which DCF is active), which are together referred as a super-frame. In the Q-PCF function, a prioritized procedure is presented and priority levels are numbered from 0 to H, with H denoting the highest priority level. A frame with priority zero will be sent via the DCF. An active station that has a flow with priority level ranging from 1 to H has a chance to join the polling list. After broadcasting a beacon and waiting for an SIFS period, the PC sends the control frame priority enquiry (PEH) to invite active stations whose priority equals H to reply to the priority response (PR) frame. On receiving the PEH frame, an active station with priority level H will acknowledge a PR frame after an SIFS period. At the end of the handshake, the PC can obtain the ternary feedback information according to stations' responses: (i) NULL: the PC does not receive any PR frames; (ii) SINGLE: the PC successfully receives a single PR frame that contains the AID of the sender, which will be placed on the polling list; and (iii) COLLISION: this event occurs if the outcome of the handshake is neither NULL nor SINGLE. If the conclusion of the current handshake is NULL (SINGLE), the PC may proceed to the next handshake by issuing the PEHK1 frame after an elapsed PIFS (SIFS). The priority probing process keeps running until the occurrence of a COLLISION. Once the PC recognizes a COLLISION event, it will send a registration enquiry (RE) frame to announce the start of the collision resolution period. During the collision resolution period, the PC executes the deterministic collision resolution procedure to discover which active stations bring the COLLISION event.

Lagkas, Papadimitriou, and Pomportsis (2006) propose an optimized MAC based on IEEE 802.11 PCF function called QAP, QoS supportive Adaptive Polling. The polling algorithm tends to poll the nodes, which are actually active, without having direct feedback about their current status. The polling algorithm takes into account the priorities of the data packets that are broadcast by the mobile nodes in order to decide which node to poll. Furthermore, every node implements a highest priority first (HPF) packet buffer discipline, which contributes in the QoS support. The proposed protocol is summarized as the following. The QAP protocol uses the POLL, NO_DATA, and ACK control packets; a single channel is assumed, where the whole provided bandwidth is available for all transmissions. Three cases are presented. First, the AP polls an inactive STA: the AP sends POLL to the STA and waits for feedback, $t_{POIL}+t_{DATA}+t_{ACK}+3t_{PROP\_DELAY}$. The STA responds with a NO_DATA packet. If the AP successfully receives this packet, it proceeds to poll another STA. In this case, it just had to wait for $t_{POIL}+t_{NO\_DATA}+2t_{PROP\_DELAY}$. Otherwise, if the AP has not successfully received the NO_DATA control packet, it has to wait for the whole $t_{POIL}+t_{DATA}+t_{ACK}+3t_{PROP\_DELAY}$ time duration before polling another STA. Either way, the STA is considered inactive. Second, the AP polls an active STA. The AP sends POLL to the STA and waits for feedback for $t_{POIL}+t_{DATA}+t_{ACK}+3t_{PROP\_DELAY}$. The STA sends a data packet (DATA) directly to the destination STA and waits for an ACK packet. The AP monitors the wireless medium during all that time. If it successfully receives one or more of these two packets (DATA, ACK), then it assumes that the polled STA is active. At the end of the waiting time, the AP polls another STA. In case the AP fails to receive one of the packets, it assumes there is a bad link between it and the mobile STA, so the STA is considered inactive. Third, the AP fails to poll the STA The AP sends POLL to the STA and waits for feedback for $t_{POIL}+t_{DATA}+t_{ACK}+3t_{PROP\_DELAY}$. If the STA fails to receive the POLL control packet, then there can be no feedback for the AP. So the latter has to wait for the maximum cycle duration before polling another STA. Also, it assumes that there is a bad link between it and the mobile STA, so the STA is considered inactive.

Yeh and Chen (2002) propose four polling schemes to be evaluated to provide service differentiation support in PCF: Round-Robin (RR), First-In-First-Out (FIFO), Priority, and Priority-Effort Limited Fair (ELF). Simulations show that all these schemes have better performance than DCF. Another scheme called Robust SuperPoll protocol (Ganz & Phonphoem, 2001) aims to improve performance of the PCF access scheme. Actually, PCF is very sensitive to lost polls. Instead of individually polling stations as in PCF, the SuperPoll mechanism sends polls (called "SuperPolls") to a group of stations. To make the scheme more robust against frame loss, each packet includes identities of remaining stations to be polled in the list. Therefore, stations have multiple opportunities to receive the poll. The observed increase in bandwidth and decrease in channel access time provide a better support for multimedia applications, especially in noisy environments.

The scheme proposed by Li and Battiti (2007), called Link adaptation and Adaptive Backoff Scheme (LABS), aims to make the system operate under the optimal operation point and at the same time achieves some predefined target service differentiation ratio between different traffic flows. In this approach, two adaptive schemes are combined: one is the so called Link Adaptation scheme, which dynamically selects an optimal modulation mode at a given time to improve the achieved system performance; and the other is the Adaptive Backoff scheme, which adaptively adjusts the minimum contention window size of each sending node to guarantee that the system operates under the optimal operation point.

A scheduler is proposed by Zhu and Yang (2006) to improve the performance of IEEE 802.11e WANs, which aims to adaptively adjust the ratio of EDCA duration to controlled access phase (CAP) duration by tracking the amounts of variable bit rate (VBR) and constant bit rate (CBR) traffics in a real time. The proposed scheme adjusts the ratio of EDCA duration to CAP duration adaptively according to the varying ratio of VBR traffics to CBR traffics of the system in a real-time manner. Meanwhile, the VBR and CBR traffics are transmitted in EDCA period and CAP period, respectively. The scheduler works as follows. In the first step, at the beginning of the next beacon, the scheduler gets the statistical amount $C_{VBR}$ and $C_{CBR}$, ($C_{VBR}$ and $C_{CBR}$ are the transmitted amount of VBR traffics and CBR traffics during one beacon period in bytes) and calculates the ratio of VBR traffic to CBR traffic. The second step is calculating the periods of EDCA and CAP. The third step is transmitting the value EDCA CAP durations to the stations by the QoS control field. Finally, when there is a new arrival, the admission control is applied. If the request TXOP is larger than the sum of the surplus available periods of EDCA and CAP, the request will be refused; otherwise, the scheduler accepts the requirement. Then if the request TXOP is larger than the surplus available period of the corresponding mode period, the scheduler will adjust the proportion of tow modes by the scheme mentioned previously to satisfy the requirement; otherwise, it allocates the TXOP directly in the corresponding mode. When the beacon interval is over, it goes to the first step.

## Call Admission Control

One of the important design aspects in wireless multimedia networks is to support guaranteed quality of services to mobile users. The call admission controller's (CAC's) main function is to decide whether a call is accepted or not based on certain conditions. Basically, CAC manages the available resources based on application QoS requirements. CAC plays an essential role in assuring the success of flow reservation scheme for connecting handover across heterogeneous networks. CAC is very important and a basic function, especially in real-time applications such as Voice over Wireless LAN (VoWLAN). To maintain connections at an acceptable QoS level in a cost-effective manner, the CAC engaged in access point (AP) must meet the following requirements (Yee, Choong, Low, Tan & Chien, 2007): (1) maximize the number of connections admitted into the network; (2) minimize the number of handoff call dropping; (3) ensure efficient bandwidth utilization; and (4) reduce the latency and overheads of both the call admission and handover computations. These four requirements can be used as well to determine the performance of the proposed CAC.

In the scheme named Conservative and Adaptive QoS (CAQoS), a CAC function is proposed (Yee et al., 2007); the basic element of this system is Statistical Reference Module (SRM), which gathers its input data (application profile, traffic patterns, network static information, etc.) from both mobiles stations and adjacent base stations over three specific time intervals (i.e., peak, moderate, and off-peak periods). Furthermore, it will issue three separate provisioning models, as it will be referenced in the future call admission process. The most important thing in this scheme is that it considers the time for decision in which the reference model is created and optimized off-line after collecting all inputs in which it will not delay or affect the admission of a new connection.

The article by Law and So (2005) proposes a soft QoS-based call admission control scheme to support the QoS requirements of multimedia traffic in IEEE 802.11e WLANs. The main purpose of the proposed algorithm is to admit the maximum number of new calls by soft QoS guarantees. In this algorithm, a so-called critical bandwidth ratio is proposed, which is defined as the relation between the QoS requirement of users and the allocated bandwidth. The algorithm works as follows: upon a new call request, if admission criterion is met, a new call is accepted in the network. When rejecting a new call, the proposed algorithm attempts to borrow the bandwidth from existing calls, based on the critical bandwidth ratio (which appears to be a fixed range of values) to allocate it to the new calls.

## Service Differentiation

Service differentiation is one of the most important methodologies used to provide QoS. The basic idea of achieving service differentiation is to allocate different access parameters set to different traffic flows. Therefore, the scheme is able to control the backoff procedures of different traffic flows, which makes it easier for traffic flows with higher priority to access channel resources. In the article by Le and Kim (2004), a differentiation mechanism is proposed to realize adaptive video transmission over WLAN based on coordination between application and MAC layer. At the application layer, Relative Priority Index (RPI) is assigned to each video packet according to its relative importance; this prioritization process is based on an application framing process, as an encoded video packet is packetized based on the group of pictures (GOB), then MSE is calculated based on the adopted error concealment scheme, which reflects the impact of packet loss. At the MAC layer, a modified version of IEEE 802.11e is used to adopt the differentiation scheme by adding four MAC queues with waiting time priority scheduling;

those queues are implemented as random early detection (RED) queue to avoid congestion by dropping packets randomly in case of overflow.

In the survey made by Ni, et al. (2004), the authors propose a scheme to classify the enhancements that have been done for MAC layer based on service differentiation schemes. This classification is based on the concept that a QoS enhancement can be supported by adding service differentiation to the MAC layer, which can be achieved by modifying the parameters that define how a station or flows should access the medium. In this survey, the criteria used are a two-level classification: at the top level, it distinguishes between the parameters, whether per-station or per-queue (priority-based); on the second level, the DCF-based (distributed control) are checked vs. PCF-based (centralized control). This will introduce four categories of MAC layer's enhancement schemes:

1.  Station-based service differentiation using DCF enhancements
2.  Station-based service differentiation using PCF enhancements
3.  Queue-based service differentiation using DCF enhancements
4.  Queue-based service differentiation using PCF enhancements

The survey also shows that most of these proposed schemes are done for the station-based service differentiation using DCF enhancements. In the following brief, a summary of the main schemes for station-based service differentiation using DCF enhancements as proposed by Ni, et al. (2004) is explored.

The scheme by Aad and Castelluccia (2001) proposes a differentiation based on different backoff increment function, DIFS and maximum frame length, which achieves good service differentiation; it works very well with UDP traffic but does not perform well with TCP traffic. Vaidya, Bahl, and Gupa (2000) presented a scheme called DFS, which is a fair scheduling algorithm defined according to packet size and flow weight. Fairness is achieved in this scheme, and the performance of high priority flows is enhanced. The implementation complexity of this scheme is high.

A virtual MAC is introduced by Veres, Campbell, Barry, and Sun (2001) to estimate delay, jitter, packet collisions, and packet losses; then it tunes the application parameters based on estimations. In this scheme, channel conditions are taken into consideration. "Virtual delay curves" can be used by the applications to tune their parameters. However, interactions between application and MAC layers introduce complexities. Sobrinho and Krishnakumar (1996) propose Blackburst scheme, in which a black burst contention period is used. It indicates the time that the station has waited to access the medium. Delay of high real-time traffic is minimized. Synchronization between high priority flows is achieved. If the two requirements on high priority flows cannot be supported, the performance will degrade. In the scheme proposed by Deng and Chang (1999), the backoff interval is divided into two parts. Then each part is combined with two IFSs yielding four priorities. Thus, the service differentiation is achieved, which ensures a good performance for high priority traffic. On the other hand, starvation of low priority stations when there are no high priority ones because they generate a long backoff.

## QoS Support in Application Layer

In literature, most researches found that supporting QoS in application layer is actually a MAC layer enhancement for a specific kind of application. Real-time application is the main target; the criterion is simply to improve the bandwidth, delay, or packet lose value according to the application needs.

VoIP is one of the most studied applications in literature (Abraham et al., 2007; Doshi et al., 2007; Lee, McGowan & Recchione, 2007). The basic technique for the wireless VoIP application is to provide an optimized MAC to reduce the delay that occurs during a voice call, since it is the key. Delay is the most important parameter for VoIP application; bandwidth is less important here. Such enhancement achieved by introducing a priority concept (service differentiation) in which a VoIP traffic will be given higher priority than other traffic flows can be classified as reactive scheme. Other researches will focus on providing an optimized Call Admission (CA) controller in order to utilize the usage of the available resource, serve as many calls as possible, and nonetheless guarantee that the admitted calls will be actually served. Some new parameters appear for CAC, such as block_on_new_call_ratio and block_on_handoff_ratio, which help to draw the CAC policy. Technique based on CA is considered a proactive mechanism. Video applications (e.g., video broadcasting, video on demand) are also targeted by research. One of the ideas to give a QoS support for video application in wireless environment is by enhancing the coding technique. It is well known that the quality of the played video will highly affect the amount of bandwidth needed to transmit this video; many transcoding techniques have been proposed in order to control the quality of the played video according to network status, and when a degrading occurs on the available bandwidth over the network, the quality of the played video will be degraded in order to reduce the amount of needed bandwidth; nevertheless, such kind of techniques won't be helpful if the bit-error or jitter is high.

In the literature, not too many works actually involve application layer in QoS support process. Ding, Ghafoor, and Bhargava (2003) combine application, transport, and data link layer to deal with a high error rate problem in the wireless environment. The main purpose of the article is error rate in wireless environment; thus, application layer in this approach is also responsible for error control. In application layer, when using the appropriate source codec to get encoded video bitstream, an error-resilient algorithm is used in encoding process. At the application layer in receiver side, an error coding algorithm is applied to correct errors, assemble fragments to a complete video frame, and buffer it until its time is up and retrieved by upper applications. This error control is added to the application layer to make sure no error will be forwarded to the upper layer. The main disadvantage of this technique is that it increases the overhead for the system.

Some other work present in literature is by providing adaptive multimedia application to improve the perceived QoS in the wireless environment. A very interesting work is presented by Ruiz and García (2002) in which the authors propose an adaptive architecture that allows applications to minimize the effect of changing the network condition. The application tries to adapt itself by reacting to what it senses from network, rather relying on nonguaranteed bandwidth reservation. This approach takes into account parameters such as codec, codec-specific parameters, frame size, and so forth, not just the ordinary network parameters.

## OPEN ISSUES

### Mobility

Wireless networks have given the ability to be connected anywhere and anytime. To support such feature, a mobility function needs to be adopted. IEEE 802.11 standard supports mobility (also known as handover in IEEE 802.11). However, handover function in IEEE 802.11 suffers from a high delay caused by three main factors: first, the discovery period or the so-called probe delay; second, the authentication delay; and third, the reassociation delay. Probe delay is considered the highest period among them, in 802.11b with 10 to 11 channels to scan, and with a 102ms beacon interval, the probe delay could be more than one second, so most of the 802.11 implementations will broadcast a probe request packet to force the APs in the neighbor to respond immediately; nevertheless, the probe delay is still high, and Ramani and Savage (2005) measured the delay between 350 and 500ms. Such a kind of delay will be very critical for delay-sensitive applications such as wireless VoIP or videoconferencing, especially while the handoff user is in the middle of a conversation.

Other delays are caused by the security function applied to the wireless network (e.g., WEP, WPA, etc.) when the wireless node is operating in a public network (e.g., hot spot) or when the handover happens while there are some delay-sensitive applications running on that node. Generally, user authentication should be performed at each AP when a mobile node moves into a new AP area; it should perform a new user authentication procedure and receive a new wired equivalent privacy (WEP) key. This authentication mechanism will impact the network performance. A fast handoff scheme based on mobility prediction in public wireless LAN is proposed by Pack and Choi (2004); this scheme is focusing on reducing the reauthentication delay needed for outdoor WLAN service. When a mobile node (MN) sends an authentication request, the AAA server authentication will send the WEP key not only for the currently used AP, but also for other APs keys in the neighbor. These multiple APs are selected by the frequent handoff region (FHR) selection algorithm based on mobility prediction. WEP-based security system is very simple, but for newer protecting methods such as Wi-Fi protection access (WPA), which is very complicated and consumes time to authenticate an MN, this technique might not be possible.

## Perceptual QoS Support

Perceptual QoS indicates user level QoS, which specifies the user perception of the media. The user's perspective concerning the presentation quality is very important since the user is the ultimate decision-maker on what preserves as good quality. For example, in lip synchronization, if data are out of synchronization, human perception tends to identify the presentation as artificial or annoying. In user perspective QoS mechanism, multimedia presentation is understood by both the user and the user's level of satisfaction. User-perception parameters need to be mapped into lower-level technology-based parameters (Gulliver & Ghinea, 2006; Jha & Hassan, 2002).

To our knowledge, little research work has discussed perceptual QoS support in wireless environment, even in any communication environment in general. Law and So (2005) investigate in their paper the effect of passing real-time multimedia contents (images and videos) over pervasive network infrastructure. In this chapter, real-time video delivery is based on a two-rank approach: subtitle ranked 1 and frame images ranked 2. The result shows that the user still can perceive the meaning of the content from the subtitles. Another study by Gulliver and Ghinea (2006), which explores the human side of the multimedia experience, shows that significant reduction in frame rate does not proportionally reduce the user's understanding of the presented media. Such studies with their rareness show that improving the network parameters only is not the only way to provide better user perception. However, research still needs to be carried out to investigate how to improve user experience in the wireless environment.

## QoS Support in Heterogeneous Networks

Recently, wireless LAN (IEEE 802.11) and cellular networks (e.g., 3G) are the most dominant wireless networks. Each of these communication methods has its strength and weak points. The network integrating different types of WLAN systems has a mobility limitation, and the network integrating 2.5G and 3G cellular networks has a bandwidth limitation and high investment cost. Therefore, there is a strong need and consensus to integrate WLANs with 3G cellular networks and develop heterogeneous mobile data networks capable of ubiquitous data services and very high data rates (Salkintzis, 2004).

The interaction among the various mobile access networks poses several challenges. One of the important challenges for a heterogeneous network is to ensure QoS; each kind of network supports different service quality to a user. Therefore, a scheme must be developed with which the heterogeneous network can manage these QoS changes with minimum effects while a mobile STA roams across the different access networks (Kim, 2006). Another important challenge is developing a seamless handoff procedure. Handoff decision criteria, handoff triggering time, and network selection criteria should be defined.

## CONCLUSION

Wireless network has gained a great deal of attention in the last years. Features such as free band license, cheap hardware, and high data rate promote IEEE 802.11 wireless LAN for a wider user base; therefore, user demands grow for more advanced applications and services. With the high development of the hardware capabilities of mobile devices, multimedia applications become more suitable; therefore, supporting QoS in a wireless environment appears as a new challenge for both academia and industry. In this chapter, we survey the QoS support for wireless LAN through the literature, providing a state of the art of the major research work. And finally, we discuss some of the remaining open topics for supporting QoS in the wireless environment and possible future research in this field, including mobility, perceptual QoS, and QoS support in heterogeneous networks.

## REFERENCES

Aad, I., & Castelluccia, C. (2001). Differentiation mechanisms for IEEE 802.11. *Proceedings of the IEEE Infocom*, Anchorage, Alaska, 209–218.

Abraham, S., Feder, P.M., Recchione, M.C., & Zhang, H. (2007). The capacity of VoIP over 802.11. *Bell Labs Technical Journal, 11*, 253–271.

Bhargava, B. (2002). Guest editorial: Quality of service in multimedia networks. *Mutimedia Tools and Applications an International Journal.*

Choi, S., & Shin, K.G. (2000). A unified wireless LAN architecture for real-time and non-real-time communication services. *IEEE/ACM Transaction on Network*, 44–59.

Deng, J., & Chang, R.S. (1999). A priority scheme for IEEE 802.11 DCF access method. *IEICE Transactions in Communications*, 96–102.

Ding, G., Ghafoor, H., & Bhargava B. (2003). Error resilient video transmission over wireless networks. *Proceedings of the IEEE Workshop on Software Technologies for Future Embedded Systems*, Hokkaido, Japan, 31–34.

Doshi, B.T., Eggenschwiler, D., Rao, A., Samadi, B., Wang, Y.T., & Wolfson, J. (2007). VoIP network architectures and QoS strategy. *Bell Labs Technical Journal, 7*, 41–59.

Ganz, A., & Phonphoem, A. (2001). Robust SuperPoll with chaining protocol for IEEE 802.11 wireless LANs in support of multimedia applications. *Wireless Networks, 7*, 65–73.

Gulliver, R.S., & Ghinea, G. (2006). Defining user perception of distributed multimedia quality. *ACM Transactions on Multimedia Computing, Communications, and Applications, 2*, 241–257.

Jha, S.K., & Hassan, M. (2002). *Engineering Internet Qos*. Norwood, MA: Artech House Inc.

Kim, S.E. (2006). *Efficient and QoS guaranteed data transport in heterogeneous wireless mobile networks* [doctoral dissertation]. Georgia Institute of Technology.

LAN MAN Standards Committee of the IEEE Computer Society. (1999). *IEEE standard 802.11-1999 wireless LAN medium access control (MAC) and physical layer (PHY) specifications*. IEEE Press.

LAN MAN Standards Committee of the IEEE Computer Society. (2003). *IEEE 802.11e/D6.0, draft supplement to part 11: Wireless medium access control and physical layer (PHY) specifications: Medium access control (MAC) enhancements for quality of service (QoS)*. IEEE.

Lagkas, T.D., Papadimitriou, G.I., & Pomportsis, A.S. (2006). QAP: A QoS supportive adaptive polling protocol for wireless LANs. *Computer Communications*, 618–633.

Law, K.L.E., & So, S. (2005). Real-time perceptual QoS satisfactions of multimedia information. *Proceedings of the 2nd ACM International Workshop on Performance Evaluation of Wireless Ad Hoc, Sensor, and Ubiquitous Networks*, Canada, 277–278.

Le, J., & Kim, J.-W. (2004). Differentiation mechanisms over IEEE 802.11 wireless LAN for network-adaptive video transmission. *Lecture Notes in Computer Science, 3090*, 553–562.

Lee, M., McGowan, W.J., & Recchione, C.M. (2007). Enabling wireless VoIP. *Bell Labs Technical Journal, 11*, 201–215.

Li, B., & Battiti, R. (2007). Achieving optimal performance in IEEE 802.11 wireless LANs with the combination of link adaptation and adaptive backoff. *International Journal of Computer and Telecommunications Networking*, 1574–1600.

Ni, Q., Romdhani, L., & Turletti, T. (2004). A survey of QoS enhancements for IEEE 802.11 wireless LAN. *Journal of Wireless Communications and Mobile Computing, 4*(5), 547–566.

Pack, P., & Choi, Y. (2004). Fast handoff scheme based on mobility prediction in public wireless LAN systems. *IEE Proceedings Communications, 151*(5), 489–495.

Raghavan, S.V, & Tripathi, S.K. (1998). *Network multimedia, concept, architecture and design, system*. Prentice Hall.

Ramani, I., & Savage S. (2005). SyncScan: Practical fast handoff for 802.11 infrastructure networks. *Proceedings of the IEEE Infocom Conference*, Miami, Florida.

Ruiz, M.P., & García, E. (2002). Adaptive multimedia applications to improve user-perceived QoS in multihop wireless ad hoc networks. *Proceedings of the IEEE International Conference on Wireless LANs and Home Networks*, Atlanta, Georgia, 673–684.

Salkintzis, K.A. (2004). Interworking techniques and architectures for WLAN/3G integration toward 4G mobile data networks. *IEEE Wireless Commun.*, 50–61.

Sobrinho, J.L., & Krishnakumar, A.S. (1996). Real-time traffic over the IEEE 802.11 medium access control layer. *Bell Labs Technical Journal*, 172–187.

Vaidya, N.H., Bahl, P., & Gupa, S. (2000). Distributed fair scheduling in a wireless LAN. *Proceedings of the Sixth Annual International Conference on Mobile Computing and Networking (Mobicom 2000)*, Boston, Massachusetts, 167–178.

Veres, A., Campbell, A.T., Barry, M., & Sun, L.H. (2001). Supporting service differentiation in wireless packet networks using distributed control. *IEEE Journal of Selected Areas in Communications (JSAC), Special Issue on Mobility and Resource Management in Next-Generation Wireless Systems*, 2094–2104.

Wu, S.-L., Fan-Jiang, S., & Chou, Z.-T. (2006). An efficient quality-of-service MAC protocol for infrastructure WLANs. *Journal of Network and Computer Applications*, 235–261.

Yee, Y.C., Choong, K.N., Low, L.Y.A., Tan, S.W., & Chien, S.F. (2007). A conservative approach to adaptive call admission control for QoS provisioning in multimedia wireless networks. *Computer Communications*, 249–260.

Yeh, J.-Y., & Chen, C. (2002). Support of multimedia services with the IEEE 802.11 MAC protocol. *Proceedings of the IEEE ICC*, New York, 600–604.

Zhu, R., & Yang, Y. (2006). Adaptive scheduler to improve QoS in IEEE 802.11e wireless LANs. *Proceedings of the First International Conference on Innovative Computing, Information and Control*, China, 1, 377–380.

## ADDITIONAL READING

Ghinea, G., & Thomas, J.P. (1998). QoS impact on user perception and understanding of multimedia video clips. *Proceedings of the Sixth ACM international Conference on Multimedia*, Bristol, UK, 49–54.

Hands, D., Bourret, A., & Bayart, D. (2005). Video QoS enhancement using perceptual quality metrics. *23*(2), 208–216.

Ito, Y., Tasaka, S., & Fukuta, Y. (2004). Psychometric analysis of the effect of buffering control on user-level QoS in an interactive audio-visual application. *Proceedings of the 2004 ACM Workshop on Next-Generation Residential Broadband Challenges*, New York, 2–10.

Salvador, P., Nogueira, A., & Valadas, R. (2007). Predicting QoS characteristics on wireless networks. *Proceedings of the Third international Conference on Networking and Services.*

Song, S., Won, Y., & Song, I. (2002). Empirical study of user perception behavior for mobile streaming. *Proceedings of the Tenth ACM International Conference on Multimedia*, Juan-les-Pins, France.

Takahashi, A., Yoshino, H., & Kitawaki, N. (2004). Perceptual QoS assessment technologies for VoIP. *IEEE Communications*, 42(7), 28–34.

# Chapter III
# Getting the Big Picture on Small Screens:
## Quality of Experience in Mobile TV

**Hendrik Knoche**
*University of College London, UK*

**M. Angela Sasse**
*University of College London, UK*

## ABSTRACT

*This chapter provides an overview of the key factors that influence the quality of experience (QoE) of mobile TV services. It compiles the current knowledge from empirical studies and recommendations on four key requirements for the uptake of mobile TV services: (1) handset usability and its acceptance by the user, (2) the technical performance and reliability of the service, (3) the usability of the mobile TV service (depending on the delivery of content), and (4) the satisfaction with the content. It illustrates a number of factors that contribute to these requirements ranging from the context of use to the size of the display and the displayed content. The chapter highlights the interdependencies between these factors during the delivery of content in mobile TV services to a heterogeneous set of low resolution devices.*

## INTRODUCTION

It is the second time around for mobile TV. In the 1980s, Seiko introduced a TV wristwatch that was capable of displaying standard TV channels on an liquid crystal display (LCD) wrist watch. It seemed like a great idea at the time. Many people wore watches, a growing number of people used LCD or digital watches, and it was possible to display anything on an LCD display. However, the watch was not a success. One of the biggest problems was high energy consumption—the watch wearer had to separately carry the battery, which was part of a box that housed the TV receiver and connected to the watch through a cable. This setup gave the wearer approximately one hour of viewing time. The screen was monochrome and had low contrast. Furthermore, watching TV while wearing the watch resulted in an unnatural wrist posture. Last but not least, the TV wristwatch was expensive.

Twenty years later, mobile TV is back. Many people now carry inexpensive mobile phones with built-in LCD screens. This allows the display of moving images, which can be received in a more energy efficient way these days, and mobile TV is making its second appearance. Today, mobile TV services are available in a number of countries. While Asian consumers already have access to broadcast services, Western countries have finished trials and are aiming to move from unicast, that is, individual delivery services, to broadcast solutions. Portable play stations and video Ipods provide alternative platforms for playing prestored content.

So far, the deployment of these services has been driven by technical feasibility and matching business models. The wireless domain is one of limited bandwidth resources, and service providers have to decide on broadcasting more content at lower quality or vice versa in search of optimal configurations for people's QoE that are financially viable. The content is produced by companies with a specific primary target medium, that is, cinema, TV, or mobile in mind. This choice influences the selection of shot types, length, and the type of programme. Cameras can be chosen from a wide selection delivering different resolutions, aspect ratios, contrast ranges, and frame rates. After post-production the content is delivered to audiences through various channels. For example, TV broadcast companies adapt cinema content to the TV and mobile service operators adapt TV content for mobile TV distribution. Uptake of existing mobile TV services lags behind expectations, possibly because customers are not willing to pay high premiums for content (KPMG, 2006). To assist service providers in improving their service offerings, we need to understand how people might experience mobile TV services in their entirety. QoE (Aldrich, Marks, Lewis, & Seybold, 2000; Jain, 2004; McCarthy & Wright, 2004) is a broad concept that encompasses all aspects of a service that can be experienced by the user. In the case of mobile TV, QoE includes the usability of the service; the restrictions inherent in the delivery; the audio-visual quality of the content; the usage and payment model; and the social context as well as possible parallel use of standard TV. According to Mäki (2005) the following four requirements are the most important for adoption of mobile TV services:

1. Handset usability and acceptance
2. Technical performance and reliability
3. Usability of the mobile TV service
4. Satisfaction with the content

We will address each of these factors in turn in more detail in the following sections in order to provide a comprehensive view on the QoE of mobile TV services.

## HANDSET INTEGRATION AND USABILITY

Currently, the mobile phone is the most likely platform for mobile TV, but personal digital assistants (PDAs), portable game consoles, and music players are attractive alternatives. In 2003 a total of 70% of the people in Europe owned or used mobile phones. The importance of mobile phones in people's lives means that most owners carry it with them wherever they go. Mobile TV consumption on mobile phones allows for privacy of consumption, because of short viewing distances and the viewing angle afforded by many mobile devices. However, people perceive the battery consumption of mobile TV as a threat to more important communication needs. The application should provide warnings when the battery is drained beyond a certain threshold (Knoche & McCarthy, 2004), and service providers should set user expectations about battery drain induced by, for example, watching live content (Serco, 2006).

The mobile TV application should not get in the way of communication but alert users of incoming calls, text, or other messaging and provide means to deal with them in a seamless manner. On inbound communication this includes automatic pausing of the TV service, if possible, and offering to resume once the user has finished communicating. Likewise, important indicators, for example, for battery status or menus should not unnecessarily obstruct the TV screen but could use semi-transparent menus as suggested in Serco (2006).

Depending on the technical realisation, having TV reception might require a second receiver unit in the handset that would allow for parallel reception of TV content and making and receiving telephone calls at the same time. A single receiver unit, for example, would not be able to record live TV content during a phone call.

## Display

The screen should have high contrast, backlight, and a high viewing angle to support viewing in different circumstances and by multiple viewers. Due to size and power constraints LCDs are currently the preferred technology to present visual information on mobile devices. LCDs come in a range of shapes, sizes, and resolutions, from video graphics array (VGA) PDAs (480 x 640 pixels) and high end third generation (3G) or digital video broadcasting-handheld (DVB-H) enabled phones (320 x 240) to more compact models with quarter common intermediate format (QCIF) size (176 x 144) and below. Users want as large a screen as possible for viewing, but they do not want their phones to be too big (Knoche & McCarthy, 2004). Landscape-oriented use of the display might be preferred (Serco, 2006) over the typical portrait mode that mobile phones are used in. In general, pictures subtending a larger visual angle in the eye of the beholder make for a better viewing experience. Results from studies on TV pictures revealed that larger image sizes are generally preferred to smaller ones (Lombard, Grabe, Reich, Campanella, & Ditton, 1996; Reeves & Nass, 1998) and are perceived to be of higher quality (Westerink & Roufs, 1989), but that there is no difference in arousal and attention between users watching content on 2" and 13" screens (Reeves, Lang, Kim, & Tartar, 1999).

Which resolutions best support the different screen sizes of mobile TV devices is subject to current research, and the pros and cons of different resolutions will be discussed in the section on video quality. Besides the size of the device, the visual impact can be increased by head-mounted displays and projection techniques. Whereas, the former results in an experience of greater immersion and requires additional equipment to be carried around, the latter reduces the anonymity of visual consumption.

## Device Use

A stand for continuous viewing is beneficial for mid- to long-term use. In public places, the use of headphones, which increase immersion (see later on), might be required. Many people already use head phones for portable music players, and standard headset jacks on mobile TV devices would make switching between devices easy. Dedicated buttons would be valuable for mobile TV access, basic playback controls, and content browsing, for example, channel switching or selecting. On touch screens many people value on-screen buttons that do not decrease the viewing area of the content instead of having to use a stylus which requires two-handed operation.

## Immersion

Users are worried about becoming too absorbed in what they are watching and thus distracted from other tasks while being on the move, for example, missing trains or stops (Knoche & McCarthy, 2004). They require a pause/mute facility to cope with likely interruptions. In the case of broadcast content, this requirement places demands on the device's storage capacity. Volume control should possible preferably without the need to access menus. The question whether a separate means to mute the volume and would let the video play in the background will be necessary or might confuse users more in conjunction with the pause button which pauses both audio and video has to be addressed by future research. An easy way to set alarms or countdowns might help mobile users to not loose touch with the world around them.

## TECHNICAL PERFORMANCE AND RELIABILITY

The way the content is delivered has a major effect on the possible uses of a mobile TV service. The perceived video and audio quality will depend on the quality of service (QoS) provided by the network that is delivering the packets that carry the content and might noticeably degrade the content by introducing errors, loss, and varying delays to those packets. For an example of how loss influences the perceived video quality of mobile TV content see Jumisko-Pyykkö, Vinod Kumar, Liinasuo, and Hannuksela (2006).

### Service Delivery

From the user point of view, TV is commonly understood as an "any time" service: turn it on and it will deliver content at any time of day. Mobile TV services implicitly suggest being available anywhere at any time. Mobile phone users have been wary of this promise (Knoche & McCarthy, 2004).

There are four content delivery models that significantly shape the experience of the mobile TV service: (1) media charger, (2) streaming (unicast), (3) broadcast, and (4) pre-cached broad- or multi-cast.

The video Ipod is an example of a *media charger*. The user has no live content but does have full playback control and can watch anywhere at any time. In order to have a supply of fresh content the user has to touch base regularly.

Many of the services like MobiTV and Slingbox (Sling Media, 2006) in the U.S. and Vodafone live! in the UK are currently offered as unicast services, which makes them relatively expensive in terms of spectrum usage and difficult to scale. With each increase in the number of receivers in a reception cell the available bandwidth per receiver decreases. The number of users receiving a unicast mobile TV stream on demand within a wireless cell is therefore limited, and the audio-visual quality degrades with the increase in receivers. However, unicast can deliver personalised content for niche interests that would not be viable through broadcasts.

Broadcast approaches like digital multimedia broadcasting (DMB) and DVB-H are more efficient in mass delivery as they support an arbitrary number of receivers at constant quality in the coverage area.

Broadcast users have no playback control unless pausing live TV and other functions available in personal video recorders (PVR) are implemented on the user terminal. However, since being on the move results in varying levels of reception people experience varying quality and service discontinuities. This poses a problem to broadcast TV services without PVR-like functionality. People might tune into the streams at times when the programmes they want to see are not being broadcast. Similar to media chargers, pre-cached services, for example, SDMB (Selier & Chuberre, 2005), can continuously display recently downloaded, that is, non-live, content at higher quality through carrousel broadcasts. This is an example of TV any time, which allows users to watch broadcast content when convenient. Mobile TV services do not have to rely solely on one of these delivery mechanisms but could mix them in order to leverage their different advantages.

The content has to be delivered through one of these transmission schemes to a range of devices with different display capabilities. There are three main ways to address the problem of multiple target solutions: (1) sending multiple resolutions, which requires more bandwidth if broadcast; (2) broadcasting at the highest resolution and resizing at the receiver side; and (3) employing layered coding schemes that broadcast a number of resolution layers from which every receiver can assemble the parts it can display.

## Resolution, Image Size, and Viewing Distance

Human perception of displayed information has been studied for a long time, see Biberman (1973) for an overview. Spatial and temporal resolution are key factors for the perceived quality of video content. Whereas, temporal resolution below 30 frames per second (fps) results in successively jerkier motion, lowering the number of pixels to encode the picture reduces the amount of visible detail. Excessive delays and loss during transmission of the content may affect both the spatial and temporal resolution resulting in visible artefacts and or skipping of frames causing the picture to freeze.

The higher the resolution in both of these dimensions, the more bandwidth is required to transmit it. Service providers only have a limited amount of bandwidth available and want to maximise the content they can offer to their customers while still delivering the quality that the customers expect. They face the trade-off between visual quality and quantity of the content.

Mobile TV will be consumed at arm's length. Paper, keyboard, and display objects are typically operated at distances ranging from 30 cm to 70 cm. Continued viewing at distances closer than the resting point of vergence—approx. 89 cm, with a 30° downward gaze—can contribute to eyestrain (Owens & Wolfe-Kelly, 1987). When viewing distances come close to 15 cm, people experience discomfort (Ankrum, 1996). Normal 20/20 vision is classified as the ability to resolve 1 minute of arc (1/60°) (Luther, 1996) and translates to 60 pixels per degree. The amount of pixels p that can be resolved by a human at a given distance d and a picture height h can be computed by the following equation:

$$p = \frac{h}{d \cdot 2\tan(1/120)}.$$

In the typical TV viewing setup at a seating distance of 3m, the benefits of high definition television (HDTV) can only be enjoyed on relatively big screens. On handheld devices, people could easily enjoy HDTV resolutions on a screen of 8 cm height. However, mobile TV does not exceed quarter video graphics array (QVGA) resolution at present. In addition, people are able to identify content that has been upscaled from low resolutions to higher resolution mobile screens. So far no research has addressed the potential effects of upscaling low broadcast resolution content to a screen with a higher resolution. Research on these topics is proprietary. Philips uses a nonlinear upscaling method called Mobile PixelPlus to fill a screen with higher resolution than the broadcast material.

Some studies have addressed the perception of low resolution content on small handheld screens (Knoche, McCarthy, & Sasse, 2005; Jumisko-Pyykkö & Häkkinen, 2006; Song, Won, & Song, 2004). Content shown on mobile devices at higher resolutions and larger sizes is generally more acceptable than lower resolutions and smaller sizes at identical encoding bitrates. However, the differences are not uniform across content types (Knoche, McCarthy, et al., 2005). All content types received poor ratings when presented at resolutions smaller than 168 x 126. Other studies have shown that low image resolution can improve task performance. For example, Horn (2002) showed that lie detection was better with a small (53 x 40) than a medium (106 x 80) video image resolution. In another study, however, smaller video resolutions (160 x 120) had no effect on task performance but did reduce satisfaction when compared to 320 x 240 image resolutions (Kies, Williges, & Rosson, 1996). In a study by Barber and Laws (1994), a reduction in image resolution (from 256 x 256 to 128 x 128) at constant image size led to a loss in accuracy of emotion detection especially in a full body view. The legibility of text has a major influence on the acceptability of the overall video quality (Knoche & Sasse, 2006) and should be sent separately and rendered at the receiving side.

## Frame Rate

Low video frame rates are common in recent mobile multimedia services especially in streamed unicast services. Frame rates as low as 5 fps and lower were avoided at all costs in a desktop computer-based study by Pappas and Hinds (1995). Another study, conducted by Apteker, Fisher, Kisimov, & Neishlos (1994) assessed the watchability of various types of video at different frame rates (30, 15, 10, 5 fps). Compared to a benchmark of 100% at 30 fps, video clips high in visual importance dropped to a range of 43% to 64% watchability when displayed at 5 fps, depending upon the importance of audio for the comprehension of the content and the static/dynamic nature of the video. Participants who saw football clips on mobile devices found the video quality of football content less acceptable when the frame rate dropped below 12 fps (McCarthy, Sasse, & Miras, 2004). Comparable displays on desktop computers maintained high acceptability for frame rates as low as 6 fps. The reason for the higher sensitivity to low frame rates on mobile devices is not yet fully understood, but highlights the importance to measure video quality in as realistic setups as possible to the real experience. The proprietary natural motion approach by Philips supposedly reduces the jerkiness of low-frame-rate content by generating intermediate frames from the broadcast set of frames at the receiver side (De Vries, 2006).

Some programmes have sign language interpreters signing to make the programme understandable for deaf people. This is one of the few applications that require high frame rates for comprehension of the visual content. Spelling sign language requires 25 frames to be able to capture all letters in at least one frame (Hellström, 1997).

## Temporal vs. Spatial Resolution

Whereas, earlier guidelines suggested the use of higher frame rates for fast moving content, for example, sports, (IBM, 2002) recent findings show that users prefer higher spatial resolution over higher frame rates in order to be able to identify objects and actors in mobile TV content (McCarthy et al., 2004). Wang, Speranza, Vincent, Martin, and Blanchfield (2003) reported on a study in which they manipulated both frame rate and quantization with an American football clip. They concluded that "quantization distortion is generally more objectionable than motion judder" and that large quantization parameters should be avoided whenever possible.

## Audio Visual Quality

A number of studies have found that the combined quality of audio-visual displays is not simply based on the sum of its parts (e.g., Hands, 2004; Jumisko-Pyykkö et al., 2006). In a study on audio-visual interactions, Winkler and Faller (2005) found that selecting mono audio for a given bitrate gives better quality ratings and that more bitrate should be allocated to the audio for more complex scenes. As a byproduct in a study on TV viewing experience Neuman, Crigler, and Bove (1991) discovered that the perceived video quality was improved by better audio. However, it was only the case for one of the three used content types. Similarly, a study by Beerends and De Caluwe (1999) using a 29 cm monitor, found that the rating of video quality was slightly higher when accompanied by CD quality audio than when accompanied by no audio. The effect, however, was small and has not been replicated with small screens. However, in the same study participants judged the two lower video quality levels (in which the video bandwidth was limited to 0.15 MHz and 0.025 MHz) worse when they were presented with audio, than without audio. Similarly, in a study by Knoche, McCarthy, et al. (2005), the visual quality of video clips displayed on mobile devices was more acceptable to participants across all video encoding bitrates when it was supported by lower (16 kbps) than with higher audio quality (32 kbps).

Synchronous playback of sound and video affects the overall AV-quality (Knoche, De Meer, & Kirsh, 2005). For 30 fps video the window of synchronisation is ±80ms (Steinmetz, 1996). The temporal window of synchronisation depends on the video frame rate (Knoche, De Meer, et al., 2005; Vatakis & Spence, in press). At lower frame rates audio-visual speech perception is more sensitive to audio coming before video and the presentation of the audio relative to the video should be delayed (Knoche, De Meer, et al., 2005).

## USABILITY OF THE MOBILE TV SERVICE

In order to understand what makes for a usable mobile TV service, we need to know about the context of the user including the motivation for use and the location. Many of the guidelines that apply to mobile application design in general equally apply to mobile TV; see Serco (2006) for an overview.

## Motivation of Use

Whereas, the drivers behind standard TV consumption are fairly well understood, we lack comparable knowledge in mobile TV. Peoples' watching of standard TV is driven by ritualistic (Taylor & Harper, 2002) and instrumental motives (Rubin, 1981) as in "electronic wallpaper" (Gauntlett & Hill, 1999), mood management (Zillman, 1988), escapism, information, entertainment, social grease, social activity, and social learning (Lee & Lee, 1995). For many of these drivers watching TV constitutes a group activity. Mobile TV is, due to its nature and limitations, more likely to be an individual consumption activity.

The restricted viewing angle of the screens, the (for some people uncomfortable) proximity with others to share it, and the fact that the mobile phone is a rather personal device might curb group usage.

## Location

According to Mäki (2005) the most common places for mobile TV use are (in descending order):

1.   In public transport
2.   At home
3.   At work

This is supported by other studies, in which many participants of mobile TV trials used the device as an additional TV set at home (Södergård, 2003). While at home, users' perception of the mobile TV service might depend on the comparison with standard TV in terms of delay (mobile broadcasts might incur additional delay due to processing or delivery, e.g., through satellite); programme availability; audio-visual quality; responsiveness; ease of use; interoperability with other media solutions including recording devices—such as PVRs—that allow for easy recording of television shows; content sharing; and user-controlled storage.

People are able to compare the different experiences of consuming TV content at home. Some might object to the inherent delay (approximately 1 minute) between the live broadcast TV signal and the mobile TV signal as currently seen in MobiTV (Lemay-Yates Associates Inc., 2005). What is more important, perhaps, is that the delay disadvantages the mobile audience in interactive game shows or betting services.

## Usage Patterns

Previous research has shown that peoples' average usage of mobile TV is less than 10 minutes long (Södergård, 2003). This window of consumption places demands both on the length of consumable content and the time that users might be willing to spend to access and navigate through it. Data from SDMB trials in Korea for example show that people use mobile TV throughout the day with peaks in the morning, at lunch time, in the early evening, and very late in the evening.

## Interactivity of the Mobile TV Service

The interface needs to provide the user with controls to use the different kinds of interactivities offered in mobile TV. Users expect the entry points to the mobile TV to be available from prominent places in the mobile phone user interface (Stockbridge, 2006).

## Participation Interactivity and Payments

One of the potentially biggest advantages of mobile TV over regular TV is the existence of a return channel with built-in billing possibilities for premium and subscription services, as well as transactions involved in interactive services such as voting and betting.

Participants in mobile TV trials favoured the flat-rate payment model, that is, a single payment for unlimited mobile TV use during a billing period (Mäki, 2005). Flat rates do not place additional barriers between the users and the content. In South Korea, early payment models greatly influenced the use of mobile TV. When mobile TV usage was billed in the amount of kilobytes received, each 1-minute part of a programme made especially for mobile TV had to be confirmed for delivery, which resulted in a discontinuous viewing experience (Knoche, 2005).

## Distribution Interactivity and Content Navigation

Taylor and Harper (2002) argued that channel surfing is inherently associated with the act of watching TV. The methods to select a programme used in traditional TV viewing depend on the time of day. But the method used generally escalates—if nothing of interest is found—to strategies that require more effort on behalf of the user. The order of strategies is:

1. Channel surfing
2. Wait or search for a TV programme announcement
3. Knowledge of weekly schedules or upcoming programmes
4. Paper-based or on-screen guides

Since mobile TV usage spurts are rather short, waiting for and searching for announcements or upcoming programmes might not be feasible. Information on what is currently playing and what will come up next might be valuable and should be easy to access.

Ideally, dedicated buttons or soft keys will allow users to switch channels. Long waiting times after a requested channel switch will result in lower user satisfaction. Tolerable switching delays between mobile TV channels have not been thoroughly researched but should be as short as possible since users are accustomed to almost instantaneous switches on standard TV. First results for digital TV indicate that 0.43 seconds might be the limit beyond which users will be increasingly dissatisfied (Ahmed, Kooij, & Brunnström, 2006). In digital TV, the switching delays depend to a large part on the video codec, for example, in Motion Picture Experts Group (MPEG)-encoded content on the occurrence of so-called key frames. Fewer key frames in a video broadcast result in smaller amounts of bandwidth required to transmit the content, but the receiver has to wait for the arrival of the next key frame in order to be able to display a newly selected channel. Service providers could exploit the fact that the human visual system is inert. An average recovery time of 780 msec between scene changes was acceptable to even the most critical observers, when visual detail was reduced to a fraction of the regular stream (Seyler & Budrikis, 1964). Further research would be needed to see if this period applies equally to channel switching on mobile devices and how which codecs could make use of this period. Displaying the logo of the upcoming channel or other tricks might perceptually shorten the wait time for users. Long wait times, for example, for downloading or on-demand streaming content should be accompanied with progress bars to help users assess the remaining time (Serco, 2006).

Because of the strong brand recognition of current TV broadcasters (e.g., CNN, BBC), it is likely that channel-centric content organisation under those brand names will prevail in mobile TV. But they could be replaced by virtual channels (Chorianopoulos, 2004) or category-centric content organisation which would group similar content from various sources under one category (e.g., news, music, movies, etc.). Because of the limited space and need for fast access, users will be interested in arranging content and channels according to their preferences. An electronic programme guide (EPG) which shows what programmes are currently available for viewing and what will come up might become a more important content navigation tool in mobile TV than in digital TV settings as reported in Eronen and Vuorimaa (2000).

Different video skipping approaches (Drucker, Glatzer, De Mar, & Wong, 2004), skimming video (Chistel, Smith, Taylor, & Winkler, 2004), and overall gist determination and information seeking (Tse, Vegh, Marchionini, & Shneiderman, 1999) have been studied in digital and standard TV settings but not in the mobile domain. When selecting from a range of programmes represented by video clips playing in parallel on mosaic pages of a digital TV study found that viewers preferred interfaces that gave fewer choices and bigger pictures (Kunert & Krömker, 2006). This would have to be traded off with the necessary navigation required between pages or scrolling in order to display all possible channels of a big bouquet. Mobile TV services, which provide a mixture of live, pre-cached, and downloadable content need to communicate these differences through the user interface.

## Information Interactivity

Accessing additional information on mobile TV programmes is a challenge to design because of the limited screen estate. While watching regular TV some people are already making use of their mobile phones by sending short message service (SMS) messages to friends to comment on what they are watching on TV. This kind of distributed co-viewing experience would be feasible on mobile TVs with large enough screens to show both the content and the textual conversation.

## Digital Rights Management (DRM)

People have a strong sense of ownership about the content that resides on their mobile devices. Many expect to be able to capture and transfer the content to and from computers for back-up purposes or for sharing with friends (Knoche & McCarthy, 2004). Restrictive DRM approaches that run against perceived user needs will affect the experience of mobile TV.

## CONTENT

The content distributed to mobile devices ranges from interactive content, specifically created for the mobile, to material that is produced for standard TV or cinema consumption. A number of studies have identified news as the most interesting content for mobile consumption(Knoche & McCarthy, 2004; Mäki, 2005). Considering the fact that many users watch mobile TV at home there is not much reason why programmes on regular TV would not be popular on mobile devices unless they prove impractical to watch on small screens. Whereas, news is of interest throughout the day, participants want to watch sports; series and general entertainment; music; and films on specific occasions (Mäki, 2005). Many people expect that their standard TV channels will be available on mobile TV (Serco, 2006). Time will tell whether relaying standard TV channels will be good enough for a mobile audience that is constrained when to watch, has short viewing periods, and small display sizes.

## Made for Mobile Content

Currently, content made especially for mobile use is expensive as the audience compared to broadcast television is relatively small. However, content producers adapt their content with respect to low resolutions and the typical use time, for example, short versions of the popular TV series 24. In sports coverage for mobile devices ESPN minimises the use of long shots in their coverage (Gwinn & Hughlett, 2005) and instead uses more highlights with close-up shots. Others produce soap operas for mobile devices that rely heavily on close-up shots with little dialogue ("Romantic drama in China soap opera," 2005). However, the gain of these changes is not fully researched or understood. Research has shown that differences in the perceived quality of shot types depend on the displayed content (Knoche, McCarthy, & Sasse, 2006). Further research is required to evaluate the potential benefits of cropping for mobile TV resolutions.

## Recoded Content

Relatively cheap in comparison to the made-for-mobile content is the pre-encoding of cinema or TV content both in length and in size. Automatic highlight extraction from TV content (Voldhaug, Johansen, & Perkis, 2005) is a promising technique that needs to be evaluated with end users on mobile devices.

Content-based pre-encoding can improve on the visual information and detail by: (1) cropping off the surrounding area of the footage that is outside the final safe area for action and titles and does not include essential information (Thompson, 1998); (2) zooming in on the area that displays the most important aspects (Dal Lago, 2006; Holmstrom, 2003); and (3) visually enhancing content, for example, by sharpening the colour of the ball in football content (Nemethova, Zahumensky, & Rupp, 2004). Research is required to rule out possible negative side effects caused by these automated approaches.

## FUTURE TRENDS

Video encoders will further reduce the amount of encoding bitrates required and will result in better perceived quality. Memory will continue to drop in price and make full PVR functionality with ample amounts of storage capacity available on mobile TV devices. Designing a mobile TV service on the edges of the coverage area might be another challenge. When viewers move in and out of the coverage area or the kind of delivery service that is provided the application will have to feature a way to gracefully switch between these different service concepts, for example, DVB-H live streams and pre-cached content in SDMB. Intelligent cropping algorithms that enlarge parts of the content might become a solution if the content depicted on mobile TV screens is too small for the viewer. Mobile phones with video camera capabilities might make for a very different mobile TV experience if peers or groups of people start providing each other with video clips on the go.

## CONCLUSION

Mobile TV is a very promising service for both customers and service providers. In order to provide the former with a satisfying QoE during potentially short interaction periods, the service provider will have to take into consideration a range of aspects in the creation, preparation, delivery, and consumption of content on a variety of mobile platforms. It will require cooperation between all involved parties to make mobile TV as appealing as the standard TV that constitutes a necessity in many households. This chapter has presented the key factors that determine QoE for mobile TV along with previous research results which can help improve the uptake of mobile TV 2.0 in a mobile and diversified market place.

## REFERENCES

Ahmed, K., Kooij, R., & Brunnström, K. (2006). Perceived quality of channel zapping. In *ITU-T Workshop on QoE/QoS 2006.*

Aldrich, S. E., Marks, R. T., Lewis, J. M., & Seybold, P. B. (2000). *What kind of the total customer experience does your e-business deliver?* Patricia Seybold Group.

Ankrum, D. R. (1996). Viewing distance at computer workstations. *Work Place Ergonomics,* 10-12.

Apteker, R. T., Fisher, A. A., Kisimov, V. S., & Neishlos, H. (1994). Distributed multimedia: User perception and dynamic QoS. In *Proceedings of SPIE* (pp. 226-234).

Barber, P. J., & Laws, J. V. (1994). Image quality and video communication. In R. Damper, W. Hall, & J. Richards (Eds.), *Proceedings of IEEE International Symposium on Multimedia Technologies & their Future Applications* (pp. 163-178). London, UK: Pentech Press.

Beerends, J. G., & De Caluwe, F. E. (1999). The influence of video quality on perceived audio quality and vice versa. *Journal of the Audio Engineering Society, 47,* 355-362.

Biberman, L. M. (1973). *Perception of displayed information.* Plenum Press.

Chistel, M., Smith, M., Taylor, C., & Winkler, D. (2004). Evolving video skims into useful multimedia abstractions. In *Proceedings of CHI '98* ACM Press.

Chorianopoulos, K. (2004). *Virtual television channels conceptual model, user interface design and affective usability evaluation.* Unpublished doctoral thesis, Greece: Athens University of Economics and Business.

Dal Lago, G. (2006). *Microdisplay emotions.* Retrieved from http://www.srlabs.it/articoli_uk/ics.htm

De Vries, E. (2006). *Renowned Philips picture enhancement techniques will enable mobile devices to display high-quality TV images.* Retrieved from http://www.research.philips.com/technologies/display/picenhance/index.html

Drucker, P., Glatzer, A., De Mar, S., & Wong, C. (2004). SmartSkip: Consumer level browsing and skipping of digital video content. In *Proceedings of the SIGCHI conference on Human factors in computing systems: Changing our world, changing ourselves* (pp. 219-226). New York: ACM Press.

Eronen, L., & Vuorimaa, P. (2000). User interfaces for digital television: A navigator case study. In *Proceedings of the Working Conference on Advanced Visual Interfaces AVI 2000* (pp. 276-279). New York: ACM Press.

Gauntlett, D., & Hill, A. (1999). *TV living: Television, culture and everyday life.* Routledge.

Gwinn, E., & Hughlett, M. (2005, October 10). Mobile TV for your cell phone. *Chicago Tribune.* Retrieved from http://home.hamptonroads.com/stories/story.cfm?story=93423&ran=38197

Hands, D. S. (2004). A basic multimedia quality model. *IEEE Transactions on Multimedia, 6,* 806-816.

Hellström, G. (1997). Quality measurement on video communication for sign language. In *Proceedings of 16th International Symposium on Human Factor inTelecommunications* (pp. 217-224).

Holmstrom, D. (2003). *Content based pre-encoding video filter for mobile TV.* Unpublished thesis, Umea University, Sweden. Retrieved from http://exjob.interaktion.nu/files/id_examensarbete_5.pdf

Horn, D. B. (2002). The effects of spatial and temporal video distortion on lie detection performance. In *Proceedings of CHI'02.*

IBM. (2002). *Functions of mobile multimedia QOS control.* Retrieved from http://www.trl.ibm.com/projects/mmqos/system_e.htm

Jain, R. (2004). Quality of experience. *IEEE Multimedia, 11,* 95-96.

Jumisko-Pyykkö, S., & Häkkinen, J. (2006). "I would like see the face and at least hear the voice": Effects of screen size and audio-video bitrate ratio on perception of quality in mobile television. In G. Doukidis, K. Chorianopoulos, & G. Lekakos (Eds.), *Proceedings of EuroITV '06* (pp. 339-348). Athens: University of Economics and Business.

Jumisko-Pyykkö, S., Vinod Kumar, M. V., Liinasuo, M., & Hannuksela, M. (2006). Acceptance of audiovisual quality in erroneous television sequences over a DVB-H channel. In *Proceedings of the Second International Workshop in Video Processing and Quality Metrics for Consumer Electronics.*

Kies, J. K., Williges, R. C., & Rosson, M. B. (1996). *Controlled laboratory experimentation and field study evaluation of video conference for distance learning applications* (Rep. No. HCIL 96-02). Blacksburg: Virginia Tech.

Knoche, H. (2005). *FirstYear report.* Unpublished thesis, University College London.

Knoche, H., De Meer, H., & Kirsh, D. (2005). Compensating for low frame rates. In *CHI'05 extended abstracts on Human factors in computing systems* (pp. 1553-1556).

Knoche, H., & McCarthy, J. (2004). Mobile users' needs and expectations of future multimedia services. In *Proceedings of the WWRF12.*

Knoche, H., McCarthy, J., & Sasse, M. A. (2005). Can small be beautiful? Assessing image resolution requirements for Mobile TV. In *ACM Multimedia* ACM.

Knoche, H., McCarthy, J., & Sasse, M. A. (2006). A close-up on mobile TV: The effect of low resolutions on shot types. In G. Doukidis, K. Chorianopoulos, & G. Lekakos (Eds.), *Proceedings of EuroITV '06* (pp. 359-367). Greece: Athens University of Economics and Business.

Knoche, H., & Sasse, M. A. (2006). Breaking the news on mobile TV: User requirements of a popular mobile content. In *Proceedings of IS&T/SPIE Symposium on Electronic Imaging.*

KPMG. (2006). Consumers and convergence challenges and opportunities in meeting next generation customer needs.

Kunert, T., & Krömker, H. (2006). Proven interaction design solutions for accessing and viewing interactive TV content items. In G. Doukidis, K. Chorianopoulos, & G. Lekakos (Eds.), *Proceedings of EuroITV 2006* (pp. 242-250). Greece: Athens University of Economics and Business.

Lemay-Yates Associates Inc. (2005). *Mobile TV technology discussion.* Lemay-Yates Associates Inc.

Lombard, M., Grabe, M. E., Reich, R. D., Campanella, C., & Ditton, T. B. (1996). Screen size and viewer responses to television: A review of research. In *Annual Conference of the Association for Education in Journalism and Mass Communication.*

Luther, A. C. (1996). *Principles of digital audio and video.* Boston, London: Artech House Publishers.

Mäki, J. (2005). *Finnish mobile TV pilot.* Research International Finland.

McCarthy, J., Sasse, M. A., & Miras, D. (2004). Sharp or smooth? Comparing the effects of quantization vs. frame rate for streamed video. In *Proceedings of CHI* (pp. 535-542).

McCarthy, J., & Wright, P. (2004). *Technology as experience.* Cambridge, MA: MIT Press.

Nemethova, O., Zahumensky, M., & Rupp, M. (2004). Preprocessing of ball game video-sequences for robust transmission over mobile networks. In *Proceedings of the CIC 2004 The 9th CDMA International Conference.*

Neumann, W. R., Crigler, A. N., & Bove, V. M. (1991). Television sound and viewer perceptions. In *Proceedings of the Joint IEEE/Audio Eng. Soc. Meetings* (pp. 101-104).

Owens, D. A., & Wolfe-Kelly, K. (1987). Near work, visual fatigue, and variations of oculomotor tonus. *Investigative Ophthalmology and Visual Science, 28,* 743-749.

Pappas, T., & Hinds, R. (1995). On video and audio integration for conferencing. In *Proceedings of SPIE—The International Society for Optical Engineering.*

Reeves, B., Lang, A., Kim, E., & Tartar, D. (1999). The effects of screen size and message content on attention and arousal. *Media Psychology, 1,* 49-68.

Reeves, B., & Nass, C. (1998). *The media equation: How people treat computers, television, and new media like real people and places.* University of Chicago Press.

Romantic drama in China soap opera only for mobile phones. (2005, June 28). *Guardian Newspapers Limited.* Retrieved from http://www.buzzle.com/editorials/6-28-2005-72274.asp

Rubin, A. M. (1981). An examination of television viewing motivations. *Communication Research, 9,* 141-165.

Selier, C., & Chuberre, N. (2005). Satellite digital multimedia broadcasting (SDMB) system presentation. In *Proceedings of 14th IST Mobile & Wireless Communications Summit.*

Serco. (2006). *Usability guidelines for Mobile TV design.* Retrieved from http://www.serco.com/Images/Mobile%20TV%20guidelines_tcm3-13804.pdf

Seyler, A. J., & Budrikis, Z. L. (1964). Detail perception after scene changes in television image presentations. *IEEE Transactions on Information Theory, 11,* 31-42.

Sling Media. (2006). *SlingPlayer mobile.* Retrieved from http://www.slingmedia.com

Södergård, C. (2003). *Mobile television—Technology and user experiences. Report on the Mobile-TV project* (Rep. No. P506). VTT Information Technology.

Song, S., Won, Y., & Song, I. (2004). Empirical study of user perception behavior for mobile streaming. In *Proceedings of the tenth ACM international conference on Multimedia* (pp. 327-330). New York: ACM Press.

Steinmetz, R. (1996). Human perception of jitter and media synchronization. *IEEE Journal on Selected Areas in Communications, 14,* 61-72.

Stockbridge, L. (2006). Mobile TV: Experience of the UK Vodafone and Sky service. Retrieved from http://www.serco.com/Images/EuroITV%20mobile%20TV%20presentation_tcm3-13849.pdf

Taylor, A., & Harper, R. (2002). Switching on to switch off: An analysis of routine TV watching habits and their implications for electronic programme guide design. *usableiTV, 1,* 7-13.

Thompson, R. (1998). *Grammar of the shot.* Elsevier Focal Press.

Tse, T., Vegh, S., Marchionini, G., & Shneiderman, B. (1999). An exploratory study of video browsing user interface designs and research methodologies: Effectiveness in information seeking tasks. In *Proceedings of the 62nd ASIS Annual Meeting* (pp. 681-692).

Vatakis, A., & Spence, C. (in press). Evaluating the influence of frame rate on the temporal aspects of audiovisual speech perception. *Neuroscience Letters.*

Voldhaug, J. E., Johansen, S., & Perkis, A. (2005). Automatic football video highlights extraction. In *Proceedings of NORSIG-05.*

Wang, D., Speranza, F., Vincent, A., Martin, T., & Blanchfield, P. (2003). Towards optimal rate control: A study of the impact of spatial resolution, frame rate and quantization on subjective quality and bitrate. In T. Ebrahimi & T. Sikora (Eds.), *Visual communications and image processing* (pp. 198-209).

Westerink, J. H., & Roufs, J. A. (1989). Subjective image quality as a function of viewing distance, resolution, and picture size. *SMPTE Journal.*

Winkler, S., & Faller, C. (2005). Maximizing audiovisual quality at low bitrates. In *Proceedings of Workshop on Video Processing and Quality Metrics.*

Zillman, D. (1988). Mood management: Using entertainment to full advantage. In L. Donohew, H. E. Sypher, & E. T. Higgins (Eds.), *Communication, social cognition, and affect* (pp. 147-172). Hillsdale, NJ: Erlbaum.

# Chapter IV
# Semantic Multimedia Information Analysis for Retrieval Applications

**João Magalhães**
*Imperial College London, UK*

**Stefan Rüger**
*Imperial College London, UK*

## ABSTRACT

*Most of the research in multimedia retrieval applications has focused on retrieval by content or retrieval by example. Since the classical review by Smeulders, Worring, Santini, Gupta, and Jain (2000), a new interest has grown immensely in the multimedia information retrieval community: retrieval by semantics. This exciting new research area arises as a combination of multimedia understanding, information extraction, information retrieval, and digital libraries. This chapter presents a comprehensive review of analysis algorithms in order to extract semantic information from multimedia content. We discuss statistical approaches to analyze images and video content and conclude with a discussion regarding the described methods.*

## INTRODUCTION: MULTIMEDIA ANALYSIS

The growing interest in managing multimedia collections effectively and efficiently has created new research interest that arises as a combination of multimedia understanding, information extraction, information retrieval, and digital libraries. This growing interest has resulted in the creation of a video retrieval track in TREC conference series in parallel with the text retrieval track (TRECVID, 2004).

*Figure 1. A typical multimedia information retrieval application*

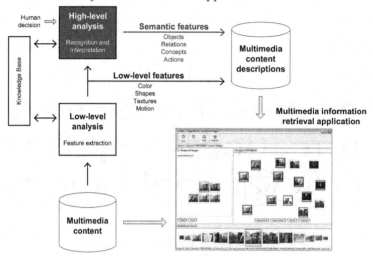

Figure 1 illustrates a simplified multimedia information retrieval application composed by a multimedia database, analysis algorithms, a description database, and a user interface application. Analysis algorithms extract features from multimedia content and store them as descriptions of that content. A user then deploys these indexing descriptions in order to search the multimedia database. A semantic multimedia information retrieval application (Figure 1) differs eminently from traditional retrieval applications on the low-level analysis algorithms; its algorithms are responsible for extracting semantic information used to index multimedia content by its semantic. Multimedia content can be indexed in many ways, and each index can refer to different modalities and/or parts of the multimedia piece. Multimedia content is composed of the visual track, sound track, speech track, and text. All these modalities are arranged temporally to provide a meaningful way to transmit information and/or entertainment. The way video documents are temporally structured can be distinguished in two levels: semantic and syntactic structure (Figure 2).

At the syntactic level, the video is segmented into shots (visual or audio) that form a uniform segment (e.g., visually similar frames); representative key-frames are extracted from each shot, and scenes group

*Figure 2. Syntactic and semantic structure of video*

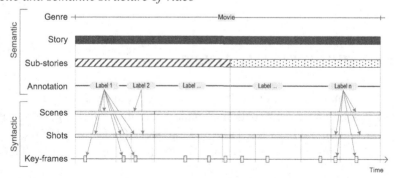

neighboring similar shots into a single segment. The segmentation of video into its syntactic structure of video has been studied widely (Brunelli, Mich, & Modena, 1999; Wang, Liu, & Huang, 2000).

At the semantic level, annotations of the key-frames and shots with a set of labels indicate the presence of semantic entities, their relations, and attributes (agent, object, event, concept, state, place, and time (see Benitez et al., 2002, for details). Further analysis allows the discovery of logical sub-units (e.g., substory or subnarrative), logical units (e.g., a movie), and genres. A recent review of multimedia semantic indexing has been published by Snoek and Worring (2005).

The scope of this chapter is the family of semantic-multimedia analysis algorithms that automate the multimedia semantic annotation process. In the following sections, we will review papers on multimedia-semantic analysis: semantic annotation of key-frame images, shots, and scenes. The semantic analysis at the shot and scene level considers independently the audio and visual modalities and then the multi-modal semantic analysis. Due to the scope of this book, we will give more emphasis to the visual part than to the audio part of the multimedia analysis and will not cover the temporal analysis of logical substories, stories, and genres.

## KEY-FRAME SEMANTIC ANNOTATION

Image analysis and understanding is one of the oldest fields in pattern recognition and artificial intelligence. A lot of research has been done since (Marr, 1983), culminating in the modern reference texts by Forsyth and Ponce (2003) and Hartley and Zisserman (2004). In the following sections we discuss different types of visual information analysis algorithms: single class models fit a simple probability density distribution to each label; translation models define a visual vocabulary and a method to translate from this vocabulary to keywords; hierarchical and network models explore the interdependence of image elements (regions or tiles) and model its structure; knowledge-based models improve the model's accuracy by including other sources of knowledge besides the training data (e.g., a linguistic database such as WordNet).

### Single Class Models

A direct approach to the semantic analysis of multimedia is to learn a class-conditional probability distribution $p(w \mid x)$ of each single keyword $w$ of the semantic vocabulary, given its training data $x$ (see Figure 3). This distribution can be obtained by using Bayes' law:

$$p(w \mid x) = \frac{p(x \mid w)p(w)}{p(x)}.$$

The data probability $p(x)$ and the keyword probability $p(w)$ can be computed straightforward, and the $p(x \mid w)$ can be computed with very different data density distribution models.

Several techniques to model the $p(x \mid w)$ with a simple density distribution have been proposed: Yavlinsky, Schofield, and Rüger (2005) used a nonparametric distribution, Carneiro and Vasconcelos (2005) a semi-parametric density estimation, Westerveld and de Vries (2003) a finite mixture of Gaussians, and Mori, Takahashi, and Oka (1999), Vailaya, Figueiredo, Jain, and Zhang (1999), and Vailaya, Figueiredo, Jain, and Zhang (2001) different flavors of vector quantization techniques.

*Figure 3. Inference of single class models*

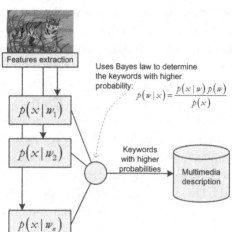

Yavlinsky et al. (2005) modeled the probability density of images, given keywords as a nonparametric density smoothed by two kernels: a Gaussian kernel and an Earth Mover's Distance kernel. They used both global and 3 × 3 tile color and texture features. The best reported mean average precision (MAP) results with tiles achieved 28.6% MAP with the dataset of Duygulu, Barnard, de Freitas, and Forsyth (2002) and 9.2% with a Getty Images dataset.

Yavlinsky et al. (2005) showed that a simple nonparametric statistical distribution can perform as well or better than many more sophisticated techniques (e.g., translation models). However, the non-parametric density nature of their framework makes the task of running the model on new data very complex. The model is the entire dataset meaning that the demands on CPU and memory increase with the training data.

Westerveld and de Vries (2003) used a finite-mixture density distribution with a fixed number of components to model a subset of the DCT coefficients:

$$p\left(x\mid\theta\right)=\sum_{m=1}^{k}\alpha_{m}\,p\left(x\mid\mu_{m},\sigma_{m}^{2}\right),$$

in which $k$ is the number of components, $\theta$ represents the complete set of model parameters with mean $\mu_{m}$, covariance $\sigma_{m}^{2}$, and component prior $\alpha_{m}$. The component priors have the constraints $\alpha_{1},...,\alpha_{k}\geq 0$ and $\sum_{m=1}^{k}\alpha_{m}=1$. Westerveld (2003) tested several scenarios to evaluate the effect (a) of the number of mixture components, (b) of using different numbers of DCT coefficients (luminance and chrominance), and (c) of adding the coordinates of the DCT coefficients to the feature vectors. The two first factors produced varying results, and optimal points were found experimentally. The third tested aspect, the presence of the coefficients position information, did not modify the results.

Marrying the two previous approaches, Carneiro and Vasconcelos (2005) deployed a hierarchy of semi-parametric mixtures to model $p(x\mid w)$ using a subset of the DCT coefficients as low-level features. Vasconcelos and Lippman (2000) had already examined the same framework in a content-based retrieval system.

The hierarchy of mixtures proposed by Vasconcelos and Lippman (1998) can model data at different levels of granularity with a finite mixture of Gaussians. At each hierarchical level *l*, the number of each mixture component $k^l$ differs by one from adjacent levels. The hierarchy of mixtures is expressed as:

$$p\left(x\mid w_i\right)=\frac{1}{D}\sum_{m=1}^{k^l}\alpha_{i,m}^l\,p\left(x\mid\theta_{i,m}^l\right).$$

The level *l=1* corresponds to the coarsest characterization. The more detailed hierarchy level consists of a nonparametric distribution with a kernel placed on top of each sample. The only restriction on the model is that if node *m* of level *l+1* is a child of node *n* of level *l*, then they are both children of node *p* of level *l-1*. The EM algorithm computes the mixture parameters at level *l*, given the knowledge of the parameters at level *l+1*, forcing the previous restriction.

Carneiro and Vasconcelos (2005) report the best published retrieval MAP of 31% with the dataset of Duygulu et al. (2002). Even though we cannot dissociate this result from the pair of features and statistical model, the hierarchy of mixtures appears to be a very powerful density distribution technique.

Even though the approaches by Carneiro and Vasconcelos (2005) and Westerveld and de Vries (2003) are similar, the differences make it difficult to do a fair comparison. The DCT features are used in a different way, and the semi-parametric hierarchy of mixtures can model classes with very few training examples.

The relationship between finite-mixture density modeling and vector quantization is a well-studied subject (see Hastie, Tibshirani, & Friedman, 2001). One of the applications of vector quantization to image retrieval and annotation was realized by Mori et al. (1999). Given the training data of a keyword, they divide the images into tiles and apply vector quantization to the image tiles in order to extract the codebook used to estimate the $p(x \mid w)$ density distribution. Later, they use a model of word co-occurrence on the image tiles in order to label the image. The words with the higher sum of probabilities across the different tiles are the ones assigned to that image.

Vailaya et al. (1999) and Vailaya et al. (2001) describe a Bayesian framework using a codebook to estimate the density distribution of each keyword. They show that the Minimum Description Length criterion selects the optimal size of the codebook extracted from the vector quantizer. The features are extracted from the global image, and there is no image tiling. The use of the MDL criterion makes this framework quite elegant and defines a statistical criterion to select every model parameter and without any user-defined parameters.

## Translation Models

All of the previous approaches employ a direct model to estimate $p(x \mid w)$ with image global features and/or image tiles features. In contrast to this, the vector quantization (usually *k*-means) approach generates a codebook of image regions or image tiles (depending on the segmentation solution). The problem then is formulated as a translation problem between two representations of the same entity: English-Esperanto, word-blob codebook, or word-tile codebook.

Inspired by machine translation research, Duygulu et al. (2002) developed a method of annotating image regions with words. First, regions are created using a segmentation algorithm like normalized cuts (Shi & Malik, 2000). For each region, features are computed, and then blobs are generated by clustering the regional image features across an image collection. The problem then is formulated as learning the correspondence between the discrete vocabulary of blobs and the image keywords. The model consists of a mixture of correspondences for each word of each image in the collection:

*Figure 4. Translation models*

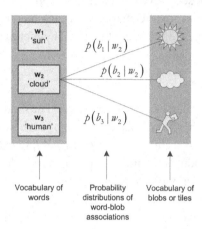

in which $p(a_{nj} = i)$ expresses the probability of associating word $j$ to blob $i$ in image $n$, and $p(w = w_{nj} \mid b = b_i)$ is the probability of obtaining an instance of word $w$ given an instance of blob $b$. These two probability distributions are estimated with the EM algorithm. The authors refined the lexicon by clustering indistinguishable words and ignoring the words with probabilities $p(w \mid b)$ below a given threshold.

The machine translation approach, the thorough experiments, and the dataset form strong points of this chapter (Duygulu et al., 2002). This dataset is nowadays a reference, and thorough experiments showed that (a) their method could predict numerous words with high accuracy, (b) increasing the probability threshold improved precision but reduced recall, and (c) the word clustering improved recall and precision.

Following a translation model, Jeon, Lavrenko, and Manmatha (2003), Lavrenko, Manmatha, and Jeon (2003), and Feng, Lavrenko, and Manmatha (2004) studied a model in which blob features $b_I^{(r)}$ of an image $I$ are assumed to be conditionally independent of keywords $w_i$, that is:

$$p(w_i, b_I) = \sum_{J \in D} P(J) P(w_i \mid J) P(b_I \mid J) = \sum_{J \in D} P(J) P(w_i \mid J) \prod_{r \in I} P\left(b_I^{(r)} \mid J\right).$$

Note that $b_I^{(r)}$ and $w_i$ are conditionally independent, given the image collection $D$ and that $J \in D$ act as the hidden variables that generated the two distinct representations of the same process (words and features).

Jeon et al. (2003) recast the image annotation as a cross-lingual information retrieval problem, applying a cross-media relevance model based on a discrete codebook of regions. Lavrenko et al. (2003) continued their previous work (Jeon et al., 2003) and used continuous probability density functions $p(b_I^{(r)} \mid J)$ to describe the process of generating blob features and to avoid the loss of information related to the generation of the codebook. Extending their previous work, Feng et al. (2004) replaced blobs with tiles and modeled image keywords with a Bernoulli distribution. This last work reports their best results, a MAP of 30%, with a Corel dataset (Duygulu et al., 2002).

Latent semantic analysis is another technique of text analysis and indexing; it looks at patterns of word distributions (specifically, word co-occurrence) across a set of documents (Deerwester, Dumais,

Furmas, Landauer, & Harshman, 1990). A matrix $M$ of word occurrences in documents is filled with each word frequency in each document. The singular value decomposition (SVD) of matrix $M$ gives the transformation to a singular space in which projected documents can be compared efficiently.

## Hierarchical Models

The aforementioned approaches assumed a minimal relation among the various elements of an image (blobs or tiles). This section and the following section will review methods that consider a hierarchical relation or an interdependence relation among the elements of an image (words and blobs or tiles).

Barnard and Forsyth (2001) studied a generative hierarchical aspect model, which was inspired by Hofmann and Puzicha's (1998) hierarchical clustering/aspect model. The data are assumed to be generated by a fixed hierarchy of nodes in which the leaves of the hierarchy correspond to soft clusters. Mathematically, the process for generating the set of observations $O$ associated with an image $I$ can be described by:

$$p(O \mid I) = \sum_{c} \left( p(c) \prod_{o \in O} \left( \sum_{l} p(o \mid l, c) p(l \mid c, I) \right) \right), \quad O = \{w_1, ..., w_n, b_1, ..., b_m\},$$

in which $c$ indexes the clusters, $o$ indexes words and blobs, and $l$ indexes the levels of the hierarchy. The level and the cluster uniquely specify a node of the hierarchy. Hence, the probability of an observation $p(o \mid l, c)$ is conditionally independent given a node in the tree. In the case of words, $p(o \mid l, c)$ assumes a tabular form, and in the case of blobs, a single Gaussian models the regions' features. The model is estimated with the EM algorithm.

Blei and Jordan (2003) describe three hierarchical mixture models to annotate image data, culminating in the correspondence latent Dirichlet allocation model. It specifies the following joint distribution of regions, words, and latent variables ($\theta$, $z$, $y$):

$$p(r, w, \theta, z, y) = p(\theta \mid \alpha) \left( \prod_{n=1}^{N} p(z_n \mid \theta) p(r_n \mid z_n, \mu, \sigma) \right) \cdot \left( \prod_{m=1}^{M} p(y_m \mid N) p(w_m \mid y_m, z, \beta) \right).$$

This model assumes that a Dirichlet distribution $\theta$ (with $\alpha$ as its parameter) generates a mixture of latent factors: $z$ and $y$. Image regions $r_n$ are modeled with Gaussians with mean $\mu$ and covariance $\sigma$, in which words $w_n$ follow a multinomial distribution with a $\beta$ parameter.

This mixture of latent factors then is used to generate words ($y$ variable) and regions ($z$ variable). The EM algorithm estimates this model, and the inference of $p(w \mid r)$ is carried out by variational inference. The correspondence latent Dirichlet allocation model provides a clean probabilistic model for annotating images with multiple keywords. It combines the advantages of probabilistic clustering for dimensionality reduction with an explicit model of the conditional distribution from which image keywords are generated.

Li and Wang (2003) characterize the images with a hierarchical approach at multiple tiling granularities (i.e., each tile in each hierarchical level is subdivided into smaller sub-tiles). A color and texture feature vector represents each tile. The texture features represent the energy in high-frequency bands of wavelet transforms. They represent each keyword separately with two-dimensional, multi-resolution hidden Markov models. This method achieves a certain degree of scale invariance due to the hierarchical tiling process and the two-dimensional multiresolution hidden Markov model.

*Figure 5. Two types of random fields*

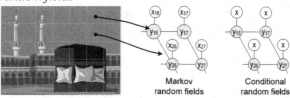

Markov random fields    Conditional random fields

## Network Models

In semantic-multimedia analysis, concepts are interdependent; for example, if a house is detected in a scene, then the probability of existing windows and doors in the scene are boosted, and vice-versa. In other words, when inferring the probability of a set of interdependent random variables, their probabilities are modified iteratively until an optimal point is reached (to avoid instability, the loops must exist over a large set of random variables [Pearl, 1988]). Most of the papers discussed next model keywords as a set of interdependent random variables connected in a probabilistic network.

Various graphical models have been implemented in computer vision to model the appearance, spatial relations, and co-occurrence of local parts. Markov random fields and hidden Markov models are the most common generative models that learn the joint probability of the observed data (X) and the corresponding labels (Y). These models divide the image into tiles or regions (other approaches use contour directions, but these are outside the scope of our discussion). A probabilistic network then models this low-level division in which each node corresponds to one of these tiles or regions and its label. The relation among nodes depends on the selected neighboring method. Markov random fields can be expressed as:

$$P(x,y) = \frac{1}{Z} \cdot \prod_i \left( \phi_i(x_i, y_i) \cdot \prod_{j \in N_i} \varphi_{i,j}(y_i, y_j) \right),$$

in which $i$ indexes the image's tiles, $j$ indexes the neighbors of the current $i$ tile, $\phi_i$ is the potential function of the current tile $x_i$, and its possible labels $y_i$, and $\varphi_{i,j}$ are the interaction functions between the current tile label and its neighbors. Figure 5 illustrates the Markov random field framework.

The Markov condition implies that a given node only depends on its neighboring nodes. This condition constitutes a drawback for these models, because only local relationships are incorporated into the model. This makes it highly unsuitable for capturing long-range relations or global characteristics.

In order to circumvent this limitation, Kumar and Herbert (2003a) propose a multi-scale random field (MSRF) as a prior model on the class labels on the image sites. This model implements a probabilistic network that can be approximated by a 2D hierarchical structure such as a 2D-tree. A multiscale feature vector captures the local dependencies in the data. The distribution of the multiscale feature vectors is modeled as a mixture of Gaussians. The features were selected specifically to detect human-made structures, which are the only types of objects that are detected.

Kumar and Herbert's (2003) second approach to this problem is based on discriminative random fields, an approach inspired on conditional random fields (CRF). CRFs, defined by Lafferty, McCallum, and Pereira (2001), are graphical models, initially for text information extraction, that are meant for visual information analysis in this approach. More generally, a CRF is a sequence-modeling framework based on the conditional probability of the entire sequence of labels (Y), given the all image (X). CRFs have the following mathematical form:

$$P(y|x) = \frac{1}{Z} \cdot \prod_i \left( \phi_i(y_i, x) \cdot \prod_{j \in N_i} \varphi_{i,j}(y_i, y_j; x) \right),$$

n which $i$ indexes the image's tiles, $j$ indexes the neighbors of the current $i$ tile, $\phi_i$ is the association potential between the current tile and the image label, and $\varphi_{i,j}$ is the interaction potential between the current tile and its neighbors (note that it is also dependent on the image label). Figure 5 illustrates the conditional random field framework. The authors showed that this last approach outperformed their initial proposal of a multiscale random field as well as the more traditional MRF solution in the task of detecting human-made structures.

He, Zemel, and Carreira-Perpiñán (2004) combine the use of a conditional random field and data at multiple scales. Their multiscale conditional random field (mCRF) is a product of individual models, each model providing labeling information from various aspects of the image: a classifier that looks at local image statistics; regional label features that look at local label patterns; and global label features that look at large, coarse label patterns. The mCRF is shown to detect several types of concepts (i.e., sky, water, snow, vegetation, ground, hippopotamus, and bear) with classification rates better than a traditional Markov random field.

Quattoni, Collins, and Darrell (2004) extend the CRF framework to incorporate hidden variables and combine class-conditional CRFs into a unified framework for part-based object recognition. The features are extracted from special regions that are obtained with the scale-invariant feature transform or SIFT (Lowe, 1999). The SIFT detector finds points in locations at scales in which there is a significant amount of variation. Once a point of interest is found, the region around it is extracted at the appropriate scale. The features from this region then are computed and plugged into the CRF framework. The advantage of this method is that it needs fewer regions by eliminating redundant regions and selecting the ones with more energy on high-frequency bands.

One should note that all these approaches require a ground truth at the level of the image's tiles/regions as is common in computer vision. This is not what is found traditionally in multimedia information retrieval datasets in which the ground truth exists rather at a global level.

## Knowledge-Based Models

The previous methods have only visual features as training data to create the statistical models in the form of a probabilistic network. Most of the time, these training data are limited, and the model's accuracy can be improved by other sources of knowledge. Prior knowledge can be added to a model either by a human expert who states the relations between concept variables (nodes in a probabilistic network) or by an external knowledge base in order to infer the concept relations (e.g., with a linguistic database such as WordNet) (Figure 6).

Tansley (2000) introduces a multimedia thesaurus in which media content is associated with appropriate concepts in a semantic layer composed by a network of concepts and their relations. The process of building the semantic layer uses Latent Semantic Indexing to connect images to their corresponding

*Figure 6. Knowledge-based models*

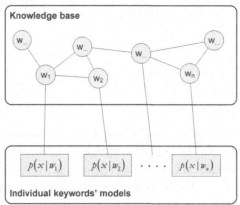

concepts, and a measure of each correspondence (image concept) is taken from this process. After that, unlabeled images (test images) are annotated by comparing them with the training images using a *k*-nearest-neighbor classifier. Since the concepts' interdependences are represented in the semantic layer, the concepts' probability computed by the classifier are modified by the others concepts.

Other authors have explored not only the statistical interdependence of context and objects but also have used other knowledge that is not present in multimedia data, which humans use to understand (or predict) new data. Srikanth, Varner, Bowden, and Moldovan (2005) incorporated linguistic knowledge from WordNet (Miller, 1995) in order to deduce a hierarchy of terms from the annotations. They generate a visual vocabulary based on the semantics of the annotation words and their hierarchical organization in the WordNet ontology.

Benitez and Chang (2002) and Benitez (2005) took this idea further and suggested a media ontology (MediaNet) to help to discover, summarize, and measure knowledge from annotated images in the form of image clusters, word senses, and relationships among them. MediaNet, a Bayesian network-based multimedia knowledge representation framework, is composed by a network of concepts, their relations, and media exemplifying concepts and relationships. The MediaNet integrates classifiers in order to discover statistical relationships among concepts. WordNet is used to process image annotations by stripping out unnecessary information. The summarization process implements a series of strategies to improve the images' description qualities, for example using WordNet and image clusters to disambiguate annotation terms (images in the same clusters tend to have similar textual descriptions). Benitez (2005) also proposes a set of measures to evaluate the knowledge consistency, completeness, and conciseness.

Tansley (2000) used a network at the concept level, and Benitez (2005) used the MediaNet network to capture the relations at both concept and feature levels. In addition, Benitez (2005) utilized WordNet, which captures human knowledge that is not entirely present in multimedia data.

## Summary

The described algorithms vary in many different aspects such as in their low-level features, segmentation methods, feature representation, modeling complexity, or required data. While some concepts require a lot of data to estimate its model (e.g., a car), others are very simple and require just a few examples (e.g., sky). So, we advocate that different approaches should be used for different concept complexities.

Single-class models assume that concepts are independent and that each concept has its own model. These are the simplest models that can be used and the ones with better accuracy (e.g., Yavlinsky et al., 2005).

Translation models, hierarchical models, and network models capture a certain degree of the concept's interdependence (co-occurrence) from the information present in the training data. The difference between the models is linked to the degree of interdependence that can be represented by the model. In practice, when interdependencies information is incorporated in the model, it also inserts noise in the form of false interdependencies, which causes a decrease in performance. So, the theoretical advantage of these models is in practice reduced by this effect.

All these models rely exclusively on visual low-level features in order to capture complex human concepts and to correctly predict new unlabeled data. Most of the time, the training data are limited, and the model's accuracy can be improved by other sources of knowledge. Srikanth et al. (2005) and Benitez (2005) are two of the few proposals that exploit prior knowledge that is external to the training data in order to capture the interdependent (co-occurrence) nature of concepts.

At this time, knowledge-based models seem to be the most promising semantic analysis algorithms for information retrieval. Text information retrieval already has shown great improvement over exclusively statistical models when external linguistic knowledge was used (Harabagiu et al., 2000). Multimedia retrieval will go through a similar progress but at a slower pace, because there is no multimedia ontology that offers the same knowledge base as WordNet offers to linguistic text processing.

## SHOT AND SCENE SEMANTIC ANNOTATION

Shot and scene semantic analysis introduces the time dimension to the problem at hand. The time dimension adds temporal frames, resulting in more information to help the analysis. To take advantage of the sequential nature of the data, the natural choices of algorithms are based on hierarchical models or network models. The section is organized by modality, and within each modality, we don't detail the algorithms by technique due to space constraints. This way, we shed some light on multimodality shot and scene semantic analysis and keep the chapter's emphasis on visual information analysis.

### Audio Analysis

Audio analysis becomes a very important part of the multimodal analysis task when processing TV news, movies, sport videos, and so forth. Various types of audio can populate the sound track of a multimedia document, the most common types being speech, music, and silence. Lu, Zhang, and Jiang (2002) propose methods to segment audio and to classify each segment as speech, music, silence, and environment sound. A $k$-nearest neighbor model is used at the frame level followed by vector quantization to discriminate between speech and nonspeech. A set of threshold-based rules is used in order to discriminate among silence, music, and environment sound. The authors also describe a speaker change detection algorithm based on Gaussian-mixture models (GMM); this algorithm continuously compares the model of the present speaker's speech with a model that is created dynamically from the current audio frame. After a speaker change has been detected, the new GMM replaces the current speaker's GMM.

In most TV programs and sport videos, sound events do not overlap, but in narratives (movies and soap operas), these events frequently occur simultaneously. To address this problem, Akutsu, Hamada, and Tonomura (1998) present an audio-based approach to video indexing by detecting speech and music independently, even when they occur simultaneously. Their framework is based on a set of heuristics over features histograms and corresponding thresholds. With a similar goal, Naphade and Huang (2000) define a generic statistical framework based on hidden Markov models (Rabiner, 1989) in order to classify audio segments into speech, silence, music, and miscellaneous and their co-occurrences. By creating an HMM for each class and every combination of classes, the authors achieved a generic framework that is capable of modeling various audio events with high accuracy.

Another important audio analysis task is the classification of the musical genre of a particular audio segment. This can capture the type of emotion that the director wants to communicate (e.g., stress, anxiety, happiness). Tzanetakis and Cook (2002) describe their work on categorizing music as rock, dance, pop, metal, classical, blues, country, hip-hop, reggae, or jazz (jazz and classical music had more subcategories). In addition to the traditional audio features, they also use special features to capture rhythmic characteristics and apply simple statistical models such as GMM and KNN to model each class' feature histogram. Interestingly, the best reported classification precision (61%) is in the same range as human performance for genre classification (70%).

All these approaches work as a single class model of individual classes/keywords. Note that the hidden Markov model is, in fact, a probabilistic network for modeling a single temporal event that corresponds to a given concept/keyword. So, even though it is a network model, it is used as a single class model.

## Visual Analysis

Many of the visual video analysis methods are based on heuristics that are deduced empirically. Statistical methods are more common when considering multimodal analysis. Most of the following papers explore the temporal evolution of features to semantically analyze video content (e.g., shot classification, logical units, etc.). Video visual analysis algorithms are of two types: (a) heuristics-based, in which a set of threshold rules decides the content class, and (b) statistical algorithms that are similar to the ones described in Section 2.

Heuristic methods rely on deterministic rules that were defined in some empirical way. These methods monitor histograms, and events are detected if the histogram triggers a given rule (usually a threshold). They are particularly adequate for sport videos because broadcast TV follows a set of video production rules that result in well-defined semantic structures that ease the analysis of the sports videos. Several papers have been published on sports video analysis, such as football, basketball and tennis, in order to detect semantic events and to semantically classify each shot (Li & Sezan, 2003; Luo & Huang, 2003; Tan, Saur, Kulkarni, & Ramadge, 2000).

Tan et al. (2000) introduced a model for estimating camera movements (pan, tilt, and zoom) from the motion vectors of compressed video. The authors further showed how camera motion histograms could be used to discriminate various basketball shots. Prior to this, the video is segmented into shots based on the evolution of the intensity histogram across different frames. Shots are detected if the histogram exceeds a predefined threshold; then, they are discriminated based on (a) the accumulated histogram of camera motion direction (fast breaks and full-court advances), (b) the slope of this histogram (fast breaks or full-court advances), (c) sequence of camera movements (shots at the basket), and (d) persistence of camera motion (close-ups).

Other heuristic methods deploy color histograms, shot duration, and shot sequences to automatically analyze various types of sports such as football (Ekin, Tekalp, & Mehrotra, 2003) and American football (Li & Sezan, 2003).

The statistical approaches reviewed previously can be applied to the visual analysis of video content with the advantage that shapes obtained by segmentation are more accurate due to the time dimension. Also, analyzing several key-frames of the same shot and then combining the results facilitate the identification of semantic entities in a given shot.

Luo and Hwang's (2003) statistical framework tracks objects within a given shot with a dynamic Bayesian network and classifies that shot from a coarse-grain to a fine-grain level. At the course-grain level, a key-frame is extracted from a shot every 0.5 seconds. From these key-frames, motion and global features are extracted, and their temporal evolution is modeled with a hierarchical hidden Markov model (HHMM). Individual HHMMs (a single-class model approach) capture a given semantic shot category. At the fine-grain level analysis, Luo and Hwang (2003) employ object recognition and tracking techniques. After the coarse-grain level analysis, segmentation is performed on the shots to extract visual objects. Then, invariant points are detected in each shape to track the object movement. These points are fed to a dynamic Bayesian network to model detailed events occurring within the shot (e.g., human body movements in a golf game).

Souvannavong, Merialdo, and Huet (2003) used latent semantic analysis to analyze video content. Recall that latent semantic analysis algorithm builds a matrix $M$ of word occurrences in documents, and then the SVD of this matrix is computed to obtain a singular space. The problem with multimedia content is that there is no text corpus (a vocabulary). A vector quantization technique ($k$-means) returns a codebook of blobs, the vocabulary of blobs from the shots' key-frames. In the singular feature space, a $k$-nearest-neighbor ($k=20$) and a Gaussian mixture model technique are used to classify new videos. The comparison of the two techniques shows that GMM performs better when there is enough data to correctly estimate the 10 components. The $k$-nn algorithm has the disadvantages of every nonparametric method—the model is the training data, and for the TRECVID dataset (75,000 key-frames), training can take considerable time.

## Multimodal Analysis

In the previous analysis, the audio and visual modalities were considered independently in order to detect semantic entities. These semantic entities are represented in various modalities, capturing different aspects of that same reality. Those modalities contain co-occurring patterns that are synchronized in a given way because they represent the same reality. Thus, synchronization and the strategy to combine the multimodal patterns is the key issue in multimodal analysis. The approaches described in this section explore the multimodality statistics of semantic entities (e.g., pattern synchronization).

Sports video analysis can be greatly improved with multimodal features; for example, the level of excitement expressed by the crowd noise can be a strong indicator of certain events (foul, goal, goal miss, etc). Leonardi, Migliotari, and Prandini (2004) take this into account when designing a multimodal algorithm to detect goals in football videos. A set of visual features from each shot is fed to a Markov chain in order to evaluate their temporal evolution from one shot to the next. The Markov chain has two states that correspond to the goal state and to the nongoal state. The visual analysis returns the positive pair shots, and the shot audio loudness is the criterion to rank the pair shots. Thus, the two modalities never are combined but are used sequentially. Results show that audio and visual modalities together improve the average precision when compared only to the audio case (Leonardi et al., 2004).

In TV news videos, text is the fundamental modality with the most important information. Westerveld, et al. (2003) build on their previous work described previously to analyze the visual part and to add text provided by an Automatic Speech Recognition (ASR) system. The authors further propose a visual dynamic model to capture the visual temporal characteristics. This model is based on the Gaussian mixture model estimated from the DCT blocks of the frames around each key-frame in the range of 0.5 seconds. In this way, the most significant moving regions are represented by this model with an evident applicability to object tracking. The text retrieval model evaluates a given $Shot_i$ for the queried keywords $Q = q_1, q_2, q_3, ...$:

$$RSV\left(Shot_i\right) = \frac{1}{|Q|} \sum_{k=1}^{|Q|} \log\left(\lambda_{Shot} p\left(q_k \mid Shot_i\right) + {}_{Scene} p\left(q_k \mid Scene_i\right) + \lambda_{Coll} p\left(q_k\right)\right).$$

This measure evaluates the probability that one or more queried keywords appear in the evaluated shot, $p(q_k \mid Shot)$, or in the scene, $p(q_k \mid Scene)$, under the prior $p(q_k)$. The $\lambda$ variables correspond to the probabilities of corresponding weights. This function, inspired by language models, creates the scene-shot structure of video content. The visual model and the text model are combined under the assumption that they are independent; thus, the probabilities are simply multiplied. The results with both modalities are reported to be better than using just one.

Naphade and Huang (2001) characterize single-modal concepts (e.g., indoor/outdoor, forest, sky, water) and multimodal concepts (e.g., explosions, rocket launches) with Bayesian networks. The visual part is segmented into shots (Naphade et al., 1998), and from each key-frame, a set of low-level features is extracted (color, texture, blobs, and motion). These features then are used to estimate a Gaussian mixture model of multimedia concepts at region level and then at frame level. The audio part is analyzed with the authors' algorithm described previously (Naphade & Huang, 2000). The outputs of these classifiers are then combined in a Bayesian network in order to improve concept detection. Their experiments show that the Bayesian network improves the detection performance over individual classifiers. IBM's research by Adams et al. (2003) extend the work of Naphade and Huang (2001) by including text from Automatic Speech Recognition as a third modality and by using Support Vector Machines to combine the classifiers' outputs. The comparison of these two combination strategies showed that SVMs (audio, visual, and text) and Bayesian networks (audio and visual) perform equally well. However, since in the latter case, speech information was ignored, one might expect that Bayesian networks can, in fact, perform better. More details about IBM's research work can be found in Naphade and Smith (2003), Natsev, Naphade, and Smith (2003), and Tseng, Lin, Naphade, Natsev, and Smith (2003).

The approach by Snoek and Worring (2005) is unique in the way synchronization and time relations between various patterns are modeled explicitly. They propose a multimedia semantic analysis framework based on Allen's (1983) temporal interval relations. Allen showed that in order to maintain temporal knowledge about any two events, only a small set of relations is needed to represent their temporal relations. These relations, now applied to audio and visual patterns, are the following: precedes, meets, overlaps, starts, during, finishes, equals, and no relation. The framework can include context and synchronization of heterogeneous information sources involved in multimodal analysis. Initially, the optimal pattern configuration of temporal relations of a given event is learned from training data by a standard statistical method (maximum entropy, decision trees, and SVMs). New data are classified with the learned model. The authors evaluate the event detection on a soccer video (goal, penalty, yellow card, red card and substitution) and TV news (reporting anchor, monologue, split-view and weather report). The differences among the various classifiers (maximum entropy, decision trees, and SVMs) appear to be not statistically significant.

## Summary

When considering video content, a new, very important dimension is added: time. Time adds a lot of redundancy that can be explored effectively in order to achieve a better segmentation and semantic analysis. The most interesting approaches consider time either implicitly (Westerveld et al., 2003) or explicitly (Snoek & Worring, 2005).

Few papers show a deeper level of multimodal combination than Snoek and Worring (2005) and Naphade and Huang (2001). The first explicitly explores the multimodal co-occurrence of patterns resulting from the same event with temporal relations. The latter integrates multimodal patterns in a Bayesian network to explore pattern co-occurrences and concept interdependence.

Natural language processing experts have not yet applied all the techniques from text to the video's extracted speech. Most approaches to extract information from text and combine this with the information extracted from audio and video are all very simple, such as a simple product between the probabilities of various modalities' classifiers.

## CONCLUSION

This chapter reviewed semantic-multimedia analysis algorithms with special emphasis on visual content. Multimedia datasets are important research tools that provide a means for researchers to evaluate various information extraction strategies. The two parts are not separate, because algorithm performances are intrinsically related to the dataset on which they are evaluated.

Major developments in semantic-multimedia analysis algorithms will probably be related to knowledge-based models and multimodal fusion algorithms. Future applications might boost knowledge-based model research by enforcing a limited application domain (i.e., a constrained knowledge base). Examples of such applications are football game summaries and mobile photo albums.

Multimodal analysis algorithms already have proven to be crucial in semantic multimedia analysis. Large developments are expected in this young research area due to the several problems that wait to be fully explored and to the TRECVID conference series that is pushing forward this research area through a standard evaluation and a rich multimedia dataset.

We believe that semantic-multimedia information analysis for retrieval applications has delivered its first promises and that many novel contributions will be done over the next years. To better understand the field, the conceptual organization by different statistical methods presented here allows readers to easily put into context novel approaches to be published in the future.

## REFERENCES

Adams, W. H. et al. (2003). Semantic indexing of multimedia content using visual, audio and text cues. *EURASIP Journal on Applied Signal Processing, 2*, 170–185.

Akutsu, M., Hamada, A., & Tonomura, Y. (1998). Video handling with music and speech detection. *IEEE Multimedia, 5*(3), 17–25.

Allen, J. F. (1983). Maintaining knowledge about temporal intervals. *Communications of the ACM, 26*(11), 832–843.

Barnard, K., & Forsyth, D. A. (2001). Learning the semantics of words and pictures. In *Proceedings of the International Conference on Computer Vision*, Vancouver, Canada.

Benitez, A. (2005). *Multimedia knowledge: Discovery, classification, browsing, and retrieval* [doctoral thesis]. New York: Columbia University.

Benitez, A. B., & Chang, S. F. (2002). Multimedia knowledge integration, summarization and evaluation. In *Proceedings of the International Workshop on Multimedia Data Mining in conjunction with the International Conference on Knowledge Discovery & Data Mining*, Alberta, Canada.

Benitez, A. B. et al. (2002). Semantics of multimedia in MPEG-7. In *Proceedings of the IEEE International Conference on Image Processing, Rochester*, NY.

Blei, D., & Jordan, M. (2003). Modeling annotated data. In *Proceedings of the ACM SIGIR Conference on Research and Development in Information Retrieval*, Toronto, Canada.

Brunelli, R., Mich, O., & Modena, C. M. (1999). A survey on the automatic indexing of video data. *Journal of Visual Communication and Image Representation, 10*(2), 78–112.

Carneiro, G., & Vasconcelos, N. (2005). Formulating semantic image annotation as a supervised learning problem. In *Proceedings of the IEEE Conference on Computer Vision and Pattern Recognition*, San Diego, CA.

Deerwester, S., Dumais, S. T., Furnas, G. W., Landauer, T. K., & Harshman, R. (1990). Indexing by latent semantic analysis. *Journal of the American Society for Information Science, 41*(6), 391–407.

Duygulu, P., Barnard, K., de Freitas, N., & Forsyth, D. (2002). Object recognition as machine translation: Learning a lexicon for a fixed image vocabulary. In *Proceedings of the European Conference on Computer Vision*, Copenhagen, Denmark.

Ekin, A., Tekalp, A. M., & Mehrotra, R. (2003). Automatic video analysis and summarization. *IEEE Transactions on Image Processing, 12*(7), 796–807.

Feng, S. L., Lavrenko, V., & Manmatha, R. (2004). Multiple Bernoulli relevance models for image and video annotation. In *Proceedings of the IEEE Conference on Computer Vision and Pattern Recognition*, Cambridge, UK.

Forsyth, D., & Ponce, J. (2003). *Computer vision: A modern approach.* Prentice Hall.

Harabagiu, S., et al. (2000). Falcon: Boosting knowledge for answer engines. In *Proceedings of the Text Retrieval Conference*, Gaithersburg, MD.

Hartley, R., & Zisserman, A. (2004). *Multiple view geometry in computer vision* (2nd ed.). Cambridge University Press.

Hastie, T., Tibshirani, R., & Friedman, J. (2001). *The elements of statistical learning: Data mining, inference and prediction.* Springer.

He, X., Zemel, R. S., & Carreira-Perpiñán, M. Á. (2004). Multiscale conditional random fields for image labeling. In *Proceedings of the IEEE International Conference on Computer Vision and Pattern Recognition*, Cambridge, UK.

Hofmann, T., & Puzicha, J. (1998). *Statistical models for co-occurrence data* (No. 1635 A. I. Memo). Massachusetts Institute of Technology.

Jeon, J., Lavrenko, V., & Manmatha, R. (2003). Automatic image annotation and retrieval using cross-media relevance models. In *Proceedings of the ACM SIGIR Conference on Research and Development in Information Retrieval*, Toronto, Canada.

Kumar, S., & Herbert, M. (2003a). Discriminative random fields: A discriminative framework for contextual interaction in classification. In *Proceedings of the IEEE International Conference on Computer Vision*, Nice, France.

Kumar, S., & Herbert, M. (2003b). Man-made structure detection in natural images using causal multiscale random field. In *Proceedings of the IEEE International Conference on Computer Vision and Pattern Recognition*, Madison, WI.

Lafferty, J., McCallum, A., & Pereira, F. (2001). Conditional random fields: Probabilistic models for segmenting and labeling sequence data. In *Proceedings of the International Conference on Machine Learning*, San Francisco.

Lavrenko, V., Manmatha, R., & Jeon, J. (2003). A model for learning the semantics of pictures. In *Proceedings of the Neural Information Processing System Conference*, Vancouver, Canada.

Leonardi, R., Migliotari, P., & Prandini, M. (2004). Semantic indexing of soccer audio-visual sequences: A multimodal approach based on controlled Markov chains. *IEEE Transactions on Circuits Systems and Video Technology, 14*(5), 634–643.

Li, B., & Sezan, I. (2003). Semantic sports video analysis: Approaches and new applications. In *Proceedings of the IEEE International Conference on Image Processing*, Barcelona, Spain.

Li, J., & Wang, J. Z. (2003). Automatic linguistic indexing of pictures by a statistical modeling approach. *IEEE Transactions on Pattern Analysis and Machine Intelligence, 25*(9), 1075–1088.

Lowe, D. (1999). Object recognition from local scale-invariant features. In *Proceedings of the International Conference on Computer Vision*, Kerkyra, Corfu, Greece.

Lu, L., Zhang, H-J., & Jiang, H. (2002). Content analysis for audio classification and segmentation. *IEEE Transactions on Speech and Audio Processing, 10*(7), 293–302.

Luo, Y., & Hwang, J. N. (2003). Video sequence modeling by dynamic Bayesian networks: A systematic approach from coarse-to-fine grains. In *Proceedings of the IEEE International Conference on Image Processing*, Barcelona, Spain.

Marr, D. (1983). *Vision*. San Francisco: W.H. Freeman.

Miller, G. A. (1995). Wordnet: A lexical database for English. *Communications of the ACM, 38*(11), 39–41.

Mori, Y., Takahashi, H., & Oka, R. (1999). Image-to-word transformation based on dividing and vector quantizing images with words. In *Proceedings of the First International Workshop on Multimedia Intelligent Storage and Retrieval Management*, Orlando, FL.

Naphade, M., et al. (1998). A high performance shot boundary detection algorithm using multiple cues. In *Proceedings of the IEEE International Conference on Image Processing*, Chicago.

Naphade, M., & Smith, J. (2003). Learning visual models of semantic concepts. In *Proceedings of the IEEE International Conference on Image Processing*, Barcelona, Spain.

Naphade, M. R., & Huang, T. S. (2000). *Stochastic modeling of soundtrack for efficient segmentation and indexing of video.* In *Proceedings of the Conference on SPIE, Storage and Retrieval for Media Databases*, San Jose, CA.

Naphade, M. R., & Huang, T. S. (2001). A probabilistic framework for semantic video indexing filtering and retrieval. *IEEE Transactions on Multimedia, 3*(1), 141–151.

Natsev, A., Naphade, M., & Smith, J. (2003). Exploring semantic dependencies for scalable concept detection. In *Proceedings of the IEEE International Conference on Image Processing*, Barcelona, Spain.

Pearl, J. (1988). *Probabilistic reasoning in intelligent systems: Networks of plausible inference.* Los Angeles: Morgan Kaufmann Publishers.

Quattoni, A., Collins, M., & Darrell, T. (2004). Conditional random fields for object recognition. In *Proceedings of the Neural Information Processing Systems Conference*, Vancouver, Canada.

Rabiner, L. R. (1989). A tutorial on hidden Markov models and selected applications in speech recognition. *Proceedings of IEEE, 77*(2), 257–286.

Shi, J., & Malik, J. (2000). Normalized cuts and image segmentation. *IEEE Transactions on Pattern Analysis and Machine Intelligence, 22*(8), 888–905.

Smeulders, A. W. M., Worring, M., Santini, S., Gupta, A., & Jain, R. (2000). Content-based image retrieval at the end of the early years. *IEEE Transactions on Pattern Analysis and Machine Intelligence, 22*(12), 1349–1380.

Snoek, C. G. M., & Worring, M. (2005). Multimedia event based video indexing using time intervals. *IEEE Transactions on Multimedia, 7*(4), 638-647.

Snoek, C. G. M., & Worring, M. (2005). Multimodal video indexing: A review of the state-of-the-art. *Multimedia Tools and Applications, 25*(1), 5–35.

Souvannavong, F., Merialdo, B., & Huet, B. (2003). Latent semantic indexing for video content modeling and analysis. In *Proceedings of the TREC Video Retrieval Evaluation Workshop*, Gaithersburg, MD.

Srikanth, M., Varner, J., Bowden, M., & Moldovan, D. (2005). Exploiting ontologies for automatic image annotation. In *Proceedings of the ACM SIGIR Conference on Research and Development in Information Retrieval*, Salvador, Brazil.

Tan, Y-P., Saur, D. D., Kulkarni, S. R., & Ramadge, P. J. (2000). Rapid estimation of camera motion from compressed video with application to video annotation. *IEEE Transactions on Circuits and Systems for Video Technology, 10*(1), 133–146.

Tansley, R. (2000). *The multimedia thesaurus: Adding a semantic layer to multimedia information* [doctoral thesis]. University of Southampton, UK.

TRECVID. (2004). *TREC video retrieval evaluation.* Retrieved November 2005, from http://www-nlpir.nist.gov/projects/trecvid/

Tseng, B. L., Lin, C-Y., Naphade, M., Natsev, A., & Smith, J. (2003). Normalised classifier fusion for semantic visual concept detection. In *Proceedings of the IEEE International Conference on Image Processing*, Barcelona, Spain.

Tzanetakis, G., & Cook, P. (2002). Musical genre classification of audio signals. *IEEE Transactions on Speech and Audio Processing, 10*(5), 293–302.

Vailaya, A., Figueiredo, M., Jain, A., & Zhang, H. (1999). A Bayesian framework for semantic classification of outdoor vacation images. In *Proceedings of the SPIE: Storage and Retrieval for Image and Video Databases VII*, San Jose, CA.

Vailaya, A., Figueiredo, M., Jain, A. K., & Zhang, H. J. (2001). Image classification for content-based indexing. *IEEE Transactions on Image Processing, 10*(1), 117–130.

Vasconcelos, N., & Lippman, A. (1998). A Bayesian framework for semantic content characterization. In *Proceedings of the IEEE Conference on Computer Vision and Pattern Recognition*, Santa Barbara, CA.

Vasconcelos, N., & Lippman, A. (2000). A probabilistic architecture for content-based image retrieval. In *Proceedings of the IEEE Computer Vision and Pattern Recognition, Hilton Head*, SC.

Wang, Y., Liu, Z., & Huang, J-C. (2000). Multimedia content analysis using both audio and visual clues. *IEEE Signal Processing, 17*(6), 12–36.

Westerveld, T., & de Vries, A. P. (2003). Experimental result analysis for a generative probabilistic image retrieval model. In *Proceedings of the ACM SIGIR Conference on Research and Development in Information Retrieval*, Toronto, Canada.

Westerveld, T., de Vries, A. P., Ianeva, T., Boldareva, L., & Hiemstra, D. (2003). Combining information sources for video retrieval. In *Proceedings of the TREC Video Retrieval Evaluation Workshop*, Gaithersburg, MD.

Yavlinsky, A., Schofield, E., & Rüger, S. (2005). Automated image annotation using global features and robust nonparametric density estimation. In *Proceedings of the International Conference on Image and Video Retrieval*, Singapore.

# Chapter V
# Modality Conversion:
## Toward the Semantic Frontier of UMA

**Truong Cong Thang**
*Information and Communications University, Korea*

**Yong Man Ro**
*Information and Communications University, Korea*

## ABSTRACT

*Content adaptation currently appears to be the key solution to support the quality of service (QoS) for multimedia services over heterogeneous environments. In this chapter, we study modality conversion as an important adaptation method. We point out two main challenging issues of the problem of modality conversion: (1) the quantification of the content value (quality) when contents are drastically scaled and/or converted to other modalities and (2) the method to accurately decide the modality and content value for each object given that quantification. Accordingly, we will present in detail the solutions as well as the open questions to these two issues. Moreover, we discuss the benefits and obstacles as well as future trends of modality conversion in realizing the goal of universal multimedia access.*

## INTRODUCTION

Multimedia contents are increasingly being created in different formats, standards, modalities, and complexities. Meanwhile, the explosive growth of the Internet and wireless networks brings about the diversity and heterogeneity of terminals and network connections. This fact results in big challenges for both providers and users in accessing and disseminating the huge amount of multimedia contents today. The concept of Universal Multimedia Access (UMA) has been introduced in the literature to address the need for solutions to these challenges (Vetro, 2004).

Content adaptation currently appears to be the key solution to support the quality of service (QoS) for multimedia services over heterogeneous environments (Chang & Vetro, 2005). In this trend, the rich multimedia contents are adapted to meet various constraints of terminals, network connections, and user preferences, so as to provide the best possible presentation to the user at anytime and anywhere. It should be noted that in the literature, the term *transcoding* sometimes implies format conversion (e.g., MPEG-2 to MPEG-4). In this chapter, *transcoding* will be used interchangeably with *content adaptation*.

Obviously, when a terminal cannot support the original modality of a content, that modality could be converted to another modality that can be displayed by the terminal. Besides, modality conversion (also called transmoding) can be used to meet some resource constraint while maximizing the quality for users. Given a bitrate constraint, the provider normally (down)scales a content to meet the constraint. However, in some cases, the quality of the scaled content is unacceptable, and a possible solution for this problem is to convert the contents into other modalities. For example, when the connection bitrate is too low, sending a sequence of "important" images would be more appropriate than streaming a scaled video of low quality. This is a typical case of video-to-image conversion.

An illustration for the video-to-image conversion is shown in Figure 1. Here, a Foreman video stream consisting of 20 frames (MPEG-4 format) is compared with a sequence of eight "important" images (JPEG format); both versions are encoded at the bitrate of 13.3kbps. We can see that both versions have the same semantics, but the visual clarity of the image sequence is much better than that of the video stream.

In this chapter, we try to provide a comprehensive picture of modality conversion. As modality conversion lies within the context of content adaptation/transcoding, we first present the key conceptual components of a content adaptation framework. Among these components, we will delve into the decision module, which can be considered as the QoS manager of the whole system. We identify the factors affecting modality conversion and show how they are technically related in a general framework. Especially, we point out two important issues of modality conversion for QoS management; namely,

*Figure. 1. Comparison of a video stream and an image sequence at 13.3kbps (Thang et al., 2004)*

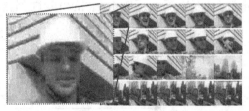

(a) Video stream

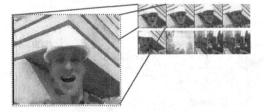

(b) Image sequence

*quality quantification* and *optimization algorithms*. Accordingly, we will discuss in detail the solutions as well as the open questions to these two issues. From our study, we show that modality conversion can be considered as part of a new trend called semantic transcoding.

The chapter is organized as follows. In the next section, we present an overview of content adaptation and then highlight modality conversion as an important technique of content adaptation. The section Modality Conversion Modeling deals with quality issue in the context of modality conversion. The section Constrained Optimization Solution focuses on the optimal algorithm to effectively make a decision on modality conversion. In the last sections, we discuss the benefits, obstacles, and future trends of the modality conversion topic.

## OVERVIEW

### Content Adaptation

As modality conversion is an inherent part of content adaptation, in this section we present an overview of content adaptation with some emphasis on the modality conversion aspect. Let us first define some basic terms used in the following. A *multimedia document* is a container of one or more *content objects* (*object* for short). An object is an entity conveying some information (e.g., a football match). Each object may have many *content versions* of different modalities and qualities. A content version is a physical instance of the object (e.g., a video or audio file reporting a football match).

In general, the key components of a content adaptation system include *content description*, *usage environment description*, *adaptation methods*, and *decision engine*. The relations among these components are illustrated in Figure 2.

1.  **Content description:** As the amount of multimedia content is enormous, adaptation systems need mechanisms to search and understand the features of the content to be adapted. The information describing multimedia contents is called metadata or content description. A large number of description tools for this purpose has been standardized in MPEG-7 (ISO/IEC, 2003) and MPEG-21 (ISO/IEC, 2004).

*Figure 2. Key components of content adaptation*

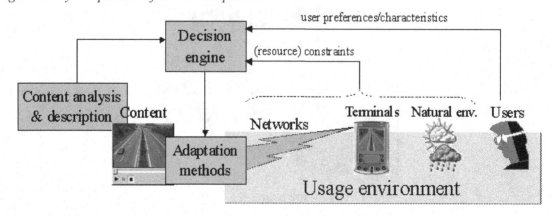

2. **Usage environment description:** The situations where users consume multimedia contents are various today. For example, a user stays in a noisy train and accesses a video streaming service via a PDA. In this case, the original video should be adapted to fit the user's display size, and the audio channel may be converted to text. All the information about the usage conditions should be standardized so different adaptation systems can understand the information in the same way (ISO/IEC, 2004).

3. **Adaptation methods:** Physical adaptation of contents can be divided into the following categories: *modality conversion* that converts content from one modality to different modalities; *content scaling* that changes the amount of resources (e.g., data size) and thus the quality of the contents without converting their modalities; *adjustment* that modifies some perceptual features of contents (e.g., contrast enhancement). More discussion on this issue will be provided in the following parts.

4. **Decision engine:** Decision engine provides the logics to make decisions on adapting multimedia contents. For this purpose, the decision engine takes as input the information from content description, usage environment, and available adaptation methods. The output decisions can be based on some rules or complex QoS optimization algorithms.

The combination of decision engine and adaptation methods constitutes the so-called content *adaptation engine*. In this chapter, we just consider two categories of adaptation methods: modality conversion and content scaling. As shown in Figure 3, the adaptation engine is composed of three modules: a decision engine, a modality converter, and a content scaler. The modality converter and the content scaler include specific (modality) conversion and (content) scaling tools in order to adapt the content objects according to instructions from the decision engine. Some contents may be passed directly to the content scaler without converting their modality; while others are passed first to the modality converter and then possibly to the content scaler.

It should be noted that the modality converter and the content scaler can be *either off-line or online*. In the off-line case, content objects are transcoded in advance into various versions of different modalities and qualities; then under certain constraints, appropriate versions are selected and sent to the user (Lum & Lau, 2002; Thang et al., 2004). In the online case, the needed versions are created on the fly.

For both online and off-line adaptation/transcodings, the decision engine must find the appropriate modality and the level of scaling for each object; that is, the functionality of the decision engine *is essentially the same for both online and offline transcodings*. In addition, the current trend is to ease online transcoding by various techniques such as employing scalable coding (Ohm, 2005) and bitstream syntax

*Figure 3. Architecture of the content adaptation engine*

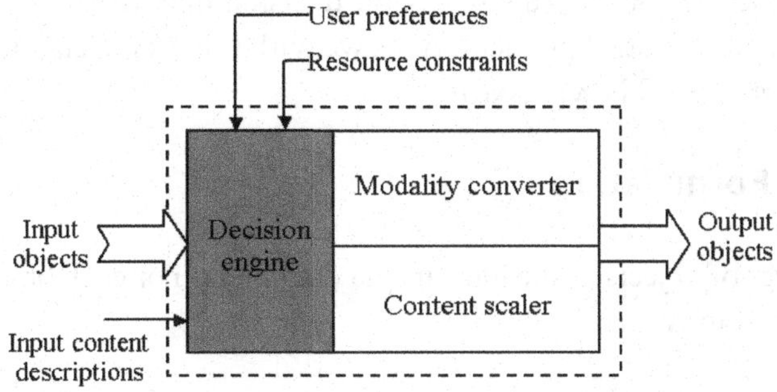

metadata (Panis et al., 2003). The mechanism of a decision engine that can make accurate decisions on modality conversion (as well as content scaling) is the very focus of this chapter.

## Modality Conversion in Content Adaptation

The *modality* concept of multimedia content actually is quite broad. It can be considered from the human senses such as visual, auditory, and tactile, which have been tackled for a long time in the field of human-computer interfaces (HCI). Modalities can also be derived from different modes of content coding (e.g., video, image, graphics for visual sense). Even different coding formats (e.g., GIF, JPEG for image) are sometimes referred to as modalities or submodalities. On the other hand, the modality of a content version may be single (e.g., video only or text only) or combined (e.g., audio+video modality combining both video and audio).

When applying modality conversion to adapt a multimedia document, the decision engine must answer for every object the following basic questions:

1. *What is the output modality of the object?*
2. *What is the quality of the object given that modality?*

The first question considers whether the original modality should be kept or converted to a specified modality, while the second one considers how much the content will be scaled within the determined modality. Obviously, if these questions are not answered, we cannot apply appropriate conversion and scaling operations (either online or offline) to the objects.

Moreover, from the preceding, we see that there are various conditions that may affect the decision on modality conversion. They can be grouped into four main factors:

- **Modality capability**, the support to display certain modalities. This factor can be determined from the characteristics of a terminal (e.g., text-only pager), surrounding environment (e.g., a too noisy place) or disability of the user (e.g., blindness).
- **User preference**, which shows the user's level of interest in various modalities.
- **Resource constraints** of terminals or networks, such as the connection bitrate or the memory size available for the requested contents. In fact, the resources of the provider/server should also be taken into account (e.g., how fast the server transcodes the contents).
- **Semantics** of the content itself. For instance, between a news video and a ballet video, the provider would be more willing to convert the former to a text stream.

In order to answer the previous two questions, the decision-making process will be represented as a traditional constrained optimization problem. Also, we will discuss in detail the roles and relationships of the preceding factors in the following parts.

## General Problem Formulation

Denote $N$ as the number of objects in the multimedia document. For each object $i$ in the document, we have the following definitions:

- $V_i$ is the content value of the object.
- $R_i = \{R_{i1}, R_{i2},..., R_{iL}\}$ is the set of resources of the object where $R_{il}$ is the amount of resource $l$ that object $i$ consumes; and $L$ is the number of resources.
- $P_i$ is the user preference for the object.
- $M = \{m_1, m_2, ..., m_Z\}$ is the *modality capability* that lists the indexes of supported modalities; $Z$ is the number of supported modalities.

The normal trend is that $V_i$ is a nondecreasing function with respect to each $R_{il}$. $V_i$ also depends on the personal evaluation of the user. In addition, when some modalities are not supported at the target terminal, the content versions of those modalities will be useless. So, $V_i$ can be represented as a function of $R_i$, $P_i$, and $M$:

$$V_i = f_i(R_i, P_i, M). \tag{1}$$

Given a set of resource constraints $R^c = \{R_1^c, R_2^c,..., R_L^c\}$, we have the problem statement as follows:

*Find $R_i$ for each object, so as to maximize the overall quality $V^O = g(V_1, ..., V_N)$ subject to,*

$$\sum_{i=1}^{N} R_{il} \leq R_l^c \text{ for all } l = 1...L \tag{2}$$

where $g()$ is the function to compute the overall quality $V^O$ from $\{V_i\}$. Usually, $g()$ is defined as

$$g(V_1, ..., V_N) = \sum_{i=1}^{N} w_i \cdot V_i \tag{3}$$

where $w_i$ is the importance value of object $i$, $0 \leq w_i \leq 1$.

In general, after solving the amounts of resources from problem (2), one can find the modality and the quality for each object using Equation (1). With the previous constrained optimization formulation, *two main challenging issues* are:

1.  The quantification of the content value (Eq. (1)) when contents are drastically scaled and/or converted to other modalities; and
2.  The method to solve problem (2) so as to accurately decide the modality and the content value for each object given that quantification.

These two issues the topics of the next two sections, respectively. In the next part, we will present a review of related literature.

## A Survey on Related Work

Many existing studies tackle specific cases of modality conversion under the constraint of modality capability. For instance, text-to-speech (TTS) technologies have long been used for many applications, such as receiving e-mails through telephones (Wu & Chen, 1997). In other cases, video-to-image conversion can be employed to send an image sequence (i.e., a video summary) to a terminal that does not support video playback (Kaup, 2002). Some recent studies use metadata to help automate the processing of conversion between specific modalities (Asadi & Dufourd, 2004; Kim et al., 2003).

Modality conversion is also an interesting topic in Human Computer Interfaces (HCI). Traditionally, HCI studies the use of multiple modalities for the interface between human and computers/terminals. As terminals become more and more heterogeneous, some HCI-related research considers the changes of modalities in the interface according to different terminal characteristics. Archambault and Burger (2001) sketch the idea of a data model that is independent of modalities so as to give the user the same experience across different interfaces. In the research of Elting, Zwickel, and Malaka (2002), users' choices of presentation modalities for different terminals are subjectively investigated, resulting in general guidelines for converting modalities in certain contexts. It should be noted that in HCI, not only content modalities but also interaction modalities (e.g., voice or keyboard) are subject to conversion (Bandelloni, Berti, and Paternò, 2004).

In addition, modality conversion could be particularly useful for disabled users to access multimedia contents (Balasubramanian & Venkatasubramanian, 2003; Thang, Yang, Ro & Wong, 2007). Currently, there is a wide variety of commercial products that read textual contents (e.g., text on PC screens) for blind users (Thang et al., 2007). Balasubramanian and Venkatasubramanian (2003) propose a systematic selection scheme of content modality depending on the user's type of disability. However, this research area is still in an initial stage.

Meanwhile, there has so far been little research on modality conversion under the resource constraint. Lum & Lau (2002) consider modality as one variable of the adaptation of a multimedia document to resource constraint, yet this approach does not show the relationship between different modalities. Mohan, Smith, and Li (1999) use the Lagrangian method for selecting content versions of different modalities. However, as shown later, if the quality is modeled by a nonconcave function of the resource, this method is not suitable to find the output modality (as well as the quality). Boll, Klas, and Wandel (1999) present a cross-media adaptation scheme, but no QoS framework has been established. Similarly, Adam, Atluri, Adiwijaya, and Banerjee (2001) propose representation and adaptation schemes of multimedia contents that may allow selection or substitution of modalities. However, the adaptation strategy in this work is quite limited. Recently, the use of modality conversion for QoS management in streaming service has been investigated through representing the qualities of different modalities with respect to the amount of resource (Thang, Yung & Ro, 2005a).

Moreover, most research related to modality conversion under the resource constraint supposes that the content quality (also called utility, content value, or quality score) is already provided by some means. The only exception is the case of video-to-image conversion where many distortion metrics have been proposed to compare an extracted image sequence with the original video stream (Chang, Sull & Lee, 1999; Lee & Kim, 2003). However, these metrics are still ad hoc and not shown to be consistent with user perception. Actually, quality is the most challenging issue in content adaptation (Chang & Vetro, 2005). Especially with modality conversion, quality must be considered across different modalities.

MPEG standards include a number of tools to support modality conversion in an interoperable manner. MPEG-7 (ISO/IEC, 2003) defines several classification schemes (CS) to describe various modalities (e.g., ContentCS, GraphicsCodingCS, etc.). MPEG-21 Digital Item Adaptation (DIA) provides Usage Environment description tools to help determine the set of supported modalities, the Conversion Preference tool to specify user preference on modalities, and the Universal Constraints description tool to define the (resource) constraints of the adaptation (ISO/IEC, 2004). Recently, a tool to manage QoS with modality conversion, named CrossConversionQoS, has been included in the amendment of MPEG-21 DIA (ISO/IEC, 2006).

## MODALITY CONVERSION MODELING

This section deals with the first issue of modality conversion, which is modeling of content value w.r.t. resources and modalities. We will also discuss how the factors of modality capability, user preference, and semantics will be incorporated into the quality. As our main concern is modality conversion, which may exist no matter what types of resources are involved, in the following we present chiefly the case of a single resource where the set of resources $R_i$ is replaced by $R_i$. The involvement with multiple resources can be treated in a similar manner (Lee, Lehoczky, Siewiorek, Rajkumar & Hansen, 1999; Lengwehasatit & Ortega, 2000).

### Overlapped Content Value Model

The process of content scaling, either online or off-line, can be represented by some "rate-quality" curve that shows the quality of a scaled content according to the bitrate (or any resource in general) (Chang & Vetro, 2005). A recent trend is to use the rate-quality curve as metadata to automate content scaling (Kim, Wang, & Chang, 2003; Mukherjee, Delfosse, Kim & Wang, 2005). Usually, the curve is obtained for a particular modality because each modality has its own scaling characteristics. Extending the concept of the rate-quality curve, we propose the overlapped content value (OCV) model to conceptually represent both the content scaling and modality conversion of each content object (Thang et al., 2005a).

The OCV model of an object consists of multiple rate-quality curves representing the content value of different modalities vs. the amount of resource. The number of curves in the model is the number of

*Figure 4. Overlapped content value model of a content object (a). The model consists of modality curves; each curve relates the content value of a modality to the amount of resource. The final content value function is the convex hull of the modality curves (b).*

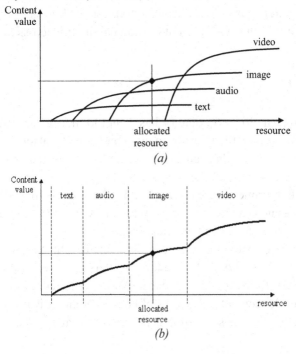

modalities the object would have. Figure 4(a) illustrates the OCV model of an object that is originally of video modality. Here, the rate-quality curve of each modality (called *modality curve*) can be assigned manually or automatically. For example, the rate-quality curve may be manually set as a log function (Mohan et al., 1999) or automatically estimated using a machine learning approach (Kim, Wang & Chang, 2003). Normally, a modality curve saturates when the amount of resource is high. Each point on a modality curve corresponds to a content version of that modality. The intersection points of the modality curves represent the conversion boundaries between the modalities. Though not really mandatory, each modality curve should cut another one, at most, at one point.

Let $VM_j(R)$ denote the rate-quality curve of modality $j$ of a content, $j = 1...J$, where $J$ is the number of modalities of the content; $R$ is the amount of resource. $VM_j(R) \geq 0 \ \forall \ j$. Also let $u_j$ denote the scale factor of modality $j$. The content value function, which is the convex hull of the modality curves in the OCV model, can be written as follows:

$$V = max\{u_j \times VM_j(R) \mid j = 1...J\} \tag{4}$$

Figure 4(b) shows the final content value function and the conversion boundaries of the content. If we know the amount of resource allocated for an object, we can find its appropriate modality and content value by mapping the amount of resource to the content value function. As the amount of resource decreases from a maximum to zero, the object's modality will be converted in an ordered manner. For instance, in Figure 4, the original video modality will be converted to image, to audio, and then to text.

## Quality Evaluation Across Modalities

By a proper estimation of content value for different modalities, we can put the modality curves into a single OCV model. Currently, there are already some standardized methods for subjective/objective evaluation of video and audio contents (ITU, 1999, 2002). However, these methods are not appropriate for multimedia applications (Watson & Sasse, 1998), especially under the various adaptations of UMA. This subsection aims at the evaluation of the content quality across different scaling levels and modalities.

### Composition of Quality

It is commonly agreed that multimedia quality has a multidimensional nature and that key quality dimensions/aspects should be identified for the application in use (Watson & Sasse, 1998). With video content scaling, the quality is normally evaluated by some measures that show the perceptual satisfaction of scaled video. In the case of video-to-image conversion, some semantic scores representing the understandability of the key-frame set are often mentioned (Chang et al., 1999; Lee & Kim, 2003). In some extreme cases such as news video converted to text, it is obviously not the perceptual quality but rather the amount of conveyed semantics that really counts.

For content adaptation, we contend that the content value (quality) *consists of both the perceptual quality (PQ) and the semantic quality (SQ)*. The former refers to a user's satisfaction in perceiving the content, regardless of what information the content contains; the latter refers to the amount of information the user obtains from the content, regardless of how the content is presented. Although one may say that *PQ* already includes *SQ*, the separation is necessary because when *PQ* is reduced (e.g., lower frame rate), *SQ* may remain unchanged (Ghinea & Thomas, 1998). Even when *PQ* is nearly zero (e.g., the previous video-to-text conversion), the value of *SQ* may still be acceptable. We then propose the composition of content value *V* as follows:

$$V = s \times PQ + (1-s) \times SQ \tag{5}$$

where *s* is the weight of *PQ*, $0 \leq s \leq 1$; *s* can be assigned by the provider depending on the particular applications (Prangl, Szkaliczki & Hellwagner, 2007). In general, if the information itself is more important than the perceptual satisfaction, then the weight of *SQ* should be higher than that of *PQ*. We assume that an average user in a normal situation would need *SQ* and *PQ* in an equal manner. So, as default, we let the value of *s* be 0.5. In the following sections, the evaluations of *SQ* and *PQ* will be presented.

## Experiments

We have carried some subjective tests to evaluate the quality across different modalities (Thang et al., 2005a). Each time during the test, the subject is presented with two content versions, the original and then the adapted one, so the subject can give the score to the adapted version with respect to the original one. As for the measures of quality, with every adapted version, we ask the subjects to give two scores: one for the "understanding" (i.e., semantic quality) and one for the perceptual quality. Each score will take an integer value in Likert-style 10-point scale, from 0 to 9. For semantic quality, 9 means the adapted version shows sufficiently the original semantics, whereas 0 corresponds to totally different semantics. For perceptual quality, 9 corresponds to a presentation quality that is the same as the original one, while 0 means a very annoying and/or totally different presentation.

In the following, the result of a typical content is presented with four modalities; namely, video, image, audio, and text. This content, which is a landscape video (without audio channel), is originally encoded in MPEG-4 format with frame size of 176x144, frame rate $f = 25$fps, quantization parameter $q=10$, and GOP structure of M=3 and N=15. To obtain the adapted video versions, the original video is scaled using a combination of frame-dropping and requantization. Image versions are obtained as sequences of key-frames of the original video using the method of Lee and Kim (2003). Extracted im-

*Table 1. List of test versions and their characteristics; the first version is the original*

| No. | Modality | Bit Rate (kbps) | Description |
|---|---|---|---|
| 1 | Video | 80.00 | Original video, 240 frames, $q = 10$, $f = 25$fps |
| 2 | Video | 45.78 | Dropping all B frames, $q = 10$, $f = 8.3$fps |
| 3 | Video | 26.63 | Dropping all B and P frames, $q=10$, $f = 1.7$fps |
| 4 | Video | 13.36 | Dropping all B frames, $q = 30$, $f = 8.3$fps |
| 5 | Video | 7.5 | Dropping all B and P frames, $q= 30$, $f =1.7$fps |
| 6 | Image | 53.33 | Sequence of 32 images, $q = 10$ |
| 7 | Image | 26.67 | Sequence of 16 images, $q = 10$ |
| 8 | Image | 13.33 | Sequence of 8 images, $q = 10$ |
| 9 | Image | 6.67 | Sequence of 4 images, $q = 10$ |
| 10 | Image | 1.66 | Sequence of 1 image, $q = 10$ |

ages are encoded in the JPEG format such that their qualities are the same as the I-frames of the original video. Text, which is the description of the original content, is created manually. Audio content is created as the speech from the text. All versions of this content are listed in Table 1.

Figure 5(a) shows the perceptual and semantic qualities w.r.t. bitrate for different modalities of the contents. We see that the relationship of $SQ$ and $PQ$, in which $SQ$ is always higher than or equal to $PQ$, is quite consistent. This is perhaps due to the fact that usually a small clue of information in a degraded presentation may be enough for the user's understanding. Especially the $PQ$ of text modality is nearly zero; however, its $SQ$ is quite significant. That is, in a critical application (e.g., aircraft communication with very low bandwidth) where the semantics is the most important thing, the conversion to text is really helpful.

In Figure 5(b), content value of each modality is obtained by averaging $PQ$ and $SQ$ (i.e., $s = 0.5$ for all modalities). From the final OCV model of the landscape content (Figure 5(b)), we find that the conversion point between video and image modalities is at 23kbps and the conversion point between image and text is at 1.7kbps. There is no conversion point related to audio modality because its content value is similar to that of text while its bitrate is rather high. The obtained OCV model confirms that modality conversion, specifically video-to-image and image-to-text, is useful for this video content. Anyway, for a blind user, video-to-audio conversion obviously would be useful to consume this video content.

*Figure 5. Subjective quality across different modalities for landscape content*

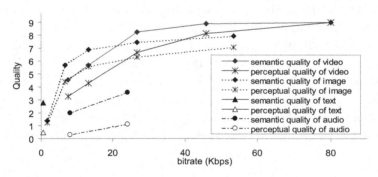

*(a) Quality curves of different modalities*

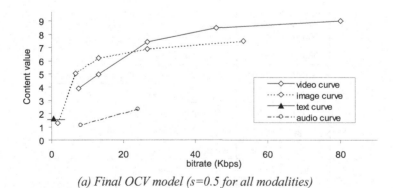

*(a) Final OCV model (s=0.5 for all modalities)*

## Discussion

Previously, we have shown that it is feasible to obtain realistic OCV models. Such a model can be directly used in the case of single content adaptation, where a decision engine can easily determine the conversion boundaries between different modalities. This result also confirms that a quality metric used for modality conversion should take into account the semantic aspect of quality. Among the two key components of content value, perceptual quality can be estimated by some established objective methods (Thang et al., 2005a), while objective estimation of semantic quality is still being investigated. With a homogeneous content (e.g., a short video shot), the semantic quality can be reliably modeled by some analytical functions (Prangl et al., 2007; Thang et al., 2005a). More discussion on semantic quality is provided in the following sections.

With the OCV model, we can easily incorporate the factors of *modality capability* and *user preference* into the decision on modality conversion. For example, when a modality is not supported by the terminal, the corresponding modality curve will be removed from the OCV model. Besides, different users may have different preferences on the "goodness" of different modalities. As implied in Equation (1), the factor of user preference can be used to adjust the quality of the content and ultimately result in a customized adaptation solution. In the context of modality conversion, the user preference can be used to adjust the OCV model, as shown in Figure 6. In this example, the OCV model of Figure 6(a) is adjusted to get the model of Figure 6(b) where the operational range of the second modality is expanded. More details on the user preference in modality conversion can be found in Thang, Jung, and Ro (2005b).

Regarding the *semantics factor*, actually this factor is already "embedded" in OCV models. For example (see Figure 7), given a textual video, the text modality curve would have similar semantic quality

*Figure 6. User preference can be used to adjust the conversion boundaries of OCV model*

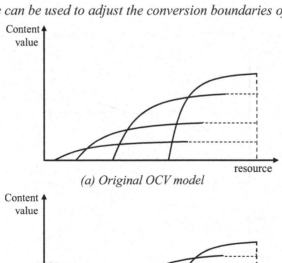

*(a) Original OCV model*

*(b) Customized OCV model*

(i.e., amplitude) to the video modality curve. Meanwhile, with a scenery video, the text modality curve would have much lower semantic quality than the video modality curve. So when the bitrate is reduced, the textual video would be more likely to be converted to text modality.

In a special case where content scaling is not applied, we can see that each modality curve is reduced to just one point. In this case, the OCV model can be represented *by some simple rules* (e.g., the orders of modalities in conversion), not explicitly based on a content value. This case is currently studied in HCI, where some display migration guidelines often result from empirical/subjective research (Elting et al., 2002).

## CONSTRAINED OPTIMIZATION SOLUTION

The previous sections have quantified the content value based on the OCV model. Now, given that we have a multimedia document consisting of multiple content objects and each object is attributed by an OCV model, we need to find some method to solve problem (2). In this section, we employ Equation (3) to compute the overall quality. Problem (2) is now rewritten as an optimization problem with a single resource as follows:

$$\text{Find } R_i \text{ for each object, so as to } maximize \ \sum_{i=1}^{N} w_i \cdot V_i \ subject \ to \ \sum_{i=1}^{N} R_i \leq R^c. \tag{6}$$

### Optimal Solution Based on the Viterbi Algorithm

We see that a content value function can be continuous or discrete. If it is continuous, it can be discretized because practical transcoding is done in the unit of bits or bytes. In the following, we implicitly sup-

*Figure 7. The dependence of OCV model on the semantics of contents*

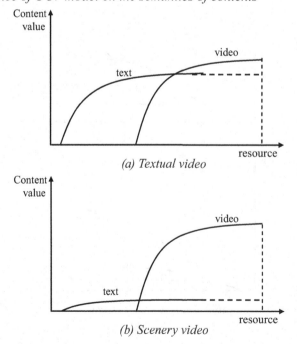

*(a) Textual video*

*(b) Scenery video*

pose a content value function is discrete, either originally or after discretization. We call a point on the content value function a *selection*. Then, a content value function will have a finite number of selections. Meanwhile, function (4), which is constituted from multiple modality curves, is inherently nonconcave. Thus, the previous optimization can be solved optimally by the Viterbi algorithm of dynamic programming (Forney, 1973; Ortega, Ramchandran & Vetterli, 1994).

The principle of the Viterbi algorithm lies in building a trellis to represent all viable allocations at each instant, given all the predefined constraints. The basic terms used in the algorithm are defined as follows (see Figure 8):

- **Trellis:** The trellis is made of all surviving paths that link the initial node to the nodes in the final stage.
- **Stage:** Each stage corresponds to an object to be adapted.
- **Node.** In our problem, each node is represented by a pair $(i, a_i)$, where $i = 0...N$ is the stage number, and $a_i$ is the accumulated amount of resource of all objects until this stage.
- **Branch:** If selection $k$ at stage $i$ has the value-resource pair $(V_{ik}, R_{ik})$, then node $(i-1, a_{i-1})$ will be linked by a branch of value $V_{ik}$ to node $(i, a_i)$ with:

$$a_i = a_{i-1} + R_{ik}, \tag{7}$$

satisfying (if not, the branch will not be linked):

$$a_i \leq R^c. \tag{8}$$

*Figure 8. Trellis diagram grown by the Viterbi algorithm*

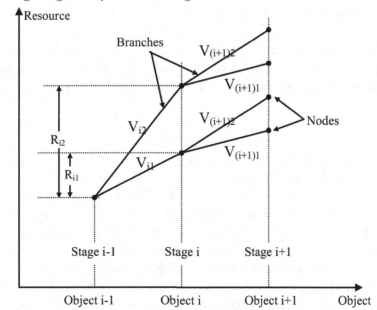

*Figure 9. Algorithm to find the optimal solution of problem (6)*

---

**Algorithm**

*Step 0: i=0. Start from the initial node (0, 0)*

*Step 1: At each stage i, add possible branches to the end nodes of the surviving paths. At each node, a branch is grown for each of the available selections; the branch must satisfy condition (8).*

*Step 2: Among all paths arriving at a node in stage i+1, the one having the highest accumulated sum of $\sum_{t=1}^{i+1} w_t \cdot V_t$ is chosen, and the rest are pruned.*

*Step 3: i=i+1. If $i \leq N$ go back to step 1, otherwise go to step 4.*

*Step 4: At the final stage, compare all surviving paths then select the path having the highest value of $\sum_{i=1}^{N} w_i \cdot V_i$. That path corresponds to the optimal set of selections for all objects.*

---

- **Path:** A path is a concatenation of branches. A path from the first stage to the final stage corresponds to a set of possible selections for all objects.

From the previous, we can immediately see that the optimal path, corresponding to the optimal set of selections, is the one having the highest weighted sum $V^0 = \sum_{i=1}^{N} w_i \cdot V_i$. We now apply the Viterbi algorithm to generate the trellis and to find the optimal path as follows (Forney, 1973; Ortega et al., 1994):

## Experiments

For experiments, we employ a multimedia document of six objects. In this part, we consider one practical resource: the datasize of each object. Originally, object 1 is a short audiovisual (AV) clip; objects 2, 3, 4, and 5 are JPEG images; and object 6 is a text paragraph. The datasizes of these objects are respectively 1500KBs, 731KBs, 834KBs, 773KBs, 813KBs, and 8KBs. The importance values $w_i$'s of the six objects are set to be 1, 0.55, 0.5, 0.6, 0.55, and 0.15. These values are subjectively decided based on the relative importance of the objects in the document. Upon the user's request, the multimedia document is adapted to meet the datasize (resource) constraint and then downloaded to the terminal as a normal Web page. In our experiments, content transcoding is simply done off-line. The OCV model of each object is obtained by curve-fitting to the empirical data provided by subjective tests. Figure 10 shows the six OCV models of the six objects. To illustrate clearly the conversion boundaries, we show only the beginning parts of the OCV models.

*Figure 10. The OCV models for the six objects of the experimental document: AV object (a); image objects (b), (c), (d), and (f); text object (f)*

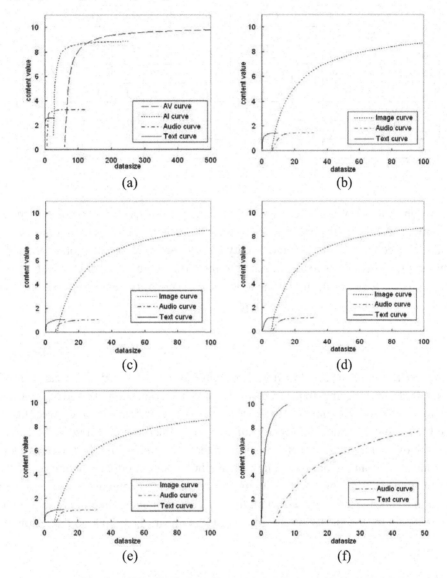

To check the response of the adaptation system, we vary the resource constraint $R^c$. The result is provided in Table 2, where each row shows one document version adapted to a value of $R^c$. In this table, the first column is $R^c$; each object has two columns representing its datasize and modality; and the last column is the total content value $V^o$ of the adapted document. We can see that as $R^c$ decreases, the amounts of resource of the objects are reduced to satisfy the resource constraint of the whole document. Also, at certain points, the modalities of the objects are converted to meet the constraint and give the highest possible total content value.

We also carry out an experiment without modality conversion in which the OCV model of each object contains only the curve of the original modality. The result is shown in Table 3. We see that

*Table 2. Results of adapted documents with modality conversion; here, Mod means modality; AV, AI, I, A, T mean "audiovisual," "audio+image," image, audio, and text modalities, respectively*

| $R^c$ | Object 1 | | Object 2 | | Object 3 | | Object 4 | | Object 5 | | Object 6 | | $V^o$ |
|---|---|---|---|---|---|---|---|---|---|---|---|---|---|
| | $R_1$ | Mod | $R_2$ | Mod | $R_3$ | Mod | $R_4$ | Mod | $R_5$ | Mod | $R_6$ | Mod | |
| 3000 | 701 | AV | 585 | I | 562 | I | 588 | I | 556 | I | 8 | T | 33.37 |
| 1000 | 264 | AV | 186 | I | 178 | I | 187 | I | 177 | I | 8 | T | 31.93 |
| 500 | 154 | AV | 87 | I | 82 | I | 87 | I | 82 | I | 8 | T | 29.68 |
| 100 | 0 | | 26 | I | 22 | I | 24 | I | 24 | I | 4 | T | 14.10 |
| 40 | 0 | | 13 | I | 12 | I | 13 | I | 0 | | 2 | T | 7.23 |
| 10 | 0 | | 0 | | 0 | | 8 | I | 0 | | 2 | T | 2.31 |

when modality conversion is not applied, some objects may be discarded as the resource constraint is reduced. In contrast, in Table 2, the objects are converted to other modalities to maintain some meaning for the user. The consequence is that when modality conversion is applied, the total content value of the adapted document is always higher than or equal to the case where only content scaling is employed. As shown in Figure 11, it can be seen that the advantage of modality conversion becomes clear as the resource constraint is reduced to below 500KBs.

## Discussion

In practice, the problem of resource allocation represented as a constrained optimization is often solved by two basic methods: the Lagrangian method and dynamic programming method (Ortega & Ramchandran, 1998). Mohan et al. (1999) adopt the Lagrangian method to find the allocated amounts of resource. However, the Lagrangian method is not really suitable with nonconcave content value functions.

The drawback of the Lagrangian method is illustrated in Figure 12 in which we have an AV object that may be converted to audio and text. The concave hull of the model is the curve (ABCD), where (BC) is a linear segment. With the Lagrangian method, the selected content version corresponds to the contact point of the concave hull with a tangent line having a slope λ, called the Lagrangian multiplier (Ortega & Ramchandran, 1998). Because segment (BC) is linear, the points on that segment, except B

*Table 3. Results of adapted documents without modality conversion; as the resource constraint is reduced, some objects are allocated with zero amount of resource (i.e., the objects are removed)*

| $R^c$ | Object 1 | | Object 2 | | Object 3 | | Object 4 | | Object 5 | | Object 6 | | $V^o$ |
|---|---|---|---|---|---|---|---|---|---|---|---|---|---|
| | $R_1$ | Mod | $R_2$ | Mod | $R_3$ | Mod | $R_4$ | | $R_5$ | | $R_6$ | Mod | |
| 3000 | 701 | AV | 585 | I | 562 | I | 588 | I | 556 | I | 8 | T | 33.37 |
| 1000 | 264 | AV | 186 | I | 178 | I | 187 | I | 177 | I | 8 | T | 31.93 |
| 500 | 85 | AI | 104 | I | 100 | I | 104 | I | 99 | I | 8 | T | 29.76 |
| 100 | 41 | AI | 22 | I | 15 | I | 16 | I | 2 | T | 4 | T | 18.42 |
| 40 | 12 | A | 18 | I | 2 | T | 2 | T | 2 | T | 4 | T | 11.77 |
| 10 | 2 | T | 2 | T | 1 | T | 1 | T | 1 | T | 3 | T | 7.76 |

*Figure 11. The total content value of the adapted document w.r.t. the resource constraint*

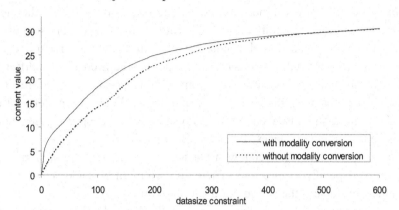

and C, are never selected. This leads to an unexpected consequence: the points below the concave hull are not selected. In particular, if a modality curve lies below the concave hull (e.g., the audio curves in Figure 12 and Figure 10(a)), that modality is never reached. Moreover, the actual range of selections is also limited (e.g., (AB) and (CD) in Figure 12). In this case, we see that the allocated resource may be either much larger or much smaller than the amount that is actually needed.

The advantage of dynamic programming is that it can work with non-concave content value functions. Its disadvantage is higher complexity than the Lagrangian method. However, through extensive experiments (Thang et al., 2005b), we have shown that the Viterbi algorithm of dynamic programming has potential for real-time computation of the decision engine.

## BENEFITS AND OBSTACLES OF MODALITY CONVERSION

The results presented in two previous sections quantitatively show that under the low resource constraint, using modality conversion in combination with content scaling would expand the operational range of QoS management. That is, from *resource usage point of view*, modality conversion provides more freedom in service provision subject to the limited resources of the Internet and wireless networks, thus giving more quality to the user.

*Figure 12: Drawback of Lagrangian method; solution range includes only segments (AB) and (CD)*

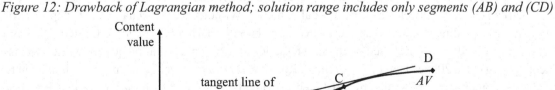
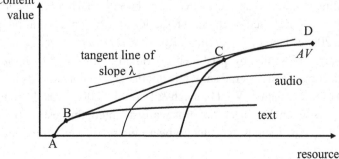

Modality conversion is useful not only from the *resource usage point of view* but also from the *accessibility point of view*. Even when the resource (e.g., bitrate) is plentiful but the modality capability is limited, good decisions on modality conversion would help the user consume the content with a similar experience as other users. It should be noted that in contrast to resource usage scenarios where the provider tries to create substitute versions of lower resource requirements (in different modalities), the accessibility scenarios may need substitute versions of higher resource requirements. For example, a substitute audio version has much higher data size than the original text version, but it would be the best conversion choice for a blind user. This is an important point in supporting the Quality of Experience (QoE) in future multimedia services (Pereira & Burnett, 2003).

Currently, the use of modality conversion in particular and content adaptation in general is still limited to some context-specific applications. There are two main obstacles in practical deployment. The first and foremost obstacle is the very quantification of quality. Actually, the most popular quality metrics used in existing content adaptation research are still MSE, MAD, and PSNR. The quality estimation across different modalities, especially semantic quality, still needs more study. Currently, most of the research focuses on detection and annotation of semantics within the contents, which facilitate semantic transcoding (Nagao, Shirai & Squire, 2001). There is little research on semantic quality measure to quantitatively guide and evaluate semantic transcoding (Thang, Jung & Ro, 2005c). The second obstacle is the wide variety of constraints that affect decision-making. In practice, the provider must consider simultaneously many types of constraints, such as bitrate, display size, color depth, complexity/energy, and so forth. Moreover, most current transcoding methods are still very complex to deploy in real-time applications. As discussed next, the trend of metadata-enabled adaptation is being promoted to overcome these obstacles.

## FUTURE RESEARCH DIRECTIONS

### Modality Conversion in the Trend of Semantic Transcoding

The previous investigation showed that semantic quality is crucial in making decisions on modality conversion. Actually, modality conversion can be considered as part of semantic transcoding (Cucchiara, Grana & Prati, 2003; Nagao et al., 2001; Thang et al., 2005c). This is a recent trend of multimedia communication that aims to remove the "semantically irrelevant" details of contents, thus better accommodating to the limited resources and/or customized consumption. However, as already mentioned, a difficulty of semantic transcoding is that it is hard to define a *semantic quality metric*.

In our opinion, there needs to be a proper representation mechanism of semantics of multimedia content, which can be used to develop a semantic quality metric. Without such a mechanism, the deployment of semantic transcoding in general and modality conversion in particular would be limited. We have proposed a general framework based on the graph theory to formulate semantic quality of multimedia content (Thang et al., 2005c; Thang, Kim, Kim & Ro, 2006). The basic idea is that both original content and adapted content are represented by attributed-relational graphs, and then the similarities between the graphs are used to compute the overall semantic quality. This approach, which is consistent with the current development of the semantic Web (Jannach & Leopold, 2005), has the potential to represent the relations between objects when the objects are drastically adapted, thus estimating the change in overall quality of the document. This issue is expected to be an interesting research topic in the near future.

## Metadata-Enabled Adaptation System

Another recent trend is to employ metadata to automate and improve multimedia systems (van Beek, Smith, Ebrahimi, Suzuki & Askelof, 2003). This approach tries to provide necessary hints and mechanisms to reduce the complexity in making adaptation decisions. For example, the quality, semantics, and adaptation behavior of multimedia contents can be obtained in advance, stored as metadata, and then used in real-time adaptation. In parallel with academic and industrial research on content adaptation, the emergence of MPEG standards, especially MPEG-21 and MPEG-7, facilitates the realization of UMA systems in an interoperable manner. Currently, MPEG-21-enabled UMA systems are being developed in many trial studies.

## Tools for Specific Conversions Between Various Modalities

The rapid development of digital technology has resulted in a wide variety of content formats and modalities. There will be a huge demand for the conversion tools that can convert one format/modality to another in an efficient and effective manner. Currently, the tools for text-to-speech and speech-to-text conversions have been well established with various commercial products. The conversion from video to text in Optical Character Reader (OCR) application (Lienhart, 2003) has also progressed a lot due to the advances in text recognition. Many other conversion tools, such as speech to animation (or visual-speech video) and 2D video to 3D video, are being under active research.

It should be noted that in the future multimedia network, the conversion tools (and scaling tools as well) can be employed in various manners. The simplest scenario is that the conversion tools are available at the server of content provider. In some cases, a tool is automatically downloaded (and paid for) from another supplier any time when a conversion is requested. In some other cases, the content itself is sent to another node to be converted and then forwarded to the content consumer.

## CONCLUSION

In this chapter, we have presented a comprehensive study on modality conversion in the context of content adaptation. We described the solutions to the challenges of modality conversion. We also discussed the main factors affecting modality conversion, showing how they are technically related in a general framework. Specifically, the main contributions of this chapter include:

- We quantitatively showed that modality conversion is an effective solution to extend the range of QoS management under limited resource conditions. Moreover, modality conversion is useful to improve multimedia accessibility, thus enhancing the quality of experience for users.
- With the optimization problem of content adaptation, we showed that the optimal solution for modality conversion should be able to handle the inherently nonconcave feature of quality-resource relationship.
- We showed that semantic quality is crucial in modality conversion. Thus, modality conversion should be put in the context of semantic transcoding and semantic Web. In particular, there needs to be a mechanism to represent the semantics of a content.

As for future work, we will investigate objective methods to quantify the content value where the graph theory can be a suitable mathematic tool. We will also focus on the automation of online transcoding in terms of both content scaling and modality conversion.

## REFERENCES

Adam, N.R., Atluri, V., Adiwijaya, I., & Banerjee, S. (2001). A dynamic manifestation approach for providing universal access to digital library objects. *IEEE Transactions on Knowledge and Data Engineering, 13*(4), 705–716.

Archambault, D., & Burger, D. (2001). From multimodality to multimodalities: The need for independent models. *Proceedings of Universal Access in Human-Computer Interaction Conference*, New Orleans, Louisiana, 227–231.

Asadi, M.K., & Dufourd, J.-C. (2004). Multimedia adaptation by transmoding in MPEG-21. *Proceedings of the International Workshop on Image Analysis for Multimedia Interactive Services*, Lisbon, Portugal.

Balasubramanian, V., & Venkatasubramanian, N. (2003). *Server transcoding of multimedia information for cross disability access. Proceedings of the ACM/SPIE Conference on Multimedia Computing and Networking*, Santa Clara, California, 45–56.

Bandelloni, R., Berti, S., & Paternò, F. (2004). Mixed-initiative, trans-modal interface migration. *Proceedings of the Mobile HCI 2004 (MHCI04)*, Glasgow, UK, 216–227.

Boll, S., Klas, W., & Wandel, J. (1999). A cross-media adaptation strategy for multimedia presentations. *Proceedings of the ACM Multimedia'99*, Orlando, Florida, 37–46.

Chang, H.S., Sull, S., & Lee, S.U. (1999). Efficient video indexing scheme for content-based retrieval. *IEEE Trans. Circ. Syst. Video Technol., 9*(8), 1269–1279.

Chang, S.-F., & Vetro, A. (2005). Video adaptation: Concepts, technologies, and open issues. *Proceedings of the IEEE, 93*(1), 148–158.

Cucchiara, R., Grana, C., & Prati, A. (2003). Semantic video transcoding using classes of relevance. *International Journal of Image and Graphics, 3*(1), 145–169.

Elting, C., Zwickel, J., & Malaka, R. (2002). Device-dependent modality selection for user-interfaces—An empirical study. *Proceedings of the International Conference on Intelligent User-Interfaces*, San Francisco, California, 55–62.

Forney, G.D. (1973). The Viterbi algorithm. *Proceedings of the IEEE, 61*(3), 268–278.

Ghinea, G., & Thomas, J.P. (1998). QoS impact on user perception and understanding of multimedia clips. *Proceedings of the ACM Multimedia*, Bristol, UK, 98, 49–54.

ISO/IEC. (2003). IS 15938-5:2001: Information Technology—Multimedia Content Description Interface—Multimedia Description Schemes.

ISO/IEC. (2004). IS 21000-7:2004 Information Technology—Multimedia Framework—Part 7: DIA.

ISO/IEC. (2006). IS 21000-7:2006 FPDAM/1: Conversions and permissions.

ITU. (1999). ITU-T recommendation P.910: Subjective video quality assessment methods for multimedia applications.

ITU. (2002). ITU-R recommendation BT.500-11: Methodology for the subjective assessment of the quality of television pictures.

Jannach, D., & Leopold, K. (2005). A multimedia adaptation framework based on semantic Web technology. *Proceedings of the 2nd European Semantic Web Conference*, Heraklion, Greece, 61–68.

Kaup, A. (2002). Video analysis for universal multimedia messaging. *Proceedings of the 5th IEEE Southwest Symp. Image Analysis and Interpretation*, Santa Fe, New Mexico, 211–215.

Kim, J.-G., Wang, Y., & Chang, S.-F. (2003). Content-adaptive utility based video adaptation. *Proceedings of the International Conference on Multimedia & Expo*, Baltimore, Maryland, 281–284.

Kim, M.B., Nam, J., Baek, W., Son, J., & Hong, J. (2003). The adaptation of 3D stereoscopic video in MPEG-21 DIA. *Signal Processing: Image Communication*, *18*(8), 685–697.

Lee, C., Lehoczky, J., Siewiorek, D., Rajkumar, R., & Hansen, J. (1999). A scalable solution to the multi-resource QoS problem. *Proceedings of the 20th IEEE Real-Time Systems Symposium*, Phoenix, Arizona, 315–326.

Lee, H.-C., & Kim, S.-D. (2003). Iterative key frame selection in the rate-constraint environment. *Signal Processing: Image Communication*, *18*(1), 1–15.

Lengwehasatit, K., & Ortega, A. (2000). Rate-complexity-distortion optimization for quadtree-based DCT coding. *Proceedings of the Conference on Image Processing*, Vancouver, Canada, 821–824.

Lienhart, R. (2003). Video OCR: A survey and practitioner's guide. In A. Rosenfeld, D. Doermann, & D. DeMenthon (Eds.), *Video mining* (pp. 155–184), Kluwer Academic Publisher.

Lum, W.Y., & Lau, F.C.M. (2002). A QoS-sensitive content adaptation system for mobile computing. *Proceedings of the Computer Software and Applications Conference*, Oxford, UK, 680–685.

Mohan, R., Smith, J. R., & Li, C.-S. (1999). Adapting multimedia Internet content for universal access. *IEEE Trans. Multimedia*, *1*(1), 104–114.

Mukherjee, D., Delfosse, E., Kim, J.-G., & Wang, Y. (2005). Optimal adaptation decision-taking for terminal and network quality-of-service. *IEEE Trans. Multimedia*, *7*(3), 454–462.

Nagao, K., Shirai, Y., & Squire, K. (2001). Semantic annotation and transcoding: Making Web content more accessible. *IEEE Multimedia*, *8*(2), 69–81.

Ohm, J.-R. (2005). Advances in scalable video coding. *Proceedings of the IEEE*, *93*(1), 42–56.

Ortega, A., & Ramchandran, K. (1998). Rate-distortion methods for image and video compression. *IEEE Signal Processing Magazine,* *15*(6), 23–50.

Ortega, A., Ramchandran, K., & Vetterli, M. (1994). Optimal trellis-based buffered compression and fast approximations. *IEEE Trans. Image Processing, 3*(1), 26–40.

Panis, G., et al. (2003). Bitstream syntax description: A tool for multimedia resource adaptation within MPEG-21. *Signal Processing: Image Communication, 18*(8), 721–747.

Pereira, F., & Burnett, I. (2003). Universal multimedia experiences for tomorrow. *IEEE Signal Processing Magazine, 20*(2), 63–73.

Prangl, M., Szkaliczki, T., & Hellwagner, H. (2007). A framework for utility-based multimedia adaptation. *IEEE Trans. Circ. Syst. Video Technol., 17*(6), 719–728.

Thang, T.C., Jung, Y.J., Lee, J.W., & Ro, Y.M. (2004). Modality conversion for universal multimedia services. *Proceedings of the International Workshop on Image Analysis for Multimedia Interactive Services*, Lisbon, Portugal.

Thang, T.C., Jung, Y.J., & Ro, Y.M. (2005a). Modality conversion for QoS management in universal multimedia access. *IEE Proc. Vision, Image & Signal Processing, 152*(3), 374–384.

Thang, T.C., Jung, Y.J., & Ro, Y.M. (2005b). Effective adaptation of multimedia documents with modality conversion. *Signal Processing: Image Communication, 20*(5), 413–434.

Thang, T.C., Jung, Y.J., & Ro, Y.M. (2005c). Semantic quality for content-aware video adaptation. *Proceedings of the IEEE MMSP2005*, Shanghai, China.

Thang, T.C., Kim, Y.S., Kim, C.S., & Ro, Y.M. (2006). Quality models for audiovisual streaming. *Proceedings of the SPIE Electronic Imaging*, San Jose, California.

Thang, T.C., Yang, S., Ro, Y.M., & Wong, K.E. (2007). Media accessibility for low vision users in the MPEG-21 multimedia framework. *IEICE Trans. Information and Systems. E90-D*(8), 1271–1278.

van Beek, P., Smith, J.R., Ebrahimi, T., Suzuki, T., & Askelof, J. (2003). Metadata-driven multimedia access. *IEEE Signal Processing Magazine, 20*(2), 40–52.

Vetro, A. (2004). MPEG-21 digital item adaptation: Enabling universal multimedia access. *IEEE Multimedia, 11*(1), 84–87.

Watson, A. & Sasse, M.A. (1998). Measuring perceived quality of speech and video in multimedia conferencing applications. *Proceedings of the ACM Multimedia98*, Bristol, UK, 55–60.

Wu, C.-H., & Chen, J.-H. (1997). Speech activated telephony email reader (SATER) based on speaker verification and text-to-speech conversion. *IEEE Trans. Consumer Electronics, 43*, 707–716.

## ADDITIONAL READING

Ahmad, I., Wei, X., Sun, Y., & Zhang, Y.-Q. (2005). Video transcoding: An overview of various techniques and research issues. *IEEE Trans. Multimedia, 7*(5), 793–804.

Batra, P. (2000). Modeling and efficient optimization for object-based scalability and some related problems. *IEEE Trans. Image Processing, 9*(10), 1677–1692.

Berretti, S., Del Bimbo, A., & Vicario, E. (2001). Efficient matching and indexing of graph models in content based retrieval. *IEEE Trans. Pattern Analysis and Machine Intelligence, 23*(1), 1089–1105.

Burnett, I., Pereira, F., Van de Walle, R., & Koenen, R. (Eds.). (2006). *The MPEG-21 book*. Chichester, UK: John Wiley & Sons.

Chandra, S., Ellis, C.S., & Vahdat, A. (2000). Application-level differentiated multimedia Web services using quality aware transcoding. *IEEE Journal on Selected Areas in Communications, 18*(12), 2544–2565.

Chen, J., Yang, Y., & Zhang, H. (2000). An adaptive Web content delivery system. *Proceedings of the International Conference on Adaptive Hypermedia and Adaptive Web-based Systems*, Trento, Italy, 284–288.

ISO/IEC. (2006). IS 21000-7:2006 FPDAM/2: Dynamic and distributed adaptation.

Lee, K., Chang, H.S., Chun, S.S., & Sull, S. (2001). Perception-based image transcoding for universal multimedia access. *Proceedings of the Conference on Image Processing*, Thessaloniki, Greece, 475–478.

Li, Z., Katsaggelos, A.K., Schuster. G., & Gandhi, B. (2005a). Rate-distortion optimal video summary generation. *IEEE Trans. on Image Processing, 14*(10), 1550–1560.

Li, Z., Schuster, G., & Katsaggelos, A.K. (2005b). MINMAX optimal video summarization and coding. *IEEE Trans. on Circuits and System for Video Technology, 15*(10), 1245–1256.

Magalhaes, J., & Pereira, F. (2004). Using MPEG standards for multimedia customization. *EURASIP Signal Processing: Image Communication, 19*(5), 437–456.

Pereira, F. (2003). Content adaptation: The panacea for usage diversity? *Proceedings of 8th International Workshop on Very Low Bitrate Video Coding*, Spain, 9–12.

Pinson, M.H., & Wolf, S. (2004). A new standardized method for objectively measuring video quality. *IEEE Trans. Broadcasting, 50*(3), 312–322.

Salembier, P., & Smith, J.R. (2001). MPEG-7 multimedia description schemes. *IEEE Trans. Circ. Syst. Video Technol., 11*(6), 748–759.

Serif, T., Gulliver, S.R., & Ghinea, G. (2004). Infotainment across access devices: The perceptual impact of multimedia QoS. *Proceedings of the ACM Symp. on Applied Computing*, Nicosia, Cyprus, 1580–1585.

Sundaram, H., Xie, L., & Chang, S.-F. (2002). A utility framework for the automatic generation of audiovisual skims. *Proceedings of the ACM Multimedia 2002*, Juan Les Pins, France, 189–198.

Thang, T.C., Jung, Y.J., & Ro, Y.M. (2003). On some QoS aspects of user profile in universal multimedia access. *Proceedings of the IEEE TENCON2003*, Bangalore, India, 591–595.

Thang, T.C., Jung, Y.J., & Ro, Y.M. (2003). Modality conversion in content adaptation for universal multimedia access. *Proceedings of International Conference on Imaging Science, Systems, and Technology*, Nevada, 434–440.

Thang, T.C., Jung, Y.J., & Ro, Y.M. (2004). Efficient modeling of video-to-image conversion for QoS management in networked video service. *Proceedings of the IEEE TENCON2004*, Thailand, 598–601.

Thang, T.C., Kang, J.W., & Ro, Y.M. (2007). Graph-based perceptual quality model for audiovisual contents. *Proceedings of the IEEE ICME2007*, Beijing.

Vetro, A. (2003). Transcoding, scalable coding & standardized metadata. *Proceedings of International Workshop on Very Low Bitrate Video*, Spain, 15–16.

Vetro, A., Christopoulos, C., & Ebrahimi, T. (Eds.). (2003). Special issue on universal multimedia access. *IEEE Signal Processing Magazine, 20*(2).

Vetro, A., Christopoulos, C., & Sun, H. (2003). An overview of video transcoding architectures and techniques. *IEEE Signal Processing Magazine, 20*(2), 18–29.

Vetro, A., Sun, H., & Wang, Y. (2001). Object-based transcoding for adaptable video content delivery. *IEEE Trans. Circ. Syst. Video Technol., 11*(3), 387–401.

Vetro, A., & Timmerer, C. (2005). Digital item adaptation: Overview of standardization and research activities. *IEEE Trans. Multimedia, 7*(3), 418–426.

# Section II
# Frameworks and Algorithms for Multimedia Transcoding in Mobile and Wireless Network

Chapter VI

# Transcoding vs. Scalability in Video Streaming for Heterogeneous Networks/Clients

**Nicola Conci**
*University of Trento, Italy*

**Francesco G.B. De Natale**
*University of Trento, Italy*

## ABSTRACT

Transcoding provides ad hoc solutions for every user's category by decompressing a video sequence and recompressing it into a different format where the frame size, colour representation, frame rate, quality, and other characteristics may change. Scalable coding allows implementing most of these operations in an easier and cheapest way, substituting decoding and re-encoding with simple selection and combination operations. In this case, the video is encoded once for all, but different users can access different instances of it according to their specific requirements, capabilities, and compatibilities. The aim of this chapter is to highlight the pros and cons of both techniques, presenting solutions based on layered coding and multiple description coding as a valuable alternative to transcoding, especially in those cases where network losses are not negligible.

## INTRODUCTION

Although the widespread use of video streaming services is rapidly increasing, some major problems are still to be solved when heterogeneous networks and terminals are concerned. Channel adaptation, storage and computational power constraints, requirements in terms of quality of service, and real-time delivery are some of the main technological challenges, but the business model that lies beyond the service provision should also be considered. In fact, in most cases, the task of managing the channel/terminal adaptation is left to service providers, which need to tailor (statically or dynamically) contents and data formats to specific user categories and billing models.

The immediate consequence is an increased complexity and the need to introduce suitable mechanisms at both the server and network levels. Among various possibilities, transcoding and scalability can represent viable solutions to adapt visual contents to different services. In the first case, the video is converted into different formats by a (possibly partial) decoding and re-encoding mechanism to match the requirements of the receiver; in the second case, the video is coded once for all in a flexible format that allows accessing it in different ways (bit-rate, frame rate, resolution, etc.). The choice of whether to choose a transcoder or a scalable video coder certainly depends on the application to be developed, and there is no ultimate solution that allows developers to rapidly select between them. The purpose of this chapter is to comparatively analyze the two strategies in order to provide readers with some hints to understand the advantages and drawbacks of either approach.

What usually happens in multimedia delivery is that a video server must grant a service to various classes of customers, which usually can be grouped into categories, depending on the channel/terminal capacity. In general, we could identify a low-level user profile with an available bandwidth below 100kbps (portable devices over 2.5G mobile, devices connected by modem over PSTN), a middle-level profile at less than 500kbps (new generation mobile and PDA over 3G, PC devices connected to low-speed xDSL), and a high-quality model for all the applications that can afford broadband services (PC and set-top boxes over high-speed xDSL, fiber, 4G mobile, Wifi/WiMax). In transcoding approaches, the streaming server converts the stream into different compression standards or into different profiles of the same standard to fit the aforementioned requirements. Adaptation capabilities are also required at the network/transport layer. This means that transcoding can be seen as an intermediate layer that receives the high quality video as input and outputs a lower quality/resolution stream. This process requires an ad hoc conversion (see transcoders T1, T2, and T3 in Figure 1) each time a stream is sent over the network.

As an alternative, scalable video coders provide coding strategies and formats able to limit the amount of data to be processed in order to support fast conversion and rate adaptation implementing

*Figure 1. Example of transcoding-based video server; Ad hoc streams are generated for each user category.*

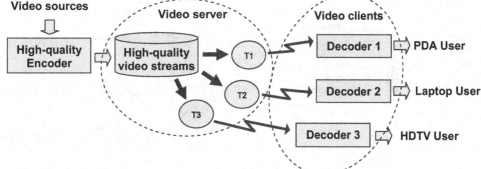

simple dataflow-selection procedures. In this context, techniques such as layered video, fine granularity or bit-plane coding, and multiple description coding could represent helpful alternatives to classical transcoding approaches, providing high flexibility and reusability of the encoded stream.

This makes it possible to optimize the adaptation layer as well, creating complementary streams capable to easily represent the visual content. The structure of a scalable coder acts on a different level if compared to a transcoder (i.e., it is a source coder that directly produces an adaptable network-ready stream, therefore without requiring additional layers and operations). In this case, of course, part of the complexity is left to the decoder, which should be capable of interpreting and managing a structured video stream (e.g., layered, progressive, multisource, etc.) and extract the best possible subset of data for decoding.

Transcoding and scalable coding are not necessarily competing techniques and can coexist in the same system. However, both can be viable solutions for the problem of channel/terminal adaptation, and it is interesting to analyze, which one can perform better. Several pros and cons in either approach can be identified, and in the following, we will revise the main arguments that are provided in literature. In particular, as can be deducted from Xin, Lin, and Sun (2005), there are some reasons why industry has not yet relied on current scalable video coding standards. At the moment, commercial applications tend to implement transcoding algorithms. In fact, they deal with well-known and consolidated standards such as the ISO-MPEG family (mainly single layer coding) because of their widespread market and user acceptance. Furthermore, transcoding makes it always possible to tune the output bit-rate as desired. A layered coder, instead, if not properly configured, might lead to incompatibilities with the transmission channel because of incorrect configuration and settings, leading either to congestion or waste of bandwidth. However, such generalizations are often inappropriate. Usually, a limited number of use-cases are taken into account, which is perfectly compatible with widely investigated scalability technologies such as layered coding. In addition, recent improvements suggest that the scalability concept is viable and, in some cases, could provide benefits with respect to transcoding.

The chapter is organized as follows: first, the streaming framework is introduced, addressing the most important features and analyzing the various types of services that are commonly delivered over the network (wired or wireless). This allows identifying the main problems that arise while setting up a streaming server. In the following section, an in-depth analysis of the solutions for adaptive video

*Figure 2. Example of scalable coder-based video server; Each user decodes the best quality stream according to the capabilities of his client.*

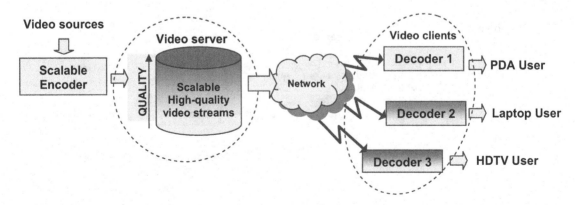

streaming based on scalable coding is proposed. For every solution, advantages and disadvantages are analyzed, focusing particularly on aspects related to complexity (e.g., computation, storage, delays), quality, and overheads. The relationships and comparisons among these techniques and relevant transcoding approaches are investigated as well. Some of the methods presented have already been standardized, while some others have not, even if they may become flexible instruments for the creation of differentiated services. Some useful notes about the level of standardization and the inclusion in up-to-date recommendations are then provided as a reference. Finally, some concluding remarks are drawn about current situations and future trends of the research in this field.

## A SHORT INTRODUCTION TO STREAMING SERVICES

Usually, with the term "streaming," people refer to the communication of multimedia content over a transmission channel, or formally to the "transmission of multimedia data over telecommunication networks" as it involves primarily the way in which media are transmitted, instead of the media themselves.

The number of applications making use of streaming technologies over wired and wireless networks has experienced a dramatic increase in the last years due to the widespread use of wideband connectivity, which target is to connect as many users as possible and to provide network services at lower costs and higher quality. Enabling users to effectively access such services is a primary target for the companies involved in multimedia content distribution, including broadcasters, pay-per-viewers, user communities, telephone providers (fixed and mobile), and so forth. The quality of the service provided may greatly vary from one application to another, from the baseline quality of a personal audiovisual communication (e.g., a mobile video call) to a very high quality of multimedia interactive services (e.g., the future high-definition TV). In between, there is a wide range of scenarios involving suitable trade-offs between quality of service (e.g., video resolution, frame rate, speech quality, etc.) and resources (maximum and average bandwidth, costs, etc.).

Moreover, additional requirements are imposed by the nature of the devices (servers and terminals) involved in the coding-decoding process. These requirements are particularly demanding in the case of mobile and nomadic applications where the terminal has to be sufficiently small, cheap, and with low power consumption, implying a reduced computational performance, limitations in the display dimension/resolution, and so forth. The typical applications covered by this kind of terminal include audio and videoconferencing, delivery of multimedia contents acquired by the onboard camera and microphone of a PDA/smartphone, broadcasting over wireless channels for entertainment purposes (e.g., sports events, TV programs), transmission of video sources grabbed by webcams for environmental monitoring, automotive applications, and many more.

The scheme in Figure 3 illustrates a very simple generalization of a streaming architecture. It is composed of a number of elements and offers several functionalities. The main blocks can be identified as a:

- Video server
  o It performs media compression and encoding (source coding).
  o It introduces application-layer error protection (resilience mechanisms, concealment).
  o It manages network adaptation (e.g., rate control)

*Figure 3. Generalization of a streaming architecture*

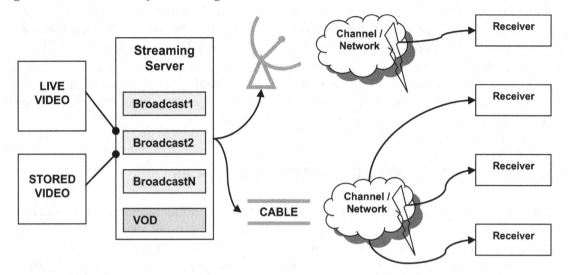

- Communication channel (including communication protocols)
  - o It is characterized by a given capacity and may introduce errors, delays, jitters, packet/data losses.
  - o It introduces communication-layer error protection (channel coding, ARQ, etc.).
- Receiver
  - o It performs stream assembly
  - o It exploits error resilience features (correction, resynchronization, concealment, etc.).
  - o It performs stream decoding.

Each component listed previously behaves differently on the basis of the streaming requirements and depending on the network capabilities. In fact, the network structure can be highly variable, presenting different problems such as delays, delay jitters, errors, packet losses, temporary blockings due to inefficient network congestion management, and media adaptation (Gou, Hofmann, Ng, Paul & Zhang, 2002; Rejaie, Handley & Estrin, 2000). Streaming technologies try to mitigate the impact of these problems on the quality perceived by the end user, thus introducing various mechanisms according to the difficulties to be faced.

## Requirements at the Client and Server Sides

Video streaming concerns the transmission of audiovisual information together with relevant side information. Video is a very important source of information in current media, even if it requires the highest amount of bandwidth. Audio tracks come immediately after in terms of bit-rate, in particular when audio is multilingual, high-quality, and possibly associated with special effects (multisource, surrounding). Moreover, audio and video need to be synchronized and associated to suitable signaling information to ensure a robust transports structure. Then, additional context information can be added, such as MIME types (revealing the type of data contained in the stream: audio, video, applications,

*Figure 4. Media types and synchronization*

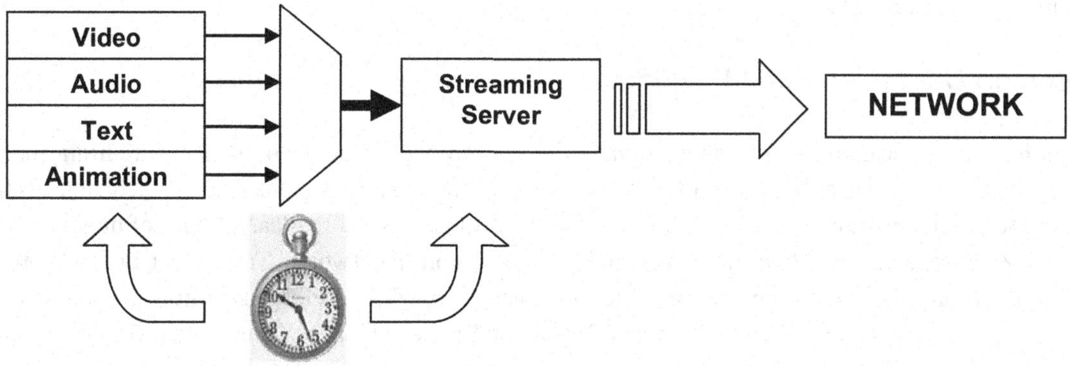

file extensions), headers, packetization, and other network-related information (addresses and ports of the end users). By suitably managing the previously listed sources of information, a number of streams can be merged to achieve a complete service; namely, a "presentation." Particular attention should be paid to the synchronization of the streams (see Figure 4). In fact, if stand-alone streams (i.e., a single audio or video stream) can be considered independent and can be decoded even with varying delay, joint audio-video-data sources require a seamless integration with the presence of a clock to temporally align the different media.

The streams described so far can be managed at the server side in two ways: on the one hand, the delivery of prestored video contents (either broadcast or sent upon demand), while on the other hand, the transmission of real-time encoded sequences. Applications such as video downloading from the Internet or video-on-demand (VoD) belong to the first category, while personal communications or live video fall into the second one. Prestored video is easier to manage, mainly because it does not need online encoding at the server side. In fact, the video server becomes a remote archive of pre-encoded visual contents that are sent over the network according to the type of service (e.g., broadcast, multicast, unicast, etc.). Live video involves instead a higher complexity at the server due to the need of encoding the video on the fly while transmitting it.

As far as the receiver is concerned, the situation is much more variable. In fact, a user may want to gather the video stream while being connected to different networks with different devices: a cell phone, a PDA, a laptop, a workstation, a TV set connected to a set-top box. Even in this case, the video can be downloaded for later playout or consumed on the fly. This high variability makes it difficult to tailor the transmission to all users at the same time because of varying computational capabilities, storage capacity, and available bandwidth. Receiver tasks will be detailed in the following. In order to be properly decoded and played, the client usually needs at least to preload a portion of the stream on a local memory buffer, which allows compensating network delays and temporary congestions, as well as bandwidth fluctuations. The size of the cyclic buffer, usually referred to as playout buffer, is set according to the specific application to cope with storage and delay constraints, and it is designed to be compliant with the target bit-rate of the incoming stream. After having filled the buffer, the video starts playing, and the incoming data replace the displayed ones. During this process, signaling information is consumed and stripped from the stream; audio, video, and other components are separated and passed to the relevant decoders. Although these operations are usually quite inexpensive in computation due to the asymmetric nature of current standard codecs, they may cause problems of real-time constraints and high volumes of data to be processed.

## Common Communication Protocols

From the communication strategies viewpoint, efficient protocols must be used to ensure high-quality service to end users. In fact, it is usually impossible to guarantee a return channel for feedback control due to the strict constraints in terms of delays and the multicast and broadcast nature of most applications. Therefore, even though the transmission is performed on IP networks, Transport Control Protocol (TCP) is seldom used to implement real-time video services, while preferring protocols such as User Datagram Protocol (UDP) (Postel, 1980) and Real Time Protocol (RTP) (Schulzrinne, Casner, Frederick & Jacobson, 2003). The absence of a return channel does not guarantee the service to be effective from a quality point of view, but it enables the on-time delivery of the media. This implies the need for a better source protection of the stream, which is usually achieved using redundancy (e.g., duplication of important information such as headers and adoption of Forward Error Correction codes) and other resilient transmission strategies such as resynchronization markers and reversible Variable Length Codes. In case of data loss, the decoder must exploit the redundant information to recover the lost information or at least reduce the impact of errors, rapidly restarting the decoding process and trying to interpolate the missing data. As RTP is one of the most adopted transmission protocols in the field of Internet streaming, a higher level protocol has been designed on top of it, which allows users to exploit some useful VCR-like functions while watching the video. The protocol is called Real Time Streaming Protocol (RTSP) (Schulzrinne, Rao & Lanphier, 1998) and was defined by the IETF standardization body; it shows some similarities with the HTTP protocol. Its main advantage is that it does not need to always keep the connection alive. The protocol is able to store the "state" of the stream and start downloading again upon a user's request.

## SCALABLE CODING TECHNIQUES FOR VIDEO DELIVERY

Scalable coding for video streaming is still an emerging methodology, which, despite the big research efforts in the last years, has still to prove its effectiveness. Main problems concern the coding efficiency (due to the introduced overhead) and implementation complexity (due to the additional mechanisms and computations required at the encoder and sometimes also at the receiver side). The purpose of this section is to introduce the fundamental concepts of scalable coding and demonstrate that this approach can solve some of the problems traditionally settled by transcoding. The former concentrates on the encoding stage, while the latter focuses on the transmission channel as the key element (Vetro, Christopoulos & Sun, 2003). Nevertheless, the two worlds do not have to be considered independent and mutually exclusive since there are cases in which transcoding and scalability are used jointly. As an example, Shanableh and Ghanabari (2005) proposes an encoder able to serve various kinds of terminals through an efficient transcoder using a scalable coder as an intermediate step between the pre-encoded video sequence and the transmitter/router. The merging procedure creates, therefore, a multipurpose coding scheme capable of facing any network and device requirement, especially thanks to the exploitation of both transcoding and layered coding.

First, we will focus on a critical analysis of transcoding approaches, assessing their features and limitations; then, we will review the most well-known scalability concepts, describing and evaluating the relevant techniques; and finally, we will conclude with a brief survey on the use of scalability principles within current international coding standards.

## Transcoding: Issues and Limitations

After the introduction of the universal media access, which made it possible for different terminals to access the Internet through different means (e.g., LAN, DSL, GPRS, UMTS), digital video transcoding (Xin et al., 2005) has become a major requirement in multimedia content delivery systems. Literally, the term implies a conversion from one compressed format to another, aiming to build a framework capable of satisfying the requirements of several categories of users. One of the main constraints is related to the computational complexity of the transcoder. Besides the concept of universal access and rate adaptation, there are many applications that would benefit from transcoding techniques; in particular, the ones related to information insertion and extraction (e.g., subtitles, watermarks, etc.), but even format and standard conversions (e.g., resolution, chromatic representation, compression techniques, etc.). Mohan, Smith, and Li (1999), for instance, address the need of adapting Web contents to different client platforms. In their paper, the content delivery is assigned to a *customizer* that chooses the resolution and definition of the Web content according to the capabilities of the receiver. Even though the paper does not deal directly with video delivery, it is useful to understand the content adaptation problem, which is strictly related to the video transcoding application. In fact, transcoding must be carried out not only on an objective basis, but also specific attention should be paid to understanding the visual content of the media, thus exploiting the a priori knowledge to optimize the rate adaptation process.

It is out of the scope of this chapter to fully review the huge literature on transcoding. We will instead introduce some concepts related to transcoding (and to the relevant technical approaches) that can be useful to understand the interconnections between it and scalable coding, therefore helping the reader in a comparative appraisal. As the term *transcoding* implies some kind of format conversion, we can state that this operation may or may not introduce a variation in the bit-rate of the output video.

If the only purpose of transcoding is a standard conversion (e.g., to make a stream compatible with different equipment), in general, different syntaxes and representation of the data are also required, which are not necessarily connected to rate adaptation. In this case, there is no easy solution to relieve this operation. More often, transcoding is operated to adapt the stream to different application domains, where the content should be tailored to different networks and media. In this case, transcoding implies a variation (usually a reduction) in the bit-rate, while not necessarily requiring significant modifications in the syntax.

Practically speaking, the reduction of the bit-rate can be achieved following different strategies, and three main branches of research can be identified in this field. A simple way to adapt the bit-rate is to work on the quantization operation. As most of the video coders deal with lossy encoding strategies, the quantization is an easy parameter to tune the output rate of the video (Assuncao & Ghanbari, 1997; Werner, 1999). Even though the requantization is probably one of the most common ways to achieve the goal, there are obviously some drawbacks, and the most important one is that the output video could be severely damaged if the rate reduction is too sharp. From the user's point of view, this means perceiving a poor quality of the displayed sequence. In order to dramatically reduce the bit-rate also, the variation in the frame rate is often adopted as a simpler alternative (Fung, Chan & Siu, 2002; Shu

& Chau, 2004). Temporal down-sampling is very effective, especially when the motion is not too high. In fact, if the video contains fast movements, the frame rate reduction will introduce motion artefacts and drifts due to two reasons. First, frame skipping lets the human eye perceive a nonfluent video, and second, the motion estimation can be affected by the lack of frames. In these cases, a re-estimation of the motion field would be necessary at the cost of an increase in computational complexity. A third common approach to reduce the rate consists in changing the video resolution. Spatial down-sampling is very effective in cutting down the bit-rate, and with respect to the methods already cited, it does not affect either motion compensation or perceived quality (provided that the display is conveniently sized). If the resize factor becomes too high with respect to the presentation device, the resulting video could be strongly damaged, leading to a significant increase in the distortion, which could be comparable or even worse than requantization.

Therefore, in order to fulfill bandwidth requirements, the process can be tuned for a specific transmission channel, trying to minimize the differences with the original video (through some rate-distortion optimization). After the video is received, the user can decide whether to enjoy the low-resolution video or expand it to the original size. In the image processing field, the problem has been faced with good results (Dugad & Ahuja, 2001; Mukherjee & Mitra, 2002; Shu & Chau, 2006). The last one in particular works directly in the transformed domain through DCT sub-band approximation, which makes the approach suitable for many image and video coding schemes that often are based on the DCT transform. The performance of the method has recently been improved (Patil, Kumar & Mukherjee, 2006) and adapted to the video coding framework. The obtained results are pretty impressive, as the implementation allows for a strong improvement in terms of both computational complexity and quality with respect to previously proposed methods.

The previous considerations allow highlighting pros and cons of transcoding. First, a transcoder is an irreplaceable instrument to convert streams among different standards, especially when the stream syntax and the data representation have to be significantly modified. In this case, the transcoder can be implemented in a straightforward way by cascading a *"standard-A"* decoder with a *"standard-B"* encoder. This structure makes it possible with minor conceptual adaptations to arbitrarily choose the input-output formats. Flexibility and inherent compliance with any standard make this approach attractive also from a commercial point of view, where industries have big interests in developing fast and efficient transcoders. The devices are usually implemented as hardware solutions for consumer applications (DV to DVD conversions for digital video cameras, DVD backup, media transportability, video streaming for heterogeneous fixed and mobile devices, etc.). On the other side, some major weakness points can be underlined.

Hardware devices capable of performing a format conversion are very efficient, but they are required to possibly manage any combination of input-output formats, causing a rapid increase in complexity and costs. Software solutions are more flexible, even though they require powerful general-purpose hardware to run the conversion at the requested speed. This kind of trouble can be managed quite smoothly in off-line scenarios, but online streaming services can pose severe problems. In fact, transcoding has to be performed at the server level, where the user's needs are not necessarily known, thus requesting real-time conversion (or in the alternative, the preconversion of the document in all possible output formats, which turns out to be very unpractical in terms of storage requirements). Real time implies very strong requirements in terms of memory and computation at the server. At the encoder, in fact, transcoding has to be performed in parallel if the number of users' categories is large. This implies having a large memory buffer at disposal in order to store the sets of frames (GOPs in MPEG terminology) used for motion field computation.

Furthermore, there are some more subtle implications that are not strictly related to the hardware or software complexity but are more focused on the context in which the transcoder is deployed. On top, the reversibility of the operation must be taken into account. In rate adaptation, high-quality sequences are transcoded to achieve lower bit-rates to fit a narrowband connection. Such conversion introduces a loss of quality that cannot be recovered from that point on (e.g., for successive transmission at higher bit-rate) unless the original video is used. Similarly, if a user desires to receive an improved version of the video he or she just enjoyed, the user must download it again completely, using a different transcoder. Another problem is connected to encryption (Schneier, 1996). When talking about encryption, we usually want to improve the robustness of a system in terms of vulnerabilities and violations. This means that we would like to restrict the access to a specific resource among a given number of authorized users. In video applications, the visual content is opportunely scrambled and hidden in order to make it inaccessible unless the user owns a specific key. The key allows achieving the undisclosed version of the document through a decryption algorithm. From a security point of view, it is natural that the key sharing is limited to the video owner and to authorized users. When transcoding, the device must instead be able to decode the sequence and encode it again in order to fulfill the receiver requirements. This implies that the secret key is shared with the transcoder, which otherwise does not have any chance to perform the task (see Figure 5). In practice, the encrypted signal is sent to the transcoder, which decrypts it, transcodes it, and finally encrypts it again in order to deliver the protected document over the network.

The inefficiency of such a scheme is twofold. On the one hand, the owner must share the key even with the streaming server, which could be a third-party company, therefore endangering the security of the system. On the other hand, this mechanism introduces further complexity into the system due to the encrypt/decrypt operations before and after transcoding.

## Scalability: Issues and Limitations

The purpose of scalability is to allow access to an encoded video stream at different quality levels without the necessity of transcoding, re-encoding, or other complex operations to be performed at the transmitter level.

This objective can be achieved in several different ways, but basically, it requires that the video stream be conveniently structured at the encoder in order to allow the decoder to extract a decodable substream at the desired quality.

Several approaches have been proposed in literature to develop a scalable coder. We will focus mainly on three methods: layered coding, fine granularity scalability, and multiple description coding. In the following sections, they are briefly reviewed.

*Figure 5. Transcoder scheme for secure applications; Need of sharing the "key."*

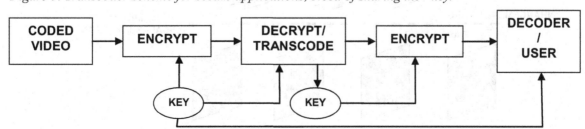

## Layered Coding

In layered coding, the stream is organized in a base layer (low-quality, low bit-rate) and one or more enhancement layers. The layers are sent over the transmission channel according to the delivery strategy in order to let the decoder always receive at least the base layer. By using this mechanism, it is possible to ensure a minimum guaranteed quality even in the presence of reduced bandwidth and high error rates, while the service can be improved in the presence of better channel performance. Alternatively, the different streams can be used to serve different user categories, which can suffer from terminal limitations in decoding speed, display resolution, or available bandwidth (Sun, Kwok & Zdepski, 1996).

There are three main options for stream layering. The first possibility is to adopt the so-called temporal scalability; in this case, the frame rate of the original video is progressively reduced to keep the bit-rate of the sequence at the desired level. The residual information is then saved on one or more additional streams, which can be transmitted according to the server policies. This means the delivery can be simultaneous on a second channel (with higher rate) or sent upon the user request at a successive time. The use of temporal prediction in the encoded sequence, typical of most current standards, makes this operation more complex, as the decoder must know the reference pictures to calculate the motion prediction. For this reason, temporal scalability is mainly applied by selectively removing less important frames (e.g., interpolated ones) and keeping in the base layer the ones used for prediction (in particular, intra frames). Taking as an example a typical group of pictures (GOP) structure, Figure 6 illustrates a possible configuration of a nonscalable stream compared to a scalable one. Intra and predicted frames are separated from interpolated ones to obtain a base and an enhancement layer. Obviously, the enhancement layer is completely useless if the base layer is lost. On the other way around, the base layer frame can be decoded even if the enhancement layer is not received.

*Figure 6. Example of temporal scalability; I-frames (in red) and P-frames (in green) are coded into the base layer; B-frames (in blue) are coded into the enhancement layer.*

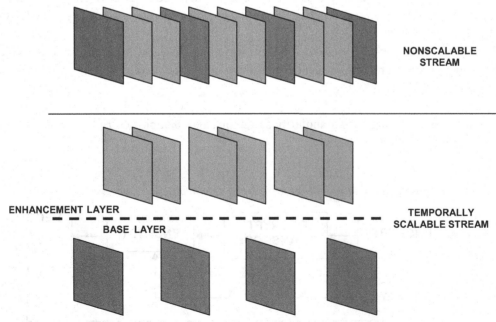

*Figure 7. Example of spatial scalability; The base layer is subsampled by an arbitrary factor; The enhancement layer contains the residual information, which is coded separately.*

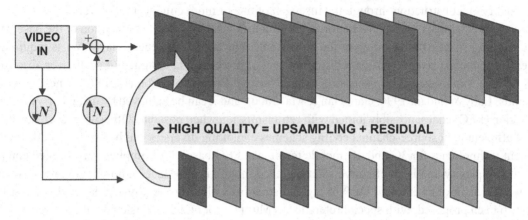

The second layering mechanism is spatial scalability. The objective here is to access the video stream at different spatial resolutions for different categories of terminals. Even in this case, there is no need of re-encoding the sequence. In Figure 7, the principle of spatial scalability is depicted. The picture is on purpose very generic and does not make any specific reference to how spatial scalability is achieved. In fact, the implementation strategies can be very different from time to time, and most standards do not force the developer to follow any specific rule, as long as the standard syntax is respected. Depending on the developers' choices, down-sampling can be performed both in the spatial domain (Dugad & Ahuja, 2001) or in the transformed domain (typically DCT or wavelet) such as Mukherjee and Mitra (2002) and Patil, et al. (2006) do. Often this process is quite heavy to perform, and it may require complex interpolation procedures, residual coding, and possibly the recalculation of the motion field.

The third common approach to scalability is quality scalability or SNR scalability (Figure 8). In this approach, the stratification is made upon a quality criterion, basically assigning a worse quantization

*Figure 8. SNR scalability; The base layer is compressed with a coarse quantization parameter; The enhancement layer contains the residual information.*

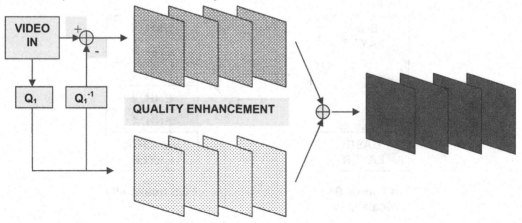

parameter to the base layer and progressively increasing the quantization step for the enhancement layers. Depending on the adopted compression standard, in some cases it is even possible to achieve a "full-quality" reconstruction through the insertion of one or more enhancement layers.

As layered coding is based on a hierarchical structure where the correct reception of the base layer is crucial for a successful decoding of the enhancement layer (and in general, layer *N-1* is required to successfully decode layer *N*), often a different level of protection is assigned to each layer according to its relative importance. This process is called Unequal Error Protection (UEP) (Albanese, Blomer, Edmonds, Luby & Sudan, 1996; Gan, Gan & Ma, 2006), and it can be achieved by using Forward Error Correction (FEC) codes, possibly joined with retransmission when possible. Otherwise, even the adoption of efficient joint source-channel coding schemes exploiting diversity can be used, as implemented in recent technologies for 3G and 4G mobile terminals. FEC-based UEP implies very limited computational complexity and is an effective solution, even though it introduces a non-negligible overhead. Solutions to achieve an implicit UEP of layered streams exploiting the physical layer characteristics have also been proposed, with special reference to Multi Carrier Code Division Multiple Access (MC-CDMA) or Orthogonal Frequency Division Multiple Access (OFDMA). Conci, Berlanda Scorza, and Sacchi (2005) achieve the target by assigning a higher number of subcarriers to the base layer in order to provide higher resilience in the framework of an SNR-scalability scheme. Costa, Eisenberg, Zhai & Katsaggelos (2004) instead develop a similar approach applying the UEP on the enhancement layers through an efficient energy control mechanism.

## Fine-Granularity Scalability (FGS)

The major limitation of layered coding lies on the definition of a predefined set of quantization steps for the different layers. This makes the system easy to implement and use, but it lacks in flexibility. In fact, the network throughput usually varies in a continuous way covering a wide range of possible values. The rate (and quality) of a layered stream varies accordingly but in a discrete way, and when sudden changes occur, the encoder (decoder) is requested to evaluate the transmission (the request) of a higher enhancement layer. Fine-Granularity Scalability (FGS) aims at solving this problem, making the quality variation seamlessly aligned to the network throughput. It relies on the so-called "progressive refinement." In practice, instead of obtaining a single enhancement layer, the idea is to create a continuum of

*Figure 9. SNR scalability VS FGS*

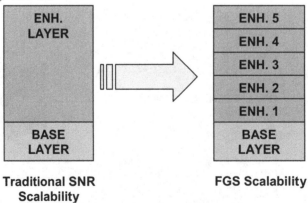

*Figure 10. Progressive refinement of an FGS-coded video frame: From left to right, base quality, first enhancement, Second enhancement.*

enhancement layers able to progressively better the video quality. This principle can be implemented in different modalities, but the basic scheme can be summarized as in Figure 9.

Useful information about FGS can be found in the works of Li (2001) and Van der Schaar (2001). From a visual point of view, we can see in Figure 10 an example of how the FGS scalability can progressively enhance the quality of the sequence.

## Multiple Description Coding

Layered coding aims at structuring the bitstream in a hierarchical cascade, such that higher layers can be properly decoded only if lower ones have been correctly received. In many situations, this constraint turns out to be unacceptable. For instance, in a distributed configuration where the video parts can be split over various servers and transmitted across different channels and subnetworks, the receiving order and integrity of the single pieces cannot be guaranteed. In such situations, UEP may be insufficient to ensure a minimum quality since the base layer may get completely lost due to server failure or channel congestion.

In order to overcome the aforementioned limitations, another interesting scalability strategy is represented by the so-called multiple description coding (MDC). In MDC, the stream is subdivided into a predefined number of independently decidable and usually balanced substreams (Wang, Reibman & Lin, 2005). The video sequence is transmitted exploiting server or path diversity according to application requirements (Apostolopoulos, 2001; Goyal, 2001) and network constraints. The independence of single substreams increments the application versatility and robustness, removing the hierarchical constraints in the decoding process. In fact, each balanced descriptor is designed to have the same weight and contribute equally to the reconstruction of the full quality video. MDC applications usually send data over $n$ (often $n=2$) independent routes and the decoder must be able to reconstruct the stream at acceptable quality for every subset of received descriptors (see Figure 11). The more the descriptors are correctly received, the higher the quality of the decoded stream. The extension of this concept to server diversity comes very easily, the only difference consisting of the download strategy of the client application.

The idea of modeling an information source by dividing its content in two or more equivalent parts is relatively old, and the first attempts were developed by Bell Labs at the end of the 1970s for telephone applications (Witsenhausen & Wyner, 1981; Wolf, Wyner & Ziv, 1980). Later on, also thanks to the

*Figure 11. Generic implementation of an MDC codec with N descriptors exploiting path diversity*

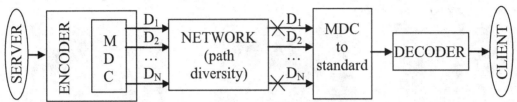

availability of more powerful processing architectures, MDC obtained renewed success, extending the application field to images and video. Notwithstanding the high variety of approaches proposed so far, the common underlying principle of MDC is to split the information content into a predefined number of equally-sized substreams, suitably structured in order to allow the decoding from any arbitrary subset of them. The main drawback of this operation is the introduction in each descriptor of an overhead, called redundancy and usually referred to as $\rho$, which is necessary to make a correct estimate of the information associated with the missing descriptors. The $\rho$ (expressed here as a percentage or as variable between 0 and 1) value is calculated as follows:

$$\rho = \frac{(\sum_N R_n) - R^*}{R^*} \cdot 100 \tag{1}$$

where $R_n$ represents the rate associated to each descriptor and $R^*$ the rate of the equivalent single description coding architecture. Typically, the overhead rapidly increases with $N$. One of the first effective applications of MDC coding, which is still a reference method nowadays, was proposed by Vaishampayan (1993). His idea of a Multiple Description Scalar Quantizer (MDSQ) was demonstrated, for the sake of generality, with application to a memoryless Gaussian source, but it turns out to be effective even for image and video coding. In particular, his example had a great impact on the development of innovative methods for video coding, as it can be observed from the literature. In the following pages, we will evaluate some of the most interesting MDC approaches that have been proposed so far and that may be considered as good alternatives to layered coding (Chakareski, Han & Girod, 2005; Lee, Kim, Altunbasak & Mersereau, 2003). We will review two main classes of methods: DCT-based and Wavelet-based.

Several approaches working in the DCT domain have been proposed in the literature. In Orchard, Wang, Vaishampayan, and Reibman (2001) and Reibman, Jafarkhani, Wang, Orchard, and Puri (2002), the authors propose an extension of the method introduced earlier by Arean, Kovacevic, and Goyal (2000) with application to audio coding. The approach is based on the introduction of a correlating transform to reintroduce some amount of correlation in the DCT coefficients. The authors demonstrate the applicability of the transform in the case of both images and video, block-coded in the DCT domain. The two descriptors are generated by applying a pairwise correlating transform (PCT) to a pair of DCT coefficients (A, B), thus obtaining the correlated PCT coefficients (C, D); namely,

$$\begin{bmatrix} C \\ D \end{bmatrix} = T \begin{bmatrix} A \\ B \end{bmatrix}, \ T = \begin{bmatrix} \sqrt{\dfrac{\cot \theta}{2}} & \sqrt{\dfrac{\tan \theta}{2}} \\ -\sqrt{\dfrac{\cot \theta}{2}} & \sqrt{\dfrac{\tan \theta}{2}} \end{bmatrix} \tag{2}$$

where the term θ is aimed at controlling the correlation between C and D on the basis of the local statistics of the macroblock. Coefficients (C, D) are assigned to the first and second descriptor, respectively. In order to avoid an excessive redundancy, the PCT is applied only to a small subset of DCT coefficients, selecting the pairs (A, B) a priori on the basis of their statistical properties and of the quantization step. The remaining coefficients are simply split into two groups in an odd-even manner. If both descriptors are received, the original coefficients can be restored by applying the inverse transform to the (C, D) pairs and alternating the remaining coefficients. When a description is lost, the missing coefficients can be recovered from the correlated ones through a linear estimation, according to:

$$\hat{D}(\widetilde{C}) = \gamma_{\hat{D}\widetilde{C}}\widetilde{C} \tag{3}$$

The coefficient $\gamma_{\hat{D}\widetilde{C}}$ takes into account the correlating properties of the PCT. In this case, the application of the inverse transform generates a pair of approximated coefficients, thus introducing signal degradation. The method is further refined by Reibman, Jafarkhani, Wang, and Orchard (2001) to produce a new scheme where a subset of the DCT coefficients is duplicated in both descriptors and the remaining ones are quantized to 1 bit and alternately embedded. The selection of the coefficients to be duplicated is based on an adaptive threshold based on the optimization of a cost functional $D+\lambda\rho$, where $D$ and $\rho$ are the distortion and overhead, respectively, and $\lambda$ is a parameter that allows tuning the overhead/distortion function. Further developments of the work proposed by Reibman, et al. (2001) are described by Matty and Kondi (2005), where the choice of the threshold is calculated by a more sophisticated cost functional. Another MDC scheme working in the DCT domain is proposed by Conci and De Natale (2007a) and further extended in Conci and DeNatale (2007b). In their works, a simple but efficient method is presented to achieve MDC coding by exploiting the natural decay in magnitude of the DCT coefficients.

In fact, the absolute value of the terms is more or less constantly decreasing while moving from the low to the high frequencies, and it is possible to estimate the missing ones by applying an interpolator at the decoder, which is capable of reconstructing (with a small error) the magnitude of the original coefficient. Coefficients are then sent over the network by splitting the non-null terms in an odd-even manner. Redundancy is introduced by replicating the most important terms. The approach could even be extended to more than two descriptors and the coefficient selection appears as in Figure 12 (three descriptors). In the example, the non-null coefficients are listed as $a_{ij}$ to be interpreted as the *j-th* coefficient in the *i-th* descriptor.

Several other approaches have been proposed working in the DCT domain. Razzak and Zeng (2001) introduce a method based on DC separation. The DC component is replicated in each descriptor and associated with a number of AC components to produce the subsignals. This is a common substrate of many MDC-DCT methods because most of the significant information is embedded in the DC component.

A major problem in MDC is how to manage the motion information in predictive coders. Being particularly important for the reconstruction of the sequence, the data are often duplicated in every descriptor, thus increasing the overhead. Furthermore, the misalignment between the transmitted mo-

*Figure 12. Coefficient selection in presence of three descriptors*

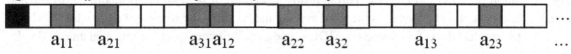

*Figure 13. Quality degradation in presence of one description loss*

*Figure 14. Examples of error propagation*

tion field (calculated on the full quality sequence) and the lower-quality reconstructions achieved from single descriptors may produce annoying artefacts in the decoded stream, such as blocking and error propagation in the successive frames. Such errors can be limited in the presence of local errors that do not prevent completely the reception of a descriptor. In Figure 13 and Figure 14, two common examples of errors occurring in the presence of channel degradation are reported. In Figure 14, the error propagation is quite strong, especially where the motion is considerably high. When no error occurs, most (or all, depending on the coding strategy) descriptors can be correctly decoded, and the highest quality is reached. The examples refer to a two-descriptor case.

Coming to wavelet-based approaches, two preliminary observations have to be formulated. First, wavelets implicitly implement scalability concepts, thus making it easier to develop layered reconstructions in terms of both resolution and SNR. Second, video coders exploiting this technology are still under investigation, and there are no standards available yet. Most of the methods have been developed for still images. Nonetheless, some studies on MDC for wavelet coding have been proposed, and they show relatively interesting performances. Among them, it is worth citing the work developed by Cai, Chen, Ma, and Mitra (2007), where the authors implement an MDC scheme by performing a dual decomposition of the visual content. Through this procedure, it is possible to identify primary and complementary parts. The former is the most crucial and contains the structural data, while the latter contains the residual data. To achieve the MDC scopes, the structural part is replicated among the descriptors, while the complementary one is split according to the number of implemented descriptors. The method is developed to work on a packet switching network, and therefore, the packet management is also considered in order to ensure the maximum resilience possible and therefore a higher image quality. Another interesting approach based on the SPIHT is proposed by Franchi, Fumagalli, Lancini, and Tubaro (2003), where the transmission of MDC streams is achieved through a poliphase transformation exploiting the motion compensation loop.

The advantage of using a wavelet approach consists in the ability of generating a large number of descriptors as it can be noticed in Miguel, Mohr, and Riskin (1999) and Servetto, Ramchandran, Vaishampayan, and Nahrstedt (2000). In these coding algorithms, the authors are able to create a huge number of descriptors (up to 20), making the streaming service extremely flexible. Even though this elasticity represents an added value to the whole system, it is often impracticable to use such a large number of substreams in a real system because of the computational complexity reasons. In fact, the receiver should be able to decode a high number of files and merge them before displaying the decoded video.

## How Scalable Coding Can Represent an Alternative to Transcoding

After having reviewed the basic concepts and techniques of scalability, we would like to summarize the main pros and cons of these approaches in order to allow a comparison with the relevant transcoding methodologies.

The main advantage of a scalable coder consists in the flexibility of the coding strategy that does not require further processing at the server (or network) side. For instance, if a server has to deliver a video stream to a set of different receivers, it is not requested to provide a different stream for each of them; it can simply select the number of layers to be sent according to the receiver characteristics. This process significantly simplifies the encoding stage, making it possible to follow the principle of "code once, decode many." The sentence means that a single encoding process can serve a wide range of decoding devices. Furthermore, when talking about transcoding, we were discussing two fundamental issues: one was related to the reversibility of the operation and the second point was dealing with the problem of data encryption. Scalable coding could be of great help in both cases. Talking about reversibility, as already said, a scalable coder does not create different sequences for all types of channels, but it simply transmits a portion of the stream according to the terminal capabilities or the channel conditions. Thanks to this principle, it is possible to request the enhancement information even after the reception of the assigned stream; for example, if the channel conditions improve or if a higher quality is expressly desired. As far as data encryption is concerned, a scalable coder would facilitate the transmission and improve the security of the application. This is possible thanks to the layered structure of the bitstream, which makes it possible to simply truncate it at the desired bit-rate without the need to reveal the key (Wee, Apostolopoulus, 2001). A simple example is provided in Figure 15: let us assume to transmit a high-quality video layered into four quality layers. If it is necessary to serve a low-bandwidth receiver, some of the layers could easily be dropped. In this way, the video sequence owner does not need to send the key to the video streaming server, which is already embedded in the received layers.

Coming to the cons, scalability has two main drawbacks: overheads (i.e., all the additional information, which is necessary to structure the video stream in order to be accessed in a scalable way), and additional complexity (i.e., the computation required at the encoder and decoder to manage the scalable structure). As far as the overhead is concerned, this is minimal in layered coding and is progressively higher in FGS and in particular MDC, where it can easily reach values over 50%. The main impact in

*Figure 15. Layered coder with data encryption*

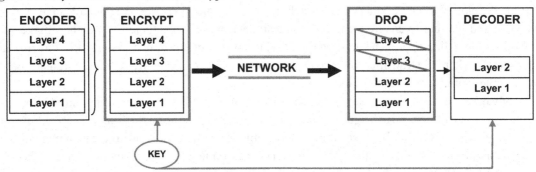

this case is on the transmission channel. The complexity is instead a problem that affects mainly the decoder. In fact, the encoding process is performed just once at the server, eventually even off-line; the decoding process requires instead online processing at the user terminal, where computational power and storage requirements may be an issue.

## SCALABLE CODING STANDARDS

Most recent video coding standards already include in their syntax the data structures to convey some form of scalable video streams. As usual, such syntaxes leave a lot of freedom to the programmer in the implementation of the scalability mechanisms. The most known scalable coding techniques are included in the MPEG standards starting from MPEG-2 and H.263+, though probably the most advanced scalability concepts are currently included in the MPEG-4 standard. Recently, scalability has been introduced even in H.264 (the extension is called SVC), which is still under standardization and involves (as the nonscalable version) the Joint Video Team (JVT), a joint teamwork between ISO and ITU committees. In this section, we will review and discuss the scalability features included in the main digital video coding standards. We will focus on layered coding and FGS, being MDC methodologies still considered immature for standardization. A short note will also be presented on object-based coding, which can be considered as a sort of high-level scalability concept.

### Scalability in MPEG-2

MPEG-2 (Tudor, 1995) includes the first ISO-IEC implementation of a scalable architecture (ISO-IEC, 1995). Even though the first version of the codec (the one used even today for DVD encoding) was not scalable and was targeted to high-quality broadcast applications, this extension was added later to cope with different channel capacities and in order to avoid transcoding operations on the video stream. MPEG-2 (like many other multimedia coding standards) is provided with a set of so-called *profiles*: simple, main, SNR-scalable, and spatial scalable. A complete review on MPEG-2 is out of the scope of this chapter; we will limit our considerations to a brief outline of the SNR and spatial scalable profiles. According to the concept of layered video, the basic scheme of an MPEG-2 compliant SNR scalable coder generates a base layer and one enhancement layer; the base layer is encoded following the nonscalable standard,

*Figure 16. MPEG-2 SNR scalable encoder*

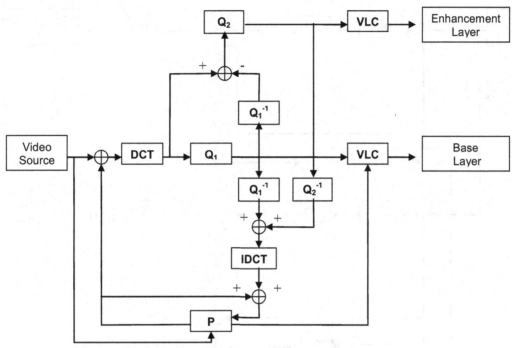

while the enhancement layer is obtained by quantizing (with a different quantization parameter) the residual between the original video and the base layer. At the receiver, the MPEG-2 decoder performs an inverse processing and can choose whether to decode only the base layer or both layers. In the second case, the streams are processed in parallel and merged together for a high-quality reconstruction. Figure 16 and Figure 17 show the encoding and decoding schemes with a single enhancement layer.

As far as the spatial scalability is concerned, MPEG-2 provides this functionality by down-sampling the original video in order to produce a lower resolution sequence. Usually this operation is performed to adapt the content to heterogeneous terminals, where the display resolution, as already said, can be

*Figure 17. MPEG-2 SNR scalable decoder*

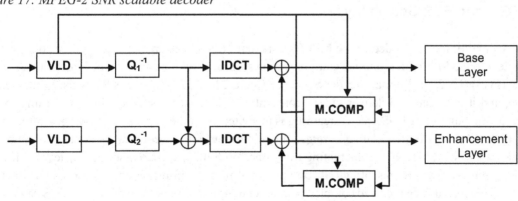

*Figure 18. MPEG-2 spatial scalable encoder*

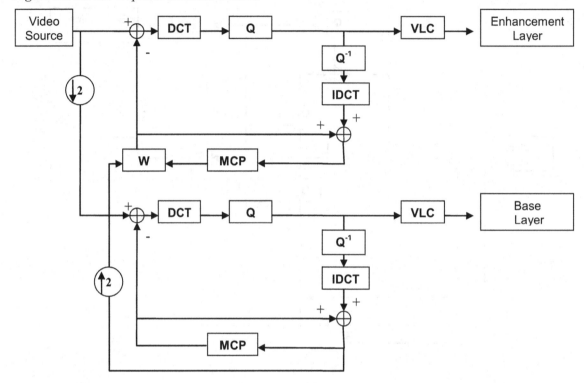

variable. The encoder structure (Figure 18) represents the addition of the down-sampler (to code the base layer) and of the up-sampler (to code the enhancement layer). The output of the latter is further used in the upper branch of the encoder to weight the coefficients in the motion compensation loop.

Temporal scalability was instead not standardized in MPEG-2, even though some implementations are available in literature.

The scalability features of MPEG-2 have not been widely adopted by commercial applications, probably because of the high bandwidth requirements. In fact, the addition of a second layer in the transmission introduces an amount of overhead, which is not negligible.

## MPEG-4 and FGS Scalability

Basic scalability tools included in the MPEG-4 standard (temporal, spatial, quality) are conceptually equivalent to the MPEG-2. An important innovation is instead the introduction of Fine Granular Scalability (FGS) (Li, 2001; Radha, Van der Schaar & Chen, 2001). FGS becomes the so-called streaming profile, and it is targeted to deliver videos constantly at the best possible quality. According to this principle, the purpose of FGS video streaming is to switch from the concept of *"coding at a given bit-rate"* to *"coding over a given bit-rate range,"* mainly because the decoder does not always know the channel capacity, which may be fluctuating over time. With the *traditional* scalability techniques, the enhancement layer was representing only an additional piece of information that, exactly as the base layer, was requested to be received completely in order to introduce any kind of benefit. FGS can always deliver the best possible quality given the bit-rate.

As in common-layered coding, the approach considers a base layer and an enhancement layer, but in this case, the latter is coded according to a bit-plane algorithm. After setting up the desired level of quality for the base layer, the residual information is sliced into bit-planes and coded accordingly. Whenever the available bandwidth is higher than the one requested for the base layer, the FGS layer is partially exploited in order to increase the quality of the stream; the enhancement occurs by progressively transmitting one or more bit-planes of the FGS layer starting from the most significant bit (MSB). To briefly explain how the FGS framework is supposed to work, we can imagine encoding the base layer at the minimum guaranteed bandwidth. The residual information is then put into the enhancement layer, which is coded according to the bit-plane strategy. In practice, if we refer to $R_{BL}$, as the necessary rate to encode the base layer, we will have $R_{max} - R_{BL}$ as the maximum amount of data left to the enhancement layer where $R_{max}$ is the maximum achievable rate for the current video. Depending on the application (unicast or multicast) and on the receiver capabilities, the rate for the enhancement layer will be set at an intermediate value $R$ in the range $(0, R_{max} - R_{BL})$.

Following this principle, it is possible for the end user to experience smooth variations in quality, therefore perceiving a more pleasant video stream. Figure 19 represents the theoretical behavior of an FGS stream over time, where the curve indicates the current available bandwidth, usually ruled by the channel conditions, and the amount of grey area indicates the portion of the enhancement layer that should be delivered.

In addition to the baseline implementation of FGS, the MPEG-4 committee added a temporal extension to the streaming profile, called FGS-T. This option aims at making the system even more flexible and suitable for a wide range of devices and application contexts, introducing a temporal down-sampling of the encoded sequence. The FGS-T compared to FGS layer structures are shown in Figure 20 and Figure 21.

As can be noticed, the temporal enhancement can be either included in the FGS layer (that will provide quality and temporal enhancement at the same time) or in a completely separate layer. In this second option, the FGS scalable coder will be composed of three layers: the base layer, the FGS layer, and the FGS-T layer.

*Figure 19. FGS stream delivery; the base layer must always be decoded, while the enhancement layer is cut on the basis of the available bandwidth*

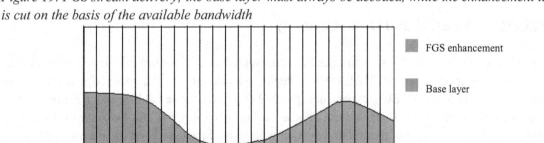

FGS enhancement

Base layer

*Figure 20. FGS scalability in MPEG-4*

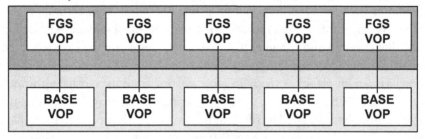

*Figure 21. FGST scalability in MPEG-4*

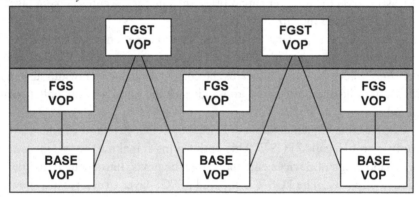

The effectiveness of the FGS streaming profile is confirmed by the interest it has gained in the scientific community. In fact, many authors have stressed the importance of the coding method by implementing different services and applications on top of it. In particular, a lot of efforts have been concentrated on the development of suitable resilience tools able to protect the FGS stream against channel impairments (Van der Schaar, 2001).

## Scalability in MPEG-4 and Object Coding

The introduction of the MPEG-4 standard has been considered as a new paradigm in the scalable video coding world (Pereira & Ebrahimi, 2002). Besides deploying and bettering the knowledge acquired during the development of the MPEG-2 experience, the ISO committee aimed at bringing a big revolution in the concept of video coding. Together with a higher coding efficiency, MPEG-4 was the first standard capable of mixing the coding of natural and synthetic elements in a scene. All these elements (audio, video, text, computer graphics objects) are considered in MPEG-4 as separate substreams in the same video. This means that each object is associated with one or more video tracks, making it possible for the user to select which objects to display on the basis of his or her requirements (bandwidth, terminal) and taste (video editing). Moreover, the developer is now able to choose a static (still image) or dynamic (video) background and add one or more objects (called video objects) previously recorded or segmented. In order to better understand the layered structure of the MPEG-4 framework, Figure 22 represents the stratification of a coded stream, which is not constrained to deal only with the audiovisual information. All the presented parts are described in detail in different sections of the standard, and specifically part 1 (standard ISO/IEC 14496-1) and part 6 (ISO/IEC 14496-6).

From a coding viewpoint, the most interesting part of the standard is for sure the compression strategy and the management of the involved video objects. A very meaningful example to show all these features is the delivery of a news program. In this kind of transmission, we could identify several processes that can then be merged into a single video stream. Figure 23 will help understand the concept.

The nature of these objects could be exploited to optimize the coding part following the principles listed next:

- Background can be considered almost static → A still image can be delivered only once when the news program is set up.
- The resolution of the monitor is smaller than the one in the main video → A lower bit-rate can be adopted for that portion of the scene.
- The speaker is the main actor in the scene and therefore requires the highest attention → The area can be coded with a higher bit-rate, even because the attention of the end user is focused on the speaker shape.
- The floating text is instead a synthetic object with low variations in terms of colors and reduced quality requirements → It can be encoded as a geometric shape or as simple text, which is very inexpensive to be coded.
- In the end, the audio part must be synchronized with the video, and the whole set of streams is finally delivered through a multiplexer.

Although very powerful and innovative, this system resulted too complex to be applied in real situations. In particular, object identification and extraction are quite difficult tasks involving sophisticated technologies such as pattern recognition and computer vision algorithms. For this reason, most MPEG-4 applications rely on a very limited subset of the opportunities offered by the standard (e.g., video recompressing). Nevertheless, MPEG-4 gave a number of useful hints that demonstrated the potential of object-based scalability in practical applications. As an example, the introduction of some graphics

*Figure 22. Abstraction of the most important layers in the MPEG-4 standard*

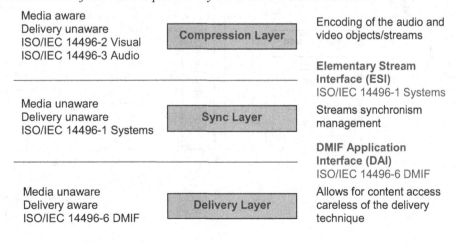

*Figure 23. Elementary streams*

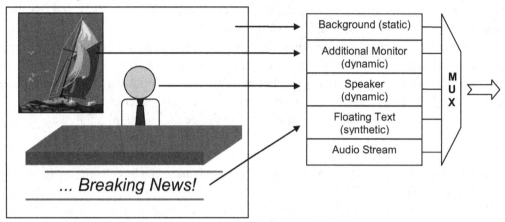

(e.g., a timestamp or a title) would require in a traditional codec the decoding, superposition, and re-encoding of the video. Furthermore, this process should be repeated if different users require different text, and definitely corrupts the video sequence. In the MPEG-4 representation, the same operation can be easily implemented by allowing graphical information to be overlaid to the video sequence, moved in any position, or discarded whenever desired (see Figure 24).

## SVC, the Scalable Extension of H.264

In 2002, after the release of MPEG-4, the Motion Picture Expert Group (MPEG) joined the ITU committee forming the Joint Video Team (JVT), with the goal of developing a new coding algorithm capable

*Figure 24. Object segmentation and multiplexing*

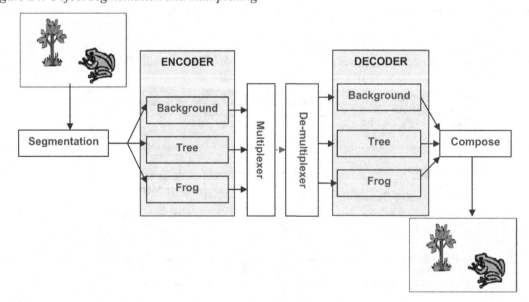

of overcoming the limitations of MPEG-4 and introducing new features that should improve the coding performances. The joint effort resulted in a new standard called H.264/AVC (in ITU terminology) and MPEG-4 part 10 (in ISO terminology) (Ostermann et al., 2004; Wiegand, Sullivan, Bjontegaard & Luthra, 2003). There are some peculiarities that characterize H.264/AVC (Advanced Video Coding) if compared to MPEG-4. H.264 has been designed in order to be efficient in terms of compression, network friendly, and suitable for interactive entertainment in broadcast, multicast, and video-on-demand (VoD) applications. Furthermore, H.264/AVC can operate in a wide range of bit-rates, making video streams suitable for a heterogeneous set of terminals and networks (Marpe, Wiegand & Sullivan, 2006). Despite some innovative tools that were not available in the previous implementations, H.264 introduces important characteristics that facilitate real-time implementation (e.g., 4x4 integer transform instead of the 8x8 DCT), improve the perceived quality through a new deblocking filter, and provide RTP packetization for easier delivery over the network. H.264 gained a lot of attention from the public, and the straightforward follow-up of this codec was the implementation of a scalable version of it.

The work toward the definition of the new Scalable Video Coding (SVC) began in 2004, and the aim was to deploy a video codec that could bring the advantages of scalability to the broad market of video services, something that unfortunately did not happen with MPEG-4. The final version of SVC is about being standardized, and for this reason, we will indicate in the following only the most common and important features that have been derived from the nonscalable H.264 standard. In Schwarz, Marpe, and Weigand (2004), the first implementation for SNR scalability is presented. This work has been further extended, and the authors have recently detailed (Schwarz, Marpe & Wiegand, 2007) the scalability features introduced in the new SVC. As expected from a scalable coder, SVC includes temporal, spatial e SNR (quality) scalability. A generalized scheme of the scalable encoder is reported for simplicity in Figure 25. One of the important advantages of SVC is that the lowest layer (i.e., the base layer with poorer quality) is compliant with the nonscalable coder (i.e., the H.264/AVC), thus ensuring backward compatibility. Even though the graphical representation in Figure 25 is dealing with spatial and quality scalability (temporal down-sampling is not reported for simplicity), the drawing demonstrates the efficiency and flexibility of the current implementation, allowing multiresolution and variable-quality coding. In this way, the user can choose the most appropriate version according to the terminal he or she is using. The whole scalability process has been revised in H.264/SVC, and some innovative aspects have been added in order to enhance efficiency and performance.

As far as temporal scalability is concerned, SVC exploits a hierarchical prediction scheme. This principle establishes that every frame can be considered as a reference picture usually following a dyadic hierarchical tree. In this way, it is possible to start from a coarse temporal resolution, while quality can be progressively refined by adding the previously discarded frames. An example with a 4 dyadic tree is reported in Figure 26.

The attempts to extend H.264 features to the scalable version are confirmed by a recent publication of Wenger, Wang, and Hannuksela (2006), where the authors propose the RTP payload format for the SVC codec. Updated information about the standardization and the features of SVC can be found at the IP-HHI Web site, as the published material is not complete and is still subject to modifications.

## FINAL REMARKS AND CONCLUSION

In this chapter, we have introduced the concept of scalability and a number of principles and techniques to develop it. Scalability was then critically compared to transcoding in the framework of adaptive

*Figure 25. Main blocks of the SVC scalable coder*

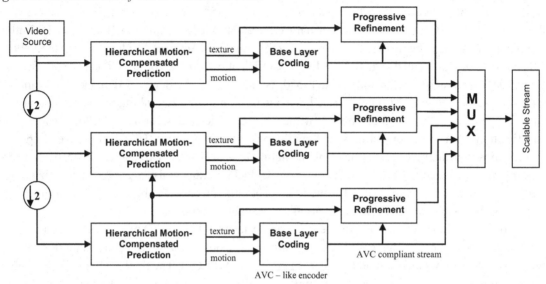

video streaming. Our aim was to show that the use of transcoding to solve the problem of channel or terminal adaptation can be a suboptimal choice, while scalable coders can achieve more flexible and convenient solutions in some of the target applications. To do this, we highlighted the pros and cons of both approaches that can be summarized in .

As we can see from Table 1, the two strategies are really contending, as they can be often seen as mutually alternative. Far from being a comprehensive study, this assessment and the relevant literature review can serve as a guideline more for system developers than researchers in order to seek the best compromise while designing new applications and services based on digital video streaming. Things will probably experience rapid changes in the near future, and therefore, new emerging technologies will take over the current coding and transcoding standards. Recent trends demonstrate that if the coding strategies are asymptotically reaching the theoretical limit of compression, there is still some room to make the coding/decoding lighter in order to maximize the efficiency for low power devices such

*Figure 26. Hierarchical temporal prediction in H.264/SVC*

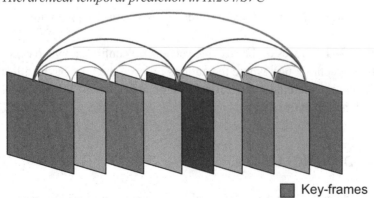

as cellular phones and PDAs. Network-oriented applications are gaining more and more attention, and therefore, interesting approaches targeted to specific applications are attracting a lot of attention such as Distributed Video Coding (Girod, Aaron, Rane & Rebello-Monedero, 2005), where the complexity (usually higher at the encoder from five to 10 times) is shared between the encoder and the decoder. These new advances will probably help solve some of the residual problems with scalable encoders and make these approaches even more appealing for future applications.

## FUTURE RESEARCH DIRECTIONS

Defining future directions in the field of multimedia standards and applications is not an easy task due to the rapid evolution of technologies and standards in all the relevant fields: networking, fixed and mobile communications, hardware and terminals, data formats, and so forth.

Narrowing the scope to video streaming and scalability approaches, one of the most interesting challenges concerns the pervasive multimedia services (i.e., the possibility of providing nomadic, high quality, interactive, personalized video services) able to fulfill the users' needs anytime, anywhere, anyhow. Forthcoming applications that will benefit such tools include healthcare/homecare systems, immersive virtual communications, entertainment, remote working, telemedicine, and so forth. To make this scenario happen, one major challenge to be faced is for sure the possibility of treating data in a network/terminal-independent way, making it possible to connect through different channels, servers, clients, and applications the higher number of users possible in any possible heterogeneous combination.

*Table 2. Comparative analysis between transcoding and scalable coding*

| Feature | Transcoding | Scalable Coding |
|---|---|---|
| Encoder complexity | **High**: a specific encoder must be developed to fit each terminal requirement | **Low**: a single encoding pass can serve any kind of terminal |
| Decoder complexity | **Low**: a standard decoder is implemented | **Medium**: it could be necessary to decode more than one stream according to the chosen policies |
| Standard conversion | **Yes:** it is the main function of transcoding | **No:** scalability is designed to work within the same standard over a range of bit-rates |
| Memory requirements | **Higher at the encoder:** in particular, if transcoding different streams in real time | **Higher at the decoder:** it may be requested to decode more than one stream in parallel |
| Data encryption management in case of rate adaptation | **Complex**: it requires to decrypt and encrypt again the sequence | **Transparent**: one or more enhancement layers can be simply dropped without affecting the base layer |
| Data encryption security | **Not secure**: the key for decoding must be shared with the transcoder | **Secure**: the key can be shared only between the owner and the end user |
| Real-time performance (encoder) | **Yes/No:** it depends on the implementation and constraints (it may be requesting a complete decoding and re-encoding) | **Yes:** it can be performed off-line once for all, according to the principle "code-once decode-many" |
| Real-time performance (decoder) | **Yes:** the decoder is unaware of the encoder complexity. It simply decodes a single stream | **Yes/No:** sometimes the decoder may be somewhat complex (e.g., some MDC schemes) |

In this context, flexible representations of multimedia data, such as scalable codes and multiple descriptors, may become powerful instruments to achieve adaptability and interoperability. Of course, the major (and still unsolved) problem is to achieve with a scalable code the same performance of a simpler code in terms of video quality, rate-distortion ratio, ease of implementation, and standardization. Furthermore, several other issues turn out to be very important for the success of new applications, and among them the possibility of jointly optimizing the scalable encoder and the network protocols (cross-layer optimization) in order to achieve optimum performance at varying network condition, streaming configuration, and parameter setting. In this context, the word "performance" is intended at large, thus including rate-distortion, power consumption, processing/storage resource consumption, user satisfaction, or, in a single word, the quality of service.

## REFERENCES

AA.VV. Scalable extension of H.264/AVC. Retrieved May 31, 2007, from http://ip.hhi.de/imagecom_G1/savce/index.htm

Albanese, A., Blomer, J., Edmonds, J., Luby, M., & Sudan, M. (1996). Priority encoding transmission. *IEEE Transactions on Information Theory*, *42*(6), 1737–1744.

Apostolopoulos, J.G. (2001). Reliable video communication over lossy packet networks using multiple state encoding and path diversity. *Proceedings of the SPIE, Visual Communications and Image Processing, VCIP 2001*, 392–409.

Arean, R., Kovacevic, J., & Goyal, V.K. (2000). Multiple description perceptual audio coding with correlating transforms. *IEEE Transactions on Speech Audio Processing, 8*(2), 140–145.

Assuncao, P.A.A., & Ghanbari, M. (1997). Transcoding of single-layer MPEG video into lower rates. *IEE Proceedings of Vision, Image and Signal Processing, 144*(6), 377–383.

Cai, C., Chen, J., Ma, K.K., & Mitra, S.K. (2007). Multiple description wavelet coding with dual decomposition and cross packetization. *Signal, Image and Video Processing, 1*(1), 53–61.

Chakareski, J., Han, S., & Girod, B. (2005). Layered coding vs. multiple descriptions for video streaming over multiple paths. *Springer Multimedia Systems*, *10*, 275–285.

Conci, N., Berlanda Scorza, G., & Sacchi, C. (2005). A cross-layer approach for efficient MPEG-4 video streaming using multicarrier spread-spectrum transmission and unequal error protection. *Proceedings of the IEEE International Conference on Image Processing, ICIP 2005*, *1*, 201–204.

Conci, N., & De Natale, F.G.B. (2007). Multiple description video coding using coefficient ordering and interpolation. *Signal Processing, Image Communication. Special Issue on Mobile Video*, *22*, 252–265.

Conci, N., & De Natale, F.G.B. (2007). Real-time multiple description intra-coding by sorting and interpolation of coefficients. *Signal Image and Video Processing, 1*(1), 1–10.

Costa, C.E., Eisenberg, Y., Zhai, F., & Katsaggelos, A.K. (2004). Energy efficient transmission of fine granular scalable video. *Proceedings of the IEEE International Conference on Communications, ICC '04, 5*, 3096–3100.

Dugad, R., & Ahuja, N. (2001). A fast scheme for image size change in the compressed domain. *IEEE Transactions on Circuit and Systems for Video Technology, 11*(4), 461–474.

Franchi, N., Fumagalli, M., Lancini, R., & Tubaro, S. (2003). Multiple description video coding for scalable and robust transmission over IP. *IEEE Transactions on Circuits and Systems for Video Technology, 15*(3), 321–334.

Fung, K.-T., Chan, Y.-L., & Siu, W.-C. (2002). New architecture for dynamic frame-skipping transcoder. *IEEE Transactions on Image Processing, 11*(8), 886–900.

Gan, T., Gan, L., & Ma, K-K. (2006). Reducing video-quality fluctuations for streaming scalable video using unequal error protection, retransmission, and interleaving. *IEEE Transactions on Image Processing, 15*(4), 819–832.

Girod, B., Aaron, A.M., Rane, S., & Rebollo-Monedero, D. (2005). Distributed video coding. *Proceedings of the IEEE, 93*(1), 71–83.

Gou, K.H., Hofmann, M.A., Ng, E., Paul, S., & Zhang, H. (2002). High quality streaming multimedia. *US PATENT 6,377,972 B1.*

Goyal, V.K. (2001). Multiple description coding: Compression meets the network. *IEEE Signal Processing Magazine, 18*(5), 74–93.

ISO/IEC. (1995). Generic coding of moving pictures and associated audio (MPEG-2). ISO/IEC 13818-2 standard.

Lee, Y.-C., Kim, J., Altunbasak, Y., & Mersereau, R.M. (2003). Layered coding vs. multiple description coded video over error-prone networks. *Signal Processing: Image Communication, 18*(5), 337–356.

Li, W. (2001). Overview of fine granularity scalability in MPEG-4 video standard. *IEEE Transactions on Circuit and Systems for Video Technology, 11*(3), 301–317.

Marpe, D., Wiegand, T., & Sullivan, G.J. (2006). The H.264 / MPEG4 advanced video coding standard and its applications. *IEEE Communications Magazine, 44*(8), 134–144.

Matty, K.R., & Kondi, L.P. (2005). Balanced multiple description video coding using optimal partitioning of the DCT coefficients. *IEEE Transactions on Circuits and Systems for Video Technology, 15*(7), 928–935.

Miguel, A.C., Mohr, A.E., & Riskin, E.A. (1999). SPIHT for generalized multiple description coding. *Proceedings of the International Conference on Image Processing, ICIP '99, 1*, 842–846.

Mohan, R., Smith, J.R., & Li, C.-S. (1999). Adapting multimedia Internet content for universal access. *IEEE Transactions on Multimedia, 1*(1), 104–114.

Mukherjee, J., & Mitra, S.K. (2002). Image resizing in the compressed domain using subband DCT. *IEEE Transactions on Circuit and Systems for Video Technology, 12*(7), 620–627.

Orchard, M.T., Wang, Y., Vaishampayan, V., & Reibman, A.R. (2001). Multiple description coding using pairwise correlating transforms. *IEEE Transactions On Image Processing, 10*(3), 351–366.

Ostermann, J., et al. (2004). Video coding with H.264/AVC: Tools, performance and complexity. *IEEE Circuit and Systems Magazine*, *4*(1), 7–28.

Patil, V., Kumar, R., & Mukherjee, J. (2006). A fast arbitrary factor video resizing algorithm. *IEEE Transactions on Circuit and Systems for Video Technology*, *16*(9), 1164–1170.

Pereira, F., & Ebrahimi, T. (2002). *MPEG-4 book.* Upper Saddle River, NJ: Prentice-Hall.

Postel, J. (1980). User datagram protocol. *IETF Request for Comments (RFC) 768.*

Radha, H., Van der Schaar, M., & Chen, Y. (2001). The MPEG-4 fine-grained scalable video coding method for multimedia streaming over IP. *IEEE Transactions on Multimedia*, *3*(1), 53–68.

Razzak, Md.A., & Zeng, B. (2001). Multiple description image transmission for diversity systems using block-based DC separation. *IEEE International Symposium on Circuits and Systems, 5*, 93–96.

Reibman, A., Jafarkhani, H., Wang, Y., & Orchard, M.T. (2001). Multiple description video using rate-distortion splitting. *Proceedings of the International Conference on Image Processing, ICIP 2001, 1*, 978–981.

Reibman, A.R., Jafarkhani, H., Wang, Y., Orchard, M., & Puri, R. (2002). Multiple-description video coding using motion compensated temporal prediction. *IEEE Transactions on Circuits and Systems for Video Technology*, *12*(3), 193–204.

Rejaie, R., Handley, M., & Estrin, D. (2000). Layered quality adaptation for Internet video streaming. *IEEE International Journal on Selected Areas in Communications*, *18*(12), 2530–2543.

Schneier, B. (1996). *Applied cryptography* (2nd edition). John Wiley & Sons.

Schulzrinne, H., Casner, S., Frederick, R., & Jacobson, V. (2003). RTP: A transport protocol for real time applications. *IETF Request for Comments (RFC) 3550.*

Schulzrinne, H., Rao,A., & Lanphier, R. (1998). Real time streaming protocol. *IETF Request for Comments (RFC) 2326.*

Schwarz, H., Marpe, D., & Wiegand, T. (2004). SNR-scalable extension of H.264/AVC. *Proceedings of the IEEE International Conference on Image Processing, ICIP '04, 5*, 3113–3116.

Schwarz, H., Marpe, D., & Wiegand, T. (2007), Overview of the scalable video coding extension of the H.264 / AVC standard. *IEEE Transactions on Circuits and Systems for Video Technology*, *17*(9), 1103–1120.

Servetto, S.D., Ramchandran, K., Vaishampayan, V.A., & Nahrstedt, K. (2000). Multiple description wavelet based image coding. *IEEE Transactions on Image Processing*, *9*(5), 813–826.

Shanableh, T., & Ghanabari, M. (2005). Multilayer transcoding with format portability for multicasting single-layered video. *IEEE Transactions on Multimedia*, *7*(1), 1–15.

Shu, H., & Chau, L.-P. (2004). Frame-skipping transcoding with motion change consideration. *Proceedings of the IEEE International Symposium Circuits Systems, ISCAS '04, 3*, 773–776.

Shu, H., & Chau, L.-P. (2006). The realization of arbitrary downsizing video transcoding. *IEEE Transactions on Circuit and Systems for Video Technology, 16*(4), 540–546.

Sun, H., Kwok, W., & Zdepski, J.W. (1996). Architectures for MPEG compressed bitstream scaling. *IEEE Transactions on Circuits and Systems for Video Technology, 6*(2), 191–199.

Tudor, P.N. (1995). MPEG-2 video compression. *Electronics and Communication Engineering Journal, 7*(6), 257–264.

Vaishampayan, V.A. (1993). Design of multiple description scalar quantizers. *IEEE Transactions on Information Theory, 39*(3), 821–834.

Van der Schaar, M., Boland, L.G., & Li, Q. (2001b). Novel applications of fine-granular-scalability: Internet & wireless video, scalable storage, personalized TV, universal media coding. *SCI2001/ISAS2001.*

Van der Schaar, M., & Radha, H. (2001a). Unequal packet loss resilience for fine-granular-scalability video. *IEEE Transactions on Multimedia, 3*(4), 381–394.

Vetro, A., Christopoulos, C., & Sun, H. (2003). Video transcoding architectures and techniques: An overview. *IEEE Signal Processing Magazine, 20*(2), 18–29.

Wang, Y., Reibman, A.R., & Lin, S. (2005). Multiple description coding for video delivery. *Proceedings of the IEEE, 93*(1), 57–70.

Wee, S.J., & Apostolopoulus, J. (2001). Secure scalable streaming enabling transcoding without decryption. *Proceedings of the International Conference on Image Processing, ICIP '01, 1,* 437–440.

Wenger, S., Wang, Y.-K., & Hannuksela, M.M. (2006). RTP payload format for H.264/SVC scalable video coding. *Journal of Zhejiang University of Science A, 7*(5), 657–667.

Werner, O. (1999). Requantization for transcoding of MPEG-2 intraframes. *IEEE Transactions on Image Processing, 8*(2), 179–191.

Wiegand, T., Sullivan, G.J., Bjontegaard, G., & Luthra, A. (2003). Overview of the H.264/AVC video coding standard. *IEEE Transactions on Circuits and Systems for Video Technology, 13*(7), 560–576.

Witsenhausen, H.S., & Wyner, A.D. (1981). Source coding for multiple descriptions II: A binary source. *Bell Systems Technologies Journal, 60*(10), 2281–2292.

Wolf, J.K., Wyner, A.D., & Ziv, J. (1980). Source coding for multiple descriptions. *Bell Systems Technologies Journal, 59*(8), 1417–1426.

Xin, J., Lin, C-W., & Sun, M.-T. (2005). Digital video transcoding. *Proceedings of the IEEE, 93*(1), 84–97.

## ADDITIONAL READINGS

Brady, N. (1999). MPEG-4 standardized methods for compression of arbitrarily shaped video objects. *IEEE Transactions on Circuits and System for Video Technology, 9*(8), 1170–1189.

Bystrom, M., & Stockhammer, T. (2004). Dependent source and channel rate allocation for video transmission. *IEEE Transactions on Wireless Communications, 3*(1), 258–268.

Carle, G., & Biersack, E.W. (1997). Survey of error recovery techniques for IP-based audio-visual multicast applications. *IEEE Network, 11*(6), 24–36.

Kim, J., Mersereau, R.M., & Altunbasak, Y. (2005). Distributed video streaming using multiple description coding and unequal error protection. *IEEE Trans. on Image Processing, 14*(7).

Neff, R., & Zakhor, A. (1997). Very low bit-rate video coding based on matching pursuits. *IEEE Transactions on Circuits System. Video Technology, 7*(1), 158–171.

Ohm, J.-R. (2005). Advances in scalable video coding. *Proceedings of the IEEE, 93*(1), 42–56.

Pereira, M., Antonini, M., & Barlaud, M. (2003). Multiple description image and video coding for wireless channels. *Signal Processing: Image Communication, 18*(10), 925–945.

Puri, R., Majumdar, A., Ishwar, P., & Ramchandran, K. (2006). Distributed video coding in wireless sensor networks. *IEEE Signal Processing Magazine, 23*(4), 94–106.

Puri, R., & Ramchandran, K. (2002). PRISM: A new robust video coding architecture based on distributed compression principles. *Proceedings of the Allerton Conference on Communication, Control, and Computing*, Allerton, Illinois.

Van der Schaar, M., & Radha, H. (2001). A hybrid temporal-SNR fine-granular scalability for Internet video. *IEEE Transactions on Circuit and Systems for Video Technology, 11*(3), 318–331.

Wang, Y., Ostermann, J., & Zhang, Y.Q. (2002). *Video processing and communications.* Upper Saddle River, NJ: Prentice-Hall.

Wang, T., Wenger, S., Wen, J., & Katsaggelos, A.K. (2000). Error resilient video coding techniques. *IEEE Signal Processing Magazine, 17*(4), 61–82.

Wyner, A.D., & Ziv, J. (1976). The rate-distortion function for source coding with side information at the decoder. *IEEE Transactions on Information Theory, 22*(1), 1–10.

Yangli, W., & Chengke, W. (2005). Low complexity multiple description coding method for networked video. *Signal Processing: Image Communication, 20*(5), 447–457.

# Chapter VII
# Extreme Rate Distributed Video Transcoding System

**Seung S. Yang**
*Virginia State University, USA*

**Javed I. Khan**
*Kent State University, USA*

## ABSTRACT

*This chapter provides a comprehensive awareness and understanding of research efforts in the field of extreme rate-distributed video transcoding. The basic concepts and theories of rate control methods such as requantization, temporal resolution reduction, spatial resolution reduction, and object-based transcoding are introduced. We will identify each rate control scheme's strengths and weaknesses and provide a distributed video transcoding system architecture that uses multiple transcoding techniques in the creation of an extreme rate video. Experimental results show that the appropriate use of multiple transcoding schemes retains a better quality video in an extreme rate control. At the end of this chapter, we will identify unsolved problems and related issues and will offer suggestions for future research directions.*

## INTRODUCTION

Video transcoding is a method that converts a compressed video signal into another signal with a different format. It also can change bit rate, frame rates, and/or frame size of the original video. Due to the irreversibility of video quality, original contents should be prepared in their highest quality, and users need to watch the videos on various devices such as HDTV, personal computers, cell phones, and so forth. There are two ways to play the original video in a target player; a target player processes the original video suitable to the target device, or the original video is transcoded into another video suitable for the target device before the video is played in the player. Most current players that are running on a computer use the first approach; however, it relies heavily on the target device's capability and cannot adapt to an environmental change such as network congestion, network bandwidth changes, and so forth. The second approach, transcoding an original video suitable to a given target player, provides wide adaptability. But if the transcoding happens in a server, it can only provide limited adaptability. It cannot quickly adapt to network resource changes. Transcoding a video on the fly provides greater adaptability and reduces burdens on a server or a player.

The prepared original content is transcoded for matching a target device's display capability and/or for the status of communication links on the fly from a video server to the display device. The diversity of the display device creates a huge gap between a high-end display device and a low-end one. Transcoding of HDTV contents to a cell phone video requires about 185 times compression (Perkins, 2002; Video Technology Magazine). The heterogeneity of communication links adds more challenges to adaptive video transcoding, especially in wireless communication networks where communication resources and characteristics keep changing. Furthermore, video transcoding is considered a computation-intensive task. A video is considered a real-time content that should be delivered and played in a timely manner. More than 0.1% of packet loss or more than 200 ms delay in transmitting a video cannot be tolerated to play the video properly.

To meet these requirements, the video transcoder reacts quickly for the network link status change and should produce the transcoded video stream on time.

Distributed video transcoding provides quick responses to the environmental changes by providing more computational power to the transcoder as well as by providing location advantages for network resource restrictions.

Extreme rate distributed video transcoding focuses on two major areas: (1) scheduling of the transcoding task to distributed transcoding nodes to provide better transcoding time and reduce jitter and (2) extreme rate control to transcoding from very high-quality original video content to a video for a device with extremely limited capability.

This chapter provides (1) basic video compression mechanism for extreme rate control, (2) speed enhancement methods in node transcoding, (3) distributed transcoding architecture, and (4) task scheduling for transcoding time and jitter reduction in distributed transcoding.

Most current video processing standards are based on discrete cosine transform (DCT) and motion vector-based video compression algorithms. This chapter describes methods based on MPEG, but they can apply to the other standards.

## BACKGROUND

### Comparison of Rate Control Methods

There are four major rate control methods: requantization, spatial resolution reduction, temporal resolution reduction, and object-based rate reduction. The requantization method changes quantization steps in the re-encoding process. A spatial resolution reduction method changes a video frame size. A temporal resolution reduction method drops some frames to reduce the bit rate of a video. An object-based rate reduction method applies requantization and/or temporal resolution reduction methods on a specific object in a video for reducing a bit rate in a video. Each method will be described in detail in the following sections.

*Figure 1. Requantization transcoder architecture*

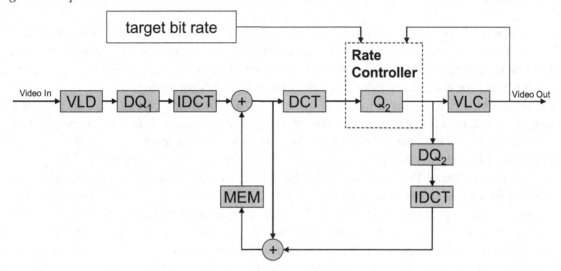

## Requantization Method

Quantization is used to reduce possible values in DCT coefficient values while still maintaining adequate image quality. Requantization changes quantization values of input video streams to reduce the required number of bits in the output video stream.

Figure 1 shows a simple requantization transcoder architecture. An input video stream is decoded by variable length decoder (VLD), and the quantized coefficient values are dequantized (DQ). The inverse discrete cosine transform (IDCT) constructs a picture frame using the dequantized coefficient. Motion compensation data are added to the frame by comparing a previous picture frame in a buffer (MEM) before the frame is processed by DCT. A rate controller in a requantization transcoder uses bit rates from the transcoder's output video stream to change its quantization value ($Q_2$) to make the output bit rate its target bit rate.

Requantization is simple, but it is a very efficient rate control method (Han & Kim, 2006; Keesman, Hellinghuizen, Hoeksema & Heideman, 1996; Shen, 2006; Sun & Zdepski, 1996). Excessive use of requantization, however, creates poor quality output by lowering signal-to-noise ratio. Shen (2006) suggests using certain selection of requantization steps that is used during the transcoding process where all coefficients are unresponsive (i.e., requantization of these coefficients is the same as a direct quantization). Han and Kim (2006) identify requantization as a key bit rate reduction technology and proposed a scheme that constructs an optimal requantization codebook iteratively for a transcoder.

Sun (1996) suggests changing a quantization value for each macro block N to maintain proper quality of a video. Each macro block N's quantization factor is derived by the last frame's quantization factor and a gain factor with cumulative bits up to macro block N-1.

Keesman, et al. (1996) use statistical properties of input video stream and required bit-rate of output video stream to decide decision levels of the transcoder's quantizer. The suggested transcoder uses statistics of DCT-coefficients from input video streams to decide the encoder's quantization threshold that can minimize the quantization error in a transcoder in the output video stream.

## Frame Skipping (Dropping)

Frame skipping or dropping is used to reduce the bit rate of an output video stream by dropping a frame. The reduction of frame rates has advantages because the human eye does not recognize the frame rate changes very well until the frame rate drops below a certain threshold. Excessive use of frame rate reduction, however, will cause a jerky video and irritate the user's perception.

There are three types of frames in MPEG video stream on which most current video encoding algorithms are based: Intra frame (I-frame), Predicted frame (P-frame), and Bidirectional frame (B-frame). I-frame contains only intra macro blocks and is used as a reference for other frames. P-frame contains data that are different from the previous I-frame. B-frame has data that are different from the previous frame and the next frame. Due to the reliance among frames, arbitrary frame dropping can reduce a bit rate of a stream, but it creates a jerky video image.

Balsree, Thawani, Gopalan, and Sridhar (2005) developed an interframe similarity based on the frame dropping method. The proposed method uses DC coefficient of luminance components of a frame and ignores chrominance components because the human eye is more sensitive to luminance than chrominance. By dropping only similar frames, it could maintain the proper bit rate of a video stream but generate only a minimal impact on the quality of the video.

## Spatial Resolution Reduction

Spatial resolution reduction can further decrease the bit rate of an output video stream by reducing frame size. The introduction of new smart devices such as PDAs, smart phones, and UMPCs require displaying the original video into an adequately sized one. A display may receive a high-quality uncustomized video and adjust the display size based on a display terminal. It uses valuable network bandwidth, however, and stores it in a network that can be used otherwise. Changing the spatial resolution not only adjusts the video stream into an adequate one, but it also reduces the bit rate to a suitable level for the network resources available. Spatially reduced video can be re-augmented on a display unit, but the reduction creates blurred images as its resolution is reduced. The entire video quality is reduced when spatial resolution has been applied to the entire frame.

For spatial resolution reduction, motion vectors cannot be reused directly. Simple approaches to calculate motion vectors have been suggested. These suggestions include averaging, finding the median, and finding the weighted median. Accurate calculations of motion vectors for spatial resolution reduction video are important to maintain high video quality.

Bhargava (1996) suggests a resolution reduction in video conferencing. Four discrete levels of frame sizes were used, and data were manipulated before they were encoded and after they were decoded.

Lei and Georganas (2002) use a DCT transformation matrix to calculate downscaled DT blocks in H.263 baseline video stream. This suggested method uses a motion refinement process that has very small search window to estimate motions. The search window of refinement is determined according to the accumulated magnitudes of all motion vectors in the downscaled frame.

Arbitrary downsizing video transcoding is suggested by Shu and Chau (2006). This proposed method determines a frame size of a video according to its bit-rate estimation process. A bit-rate of a video stream is estimated by the ratio of its original size and its transcoded size times the estimated bits for motion vector, residue, and header with quantization factor Q.

*Figure 2. Object-oriented transcoder architecture*

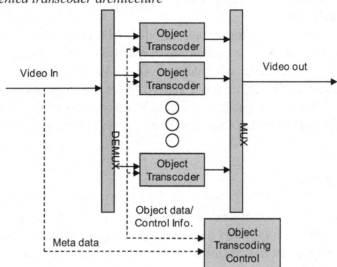

## Object-Based Rate Reduction

Unlike the other rate reduction method, the object-based rate reduction controls the shape information in each object and contains it within the input bit stream. Each object can have a different target rate than others in object-based rate reduction and be assigned to a separate transcoder. The transcoded outputs are mixed together and combined into a video stream. By controlling each object bit rate, this method can reduce the overall bit rate of the video stream while maintaining quality in important objects (Puri & Eleftheriadis, 1998; Vetro, Sun & Wang, 2001). Because the object-based video transcoding separates object shape information from texture data, the shape data cannot be removed from the video stream, and the shape data should be transcoded before they are displayed, which requires processing the power in a target device.

Vetro, et al. (2001) use an object-based transcoding with two types of strategies: conservative and aggressive. A traditional PSNR-like video quality measurement is used in the conservative approach where all areas of a video are considered equally important. In the aggressive approach, a perceptual video quality measurement is used to generate adaptive transcoding where some objects are more important than others. Therefore, in an aggressive approach, some objects may have different video encoding rates or may not appear at all in the output video stream.

## In Node Transcoding Speed Enhancement

### Frequency Domain Transcoder

DCT/IDCT and motion compensation processes in encoding are known as a computation-intensive task. A compressed video, however, already has DCT/IDCT information in it, which means the DCT/IDCT can get the information from the compressed input video. The primary reason for transcoding in a pixel domain is to get motion compensation. The frequency domain transcoder enhances the transcoding speed by producing motion compensation information in the DCT domain (Assuncao & Ghanbari, 1998; Kalva, Petljanski & Furht, 2005).

Kalva, et al. (2005) suggest the method of transcoding of a MPEG-2 video to MPEG-4 video by using directional estimates in DCT blocks. The method uses decoded motion vectors with motion compensated DCT coefficients to estimate prediction of modes and prediction block sizes for H.264 video.

Assuncao and Ghanbari (1998) replace IDCT and DCT with a field/frame DCT conversion function and MC-DCT function. The field/frame DCT conversion function converts the input filed DCT code into a frame DCT format. The MC-DCT function finds motion vectors for motion compensation in a DCT domain.

### Pixel Domain Transcoder

A frame buffer is required to perform motion compensation. DCT/IDCT is used to produce a frame buffer in video transcoding. The fast pixel domain cascaded transcoding method uses the DCT coefficient from IDCT through an inverse quantization process, but still performs a motion compensation process (Youn & Sun, 2000).

## EXTREME RATE DISTRIBUTED TRANSCODING ARCHITECTURE

As technology improves, the variations of display capability become more extensive. Needless to say, desktop computers have a very high resolution screen; television broadcasting systems also have high definition capability, while smart phones equipped with a video playback feature have low resolution such as 128x128. Any single video transcoding scheme cannot provide the desired extreme transcoding ratio such as transcoding the contents of an HDTV quality video stream into a cellular phone quality video stream. Requantization of only rate control can only reduce up to 1:5 of transcoding ratio due to the structural overhead of a video stream (Khan, 2003). Extensive use of frame skipping can easily cause a rough display. Spatial resolution reduction can further cut down on the bit rate and the requantization-based bit rate reduction, but the quality of the video is sharply reduced if the target device has low resolution. Object-based rate reduction is perceptually better than the other methods, but the input video stream should have object information or it will require heavy computation to find the object in the video stream. Multiple schemes, therefore, should be applied to achieve extreme rate transcoding.

The key of extreme rate transcoding is providing a quality video at extreme rate, which could be achieved by using multiple schemes in video transcoding. Due to the use of multiple schemes, using a distributed transcoding method may enhance transcoding speed.

In the suggested system, requantization, temporal resolution, and spatial resolution reduction methods are used to reduce bit rate of a video with the hybrid of a pixel/frequency domain transcoding the speed enhancements. The system uses a two-phase rate reduction algorithm to generate a better quality video. The system logically has five components: decoder, demultiplexer, encoder, and multiplexer. The demultiplexer is used as a scheduler that manages transcoding mechanisms to apply and select a transcoding path to reduce jitter with the help of closed status feedback architecture. By using the feedback information from a display device and its multiplexer, it can gradually adapt to its current environment.

*Figure 3. Simple video transcoder*

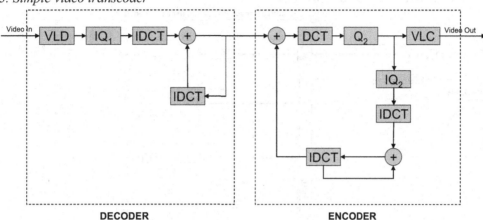

## Distributed Transcoding

The purpose of distributed transcoding is to achieve a faster transcoding result. The challenge in distributed transcoding is how to divide a transcoding task into small subtasks and schedule them properly. Due to the data dependency, segments of input video stream should be properly delivered to its corresponding transcoder.

Figure 3 shows a simple video transcoding, which includesthree steps: decoding of the input compressed video stream into a pixel-domain video, processing the pixel-domain video with appropriate parameters, and recompressing the processed video into an output format video. Decoding of the input compressed video stream is a relatively faster process, but the location of the segment cannot be known before decoding it from the beginning. So the decoding process remains a single process. The encoding process is considered a computation-intensive process. In distributed transcoding, it utilizes multiple computational nodes to execute many encoders to process a video stream. Typically, a GOP is used as a source video segment unit. A group of GOPs is assigned to a transcoding task (Sambe, Watanabe, Yu, Nakamura & Wakamiya, 2005).

A task assignment in distributed transcoding is to reduce transcoding time and jitter. Because of the data dependency, a segment of video stream should be transmitted to its transcoder node. Scheduling of the video transcoding is critical because the input of the encoder in the transcoder is typically in pixilated domain data, and the size of the data is not negligible. The scheduling of the video transcoding should consider not only the computation of the available transcoding nodes but also the communication resources given to reduce the jitter and buffer size of the network (Khan, 2003).

The suggested extreme rate transcoder is based on the distributed video transcoder. Figure 4 shows a diagram for extreme rate transcoding architecture. The variable length decoder (VLD) decodes a compressed domain video and produces a frequency-based decoded frame. The decoded frame data are delivered to encoders via a demultiplexer (DEMUX). The role of a DEMUX is to send a segmented video stream to an encoder where estimated transcoding time satisfies time restriction for the video segment. DEMUX also sends transcoding parameters and matches the required transcoding ratios for display adaptation and available network resources. The encoder receives a video stream segment with parameters that indicate transcoding methods that should apply to the segment. The encoder has

*Figure 4. Extreme rate distributed transcoder*

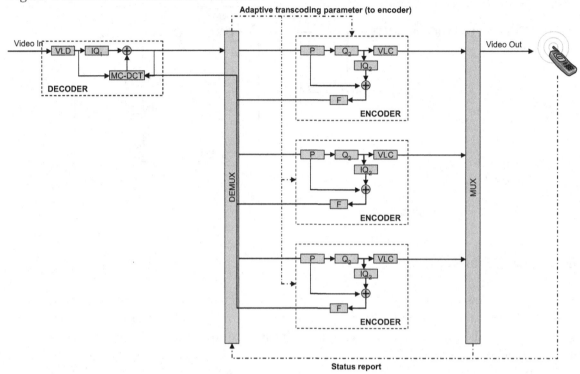

a preprocessor (P) that applies spatial and/or temporal resolution reduction. Requantization is applied in Q2 based on adaptation parameters from DEMUX. The multiplexer (MUX) monitors the transcoding time that includes decoded video data transmission time and computation time for that selected transcoder. A display device also informs the status of received video stream to DEMUX for access link resource adaptation.

By applying dynamic transcoding time estimation and multiple rate control schemes, the extreme rate distributed transcoder provides an extreme low bit rate video stream with minimal delay and jitter.

## EXTREME RATE CONTROL METHOD

Before a rate control method is suggested, the proper meaning of video quality should be defined. The proposed system measures a video quality based on a target device playing the video. Even high-quality DVD video that is delivered to a cell phone without any changes made to its quality should change its resolution from the player before it is played. To the user, there is no noticeable difference in the quality of the original video and the quality of the transcoded video that has the image resolution of the user's cell phone with its maximum quality. The second method, however, saves many communication resources during its transmission as well as saves storages and processing powers in the cell phone due to a smaller resolution video that requires less data size.

Based on the user's perspective, the suggested transcoder applies different transcoding methods in the following sequence:

1.  Spatial reduction
2.  Temporal reduction
3.  Requantization

The spatial reduction method effectively reduces the required bit rate while maintaining the proper quality on video until the resolution of a target device. After it reaches the target device resolution, video quality reduction is magnified because the video should be enlarged to match the target device resolution. Human perception is not very sensitive to temporal reduction until it reaches its threshold. The temporal reduction method can be further used to reduce the bit rate before its predefined threshold. A video could produce jerky images if a temporal reduction method drops frames randomly. In this suggested system, a full transcoder is used to reduce temporal resolution to keep better quality. After applying those two methods, a requantization method will be applied in all areas or specific areas of a frame. For extreme rate reduction, a two-phase reduction mechanism is shown in Figure 5.

In the first phase, rate reductions are applied with an acceptable video quality. The second phase of rate reductions will be applied if a desired bit rate is not achieved after the first phase of bit rate reduction. In the second phase, requantization methods are applied, and temporal and spatial reductions follow. Requantization more effectively reduces the bit rate when compared to the other two reduction methods and retains a better quality of a video than the other methods.

As the transcoding processes an input video, the DEMUX sends configuration information to transcoders based on the status information gathered from its MUX and the player.

## DISTRIBUTED TRANSCODING TASK SCHEDULING

In distributed transcoding, selecting a proper encoder is critical to the overall system's delay and jitter. Task scheduling of the distributed transcoder is selecting the best transcoding path according to the

*Figure 5. Two-phase rate reduction algorithm*

```
rate_reduction(target_bitrate) {
    return any time when target_bitrate <= current_bitrate;

    // phase 1 rate reduction with resonable quality
    if (target_resolution < current_resolution)
        spatial_resolution_reduction(target_resolution);
    if (temporal_resolution > temporal_threshold)
        temporal_resolution_reduction(temporal_threshold);
    if (quality_of_video > quality_threshold)
        requantization();

    // phase 2 aggressive rate reduction
    while (target_bitrate >= current_bitrate) {
        requantization();
        temporal_resolution_reduction();
        spatial_resolution_reduction();
    }
}
```

current load of each of the encoders, its transcoding capability, and the network resources in the path. A transcoding path is a path from the DEMUX to the MUX through a selected encoder.

Let $\tilde{d}_{g,p}^{de}$ as expected transmission delay from the DEMUX to an encoder for a given picture group, $g$, on path $p$, $\tilde{d}_{g,p}^{em}$ as the expected transmission delay from the encoder to the MUX for the given picture group, and $\tilde{d}_{g,p}^{E}$ as the expected transcoding delay on the encoder. Equation (1) shows the estimated delay of each transcoding path, $\tilde{d}_{g,p}$.

$$\tilde{d}_{g,p} = \tilde{d}_{g,p}^{de} + \tilde{d}_{g,p}^{E} + \tilde{d}_{g,p}^{em} \tag{1}$$

The average of the previous transmission delays of the path are used to estimate the transmission delay $\tilde{d}_{g,p}^{de}$ and $\tilde{d}_{g,p}^{em}$. Let $i$ be the index of the previous group of pictures transcoded in the path, then $\tilde{d}_{g,p}^{de}$ and $\tilde{d}_{g,p}^{em}$ can be represented in equations (2) and (3).

$$\tilde{d}_{g,p}^{de} = \frac{\sum_{k=1}^{i} d_{k,p}^{de}}{i} \tag{2}$$

$$\tilde{d}_{g,p}^{em} = \frac{\sum_{k=1}^{i} d_{k,p}^{em}}{i} \tag{3}$$

The average of the previous computing delays and estimated queuing delay of the path are used to estimate the computation delay $\tilde{d}_{g,p}^{E}$. Let $c_{g,p}^{E}$ be the computation delay for a group g. Equation (4) shows the estimated computation delay for $\tilde{d}_{g,p}^{E}$.

$$\tilde{d}_{g,p}^{E} = \frac{\sum_{k=1}^{i} c_{k,p}^{E}}{k} + \tilde{q}_{g,p}^{E} \tag{4}$$

Let $w$ be the number of jobs in queue of the path, $T_c$ as the current time, and $T_s^c$ as the start time of a current job. Equation (5) shows the estimated queuing delay for $\tilde{d}_{g,p}^{E}$.

$$\tilde{q}_{g,p}^{E} = \tilde{c}_{c,p}^{E} - (T_c - T_s^c) + \sum_{w \in W} \tilde{c}_{w,p}^{E} \tag{5}$$

After calculating the estimated path delay $\tilde{d}_{g,p}$ for all available paths, the DEMUX selects a path that provides the lowest delay and jitter, and schedules the picture group, $g$, to the path. A detailed explanation is provided in Javed (2003).

## EVALUATION/EXPERIMENT ANALYSIS

The developed system is based on the publicly available MPEG 2 decoding and encoding source code from MPEG Software Simulation Group (MSSG). The testing video is captured from the Terminator

*Figure 6. Temporal resolution reduction*

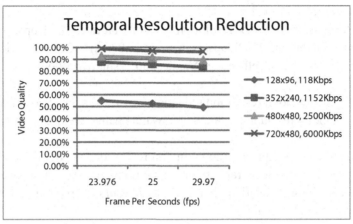

*Figure 7. Spatial resolution reduction*

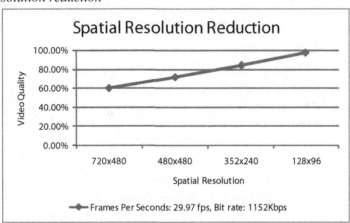

*Figure 8. Requantization reduction*

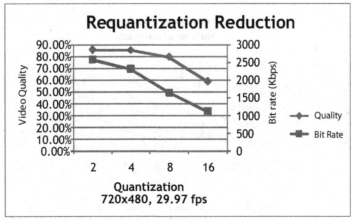

3 DVD in a widescreen format with a frame size of 720x416, a bit rate of 27123Kbps and a frame rate of 29.97fps in an uncompressed format.

The used output formats are in DVD (resolution 720x480, bit rate 6000Kbps, frame rate 29.97fps), SVCD (resolution 480x480, bit rate 2500Kbps, frame rate 29.97fps), VCD (resolution 352x240, bit rate 1152Kbps, frame rate 29.97fps), and cell phone (Nokia 6230: resolution 128x96, bit rate 118Kbps, frame rate 25.00fps).

Figure 6 shows that the temporal resolution reduction only results for various frame size videos. As shown in the figure, temporal resolution reduction does not change the quality much or the bit rate of the videos.

Spatial resolution reduction results are shown in Figure 7. Video quality dramatically increased on a smaller sized video when the same bit rate and the same frame per second rate were used. Therefore, if the display device has a lower resolution, then the spatial resolution reduction method could provide a lower bit rate without losing its quality.

*Figure 9. Extreme rate reduction*

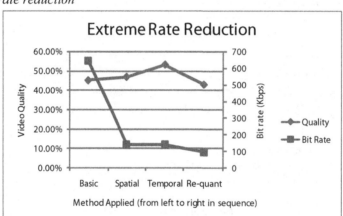

*Figure 10. Performance comparison on distributed transcoding*

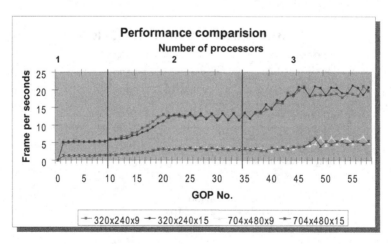

*Figure 11. Jitter controls in distributed transcoder*

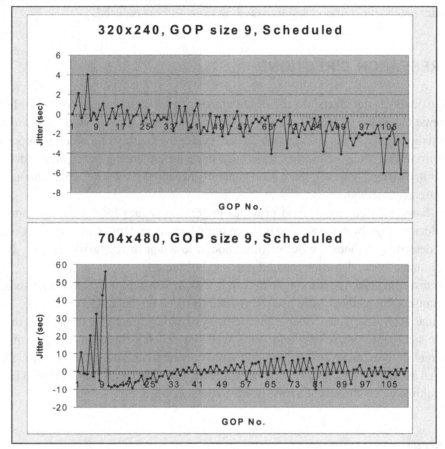

The requantization method is one of most frequently used methods for rate reduction. As seen in Figure 8, the bit rate could be controlled by changing the quantization scale. The quality of video, however, is dramatically reduced along with its bit rate.

Figure 9 shows the rate reduction by applying multiple reduction techniques. It assumes that a high-quality video, 720x480 resolution, 29.97fps, 27123Kbps bit rate, is transcoded into a low-quality video, 128x96 resolution, 23.976fps, 118Kbps bit rate. This basic method transcodes the video without applying any bit rate reduction scheme. It maintains a high bit rate with dramatic reduction of its video quality. By applying a spatial reduction method, bit rate is down at the desired level, and even better video quality is achieved. By applying a temporal resolution reduction method, the video quality can be enhanced with the same bit rate. Furthermore, the bit rate reduction can be possible by applying a requantization method without the loss of video quality. The system maintains its video quality but with a lower bit rate.

A performance comparison on distributed transcoding is shown in Figure 10. The top portion of the figure indicates the number of video transcoders. As expected, a small frame size video can be transcoded faster than a larger frame size video. Also, as the number of available transcoders increases, the number of frames it can transcode also increases.

The jitter controls in the distributed transcoding system is shown in Figure 11. As the system learns each transcoder path's transmission and transcoding time, jitter is reduced.

## FUTURE RESEARCH DIRECTIONS

Because video quality is not reversible, the stored videos in a server are prepared in their highest video quality. Extreme rate video transcoding supports a user who wants to see a video that was prepared in a very high quality format on its less capable device. Perceptive quality of a video is important in such a limited environment. Many researches have been done for enhancing perceptual video quality. To the best of our knowledge, however, there is no generally accepted standard for perception-based video quality measurement method.

An object-based transcoding method provides better approaches for the perception-based video transcoding. Identifying objects in a video is still relying heavily on human intervention, and machine-based object detection methods are not mature enough to adapt in real-world usages. Therefore, an intelligent automatic object detection method needs to be studied.

A video transcoding task is not a simple task. It is known as one of the computation-oriented tasks. Distributed transcoding methods have been suggested to speed up the transcoding time. The next step is to create a massively distributed video transcoding system that effectively transcodes multiple video streams at the same time. Many of World Wide Web sites, such as broadcasting system companies, online video rental stores, and YouTube, provide video content to massive users. As the video contents are downloaded and played on a variety of devices, an effective video transcoding system that massively transcodes multiple video streams at a time needs to be developed.

## CONCLUSION

Extreme rate video transcoding requires multiple methods applied to a video stream to get a proper bit rate with a reasonable quality. In this chapter, we reviewed rate control methods and transcoding speed up methods. We suggest an algorithm that uses multiple transcoding methods to retain a better quality video in an extreme rate control. A distributed transcoding method also is included to achieve a better transcoding speed for adjusting a bit rate in real time. The qualities of videos are compared in experiments. Experimental results support that applying multiple transcoding methods does achieve a better video quality under the same bit rate constraints than a single rate control method.

An object-based transcoding method is important, but identifying an object in a video relies heavily on human intervention. A machine-based object detection method is getting better, but still objects that a user wants to see are very subjective. A better perceptual video quality can be achieved if an object-based transcoding method is integrated with a system by using perception information from a user through a player. A frequency domain video transcoding enhances the speed of a video transcoding at the cost of scarifying a video quality. Providing a frequency domain video transcoding method with a same level of the video quality in a pixel domain transcoding would create a massive video transcoding system that could replace the current broadcasting systems in the future.

## REFERENCES

Assuncao, P., & Ghanbari, M. (1998). A frequency-domain video transcoder for dynamic bit-rate reduction of MPEG-2 bit streams. *IEEE Transactions on Circuits and Systems for Video Technology, 8*(8).

Balsree, R., Thawani, A., Gopalan, S., & Sridhar, V. (2005). Inter-frame similarity based video transcoding. *Proceedings of the Seventh IEEE International Symposium on Multimedia.*

Bhargava, B. (1996). Adaptable software for communications in video conferencing. *Proceedings of the IETE International Conference on Multi-media Information Systems (MULTIMEDIA 96)*, New Delhi, India.

Han, J., & Kim, H. (2006). Optimization of requantization codebook for vector quantization. *IEEE Transactions on Image Processing, 15*(5).

Kalva, H., Petljanski, B., & Furht, B. (2005). Complexity reduction tools for MPEG-2 to H.264 video transcoding. *WSEAS Transactions on Information Science & Applications, 2*, 295–300.

Keesman, G., Hellinghuizen, R., Hoeksema, F., & Heideman, G. (1996). Transcoding of MPEG bitstreams. *Signal Processing Image Communication, 8.*

Khan, J., & Patel, D. (2003). Extreme rate transcoding for dynamic video rate adaptation. *Proceedings of the 4th International Conference on Wireless and Optical Communication.*

Khan, J., & Yang, S. (2003). Delay and jitter minimization in high performance Internet computing. *Proceedings of the International Conference on High Performance Computing*, Hyderabad, India.

Lei, Z., & Georganas, N. (2002). H.263 video transcoding for spatial resolution downscaling. *Proceedings of the International Conference on Information Technology.*

Puri, A., & Eleftheriadis, A. (1998). MPEG-4: An object-based multimedia coding standard supporting mobile applications. *Mobile Networks and Applications, 3*(1).

Sambe, Y., Watanabe, S., Yu, D., Nakamura, T., & Wakamiya, N. (2005). High-speed distributed video transcoding for multiple rates and formats. *IEICE Transactions on Information and Systems, E88-D*(8).

Shen, B. (2006). Optimal requantization-based rate adaptation for H.264. *Proceedings of the IEEE ICME*, 317–320.

Shu, H., & Chau, L. (2006). The realization of arbitrary downsizing video transcoding. *IEEE Transactions on Circuits and Systems for Video Technology, 16*(4).

Sun, W., & Zdepski, J. (1996). Architecture for MPEG compressed bitstream scaling. *IEEE Transactions on Circuit Systems Video Technology, 6*(2).

Vetro, A., Sun, H., & Wang, Y. (2001). Object-based transcoding for adaptable video content delivery. *IEEE Transaction on Circuits and Systems for Video Technology, 11*(3).

Video Technology Magazine. Retrieved September 28, 2007, from http://www.videotechnology. com/0904/formats.html

Xin, J., Lin, C., & Sun, M. (2005). Digital video transcoding. *Proceedings of the IEEE, 93*(1).

Youn, J., & Sun, M. (2000). Video transcoding with H.263 bit-streams. *Journal of Visual Communication and Image Representation, 11*(4).

## ADDITIONAL READING

Acharya, S., & Smith, B. (1998). Compressed domain transcoding of MPEG. *Proceedings of the IEEE International Conferences on Multimedia Computing and Systems*, Austin, Texas.

Amir, E., McCanne, S., & Katz, R. (1998). An active service framework and its application to real-time multimedia transcoding. *Proceedings of the ACM Special Interest Group on Data Communication (SIGCOMM) 98*, Vancouver, British Columbia.

Brandt, J., & Wolf, L. (2007). Multidimensional transcoding for adaptive video streaming. *Proceedings of the ACM 17th International Workshop on Network and Operating Systems Support for Digital Audio & Video*, Urbana-Champaign, Illinois.

Brewer, E., et al. (1998). A network architecture for heterogeneous mobile computing. *IEEE Personal Communications, 5*(5).

Chang, S. (2002). Optimal video adaptation and skimming using a utility-based framework. *Proceedings of the International Thyrrhenian Workshop on Digital Communication,* Calcutta, India.

Cornea, R., Mohapatra, S., Dutt, N., Nicolau, A., & Venkatasubramanian, N. (2003). Managing cross-layer constraints for interactive mobile multimedia. *Proceedings of the IEEE Workshop on Constraint-Aware Embedded Software*, Cancun, Mexico.

Guo, J., Chen, F., Bhuyan, L., & Kumar, R. (2003). A cluster-based active router architecture supporting video/audio stream transcoding service. *Proceedings of the 17th International Symposium on Parallel and Distributed Processing*, Nice, France.

Harville, M., Covell, M., & Wee, S. (2003). An architecture for componentized, network-based media services. *Proceedings of the International Conference on Multimedia and Expo*, Baltimore, Maryland.

Holub, P., & Hejtmanek, L. (2004). Distributed encoding environment based on grids and IBP infrastructure. *Proceedings of the Terena Networking Conference*, Rhodes, Greece.

Jammeh, E., Fleury, M., & Ghanbari, M. (2004). Smoothing transcoded MPEG-1 video streams for Internet transmission. *IEE Proceeding Vision, Image and Signal Processing, 151*(4).

Koenen, R. (2002). MPEG-4 overview. ISO/IEC JTC1/SC29/WG11 N4668.

Kwok, T. (2007). Wireless networking requirements of multimedia applications. *Proceedings of the IEEE International Conference on Universal Personal Communications*, Florence, Italy.

Lei, Z., & Georganas, N. (2002). Rate adaptation transcoding for precoded video streams. *Proceedings of the Tenth ACM International Conference on Multimedia*, Juan-les-Pins, France.

Lei, Z., & Georganas, N.D. (2002). A frame layer bit-allocation for H.263+ based video transcoding. *Proceeding of the 21st Biennial Symposium on Communications*, Kingston, Ontario.

Lei, Z., & Georganas, N. (2003). Video transcoding gateway for wireless video access. *Proceedings of the Canadian Conference on Electrical and Computer Engineering*, Montréal, Canada.

Lienhart, R., et al. (2003). Challenges in distributed video management and delivery. In *Handbook of video databases* (pp. 961–990), Boca Raton, Florida: CRC Press.

Liu, S., & Bovik, A. (2005). Foveation embedded DCT domain video transcoding. *Journal of Visual Communication and Image Representation, 16*(6).

Lu, M., Steenkiste, P., & Chen, T. (2007). A time-based adaptive retry strategy for video streaming in 802.11 WLANs. *Wireless Communications & Mobile Computing, 7*(2).

Roy, S., Shen, B., Sundaram, V., & Kumar, R. (2003). Application level handoff support for mobile media transcoding sessions. *Proceedings of the 12th International Workshop on Network and Operating Systems Support for Digital Audio and Video*, Miami, Florida.

Shanmugham, S. (2006). *Perceptual video quality measurement for streaming video over mobile networks* [master's thesis]. Department of Electrical Engineering and Computer Science, University of Kansas.

Smith, J., Mohan, R., & Li, C. (1998). Transcoding Internet content for heterogeneous client devices. *Proceedings of the IEEE International Symposium on Circuits and Systems*, Monterey, California.

Vass, J., Zhuang, S., Yao, J., & Zhuang, X. (1999). Efficient mobile video access in wireless environments. *Proceedings of the Wireless Communications and Networking Conference*, New Orleans, Louisiana.

Vetro, A., & Huifang, S. (2001). Media conversions to support mobile users. *Proceedings of the Canadian Conference on Electrical and Computer Engineering*, Toronto, Ontario, Canada.

Wee, S., & Apostolopoulos, J. (2001). Secure scalable video streaming for wireless networks. *Proceedings of the IEEE International Conference on Acoustics, Speech, and Signal Processing*, Salt Lake City, Utah.

Youn, J., Sun, M., & Lin, C. (1999). Motion vector refinement for high-performance transcoding. *IEEE Transactions on Multimedia, 1*(1).

Zhang, J., Perkis, A., & Georganas, N.D. (2004). H.264/AVC and transcoding for multimedia adaptation. *Proceedings of the 6th COST 276 Workshop*, Thessaloniki, Greece.

Chapter VIII

# Semantic–Based Video Transcoding Architectures for Quality of Service Applications in Mobile and Wireless Video Communication

**Ashraf M.A. Ahmad**
*Princess Sumaya University for Technology, Jordan*

## ABSTRACT

*Delivering streaming video over wireless networks is an important component for most interactive multimedia applications running on personal wireless handset devices. Such personal devices have to be inexpensive, compact, and lightweight. Wireless channels have limited bandwidth and a high channel bit error rate and limited bandwidth. Delay variation of packets due to network congestion with the high bit error rate lessens the quality of video at the handheld device. Mobile access to multimedia content requires video transcoding functionality at the edge of the mobile network for interworking with heterogeneous networks and services. Under certain conditions, the bandwidth of a coded video stream needs to be drastically reduced. We present several efficient mechanisms for improving the quality of service (QoS) delivered to the client by deploying content-based transcoding schemes. The proposed approaches are performing the required transcoding based on the video content. Some approaches study the texture and temporal features. Other approaches perform object detection in order to determine the important objects to achieve semantic transcoding. The quality of the reconstructed images is remarkably similar to results that have been processed by the expensive and high performance transcoding approach. Exceptional performance is demonstrated in the experiment results. Extensive experiments have been conducted, and the results of various video clips with different bit rates and frame rates have been provided.*

## INTRODUCTION

Recent advances in mobile communications and portable client devices enable us to access multimedia content ubiquitously. However, when multimedia content becomes richer, including video and audio, it becomes more difficult for wireless access to communicate due to many practical restrictions. Most important of all, wireless connections usually have a much lower bandwidth compared to wired ones, and communication conditions change dynamically due to the effect of fading. Another practical factor is that portable client devices are equipped with limited computing and display capabilities. Most portable devices are not suitable for high-quality video decoding and displaying.

Concerning the heterogeneity issue, the previous era has seen a variety of developments in the area of multimedia representation and communication. In particular, we are beginning to see delivery of various multimedia data for all types of users and conditions. In a diverse and heterogeneous world, the delivery path for multimedia content to a multimedia terminal is not straightforward, especially in the mobile communication environment. Access networks vary in nature, sometimes limited, and differ in performance. The characteristics of end-user devices vary increasingly in terms of storage, processing capabilities, and display qualities. Finally, users are different by nature, showing dissimilar preferences, special usage, disabilities, and so forth.

However, the major traffic component in multimedia services is undoubtedly due to visual information encoded and delivered either as video frames or visual components.

In order to cope with the current heterogeneous communication infrastructure and the diversity of services and user terminals, different transcoding mechanisms are necessary at Internet working nodes (Han, Bhagwat, LaMaire, Mummert, Perret & Rubas, 1998; Warabino, Ota, Morikawa & Ohashi, 2000).

Whenever a client terminal or its access channel does not comply with the necessary requirements, media transcoding must be triggered to allow interoperability. This is basically an adaptation function operating on coded streams such as MPEG1/2 (ISO/IEC 11 172, 1993; ISO/IEC 13 818, 1995) for matching a set of new constraints, different from those assumed when the signals were originally encoded. Since many multimedia services are not specifically meant for mobile systems, in general the channel bandwidth required for transmission as well as the coded signal format do not match mobile applications (Correia, Faria & Assuncao 2001; Shanableh & Ghanbari, 2000). Because of traffic characteristics such as high bit rate, video will be the dominant traffic in multimedia streams; hence, it needs to be managed efficiently. Obviously, for efficient utilization of network resources, video must be compressed to reduce its bandwidth requirement. Although several compression techniques exist, MPEG (Han et al., 1998; ISO/IEC 13 818, 1995; Warabino et al., 2000) is one of the most widely used compression algorithms for network video applications. A wireless handset device (e.g., personal data assistant) can integrate voice, video, and data into one device. In contrast to solely text information, multimedia data can tolerate a certain level of error and fading. Therefore, although a wireless network has a high bit error rate when compared to a wireline one, it is possible in a cost-effective manner to transmit multimedia over wireless networks with an acceptable quality.

As mentioned earlier, although the constraints imposed by the heterogeneous nature of the communication network are quite different from those arising from the diversity of user terminals and the problem of fading and error in wireless channels, all of them may be dealt with using the so-called transcoding mechanism. In this work, we address the problem of MPEG stream video transcoding where the bandwidth of a coded video stream must be drastically reduced in order to cope with a highly constrained transmission channel. Particularly, we work on the MPEG-2 compressed digital video content, as MPEG-2 is being used in a number of products, including DVDs, camcorders, digital TV, and HDTV. In addition, vast MPEG2 data have already been stored in different accessible multimedia servers. The ability to access this widely available MPEG-2 content on low-power, end-user devices such as PDAs and mobile phones depends on effective techniques for transcoding the MPEG-2 content to a more appropriate, low bit-rate video.

In the subject where video is concerned, transcoding may be needed to convert precoded high-quality videos into lower quality ones to display on handheld devices. Video transcoding deals with converting a previously compressed video signal into another one with a different format, such as different bit rate, frame rate, frame size, or even compression standard. With the expansion and diversity of multimedia applications and the present communication infrastructure comprising different underlying networks and protocols, there is a growing need for internetwork multimedia communications over heterogeneous networks and devices. Especially in applications where pre-encoded videos are spread to users through different connections, such as video on demand or streaming of pre-encoded videos, the end transmission channel conditions are generally unknown when the video is originally encoded. By means of transcoding, pre-encoded videos can be converted on the fly as they are transmitted. Similar to source encoders, video transcoders can modulate the data they produce by adjusting a number of parameters, including quality, frame rate, or resolution. However, using transcoders gives us another chance to dynamically adjust the video format according to channel bandwidth and end devices. This is particularly useful when there are time variations in the channel characteristics.

## HANDHELD AND WIRELESS AND MOBILE TECHNOLOGIES

### Handheld Features

The handheld device involved in mobile communication is supposed to have some specific features:

1. Inexpensive
2. Compact
3. Lightweight
4. Power consumption
5. Limited display capabilities

### Wireless Wide Area Networks

After the first-generation analog mobile systems, the second-generation (2G) mobile digital systems were introduced, offering higher capacity and lower costs for network operators, while for the users, they offered short messages and low-rate data services added to speech services. An important evolution of the 2G systems, sometimes known as 2.5G, is the ability to use packet-switched solution in General Packet Radio System (GPRS). The main investment for the operators lies in the new packet-switched core network, while the extensions in the radio access network mainly are software upgrades.

## Wireless and Mobile Network Features

In general, wireless and mobile network have some limitations:

1. Limited bandwidth
2. High channel bit error rate
3. Wireless connections much lower bandwidth compared to wired ones
4. Communication conditions change dynamically due to the effect of fading

To address the technical solutions, several mechanism and technologies have been deployed, such as Wideband CDMA, CDMA 2000, Time Division-Synchronous CDMA (TD-SCDMA), Digital Enhanced Cordless Telecommunications (DECT), and UWC-136.

## Issues of Viewing a Video Stream in a Mobile Environment

Although the constraints imposed by the heterogeneous nature of the communication network are quite different from those arising from the diversity of user terminals, both of them may deal with transcoding systems. In this work, we address the problem of MPEG stream video transcoding where the bandwidth of a coded video stream must be drastically reduced in order to cope with a highly constrained transmission channel such as mobile. The variety in mobile devices also increases the difficulty of accessing content. For example, mobile devices are conveniently sized to fit in a pocket, but this size constrains their display area. Creating arbitrary trimmed versions of content could get around this constraint, but differences in display capabilities would easily make a device-specific authoring approach too costly to be practical and would lower quality of service in some cases. Examples of device differences include screen sizes ranging from a few hundred to thousands of pixels, and color depths ranging from two-line black-and-white displays to full-color displays. Video content can also be encoded in many different modes, such as MPEG-X series, H26X series, and so forth.

In these cases, transcoders can be used to transform multimedia content to an appropriate video format and bandwidth for wireless mobile streaming media systems. A conceptually simple and straightforward method to perform this transcoding is to decode the original video stream, downsample the decoded frames to a smaller size, and re-encode the downsampled frames at a lower bit rate. However, a typical CCIR601 MPEG-2 video requires almost all the cycles of a 300Mhz CPU to perform real-time decoding. Encoding is significantly more complex and usually cannot be accomplished in real time without the help of dedicated hardware or a high-end PC. These factors render the conceptually simple and straightforward transcoding method impractical. Furthermore, this simple approach can lead to significant loss in video quality. In addition, if transcoding is provided as a network service in the path between the content provider and content consumer, it is highly desirable for the transcoding unit to handle as many concurrent sessions as possible. This scalability is critical to enable wireless networks to handle user requests that may be very intense at high load times. Therefore, it is very important to develop fast algorithms to reduce the compute and memory loads for transcoding sessions.

In this section, we identify issues involved in viewing a video stream in a mobile computing environment and propose methods of handling these issues. Video streams encoded by a high bit-rate compression method (e.g., MPEG-1) require several megabits per second of bandwidth and are not suitable for a strictly band-limited environment. Therefore, video streams should be encoded by a low bit-rate compression method (e.g., MPEG-4). MPEG-4 is appropriate for mobile access because it is robust to channel errors. From this point of view, some MPEG-4 codec large-scale integrations for mobile devices are under development, and MPEG-4 is apparently becoming the mainstream technique for mobile video usage. When communication conditions get worse and error rate increases in a wireless link, transmission jitter increases because error packets are retransmitted based on Radio Link Control protocol located at the data link layer. If any packets are not recovered by retransmission using a reliable transport protocol such as Transmission Control Protocol (TCP), error packets are retransmitted end to end. Consequently, this causes more transmission jitter and throughput reduction. Also, if an unreliable transport protocol such as User Datagram Protocol (UDP) is used, packets not recovered by retransmission and flooded by congestion on the communication link will be discarded so the rate of packets that arrive at the client decreases. As a result, in both cases, the application layer throughput reduces, and video data cannot be transferred stably. Therefore, the data rate of a video stream needs to be adapted in accordance with communication conditions. In addition, jitter can be absorbed by preserving some video data on the client buffer. As far as client device capabilities are concerned, display size, processing power, and memory size have to be taken into account. Since the display size of portable devices is small (on cellular phones both width and height are about 100 pixels at most), a video stream may be larger than the display size and is not easily viewed by mobile users. Hence, both the width and height of a video frame have to be fitted to the display size. In another method, the size may be reduced on the user client. However, it places an extra load on the user client and is undesirable for mobile where the processing power of the client device is low. If the client device does not have enough real-time video stream decoding power, a mobile user cannot fully view video streams. The amount of processing required for decoding is related to the number of video frames in one second (frame rate) and total number of pixels in one frame (frame size). Therefore, the frame rate and frame size need to be adjusted according to the processing power of the client device. As for memory size, the client device needs to have sufficient memory to preserve several decoded frames, because in encoding methods such as MPEG-4, the decoding process requires a few frames before and after the frame that is actually being decoded.

## RELATED WORK

Converting a previously compressed video bit stream to a lower bit rate through transcoding can provide finer and more dynamic adjustments of the bit rate of the coded video bit stream to meet various channel situations (Assunçno & Ghanbari, 1996; Eleftheriadis & Anastassiou, 1995; Keesman, Hellinghuizen, Hoekesma & Heidman, 1996; Morrison, Nilsson & Ghanbari, 1994; Safranek, Kalmanek & Garg, 1995; Sun, Kwok & Zdepski, 1996; Tudor & Werner, 1997). Depending on the particular strategy that is adopted, the transcoder attempts to satisfy network conditions or user requirements in various ways. In the context of video transmission, compression standards are needed to reduce the amount of bandwidth required by the network. Since the delivery system must accommodate various transmission and load constraints, it is sometimes necessary to further convert the already compressed bitstream before transmission.

Depending on these constraints, conventional transcoding techniques can be classified into three major categories: bit-rate conversion or scaling, resolution conversion, and syntax conversion (Assunçno & Ghanbari, 1996; Keesman et al., 1996). Bit-rate scaling can accommodate deficiency in available bandwidth. Resolution conversion can also accommodate bandwidth limitations but is primarily used

*Figure 1. Typical transcoder architecture*

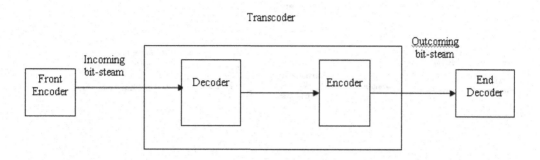

to account for known limitations in the user device (Correia et al., 2001; Eleftheriadis & Anastassiou, 1995; Tudor & Werner, 1997), such as processing power, display constraints, or memory capability. To ensure adaptability across hybrid networks, syntax conversion at the protocol layer is required (Chang & Messerschmidt, 1995; Sun, Vetro, Bao & Poon, 1997). Syntax conversions may also be considered at the compression layer to ensure receiver compatibility.

The simplest way to develop a video transcoder is by directly cascading a source video decoder with a destination video encoder known as the cascaded pixel domain transcoder (Youn & Sun, 2000). Without using common information, this direct approach needs to fully decode input video and re-encode the decoded video by an encoder with different characteristics, as described in Figure 1. Obviously, this direct approach is usually computationally intensive. The architecture is flexible because the compressed video is first decoded into raw pixels; hence, many operations can be performed on the decoded video. However, as we mentioned earlier, the direct implementation of the Cascaded Pixel Domain Transcoder is not desirable because it requires high complexity of implementation.

The alternative architecture for transcoding is an open-loop transcoding in which the incoming bitrate is downscaled by modifying the discrete cosine transform (DCT) coefficients. For example, the DCT coefficients can be truncated, requantized, or partially discarded in the optimal sense to achieve the desirable lower bit rate (Eleftheriadis & Anastassiou, 1995; Sun et al., 1997). In the open-loop transcoding, because the transcoding is carried out in the coded domain where complete decoding and

*Figure 2. General scheme for motion vector reuse transcoding*

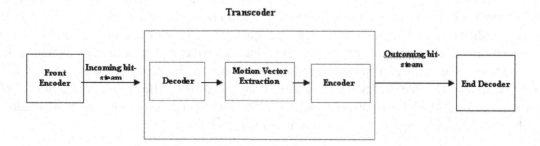

*Figure 3. Video transcoding scheme for partial motion vector estimation*

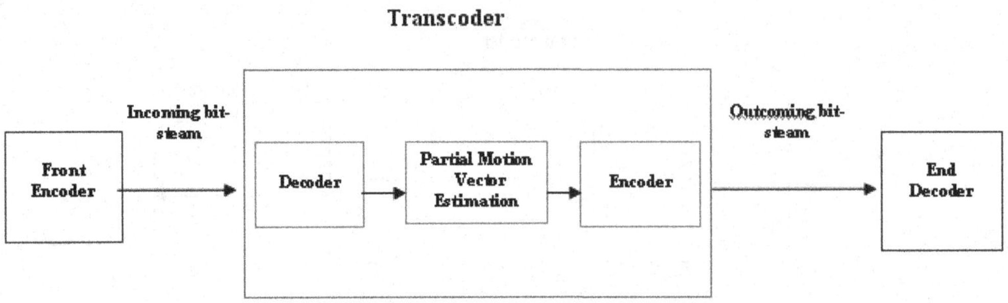

re-encoding are not required, it is possible to construct a simple and fast transcoder. However, open-loop transcoding can produce "drift" degradations due to mismatched reconstructed pictures in the front-encoder and the end-decoder, which often result in an unacceptable video quality.

Drift-free transcoding is possible by the direct cascade of a decoder and an encoder. Although this transcoder has a higher complexity than the open-loop transcoder, some information extracted from the incoming video bit stream after the decoding can be used to significantly reduce the complexity of the encoder. Thus, the complexity may not be as bad as it looks.

In transcoding, full motion estimation is usually not performed in the transcoder because of its computational complexity. Instead, motion vectors extracted from the incoming bit stream are reused. Since a great deal of bit rate reduction is required, traditional transcoding methods based on simply reusing the motion vectors extracted from an incoming video bit stream are not adequate (Assunçno & Ghanbari, 1997; Bjork & Christopoulos, 1998; Youn & Sun, 1998). Figure 2 states the basic scheme of these approaches. They would produce an unacceptable texture distortion in the reconstructed signals (i.e., very low quality of service (QoS) delivered to the end user, which may not result in the best quality). Although an optimized motion vector can be obtained by full-scale motion estimation, this is not desirable because of its high computational complexity.

Another related work was suggested by Youn, Sun, and Lin (1999), as they proposed to partially estimate the motion vectors based on predefined search area. Their constructed images quality was relatively good. The performance of video transcoding was boosted, but on the other hand, they still have high computation complexity as they need to perform motion estimation even partially. For further description, the basic scheme of their proposed approach is shown in Figure 3.

In this chapter, we consider the cascaded architecture as a framework for high-performance transcoding. The cascaded transcoder is very flexible and easily extendible to various types of transcoding such as temporal or spatial resolution conversions. We will investigate techniques that can reduce the complexity while maintaining the same level of video quality. In transcoding, motion estimation is usually not performed in the transcoder because of its computational complexity. Instead, motion vectors extracted from the incoming bit stream are reused. However, this simple motion-vector reuse scheme may introduce considerable quality degradation in many applications (Bjork & Christopoulos, 1998; Youn et al., 1999). Although an optimized motion vector can be obtained by full-scale motion estimation, this is not desirable because of its high computational complexity.

Therefore, in this chapter, we propose a new semantic and content-based transcoding scheme using the MPEG1/2 encoded bit streams (ISO/IEC 11 172, 1993; ISO/IEC 13 818, 1995). This scheme consists of several components to achieve the semantic transcoding, which includes:

1. Feature extraction
2. Temporal analysis
3. Texture and edge analysis
4. Transcoding control
5. Video transcoder

## TRANSCODING FUNCTIONS

To overcome the aforementioned limitations and obstacles in viewing video steams in wireless and mobile networks, an effective transcoding mechanism is required. Building a good video transcoding for mobile devices poses many challenges. To overcome these challenges, a various kind of transcoding function is provided. The following paragraphs will describe these functions in detail.

The first function is bit rate adaptation. Bit rate adaptation has been the most significant function of video transcoding techniques. The idea of compressed video bit rate adaptation is initiated by the applications of transmitting pre-encoded video streams over heterogeneous networks. When connecting two transmission media, the channel capacities of the outgoing channel may be less than those of the incoming channel, so bit rate adaptation is necessary before sending the video bit stream over heterogeneous channels. In applications such as video on demand where video is off-line encoded for later transmission, the channel characteristics through which the resulting bit stream will be transmitted might be unknown. Through video transcoding, the bit rate of pre-encoded videos can be dynamically adapted to the obtainable bandwidth and variable communication circumstances. In most bit adaptation cases, a pre-encoded video with high bit rate and fine visual quality will be converted into low bit rate video with elegantly degraded visual quality.

The second function is frame size conversion. Video spatial resolution downscaling is significant since most current handheld devices are characterized by limited screen sizes. By inserting a downscaling filter in the transcoder, the resolution of the incoming video can be reduced. Because of downscaling the video into lower spatial resolution, motion vectors from the incoming video cannot be reused directly but have to be resampled and downscaled. Based on the updated motion vectors, predictive residues are recalculated and compressed.

The third function is frame rate conversion. To transcode an arriving compressed video bitstream for a low bandwidth outgoing channel such as a wireless network, a high transcoding percentage is often necessary. However, high transcoding ratios may result in intolerable video quality when the arriving bitstream is transcoded with the full frame rate as the arriving bitstream. Frame-rate conversion or frame-dropping is often used as an efficient scheme to assign more bits to the remaining frames so acceptable quality can be maintained for each frame. In addition, frame-rate conversion is also needed when an end system can play video only at a lower frame rate due to the processing power limit. Frame rate conversion can be accomplished simply by random frame dropping. For instance, dropping every other frame in a sequential order leads to a half rate reduction in the transcoded sequence. When frames are dropped, motion vectors from the arriving video cannot be reused directly because they are

*Figure 4. Overview of video transcoding system architecture*

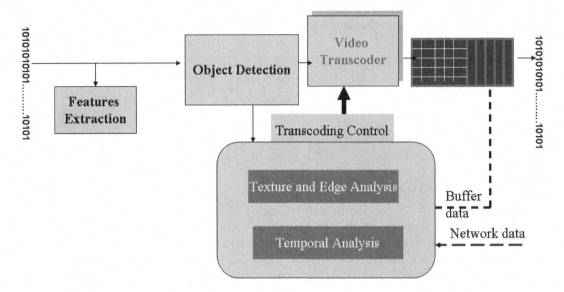

pointed to the immediately previous frame. If the previous frame is dropped in the transcoder, the link between two frames is broken, and the end decoder will not be able to reconstruct the picture by these motion vectors. Therefore, the transcoder is in charge of calculating new motion vectors that point to the previous undropped frames.

## VIDEO TRANSCODING SYSTEM ARCHITECTURE

In this section, a full description of video transcoding is presented. The proposed transcoding scheme is shown in Figure 4. In this figure, we capture video stream in MPEG format from the front encoder, then we extract the desired features needed to perform the texture and temporal analysis and the object detection. Then the transcoding control is in charge of providing the video transcoder with the necessary decisions.

### Features Extraction

In order to start our system, we should extract the desired features, which are described in this section. The compressed video provides one MV for each macroblock of size 16x16 pixels, which means that the MVs are quantized to one vector per 16x16 block. The MVs are not the true MVs of a particular pixel in the frame. Our object detection algorithm requires MVs of each P-frame from the video streams. Our system takes the sparse MVs from the compressed video stream as the only input. For the computational efficiency, only the MVs of P-frames are used for object detection algorithm since, in general, in a video with 30fps, consecutive P-frames separated by two or three B-frames are still similar and would not vary too much. Besides, it must be noted that B-frames are just "interpolating" frames that hinge on the hard motion information provided in P-frames, and therefore, using them for the concatenation of displacements would be redundant. Therefore, it is sufficient to use the motion information of P-frames only to detect the objects. In addition, we need to extract the DCT information from I-frames; this information is readily available in MPEG stream, and thus we are not demanded to spend too much time decoding the MEPG stream. Hence, our approach can fit for the real time application environment.

## Object Detection

An object detection algorithm is used to detect potential objects in video shots. Initially, undesired MVs are eliminated. Subsequently, MVs that have similar magnitude and direction are clustered together, and this group of associated macroblocks of similar MVs is regarded as a potential object. Details are presented in the object detection algorithm.

### The Object Detection Algorithm

Input: P-frames of a video clip

Output: object sets {Obj1 , Obj2 , … ObjN } where N is total number of regions in P-frame and Objn means the nth object of the P-frame. Each object size is measured in terms of number of macroblocks.

1. Cluster MVs that are of similar magnitude and direction into the same group with region growing approach.

1.1 Set search windows (W) size 3x3 macroblocks.

1.2 Search all macroblocks (MB) within W and compute the difference ( and ) of MV magnitude ( ) and direction ( ) between center and its neighboring eight MVs within W.

where k [1,8] and it is the MV in the center position of W
 MVs within W except
For all $1 \geq k \geq 8$, flag

where is the predefined threshold for MV magnitude and is the threshold for MV direction.

If , mark of as 1, where is the flag of the center MV within W.
Otherwise, set all flags within W to 0.

1.3 Go to step 1.2 until all MBs are processed.
1.4 Group MBs that are marked as 1 into the same cluster.
1.5 Compute each object center and record its associated macroblocks.

## Texture and Edge Analysis

To assist the texture and edge module in making a decision, texture metric should be calculated. A novel mechanism is proposed and justified in this chapter. We will extract the DCT coefficients from

I-frames; these coefficients include the DC coefficient as well as the AC components. Then we will pass the DCT coefficients into a module to calculate the energy values "texture" of each frame, after which we will propagate these "texture information" values into P-frames using construction of DC image module. We pass both I-frame and P-frame texture information into scaling module along with feedback information from the client side to decide the suitable scaling mechanism.

## Energy Computation

The video analysis is performed directly in the DCT compressed domain using the intensity variation encoded in the DCT domain. Therefore, only a very small amount of decoding is required. In some applications, researchers do use either the horizontal intensity variation or vertical intensity variation. For example, in the text detection, it is generally approved that text regions possess a special texture because text usually consists of character components, which contrast the background and at the same time show a periodic horizontal intensity variation due to the horizontal alignment of characters. In addition, character components form text lines with approximately the same spacing. As a result, text regions can be segmented using texture features.

The DCT coefficients in MPEG video, which capture the directionality and periodicity of local image blocks, are used as measures to identify high texture regions. Therefore, we will be able to treat block accordingly. Each unit block in the compressed images is classified based on local horizontal, vertical, and diagonal intensity variations.

*Figure 5. Flowchart of texture calculation on frame level*

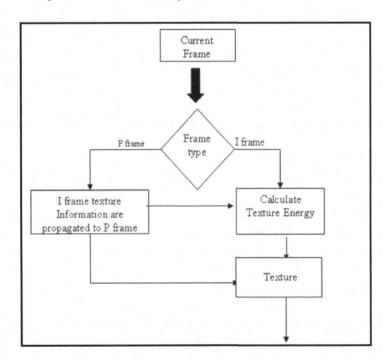

*Figure 6. Redefined texture energy map*

| $C_0$ | $C_1$ | $C_2$ | | | | | $C_7$ |
|---|---|---|---|---|---|---|---|
| $C_8$ | $C_9$ | $C_{10}$ | | | | | $C_{15}$ |
| $C_{16}$ | $C_{17}$ | $C_{18}$ | | | | | |
| | | | $C_{27}$ | $C_{28}$ | | | |
| | | | | $C_{36}$ | | | |
| | | | | | $C_{45}$ | | |
| | | | | | | $C_{54}$ | $C_{55}$ |
| $C_{56}$ | $C_{57}$ | | | | | $C_{62}$ | $C_{63}$ |

For texture and edge calculation, a mathematical model has been proposed for providing texture information. The details of the approach are presented herein. First, the energy map is defined according to Figure 6. Energy detentions are introduced.

- Atot: Total Energy
- AD: Diagonal Energy
- AH: Horizontal Energy
- AV: Vertical Energy
- AFin: Final Energy

Energy calculation is based on the redefined texture energy map as show in Figure 6.

$$A_V = C_{16\text{-}17}^2 + C_{24\text{-}25}^2 + C_{32\text{-}33}^2 + C_{40\text{-}41}^2 + C_{48\text{-}49}^2 + C_{56\text{-}57}^2$$
$$A_{Fin} = C_{57}^2 + C_{45}^2 + C_{15}^2$$
$$A_{tot} = A_H + A_V + A_H$$
$$A_D = C_{45}^2 + C_{44}^2 + C_{36}^2 + C_{37}^2 + C_{28}^2 + C_{27}^2 + C_{26}^2 + C_{19}^2 + C_{18}^2$$
$$A_H = C_{2\text{-}7}^2 + C_{10\text{-}15}^2$$

To make a decision regarding the texture of each macroblock, the following procedure is deployed.

(1) IF $(A_D/A_{tot})$ > Threshold$_1$ Then
High contrast → Fine Else
Low Contrast → Texture End IF
(2) IF $(A_H/(A_H + A_V))$ > Threshold$_2$ Then
Vertical Edge Else
Edge or "texture or coarse area" End IF


(3) IF $(A_V/(A_V + A_H))$ > Threshold$_3$ Then
Horizontal Else
Texture or Coarse Area End IF
(4) IF $(A_{Fin}/A_{tot})$ > Threshold$_4$ Then
Coarse Else
Texture End IF
Threshold$_{1-4}$ are decided by experiments


## Temporal Analysis

To perform the temporal analysis, the motion vectors are needed. Temporal analysis component is designed based on the temporal adjacent neighborhood of a macroblock. The main idea is that a "fine" motion vector should not have its direction altered in a drastic manner.

Figure 7 states the relation among the current, successive, and precedent frames. Motion vectors in these frames are temporally correlated. Each frame is affected by its successive and precedent frames. The closer the frame, the more correlated and contributing to its neighbor, so MVN+1 is twice as important as MVN+2 to current motion vector MVN.

*Figure 7. Relation among the current fame and other frames in temporal domain*

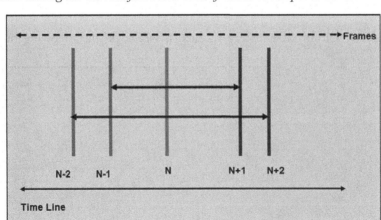

## TRANSCODING CONTROL

The control module is responsible for creating a transcoding scheme according to the user profile and other information. The transcoding scheme will include some transcoding parameters. In order to decide appropriate transcoding parameters, decisions must be made by considering all of the factors adaptively. For example, when connection throughput is low, the bit rate of the video needs to be converted. At the same time, in order to ensure video quality, the frame rate of the video also needs to be reduced. In so doing, each frame will have enough bit budgets to maintain tolerable visual quality.

## VIDEO TRANSCODER

The video transcoder is the actual conversion engine of a video stream. It decodes a video stream, which is pre-encoded at high quality and stored in the video source, and then performs transcoding according to our proposed scheme. According to the result we present in section 6, our proposed scheme has a very high performance in terms of visual quality. They are comparable to results that can be achieved by full-scale motion estimation-based transcoding. When fast transcoding architectures are used, it is possible to execute transcoding in real time. Thus, we can provide the handheld device user a smooth, online video presentation. In short, video transcoder is in charge of performing the early mentioned transcoding functions.

## RESULT AND DISCUSSION

We have designed an experiment in order to verify the performance of the proposed scheme. The experiment has been designed to test the proposed scheme on several video clips. These video clips are in MPEG format and are part of the MPEG7 testing dataset and other video clips, which have been widely used in such applications performance evaluation.

In all the simulations presented in this chapter, test sequences of QCIF (176 144) were encoded at high bit rate using a fixed quantization parameter. At the front-encoder, the first frame was encoded as an intraframe (I-frame), and the remaining frames were encoded as interframes (P-frames). These picture-coding modes were preserved during the transcoding. In our simulations, bidirectional predicted frames (B-frames) were not considered. In general, in a video with 30fps, consecutive P-frames separated by two or three B-frames are still similar and would not vary too much. Besides, it must be noted that B-frames are just "interpolating" frames that hinge on the hard motion information provided in P-frames, and therefore, using them for the concatenation of displacements would be redundant. Therefore, it is sufficient to use the motion information of P-frames only in our experiment design. However, the idea of the proposed scheme can also be applied to B-frames.

Group A using object-based streaming only (Correia et al., 2001; Shanableh & Ghanbari, 2000), group B using motion vector-based streaming, Group C using no content scaling, and group D our system, comparison is held among four types of work that are transcoding scheme using full-scale motion estimation (A), transcoding scheme using proposed architecture (D), transcoding scheme using reuse motion vector (C), and transcoding using partial-scale motion estimation (B).The peak signal-to-noise ratio (PSNR) is taken to measure the video quality. We choose PSNR because it is most commonly used to evaluate such system performance (Huang & Hui, 2003; Safranek et al., 1995; Sun et al., 1996; Youn et al., 1999).

Assume we are given a source image that contains N by N pixels and a reconstructed image reconstructed by decoding the encoded version. First, we compute the mean squared error (MSE) of the reconstructed image as follows:

$$MSE = \frac{\sum \left[ f(x,y) - \tilde{f}(x,y) \right]^2}{N^2} \tag{1}$$

Based on each mean-square error (MSE), the PSNR for each color component (Y, Cb, Cr) luminance and chrominance component is separately calculated. The equation for PSNR calculation in decibels (dB) is computed as follows:

$$PSNR = 20 \log_{10} \left( \frac{255^2}{\sqrt{MSE}} \right) \tag{2}$$

In our result, we present the PSNR values for Y components due to paper space and readability issues. As we are emphasizing the processing performance and its importance to the handheld device, we measure the speed-up result according to the following equation.

$$Speed - up = \frac{Excution - Time(Y)}{Excution - Time(x)} \tag{3}$$

For comprehensive description sake, we provide simulation environment Table 1. The CPU, memory, and hard-disk capability have been listed under Hardware. The operating system, programming environment, and profiler tool have been listed under Software.

Figure 8 and Figure 9 show the simulation results of the different schemes at different frame-rates for "Mother and Daughter" and "Claire" sequences.

According to the presented results, one can infer the advantages of deploying our scheme in described applications in both wireless platform and future work. The figure 12's results are conducted on mother

*Table 2. Simulation environment*

| Table Head | | | Table Column Head | | |
|---|---|---|---|---|---|
| CPU | Memory | Hard disk | OS | Programming Language | Profiler Tool |
| P3 1GH | 256 SDRAM | 10025 RPM | XP Pro. | ANSI C | NuMega TrueTime 2.1 |

*Figure 8. Performance of the proposed scheme against related works in "mother and daughter" clip*

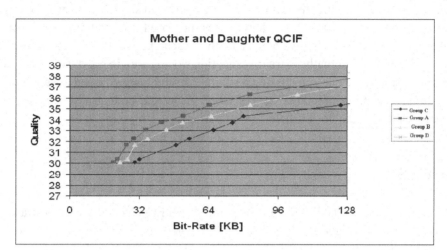

*Figure 9. Performance of the proposed scheme against related works in "Claire" clip*

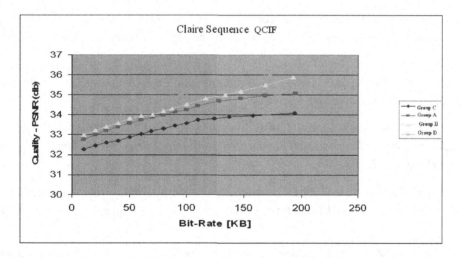

and daughter video clip. Our approach is gaining in average around 1 to 2 DBs, while keeping remarkable resources utilization as proved in rest of this section. Similarly, the presented results in Figure 13 state the clear advantage from deploying our scheme in video transcoding.

## CONCLUSION AND FUTURE WORK

In this chapter, we have discussed a content-based scheme for high-performance video transcoding. Since a great deal of bit rate reduction is required, traditional transcoding methods based on simply reusing the motion vectors that are extracted from an incoming video bit stream are not adequate. They would produce unacceptable texture distortion in the reconstructed signals. However, by applying our proposed scheme, good results have been achieved. The proposed transcoding mechanism has been applied in MPEG domain videos only; we believe further researches should be conducted in different video domains such as H.263. Actually, extra investigation would result in good description for generic transcoding mechanism in any video processing domain. Currently, a good trend toward the mobile TV has been brought to academia and industries. Therefore, video transcoding will be a very interesting issue to be addressed for the mobile TV field.

# REFERENCES

Assunçno, P., & Ghanbari, M., (1996). Post-processing of MPEG-2 coded video for transmission at lower bit-rates. *Proceedings of the IEEE International Conference on Acoustics, Speech and Signal Processing*, Atlanta, Georgia.

Assuncao, P., & Ghanbari, M. (1997). Congestion control of video traffic with transcoders. *Proceedings of the IEEE International Conference on Communications, ICC'97*, Montreal, Canada, 523–527.

Bjork, N., & Christopoulos, C. (1998). Transcoder architectures for video coding. *Proceedings of the IEEE International Conference on Acoustics, Speech and Signal Processing*, Seattle, Washington, 2813–2816.

Chang, S.F., & Messerschmidt, D.G. (1995). Manipulation and compositing of MC-DCT compressed video. *IEEE J. Select. Areas Commun., 13*, 1–11.

Correia, P., Faria, S.M., & Assuncao, P.A. (2001). Matching MPEG-1/2 coded video to mobile applications. *Proceedings of the 4th International Symposium on Wireless Personal Multimedia Communications*, Aalborg, Denmark, 2, 699–704.

Eleftheriadis, A., & Anastassiou, D. (1995). Constrained and general dynamic rate shaping of compressed digital video. *Proceedings of the IEEE International Conference on Image Processing*, Washington, DC.

Han, R., Bhagwat, P., LaMaire, R., Mummert, T., Perret, V., & Rubas, J. (1998). Dynamic adaptation in an image transcoding proxy for mobile Web browsing. *IEEE Personal Communications*, 8–17.

Huang, Y., & Hui, L. (2003). An adaptive spatial filter for additive Gaussian and impulse noise reduction in video signals. *Proceedings of the ICICS PCM 2003*, 402–406.

ISO/IEC 11 172. (1993). Information technology—Coding of moving pictures and associated audio for digital storage media at up to about 1.5 Mbit/s. .

ISO/IEC 13 818. (1995). Information technology—Generic coding of moving pictures and associated audio information.

Keesman, G., Hellinghuizen, R., Hoekesma, F., & Heidman, G. (1996). Transcoding of MPEG bitstreams. *Signal Process. Image Comm., 8*, 481–500.

Kim, N.W., Kim, T.Y., & Choi, J.S. (2002). Motion analysis using the normalization of motion vectors on MPEG compressed domain. *Proceedings of the ITC-CSCC2002*, 1408–1411.

Morrison, D.G., Nilsson, M.E., & Ghanbari, M. (1994). Reduction of the bit-rate of compressed video while in its coded form. *Proceedings of the Sixth International Workshop Packet Video*, Portland, Oregon.

Safranek, R.J., Kalmanek, C., & Garg, R. (1995). Methods for matching compressed video to ATM networks. *Proceedings of the International Conference on Image*, Washington, DC.

Shanableh, T., & Ghanbari, M. (2000). Heterogeneous video transcoding to lower spatio-temporal resolutions and different encoding formats. *IEEE Transactions on Multimedia, 2*(2), 101–110.

Sun, H., Kwok, W., & Zdepski, J.W. (1996). Architecture for MPEG compressed bitstream scaling. *IEEE Trans. Circuits Syst. Video Technol., 6*, 191–199.

Sun, H., Vetro, A., Bao, J., & Poon, T. (1997). A new approach for memory-efficient ATV decoding. *IEEE Trans. Consumer Electron., 43*, 517–525.

Tudor, P.N., & Werner, O.H. (1997). Real-time transcoding of MPEG-2 video bit streams. *Proceedings of the International Broadcasting Convention*, Amsterdam, The Netherlands, 286–301.

Warabino, T., Ota, S., Morikawa, D., & Ohashi, M. (2000). Video transcoding proxy for 3Gwireless mobile Internet access. *IEEE Communications Magazine*, 66–71.

Youn, J., & Sun M.-T. (1998). Motion estimation for high performance transcoding. *Proceedings of the IEEE International Conference on Consumer Electronics*, Los Angeles, California.

Youn, J., & Sun, M.-T. (2000). Video transcoding with H.263 bit-streams. *Journal of Visual Communication and Image Representation, 11*.

Youn, J., Sun, M.-T., & Lin, C.-W. (1999). Motion vector refinement for high-performance transcoding. *IEEE Transactions on Multimedia, 1*(1), 30–41.

## ADDITIONAL READING

Cao, G., Lei, Z., Li, J., Georganas, D.N., & Zhu, Z. (2004). A novel DCT domain transcoder for transcoding video streams with half-pixel motion vectors. *Real-Time Imaging, 10*(5), 331–337.

Chiou, H.-J., Lee, Y.-R., & Lin, C.-W. (2005). Content-aware error-resilient transcoding using prioritized intra-refresh for video streaming. *Journal of Visual Communication and Image Representation, 16*(4-5), 563–588.

Lei, Z., & Georganas, D.N. (2003). An accurate bit-rate control algorithm for video transcoding. *Journal of Visual Communication and Image Representation, 14*(3), 321–339.

Xin, J., Lin, C.-W., & Sun, M.-T. (2005). Digital video transcoding. *Proceedings of the IEEE*, 84–97.

# Chapter IX
# Adaptation and Personalization of Web–Based Multimedia Content

**Panagiotis Germanakos**
*National & Kapodistrian University of Athens, Greece*

**Constantinos Mourlas**
*National & Kapodistrian University of Athens, Greece*

## ABSTRACT

*A traditional multimedia system presents the same static content and suggests the same next page to all users, even though they might have widely differing knowledge of the subject. Such a system suffers from an inability to be all things to all people, especially when the user population is relatively diverse. The rapid growth of mobile and wireless communication allowed service providers to develop new ways of interactions, enabling users to become accustomed to new means of multimedia-based service consumption in an anytime, anywhere, and anyhow manner. This chapter investigates the new multi-channel constraints and opportunities emerged by these technologies, as well as the new user-demanding requirements that arise. It further examines the relationship between the adaptation and personalization research considerations, and proposes a three-layer architecture for adaptation and personalization of Web-based multimedia content based on the "new" user profile, with visual, emotional, and cognitive processing parameters incorporated.*

## INTRODUCTION

Since 1994, the Internet has emerged as a fundamental information and communication medium that has generated extensive enthusiasm. The Internet has been adopted by the mass market more quickly than any other technology over the past century, and is currently providing an electronic connection between progressive entities and millions of users whose age, education, occupation, interest, and income demographics are excellent for sales or multimedia-based service provision.

The explosive growth in the size and use of the World Wide Web, as well as the complicated nature of most Web structures, may lead in orientation difficulties, as users often lose sight of the goal of their inquiry, look for stimulating rather than informative material, or even use the navigational features unwisely. To alleviate such navigational difficulties, researchers have put huge amounts of effort to identify the peculiarities of each user group, and design methodologies and systems that could deliver an adapted and personalized Web-content. To this date, there has not been a concrete definition of personalization. However, the many solutions offering personalization features meet an abstract common goal: to provide users with what they want or need without expecting them to ask for it explicitly (Mulvenna, Anand, & Buchner, 2000). A complete definition of personalization should include parameters and contexts such as user intellectuality, mental capabilities, socio-psychological factors, emotional states, and attention-grabbing strategies, since these could affect the apt collection of users' customization requirements, offering in return the best adaptive environments to the user preferences and demands.

With the emergence of wireless and mobile technologies, new communication platforms and devices, apart from PC-based Internet access, are now emerging, making the delivery of content available through a variety of media. Inevitably, this increases user requirements which are now focused upon an *"anytime, anywhere, and anyhow"* basis. Nowadays, researchers and practitioners not only have to deal with the challenges of adapting to the heterogeneous user needs and user environment issues such as current location and time (Panayiotou & Samaras, 2004), but they also have to face numerous considerations with respect to multi-channel delivery of the applications concerning multimedia, services, entertainment, commerce, and so forth. To this end, personalization techniques exploit Artificial Intelligence, agent-based, and real-time paradigms to give presentation and navigation solutions to the growing user demands and preferences.

This chapter places emphasis on the adaptation of the Web-based multimedia content delivery, starting with an extensive reference to the mobility and wireless emergence that sub-serves the rapid development of the multi-channel multimedia content delivery, and the peculiarities of the user profiling that significantly vary from the desktop to the mobile user. Furthermore, it approaches the existing adaptation (adaptive hypermedia) and personalization (Web personalization) techniques and paradigms that could work together in a coherent and cohesive way, since they are sharing the same goal, to provide the most apt result to the user. Lastly, having analyzed the aforementioned concepts, it defines a three-layer adaptation and personalization Web-based multimedia content architecture that is based on the introduction of a "new" user profile that incorporates user characteristics such as user perceptual preferences, on top of the "traditional" ones, and the semantic multimedia content that includes, amongst others, the perceptual provider characteristics.

## MOBILITY EMERGENCE

The rapid development of the wireless and mobile advancements and infrastructures has evidently given "birth" to Mobile Internet. It is considered fundamental to place emphasis on its imperative existence, since statistics show that in the future the related channels will take over as the most sustainable mediums of Web-based (multimedia) content provision. Mobile Internet could be considered as a new kind of front-end access to Web-based content with specific capabilities of delivering on-demand real-time information. Nowadays, many sectors (governmental, private, educational, etc.) start to offer multimedia-based services and information via a variety of service delivery channels apart from the Web (Germanakos, Samaras, & Christodoulou, 2005). Two of these mobile multimedia-based service delivery channels are mobile telephony and PDAs. These channels become more important considering the much faster growth of the mobile penetration rate compared to desktop-based Internet access. The most significant future development will be the growth of mobile broadband multimedia-based services, once the potential of third generation mobile (3G) and its enhancements, as well other wireless technologies, including W4, RLAN, satellite, and others, is realized. The dissemination of these technologies represents a paradigm shift that enables the emergence of new data multimedia-based services, combining the benefits of broadband with mobility, delivered over high-speed mobile networks and platforms.

## Multi-Channel Web-Based Content Delivery Characteristics

"To struggle against the amplification of the digital divide and therefore to think 'user interaction' whatever the age, income, education, experience, and the social condition of the citizen" (Europe's Information Society, 2004).

The specific theme above reveals exactly the need for user-centered multimedia-based service development and personalized content delivery. In many ways, the new technology provides greater opportunities for access. However, there are important problems in determining precisely what users want and need, and how to provide Web-based content in a user-friendly and effective way. User needs are always conditioned by what they already get, or imagine they can get. A channel can change the user perception of a multimedia application; when users have a free choice between different channels to access an application, they will choose the channel that realizes the highest relative value for them. However, separate development of different channels for a single multimedia content (multi-channel delivery) can lead to inconsistencies such as different data formats or interfaces. To overcome the drawbacks of multiple-channel content delivery, the different channels should be integrated and coordinated.

Since successful multimedia-based service delivery depends on a vast range of parameters, there is not a single formula to fit all situations. However, there have been reported particular steps (IDA, 2004) that could guide a provider throughout the channel selection process. Moreover, it should be mentioned that the suitability and usefulness of channels depends on a range of factors, out of which technology is only one element. Additional features that could affect the service channels assessment could be: directness, accessibility and inclusion, speed, security and privacy, and availability. To realize though their potential value, channels need also to be properly implemented and operated.

The design and implementation complexity is rising significantly with the many channels and their varying capabilities and limitations. Network issues include low bandwidth, unreliable connectivity, lack of processing power, limited interface of wireless devices, and user mobility. On the other hand, mobile devices issues include small size, limited processing power, limited memory and storage space, small screens, high latency, and restricted data entry.

## Initial Personalization Challenges and Constraints

The needs of mobile users differ significantly from those of desktop users. Getting personalized information "*anytime, anywhere, and anyhow*" is not an easy task. Researchers and practitioners have to take into account new adaptivity axes, along which the personalized design of mobile Web-based content would be built. Such applications should be characterized by flexibility, accessibility, quality, and security in a ubiquitous interoperable manner. User interfaces must be friendlier enabling active involvement (information acquisition), giving the control to the user (system controllability), providing easy means of navigation and orientation (navigation), tolerating users' errors, supporting system-based and context-oriented correction of users' errors, and finally enabling customization of multi-media and multi-modal user interfaces to particular user needs (De Bra, Aroyo, & Chepegin, 2004; De Bra & Nejdl, 2004). Intelligent techniques have to be implemented that will enable the development of an open Adaptive Mobile Web (De Bra & Nejdl, 2004), having as fundamental characteristics the directness, high connectivity speed, reliability, availability, context-awareness, broadband connection, interoperability, transparency and scalability, expandability, effectiveness, efficiency, personalization, security, and privacy (Lankhorst, Kranenburg, Salden, & Peddemors, 2002; Volokh, 2000).

## PERSONALIZATION CONSIDERATIONS IN THE CONTEXT OF DESKTOP AND MOBILE USER

The science behind personalization has undergone tremendous changes in recent years while the basic goal of personalization systems was kept the same, to provide users with what they want or need without requiring them to ask for it explicitly. Personalization is the provision of tailored products, multimedia-based services, Web-based multimedia content, information, or information relating to products or services. Since it is a multi-dimensional and complicated area (covering also recommendation systems, customization, adaptive Web sites, Artificial Intelligence), a universal definition that would cover all its theoretical areas has not been given so far. Nevertheless, most of the definitions that have been given to personalization (Kim, 2002; Wang & Lin, 2002) are converging to the objective that is expressed on the basis of delivering to a group of individuals relevant information that is retrieved, transformed, and/or deduced from information sources in the format and layout as well as specified time intervals.

### Comprehensive User Requirements and the Personalization Problem

The user population is not homogeneous, nor should be treated as such. To be able to deliver quality knowledge, systems should be tailored to the needs of individual users providing them personalized and adapted information based on their perceptions, reactions, and demands. Therefore, a serious analysis of user requirements has to be undertaken, documented, and examined, taking into consideration their multi-application to the various delivery channels and devices. Some of the user (customer) requirements and arguments anticipated could be clearly distinguished into Top of the Web (2003) and CAP Gemini Ernst & Young (2004): (a) General User Service Requirements (flexibility: anyhow, anytime, anywhere; accessibility; quality; and security), and (b) Requirements for a Friendly and Effective User Interaction (information acquisition; system controllability; navigation; versatility; errors handling; and personalization).

Although one-to-one multimedia-based service provision may be a functionality of the distant future, user segmentation is a very valuable step in the right direction. User segmentation means that the user population is subdivided, into more or less homogeneous, mutually-exclusive subsets of users who share common user profile characteristics. The subdivisions could be based on: demographic characteristics (i.e. age, gender, urban- or rural-based, region); socio-economic characteristics (i.e. income, class, sector, channel access); psychographic characteristics (i.e. life style, values, sensitivity to new trends); individual physical and psychological characteristics (i.e. disabilities, attitude, loyalty).

The issue of personalization is a complex one with many aspects and viewpoints that need to be analyzed and resolved. Some of these issues become even more complicated once viewed from a moving user's perspective, in other words when constraints of mobile channels and devices are involved. Such issues include, but are not limited to: what content to present to the user, how to show the content to the user, how to ensure the user's privacy, how to create a global personalization scheme. As clearly viewed, user characteristics and needs, determining user segmentation, and thus provision of the adjustable information delivery, differ according to the circumstances and change over time (Panayiotou and Samaras, 2004).

There are many approaches to address these issues of personalization, but usually, each one is focused upon a specific area, that is, whether this is profile creation, machine learning and pattern matching, data and Web mining, or personalized navigation.

## Beyond the "Traditional" User Profiling

One of the key technical issues in developing personalization applications is the problem of how to construct accurate and comprehensive profiles of individual users and how these can be used to identify a user and describe the user behavior, especially if they are moving (Adomavicious & Tuzhilin, 1999). According to Merriam-Webster dictionary, the term profile means "a representation of something in outline". User profile can be thought of as being a set of data representing the significant features of the user. Its objective is the creation of an information base that contains the preferences, characteristics, and activities of the user. A user profile can be built from a set of keywords that describe the user-preferred interest areas compared against information items.

User profiling is becoming more and more important with the introduction of the heterogeneous devices used, especially when published contents provide customized views on information. User profiling can either be static, when it contains information that rarely or never changes (e.g. demographic information), or dynamic, when the data change frequently. Such information is obtained either explicitly, using online registration forms and questionnaires resulting in static user profiles, or implicitly, by recording the navigational behavior and/or the preferences of each user. In the case of implicit acquisition of user data, each user can either be regarded as a member of a group and take up an aggregate user profile or be addressed individually and take up an individual user profile. The data used for constructing a user profile could be distinguished into: (a) the Data Model which could be classified into the demographic model (which describes who the user is), and the transactional model (which describes what the user does); and (b) the Profile Model which could be further classified into the factual profile (containing specific facts about the user derived from transactional data, including the demographic data, such as "the favorite beer of customer X is Beer A"), and the behavioral profile (modeling the behavior of the user using conjunctive rules, such as association or classification rules. The use of rules in profiles provides an intuitive, declarative, and modular way to describe user behavior (Adomavicious & Tuzhilin, 1999)). Additionally, in the case of a mobile user, by user needs is implied both the thematic preferences (i.e., the traditional notion of profile) as well as the characteristics of their personal device called "device profile". Therefore, here, adaptive personalization is concerned with the negotiation of user requirements and device abilities.

But, could the user profiling be considered complete incorporating only these dimensions? Do the designers and developers of multimedia-based services take into consideration the real user preferences in order to provide them a really personalized Web-based multimedia content? Many times this is not the case. How can user profiling be considered complete, and the preferences derived optimized, if it does not contain parameters related to the user perceptual preference characteristics? We could define User Perceptual Preference Characteristics as all the critical factors that influence the visual, mental, and emotional processes liable of manipulating the newly received information and building upon prior knowledge, that is different for each user or user group. These characteristics determine the visual attention, cognitive, and emotional processing taking place throughout the whole process of accepting an object of perception (stimulus) until the comprehensive response to it. It has to be noted at this point that the user perceptual preference characteristics are directly related to the "traditional" user characteristics since they are affecting the way a user approaches an object of perception.

It is true that nowadays, there are not so many researches that move towards the consideration of user profiling to incorporate optimized parameters taken from the research areas of visual attention processing and cognitive psychology. Some serious attempts have been made on approaching e-learning systems providing adapted content to the students, but most of them are lying to restricted analysis and design methodologies considering particular cognitive learning styles, including Field Independence vs. Field Dependence, Holistic-Analytic, Sensory Preference, Hemispheric Preferences, and Kolb's Learning Style Model (Yuliang & Dean, 1999), applied to identified mental models, such as concept maps, semantic networks, frames, and schemata (Ayersman & Read, 1999). In order to deal with the diversified students' preferences, they are matching the instructional materials and teaching styles with the cognitive styles, and consequently they are satisfying the whole spectrum of the students' cognitive learning styles by offering a personalized Web-based educational content.

## A COMPREHENSIVE OVERVIEW OF ADAPTATION AND PERSONALIZATION TECHNIQUES AND PARADIGMS: SIMILARITIES AND DIFFERENCES

When we are considering adaptation and personalization categories and technologies, we refer to Adaptive Hypermedia and Web Personalization respectively, due to the fact that together these can offer the most optimized adapted content result to the user.

### Adaptive Hypermedia Overview

Adaptive Hypermedia is a relatively old and well-established area of research counting three generations: The first "pre-Web" generation of adaptive hypermedia systems explored mainly adaptive presentation and adaptive navigation support and concentrated on modeling user knowledge and goals. The second "Web" generation extended the scope of adaptive hypermedia by exploring adaptive content selection and adaptive recommendation based on modeling user interests. The third "New Adaptive Web" generation moves adaptive hypermedia beyond traditional borders of desktop hypermedia systems embracing such modern Web trends as "mobile Web", "open Web", and "Semantic Web" (Brusilovsky & Maybury, 2002).

Adaptivity is a particular functionality that alleviates navigational difficulties by distinguishing between interactions of different users within the information space (De Bra & Nejdl, 2004; Eklund &

Sinclair, 2000). Adaptive Hypermedia Systems employ adaptivity by manipulating the link structure or by altering the presentation of information, based on a basis of a dynamic understanding of the individual user, represented in an explicit user model (Brusilovsky, 1996; De Bra et al., 1999; Eklund, & Sinclair, 2000). In 1996, Brusilovsky identified four user characteristics to which an Adaptive Hypermedia System should adapt. These were: user's knowledge, goals, background and hypertext experience, and user's preferences. In 2001, further two sources of adaptation were added to this list, user's interests and individual traits, while a third source of different nature having to deal with the user's environment had also been identified.

Generally, Adaptive Hypermedia Systems can be useful in application areas where the hyperspace is reasonably large and the user population is relatively diverse in terms of the above user characteristics. A review by Brusilovsky has identified six specific application areas for adaptive hypermedia systems since 1996 (Brusilovsky, 2001). These are: educational hypermedia, on-line information systems, information retrieval systems, institutional hypermedia, and systems for managing personalized view in information spaces. Educational hypermedia and on-line information systems are the most popular, accounting for about two-thirds of the research efforts in adaptive hypermedia. Adaptation effects vary from one system to another. These effects are grouped into three major adaptation technologies: adaptive content selection (De Bra & Nejdl, 2004), adaptive presentation (or content-level adaptation), and adaptive navigation support (or link-level adaptation) (Brusilovsky, 2001; De Bra et al., 1999; Eklund & Sinclair, 2000) and are summarized in Figure 1.

As mentioned earlier, successful adaptation attempts have been made in the e-learning research field to provide the students with adapted content according to their different learning styles or knowledge

*Figure 1. Adaptive hypermedia techniques*

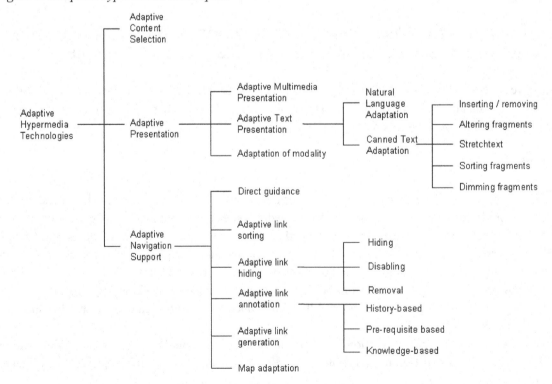

*Figure 2. INSPIRE's components and the interaction with the learner*

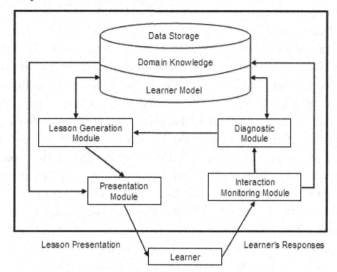

level and goals. A typical case of such a system could be considered the INSPIRE (Intelligent System for Personalized Instruction in a Remote Environment) architecture, see Figure 2, where throughout its interaction with the learner, the system dynamically generates lessons that gradually lead to the accomplishment of the learning goals selected by the learner (Papanikolaou, Grigoriadou, Kornilakis, & Magoulas, 2002). INSPSIRE architecture has been designed so as to facilitate knowledge communication between the learner and the system and to support its adaptive functionality.

INSPIRE comprises of five different modules: (a) the *Interaction Monitoring Module* that monitors and handles learner's responses during his/her interaction with the system, (b) the *Learner's Diagnostic Module* that processes data recorded about the learner and decides on how to classify the learner's knowledge, (c) the *Lesson Generation Module* that generates the lesson contents according to learner's knowledge goals and knowledge level, (d) the *Presentation Module* which functions to generate the educational material pages sent to the learner, and (e) the *Data Storage*, which holds the *Domain knowledge* and the *Learner's Model*.

## Web Personalization Overview

Web Personalization refers to the whole process of collecting, classifying, and analyzing Web data, and determining based on these the actions that should be performed so that the information is presented in a personalized manner to the user. As inferred from its name, Web Personalization refers to Web applications solely (with popular use in e-business multimedia-based services), and generally is a relatively new area of research. Web personalization is the process of customizing the content and structure of a Web site to the specific needs of each user by taking advantage of the user's navigational behavior. Being a multi-dimensional and complicated area, a universal definition has not been agreed to date. Nevertheless, most of the definitions given to Web personalization (Cingil, Dogac, & Azgin, 2000; Kim, 2002) agree that the steps of the Web personalization process include: (1) the collection of Web data, (2) the modeling and categorization of these data (pre-processing phase), (3) the analysis of the collected data, and the determination of the actions that should be performed. Moreover, many argue that emotional or mental needs, caused by external influences, should also be taken into account.

Web Personalization could be realized in one of two ways: (a) Web sites that require users to register and provide information about their interests, and (b) Web sites that only require the registration of users so that they can be identified (De Bra et al., 2004). The main motivation points for personalization can be divided into those that are primarily to facilitate the work, and those that are primarily to accommodate social requirements. The former motivational subcategory contains the categories of enabling access to information content, accommodating work goals, and accommodating individual differences, while the latter contains the categories of eliciting an emotional response and expressing identity.

Personalization levels have been classified into: Link Personalization (involves selecting the links that are more relevant to the user, changing the original navigation space by reducing or improving the relationships between nodes), Content Personalization (user interface can present different information for different users providing substantive information in a node, other than link anchors), Context Personalization (the same information (node) can be reached in different situations), Authorized Personalization (different users have different roles and therefore they might have different access authorizations) and Humanized Personalization (involves human computer interaction) (Lankhorst et al., 2002; Rossi, Schwade, & Guimaraes, 2001). The technologies that are employed in order to implement the processing phases mentioned above as well as the Web personalization categories are distinguished into: Content-Based Filtering, Rule-Based Filtering, Collaborative Filtering, Web Usage Mining, Demographic-Based Filtering, Agent Technologies, and Cluster Models (Mobasher, 2002; Pazzani, 1999; Perkowitz & Etzioni, 2003).

The use of the user model is the most evident technical similarity of Adaptive Hypermedia and Web Personalization to achieve their goal. However, the way they maintain the user profile is different; Adaptive Hypermedia requires a continuous interaction with the user, while Web Personalization employs algorithms that continuously follow the users' navigational behavior without any explicit interaction with the user. Technically, two of the adaptation/personalization techniques used are the same. These are adaptive-navigation support (of Adaptive Hypermedia and else referred to as link-level adaptation) and Link Personalization (of Web Personalization) and adaptive presentation (of Adaptive Hypermedia and else referred to as content-level adaptation) and Content Personalization (of Web Personalization).

An example of a Web personalization application for the wireless user is the mPERSONA system, depicted in Figure 3. The mPERSONA system architecture combines existing techniques in a component-based fashion in order to provide a global personalization scheme for the wireless user. The mPERSONA is a flexible and scalable system that focuses towards the new era of wireless Internet and the moving user. The particular architecture uses autonomous and independent components avoiding this way tying up to specific wireless protocols (e.g., WAP). To achieve a high degree of independence and autonomy, mPERSONA is based on mobile agents and mobile computing models such as the "client intercept model" (Panayiotou & Samaras, 2004).

The architectural components are distinguished based on their location and functionality: a) the *Content description* component (Figure 3: 2 & 6), creates and maintains the content's provider metadata structure that describes the actual content, (b) the *Content selection* component (Figure 3: 1 & 7), selects the content that will be presented to the user when "applying" his profile, (c) the *Content reform* component (Figure 3: 3 & 4), reforms and delivers the desired content in the needed (by the user's device) form, and (d) the *User profile management* component (Figure 3: 5), registers and manages user profiles. The user's profile is split into two parts: the device profile (covers the user's devices) and the theme profile (preferences).

*Figure 3. Detailed view of the mPERSONA architecture*

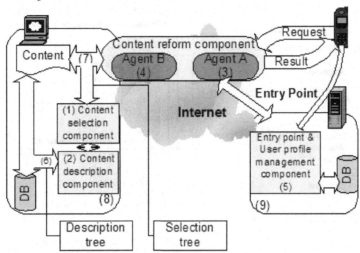

# A THREE-LAYER ARCHITECTURE FOR ADAPTATION AND PERSONALIZATION OF WEB-BASED MULTIMEDIA CONTENT

Based on the above considerations, a three-layer architecture for adaptation and personalization of Web-based multimedia content will now be presented, trying to convey the essence and the peculiarities encapsulated, and further answering the question why adaptation and personalization of Web-based content is considered vital for the sustainable provision of quality multi-channel Web-based multimedia content/multimedia-based services.

The current architecture, depicted in Figure 4, Adaptation and Personalization of Web-based Multimedia Content Architecture, is composed of three interrelated parts/layers. Each *layer* for the purpose of the infrastructure functionality may be composed of *components*, and each component may be broken down into *elements*, as detailed below:

## Front-End Layer (Entry Point and Content Reconstruction)

The front-end layer is the primary layer, and it is the user access interface of the system. It is called "Entry Point and Content Reconstruction", and it accepts multi-device requests. It enables the attachment of various devices on the infrastructure (such as mobile phones, PDAs, desktop devices, tablet PC, satellite handset, etc.) identifying their characteristics and preferences as well as the location of the user currently active (personalization/locationbased). It also handles multi-channel requests. Dut to the variety of multi-channel delivery (i.e., over the Web, telephone, interactive kiosks, WAP, MMS, SMS, satellite, and so on), this layer identifies the different characteristics of the channels. It directly communicates with the middle layer exchanging multi-purpose data. It consists of two components, each one assigned for a different scope:

- **Adaptation:** This component comprises of all the access-control data (for security reasons) and all the information regarding the user profile. These might include user preferences, geographical

*Figure 4. Adaptation and personalization of Web-based multimedia content architecture*

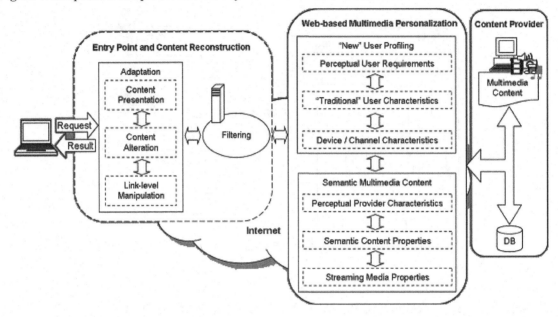

data, device model, age, business type, native language, context, and so forth. It is the entry point for the user, enabling the login to the architecture. This component is directly communicating with the middle layer where the actual verification and profiling for the user is taking place. Once the whole processing has been completed, it returns the adapted results to the user. It is comprised of three elements:

- **Content Presentation (or Adaptive Presentation):** It adapts the content of a page to the characteristics of the user according to the user profile and personalization processing. The content is individually generated or assembled from pieces for each user, to contain additional information, pre-requisite information, or comparative explanations by conditionally showing, hiding, highlighting, or dimming fragments on a page. The granularity may vary from word replacement to the substitution of pages to the application of different media.

- **Content Alteration (or Adaptive Content Selection):** When the user searches for a particular content, that is, related information to his/her profile, the system can adaptively select and prioritize the most relevant items.

- **Link-Level Manipulation (or Adaptive Navigation Support):** It provides methods that restrict the user's interactions with the content or techniques that aid the user in their understanding of the information space, aiming to provide either orientation or guidance (i.e. adaptive link, adaptive link hiding/annotation). Orientation informs the user about his/her place in the information space, while guidance is related to a user's goal.

- **Filtering:** This component is considered the main link of the front-layer with the middle layer of the architecture. It actually transmits the data accumulated both directions. It is responsible for making the the low-level reconstruction and filtering of the content, based on the personalization rules created, and to deliver the content for adaptation.

## Middle Layer (Web-Based Multimedia Personalization)

The middle layer is the main layer of the architecture and it is called "Web-Based Multimedia Personalization". At this level all the requests are processed. This layer is responsible for the custom tailoring of information to be delivered to the users, taking into consideration their habits and preferences, as well as, for mobile users mostly, their location ("location-based") and time ("time-based") of access. The whole processing varies from security, authentication, user segmentation, multimedia content identification, to provider perceptual characteristics, user perceptions (visual, mental and emotional), and so forth. This layer accepts requests from the front-end and, after the necessary processing, either sends information back or communicates with the next layer (back-end) accordingly. The middle layer is comprised of the following two components:

- **"New" User Profiling:** It contains all the information related to the user, necessary for the Web Personalization processing. It is directly related to the Semantic Multimedia Content component and is composed of three elements:
- **Perceptual User Requirements:** This is the new element/dimension of the user profile. It contains all the visual attention and cognitive processes (cognitive and emotional processing parameters) that completes the user perception and fulfills the user profile. It is considered a vital element of the user profile since it identifies the aspects of the user that is very difficult to be revealed and measured but, however, might determine his/her exact preferences and lead to a more concrete, accurate, and optimized user segmentation.
- **"Traditional" User Characteristics:** This element is directly related to the Perceptual User Requirements element and provides the so-called "traditional" characteristics of a user: knowledge, goals, background, experience, preferences, activities, demographic information (age, gender), socio-economic information (income, class, sector, etc.), and so forth. Both elements are completing the user profiling from the user's point of view.
- **Device/Channel Characteristics:** This element is referring to all the characteristics that referred to the device or channel that the user is using and contains information like: bandwidth, displays, text-writing, connectivity, size, power processing, interface and data entry, memory and storage space, latency (high/low), and battery lifetime. These characteristics are mostly referred to mobile users and are considered important for the formulation of a more integrated user profile, since it determines the technical aspects of it.
- **Semantic Multimedia Content:** This component is based on metadata describing the content (data) available from the Content Provider (back-end layer). In this way, a common understanding of the data, that is, semantic interoperability and openness is achieved. The data manipulated by the system/architecture is described using metadata that comprises of all needed information to unambiguously describe each piece of data and collections of data. This provides semantic interoperability and a human-friendly description of data. This component is directly related to the "New" User Profile component, providing together the most optimized personalized Web-based multimedia content result. It is consisted of three elements:
- **Perceptual Provider Characteristics:** It identifies the provider characteristics assigned to the Web-based multimedia content or multimedia based service. They are involving all these perceptual elements that the provider has been based upon for the design of the content (i.e., actual content/data of the service, layout preferences, content presentation, etc.)

- **Semantic Content Properties:** This element performs the identification and metadata description of Web-based multimedia content or multi-media-based service based on predetermined ontologies. It is implemented in a transparent manner, removing data duplication and the problem of data consistency.
- **Streaming Media Properties:** It contains data transition mechanisms and the databases. These databases contain the Web-based multimedia content or multimedia-based services as supplied by the provider (without at this point being further manipulated or altered).

## Back-End Layer (Content Provider)

This is the last layer of the architecture and is directly connected to the middle layer. It contains transition mechanisms and the databases of Web-based multimedia content or multimedia-based services as supplied by the provider without been through any further manipulation or alteration.

The proposed three-layer architecture for adaptation and personalization of Web-based multimedia content will allow users to receive the Web-based multimedia content or multimedia-based service which they access in an adapted style according to their preferences, increasing in that way efficiency and effectiveness of use.

## Implementation Considerations

So far, the functionality and interrelation of three-layer achitecture components that provide adapted and personalized Web-based content have been extensively investigated This section will focus on the concepts and parameters that take part in the construction of a comprehensive user profile, and how these could be used in order to collect all the relevant information. As it has already been mentioned, a lot of research has been done for the implementation of the "traditional" user profiling. Many adaptation and personalization techniques have been developed, and common semantic libraries have been set up that give basically specific and ad-hoc solutions.. However, to our knowledge, implementations that incorporate visual attention, cognitive, and emotional processing parameters to the user profile have not been reported as yet, and such parameters would definitely lead to a comprehensive accumulation of user perceptual preference characteristics and hence, provide users with more sustainable personalized content. Therefore, main emphasis in the following section is given to the construction of the "new" comprehensive user profiling, incorporating these user perceptual preference characteristics mentioned above.

Further examining the middle layer of the proposed architecture and the Perceptual User Requirements element of the "New" User Profiling component, we can see that the User Perceptual Preference Characteristics could be described as a continuous mental processing starting with the perception of an object in the users' attentional visual field (stimulus) and going through a number of cognitive, learning, and emotional processes giving the actual response to that stimulus. This is depicted in Figure 5.

These processes formulate a three-dimensional approach to the problem, as depicted in Figure 6. The three dimensions created are the Learning Styles, the Visual and Cognitive Processing, and the Emotional Processing dimensions.

The *User Learning Processing* dimension is a selection of the most appropriate and technologically feasible learning styles, such as Witkin's Field-Dependent and Field-Independent and Kolb's Learning Styles, being in a position to identify how users transform information into knowledge (constructing new cognitive frames) and if they could be characterized as a converger, diverger, assimilator, accommodator, wholist, analyst, verbalizer, or imager.

The *Visual and Cognitive Processing* dimension is being distinguished from:

- **Visual Attention Processing:** It is composed from the pre-attentive and the limited-capacity stage; the pre-attentive stage of vision subconsciously defines objects from visual primitives, such as lines, curvature, orientation, color, and motion, and allows definition of objects in the visual field. When items pass from the pre-attentive stage to the limited-capacity stage, these items are considered as selected. Interpretation of eye movement data is based on the empirically-validated assumption that when a person is performing a cognitive task, while watching a display, the location of his/her gaze corresponds to the symbol currently being processed in working memory and, moreover, that the eye naturally focuses on areas that are most likely to be informative.
- **Control of Processing:** It refers to the processes that identify and register goal-relevant information and block out dominant or appealing but actually irrelevant information.
- **Speed of Processing:** It refers to the maximum speed at which a given mental act may be efficiently executed (cognitive processing efficiency).
- **Working Memory:** It refers to the processes that enable a person to hold information in an active state while integrating it with other information until the current problem is solved.

The *Emotional Processing* dimension is composed of these parameters that could determine a user's emotional state during the whole response process. This is vital so as to determine the level of adaptation (user needs per time interval) during the interaction process. These parameters include:

- **Extroversion:** Extraverts are sociable, active, self-confident, and uninhibited; while introverts, are withdrawn, shy, and inhibited.
- **Conscientiousness:** Conscientious individuals are organized, ambitious, determined, reliable, and responsible; while individuals low in conscientiousness are distractible, lazy, careless, and impulsive.
- **Neuroticism:** Individuals high in neuroticism are confident, clear- thinking, alert, and content.
- **Open to experience:** Individuals who are open to experience are curious and with wide interests, inventive, original, and artistic; individuals who are not open to experience are conservative, cautious, and mild.
- **Understanding of emotions:** It is the cognitive processing of the emotions; it is the ability of understanding and analysis of the complex emotions and the chain reactions of the emotions, that is, how one emotion generates another.
- **Regulation of emotions:** It is the control and regulation of personal and other people's emotions for the emotional and intellectual development; it is the human's ability to realize what is hidden behind an emotion, like fear, anxiety, anger, or sadness, and to find each time the most suitable ways to confront them.
- **Self control:** It includes processes referring to the control of attention, the provision of intellectual resources, and the selection of the specialized procedures and skills liable for the evaluation of a problem's results or a decision's uptake; it is a superior control system that coordinates the functioning of other, more specialized control systems.

*Figure 5. User perceptual preference characteristics*

*Figure 6. Three-dimensional approach*

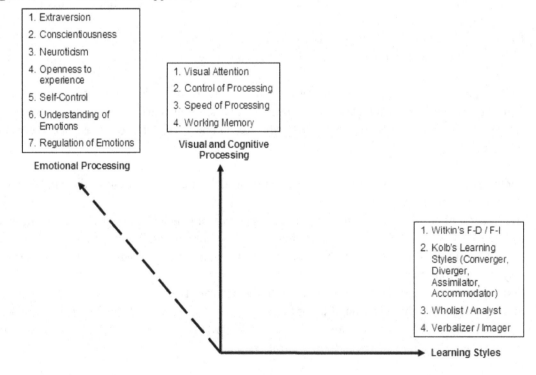

These parameters must be filtered even more so that the final optimized model is achieved. Once this is established, a series of tests (some in the form of questionnaires and others with real-time interaction metrics) will be constructed which will attempt to reveal users' perceptual preference characteristics. These features, along with the *"Traditional" User Characteristics*, could complete the "New" User Profile, and therefore adaptation and personalization schemes could be adjusted to deliver even more personalized Web-based content accordingly. The next step is to identify what is the correlation between the various users and/or user groups (i.e., to investigate similarities and differences between them) and if it would be feasible to refer to the term "users' segmentation" (i.e., users sharing similar "new" user profiling characteristics). In case the latter is true, personalization mechanisms will be based upon these parameters and considering users' device/channel characteristics, and the semantic content will provide them with the corresponding adapted result. Eventually, this methodology will be implemented with personalization algorithms and paradigms so to automatically gather all the related information and construct the "new" user profiling, giving the users the adapted and personalized result without their actual intervention.

## SUMMARY AND FUTURE TRENDS

When referring to adapted multimedia-based services or Web-based multimedia content provision, it is implied that the content adaptation and personalization is based not only on the "traditional" user characteristics, but on a concrete and comprehensive user profiling that covers all the dimensions and parameters of the users preferences. However, knowing the user traditional characteristics and channel/device capabilities, providers can design and offer an apt personalized result. Most of the times, though the providers tend to design multimedia applications based on their own preferences and what they think should be offered. However, the concept of adaptation and personalization is much more complicated than that. This is the reason why until today there is not any sustainable related definition of personalization. A profile can be considered complete when it incorporates the users' perceptual preference characteristics that mostly deal with intrinsic parameters and are very difficult to be technologically measured. Visual attention (that can be thought of as the gateway to conscious perception and memory) and cognitive psychology processes (cognitive and emotional processing parameters) should be in combination investigated and analyzed in a further attempt to complete the desktop and mobile users' preferences.

This chapter made an extensive reference to the mobility emergence and the extensive use of the new channels that tend to satisfy the new user requirements (desktop and mobile) for *"anytime, anyhow, and anywhere"* multimedia-based services and Web-based multimedia content provision in general. The problem of personalization as well as challenges created has been investigated supporting the view of why the provision of adapted content, based on a comprehensive user profile, is considered critical nowadays. Moreover, an Adaptation (Adaptive Hypermedia) and Personalization (Web Personalization) categories and paradigms review has been presented identifying common grounds and objectives of these two areas. Eventually, a three-layer architecture for the adaptation and personalization of Web-based multimedia content was reviewed, making use of the aforementioned adaptation and personalization concepts and technologies, the new user profiling (that incorporates the user perceptual preference characteristics), as well as the semantic multimedia content..

The basic objective of this chapter was to introduce a combination of concepts coming from different research areas, all of which focus upon the user. It has been attempted to approach the theoretical considerations and technological parameters that can provide the most comprehensive user profiling, supporting the provision of the most apt and optimized adapted and personalized multimedia result.

## REFERENCES

Adomavicious, G., & Tuzhilin, A. (1999). User profiling in personalization applications through rule discovery and validation. *Proceedings of the ACM Fifth International Conference on Data Mining and Knowledge Discovery (KDD'99)* (pp. 377-381).

Ayersman, D. J., & Reed, W. M. (1998). Relationships among hypermedia-based mental models and hypermedia knowledge. *Journal of Research on Computing in Education, 30*(3), 222-238.

Brusilovsky, P. (1996). Adaptive hypermedia: An attempt to analyze and generalize. In P. Brusilovsky, P. Kommers, & Streitz (Eds.), *Multimedia, hypermedia, and virtual reality* (pp. 288-304). Berlin: Springer-Verlag.

Brusilovsky, P. (1996). Methods and techniques of adaptive hypermedia. *User Modeling and User Adapted Interaction, 6*(2-3), 87-129.

Brusilovsky, P. (2001). Adaptive hypermedia. *User Modeling and User-Adapted Interaction, 11*, 87-110.

Brusilovsky, P., & Maybury, M. T. (2002). From adaptive hypermedia to the adaptive Web. In P. Brusilovsky & M. T. Maybury (Eds.), *Communications of the ACM, 45*(5), *Special Issue on the Adaptive Web*, 31-33.

CAP Gemini Ernst & Young. (2004). Online availability of public services: How is Europe progressing? *European Commission DG Information Society.*

Cingil, I., Dogac, A., & Azgin, A. (2000). A broader approach to personalization. *Communications of the ACM, 43*(8), 136-141.

De Bra, P., Aroyo, L., & Chepegin, V. (2004). The next big thing: Adaptive Web-based systems. *Journal of Digital Information, 5*(1), Article no. 247.

De Bra, P., Brusilovsky, P., & Houben, G. (1999). Adaptive hypermedia: From systems to framework. *ACM Computing Surveys, 31*(4es), 12.

De Bra, P., & Nejdl, W. (2004). Adaptive hypermedia and adaptive Web-based systems. *Proceedings of the Third International Conference (AH 2004)*, Springer Lecture Notes in Computer Science, 3137.

Eklund, J., & Sinclair, K. (2000). An empirical appraisal of the effectiveness of adaptive interfaces of instructional systems. *Educational Technology and Society, 3*(4), 165-177.

Europe's Information Society. (2004). *User interaction.* Retrieved from http://europa.eu.int/information_society/activities/egovernment_research/focus/user_interaction/index_en.htm

Germanakos, P., Samaras, G., & Christodoulou, E. (200510-12). Multi-channel delivery of services—the road from e-government to m-government: Further technological challenges and implications. *Proceedings of the 1st European Conference on Mobile Government (Euro mGov 2005)*, Brighton (pp. 210-220).

Interchange of Data between Administrations. (2004). *Multi-channel delivery of e-government services*. Retrieved from http://europa.eu.int/idabc/

Kim, W. (2002). Personalization: Definition, status, and challenges ahead. *JOT, 1*(1), 29-40.

Lankhorst, M. M., Kranenburg, Salden, A., & Peddemors A. J. H. (2002). Enabling technology for personalizing mobile services. *Proceedings of the 35th Annual Hawaii International Conference on System Sciences (HICSS-35'02): Vol. 3*(3) (p. 87).

Mobasher, B., Dai, H., Luo, T., Nakagawa, M., & Wiltshire, J. (2002). Discovery of aggregate usage profiles for Web personalization. *Data Mining and Knowledge Discovery, 6*(1), 61- 82.

Mulvenna, M. D., Anand, S. S., & Buchner, A. G. (2000). Personalization on the net using Web mining. *Communications of the ACM, 43*(8), 123-125.

Panayiotou, C., & Samaras, G. (2004). mPersona: Personalized portals for the wireless user: An agent approach. *Journal of ACM/ Baltzer Mobile Networking and Applications (MONET), Special Issue on Mobile and Pervasive Commerce, 9*(6), 663-677.

Papanikolaou, K.A., Grigoriadou, M., Kornilakis, H., & Magoulas, G.D. (2002). INSPIRE: An intelligent system for personalized instruction in a remote environment. In S. Reich, M. M. Tzagarakis, & P. M. E. De Bra (Eds.), *OHS/SC/AH 2001, LNCS 2266* (pp. 215-225). Springer-Verlag.

Pazzani, J. M. (1999). A framework for collaborative, content-based, and demographic filtering. *Artificial Intelligence Review, 13*(5-6), 393-408.

Rossi, G., Schwade, D., & Guimaraes, M. R. (2001). Designing personalized Web applications. *ACM Proceedings of the 10th International Conference on World Wide Web* (pp. 275-284).

Top of the Web (2003). Survey on quality and usage of public e-services. Top of the Web. Retrieved from http://www.idt.unisg.ch/org/idt/ceegov.nsf/0/1ae4025175a16a90c1256df6002a0fef/$FILE/Final_report_2003_quality_and_usage.pdf

Volokh, E. (2000). Personalization and privacy. *The Communications of the Association for Computing Machinery, 43*(8), 84.

Wang, J., & Lin, J. (2002). Are personalization systems really personal? Effects of conformity in reducing information overload. *Proceedings of the 36th Hawaii International Conference on Systems Sciences (HICSS'03)*. 0-7695-1874-5/03.

Yuliang, L., & Dean, G. (1999). Cognitive styles and distance education. *Online Journal of Distance Learning Administration, 2*(3), Article 005.

# Chapter X
# QoE for Mobile TV Services

**Florence Agboma**
*University of Essex, UK*

**Anotonio Liotta**
*University of Essex, UK*

## ABSTRACT

*This chapter discusses the various issues that surround the development stage of mobile TV services. It highlights the importance of Quality of Experience (QoE), which is a shift in paradigm away from the widely studied Quality of Service (QoS). We discuss the factors affecting QoE and the types of assessment methods used to evaluate QoE. A QoE-layered model is presented with the aim of ensuring end-to-end user satisfaction. Using a case study, we develop a QoE management framework. We argue that gaining an understanding of users' perceptions and their service quality expectations may assist in the development of QoE models that are user centric.*

## INTRODUCTION

The delivery of TV materials (i.e., mobile TV and video on demand) onto mobile devices is a fast-evolving technology. It is also a very active research area. Mobile TV services provide a different user experience, which is a big shift away from the traditional TV experience. Although mobile TV services have the advantage of content ubiquity, they have shortcomings such as small screen size, low transmission bandwidth, high error rates, and poor network type and coverage. These shortcomings lead to unimpressive viewer experiences. To improve user experience and acceptance of mobile TV services, these drawbacks need to be properly addressed.

The novelty of mobile technology has been the driving force behind the development and introduction of new services. Providers of mobile multimedia services have increasingly realized that the newness of this technology is not the only influential factor responsible for the success of a new service. Of immense importance are the user's opinions, expectations, and service preferences. This realization is mainly due to low uptake of some of the services and stiff competition in the telecommunication industries. The rapid increase in the number of mobile services, some of which were hurriedly offered to customers, has led to some commercial failures. A notable example was the WAP services, where users experienced difficulty in navigating to specific part of the service because of the design being adopted from traditional Web design. It was time-consuming even in accomplishing the simplest trivial tasks. This has taught the important lesson that the success of mobile TV services depends on their ability to meet user expectations and provide a satisfactory user experience.

This chapter discusses the various issues that can influence the user's experience when using mobile TV services. It demonstrates how to ensure end-to-end user satisfaction and also discusses the types of assessment methods used to evaluate the user's experience. A case study is presented by considering mobile user requirements, which assist in ensuring that the user's expectations of service quality are met. We advocate the management of Quality of Experience (QoE) in addition to the more widely studied Quality of Service (QoS).

QoS is a metric commonly used to represent the capability of a network to provide guarantees to selected network traffic. QoS considers parameters of a network that can be easily measured but do not tell how the service is perceived by users. Therefore, QoE represents a shift in paradigm from the traditional QoS. There are different definitions of QoE (David, Man & Renaud, 2006; Empririx, 2003; Nokia, 2004), but all have the same concept, which translates to user satisfaction. QoE is defined in David, et al. (2006) as the perception of the user about the quality of a particular service or network. QoE depends largely on the expectations of the users on the offered service. QoS metrics (e.g., packet loss, jitter) measured in the network may not linearly map to user satisfaction; hence, the need to understand QoE in order to use QoS efficiently. The next section explains what constitutes a good QoE in mobile TV services.

## BEHIND THE SCENES OF QoE

There are many factors that constitute producing a good QoE. Measuring and ensuring QoE for multimedia services in a mobile environment is very subjective in nature and includes a variety of factors such as terminal type, usability, content type, cost, delivery method, and quality of service. These factors are discussed next.

### Terminal Type

Various mobile devices such as mobile phones, personal digital assistants (PDAs), and laptops have the capability to play back multimedia content. The content formats for these devices are different due to their intrinsic small screen sizes. Thus, the QoE of a user watching a football game on a laptop might differ from another user watching that same football game on a mobile phone. In a mobile TV environment, the quickest and most cost-effective way to deliver these materials is to encode existing TV materials for the mobile terminals. This approach would hardly satisfy the user watching a football match from the mobile phone, because the different shot types usually found within a video for traditional TV consumption may not be suitable for a small screen.

Knoche, McCarthy, and Sasse (2008) carried out a study to determine the effect of shot types at low resolutions. The results in Knoche (2008) indicate that the subject's acceptability of shot types for mobile TV consumption depends on the type of content and the resolution at which the content was displayed. The authors concluded that the use of extreme long shots is only favorable for resolutions of 240x180 and higher. To provide good QoE for mobile video, content should be specifically tailored to accommodate the differences in screen sizes and resolutions.

## Usability

Mobile phones were primarily used for voice communication, but more applications are being integrated into them. In ISO 9241-11 (1998), usability is defined as the extent to which a product can be used by specified users to achieve specified goals with effectiveness, efficiency, and satisfaction in a specified context of use. In the context of mobile handsets, Ketola and Röykkee (2001) categorized the concept of usability into the user interface, the external interface, and the service interface. Pertaining to the service interface, it is essential that mobile TV service is easy to use. A survey carried out by Olista (2007) found that 55% of first-time users abandoned the value added service of mobile data offered by mobile operators because of usability problems. These problems include difficulty navigating through the menus, inability to find downloaded content, and confusion in terminology such as streaming and download.

Mobile TV acceptance strongly depends on the design of its interface. In Lucy and Sara (2006), usability guidelines based on a user-centered approach for the design of mobile TV were suggested. Mobile TV services must not impede the phone functionalities and vice versa. They should be integrated to provide a seamless interoperability. For example, incoming calls should "pause" mobile TV application for the duration of the call, and the user should have the choice to resume once the call is ended. There should also be ease in navigation with the use of minimal keypad interaction, possibly using a "soft key." Finally, there should be the provision of Electronic Program Guide (EPG), informing the user of content available on the channels, "now" and "next" program listings, time duration for each content, and so forth. If the user's interaction with the service is poor, the outcome will be a decreased use of the service. Ease and intuitive service usability provides a foundation for the adoption of mobile TV service (Nokia, 2005).

## Content Type

The choice of available and quality content is a key factor in determining the success of mobile TV services. A survey carried out by Gilliam (2006) to determine the types of content consumers desire to watch on their mobile devices, revealed that consumers do have preferences as to the type of content they are interested in and would like to watch on their mobile devices. Examples of these contents in order of preference are news, movies, comedy, sports, and travel. The question on the duration of the content is still not well defined because of the issue of battery performance and user's behavior of watchability on a small screen. Will a user watch a full movie of about 90 minutes on a small screen? Studies carried out by Knoche, McCarthy, and Sasse (2005) and Sodergard (2003) suggest that the watching time of mobile television is likely to be very short, usually within 2 to 5 minutes. Content providers and aggregators are faced with the challenge of determining what type of mobile TV service to provide; whether to offer linear transmission of TV channels; repurpose existing TV materials; or produce short, custom-made content for mobile viewing. The type of mobile TV service that will be popular with users still remains an open issue. Currently, content providers offer a mixture on the types of mobile TV service.

## Delivery Method

The delivery of mobile TV services to mobile terminals can be achieved via three approaches; namely, unicast, multicast, and broadcast. In unicast delivery, a video stream is transmitted from a single source to a single user. This works well for 3G networks since the infrastructure is already available. But with simultaneous users, the quality degrades as the bandwidth is shared by all users in the cell. This approach will not scale well with mass market volume because the problem of bandwidth contention arises.

In the multicast delivery approach, the same video stream is transmitted from a single source to selected groups of users (multicast group). A multicast group could be users with similar interests such as sports or stock news contents. Examples of multicast technologies are MBMS and mobile WiMAX, which can be operated in unicast node as well.

The last approach is broadcast delivery, where the same video stream is transmitted to every user. Users who have a broadcast-enabled receiver handset and are within the coverage area can watch the video stream. There are several broadcast standards (DVB-H, ISDB-T, DAB-IP, DMB, MediaFLO™) currently being deployed in various parts of the world. Broadcasting does not depend on the number of users as the case would be for unicast delivery, but it is limited to the number of channels it can transmit.

The three delivery approaches have their various weaknesses as already mentioned. But they can be combined to complement each other to ensure that the user experience with mobile TV service is not compromised. Thus, the most popular content can be broadcast, while video-on-demand streams and users outside the broadcast coverage area can use unicast or multicast delivery.

## Cost

Pricing is crucial to the success of mobile TV services. Multimedia Messaging Service (MMS) uptake was slow initially due to the high pricing and interoperability issues among handsets and networks. The long-established practice of judging quality by price implies that expectations are price-dependent (Robert, 1986). If the cost is relatively high and the user's expectations are not met, it might cause users to stop using the service. Another barrier for the adoption of mobile TV services also lies in the cost of the mobile handsets. Once a user has acquired a mobile TV handset, the key problem will be to price the services, because users perceive services as something free on the Internet. A study by comScore (2007) reveals that 71% of their respondents said "cost" is a top consideration for the adoption of mobile TV service. There are four pricing strategies available for mobile TV services: subscription, pay-per-view, one-time fee[1], and ad-based TV[2] (Sodergard, 2003). Results from initial field trials suggest that users preferred pay monthly subscriptions (Lloyd, Maclean & Stirling, 2006; Nokia, 2005). Affordable cost of using mobile TV service is crucial for service uptake.

## Quality of Service

There are several parameters that affect the visual quality of the displayed content. These parameters can be grouped into two categories: Application-level Quality of Service (AQoS) and Network-level Quality of Service (NQoS). The former is concerned with the control of parameters such as content resolution, frame rate, color depth, codec type, layering strategy, sampling rate, and number of channels. The latter deals with parameters such as service coverage, bandwidth, packet loss, jitter, and so forth.

## Application-Level Quality of Service (AQoS)

On the application level, QoS is driven by human perception of audio and video. Good audio quality tends to produce a better video quality experience (Joly, Nathalie & Marcel, 2001; Reeves & Nass, 1998). There have been studies on the influence of audio on video and vice versa on the overall audiovisual quality. The integration of audio and video quality tends to be content-dependent (Hands, 2004), where for less complex scenes (e.g., head and shoulder content), the importance of audio quality is slightly more important than video quality. By contrast, for high motion content, video quality is significantly more important than audio quality. The results from Winkler & Faller (2005) also suggest that the optimum audio/video bit rate allocation depends on scene complexity. For instance, visually complex scenes would benefit from the allocation of a higher bit rate with relatively more bits allocated toward audio because a high audio bit rate seemed to produce the best overall quality (Winkler & Faller, 2005).

Frame rate also plays an important role in the perceived video quality. It influences judgment as video jerkiness if the video has been encoded with a lower frame rate with respect to the terminal type and capability. Apteker, Fisher, Kisimov, and Neishlos (1995) studied the effect of frame rate on the watchability of various classifications of video within a multitasking environment. In this context, it was observed that subjects perceived video of a high temporal nature more acceptable at a lower frame rate than video of a low temporal nature. The effects of reduced frame rate were more noticeable for low temporal video. This is consistent with another experiment carried out by Ghinea, Thomas, and Fish (1999) to investigate the interaction between quality of perception and quality of service. In Ghinea, et al. (1999), a reduction in frame rate did not proportionally reduce the subject's perception and assimilation of the multimedia materials. However, in some cases, users seem to assimilate more information. McCarthy, Sasse, and Miras (2004) found that subjects were more sensitive to reductions in frame quality than to changes in frame rates in the case of small screens.

The minimum acceptability of image resolution for mobile TV consumption was investigated by Knoche, et al. (2008). Acceptability of image resolution was notably lower for images smaller than 168x126. For QoE management, Agboma and Liotta (2007) found that users are less tolerant to quality improvement than degradations (i.e., if the user is presented with higher-than-needed quality at the start of service, it will then be possible to degrade the quality gradually down to a threshold lower than the one found if the process is reversed).

## Network-Level Quality of Service (NQoS)

Different types of traffic demand different NQoS requirements. For example, real-time multimedia require more stringent delay constraints compared to e-mail and Internet browsing applications. NQoS is concerned with network parameters such as bandwidth, jitter, packet loss that affect the quality of multimedia services and applications.

The nature of mobile wireless networks makes them more susceptible to transmission errors due to interference and challenges in mobility, which could cause part of the data to be lost during transmission. Jumisko-Pyykkö, Vadakital, Liinasuo, and Hannuksela (2006) investigated the acceptance of error rates for DVB-H networks in terms of the overall audiovisual quality and found the acceptance threshold lies between error rates of 6.9% and 13.8%. The performance evaluation of IEEE 802.11b (WiFi) under different load conditions taken as an example of possible deployment on a commercial basis for live streaming video was studied by Koucheryavy, Moltchanov, and Harju (2003). Their result concludes that in the presence of competing traffic, channel conditions greater than 40dB are needed to support live streaming service.

An empirical study was carried out by Murphy, Searles, Rambeau, and Murphy (2004) to determine how packet loss and jitter impact quality for different types of video content. Their results illustrate that the different content types (e.g., news, music video, movie trailer) performed differently under the same network conditions, with the movie trailer being affected the most. The effect of packet loss tends to be the dominant factor that affects multimedia services. Packet loss that occurs in a long video stream is more tolerant to what occurs in a short video stream (Teyeb, Sorensen, Morgensen & Wigard, 2006). In another study carried out by Claypool and Tanner (1999), it was concluded that jitter can be nearly as important as packet loss in influencing perceptual video quality.

In spite of the various issues that are concerned with NQoS, reliability and a good coverage of the service is crucial, as users will want mobile TV service available anytime, anywhere, and from any terminal. Mobile TV service coverage will need to match that of cellular phone coverage for indoor usage in order to provide acceptable service quality.

## THE LAYERS OF QoE

In the section "Behind the Scenes of QoE," we recapped the factors that need to be addressed in order to produce good QoE for mobile TV services. Delivering high QoE depends on gaining an understanding of the factors that contribute to the user's perception of service quality. Existing systems concentrate on managing either network or application parameters but fail to consider the user's perception of service quality as a whole. QoE captures both the QoS and psychological factors (e.g., user expectations and requirements) as well as the overall performance of the service as perceived by the end user. These different factors can be combined in one integrated QoS/QoE layered model (Siller, 2006; Siller & Woods, 2003; Zapater & Bressan, 2007), as illustrated in Figure 1.

**The service level** is like a pseudo layer where the user experience of the overall performance of the service can be measured (Siller, 2006). The user experience with the service can include cost, usability, visual quality, type of content, and the terminal type on which the service is presented. This is the level where QoE assessments (subjective and objective) are carried out, as described in the following sections.

**The application level** enables AQoS management, which is driven by human perception of audio and video. Understanding the user requirements at the AQoS could further lead to better resource management at the network level.

*Figure 1. QoS/QoE layered model*

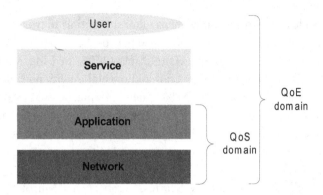

**The network level** addresses both soft (prioritization) and hard (resource reservation) QoS so as to mitigate the effect that jitter, delay, and packet loss could have on the service when presented to the application level. The network resources also need to be managed to achieve network optimization while adhering to QoE requirements.

Taking these layers as a whole unit rather than individual entities might achieve a better QoE. In other words, the different mechanism across the layers should be made to interact via a single portal to meet the end user requirements (Siller, 2006). The QoS/QoE layered model is designed to help ensure end-to-end user satisfaction.

In mobile TV services, video quality is perceived to be the most significant factor affecting QoE as this is the physical aspect of the service that is displayed to the user. The visual quality of the video can be affected by impairments due to conversions between analog and digital formats, compression, coding, and transmission channels errors (ITU-T Rec. P.930, 1996). Examples of these impairments include blockiness, blurring, smearing, staircase effect, ringing, false edges, mosquito noise, flickering, aliasing, among others (Winkler, 2005). There are two assessment methods used to evaluate the quality of a video; namely, subjective and objective assessment.

## SUBJECTIVE VIDEO QUALITY ASSESSMENT

In this case, human viewers (or subjects) are used to evaluate the video quality. Subjects watch a video clip and rate its quality using quality scores. Quality scores are then averaged to produce the Mean Opinion Score (MOS). The International Telecommunications Union (ITU) has recommendations guidelines on how to carry out subjective assessments intended for audio systems (ITU-R Rec. BS.1116; ITU-R Rec. BS.1679), voice (ITU-T Rec. P.800, 1996), television picture quality (ITU-R Rec. BT.500, 2002), and multimedia applications (ITU-T Rec. P.910, 1999; ITU-T Rec. P.911). These recommendations were formalized in order to maintain consistency in data being analyzed from different subjective quality assessments. The focus here is on television picture quality and multimedia applications.

The two methods of assessment currently used for subjective video quality evaluation are single stimulus and double stimulus. A third method of assessment, multi stimulus (Subjective Assessment Methodology for VIdeo Quality [SAMVIQ]) is currently being standardized (EBU, 2003).

## Single Stimulus

In this method, the viewer sees and rates only the quality of the impaired video. Depending on the method implemented, the viewer rates the quality of each video sequence individually, or continuously rates the quality of a long video sequence. Examples of single stimulus methods are Single Stimulus Continuous Quality Evaluation (SSCQE) (ITU-R Rec. BT.500, 2002) and Absolute Category Rating (ACR) (ITU-T Rec. P.910, 1999; ITU-T Rec. P.911).

## Double Stimulus

In this method, the viewer is shown the original and impaired video. Depending on the application purpose, the viewer rates the quality of the original and the impaired video separately, or rates the difference in quality between the impaired video and the original video. Examples of this method are Double Stimulus Continuous Quality Evaluation (DSCQE), Double Stimulus Impairment Scale (DSIS), Single Double Stimulus for Continuous Evaluation (SDSCE), Double Stimulus Comparison Scale (DSCS), (ITU-R Rec. BT.500, 2002), and Degradation Category Rating (DCR) method (ITU-T Rec. P.910 & P.911).

## Multi Stimulus

SAMVIQ is a new test methodology developed by the European Broadcasting Union (EBU) to assess perceptual quality of multimedia content. In this method, video sequences are shown in multistimulus form, thus allowing the viewer to choose the order of tests and adjust their quality ratings as many times as necessary. In SAMVIQ methodology, quality evaluation is carried out scene after scene, with each scene comprising an explicit reference, hidden reference, and impaired video sequences. The viewer compares the quality of the video sequences among themselves and against the explicit reference, allowing the viewer to modify quality ratings accordingly. SAMVIQ has been designed specifically for multimedia content, taking into account codec types, image format, bit rates, packet loss, and so forth (EBU, 2003).

## Psychophysics Methods

There has been another subjective assessment where authors (Agboma, (2008); Knoche et al., 2005; McCarthy et al., 2004) have adopted the psychophysics threshold of stimuli to determine the subject's acceptability of video quality. Video quality is gradually increased and decreased to determine the threshold where quality becomes acceptable or unacceptable. There is no fixed threshold[3] as these differ among individuals, but the threshold is found between two sets of parameters in the form of a psychometric function, as illustrated in Figure 2.

Hands (2004) and Jumisko-Pyykkö et al. (2006) have also used the subjective rating of acceptance to determine acceptance thresholds of quality. The binary response of "Yes" for "Acceptable" or "No"

*Figure 2. A psychometric function of threshold detection*

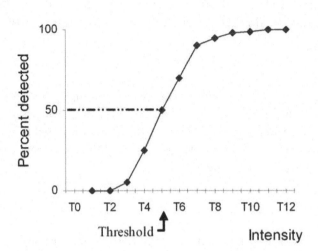

for "Not Acceptable" is used by subjects to indicate when the video quality becomes unacceptable. The common goal among these authors is to determine the minimum level of quality that subjects find acceptable.

## Strength and Weaknesses of Subjective Assessment

Subjective assessments of video quality provide accurate results because they produce quality ratings as perceived by the viewer. The results are also used as a reference in building and evaluating the performance of Video Quality Metrics (VQM) used in objective video quality assessments. However, subjective assessments, which require immense planning and design so as to produce reliable subjective quality ratings, are time-consuming and expensive to carry out. Based on these weaknesses, the use of objective video quality metrics is often desirable.

## OBJECTIVE VIDEO QUALITY ASSESSMENT

In this assessment, an algorithm is used to evaluate the quality of the video automatically. Objective quality assessment can be classified into three categories based on the availability of the original input video: Full Reference (FR) metrics, Reduced Reference (RR) metrics, and No Reference (NR) metrics.

## FR Metrics

The original input video, which is considered to be of high quality, is used as a reference to compare the difference in quality (pixel by pixel) with the impaired output video. Examples of FR metrics are the Peak Signal to Noise Ratio (PSNR) and the Mean Square Error (MSE). These are widely used because they are simple to implement and have clear physical meanings, using the assumption that a high

PSNR value usually indicates high quality and a low PSNR value specifies low quality. This precise computation does not necessarily correlate with subjective ratings (Richardson, 2003; Winkler, 2005) because it does not take into account the region of interest that might be less sensitive to the viewer. This drawback has led to the development of more complex measures based on the Human Visual System (HVS) to produce a prediction that is close to the human perception (Voelcker, Hands, Davis, Bourret & Bayart, 2003; Watson, Hu & McGowan, 2001; Webster, Jones & Pinson, 1993). The performance of HVS-based objective video quality assessment outperforms PSNR and MSE in terms of correlating with subjective ratings but has high computational complexity. Standards for objective perceptual metrics for digital cable television and standard definition digital broadcast television can be found in ITU-T J.144 (2004) and ITU-R BT.1683 (2004). As yet, there is no standardized perceptual model specifically for mobile terminals. Experts from various international organizations (ITU-T, ITU-R, and VQEG) are in the process of evaluating perceptual quality models suitable for digital video quality measurement in multimedia applications for QCIF, CIF, and VGA formats (VQEG, 2007).

## RR Metrics

In RR metrics, only partial features of the original input video are compared with the impaired output video. The partial features extracted from the original input video will need to match the same partial features of the output video in order to perform quality measurement. RR metrics are used when the full original input video is not available because of limitations in transmission bandwidth. Studies on RR video quality metrics can be found in Callet, Viard-Gaudin, and Péchard (2006) and Wolf and Pinson (2005). As yet, there is no standardized model for implementing RR metrics.

## NR Metrics

In NR metrics, the original input video is not available or may not exist, for instance, at the output of the capture chip of a camera (Winkler & Faller, 2005). The calculation of the quality metric is performed only on the impaired video output. This could lead to inaccurate quality predictions because of the limited understanding of the HVS and the unavailability of the reference for comparison. NR metrics are suitable for measuring blur and blocking artifacts. Studies on NR video quality metrics can be found in Winkler and Campos (2003), Winkler and Dufaux (2003), and Yang, Wan, Chang, and Wu (2005). As yet, there is no standardized model for implementing NR metrics.

## Subjective vs. Objective Assessment

We have discussed the assessment methods that are used in evaluating the visual quality of video. The objective metrics discussed herein eliminate the importance of the audio counterpart that usually comes with the video. Thus, these metrics produces less accurate results compared to subjective assessment. Previous studies (Joly et al., 2001; Reeves & Nass, 1998) have suggested that good audio quality tends to increase subjective ratings of video quality; Hands (2004) and Winkler and Faller (2005) concluded that the integration of audio and video quality tends to be content-dependent. Also, these objective metrics do not indicate the impact of different monitors (e.g., mobile video phone, PDA, etc.). Subjective assessments remain the most accurate and reliable way to evaluate the quality of a video because it produces quality ratings as perceived by the viewer.

## QoE MANAGEMENT: A CASE STUDY

In this section, we illustrate a case study showing the potential and applicability of one of the aforementioned techniques. Subjective assessment is adopted to develop a QoE management framework. The purpose of this study is to determine acceptability thresholds of video quality across different content types for three mobile terminals; namely, 3G mobile phone, PDA, and a laptop. Knowing the acceptability thresholds will enable us to define the user's requirements and ensure that the user's expectations of video quality for mobile TV services are met. On the other hand, this knowledge can be applied in managing network resources.

The classical psychophysics method of threshold is used to determine the minimum level of video quality that users find acceptable. The method implemented in this study is known as Methods of Limits, which was proposed by Fechner (1966). It is used to detect thresholds by changing a single stimulus in successive discrete steps either in ascending or descending series. A series terminates when the intensity of the stimulus becomes detectable. The subject gives a binary response of "Yes" or "No" when the stimulus is perceived. The use of classical psychophysics methods can be found in research laboratories, where they are used to determine thresholds; they are also used for measuring people's hearing aids when testing for possible hearing loss and so forth.

### Quantifying Acceptability Thresholds of Video Quality

By adapting the classical psychophysics method, the acceptability thresholds of video quality can be determined. The selections of test materials used in this study were chosen as a representative set of multimedia contents provided for mobile terminals, which, according to a survey carried out by Gilliam (2006), are also the types of content consumers desire to watch on their mobile devices. The characteristics of the test materials in terms of spatial and temporal information are illustrated in Figure 3.

Scenes having substantial motion activity are found toward the top of the temporal information axis, while those with minimal motion activity are found toward the bottom. Along the spatial information axis toward the right are scenes with the most spatial details; toward the left are scenes with minimal spatial details.

### Experimental Design

In this study, we emulated linear transmission of TV materials by using recordings from television programs. A full matrix of tests was carried out by varying video parameters independently. For the 3G mobile phone, Helix mobile producer was used to encode for the mobile phone (*video codec: MPEG 4 and audio codec: AMR-NB*), while for the PDA and laptop[4], Windows Media Encoder series 9 (*video codec: windows media video 9 and audio codec: windows media audio 9.1*) was chosen.

This experiment was divided into two sessions for each terminal. In the first session, we gradually decreased frame rate, keeping the video encoding bit rates constant. The video encoding bit rates was relatively of high quality, which is rarely manageable in the current mobile wireless networks. The reason for this is to enable us to arrive at a strong conclusion as to why the quality became unacceptable.

In the second session, we gradually decreased video encoding bit rates, keeping the frame rate constant. Frame rate was relatively high as well in order to allow us to attain an unbiased result. The experimental design is illustrated in Table 1.

*Figure 3. Spatial-temporal plots of test materials*

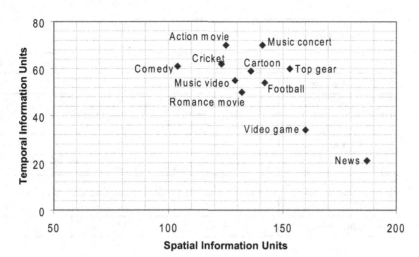

The audio parameters were kept constant because audio consumes less bandwidth relative to video. Also, previous research on audiovisual quality suggests that better audio increases subjective quality ratings. The Method of Limits has been successfully implemented in Agboma and Liotta (2007), Knoche, McCarthy, and Sasse (2005), and McCarthy, Sasse, and Miras (2004).

## Specifications of Mobile Terminals

(i) Nokia N70 3G mobile phone with display of 28×35mm, 18-bit color depth, resolution of 176×220 pixels and a Nokia HS-3 headphone for audio playback.

(ii) HP Ipaq rx1950 PDA with display type of 3.5 in TFT active matrix, 16-bit color support, maximum resolution of 320×240 pixels and Goodmans PRO CD 3100 headphone for audio playback.

(iii) Sony FR315B laptop with a 15-inch TFT display, screen resolution of 1024×768 pixels, but the actual used image size was 640×480 pixels, and Goodmans PRO CD 3100 headphone for audio playback.

## Subjective Assessment

Seventy-two subjects (30 female, 42 male) participated in the study. Their ages ranged from 19 to 36 years. Prior to the test sessions, each subject completed and passed a two-eyed Snellen test for 20/20 vision and an Ishihara test for color blindness.

A training session was also given to make sure subjects understood what was required. Subjects had no idea of the combination parameters. They were told to click on the "Not Accept" button to indicate when the quality was unacceptable. The subjects also had the option to click on the "Accept" button if, when they got to the end of the video, they still found the video quality to be acceptable. Subjects rated the video quality in the first session, had a short break, and then rated the video quality in the second session.

*Table 1. Experimental design combination*

| Target Device Image size | Matrix Order | Encoding properties | | |
|---|---|---|---|---|
| | | Video (kbps) | Audio (kbps) | Frame rates (FPS) |
| 3G Mobile Phone 176 x 144 pixels | First session | 384 | 12.2 | 25 → 3 |
| | Second session | 384→ 32 | 12.2 | 25 |
| PDA 240 x 220 pixels | First session | 448 | 32 | 25 → 6 |
| | Second session | 448→ 32 | 32 | 25 |
| Laptop 640 x 480 pixels | First session | 512 | 32 | 29 →10 |
| | Second session | 512→ 32 | 32 | 29 |

Customized media players were created for each mobile terminal to collect the subjects' details and ratings. An illustration of these is shown in Figure 4.

## Result and Analysis

The MOS of subjects' acceptability thresholds for frame rates are illustrated in Figure 5. At these thresholds, video quality became unacceptable. As expected for the mobile phone, frame rate requirements were significantly reduced due to the small screen inherently found in them. The graph clearly shows that a subject's sensitivity to frame rates is based on the type of content and the terminal type used to display the content. The qualitative results obtained from subjects concerning the quality were lack of synchronization between audio and video, jerkiness, and loss of visual details, especially for the mobile phone. In the case of cricket, seeing the ball was difficult for the subjects, and most of them

*Figure 4. Screenshots of the customized media player for the mobile phone and the PDA*

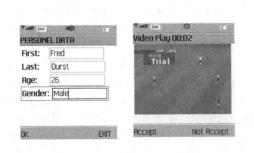

*Figure 5. Acceptability of frame rates; the error bars indicate the 95% confidence intervals*

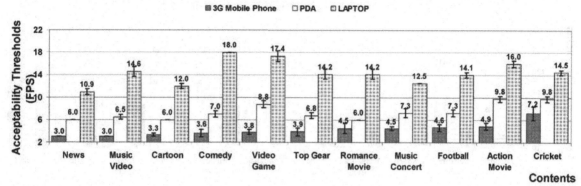

said they could only guess where the ball was. The subjects also found it difficult to identify the teams that were playing.

For the cricket and action movies, jerkiness during panning of the camera led to video quality being generally unacceptable. But this was different for football, as subjects preferred low frame rates (to some extent) because this enabled them to watch the game easily.

The MOS of subjects' acceptability thresholds for video bit rates is illustrated in Figure 6. At these thresholds, video quality became unacceptable. The variations of acceptability thresholds for the laptop were first puzzling. But when asked about their ratings for the laptop, responses were for the news, and their primary interest was audio quality. The responses from subjects concerning the content with intrinsically high thresholds of acceptability were the inability to identify facial expressions and region of interests due to the smearing effect and pixelation.

## DISCUSSION

This simple scenario helps to identify the potential of QoE management as opposed to QoS management by initially capturing the users' expectations and subsequently identifying the users' requirements of video quality. A number of unexpected results illustrate how "subjective" studies help capture psychological factors along with technical factors. Under some circumstances, our subjects were more satisfied by the quality achieved when using a mobile phone as apposed to the PDA. This was peculiar, since the PDA had a larger screen. Analysis of the users' responses led to the identification of an important psychological effect. User expectations from a mobile phone were lower, so they responded more generously. The same considerations apply to the study of the effect that content type may have on a user's QoE. We found that content such as football or a music concert on mobile phones is particularly critical and does need further attention.

Another lesson learned from our study is that media adaptation cannot be achieved merely by acting on encoding parameters, compression ratio, frame rate, and so forth. Content must be edited specifically (e.g., larger text size for smaller screen size) for the type of terminal that will be used to access the content. This is a further level of optimization that can make a significant difference to the end user. During our experiments, we used recordings from existing TV materials. This approach would hardly satisfy

*Figure 6. Acceptability of video bit rates; the error bars indicate the 95% confidence intervals*

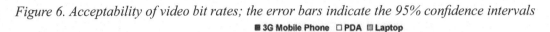

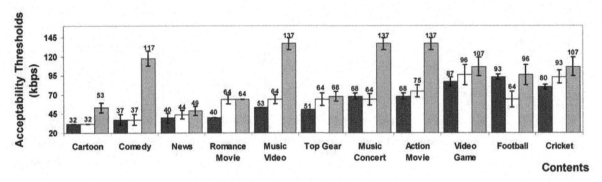

the user watching; for instance, a football game from a mobile terminal. The loss of visual details and the difficulty in identifying players or in detecting ball movement are bound to substantially decrease user satisfaction. We found that this could be improved by editing the content specifically for mobile phones. We also found that zooming out content did not lead to a measurable improvement in QoE, since screen size did not allow for the identification of details. Increasing usage of closeup shots and optimized textual rendering in mobile video will allow for a TV-like experience on small screens.

Our findings can find immediate application for the improvement of QoE and minimization of the consumed network resource. For instance, service providers can use this knowledge to determine the best tradeoff and to what thresholds (based on the type of contents and terminal being used) to gradually reduce the parameters of video quality without considerably affecting the user's QoE. Thresholds of acceptance can also enable a flexible pricing scheme, thereby enabling user-centric SLAs. A service provider might decide to offer three pricing schemes of "bronze," "silver," and "gold," depending on the quality level required by the user. For example, a football fan requiring the highest possible video quality can opt for the "gold" pricing scheme; in turn, the service provider has to ensure that those quality requirements are adequately met.

## SUMMARY OF KEY POINTS

In this chapter, we highlight the importance of QoE as opposed to simpler forms of resource management based on QoS parameters. Delivering high QoE depends on gaining an understanding of the user requirements and expectations, and then applying that knowledge in defining models that are user-centric. These models may enable a long-term adoption of mobile TV services.

The relationship between QoE and QoS are mutually dependent because QoS forms the fundamental building block for providing QoE. From the network perspective, QoS is a metric used by network operators to provide guarantees to selected network traffic. However, a better QoS may not consistently measure up to a better QoE; for instance, in the flawless transmission of packets. This is because adhering to the minimal specification of packet loss that can occur in a transmission session might not linearly map to a satisfied user because it may include other factors as discussed in the section "Behind the Scenes of QoE." Thus, the user perception of the service quality needs to be explicitly understood in order to use QoS efficiently. In other words, the concepts of QoS and QoE need to be studied in a unified manner in order to ensure that the end-user experience with mobile TV services is positive and not compromised.

## FUTURE RESEARCH DIRECTIONS

Our immediate target is to extend the work presented here in a peer-to-peer streaming environment. The results presented in this chapter pave the way toward the realization of a QoE model that could be based on the classification of video contents in the spatio-temporal domain. It is still necessary to investigate the interrelationship between acceptability thresholds and the ITU-T Recommendations (P.910) of subjective video quality assessments for multimedia applications.

## REFERENCES

Agboma, F., & Liotta, A. (2007).. Addressing user expectations in mobile content delivery. *Mobile Information Systems Journal 3(3-4),* 153-164..

Apteker, R.T., Fisher, J.A., Kisimov, V.S., & Neishlos, H. (1995). Video acceptability and frame rate. *IEEE Transaction Multimedia, 3*(3), 32–40.

Callet, L.P., Viard-Gaudin, C., & Péchard, S. (2006). No reference and reduced reference video quality metrics for end to end QoS monitoring. *IEICE Transactions on Communications, 89*(3), 289–296.

Claypool, M., &Tanner, J. (1999). The effects of jitter on the perceptual quality of video. *Proceedings of the ACM Multimedia,* 115–118.

comScore. (2007). comScore study reveals that mobile TV currently most popular among males and younger age segments [press release].

David, S., Man, L., & Renaud, C. (Eds.). (2006). *QoS and QoE management in UMTS cellular Systems.* Wiley.

EBU. (2003). BPN 056:SAMVIQ—Subjective assessment methodology for video quality.

Empririx. (2003). *Assuring QoE on next generation networks* [white paper].

Fechner, G.T. (1966). *Elements of psychophysics.* Holt Rinehart & Winston.

Ghinea, G., Thomas, J.P., & Fish, R.S. (1999). Multimedia, network protocols and users—Bridging the Gap. *Proceedings of the ACM Multimedia, 1,* 473–476.

Gilliam, D. (2006). The appeal of mobile video: Reading between the lines. Retrieved from http://www.tdgresearch.com/tdg_opinions_the_appeal_of_mobile_video.htm

Hands, D.P. QoS for mobile multimedia, BTexact Technologies. Retrieved from http://www.iee.org/on-comms/pn/visualinformation/%20P-Qos_For_Mobile_Multimedia.pdf

Hands, D. (2004). A basic multimedia quality model. *IEEE Transaction on Multimedia, 6*(6), 806–816.

ISO 9241-11. (1998). Ergonomic requirements for office work with visual display terminals (VDTs)—Part 11: Guidance on usability.

ITU-R. (1997). Recommendation BS.1116. Methods for the subjective assessment of small impairments in audio systems including multichannel sound systems.

ITU-R. (2002). Recommendation BT500, methodology for the subjective assessment of the quality of television pictures.

ITU-R. (2004). BT 1683, objective perceptual video quality measurement techniques for standard definition digital broadcast television in the presence of a full reference.

ITU-T. (1996). Recommedation P.800, methods for subjective determination of transmission quality.

ITU-T. (1999). Recommedation P.910, subjective video quality assessment methods for multimedia applications.

ITU-T. (2004). J.144, objective perceptual video quality measurement techniques for digital cable television in the presence of a full reference.

ITU-T Recommendation. P.930. (1996). Principles of a reference impairment system for video.

Joly, A., Nathalie,M., & Marcel, B. (2001). Audio-visual quality and interactions between television audio and video. *Proceedings of the International Symposium on Signal Processing and its Applications*, Malaysia.

Jumisko-Pyykkö, S., Vadakital,V., Liinasuo, M., & Hannuksela, M.M. (2006). Acceptance of audiovisual quality in erroneous television sequences over a DVB-H channel. *Proceedings of the Workshop in Video Processing and Quality Metrics for Consumer Electronics*, 1–5.

Ketola, P., & Röykkee, M. (2001). The three facets of usability in mobile handsets. *Proceedings of the CHI Workshop, Mobile Communications: Understanding Users, Adoption & Design*. Seattle, Washington.

Knoche, H., McCarthy, J., & Sasse, M.A. (2005). Can small be beautiful? Assessing image resolution requirements for mobile TV. *Proceedings of the ACM Multimedia*, 829–838.

Knoche, H., McCarthy, J., & Sasse, M.A. (2008). How low can you go? The effect of low resolutions on shot types in mobile TV. *Personalized and Mobile Digital TV Applications in Springer Multimedia Tools and Applications Series, 36(1-2),* 145-166.

Koucheryavy, Y., Moltchanov,D., & Harju, J. (2003). Performance evaluation of live video streaming service in 802.11b WLAN environment under different load conditions. *Proceedings of the MIPS*, Italy, 30–41.

Levine, W.M., & Shefner, J.M. (2000). *Fundamentals of sensation and perception* (3rd ed.). Oxford University Press.

Lloyd, E., Maclean,R., & Stirling, A. (2006). Mobile TV—Results from the BT Movio DAB-IP pilot in London. *EBU Technical Review*. Retrieved from http://www.ebu.ch/en/technical/trev/trev_frameset-index.html

Lucy, S., & Sara, K. (2006). *Usability guidelines for mobile TV design*. Serco.

McCarthy, J., Sasse, M.A., & Miras, D. (2004). Sharp or smooth? Comparing the effects of quantization vs. frame rate for streamed video. *Proceedings of the SIGCHI*, 535–542.

Murphy, S., Searles, M., Rambeau, C., & Murphy, L. (2004). Evaluating the impact of network performance on video streaming quality for categorised video content. *Proceedings of the Packet Video Workshop*.

Nokia. (2004). *Quality of experience (QoE) of mobile services: Can it be measured and improved?* White Paper No. 11212-1004. Finland.

Nokia. (2005). Finnish mobile TV: Pilot results. Retrieved from http://www.mobiletv.nokia.com/download_counter.php?file=/onAir/finland/files/RIPress.pdf

Olista. (2007). Live trials by Olista with European mobile operators demonstrate common barriers for mobile data services [press release 120207-1].

Reeves, B., & Nass, C. (1998). *The media equation: How people treat computers, television, and new media like real people and places*. University of Chicago Press.

Richardson, I.E.G. (2003). *H.264 and MPEG-4 video compression: Video coding for next generation multimedia*. Wiley.

Robert, E.M. (1986). On judging quality by price: Price dependent expectations, not price dependent preferences. *Southern Economic Journal, 52*(3), 665–672.

Siller, M. (2006). *An agent-based platform to map quality of service to experience in active and conventional networks* [doctoral thesis]. Colchester, England: University of Essex.

Siller, M., & Woods, J.C. (2003). QoS arbitration for improving the QoE in multimedia transmission. *Proceedings of IEE Visual Information Engineering*, 238–241.

Sodergard, C. (2003). Mobile television—Technology and user experiences report on the mobile-TV project. VTT Information Technology.

Teyeb, O., Sørensen, T,B., Mogensen, P., & Wigard, J. (2006). Evaluation of packet service performance in UMTS and heterogeneous networks. *Proceedings of the ACM Workshop on Quality of Service & Security for Wireless and Mobile Networks*, 95–102.

Voelcker, R., Hands, D., Davis, A., Bourret, A., & Bayart, D. (2003). Video quality measurement—Predicting subjective quality using perceptual models. *Journal of the Communications Network, 1*(3).

VQEG. (2007). VQEG multimedia test plan. Retrieved from http://www.vqeg.org

Watson, A.B., Hu, J., & McGowan III,,J.F. (2001). DVQ: A digital video quality metric based on human vision. *Journal of Electronic Imaging, 10*(1), 20–29.

Webster, A.A., Jones, C.T., & Pinson, M.H. (1993). An objective video quality assessments system based on human perception. *Proceedings of the SPIE, 1913,* 15–26.

Winkler, S. (2005). *Digital video quality: Vision models and metrics.* John Wiley & Sons, Ltd.

Winkler, S., & Campos, R. (2003). Video quality evaluation for Internet streaming applications. *Proceedings of the SPIE: Human Vision and Electronic Imaging, 5007,* 104–115.

Winkler, S., & Dufaux, F. (2003). Video quality evaluation for mobile applications. *Proceedings of the SPIE: Visual Communications and Image Processing, 5150,* 593–603.

Winkler, S., & Faller, C. (2005). Maximizing audiovisual quality at low bitrates. *Proceedings of the Workshop on Video Processing and Quality Metrics.*

Wolf, S., & Pinson, M.H. (2005). Low bandwidth reduced reference video quality monitoring system. *Proceedings of the Workshop on Video Processing and Quality Metrics for Consumer Electronics.*

Yang, F., Wan, S., Chang, Y., & Wu, H.R. (2005). A novel objective no-reference metric for digital video quality assessment. *IEEE Signal Processing Letters, 12*(10), 685–688.

Zapater, M.N., & Bressan,G. (2007). A proposed approach for quality of experience assurance for IPTV. *Proceedings of the IEEE Digital Society.*

## ADDITIONAL READING

David, S., Man, L., & Renaud, C. (Ed.). (2006). *QoS and QoE management in UMTS cellular systems.* Wiley.

Fechner, G.T. (1966). *Elements of psychophysics* (trans. H.E. Alder). Holt Rinehart & Winston.

Jain, R. (2004). Quality of experience. *IEEE Multimedia, 11,* 95–96.

Nokia. (2004). *Quality of experience (QoE) of mobile services: Can it be measured and improved?* [white paper No. 11212–1004]. Finland

Richardson, I.E.G. (2003). *H.264 and MPEG-4 video compression: Video coding for next generation multimedia.* Wiley.

Sadka, A.H (2002). *Compressed video communications.* John Wiley & Sons.

Winkler, S. (2005). *Digital video quality: Vision models and metrics*: John Wiley & Sons, Ltd.

## ENDNOTES

[1] One-time fee is described in Sodergard (2003) as a direct fee that is payable to the service provider when accessing a new service for the first time or that allows a lifetime access to mobile TV service. A one-time fee can also be an indirect fee hidden in the price for new hardware and thus sometimes invisible to the customer.

[2] In ad-based TV (Sodergard, 2003), the cost of using mobile TV service is financed completely

by sponsors or advertisers if the user is willing to receive advertisements on his or her mobile phone.

[3]     Threshold is defined in Levine and Shefner (2000) as the stimulus intensity corresponding to 50% detection on the psychometric function.

[4]     An image size of 640x480 pixels was used to represent mobile terminals with a VGA resolution.

# Chapter XI
# HSM:
# A Hybrid Streaming Mechanism for Delay–Tolerant Multimedia Applications

**Annanda Thavymony Rath**
*Institute of Technology of Cambodia, Cambodia*

**Saraswathi Krithivasan**
*India Institute of Technology, Bombay*

**Sridhar Iyer**
*India Institute of Technology, Bombay*

## ABSTRACT

*Traditionally, Content Delivery Networks (CDNs) deploy proxy servers at strategic locations at the edge of the network to efficiently serve client requests. With the tremendous growth in multimedia applications and the number of clients accessing such applications, an edge proxy server may serve clients connected to it through a multihop network of heterogeneous links. Further, a special class of multimedia applications that can tolerate startup delays is emerging. In such applications, clients require a minimum acceptable quality (loss-free transmission at a minimum encoded rate $r_i$) and the start of playback at a specific time $(t + d_i)$ where t is the current time and $d_i$ is the delay tolerance acceptable to client i. Our work deals with enhancing performance of such networks through a Hybrid Streaming Mechanism (HSM). In HSM, a client's request triggers the selection of an intermediate node as a streaming point to which multimedia contents are dynamically transferred from the proxy/source, and this streaming point streams the contents to the client. Transferred contents are temporarily cached at the streaming point to service future requests for the same content. HSM helps a Content Service Provider's objective of satisfying as many client requests as possible and providing enhanced quality to clients given their delay tolerance. Simulation results demonstrate that by leveraging the delay tolerance of clients and by combining the dynamic download and streaming mechanisms, HSM performs better than directly streaming from edge servers, serving on average 40% more client requests.*

## INTRODUCTION

For large-scale multimedia data dissemination, Content Delivery Networks (CDNs) are used to overcome the limitation of streaming server capacity and link bandwidth constraints in the network. The main objectives of CDNs are to (i) minimize the startup latency (the time it takes for a client to start the playback), (ii) reduce network congestion, and (iii) reduce the load on the central server (Frossard & Verscheure, 2002; Qian Zhang & Zhang, 2001; Shen, Lee & Basu, 200; Yang-Sao, 2003). CDNs achieve these objectives through strategic deployment of proxy servers where contents are cached in anticipation of future requests. Each proxy server serves as a source for clients connected to it through a multihop network of heterogeneous links.

In addition, streaming media applications are emerging where multiple clients access the contents at specific times according to their convenience. In these special classes of multimedia applications, termed *delay-tolerant* applications (Krithivasan & Iyer, 2006), clients request the multimedia content, specifying their requirements: (i) stream *quality*: a minimum rate at which they want to receive the stream, and (ii) *delay tolerance*: the time they will wait for the play out of the stream. Universities offering their courses to a set of global subscribers and multinational corporations providing training to employees across cities are some examples. Note that mechanisms proposed in the literature to efficiently serve requests for multimedia content, including CDNs, propose ways to *minimize* the startup delay (Hua, Cai & Sheu, 1998; Jiangchuan, Chu & Xu, 2003; Sen, 2000; Shen et al., 2000; Su & Wu, 2005), whereas we deal with applications that may *require* startup delay.

In this chapter, we present a Hybrid Streaming Mechanism (HSM) to increase the efficiency of Content Service Providers (CSPs) by using a combination of dynamic download and streaming mechanisms. In HSM, a client's request triggers the selection of an intermediate node to which multimedia contents are *dynamically* transferred from the source, and this *streaming point* streams the contents to the client. Transferred contents are temporarily cached at the streaming point to service future requests for the same content until the contents need to be evicted.

Simulation results of HSM show that by leveraging the delay tolerance of clients and by combining the dynamic download and streaming mechanisms intelligently, HSM performs better than direct streaming from edge servers, serving on average 40% more client requests. In the next section, we present a motivating example. We present the HSM algorithm in Section 3 and present our experimental analysis in Section 4. Related works in the area are presented in Section 5. Section 6 presents the conclusions of our work.

## MOTIVATING EXAMPLE

We consider a network modeled as a tree, with source S at the *root* and clients $C_1, C_2,...,C_{14}$ at the *leaves*, as shown in Figure 1.

All other intermediate nodes serve as *relay nodes*. A relay node that directly serves a group of clients is termed a *region node*. We use the term *region* to refer to the subtree that contains the region node and the clients it serves. For example, in Figure 1, the network has five regions with nodes 7, 9, 10, 11, and 12 serving as region nodes. We refer to the network from S to the region nodes as the *backbone* of the content dissemination network. While most existing research focuses on the Internet (best effort

*Figure 1. Sample tree network topology*

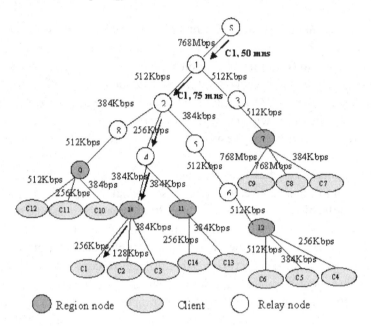

network) as the underlying network (Sen, 1999), we assume that the backbone is *provisioned* (using Multi-Protocol Label Switching [MPLS]) to support multimedia content dissemination.

Consider a stream of playout duration two hours. Client arrival times and requirements are shown in Table 1.

Let us consider the case when S is streaming:

*   C1 arrives at time zero. It gets 320Kbps (equation used is derived in Section 3.2), which flows along the path (S-1-2-4-10-C1).

*Table 1. Details of clients requesting the stream*

| Clients | Request arrival time (λ) (Mins.) | Client requirements | |
| --- | --- | --- | --- |
| | | Minimum rate (α) (Kbps) | Delay tolerance (δ) (Mins.) |
| C1 | 0 | 256 | 30 |
| C14 | +10 | 256 | 60 |
| C6 | +75 | 256 | 30 |
| C9 | +75 | 480 | 15 |
| C12 | +75 | 256 | 30 |

- This path is occupied for two hours at 320Kbps. Some links are underutilized in this case. The underutilized links and their unused bandwidths are given next: (i) Link (S –1): 448Kbps; (ii) Link (1-2): 192Kbps, and (iii) Link (4-10): 64Kbps.
- C14 joins the network at time t=10. Since C14 shares links (S-1-2-4) with C1, its request cannot be serviced.
- Client C6 joins network at t=75. It shares links (S-1-2) with C1. Given its delay tolerance, C6 can get only a stream rate of 240Kbps. Since this rate is below C6's minimum required rate, request from C6 is also rejected.
- Similarly, clients C9 and C12 also get rejected.

Thus, when the source streams directly, only one out of five clients is serviced by the CSP.

Suppose HSM is used. When a request arrives at the central server, it determines the stream rate that can be provided to the client given the client's delay tolerance requirement and the location of the streaming server, termed *streaming point*. The central server then starts downloading the data to the chosen streaming point and allows it to stream the contents to the clients. The data sent by source to the streaming point is also cached at that node for a short duration in the interest of future requests for the same content. A detailed discussion of HSM algorithm is presented in Section 3. In the rest of the chapter, we use the term *Pure Streaming Mechanism* (PSM) to refer to direct streaming from the source.

- As before, the deliverable stream rate at C1 is 320Kbps. But now we choose node 4 as the streaming point. (Details of streaming point selection are presented in Section 3.3.)
- Data are transferred from the source to the streaming point along the path (S-1-2-4). Note that all links except link (4-10) are fully utilized in this case.
- C14 joins the network 10 minutes after C1. Since C14 shares links (S-1-2-4) with C1, it is not possible for C14 to immediately initiate a new stream from S. However, since C14 is requesting for the same streaming object, as the object is being cached at node 4, its request can be serviced from node 4. C14 gets the stream at 320Kbps, which is greater than its minimum rate requirement.
- Clients C6, C9, and C12 join the network at time t=75. Before t=75, C1's transmission across links S-1 and 1-2 are finished, and these links become free. All three clients, C6, C9, and C12, get serviced with a stream rate of 480Kbps, their streaming points being at nodes 5, 1, and 8, respectively.

*As a result, under HSM, all five clients can be serviced.*

Thus, we observe that HSM performs better than PSM in terms of number of serviced clients. This is because in HSM, links from the source to the streaming point are freed sooner than PSM, as the link bandwidth is fully utilized. Another important feature of HSM is that future requests for the same content from other clients in the subtree can be serviced from the cache at the streaming point. We use a simple caching mechanism requiring limited memory and a simple cache eviction policy with very little overhead. This property allows HSM to further improve the number of serviced clients.

## DETAILS OF HSM

In this section, we first present the HSM algorithm in Section 3.1. We present details of the algorithm, including (i) streaming point selection and (ii) expressions used in HSM, in Sections 3.2 and 3.3, respectively.

## HSM Algorithm

When a request from a client is received, source S invokes the HSM algorithm. The main idea of the algorithm is as follows: find the best rate at which the client can be serviced given its delay tolerance and the link bandwidths in the path from the source to the client. A feasibility check is made to ensure that the client can be serviced with its minimum rate requirement. Then, if the links are free, find the streaming point, transfer the contents to the streaming point, and start streaming from the streaming point. Time to Live of the Content (TTLC) is initialized. Otherwise, check to see if any node in the client's path (selected as streaming point for a previously admitted client) has the content in its cache. If cached content is available, the TTLC is updated, and content is streamed to the client; otherwise, the client's request is rejected. The algorithm is outlined in Figure 2.

## Expressions Used in HSM

In this section, we present the equations for the time to transfer the file from the source to the streaming point and the deliverable rates at clients. We use Figure 3 to derive the expressions.

*Figure 2. HSM algorithm (invoked by the Source S)*

```
When a client's request arrives,
  /* client specifies minimum rate required (α) and its delay tolerance(δ) */
  Given, α and δ, and the streaming duration SD and the weakest link L_min in the client's path, determine the
  deliverable stream rate at the client :  SR = L_min + ( L_min * δ/SD)
                                          /* Equation (1) from Section 3.2.1 is used */
If SR < α
        Reject request
Else
        If link is free
              /*Streaming point (SP) selection*/
                  Find the bandwidth of weakest link in the client's path from source to region node, B_min
                  If SR <= B_min
                        Choose SP as the relay node with maximum number of outgoing links
                  Else
                        Choose SP as the node below B_min
                  End
                  Find time to transfer the contents to SP, T_t=filesize/B_min
                                          /* Equation (2) from Section 3.2.2 is used */
                  Update the client's delay tolerance and calculate the deliverable stream rate.
                  Transfer contents from S to the selected SP and start streaming
                  Intialize Time to Live of the Content (TTLC)  /* Refer to Section 3.2.3 */
        Else
                  If the requested content is already cached at SP
                        Update Time to Live of the Content (TTLC)  /* Refer to Section 3.2.3 */
                        Accept request and stream from cache
                  Else
                        Reject request
                  End
        End
End
```

*Figure 3. Example used to illustrate the derivations*

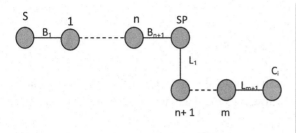

| **S** | Source |
|---|---|
| **SP** | Streaming Point |
| **C$_i$** | Client i |
| **1,...,n, n+1,...,m** | Relay nodes |
| **B$_i$** | Link bandwidth of link i from S to SP |
| **L$_i$** | Link bandwidth of link i from SP to C$_i$ |

## Equation for Deliverable Stream Rate at a Client

With reference to Figure 3, let $L_{min}$ be the minimum of link bandwidths $L_1$, $L_2$,...., $L_{m+1}$ in the path between SP and client $C_i$. Let $d_i$ be the delay tolerance of $C_i$, and let SD be the total duration of the stream. The deliverable stream rate at client $C_i$ is given by the expression:

$$SR_i = L_{min} + (L_{min} * d_i / SD) \qquad (1)$$

We derive the expression as follows:

- When the stream is encoded at $L_{min}$, $C_i$ receives it without any loss.
- However, Ci waits for a time $d_i$ before the playout starts. During this waiting time, an amount of data can be streamed to $C_i$ given by $L_{min} * d_i$.
- The amount of extra data that $C_i$ gets per second is $L_{min} * d_i / SD$. Thus, the delivered stream rate at $C_i$ is $SR_i = L_{min} + (L_{min} * d_i / SD)$.

## Time to Transfer to Streaming Point

As shown in Figure 3, let there be n relay nodes 1, 2,..., n from source S to the streaming point SP. Let $B_1$, $B_2$, ..., $B_{n+1}$ be the link bandwidths in the path from S to SP. Time to transfer the file from S to SP is dictated by the weakest link in the path between S and SP, $B_{min}$ and is given by:

$$T_t = filesize / B_{min} \qquad (2)$$

## Time to Live of Content (TTLC) in the Cache

We use a simple method to determine the value of Time to Live of Content (TTLC) such that the cache management has very little overhead unlike the replication strategies used by CDNs in their core network (Sivasubramanian, Szymaniak, Pierre & Steen, 2004).

Consider $C_i$ with delay tolerance $d_i$ requesting for a stream with duration SD.

- The client's transmission starts at time $= t_0 + d_i$.
- The client finishes its transmission at $(t_0 + d_i + SD)$.
- Hence the stream needs to be active for the duration $d_i + SD$.

We choose this value as the TTLC for the stream in the cache at SP. When multiple clients access the same stream at the same time, we choose the maximum of the delay tolerance values of the clients in the previous expression.

When there is a new request for the same stream before the TTLC expires, it is extended to $T_c + d_k - (T_c - t_k) + SD$, where $T_c$ is the TTLC of the current content, $t_k$ is the time when $C_k$'s request arrives, and $d_k$ is the delay tolerance of $C_k$.

## Streaming Point Selection

In HSM, a selected relay node serves as the streaming point for all the clients in its subtree instead of the central server. Several methods have been proposed for caching proxy locations in the context of a CDN (Xu, Li & Lee, 2002). Here we select the streaming point based on the following criteria: (i) streaming point should help to improve the number of serviced clients, and/or (ii) the position of the streaming point should help to improve the stream rate for other requests that come from the region serviced by that streaming point.

Let $SR_i$ be the deliverable stream rate at client $C_i$ having requirements: minimum rate of $\alpha$ Kbps and delay tolerance of $\delta$ minutes. Let $R_i$ be the region node serving $C_i$. Let $B_{min}$ be the bandwidth of the weakest link in the path from S to $R_i$.

**Case 1:** When $SR_i$ is less than or equal to $B_{min}$, we select the relay node in the client's path from S to $R_i$ with the most number of outgoing links as the streaming point. Rationale for this strategy is as follows:

- In this case, the stream will flow without introducing any delay up to $R_i$. Hence, any node in the client's path can be chosen as the streaming point.
- However, when the relay node with most outgoing links is chosen, more clients can be serviced concurrently.

**Case 2:** When $SR_i$ is greater than $B_{min}$, one of the nodes below $B_{min}$ in the client's path from S to $R_i$ is chosen as the streaming point. Rationale for this strategy is as follows:

- Weak link in a client's path uses up the client's delay tolerance.
- When one of the nodes below $B_{min}$, is chosen as the streaming point, other clients' requests in the subtree made within TTLC may be serviced with better stream rates, as the stream's flow is not subjected to this weak link.
- As in case 1, while selecting a node below $B_{min}$, the node with most outgoing links is chosen.

*Table 2. Details of clients requesting the stream*

| Clients | Request arrival time ($\lambda$) (Mins.) | Client Requirements | |
| --- | --- | --- | --- |
| | | Minimum Rate ($\alpha$) (Kbps) | Delay Tolerance ($\delta$) (Mins.) |
| C2 | 0 | 128 | 90 |
| C4 | +15 | 128 | 30 |
| C11 | +15 | 128 | 30 |
| C14 | +15 | 128 | 60 |

## An Illustration of Streaming Point Selection

We consider the same simple network model given in Figure 1.

With reference to Table 1, consider the request from $C_1$ arriving at time zero.

- C1 allows a delay tolerance of 30 minutes.
- The deliverable stream rate $SR_1$ for C1 is 320Kbps.
- This rate is greater than $B_{min1}$, 256Kbps in the path from source to the region node 10 serving C1. Hence, we choose the streaming point at node 4.

As explained in Section 2, all five clients are serviced when node 4 is chosen as the streaming point.

Table 2 provides another instance of client arrivals and their requirements. Consider the request from C2 arriving at time zero.

- C2 specifies a delay tolerance value of 90 minutes.
- Stream rate $SR_2$ that can be delivered to this client is 224Kbps.
- This rate is less than $B_{min2}$ (256Kbps) in the path from source to the region node 10 serving C2. Hence, we choose the streaming point at node 2.

When node 2 is chosen as the streaming point, requests from clients C4, C11, and C14 arriving 15 minutes later can be serviced concurrently from the cache at node 2, even though the links (S-1) and (1-2) are occupied by the stream serving C2.

## PERFORMANCE EVALUATION

In this section, we present the results of simulations evaluating the performance of HSM. We compare HSM with the *Pure Streaming Mechanism* (PSM), the term we use to refer to direct streaming from the source, under various network topologies and client requirements using Matlab. The following performance metrics are used: (i) the number of serviced clients and (ii) percentage improvement of client's stream rate as compared with its minimum rate requirement.

## Simulation Parameters

The following parameters remain the same across all our experiments: (i) multimedia playout duration is set to two hours; (ii) without loss of generality, queuing delay and propagation delay are set to zero; and (iii) period over which client arrivals are monitored, termed *observation period*, is set to four hours.

The key factors that affect the performance of streaming mechanisms are (i) network topology with specific link bandwidths, (ii) client request arrivals, and (iii) clients' requirements. To understand the impact of these factors, we consider 100 topologies. For these topologies, we first keep the client requirements constant and vary their arrival rates; then we keep the arrival rate constant and vary their delay tolerance requirements.

- The first 50 topologies termed as *Class 1* have high link bandwidths from source to region node. The bandwidths are chosen randomly from the range (256Kbps – 768Kbps).
- The next 50 topologies, termed *Class 2*, have low bandwidth (weak links) in the backbone, from source to region node. The bandwidths are chosen randomly from the range (128Kbps – 256Kbps).
- All topologies have a total number of nodes in the range 100 to 500, where the number of nodes is selected randomly.

## Details of Experiments

We study the impact of the key factors on the two metrics—the number of serviced clients and percentage improvement of client's stream rate—under PSM and HSM, as discussed next.

**Uniform Client Delay Tolerance Values, Varying Client Arrivals.** Clients' delay tolerance values are set to 30 minutes. Arrival rate of the clients' requests is varied from one to 30 per minute. Clients' minimum rates are set to 128Kbps.

We observe both the parameters (number of serviced clients and stream rate improvement at the clients) in Figure 4. In this figure, X-axis represents the number of client requests per minute; Y-axis (on the left) represents the percentage of clients serviced, and secondary Y-axis (on the right) represents percentage of stream rate improvement, when Class 1 topologies are used. Figure 4 shows that when the request rate increases, the number of serviced clients decreases for both the mechanisms. This is as expected. However, the decrease is more pronounced in PSM compared to HSM. For example, when the request rate is 10 per minute, HSM services around 80% of the requests, while PSM services only around 50%. Note that the difference between the number of serviced clients in PSM and HSM keeps widening as the number of requests increases. These results show that HSM is attractive for a CSP.

While comparing the percentage improvement in stream rates with reference to Figure 4, we observe that PSM appears to provide clients with better stream rates compared with HSM. This is because percentage improvement in stream rates is calculated only for the serviced clients. Since PSM rejects 78% of client requests (compared with only 30% for HSM), its stream rate improvement seems better still only marginally.

Figure 5 presents similar results for Class 2 topologies. We observe that HSM performs marginally better than PSM. In Class 2 topologies, links from the source to the region nodes have low bandwidths. In this case, transferring the file to a relay node does not provide any advantage, as the time for transferring the file is the same, even when the streaming server is placed at the source. The main advantage

*Figure 4. Percentage of serviced clients vs. percentage of stream rate improvement (class 1)*

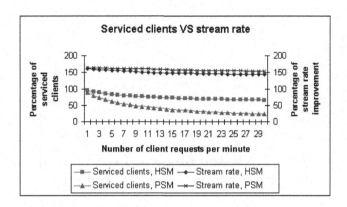

*Figure 5. Percentage of serviced clients vs. percentage of stream rate improvement (class 2)*

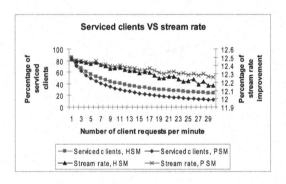

of HSM is that by choosing a streaming point appropriately, future requests from clients for the same content can be serviced from the cached contents, which contributes to the slightly better performance of HSM.

**Uniform Arrival Rate, Varying Client Delay Tolerance Values.** Client arrival rate is kept constant at one request per second. Delay tolerance values are set to 30, 60, 90, and 120 minutes, respectively, for the experiments. Clients' minimum rates are set to 128Kbps.

Due to space limitation, we only present results for Class 1 topologies in order to evaluate the impact of clients' delay tolerance on the number of serviced clients using PSM and HSM. Results in Figure 6 demonstrate that as clients' delay tolerance increases, the performance of HSM gets better. When the client delay tolerance is equal to the streaming duration, HSM services nearly 100% of the clients' requests. In the case of PSM, as shown in Figure 7, client delay tolerance has very little effect on the number of client requests serviced. This is an interesting observation that HSM is especially beneficial

*Figure 6. Impact of client delay tolerance values on HSM (Class1)*

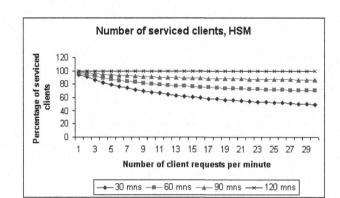

*Figure 7. Impact of client delay tolerance values on*

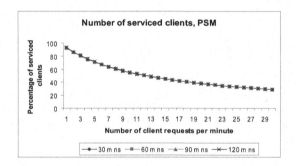

for delay-tolerant multimedia applications where the CSP's backbone has provisioned links, as the available bandwidth is better utilized in this mechanism.

## Case Study: Gnutella Peer Network

In this section, we present a case study on the Gnutella Peer Network (Geography of Cyberspace). We simplify the original network topology to a tree-based network by removing cycles in the topology shown in Figure 8[1]. Our approximated Gnutella Peer Network backbone contains 510 nodes. In this simulation, we set the clients' minimum rate to 128Kbps and delay tolerance values to 30 minutes for all clients. We observe the number of serviced clients and the percentage of clients' stream rates improvement under PSM and HSM. The result given in Figure 9 is an average across the 100 times simulation with different client request time for the Gnutella Peer network.

Figure 9 displays the number of serviced clients and the percentage of stream rate improvement. With the given results, we observe that HSM performs better than PSM in terms of number of serviced clients. Note that when the number of client requests reaches 30 per minute, HSM performs 20% better than PSM. While PSM rejects more client requests, it provides stream rates that are on average 5% better than HSM.

*Figure 8. Gnutella peer network*

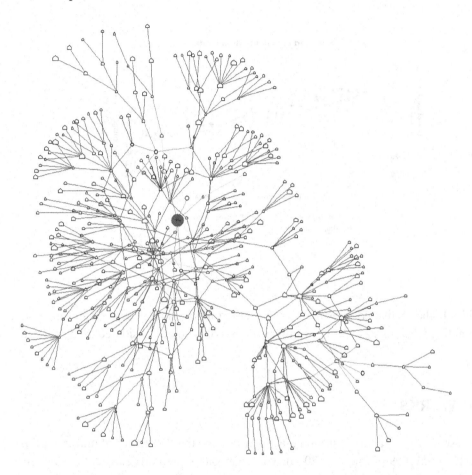

## Analysis of Results

Performance of HSM depends on the following factors: (i) network topology with specific link bandwidths and (ii) clients' requirements. We observe that for Class 1 topologies where the link bandwidths are provisioned such that the upper links from the source to the region nodes have high bandwidth, HSM is a better scheme as the available bandwidth can be better utilized with this mechanism. In Class 2 topologies, links from the source to the region nodes have low bandwidths. In this case, using FTP to transfer the file to a relay node does not provide any advantage, as the time for transferring the file is the same even when the streaming server is placed at the source. The only advantage of HSM is that by choosing a streaming point appropriately, requests from clients for the same content can be serviced from the cached contents. Thus, we observe only marginal improvement in the number of clients serviced with such topologies.

To summarize, HSM works well with Class 1 topologies because available bandwidths are fully utilized to transfer data to the streaming point. If the dissemination network falls in Class 2 category,

*Figure 9. Percentage of serviced clients vs. percentage of stream rate improvement (Gnutella)*

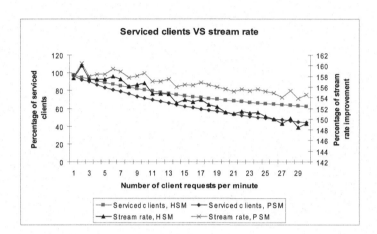

HSM provides higher delivered rates due to the caching mechanism. However, in this case, costs involved in enabling relay nodes with streaming capability have to be considered to make an appropriate decision.

## RELATED WORKS

Most of the research in the area of multimedia dissemination treats delivery of multimedia as real time application (Hua et al., 1998; Yang-Sae, 2003), which can tolerate a small delay for the purpose of solving the delay jitter problem. Mechanisms proposed in the literature focus on minimizing this startup delay (Hua et al., 1998). When we considered multimedia delivery over the Internet, there were reasons for using streaming with minimal startup delay: (i) caching or buffering the content was high due to the size of multimedia files; many mechanisms (Dan, 1995; Sen, 1999; Shen et al., 2000; Sivasubramanian et al., 2004) have been proposed for efficient content management; and (ii) price of Internet connection was high; many mechanisms have been proposed for effective use of bandwidth (Jiangchuan et al., 2003; Qian Zhang & Zhang, 2001; Sen, 1999; Xu et al., 2002).

Resource sharing strategies increase the number of serviced clients by exploiting the high skewness in video access patterns. These strategies can be classified into five main categories: batching, patching (Dan, 1995; Jiangchuan et al., 2003; Sen, 1999), piggybacking, broadcasting, and interval caching (Sen, 1999; Yang-Sae, 2003). Batching off-loads (Dan, Sitaram & Shahabuddin, 1994) the storage subsystem and uses server bandwidth and network resources efficiently by accumulating requests for the same video and serving them together by utilizing the multicast facility. Patching is similar to batching, but it expands the multicast tree dynamically to include new requests, thereby improving resource sharing; but it requires additional bandwidth and buffer space at the client. Piggybacking offers similar advantages to patching, but it adjusts the playback rate so the request catches up with a preceding stream, resulting in a lower-quality presentation of the initial part of the requested video. Broadcasting techniques divide each popular video into multiple segments and broadcast each segment periodically. The improved resource sharing here comes at the expense of requiring very high additional bandwidth and buffer space at the client. Interval caching caches interval between successive streams for the same video in the main memory of the server. It does not sacrifice the quality of playback, does not lengthen the waiting time, and does not expect much resource from the client. It has also become more cost-effective with the falling prices of semiconductor memories.

In the recent literature, an optimal chaining scheme proposed in Qian Zhang and Zhang (2001) and Chan, Su, Huang, and Wang (2005) for a video-on-demand application uses the concept of collaborative networks. In this mechanism, clients store fragments of streaming content shared between them. This mechanism is not realistic when the Internet is used in the dissemination network. Multipath routing for video delivery over bandwidth-limited networks (Hua et al., 1998) is another mechanism in which quality of streaming service and the number of serviced clients is improved as data are sent faster than one-way routing. In this mechanism, links are freed sooner, allowing other clients to get the services. But this scheme has a drawback of high computational overhead when the number of client requests increases, as the streaming server also performs the scheduling function.

Mechanisms proposed in Xu et al. (2002) and Krishnan and Shavitt (2000) explore the caching location problem and propose strategies to reduce the traffic in the network and improve the efficiency of streaming service. The following techniques are proposed: prefix caching, full object and permanent caching, and object caching based on its popularity (Sen, 1999). However, these techniques lead to high storage requirement, given the size of the streaming content. In our proposed scheme, we introduce a caching mechanism with a small overhead; the content is cached in the cache memory at the relay node for a period of time equivalent to the streaming duration for servicing any new request for the same object. We also introduce the possibility to extend the time to live of the content in the cache when new requests are made for the same content.

In recent times with the drop in the prices of memory and connectivity and the abundance of network bandwidth, clients demand convenience while accessing content. Today's content dissemination networks exhibit heterogeneous characteristics, as networks have combinations of satellite, terrestrial, and Internet links from the source to the clients. Our work focuses on such heterogeneous networks and explores ways to combine different mechanisms for effective and efficient content dissemination when clients specify their delay tolerance.

## CONCLUSION AND FUTURE WORK

Typically in a content dissemination network controlled by a CSP, weak links are at the edge of the network closer to the clients. By using a combination of dynamic download and streaming mechanisms, provisioned links in the CSP's backbone can be fully utilized, serving more client requests when compared to a centralized server handling all the streaming requests. HSM, the proposed hybrid streaming mechanism, uses this idea to improve the performance and, hence, the revenue for a CSP, leveraging the delay tolerance specified by the clients. We have shown that by choosing appropriate relay nodes as streaming points, 40% more requests on average can be serviced using HSM as compared with PSM.

Our ongoing research includes efficient utilization of combination of resources such as streaming servers, buffers, and transcoders to maximize revenues for a CSP in delay tolerant multimedia applications. Another interesting problem is the placement of the streaming object at the nodes in the network.

The idea is to divide the streaming object into segments distributed at the nodes close to the streaming point. Distribution of the streaming object segments depends on the link bandwidths and the number of hops from the chosen nodes to the streaming point. Objectives include maximizing available bandwidth usage to serve a maximum number of clients and minimize storage. The placement of the streaming object segment must utilize available resources efficiently, leveraging the delay tolerance of the clients.

## REFERENCES

Almeida, J., Eager, D., & Vernon, M. (2001). A hybrid caching strategy for streaming media files. *Proceedings of the SPIE/ACM Conference on Multimedia Computing and Networking*, 4312, 200–212.

Chan, C.-L., Su, T.-C., Huang, S.-Y., & Wang, J.-S. (2005). Optimal chaining scheme for video-on-demand applications on collaborative networks. *IEEE Transactions on Multimedia*, 7(5), 972–980.

Dan, A., Dias, D.M., Mukherjee, R., Sitaram, D., & Tewari, R. (1995). Buffering and caching in large-scale video servers. *Proceedings of the IEEE International Computer Conference*, 217–225.

Dan, A., Shahabuddin, P., Sitaram, D., & Towsley, D. (1995). Channel allocation under batching and VCR control in movie-on-demand servers. *Journal of Parallel and Distributed Computing*, 30(2), 168–179.

Dan, A., Sitaram, D., & Shahabuddin, P. (1994). Scheduling policies for an on-demand video server with batching. *Proceedings of the ACM Conference on Multimedia*, 391–398.

Frossard, P., & Verscheure, O. (2002). Batched patch caching for streaming media. *IEEE Communication Letter*, 6(4), 159–161.

Geography of Cyberspace Directory. http://www.cybergeography.org/

Hua, K.A., Cai, Y., & Sheu. S. (1998). Multicast technique for true video-on-demand services. *ACM Multimedia*, 191–200.

Jiangchuan, L., Chu, X., & Xu, J. (2003). Proxy cache management for grained scalable video streaming [technical report]. Chinese University of Hong Kong.

Krishnan, D.R.P., & Shavitt, Y. (2000). Caching location problem. *IEEE/ACM Transactions Networking*, 8(5), 795–825.

Krithivasan, S., & Iyer, S. (2006). Strategies for efficient streaming in delay-tolerant multimedia applications. *Proceedings of the IEEE ISM 2006*, 419–426.

Moon, Y.-S., Lee, S.-H., Whang, K.-Y., & Song, W.-S. (2003). Dynamic buffer allocation in video-on-demand systems. *IEEE Transactions on Knowledge and Data Engineering*, 15(6), 1535–1551.

Pallis, G., & Vakali, A. (2006). Insight and perspectives for content delivery networks. *Communications of the ACM*, 49(1), 101–106.

Qian Zhang, W.Z., & Zhang, Y.-Q. (2001). Resource allocation for multimedia streaming over the Internet. *IEEE Transaction on Multimedia*, 3(3), 339–355.

Sen, J.R.S., & Towsley, D. (1999). Proxy prefix caching for multimedia streams. *IEEE Transaction on Multimedia*, 1310–1318).

Sen, S., Rexford, J., & Towsley, D. (1999). Proxy prefix caching for multimedia streams. *Proceedings of the Eighteenth Annual Joint Conference of the IEEE Computer and Communications Societies, 3*(3), 310–1319.

Shen, B., Lee, S-J., & Basu, S. (2000). Caching strategies in transcoding-enabled proxy systems for streaming media distribution networks. *IEEE Transaction on Multimedia, 6*(2), 375–386.

Sivasubramanian, S., Szymaniak, M., Pierre, G., & Steen, M. (2004). Replication for Web hosting systems. *ACM Computing Surveys, 36*(3), 291–334.

Su, G-M., & Wu, M. (2005). Efficient bandwidth resource allocation for low-delay multi-user video streaming. *IEEE Transaction for Circuits and Systems for Video Technology, 15*(9), 1124–1137.

Survey of Content Delivery Networks/. http://cgi.di.uoa.gr/~grad0377/cdnsurvey.pdf

Wu, D., Hou, Y.-T., Zhu, W., Zhang, Y.-Q., & Peha, J.-M. (2001). Streaming approach over Internet—Approaches and directions. *IEEE Transaction on Circuits and Systems for Video Technology, 11*(3), 282–300.

Xu, J., Li, B., & Lee, D.L. (2002). Placement problem for transparent data replication proxy services. *IEEE Journal on Selected Areas in Communications, 20*(7), 1383–1398.

## ADDITIONAL READING

Chen, S., Shen, B., Wee, S., & Zhang, X. (2003). Adaptive and lazy segmentation based proxy caching for streaming media delivery. *Proceedings of the ACM NOSSDAV, 3*, 21–31.

Dey, J.K., Sen, S., Kurose, J.F., Towsley, D., & Salehi, J.D. (1997). Playback restart in interactive streaming video applications. *Proceedings of the IEEE Conference on Multimedia Computing and Systems,* 458–470.

Jung, J., Lee, D., & Chon, K. (2000). Proactive Web caching with cumulative prefetching for large multimedia data. *Proceedings of World Wide Web, 33*, 645–655.

Khan, J.I., & Tao, Q. (2001). Partial prefetch for faster surfing in composite hypermedia. *Proceedings of the 3rd USENIX Symposium on Internet Technologies and Systems, 9*, 389–406.

Miao, Z., & Ortega, A. (2002). Scalable proxy caching of video under storage constraints. *IEEE Journal on Selected Areas in Communications, 7*, 1315–1327.

Rejaie, R., Handley, M.,Yu, H., & Estrin, D. (1999). Proxy caching mechanism for multimedia playback streams in the Internet. *Proceedings of the International Web Caching Workshop, 2*, 980–989.

Rejaie, R., Handely, M.,Yu, H., & Estrin, D. (2000). Multimedia proxy caching mechanism for quality adaptive streaming applications in the Internet. *Proceedings of IEEE INFOCOM, 2*, 980–989.

Wu, K., Yu, P.S., & Wolf, J. (2001). Segment-based proxy caching of multimedia streams. *Proceedings of the World Wide Web,* 8, 243–256.

## ENDNOTE

[1]    Source: http://www.cybergeography.org/

# Chapter XII
# An H.264/AVC Error Detection Algorithm Based on Syntax Analysis

**Luca Superiori**
*Vienna University of Technology, Austria*

**Olivia Nemethova**
*Vienna University of Technology, Austria*

**Markus Rupp**
*Vienna University of Technology, Austria*

## ABSTRACT

*In this chapter, we present the possibility of detecting errors in H.264/AVC encoded video streams. Standard methods usually discard the damaged received packet. Since they can still contain valid information, the localization of the corrupted information elements prevents discarding of the error-free data. The proposed error detection method exploits the set of entropy coded words as well as range and significance of the H.264/AVC information elements. The performance evaluation of the presented technique is performed for various bit error probabilities. The results are compared to the typical packet discard approach. Particular focus is given on low-rate video sequences.*

## INTRODUCTION

H.264/AVC (Advanced Video Coding) (H.264/AVC, 2005) is the recent video coding standard, defined by the ITU-T Video Coding Experts Group (VCEG) together with the ISO/IEC Moving Picture Experts Group (MPEG) as the product of a collective partnership effort known as the Joint Video Team (JVT). This standard is especially suitable for low data rate applications as it provides substantially better video quality at the same data rates compared to previous standards (MPEG-2, MPEG-4, H.263), with only a moderate increase of the complexity. Moreover, H.264/AVC has been designed to support a wide variety of applications and operate over several types of networks and systems.

Video telephony and video streaming over Internet Protocol (IP) packet networks are quite challenging applications due to their requirements on delay and data rates. A video stream is encoded and encapsulated in Real Time Protocol (RTP) packets. These packets are typically transported end-to-end within the User Datagram Protocol (UDP). Unlike the Transmission Control Protocol (TCP), UDP does not provide any retransmission control mechanisms. Nevertheless, it has been widely adopted for video streaming and video telephony, since end-to-end retransmissions would cause unacceptable delays. Thus, in such real-time applications, transmission errors cannot be completely avoided.

To allow for applications even in error-prone environments like mobile networks, apart from the improved compression performance, H.264/AVC provides several error resilience features. Therefore, the 3rd Generation Partnership Project (3GPP), standardizing the Universal Mobile Telecommunications Network (UMTS), has approved the inclusion of H.264/AVC as an optional feature in Release 6 of its mobile multimedia telephony and streaming services specifications (TS 26.234, 2005; TS 26.235, 2005).

To facilitate error detection at the receiving entity, each UDP datagram is provided with a simple 16 bits long checksum. The packets with detected errors are typically discarded (TS 26.234, 2005; Wenger, 2003), and missing parts of the video are subsequently concealed. The reason for this handling is the Variable Length Coding (VLC). The H.264/AVC standard supports a Context Adaptive VLC (CAVLC) in all its profiles. After a bit error, CAVLC may easily desynchronize, making the correct distinction between the following codewords impossible. Therefore, without any resynchronization mechanism and/or additional detection/decoding mechanism (Nemethova, Canadas & Rupp, 2005; Chen, He & Lagendijk, 2005; Weidmann & Nemethova, 2006), the decoding of such stream may result in considerable visual impairments or may become even impossible (due to the nonexisting codewords, too many or too few bits left for decoding). The detection of errors allows utilizing the correctly received parts of the packet for the decoding. Since a packet usually contains a rather large picture area, it may considerably improve the quality of reconstruction at the receiver. The structure of the bit streams (the syntax of its information elements) may also provide some means to detect errors. For H.263 codecs, the performance of a simple syntax check method was evaluated in Barni, Bartolini, and Bianco (2000). However, the structure of the H.264/AVC bitstream and the CAVLC differs considerably from the structure and coding functionalities of the H.263 bitstream.

We investigate the possibility of detecting errors in H.264/AVC encoded video stream. We propose a method for error detection exploiting the codewords, as well as range and significance of the H.264/AVC information elements. We evaluate its performance and compare it to the typical packet discarding approach. The focus of this work is given on the baseline profile (targeting video conferencing, streaming, and especially mobile applications), and thus, we work with CAVLC rather than with context adaptive binary arithmetic coding (CABAC), mainly designed for storage applications. We do not take into account error detection within the RTP/UDP/IP header. Errors within the header could also be detected by other means (e.g., UDP-lite) (IETF RFC 3828, 2004), or using the information from lower layers, depending on the underlying system.

This chapter is organized as follows. After this introduction, we will briefly introduce the architecture of the H.264/AVC codec. Afterwards, the structure of the H.264/AVC RTP bitstream is described and the individual information elements analyzed. After presenting the way in which the syntax information may be used to detect errors, the results of the performance evaluation and comparison with alternative methods are provided.

## H.264/AVC DESIGN CHARACTERISTICS

H.264/AVC defines a hybrid block-based video codec. Despite a significant increase of performance, compared to its predecessors of both the ISO and the ITU-T family, there is no single element of the coding process granting the majority of the improvement; the enhancements are rather gained using a plurality of single improved features.

Depending on the applications, H.264/AVC defines seven profiles: baseline (conversational services), main (broadcast and storage application), extended (Internet streaming), and four high profiles (broadcast for High Definition Television [HDTV]). The 3GPP specification for transparent end-to-end packet switched streaming service (TS 26.234, 2005) as well as the ITU-T specification for 3G terminals (ITU-T H.324, 1998; Lindberg, 1996) suggest the client to be compatible with the H.264/AVC baseline profile. Therefore, in the following we will refer to the set of features supported by the baseline profile.

Similarly to its precursors, the H.264/AVC encoding process is characterized by a hierarchical structure. The video sequence consists of the succession of still pictures called frames. Each frame is segmented into MacroBlocks (MBs) of 16×16 pixels. A macroblock could be further subdivided into smaller blocks up to 4×4 pixels.

H.264/AVC in baseline profile allows two frame encoding strategies: intra and inter. Intra (I) frames are encoded exploiting spatial correlation. The already encoded neighboring macroblocks can be used as a reference to predict the macroblock to be encoded. Inter predicted (P) frames exploit the temporal correlation by referencing the MBs from previous frames (motion compensation) contained in a buffer (reference list).

For I and P coding, given an MB to be encoded, the algorithm looks for its best prediction in time and space, respectively. This predicted block is then subtracted from the original one, obtaining the residual block. The residual block is transformed by means of a modified Discrete Cosine Transforma-

*Figure 1. H.264/AVC conceptual layers*

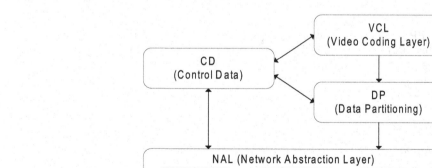

tion (DCT) (Bjontegaard & Lillevold, 2002) and quantized using a certain quantization parameter (QP), obtaining the block of quantized coefficients called levels. These levels are then zig-zag scanned and entropy encoded.

I frames are used to refresh the sequence. They enable random access and, in case of error-prone transmission channels, limit the propagation of errors in time. The set of frames from an I frame up to the P frame preceding the next I frame is defined as Group of Pictures (GOP). Intercoding requires much less associated information elements than intracoding to encode a frame. Therefore, for a given sequence, the resulting data rate depends strongly on the GOP size and on the quantization parameter.

H.264/AVC is conceptually separated into a Video Coding Layer (VCL) and a Network Abstraction Layer (NAL), as depicted in Figure 1.

The VCL is responsible for the core block-based hybrid coding functions; the NAL provides network friendliness by allowing the output bitstream to be transmitted over different transport layer protocols. The encoded video data produced by the VCL are segmented by the NAL in a stream of information units called Network Abstraction Layer Unit (NALU).

There are two types of NAL units: non-VCL and VCL NALUs. Non-VCL NALUs contain information associated to the sequence characteristics. To this category belong Sequence Parameter Set (SPS) (defining profile, resolution, and other information associated to the whole sequence) and Picture Parameter Set (PPS) (containing type of entropy coding, slice group, and quantization properties). VCL NALUs contain the data associated to the video slice; each VLC NALU refers to a non-VCL NALU, as shown in Figure 2.

The NAL is responsible for the arrangement of encoded MBs into a NALU. Given a frame to be encoded, the NAL segments the frame in groups of MBs, called video slices. The number of MBs contained in a slice depends on the proper encoding settings.

In a packet-oriented environment, each packet contains one NALU. Figure 3 shows the encapsulation hierarchy of a video slice for a transmission over IP.

Since the packets have fixed size, each NALU should fit the appropriate protocol packet payload. Therefore, the number of MBs stored in a video slice depends on frame content and on the encoding strategy. The MBs contained in a VCL NALU cannot contain references to macroblocks of the same frame but belonging to a different slice. This is intended to limit the impact of damaged or even not received packets on the quality of the decoded stream.

*Figure 2. NAL unit sequence*

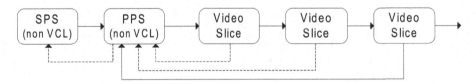

*Figure 3. NAL unit encapsulation*

| IP | UDP | RTP | NAL - Unit |
|----|-----|-----|------------|

In this chapter, we propose a syntax analysis performed on VCL NALUs, assuming that non-VCL NALUs are not transmitted within the RTP payload, but provided in the Session Description Protocol (SDP) (TS 26.234, 2005; TS 26.235, 2005).

## VCL NALU BITSTREAM STRUCTURE

This section offers a brief overview of the H.264/AVC syntax, as produced by the Joint Model (JM) reference software (JM H.264/AVC, 2005) ver. 10.2 in baseline profile and described in the standard H.264/AVC (2005).

The standard H.264/AVC (2005) defines various binarization strategies for each of the information elements. Besides Fixed Length Codes (FLC), several variable length coding strategies are used. The residuals are encoded in the baseline profile by means of CAVLC. A variable length coding reduces the entropy of the source by assigning shorter code words to the most frequent symbols. This allows on the one hand bit-rate saving, but on the other hand, it results as sensitive to the loss of synchronization at the decoder.

Figure 4 shows the structure of the considered VCL NALU payload, composed by a Slice Header (SH) and the encoded macroblocks.

The slice header contains the basic characteristics of the slice, such as the slice index, the frame index, and the macroblock prediction type. Since the information contained within the slice header determines the decoding of the contained macroblocks, an error in SH can make the entire slice undecodable.

After the slice header, the VCL-NALU contains the encoded macroblocks belonging to the slice. The VLC decoding is restarted at the beginning of each NALU since there is no resynchronization point within a NALU. The information elements associated to the macroblock are encoded depending on the prediction type (inter or intra).

Without loss of information, we decided to subdivide the entropy coding strategies into the following four groups.

- **Exp-Golomb (EG) coded code words.** The exponential Golomb code (Golomb, 1996) (or simply exp-Golomb code) is a parametric ($k$) universal code. H.264/AVC uses a special type of the exp-Golomb codes; the parameter $k$ is set to 0, also known as Elias-$\gamma$ encoding (Elias, 1975). Exp-Golomb encoded words are characterized by a regular logical structure consisting of a predetermined code

*Figure 4. Structure of a VCL NAL unit*

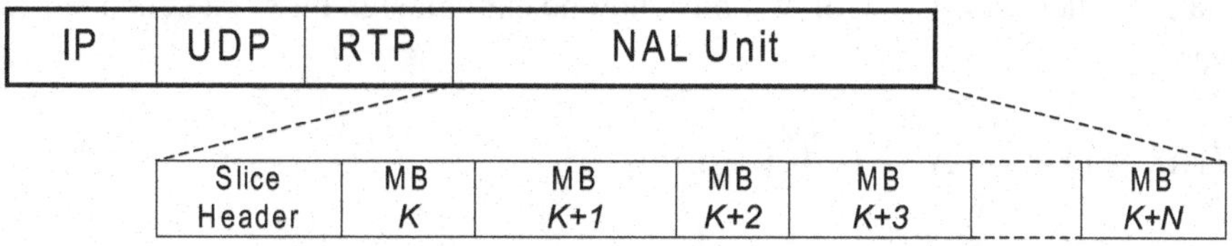

pattern without requirement of decoding tables. Each exp-Golomb code word embodies the following elements:

$$\underbrace{0_1 \ldots 0_M}_{M} 1 \underbrace{b_1 \ldots b_M}_{M}.$$

The first $M$ zeros and the middle one are regarded as a prefix, while the following $M$ bits represent the info field. In the prefix, the value of the length $M$ is unary encoded. The exp-Golomb field codeNum is obtained as

$$\text{codeNum} = 2^M + \text{info} - 1.$$

The encoded value is derived from the codeNum depending on the chosen exp-Golomb coding style (unsigned, signed, and truncated). An error affecting the leading zeros or the middle "one" affects the decoding by modifying the value of $M$, therefore causing the misinterpretation of the codeword boundaries and, consequently, the desynchronization of the decoding process. An error in the info field causes deviation of the decoded parameter value and may affect the following elements, but does not cause desynchronization directly.

- **CAVLC level (VL) codewords.** The context-adaptive variable length coding style is characteristic for encoding the levels. The levels are zig-zag ordered from the highest to the lowest frequency, and then they are encoded using a VLC-$N$ procedure, where $N$ is a parameter depending on the value of the previously encoded levels. The standard defines integer values of $N$ in the range [0,6]. The first level of each macroblock is encoded using the VLC-0; the resulting codeword has the following structure:

$$\underbrace{0_1 \ldots 0_M}_{M} 1,$$

where the parameter $M$ embodies both absolute value and sign of the level.

For increasing encoded residual values, the procedure is adapted in order to assign shorter codewords to the predicted level values. A codeword encoded with a VLC-$N$ ($N>0$) procedure has the form:

$$\underbrace{0_1 \ldots 0_M}_{M} 1 \underbrace{i_1 \ldots i_{N-1}}_{N-1} s.$$

Similarly to exp-Golomb codes, the codeword starts with a sequence of $M$ leading zeros followed by a one, an info field consisting of $N-1$ bits and one explicit sign bit $s$. The encoded value is then obtained as

$$(-1)^s \cdot ((M + 1) << (N - 1) + 1 + \text{info}),$$

where $<<$ represents the left bitwise shift operation.

The VLC-0 codewords are highly susceptible to errors since the whole information is contained in the leading zeros. For VLC-$N$, the first $M+1$ bits are critical; errors lying in the info field or sign do not cause desynchronization but affect only the decoded level. Errors in the info field may also cause the use of a false VLC procedure for the next decoded items.

- **Tabled (TE) codewords.** This category includes the VLC words to be found in a lookup table. H.264/AVC defines several VLC tables for different syntax elements (e.g., zero runs) and contexts (e.g., number of remaining zeros to be encoded). Errors may result in both deviation of the decoded value and decoding desynchronization.

## PROPOSED MECHANISM FOR ERROR HANDLING

In this section, we discuss the effects of errors during the decoding of H.264/AVC encoded data streams. The consequences of an error are twofold. We observe direct effects, since errors cause the misinterpretation of the encoded parameter value and, therefore, affect the reconstruction of the considered macroblock. At the same time, bitstreams containing VLC-encoded information are prone to desynchronization. Due to errors, the decoder segments the stream in an improper way, causing the following codewords to be misinterpreted as well. The error affecting a parameter in a given macroblock is therefore not necessarily limited to the affected MB but can propagate until the end of the slice degrading a wide frame area (spatial error propagation).

The spatial propagation is particularly critical in I frames. Even if the code associated to a certain macroblock does not contain errors, each macroblock is usually spatially predicted, referencing to the surrounding macroblocks. If one of the referencing MBs is incorrectly decoded, then the macroblock referencing to it will be flawed as well. In P frames, the spatial error propagation is caused by decoding desynchronization and by wrong motion prediction.

Besides spatial propagation, in case of errors, we also experience temporal propagation. In P frames, each macroblock is predicted by means of motion compensation from a macroblock belonging to a previous frame. If the reference picture area is distorted, the reconstructed macroblock will result in distortion as well. Such effect is called temporal error propagation. Errors in an I frame can propagate all over the GOP.

In order to limit the error propagation in time and space, we propose a syntax check mechanism capable of spotting errors during the decoding of the stream. The syntax check limits in H.263, discussed by Barni, et al. (2000), are in H.264/AVC even more evident. H.264/AVC makes extensive use of variable length coding and additionally differs from H.263 since it does not provide synchronization words between Groups of Blocks (GOB).

In the following, we will discuss our proposed error detection mechanism and its application to the encoded information elements of I and P frames as well as the slice header.

### Syntax Analysis Rules

In order to suite the structure of the JM reference software, we subdivided the macroblocks decoding process into two main blocks, as depicted in Figure 5. During the *READ* phase, the raw bitstream is read and partitioned in codewords. During the *DECODE* phase, these codewords are interpreted as Information Elements (IE) and used to reconstruct the slice.

*Figure 5. Conceptual scheme of parameter decoding*

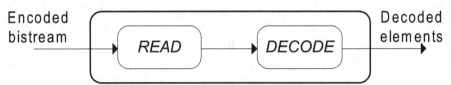

Since the length of the codewords is inferred by the bistream structure and by the expected parameter, possible desyncronizations occur during the *READ* phase.

We subdivide the possible decoding errors into three main categories, depending on their characteristics:

- **Illegal Codeword (IC):** An IC arises when the codeword does not find correspondence in the appropriate lookup table. IC occurs during the *READ* process for tabled codewords.
- **Out-of-Range (OR) Codeword:** An OR results when the decoded value lies outside the legal range. It appears during *READ* process for all types of codewords. If the decoded parameter can only take values between [-K,K], an error is produced if the absolute value of the read parameter is greater than K.
- **Contextual Error (CE):** A CE occurs when the decoded word leads the decoder to illegal actions. It arises during the *DECODE* phase for all types of encoded parameters.

The presented errors are not strictly related to current bitstream failures, but rather to the detectable anomalies, possibly caused by propagation of previously undetected errors.

The three classes of errors are detected by our decoder implementation. Our error detection mechanism cannot lead to false detections. However, it may happen that an error is detected after its true occurrence.

## Syntax Elements Analysis

After describing the encoding techniques and detectable error categories, the characteristics of the elements contained in VCL NALUs will be introduced.

The parameters encoded in I slices, P slices, and slice headers are presented as generated in the encoding trace file of the JM 10.2. Apart from the slightly different nomenclature, they correspond to the structure described in the standard H.264/AVC (2005).

For each of the considered fields, the encoding style and the possible error category are outlined. Additionally, where useful, a brief investigation of the error characteristics is provided.

*I Frames*

| Element Name | *Enc.* | **Err.** |
|---|---|---|
| mb_type | *EG* | **OR** |
| intra4x4_pred_mode | *TE* | **CE** |
| | Since the spatial prediction uses reference to the surrounding macroblocks, if they are not available, not yet decoded or belonging to another slice, a contextual error is produced. | |
| intra_chroma_pred_ mode | *EG* | **OR** |
| coded_block_pattern | *EG* | **OR** |
| mb_qp_delta | *EG* | **OR** |
| Luma(Chroma) # c & tr.1s | *TE* | **IC** |
| | The lookup table used to decode this value is not complete. The decoded codeword could not find reference to any legal value. | |
| Luma(Chroma) trailing ones sign | *EG* | |
| | The signs of the trailing ones are fixed length encoded and do not influence any of the following parameters. By means of syntax check, it is not possible to detect such errors. | |
| Luma(Chroma) lev | *VL* | **OR/CE** |
| | Decoded macroblock pixels can only take values lying in the range [0,255]. During *READ* phase, values outside the bounds are immediately associated to errors. During *DECODE* phase, the residuals are added to the predicted values and the contextual check is performed. An extended range $[-\varepsilon, 255+\varepsilon]$ is considered due to possible quantization offset. The value of $\varepsilon$ depends on the quantization parameter used. | |
| Luma(Chroma) totalrun | *TE* | **IC** |
| Luma(Chroma) run | *TE* | **IC/OR** |
| | Depending on the number of remaining zeros, a VLC lookup table is chosen. For more than six remaining zeros, a single table covering the zero run range [0,14] is used. Therefore, the decoder is exposed to out-of-range errors. | |

*P Frame*

Many of the parameters encoded in P frames are equivalent to those used to describe an I frame. In the following, only the parameters exclusive for P frames are discussed.

| mb_skip_run | *EG* | **OR/CE** |
|---|---|---|
| | The number of skipped macroblocks cannot be greater than the total number of MBs in frame minus the number of the already decoded MBs. | |
| sub_mb_type | *EG* | **OR** |
| ref_idx_l0 | *EG* | **OR/CE** |
| | The index of the reference frame cannot be greater than the actual reference buffer size. | |
| mvd_l0 | *EG* | **CE** |

*Slice Header*

| | | |
|---|---|---|
| first_mb_in_slice | *EG* | **OR** |
| pic_parameter_set_id | *EG* | **OR/CE** |
| | The VCL-NALU cannot refer to a PPS index greater than the number of available PPSs. | |
| slice_type | *EG* | **OR** |
| frame_num | *EG* | **OR** |
| | Depending on the GOP structure, an out-of-range error can be detected. | |
| pic_order_cnt_lsb | *EG* | **OR** |
| slice_qp_delta | *EG* | **OR** |

## Error Handling

In this work, we test two standard error handling strategies and compare them with our syntax check-based method. Since the focus of this work was given on the comparison of error handling strategies and detection performance rather than on the concealment results, detected errors are concealed by means of zero motion temporal error concealment. It simply replaces each corrupted macroblock in the current frame $MB_f(i, j)$ with the spatially corresponding one in the previous frame $MB_{f-1}(i, j)$.

## Straight Decoding (SD)

The straight decoding represents the plain decoding strategy where the errors are not detected and, therefore, not concealed. Since the reference software JM H.264/AVC (2005) cannot handle the error categories previously described, we modified the JM letting damaged bitstream be decoded. Each erroneous parameter value is replaced with the most similar legal one (for out-of-range and illegal codewords) or to the safest one (for contextual error).

Figure 8a shows a corrupted frame decoded using the error handling strategy SD. The different slices are separated by means of the semitransparent dark lines. An error is inserted into macroblock 32 (red square). Since no concealment routine is called, the rest of the slice is decoded using desynchronized VLC codewords, causing wide artefacts until the end of the slice.

## Slice Level Concealment (SLC)

This strategy relies on the checksum information provided by the lower layer protocols. For wireless transmission, the UDP protocol is used. The checksum information is calculated over the entire NALU and its RTP header. Each error, regardless of its position and effect on the decoding, results in the slice rejection and concealment. A block diagram of this approach is depicted in Figure 6.

The same error considered in the previous handling strategy, produces a concealed frame as shown in Figure 8b.

*Figure 6. Block scheme of the slice level concealment handling*

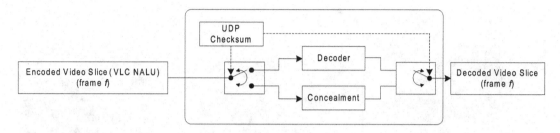

## Macroblock Level Concealment (MBLC)

Macroblock level concealment represents our proposal for an efficient error handling strategy. The first presented strategy, SD, is not aware of errors, and therefore, an error propagates spatially until the end of the slice. On the other hand, the SLC approach appears to be exceedingly coarse. As shown in the previous discussion, some errors do not influence the decoding process radically. Moreover, the slice rejection mechanism causes the discarding of the error-free macroblocks preceding the error. These macroblocks can be correctly decoded. Therefore, in contrast to the slice level concealment, our error handling mechanism is performed at macroblock level.

The proposed approach consists of the implementation of the presented error detection mechanism based on the syntax analysis. We detect errors belonging to the classes previously defined. Once one of these errors arises during the decoding, the affected macroblock and all the following (until the end of the slice) are concealed. This mechanism is depicted in Figure 7.

Figure 8 displays the result of the MBLC applied to the frame affected by an error in MB 32 as before. Using MBLC, the error is detected in macroblock 33 (green square); the macroblocks from 33 up to the end of slice MB 38 are concealed.

Further analysis shows that conceptual errors can arise also at the slice level. Due to desynchronization, the code length can be too small or too large. If the bitstream is too short to decode the whole slice, a concealment method is called for the remaining macroblocks. On the other hand, the number of decoded macroblocks can exceed the number of macroblocks originally belonging to the slice. The

*Figure 7. Block scheme of the macroblock level concealment handling*

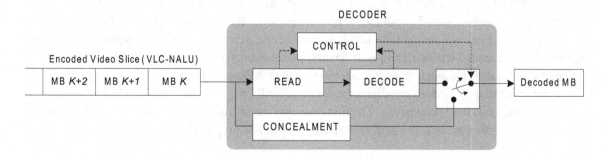

*Figure 8. Corrupted frame decoding*

(a) SD           (b) SLC           (c) MBLC

slice header contains a parameter named first_mb_in_slice, indicating the index of the first macroblock contained within the slice. Under the assumption of correctness of the slice header, if the decoded value is lower than the number of previously decoded macroblocks, the exceeding macroblocks are overwritten with the correct MB.

## PERFORMANCE ANALYSIS

To evaluate the performance of the three presented error handling methods, we performed experiments with corrupted H.264/AVC encoded video sequences.

For our simulations, we used the encoder and decoder of Joint Model H.264/AVC v.10.2 (JM H.264/AVC, 2005) adapted to our needs by introducing the following additions:

- The decoder is able to read external text files containing error patterns and modify at NAL level the bits to be corrupted.
- If a read codeword or a decoded parameter assumes an illegal value, its value is restored to the most similar legal one (SD). Additionally, two error flags, one at macroblock level and one at slice level, are forced to one (and used for error handling at macroblock level).

The sequence used for the simulations is "Foreman" in QCIF (176×144 pixels) resolution. The total length of the sequence is 400 frames, played at 30 frames per second. The sequence was encoded in baseline profile; the selected GOP size was 10. The slicing mode was chosen fixing the maximum number of bytes per slice to 700 bytes. Flexible macroblock ordering, rate control, and rate-distortion optimization were not applied. The number of reference frames for motion estimation was set to five. In order to analyze the behavior of the error handling mechanism as a function of the compression rate, the sequences were encoded with different quantization parameters; namely, 20, 22, 24, 26, 28, and 30.

For all quantization parameters, we considered various Bit Error Rates (BER) in the range from $10^{-2}$ to $10^{-7}$. We generated 75 random error patterns for each BER.

We performed two kinds of analysis. The first concerns the resulting end-to-end quality. The second investigation is performed over the detection capabilities of our proposed method.

*Figure 9. Performance of the different error handling strategies*

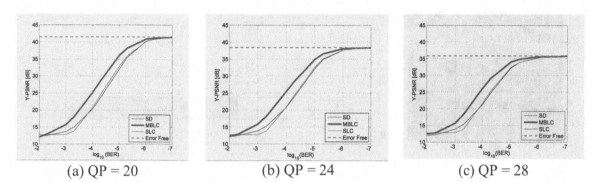

(a) QP = 20     (b) QP = 24     (c) QP = 28

## End-to-End Quality Results

We simulated transmission over a binary symmetrical channel by inserting errors in the positions indicated by the error patterns. The degraded streams were decoded using the three approaches described.

The quality was expressed as the Peak Signal-to-Noise Ratio of the luminance component (Y-PSNR). Given the luminance component $\mathbf{DY}_f$ of a degraded sequence (at frame $f$) and the luminance component $\mathbf{OY}_f$ of the original noncompressed (nondegraded) sequence, then we calculate the Mean Square Error (MSE) and Y-PSNR as

$$\text{MSE}(f) = \frac{1}{N \cdot M} \sum_{i=1}^{N} \sum_{j=1}^{M} [\mathbf{OY}_f(i,j) - \mathbf{DY}_f(i,j)]^2,$$

$$\text{Y-PSNR}(f) = 10 \cdot \log_{10} \frac{255^2}{\text{MSE}(f)}.$$

The resolution of the frame is $N \times M$, and indexes i and j address particular luminance values within the frames. For a given BER, the quality in Y-PSNR was averaged over the 400 frames and over the 75 decoded sequences.

The comparison is performed over the quality performance of the three approaches together with the error-free decoded sequence as a reference. The results of the simulations are plotted in Figure 9.

The results confirm the assumptions we made. The proposed approach clearly outperforms both classical approaches, with quality improvement up to 4dB in the middle of the considered BER range. For high BER ($10^{-2}$, $10^{-4}$), the slice rejection mechanism performs even worse than the straight decoding since statistically, one error is inserted in each slice. For decreasing BER, SLC slightly outperforms the SD.

Remaining undetected errors are not concealed and, therefore, result in artefacts. These, however, remain local if the error is detected in some successive information elements. A graphical interpretation of the results is provided in the following.

Using the proposed approach, the decoding of a slice can be described by subdividing it into three intervals, as shown in Figure 10.

The figure considers only the slice affected by the error. The characteristics of each interval are described in the following:

*Figure 10. Macroblock level concealment: The decoding*

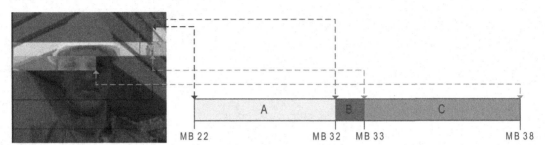

- **Interval A.** MB [22,32), the slice is correctly decoded from its beginning (MB 22) up to the error appearance (MB 32). These macroblocks were not affected by errors and are thus correctly decoded.
- **Interval B.** MB [32,33), the error (appeared in MB 32) remains undetected until MB 33. These macroblocks were decoded incorrectly and result in artefacts in the decoded frame.
- **Interval C.** MB [33,38], the macroblocks starting from MB 33, where the error was detected, until the end of the slice (MB 38) are concealed.

The efficiency of the proposed approach in comparison to SLC and SD lies in the interval [22,32] and [33,38], respectively. SD, by discarding the whole slice, does not exploit the macroblocks that were not affected by errors. This fraction of the slice can be significant. For the considered error concealment method, the improvement is even higher in the sequences with faster motion, resp. in the sequences with reduced frame rate, since in such cases the performance of error concealment decreases. The macroblocks decoded in the interval B cause errors with higher magnitude. However, assuming a small delay between error appearance and error detection, the effect of the artefacts is limited. Using the proposed method, only the macroblocks following the error detection are concealed. This clearly prevails the straight decoding, where the macroblocks in the interval C are incorrectly decoded, resulting in the wide artefact shown in Figure 11.

*Figure 11. Y-PSNR over frame number for SD, SLC, and MBLC*

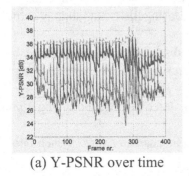

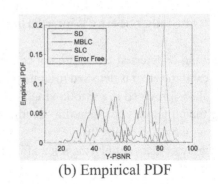

(a) Y-PSNR over time          (b) Empirical PDF

As final results, the average Y-PSNR over time (frame number) is shown in Figure 11 for the three investigated methods compared to the error-free decoded sequence. Averaging was performed over sequences encoded with QP 28 and decoded with BER of $10^{-5}$. For the same BER, Figure 11 shows the histogram of the decoded frame quality for the considered method. In both graphs, the improvement brought by the utilization of the proposed method can be observed.

The frames in the range [250,350] of the Foreman sequence are characterized by the fast camera movement. In Figure 11, we can distinguish the degradation of SLC performance in this interval.

## Detection Performance

Furthermore, we investigated the detection capabilities of the proposed method. The tests were performed choosing a quantization parameter of 28 and inserting one error per slice during the decoding.

The performance was tested separately for I and P frames. The I frames syntax presents significant differences to the P frames.

The first main difference is the size of the code associated to a frame. Considering a quantization parameter of 28 and slice dimension of 700 bytes, the majority of the P frames are contained within one NALU, whereas an I frame usually consists of more than four slices. This reflects on different effects of errors propagation and concealment, since in P frames the end of the slice usually corresponds to the end of the frame. This also explains why the SLC approach performs poorly for P frames.

Additionally, the parameters encoded in I frames are usually more sensitive to errors, improving the performance of our detection mechanism. Bit errors in P frames, the parameters of which consist mainly of motion vectors, yield less frequently to desynchronization.

For both frame types, we first calculate the detection probability. More than 60% of the errors inserted in I frame are detected; for P frames, the percentage is 47%. The following discussion will help the understanding of these values.

For the detected errors, we calculate the detection delay that is the distance expressed in number of macroblocks between the error appearance and the error detection. Figure 12 shows the histogram for I and P frames.

As expected, the range of detection distance for I frames is much smaller than the one for P frames. For I frames, we obtained excellent results. The average detection delay is 1.39MB, and more than 85% of

*Figure 12. Detected errors: Detection distance*

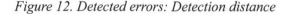

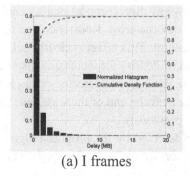

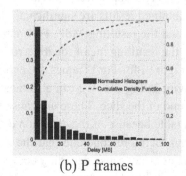

(a) I frames                           (b) P frames

*Figure 13. Undetected errors: Distance between error appearance and end of slice*

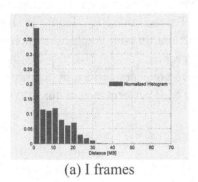

(a) I frames

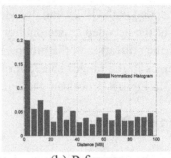

(b) P frames

the errors are detected within 2MBs. The interval B in Figure 13, where the macroblocks are incorrectly decoded, is therefore extremely narrow. For P frames, the average detection delay is bigger: 15MBs.

For the undetected errors, we performed a different analysis. We measured the distance, expressed in macroblocks, between the error appearance and the end of the slice. Besides undetectable errors, errors that cannot be detected at all by our detection approach, we assumed that missed error detections also occur if the errors arise near the end of the slice, and therefore, the decoder reaches the end of the slice before the error could be detected. Figure 13 shows the results of these measurements.

The obtained results appear to be fully compatible with our assumption. For both I and P frames, we observe peaks of the histogram for distances smaller than the average detection delays. These missed detections can be reasonably attributed to the errors arising near the end of the slice. In the remaining range, the histogram is uniformly distributed, representing the undetectable errors. For I frame, we notice decreasing occurence of undetected errors for increasing distance. This effect could be justified considering that in the simulations scenario, an I frame (99MBs) consists, on average, of five slices. Bigger I slices occur rarely; therefore, the number of occurrences of I slices decreases with increasing slice dimension (in MB), as well as the number of undetected errors.

We conclude the performance analysis by examining the effects of undetected errors. Since undetected errors result in artefacts, we observed their impact on the quality measured in terms of MSE of such missed detection. The mean square error is calculated with respect to the same frame index belonging to an error-free decoded stream. In Figure 14, we plotted the resulting MSE as a function of the distance between the error appearance and the end of the slice.

The obtained results are significant. The graphs do not show any direct proportionality between the distance and the resulting MSE. For increasing distance between the error occurrence and the end of the slice, the resulting mean square error remains roughly constant. This effect is clearly notable for P frames (Figure 14b). For I frames, we explain the decreasing MSE density for increasing distance as for the behavior in Fig 14a. We can also measure the highest MSE peaks for undetected errors appearing near the end of the slice. These are caused by errors occurring near the end of the slice and, therefore, not detectable because of the detection distance, as discussed previously.

We can therefore conclude that the errors that cannot be detected by the proposed algorithm are those that does not cause decoding desynchronization. Moreover, we can infer that they do not lead to significant quality degradation.

*Figure 14. Undetected errors: Resulting MSE*

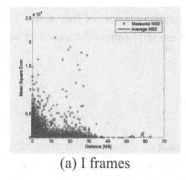

(a) I frames

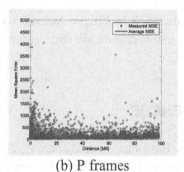

(b) P frames

## CONCLUSION

Three error handling strategies have been compared in this chapter. As first the common packet discard approach is investigated, the whole packet failing the UDP checksum is discarded, and the associated macroblocks are concealed. Afterwards, the performance of a modified H.264/AVC decoder, able to decode damaged sequences, was evaluated. Subsequently, the proposed method based on syntax analysis is presented. The localization of errors occurs during the reading and decoding of the information elements at macroblock level. Only those macroblocks that are recognized as erroneous are concealed.

The simulations showed noteworthy benefits by using the proposed macroblock level concealment strategy. Since the syntax analysis does not require much complexity, we can conclude that it is beneficial to implement it as an alternative to the widely adopted packet discard method.

## FUTURE RESEARCH DIRECTIONS

As shown in this work, the localization of transmission errors represents a promising strategy to improve the quality of damaged sequences. However, some challenging questions remain open. The precision of the localization, in terms of detection distance, still remains, for P frame, a critical point. Moreover, some of the detected syntax errors do not result in annoying impairments when decoding the damaged macroblocks by means of straight decoding. In order to overcome these limits, Superiori (2007) proposed a hybrid transmission impairments detection mechanism. Together with the information given by the syntax analysis, a further investigation is performed in the pixel domain. The artifacts remaining after the syntax analysis, in fact, possess some characteristic features that allow for designing a visual impairments detection mechanism. The frame decoded after the syntax analysis is evaluated in terms of pixelwise difference with the previous one and edginess of the macroblocks. A combined analysis of such features facilitates the localization of the artifacts in the decoded picture. Moreover, the method can be used to detect only those syntax errors that really result in visible impairment, avoiding over-concealment of consistent macroblocks.

## ACKNOWLEDGMENT

The authors thank Mobilkom Austria AG for technical and financial support of this work. The views expressed in this chapter are those of the authors and do not necessarily reflect the views of Mobilkom Austria AG.

## REFERENCES

Barni, M., Bartolini, F., & Bianco, P. (2000). On the performance of syntax-based error detection in H.263 video coding: A quantitative analysis. *Proceedings of Image and Video Communication, SPIE, 3974*, 949–956.

Bjontegaard, G., & Lillevold, K. (2002). Context-adaptive VLC (CVLC) coding of coefficients. *Proceedings of the JVT-C028 Joint Video Team Meeting*, Fairfax, Virginia.

Chen, M., He, Y., & Lagendijk, R.L. (2005). A fragile watermark error detection scheme for wireless video communications. *IEEE Transaction on Multimedia, 7*(2), 201–211.

Elias, P. (1975). Universal codeword sets and representations of the integers. *IEEE Transaction on Information Theory, 21*(2).

Golomb, S.W. (1996). Run-length encodings. *IEEE Transaction on Information Theory, 12*, 399–401.

H.264/AVC ITU-T Recommendation H.264 and ISO/IEC 11496-10 (MPEG-4). (2005). AVC: Advanced video coding for generic audiovisual services, version 3.

IETF RFC 3828. (2004). The lightweight user datagram protocol (UDP-Lite).

ITU-T Rec. H.324. (1998). Terminal for low bit-rate multimedia communication.

JM H.264/AVC Software Coordination, Joint Model Software, ver. 10.2. (2005). http://iphome.hhi.de/suehring/tml/

Lindberg, D. (1996). The H.324 multimedia communication standard. *IEEE Communication Magazine, 34*, 46–51.

Nemethova, O., Canadas, J., & Rupp, M. (2005). Improved detection for H.264 encoded video sequences over mobile networks. *Proceedings of the International Symposium on Communication Theory and Application*, Ambleside, UK.

TS 26.234 3rd Generation Partnership Project, Technical Specification Group Services and System Aspects. (2005).Transparent end-to-end packet-switched streaming service (PSS); Protocol and codecs, ver. 5.7.0. http://www.3gpp.org/

TS 26.235 3rd Generation Partnership Project, Technical Specification Group Services and System Aspects. (2005). Packet switched conversational multimedia applications; Default codecs (Release 6), ver. 6.4.0. http://www.3gpp.org/

Weidmann, C., & Nemethova, O. (2006). Improved sequential decoding of H.264 video with VLC resynchronization. *Proceedings of the IST Mobile Summit 2006*, Myconos, Greece.

Wenger, S. (2003). H.264/AVC over IP. *IEEE Transactions on Circuits and Systems for Video Technology, 13*(7), 645–656.

## ADDITIONAL READING

Corbera, J.R., Chou, P.A., & Regunathan, S.L. (2003). A generalized hypothetical reference decoder for H.264/AVC. *IEEE Transaction on Circuits and Systems for Video Technology, 13*(7), 574–587.

Cote, G., Shirani, S., & Kossentini, F. (2000). Optimal mode selection and synchronization for robust video communications over error-prone networks. *IEEE Journal on Selected Areas in Communications, 18*(6), 952–965.

Larzon, L.A., Degermark, M., Pink, S., Johnsson, L.E., & Fairhurst, G. (2004). The lightweight user datagram protocol (UDP-Lite), RFC 3828.

Nemethova, O., Forte, G.C., & Rupp, M. (2006). Robust error detection for H.264/AVC using relation based fragile watermarking. *Proceedings of the International Conference on Systems, Signals and Image Processing (IWSSIP)*, Budapest, Hungary.

Nguyen, H., & Duhamel, P. (2005). Robust source decoding of variable-length encoded video data taking into account source constraints. *IEEE Transaction on Communications, 53*(7), 1077–1084.

Postel, J. (1980). User datagram protocol, RFC 768.

Sayood, K., Out, H.H., & Demir, N. (2000). Joint source/channel coding for variable length codes. *IEEE Transaction on Communications, 48*(5), 787–794.

Stockhammer, T., & Hannuksela, M.M. (2005). H.264/AVC video for wireless transmission. *IEEE Magazine on Wireless Communications, Special Issue: Advances in Wireless Video, 12*(4), 6–13.

Superiori, L., Nemethova, O., & Rupp, M. (2007). Detection of visual impairments in the pixel domain. *Proceedings of the Picture Coding Symposium (PCS)*, Lisbon, Portugal.

Takishima, Y., Wada, M., & Murakami, H. (1994). Reversible variable length codes. *IEEE Transactions on Communications, 42*(2/3/4).

TS 26.937 3rd Generation Partnership Project, Technical Specification Group Services and System Aspects. (2003). Transparent end-to-end packet switched streaming service (PSS); Real-time transport protocol (RTP) usage model, ver. 5.0.0.

Weidmann, C., Kadlec, P., Nemethova, O., & Al-Moghrabi, A. (2004). *Combined sequential decoding and error concealment of H.264 video.* IEEE Workshop on Multimedia Signal Processing (MMSP), Siena, Italy.

Wen, J., & Villasenor, J.D. (1998). *Reversible variable length codes for efficient and robust image and video coding.* IEEE Data Compression Conference, Snowbird, Utah.

Wenger, S. (2003). H.264/AVC over IP. *IEEE transaction on circuits and systems for video technology,* *13*(7), 645–657.

Zheng, H., & Boyce, J. (2001). An improved UDP protocol for video transmission over Internet-to-Wireless networks. *IEEE Transaction on Multimedia, 3*(3) 356–365.

# Section III
# Applications for using Multimedia Transcoding

# Chapter XIII
# Wireless Collaborative Virtual Environments Applied to Language Education

**Miguel A. Garcia-Ruiz**
*University of Colima, Mexico*

**Samir A. El-Seoud**
*Princess Sumaya University for Technology, Jordan*

## ABSTRACT

*This chapter provides an overview of second language learning and an approach on how wireless collaborative virtual reality can contribute to resolving important pedagogical challenges. Second language learning provides an exceptional opportunity to employ mobility and multimedia in the context of just-in-time-learning in formal learning situations, or ubiquitous and lifelong learning in more informal settings. We hypothesize that virtual reality is a tool that can help teach languages in a collaborative manner in that it permits students to use visual, auditory, and kinesthetic stimuli to provide a more "real-life" context, based in large part on Computer-Supported Collaborative Learning. Studies are being conducted in which we assess usability, wireless multimedia technology, and collaborative learning aspects to discover how virtual reality can help students overcome language and anxiety barriers. Furthermore, we suggest carrying out longitudinal studies to determine to what extent wireless, mobile, and collaborative virtual reality can contribute to language instruction.*

## INTRODUCTION

The concept of education has greatly evolved over the last 30 years. Traditionally, the educational setting was confined to the classroom, libraries, or specific spaces set aside at home for doing homework. Technology, however, has significantly changed educational practices and has helped expand the confines of the classroom. Today, instructional settings are no longer limited to the physical structure defined by walls, and the time for learning is no longer limited to the school day or traditional times set aside for study and homework.

Wireless technologies provide information and learning opportunities for people, regardless of when or where they are physically located (Wagner, 2005). Different modalities of mobile learning such as just-in-time-learning offer dynamic, flexible learning opportunities on demand, according to the individual needs of the learner (Johnson & Johnson, 1994). Consequently, wireless network technologies, combined with information retrieval systems and multimedia applications, will soon provide an interesting option for lifelong learning. As wireless mobile devices become increasingly smaller and more powerful, they contribute to ubiquitous learning, which is one of the most common, effective, and persistent forms of learning (Holzinger, Nischelwitzer & Meisenberger, 2005).

Second or foreign language learning provides an exceptional opportunity to combine the elements of mobility and multimedia in the context of just-in-time-learning in formal learning situations, or ubiquitous and lifelong learning in more informal settings. Also, because learning and producing language depends on extensive and varied sensory input, virtual reality (VR) and future mobile delivery services represent a combination of technologies that can meet learner needs, based on sound pedagogical and technological foundations.

## TRADITIONAL MULTIMEDIA

Multimedia has been used in education almost since the introduction of personal computers in classrooms and households. This technology can be defined as the combination of media elements of video, audio, images, text, and graphics in an interactive computer interface (Mishra & Sharma, 2005). Since the early 1990s, educational multimedia programs have been distributed using CD-ROMs, and more recently, the World Wide Web has become a powerful and practical way to distribute educational multimedia content in quasi-real time to a worldwide audience. Another reason is that Web-based multimedia learning offers synchronous, or real-time (e.g., audio and video conference, instant text messaging) and asynchronous, or non-real-time (e.g., e-mail, blogs, discussion forums) collaboration between students. Regardless of whether they are located in the same classroom or in different parts of the world, persons can communicate and share media content such as images or sound files (Shirmohammadi, El Saddik, Georganas & Steinmetz, 2001).

A number of research institutions around the world have developed and tested networked collaborative virtual environments since the early 1990s (Carlsson & Hagsand, 1993; Macedonia, Zyda, Pratt & Barnham, 1994). Until recently, however, there was insufficient computer and network power or adequate codification-decodification algorithms (codecs) to carry out smooth communications and immersion of participants in CVREs. Therefore, the result until recently has been a trade-off between realism and speed, as well as limited modality interactions that have focused almost exclusively on the exchange of visual and auditory information.

## VIRTUAL REALITY ENVIRONMENT

Virtual reality (VR), a computer-based technology capable of generating a 3D space (also called virtual environment) that is multisensorial, interactive, and integrally engages its users (Vince, 2004), is today considered one of the new frontiers in Computer-Assisted Language Learning (CALL). The use of VR is indicated for language learning and practice as it simulates reality, while offering a nonthreatening and stimuli-rich environment for language students. In addition, research indicates that collaborative virtual reality environments can lower anxiety, which has been negatively correlated to language learning. The purpose of this chapter is twofold: to provide an introduction and theoretical background to 3D computer interfaces and virtual reality applications to CALL, and to describe the implementation of a Collaborative Virtual Reality Environment (CVRE) running on a wireless network.

Presently, VR technology offers students the opportunity to immerse themselves in more real-life language learning contexts. VR can be defined as a technology that creates a computer-generated graphical space, also called a virtual environment, where users can interact as they use various senses within a multimodal interface (Sherman & Craig, 2003). A virtual environment can be defined as a graphical representation of a particular context that is rich and diverse in stimuli. One of the main features of VR is that it produces an effect in participants called "immersion," where users feel as if they are actually "there" as they interact from inside the virtual environment (Burdea & Coiffet, 2003; Sherman & Craig, 2003). According to Dede, Salzman, Loftin, and Ash (1997), both immersion and multimodality in VR are important because students receive different stimuli within a virtual environment, which promotes learning according to stimuli and constructionist learning theories. Early studies of collaborative virtual reality environments (CVRE) show the potential of this technology to engage a group of students in meaningful learning tasks (Jackson, Taylor & Winn, 1999).

A collaborative (also called multi-user or distributed) virtual reality environment (CVRE) is a shared virtual environment where people can meet and communicate via chat, live, synchronous voice, and gestures; and navigate (Burdea & Coiffet, 2003; Preece, Rogers & Sharp, 2002), which is based on Computer-Mediated Communication (CMC) theories. Each person is represented in the virtual environment as an *avatar* (the "incarnation of a god" in Hindu mythology), a graphical personification that represents a person's gestures, navigates, and transmits real-time voice. The sounds and events activated in the virtual environment can also be shared.

Literature reports successful research and applications on Computer-Supported Collaborative Learning (CSCL) in the context of foreign language learning (Dlaska, 2002; Hudson & Bruckman, 2002; Zurita & Nussbaum, 2004), but very little has been done on collaborative virtual reality environments, in part because until recently, personal computers and their graphics video cards and network infrastructure were not fast, powerful, or efficient enough to support CVREs.

A number of collaborative virtual reality software applications have been developed in various research centers and commercially around the world. One of them is Distributed Interactive Virtual Environments (DIVE), an open source software for displaying virtual reality environments developed at the Swedish Institute of Computer Science (Carlsson & Hagsand, 1993). DIVE is versatile and has been used in a variety of operating systems, including IRIX, Linux, and Windows, among others. Through DIVE, users can share a virtual environment using a local area network (LAN) or the Internet. DIVE has a 3D graphical interface where a virtual environment is shown. In DIVE, users can communicate with each other either by microphone (Voice-over IP [VoIP]) and/or text messages. To ease identification, each participant is represented by an avatar, a personification, or a cartoonlike representation of the users participating in the virtual environment. It is also possible to hear almost real-life 3D (spatial) sounds in DIVE, and even the participants' voices in real time. In addition, avatars can be programmed to communicate with gestures, an important element in nonverbal communication. DIVE can work as a stand-alone program, or it can be distributed as a virtual environment over a network using a multicast protocol. It is necessary, however, to install a DIVE server and a proxy to work as the carrier of the peer-to-peer communications between the computers that share the virtual environment over the network.

DIVE has been used at the University of Colima in Mexico for various research projects related to collaborative virtual environments. For instance, a CVRE was created to show bone foot trauma to a pilot group of medical students (Cervantes Medina & Garcia Ruiz, 2004). Participants in the study communicated using their own voices over IP (VoIP) and text messages using a chat window, both of which are provided by DIVE. The results of this research showed that the CVRE helped students overcome language barriers, effectively facilitating oral and written clinical diagnosis about the bone injury simulation they had to clinically diagnose in the virtual environment.

## WIRELESS VIRTUAL REALITY

One of the purposes of the paradigm of Computer-Supported Collaborative Learning (CSCL) is to provide technological tools for students to work together to achieve an academic goal, where students may be present in the same physical learning space, collaborate synchronously or asynchronously on a local area network, or interact remotely through the Internet (McManus, 1997). There have been significant advancements in CSCL regarding student collaboration on wireless networks and the integration of mobile devices such as laptops and handheld devices into educational delivery systems.

The concept of "anytime, anywhere" learning has been expanded by handheld devices (e.g., personal digital assistants [PDAs]), which has been termed Mobile Computer Supported Collaborative Learning (mCSCL) (Zurita & Nussbaum, 2004). In mCSCL, the mobile devices can be either wireless or stand-alone, making access to educational services and content very portable. However, contrary to laptops, PDAs suffer from important limitations, including their small screen display size, limited screen resolution, and relatively limited computer power. In particular, the limited computer power of PDAs severely limits how virtual environments are displayed and minimizes actual immersion, especially if the VR application involves 3D simulations for the sciences, or when high-level spatial reasoning is involved. A solution to these visualization constraints is to represent the information through other sensory channels (Brewster, 2002). 3D graphical virtual reality environments have been successfully implemented and tested in PDAs since the early 1990s (Fitzmaurice, Zhai & Chignell, 1993) and more recently by Grimstead, Avis, and Walker (2005). The technological challenge today, however, is how to seamlessly integrate graphical, auditory, and tactile information in a virtual reality environment and distribute this multimodal information wirelessly in small mobile devices (i.e., PDAs).

In the context of virtual reality, a wireless virtual reality environment (WVRE) is a mobile application of a collaborative virtual environment using a wireless network. Since many CVEs function with peer-to-peer and client-server protocols, the core, traffic handling controls and network access, and the description database of virtual objects of the CVRE all reside in a computer server. This server can be accessed by a mobile computer such as a laptop or PDA using a wireless local area network (LAN) or wide area network (WAN), depending on the network protocols and equipment configuration. Presently, however, although much work has been done in the area of programming, protocols, and hardware, little research has been carried out regarding potential of mobile WVREs.

Because WVRE development and applications are now in the early stages of research and development, it is difficult to predict their medium and large-term pedagogical contributions. However, the developments described in this chapter confirm that it is economically and technologically feasible to set up WVREs with actual computer and network characteristics that can be used by engineering-level students to carry out CSCL satisfactorily. Creating wireless semi-immersive environments does not require investing large sums in computer hardware or software since the CVRE can be open source (i.e., DIVE) and can work with almost any recent-model laptop computer functioning on a wireless network of at least 10Mbps, thus eliminating the need for investing in cabling all the network peers.

## SECOND LANGUAGE INSTRUCTION

Second language learning potentially provides an extremely fruitful area of application for VR technology. However, despite being used in a variety of educational contexts, VR has still been used more for modeling abstractions or simulating situations that are difficult to experience in the real world (Burdea & Coiffet, 2003). Still, language learning does require certain criteria to be met; criteria that VR may be able to effectively provide. According to Edwards (2005), language learning shares important characteristics with VR in that it is the following:

- **Collaborative.** The communicative act requires the participants to be actively involved in negotiating meaning and turn-taking, among other things, as they carry out communicative functions such as agreeing, disagreeing, asking, answering, and so forth.
- **Experiential.** Language learning requires persons to have "real-life" experiences with the language in order to use and experiment with it in different contexts. Experiencing a language makes language learning more meaningful, thus contributing to motivation.
- **Situational.** Communication is realized in very specific physical (i.e., time, place, etc.) and socioemotional contexts. Because language use can differ greatly according to the specific needs of a situation, language learning implies presenting students with a variety of real-life situations.
- **Self-Directed.** Learners recognize their individual needs and motivations. Thus, language learning requires flexibility as to how individual learners receive input and an understanding of how learners processes information and produce language. Consequently, effective language learning is led by the student and supported by the instructor and materials.
- **Purposeful.** Humans communicate out of pragmatic need. The speech act is almost always accompanied by a purpose, be it to convince, ask for permission, inform, compliment, and so forth.

Virtual reality is also supported by many of the most recent language instructional methodologies, which are based on some of the following premises (Larsen-Freeman, 2000):

- Language is used within a context, and language learning often involves transferring what one knows to new contexts.
- Meaningful practice without repetition is important because meaningless repetition reduces motivation. Motivation theory states that it is important for students to feel success and low anxiety to facility learning. Novelty is motivating.
- Self-correction is a powerful tool that is nonthreatening.
- Learning is facilitated in a physically, psychologically, and socioemotionally relaxed environment.

- In an atmosphere characterized by play, the conscious attention of the learner does not focus on the grammar, vocabulary, or syntactic structure (linguistic forms), but on how to achieve the goal or objective that makes the game fun. Language learning is more effective when it is fun.
- Meaning in the target language can often be conveyed through actions.
- Students can learn through observing actions as well as by performing the actions themselves.
- Memory is activated through learner physical and affective responses.
- The imperative is a powerful linguistic device through which the teacher can direct student behavior.
- Students must develop flexibility in understanding novel combinations of target language chunks. They need to understand more than the exact sentences used in training.
- Communicative interaction encourages cooperative relationships (collaborative learning).
- Language learning is facilitated when the learner employs multiple sensory inputs.

Thus, employing VR in foreign language instruction is based on strong linguistic and methodological foundations, but more research has to be done regarding its actual application in second language instruction.

## VR APPLIED TO FOREIGN LANGUAGE INSTRUCTION

One of the first and relevant applications of VR to foreign language learning is the Zengo Sayu Project (Rose & Billinghurst, 1996) carried out at the Human Interface Technology Laboratory of the University of Washington. The main research goals of this project were to determine if desktop virtual reality significantly contributed to learning, to comparing the proposed system to other Japanese teaching methods, and to determining the positive effects on student motivation and attitude toward learning Japanese. Although results from the study were inconclusive, the authors reported that the students were able to learn with Zengo Sayu and that the virtual desktop VR application allowed students to learn at their own pace and explore the virtual environment independently, thus promoting more active participation by the students.

Zohrab (1996) developed virtual models of ancient Greek and Roman buildings to be used in a distance-education classical studies course. He used Virtus WalkThrough Pro (a freeware program) for editing virtual environments. Although the virtual models were initially distributed on diskettes between the participants of the distance education course, this researcher planned to deliver the virtual models on the Internet. Zohrab considered virtual reality as "potentially the very best method available to teach a language outside the geographical and/or historical environment where it is/was used most commonly for communication" (Zohrab, 1996). He also emphasized the importance of networked virtual reality (he called it mutual reality) for second language learning. He and his development team hypothesized that an immersive virtual reality environment (including sounds, smells, and tastes) could take students on virtual field trips, allowing them to listen to a foreign language as spoken within a contextually rich virtual village.

Virtual reality has been used to teach business Chinese to intermediate and advanced Chinese learners. De Paepe, et al. (1998) constructed a series of virtual environments to develop listening, comprehension, vocabulary, and grammar skills. The environments were specific to each lesson and included representations of cultural situations and objects, as well as Chinese ideograms and narrations. The

VR system also evaluated the progress of participants by testing them after each lesson. If students had questions, they could communicate with the teacher and other students using a chat tool provided by the system. The researchers pointed out that the guiding principles of this project were creativity and self-exploration.

Another Internet-based application of collaborative virtual reality applied to second language education was developed by Milton and Garbi (2000), who developed virtual representations of a zoo, towns, and a shopping center, for foreign language teaching of primary school students. In the virtual environments, learners collaborated in activities using avatars (graphical personifications of the students) and chat rooms to communicate. The researchers reported that the participants in the study realized activities in a "relatively naturalistic way," and their communication was unforced.

An ongoing attempt to incorporate VR into foreign language instruction is the Rapid Tactical Training System for Learning Arabic (Johnson et al., 2004) funded by the Defense Advanced Research Projects Agency (DARPA) of the United States. The objective of this project is to teach United States military personnel the communicative skills and socioemotional awareness necessary for them to establish the rapport needed to help them accomplish a variety of missions, including postwar reconstruction in Iraq. The system consists of a simulated village with a pedagogical agent that accompanies each learner through a variety of situations and corresponding speech acts. This project reported useful feedback on learner performance within a multimodal interface that provided a contextually rich setting that helped motivate and engage language learners. Participants reported confidence and interest when interacting with the virtual environment, stating that they felt like they were playing a video game.

Although most of the research projects reviewed in this chapter used high-end graphics, textures (images), and some integrated sounds, none of them reported technical configurations or encodings of multimedia elements, not even descriptions or discussions on network issues, such as multimedia transcoding or data transfers. Some of the virtual environments have been programmed in C++ and OpenGl. Although these languages are very effective for 3D graphics projection, only skilled programmers and technicians can effectively exploit their versatility. Additionally, this type of programming is not the most appropriate for virtual reality network applications, especially if there is a need for rapid prototyping. Furthermore, high-level languages such as DIVE, Java 3D, Python, and Tcl/TK better support multimedia encoding and are easier to program.

## TECHNICAL ASPECTS OF MEDIA TRANSMISSION

The implementation and application of collaborative virtual reality faces important technical challenges. Audio files; images (called textures); the description, position, and orientation of virtual graphical objects; and sometimes video streams form part of a virtual reality environment. All of this information has to be distributed in a local computer network and the Internet, preferably using a highly effective transmission rate of at least 100Mbps for LANs, according to recent router and switching hardware specifications, while maintaining network size and mobility at a minimum. Simulation latency, which is greatly affected by network latency, is very important in virtual reality environments because it affects the synchronicity of interaction that is necessary for immersion. This type of latency is perceived as delayed feedback received by the user employing the virtual environment. Burdea and Coiffet (2003) recommend a visual latency of less than 100ms in order to provide acceptable user interaction. Additionally, in CVRE, since all users can interact with and alter the virtual environment, it is necessary to quickly communicate and update participant interactions to all those participating in any given activity.

Multimodal virtual reality environment generally contains descriptions of 3D graphics, images, and text, accompanied by a sound and video stream projected onto a virtual object (Burdea & Coiffet, 2003). Literature also reports that tactile applications are also being incorporated into CVREs, employing force-feedback joysticks in virtual reality video games (Sherman & Craig, 2003). Although visual and auditory modalities will probably continue to predominate in CVREs, in the near future, other senses will be employed to convey information and provide more diverse interaction. For example, there is a growing body of knowledge that studies the design, development, and application of tactile (haptic) interfaces, including their distributed use through local area networks and the Internet (Burdea & Coiffet, 2003; Sherman & Craig, 2003). Furthermore, although the design and development of olfactory and gustatory interfaces are still in their infancy, there have been significant developments in this area. Recent developments (Dinh, Walker, Song, Kobayashi & Hodges, 1999; Nakaizumi, Yanagida, Noma & Hosaka, 2006) show that computer interfaces can effectively generate specific odors. Bodnar, Corbett, and Nekrasovski (2004) carried out a test comparing the efficiency and disruptiveness of visual, auditory, and olfactory information, delivered by a multimodal messaging notification system. Their results show that the olfactory sense was the least disruptive of the three modalities. In addition, the use of "olfactory icons" to aid information searches has been studied by Kaye (2004) and Brewster, et al. (2006). Currently, a handful of commercial applications is beginning to transmit odors over the Internet, including Trisenx (www.trisenx.com). Multimodal devices have recently been developed to simulate the texture of objects when being bitten (Iwata, Yano, Uemura & Moriya, 2004), but there are no reported developments on flavor delivery for representing meaningful information.

Haptic, olfactory, and gustatory information can be represented by numeric values and their position coordinates programmed into the virtual environment. However, the olfactory and gustatory information format is only a speculation and does not fall within the scope of this chapter. Thus, because of their relatively large file sizes, most present research concentrates on the encoding of video and sound compression, primarily because these slow the performance of virtual environments and increase virtual reality and network latency (Frecon, Smith, Steed, Stenius & Stahl, 2001). Consequently, choosing the optimal video and sound codecs is of extreme importance, as the time needed to code and decode

*Table 1. Audio encoding methods used by DIVE*

| Encoding Method | Characteristics |
| --- | --- |
| ULaw8 | 8 bits / sample, 64kbits/s |
| Linear8 | 8 bits / sample, 64kbits/s |
| Linear16 | 16 bits / sample, 128kbits/s |
| Linear24 | 16 bits / sample, 192kbits/s |
| Alaw8 | 8 bits / sample, 64kbits/s |
| GSM | 264 bits, 160 samples, 13.2kbits/s |
| Intel DVI ADPCM | 4 bits / simple, 32kbits/s |

*Figure 1. Percentages of file sizes of each sensory modality*

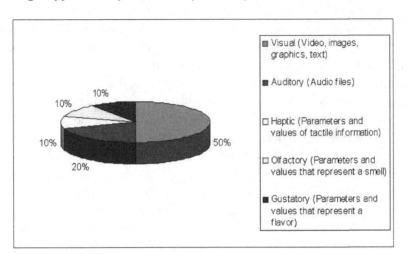

may be significant. CVRE programs like DIVE (Carlsson & Hagsand, 1993) uses the audio encoding shown in Table 1.

The audio and MPEG-like video encodings used in DIVE are described in more detail in Adler (1996) and Frecon, et al. (2001).

The Ulaw8 codec was informally tested in a DIVE CVRE with two participants, one in Murcia, Spain, and the other in Colima, Mexico. The participants shared and manipulated virtual objects together and communicated for about 10 minutes via voice over IP (VoIP) (provided by DIVE), without noticing any significant delay or voice degradation (Garcia-Ruiz & Alvarez-Cardenas, 2005). This shows that DIVE has potential for future collaborative educational applications between two distant areas.

Figure 1 describes what we consider approximate percentages of file sizes of each sensory modality, to be transmitted in a collaborative virtual environment.

Fully fledged multimodal CVREs may occupy significant bandwidth in actual LANs and WANs (100Mbs-1Gbs). However, Internet2 is a viable option for multimodal CVREs. Internet2 is a global consortium of universities, research institutions, government bodies, and companies that carries out research and development of very high-speed network connections (using an Ethernet backbone with a bandwidth in the order of tens of Gigabits) and academic applications, linking universities and research centers across the world (Fowler, 1999; Matlis, 2006).

## DEVELOPMENT

Having outlined some of the technological and educational theories and aspects of CVREs, we are currently researching whether CVREs applied to CALL on a wireless network using a multicast algorithm can be effectively used to assist students practicing foreign language listening comprehension. We believe that fully immersive VR applications using expensive equipment in traditional VR laboratories

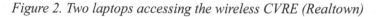

*Figure 2. Two laptops accessing the wireless CVRE (Realtown)*

can successfully be modified to meet the demands of computer laboratories and traditional classroom settings using semi-immersive virtual reality.

To test our research questions, we created a CVRE that represents a small and typical town, called Realtown, which contains an entire city of virtual buildings, including a supermarket, schools, a pharmacy, a bank, and so forth. Realtown contains background sounds and can be played through hi-fi headphones or speakers to help increase realism. Some of these sounds include traffic, children playing, sirens, and other common environmental noises. What makes Realtown interesting is that students simultaneously perceive and interpret three stimuli to help them incorporate their knowledge: visual, auditory, and kinesthetic.

Realtown runs on a DIVE server, which in this study is a Dell Poweredge 1800 computer with two 3.2GHz processors running in parallel and 2 gigabytes of RAM, using an Ubuntu Linux operating system connected to the Internet. Three 3GHz laptops with Windows XP and 512Mb of memory were wirelessly connected through a local area network (LAN) based on a Linksys wireless router model BEFW11S4 with a data transfer rate of 11Mbps and connected to the Internet. For our tests, the router was placed in the same room as the laptops at a distance of 8 meters. Interestingly, the setup used in this research operates across operating systems as the server functioned with Linux and the laptops used Windows.

Figure 2 depicts laptops employing a basic WVRE configuration running locally with a DIVE client interface. In this configuration, the laptop on the right works both as a server and as a peer (participant) of the collaborative virtual environment. Both laptops (peers) share the same virtual environment, and both peers update all the interactions and navigations made by each participant, respectively. Each participant is represented as an avatar that can be easily identified in DIVE as each avatar has a different color and the student's name or nickname written over the avatar's head. The router, or access point, shown between the laptops controls the network traffic wirelessly, thus connecting the laptops via their wireless network cards. Interestingly, preliminary results show that the Realtown CVRE can be accessed synchronously among peers working with the router's network signal. This aspect is interesting and can have particular relevance in rural settings that have no access to traditional or wireless Internet infrastructure.

Usability studies (Dumas & Redish, 1999) are currently being carried out to measure efficiency, efficacy, and user satisfaction of the Realtown CVRE, as well as to assess collaborative learning aspects related to student interaction. Additionally, the hardware needed to run the CVRE is being studied, particularly from a multicast peer-to-peer perspective where the actual setup is comprised of laptops and a server. One of the first tests conducted in this project was carried out by Hernández Díaz and Yánez García (2007).

## PRELIMINARY USABILITY STUDY TO EVALUATE NAVIGATION

A limited usability study of the CVRE has been carried out to assess navigation issues in the virtual environment. This is important because in order to have an easy-to-use virtual reality interface in a virtual town, users need to seamlessly "walk through" the virtual streets without cumbersome input devices that negatively affect navigation and create distractions. The navigation characteristics of a conventional mouse, keyboard, computer game joystick, and wireless mouse were evaluated and compared to determine which was the most appropriate for controlling navigation within a CVRE.

### Method

The Think Aloud Protocol usability method (Preece, Rogers, Sharp, Benyon, Holland & Carey, 1994) was used for this study. This usability method permits users to explore a particular computer interface and receive qualitative data about its use. In this method, the user is asked to say out loud what he or she is thinking and doing when selecting or conducting any specific activity (task) in the interface. Qualitative interview comments were recorded on paper for further analysis.

### Materials

A wireless laptop, part of the CVRE described in this chapter, was used for this study. A conventional mouse and a Genius MaxFigther F31U computer game joystick (shown in Figure 3) were also used.

### Participants

Participants in this study included four telematics engineering undergraduates, three males and one female, with an average age of 21 years. Only one male had extensive experience in playing video games, particularly in using game joysticks.

### Procedure

Each participant received an explanation about the purpose of the test, how DIVE might be applied to CVRE, and how to navigate in DIVE using a mouse, keyboard arrows, or a joystick. The main task of the participants was to navigate around a virtual house using the keyboard arrows, the mouse, and the

*Figure 3. Joystick used in the pilot usability test*

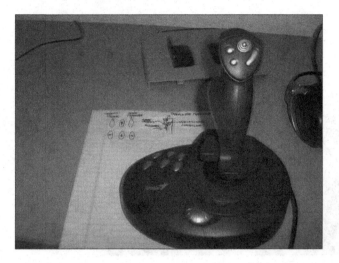

*Figure 4. A participant using the joystick for navigating in the CVRE*

joystick separately, one device at a time. Participants had unlimited time to do the tests. Figure 4 shows a participant testing the joystick in the wireless laptop. Participants' verbal comments were recorded on interview sheets.

## Results of the Preliminary Study

According to qualitative data provided by participant responses and researcher observations, the keyboard arrow keys were the easiest to use for navigating in the CVRE, and all participants felt comfortable using them. However, subjects reported they could make more precise turns with the mouse than with

*Figure 5. A participant testing the wireless mouse*

any other device. The wireless mouse showed the poorest performance. Participants commented that they tired after a few minutes because they had to hold the wireless mouse in the air, without support. The wireless mouse also proved to be overly sensible, which made the students uncomfortable when changing direction or realizing turns within Realtown. Additionally, the study participants consistently reported difficulties with the wireless mouse, and most subjects had to hold the wireless mouse using both hands. Comments about the joystick were more positive than those about the wireless mouse, but not as positive as those about the direction keys. As expected, the participant with greatest previous experience with video games and joysticks proved to be the most skillful navigator, regardless of the navigation input device used. All participants reported feeling motivated when using the CVRE, declaring they considered it much like a video game. This is particularly significant since game playing lowers anxiety, which has been negatively correlated to language learning (MacIntyre & Gardner, 1991).

## CONCLUSION

We hypothesize that virtual reality can function to teach languages in a collaborative manner in that it permits the student to use visual, auditory, and kinesthetic stimuli to place the learner nearer to the "real-life" context, also based on benefits of Computer-Supported Collaborative Learning principles, such as lowering student inhibition. Pilot usability studies are being planned in which we will assess usability and collaborative learning aspects, particularly to see how virtual reality can help them overcome language and anxiety barriers. Further, we need to carry out longitudinal studies to see whether virtual reality could cause a positive effect in students' learning.

The preliminary usability study of navigation described in this chapter served to find out that the keyboard arrows and a game joystick are usable and can be used for navigating effectively in the CVRE.

Moreover, it paves the way for more extensive usability studies about actually performing more complex cognitive tasks about the navigation in Realtown, which will be integrated into second language learning exercises.

This is work in progress done at the School of Telematics in conjunction with the University English Language Program of the University of Colima, Mexico.

## FUTURE RESEARCH DIRECTIONS

A future application to this research is to apply our Realtown virtual environment in a traditional classroom, where students will use their laptops on a local wireless network as a tool for learning a second language in regular courses. Additionally, we will conduct a usability study where students will use their laptops connected to a wireless virtual environment outside the classroom (but within the same installations) to see how Realtown is used in a mobile environment and how the wireless network responds to it. The in-class and outside-class application assessments of Realtown are necessary for ensuring ecological validity of the tests. We will carry out the network assessments by conducting usability studies and analyzing the wireless network performance, particularly analyzing packet loss, bandwidth occupancy, and wireless signal intensity, among other parameters. It is also necessary to apply various usability methods (using interface design experts as well) to triangulate the results and thus make further improvements and applications of Realtown.

Another future research is to analyze and test the WVRE under different types of access points running at different data transfer speeds (11Mbit/s, 54Mbit/s, and 540Mbit/s, according to the 802.11b, 802.11g, and 802.11n standards, respectively, and at different frequency channels (within the 2.4GHz range) to see how the wireless network behaves under different network characteristics, particularly to study how packet loss is affected.

We believe data transfer speeds will directly affect the 3D graphical and audio transmission of the WVRE, especially if the clients (the students accessing the WVRE with their laptops) are at a significant distance (more than 100 meters) from the access point. It will be interesting to see if this may cause a noticeable virtual environment lag (the delay caused when playing and refreshing the graphics and sounds of the WVRE in real time).

A future study with Realtown will be centered on the video and audio encoding algorithms that can be best used for playing video streams and sounds in the Realtown WVRE according to the wireless network characteristics, particularly its data transfer speed, since some encoding algorithms may compromise the sound and video quality and presentation speed in a WVRE, especially if the virtual environment is running over a congested wireless network.

## ACKNOWLEDGMENT

We would like to thank Miguel Hernández and Karla Yánez, students of Telematics Engineering of the University of Colima, Mexico, for their support. This chapter includes concluded work of their engineering thesis.

# REFERENCES

Adler, D. (1996). Virtual audio—Three-dimensional audio in virtual environments. *Internal Report ISRN SICS-T--96/03-SE.* Swedish Institute of Computer Science (SICS).

Bodnar, A., Corbett, R., & Nekrasovski, D. (2004). AROMA: Ambient awareness through olfaction in a messaging application. *Proceedings of the ICMI'04,* ACM.

Brewster, S.A. (2002). Overcoming the lack of screen space on mobile computers. *Personal and Ubiquitous Computing, 6*(3), 188–205.

Burdea, G., & Coiffet, P. (2003). *Virtual reality technology.* (Second edition). New York: John Wiley and Sons.

Carlsson, C., & Hagsand., D. (1993). DIVE—Multi-user virtual reality system. *Proceedings of the VRAIS '93, IEEE Virtual Reality Annual International Symposium.*

Cervantes Medina, L.A., & Garcia Ruiz, M.A. (2004). Development of a collaborative virtual reality environment for the medical diagnosis of bone trauma (in Spanish). *Proceedings of the Encuentro Internacional de Ciencias de la Computación, Taller de Computación Clínica e Informática Médica,* University of Colima, Mexico.

Dede, C., Salzman, M., Loftin, R.B., & Ash, K. (1997). *Using virtual reality technology to convey abstract scientific concepts.* Hillsdale, NJ: Lawrence Erlbaum.

De Paepe, T., et al. (1998). A virtual environment for learning Chinese. *VR in the Schools, 1*(4).

Dinh, H.Q., Walker, N., Song, C., Kobayashi, A., & Hodges, L.F. (1999). Evaluating the importance of multi-sensory input on memory and the sense of presence in virtual environments. *Proceedings of the IEEE Virtual Reality '99,* 222–228.

Dlaska, A. (2002). Sites of construction: Language learning, multimedia, and the international engineer. *Computers and Education, 39.*

Dumas, J.S., & Redish, J.C. (1999). *A practical guide to usability testing.* Exeter, England: Intellect.

Edwards, A. (2007). Unpublished manuscript.

Fitzmaurice, G.W., Zhai, S., & Chignell, M.H. (1993). Virtual reality for palmtop computers. *ACM Transactions on Information Systems, 11*(3). 197–218.

Fowler, D. (1999). The next Internet. *NetWorker, 3*(3), 20–29.

Frecon, E., Smith, G., Steed, A., Stenius, M., & Stahl, O. (2001). An overview of the COVEN platform. *Presence, 10*(1).

Garcia-Ruiz, M.A., & Alvarez-Cardenas, O. (2005). Application of virtual reality in collaborative work of small and medium enterprises. *Proceedings of the Sixth International Congress of Computer Science,* Colima, Mexico.

Grimstead, I.J., Avis, N.J., & Walker, D.W. (2005). Visualization across the pond: How a wireless PDA can collaborate with million-polygon datasets via 9,000km of cable. *Proceedings of the Tenth International Conference on 3D Web Technology*, Bangor, United Kingdom, 47–56.

Hernández Díaz, M., & Yánez García, K. (2007). *Technical aspects of the implementation of a haptic device for its use in an educational virtual environment* [unpublished telematics engineering thesis]. School of Telematics, University of Colima, Mexico.

Holzinger, A., Nischelwitzer, A., & Meisenberger, M. (2005). Lifelong-learning support by m-learning: Example scenarios. *eLearn,* 11.

Hudson, J.M., & Bruckman, A. (2002). Disinhibition in a CSCL environment. *Proceedings of Computer Support for Collaborative Learning (CSCL)*, Boulder, Colorado, 629–630.

Iwata, H., Yano, H. Uemura, T., & Moriya, T. (2004). Food simulator: A haptic interface for biting. *Proceedings of the IEEE Virtual Reality Conference* VR'04.

Jackson, R.L., Taylor, W., & Winn, W. (1999). Peer collaboration and virtual environments: A preliminary investigation of multi-participant virtual reality applied in science education. *Proceedings of the ACM 1999 Symposium on Applied Computing*, San Antonio, Texas, 121–125.

Johnson, D.W., & Johnson, R.T. (1994). Learning together. In S. Sharan (Ed.), *Handbook of cooperative learning methods*. Westport, CT: Greenwood Press.

Johnson, W.L., et al. (2004). Tactical language training system: An interim report. *Proceedings of the 7th International Conference on Intelligent Tutoring Systems*, Maceio, Brazil.

Kaye, J. (2004). Making scents: Aromatic output for HCI. *Interactions.*

Larsen-Freeman, D. (2000). *Technique and principles in language teaching*. Oxford, UK: Oxford University Press.

Macedonia, M.R., Zyda, M.J., Pratt, D.R., & Barnham, P.T. (1994). NPSNET: A network software architecture for large-scale virtual environments. *Presence; Teleoperators and Virtual Environments, 3*(4).

MacIntyre, P., & Gardner, R. (1991). Methods and results in the study of foreign language anxiety: A review of the literature. *Language Learning, 41*, 25–57.

Matlis, J. (2006). Internet2. *Computerworld.*

McManus, M.M. (1997). Computer supported collaborative learning. *SIGGROUP Bull, 18*(1), 7–9.

Mishra, S., & Sharma, R.C. (2005). *Interactive multimedia in education and training*. Hershey, PA: Idea Group.

Moody, L., & Schmidt, G. (2004). Going wireless: The emergence of wireless networks in education. *J. Comput. Small Coll, 19*(4), 151–158.

Nakaizumi, F., Yanagida, Y., Noma, H., & Hosaka, K. (2006). SpotScents: A novel method of natural scent delivery using multiple scent projectors. *Proceedings of IEEE Virtual Reality 2006*, Alexandria, Virginia.

Preece, J., Rogers, Y., & Sharp, H. (2002). *Interaction design: Beyond human computer interaction.* New York: John Wiley and Sons.

Preece, J., Rogers, Y., Sharp, H., Benyon, D., Holland, S., & Carey, T. (1994). *Human-computer interaction.* Wokingham, UK: Addison-Wesley.

Rose, H., & Billinghurst, M. (1996). Zengo sayu: An immersive educational environment for learning Japanese [technical report]. Human-Interface Technology Laboratory, University of Washington.

Sherman, W.R., & Craig, A.B. (2003). *Understanding virtual reality.* San Francisco, CA: Morgan Kauffman.

Shirmohammadi, S., El Saddik, A., Georganas, N.D., & Steinmetz, R. (2001). Web-based multimedia tools for sharing educational resources. *J. Educ. Resour. Comput, 1*(1es), 9.

Vince, J. (2004). Introduction to virtual reality. London, UK: Springer.

Wagner, D. (2005). Enabling mobile learning. *Educause Review, 40*(3), 41–52.

Zohrab, P. (1996). Virtual language and culture reality (VLCR). *VR in the Schools, 3*(4).

Zurita, G., & Nussbaum, M. (2004). Computer supported collaborative learning using wirelessly interconnected handheld computers. *Computers in Education, 42.*

Zurita, G., & Nussbaum, M. (2004). mCSCL: Mobile computer supported collaborative learning. *Computers & Education, 42*(3), 289–314.

## ADDITIONAL READING

Alena, R., Evenson, D., & Rundquist, V. (2002). Analysis and testing of mobile wireless networks. *Proceedings of the Aerospace Conference, 3.*

Amir, E., McCanne, S., & Katz, R. (1998). An active service framework and its application to real-time multimedia transcoding. *Proceedings of the ACM SIGCOMM '98 Conference on Applications, Technologies, Architectures, and Protocols for Computer Communication, SIGCOMM '98.* 178–189.

Burke, P., et al. (2005). Writing the BoK: Designing for the networked learning environment of college students. *Proceedings of the 2005 Conference on Designing for User Experience.* 135, 32.

Chi, C., & Cao, Y. (2002). Progressive proxy-based multimedia transcoding system with maximum data reuse. *Proceedings of the Tenth ACM International Conference on Multimedia, MULTIMEDIA '02.* 425–426.

Churchill, E.F., Snowdon, D.N., & Munro, A.J. (Eds.). (2001). *Collaborative virtual environments.* Heidelberg, Germany: Springer-Verlag.

Colandairaj, J., Scanlon, W., & Irwin, G. (2005). Understanding wireless networked control systems through simulation. *Computing & Control Engineering Journal, 16*(2), 26–31.

Dede, C. (2004). Enabling distributed learning communities via emerging technologies, part one. *T. H. E. Journal, 32*(2).

Dede, C. (2004). Enabling distributed learning communities via emerging technologies, part two. *T. H. E. Journal, 32*(3).

Hee L., Djoko, S., Hua J., Subramanian, S., & Basu, K. (1999). Wireless networks self engineering engine. *Proceedings of the IEEE Symposium on Application-Specific Systems and Software Engineering and Technology*, ASSET '99, 258–263.

Jacko, J., & Sears, A. (2003). *The human-computer interaction handbook*. Mahwah, NJ: Lawrence Erlbaum.

Jackson, R.L., & Fagan, E. (2000). Collaboration and learning within immersive virtual reality. *Proceedings of the Third International Conference on Collaborative Virtual Environments*, San Francisco, California.

Karnik, A., & Passerini, K. (2005). Wireless network security—A discussion from a business perspective. *Proceedings of the Wireless Telecommunications Symposium, 261–267.*

Li, H., & Chen, G. (2004). Wireless LAN network management system. *Proceedings of the Industrial Electronics, 2004 IEEE International Symposium, 1, 615–620.*

Liu, K., & Chen, H. (2005). Exploring media correlation and synchronization for navigated hypermedia documents. *Proceedings of the 13th Annual ACM International Conference on Multimedia, MULTIMEDIA '05, 61–70.*

McCarty, S. (2005). Cultural, disciplinary and temporal contexts of e-learning and English as a foreign language. *ELearn, 4*(1).

Nielsen, J. (1992). *Usability engineering*. New York: Academic Press.

Roschelle, J., Chan, T., Kinshuk, D., & Yang, S.J.H. (Eds.). (2004). *Proceedings of the 2nd IEEE International Workshop on Wireless and Mobile Technologies in Education*, JungLi, Taiwan.

Ruay-Shiung, C, Wei-Yeh, C., & Yean-Fu, W. (2003). Hybrid wireless network protocols. *IEEE Transactions on Vehicular Technology, 52*(4), 1099–1109.

Sagduyu, Y.E., & Ephremides, A. (2005). Crosslayer design for distributed MAC and network coding in wireless ad hoc networks. *Proceedings of the Symposium on Information Theory, 1863–1867.*

Sanchez-Segura, M.A. (Ed.). (2005). *Developing future interactive systems*. Hershey, PA: Idea Group Publishing.

Schwienhorst, K. (1999). Teacher autonomy in multiple-user domains: Supporting language teaching in collaborative virtual environments. *Journal of Information Technology for Teacher Education, 8*(2).

Stanney, K.M. (Ed.). (2002). *Handbook of virtual environments: Design, implementation, and applications*. Mahwah, NJ: Lawrence Erlbaum Associates.

Wagner, M., & Kellerer, W. (2004). Web services selection for distributed composition of multimedia content. *Proceedings of the 12th Annual ACM International Conference on Multimedia, MULTIMEDIA '04*, 104–107.

Winograd, D., & Dede, C. (2005). On emerging technologies that enable distributed-learning communities. *TechTrends: Linking Research & Practice to Improve Learning, 49*(1), 39–40.

Zhu, Y. (1996). Research on mobile wireless network planning. *Proceedings of the International Conference on Communication Technology Proceedings, ICCT'96*, 1, 342–346.

# Chapter XIV
# Multimedia Transcoding in Mobile and Wireless Networks:
## Secure Multimedia Transcoding for Scalable Video Streams

**Shiguo Lian**
*France Telecom R&D Beijing Center, China*

## ABSTRACT

*Secure multimedia transcoding is a challenge that operates the encrypted multimedia content directly. For example, the encrypted multimedia data's bit rate is changed directly in order to adapt a narrow channel. However, since it avoids the triple operations decryption-transcoding-re-encryption, it is suitable for the application scenarios requiring low cost operations, such as wireless or mobile multimedia communication. In this chapter, the secure transcoding scheme for scalable video coding is proposed and analyzed, together with the introduction to scalable video coding and multimedia encryption, the overview of existing secure transcoding schemes, and some open issues in this field. The chapter is expected to provide researchers or engineers valuable information on secure multimedia transcoding and communication.*

## INTRODUCTION

With the development of multimedia technology and network technology, multimedia data are used more and more widely in a human's daily life, such as mp3 sharing, video conference, video telephone, video broadcasting, video-on-demand, p2p streaming, and so forth. For multimedia, data may be in relation with privacy, profit, or copyright, and multimedia content protection becomes necessary and urgent. It permits that only the authorized users can access and read the multimedia data.

Additionally, with the development of wireless network, mobile multimedia communication becomes more and more popular in a human's daily life. Due to the diversity of mobile devices or wireless services, the transmission bandwidth is not certain in the mobile/wireless environment. Thus, it is necessary to transcode the multimedia content in order to adapt different transmission channels. Generally, multimedia transcoding is implemented by routers or mobile agents, not by the sender or receiver. It is a challenge to protect media content against routers or mobile agents since media content is often leaked out during transcoding.

Generally, multimedia content is encrypted (Qiao & Nahrstedt, 1998) and transmitted by the sender, then decrypted by the receiver. Intuitively, for media content is always in cipher form during transmission, routers or mobile agents should be decrypted, transcoded, and re-encrypted in order. However, this is not practice in mobile or wireless communication for two reasons: (1) After decryption, media content is known to routers or mobile agents; and (2) The decryption-transcoding-re-encryption operations increase the loading of the energy-constraint devices.

Alternatively, there are some solutions for progressive media streams. A progressive media stream is often composed of the substreams corresponding to different layers. For example, MPEG2 stream (MPEG2, 1994) is composed of base layer and enhancement layer, and JPEG2000 stream (ISO, 2000) is composed of various passes. Wee and Apostolopoulos (2001, 2003) proposed the scheme to encrypt a progressive stream segment by segment in which the stream's bit rate can be changed by cutting the segments directly from the end. Lian, Sun, Zhang, and Wang (2004d) proposed the scheme to encrypt JPEG2000 stream pass by pass in which the stream's bit rate can be changed by cutting some passes directly from the end.

MPEG4 SVC (Scalable Video Coding) (Li, 2001) is a standard published recently that provides a framework for constructing scalable streams. In a scalable video stream, the substreams are arranged according to spatial scalability, temporal scalability, and Peak Signal-to-Noise Ratio (PSNR) scalability. Each substream is composed of some Network Abstract Layer (NAL) units. The video stream's bit rate is changed by removing or cutting some NAL units directly. Scalable video coding provides more refined streams by introducing more scalable parameters. Secure transcoding for SVC streams is more challenging than for progressive streams because of the scalable parameters. For example, removing or cutting NAL units are not directly done from the end. They should be controlled by the scalable parameters so that the result stream can be decrypted successfully. Additionally, some means should be taken to assign NAL units subkeys, which make it easy to synchronize the decryption subkeys with the encryption subkeys.

In the following content, we introduce some related work in scalable video coding and multimedia encryption, review the existing secure transcoding schemes, propose a secure transcoding scheme for scalable video coding, analyze the scheme's performances, and present some open issues in this research field.

## SCALABLE VIDEO CODING

Scalable coding provides a unique bitstream whose syntax enables a flexible and low complexity extraction of the information so as to match the requirements of various devices and networks.

To date, several video coding methods supporting scalability have been proposed, which can be classified into four types: layered scalable coding, MPEG4 FGS, wavelet based codecs, and MPEG4 SVC.

## Layered Scalable Coding

Compared with the nonscalable video coder that generates one compressed bitstream, a scalable video coder compresses video data into multiple layers. The compressed layers are classified into two types: base layer and enhancement layer. Among them, the base layer can be independently decoded and provides coarse visual quality, while enhancement layers can only be decoded referencing to the base layer and can provide better visual quality. If all the layers are decoded, the result video will get the highest quality. Otherwise, decoding the base layer or multiple layers will get the video with degraded quality, a smaller image size, or a lower frame rate. Here, the scalabilities of quality, image sizes, or frame rates refer to signal-to-noise (SNR) ratio, special, or temporal scalability, respectively. For example, MPEG-2 or MPEG-4 (MPEG-4, 2001) provides layered scalable coding. Generally, in layered scalable coding, the enhancement layer itself is not scalable; thus, it is either entirely decoded or not decoded.

## MPEG4 FGS (Fine Granularity Scalability)

Different from layered scalable coding, MPEG4 FGS (Fine Granularity Scalability) (Li, 2001) generates a nonscalable base layer and a scalable enhancement layer. The base layer is encoded with the traditional nonscalable coder. The enhancement layer denotes the difference between the original frame and the reconstructed frame, which is encoded by bit-plane encoding of DCT coefficients. In bit rate conversion, the bitstream of the enhancement layer can be truncated into any number of bits directly. The decoder can reconstruct the video from the base layer and the truncated enhancement layer. The decoded video's quality is proportional to the number of bits decoded in the enhancement layer. Additionally, FGS is combined with temporal scalability to support both quality scalability and temporal scalability.

## Wavelet-Based Codecs

Discrete Wavelet Transform (DWT) has space-frequency decomposition properties and can be used to generate resolution scalable bitstream. The typical codecs based on DWT include Embedded Zero-tree Wavelet (EZW) (Shapiro, 1992), Set Partitioning in Hierarchical Tree (SPIHT) (Said, 1996), and JPEG2000 (Taubman, 2000; Taubman, Ordentlich, Weinberger & Seroussi, 2001). Among them, EZW and SPIHT algorithms produce the distortion-progressive bitstream based on the zero-tree's downward dependencies in multilevel DWT. The disadvantage is that the bitstream cannot be reordered after compression. Differently, JPEG2000 generates the reordered bitstream with both resolution scalability and SNR scalability. In this codec, the image is transformed with octave-band decomposition, divided into blocks, and quantized and encoded with bit-plane encoding.

## MPEG4 SVC (Scalable Video Coding)

MPEG4 SVC (Scalable Video Coding) generates the bitstream with various scalabilities, including spatial scalability, temporal scalability, and SNR scalability. Compared with MPEG4 SVC, the previous reported codecs generate only partially scalable streams. It is a scalable extension of H.264/AVC (Reichel, Hanke & Popescu, 2004a; Reichel, Wien & Schwarz, 2004b), as shown in Figure 1. In order to achieve the temporal scalability, the AVC-based approach adopts the technique of Motion Compensated Temporal Filtering (MCTF). In addition, to achieve the SNR scalability with fine granularity, the AVC-

*Figure 1. Architecture of scalable video coding based on H.264/AVC*

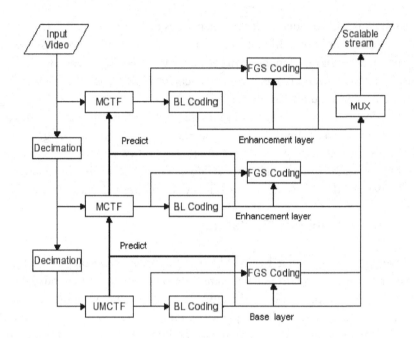

based scheme uses a context-adaptive bit-plane coding (Reichel et al., 2004b; Ridge, Bao, Karczewicz & Wang, 2005). As for the spatial scalability, the AVC-based scheme exploits the layered coding concept used in MPEG-2, H.263, and MPEG-4. In detail, to facilitate the spatial scalability, the input video is decimated into various spatial resolutions and the sequence in each spatial resolution is coded in a separated layer using AVC/H.264. Within each spatial layer, the motion compensated temporal filtering (MCTF) is employed in every group of pictures (GOPs) to provide the temporal scalability. In addition, to remove the redundancy among different spatial layers, a large degree of interlayer prediction is incorporated. The residual frames after the interlayer prediction are then transformed and successively quantized for the SNR scalability. Generally, the bitstream is packaged into Network Abstract Layer (NAL) Units, and the scalability information is stored in the Supplemental Enhancement Information (SEI) messages.

## MULTIMEDIA ENCRYPTION

### Some Multimedia Encryption Schemes

Data encryption transforms original data into unintelligible forms in order to protect the confidentiality against unauthorized customers. For multimedia data, partial encryption (Qiao & Nahrstedt, 1998) can be used to reduce the encrypted data volumes, which obtains high time efficiency. Additionally, the

*Figure 2. An example of partial encryption method*

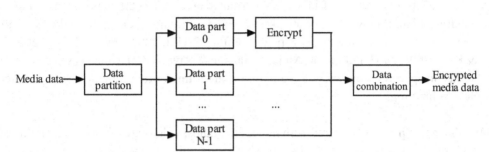

encryption algorithm keeps the file format unchanged, which can be used to synchronize the transmission process, especially in a wireless/mobile environment where transmission errors often happen. The key point of partial encryption is encrypting only the significant parameters in multimedia data while leaving other ones unchanged. Figure 2 gives an example for partial encryption in which media data are partitioned into N data parts; only the first data part is encrypted, while other parts are left unencrypted. The data part may be a block or a region of the image, a frame of the video sequence, a bit-plane of the image pixels, a parameter of the compression codec or a segment of the compressed data stream, and so forth. The encrypted data part (Data part 0) and the other data parts are then combined together to generate the encrypted media data. The significance of the encrypted data part determines the security of the encryption scheme.

For multimedia, data are often compressed before stored or transmitted; partial encryption often combines with compression codecs (Liu & Eskicioglu, 2003); that is, for different encoding codec, a different partial encryption algorithm will be designed. During the past decade, some partial encryption algorithms have been proposed, which can be classified as follows according to the type of multimedia data or the codec.

**Partial audio encryption.** Based on audio or speech codecs, some partial encryption algorithms have been proposed. For example, an algorithm based on G.729 (Servetti & Martin, 2002a, 2002b) is proposed to encrypt telephone-bandwidth speech. This algorithm partitions the bitstream into two classes:, the most perceptually relevant one and the other one. Among them, the former one is encrypted while the other one is left. It is reported that encrypting about 45% of the bitstream achieves content protection equivalent to full encryption. In another method (Sridharan, Dawson & Goldburg, 1991), only the parameters of Fast Fourier Transformation are encrypted during speech encoding, and the correct parameters are used to recover the encrypted data in decryption. For MP3 music (Gang, Akansu, Ramkumar & Xie, 2001; Servetti, Testa, Carlos & Martin, 2003), only the sensitive parameters of MP3 stream are encrypted, such as the bit allocation information, which saves much time or energy cost.

**Partial image encryption.** Some means are proposed to encrypt images partially or selectively. For raw images, only some most significant bit-planes are encrypted for secure image transmission in the mobile environment (Podesser, Schmidt & Uhl, 2002). Another image encryption algorithm (Scopigno & Belfiore, 2004) is proposed, which encrypts only the edge information in the image decomposition that produces three separate components: edge location, gray-tone or color inside the edges, and residuum "smooth" image. For JPEG images, some significant bit-planes of DCT coefficients in JBIG are encrypted (Pfarrhofer & Uhl, 2005), or only DCT blocks are permuted and DCT coefficients' signs are encrypted in JPEG encoding (Lian, Sun & Wang, 2004a). In JPEG2000 image encryption, only the significant streams in the encoded data stream are encrypted (Pommer & Uhl, 2003; Norcen & Uhl, 2003; Ando, Watanabe & Kiya, 2001, 2002; Fukuhara, Ando, Watanabe & Kiya, 2002), which is selected according to the scalability in space or frequency domain. These algorithms often remain secure in perception and efficient in computing.

**Partial video encryption.** Compared with images or audios, videos are often of higher redundancy, which are compressed in order to save the transmission bandwidth. Among the video codecs, MPEG1/2, MPEG4, and H.264/AVC are more popular. Combined with them, some video encryption algorithms have been proposed, which saves time cost by encrypting the compressed video data selectively or partially.

In MPEG1/2 codec, the signs of DCT coefficients are encrypted with the Video Encryption Algorithm (VEA) (Shi & Bhargava, 1998a), the signs of DCs and motion vectors are encrypted with a secret key (Shi & Bhargava, 1998b), the base layer is encrypted while the enhancement layer is left unencrypted (Tosun & Feng, 2001), the DCT coefficients are permuted (Tang, 1996; Lian, Wang & Sun, 2004e), or the VLC tables are modified by rearranging, random bit-flipping, or random bit-insertion (Wu & Kuo, 2000, 2001).

In MPEG4 codec, the Minimal Cost Encryption Scheme (Kim & Shin, 2005) is proposed to encrypt only the first 8 bytes in the MBs of a Video Object Plane (VOP). It is implemented and proved suitable for wireless terminals. A format-compliant configurable encryption framework (Wen, Severa, Zeng, Luttrell & Jin, 2002) is proposed for MPEG4 video encryption, which can be reconfigured for a given application scenario, including wireless multimedia communication.

In H.264/AVC codec, the intraprediction mode of each block is permuted with the control of the key (Ahn, Shim, Jeon & Choi, 2004), which makes the video data greatly degraded. Some other algorithms (Lian, Liu & Ren, 2005; Lian, Liu, Ren & Wang, 2006a) encrypts the DCT coefficients and motion vectors with sign encryption. Since these algorithms encrypt both the texture information and motion information, they often obtain high security in human perception.

## Performance Requirement

Multimedia data are often of high redundancy, large volumes, and real-time operations, and the compressed data are of a certain format. All these properties require that multimedia encryption algorithms should satisfy some requirements (Lian et al., 2006a; Furht & Kirovski, 2006).

**Security.** In multimedia encryption, the security means content security. Generally, an encryption algorithm is regarded as secure if the cost for breaking it is no smaller than the one paid for the multimedia content's authorization. For example, in broadcasting, the news may be of no value after an hour. Thus, if the attacker cannot break the encryption algorithm during an hour, then the encryption algorithm may be regarded as secure in this application. Thus, according to this case, encrypting only significant parts of multimedia data may be reasonable.

**Efficiency.** The efficiency refers to both time efficiency and energy-consumption efficiency. Since real-time transmission or access is often required by multimedia related applications, multimedia encryption algorithms should be time-efficient so they don't delay the transmission or access operations.

**Compression ratio.** Multimedia data are often compressed in order to reduce the storage space or transmission bandwidth. In this case, multimedia encryption algorithms should not change the compression ratio.

**Format compliance.** In multimedia data, format information such as file header, frame header, file tail, and so forth, will be used by the decoder to realize synchronization. Encrypting multimedia data except the format information will keep the encrypted data stream format-compliant. This property makes the encryption algorithm suitable for the application in error environment.

**Communication compliance.** In wireless or mobile environment, transmission errors such as channel error, loss, delay, or jitter often happen. The good encryption algorithms should not cause error propagation. Thus, the error conditions will also be considered when designing a wireless/mobile multimedia encryption algorithm.

**Direct operation.** If the encrypted multimedia data can be operated directly, the decryption-operation-encryption triples can be avoided, and the efficiency can also be improved. A typical example is to support direct bit rate conversion; that is, the encrypted bitstream can be cut off directly in order to adapt the channel bandwidth. This property brings convenience to the applications in wireless/mobile environment.

## EXISTING SECURE MULTIMEDIA TRANSCODING SCHEMES

To operate the encrypted multimedia data directly without decryption is challenging while being cost-efficient and very suitable for real-time applications. Especially in wireless/mobile environment, no decryption and re-encryption operations are required, which saves much cost. To date, some solutions have been proposed to realize direct transcoding, which are introduced as follows.

### Decomposition-Based Secure Transcoding

A secure transcoding scheme is proposed by Chang, Han, Li, and Smith (2004). In this scheme, the multimedia data are decomposed into multiple streams at the source, each stream is encrypted independently, and each stream is annotated with clear-text metadata. In transcoding, lower priority streams are dropped directly based on the clear-text metadata. The receiver can decrypt the remaining streams and recombine them into the transcoded output stream. The key problem in this scheme is how to decompose the media data and prioritize the data streams. In this solution, it is proposed to prioritize the data streams based on color, spatial size, or compression.

*Figure 3. Scalable encryption scheme for MPEG2 video*

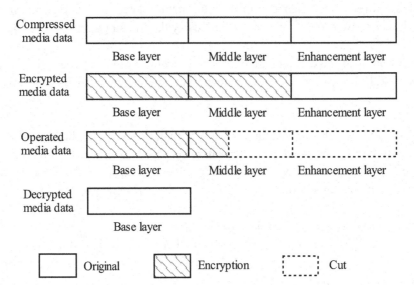

## Layered Encryption

In layered encryption schemes, the scalable data stream composed of several layers (i.e., base layer, middle layer, and enhance layer), which are encrypted layer by layer. For example, Tosun and Feng (2000, 2001) proposed the algorithm that encrypts only the base layer and middle layer in the three layers of a MPEG2 video stream, as shown in Figure 3. Yu and Yu (2003) proposed the algorithm that encrypts the pixel's bits from the most significant one to the least significant one selectively. Kunkelmann and Horn (1998) proposed the algorithms that encrypt a particular subset of important DCT coefficients in scalable MPEG2 video streams. According to the property of layered scalable coding, although the middle layer is not completely cut off, as shown in Figure 3, it cannot be decrypted, and only the base layer can be decrypted.

## MPEG4 FGS Encryption

Yuan, Zhu, Wang, Li, and Zhong (2003) and Zhu, Yuan, Wang, and Li (2005) proposed the encryption algorithms for MEPG-4 FGS that encrypt the base layer and also the sign bits of DCT coefficients in the enhancement layer to enable full scalability for the encrypted video. As shown in Figure 4, different from layered encryption, if the encrypted enhancement layer is partially cut off, the remaining part of the enhancement layer can still be decrypted.

## Multimedia Encryption in Wavelet Domain

Due to wavelet transform's property of scalability, wavelet-based codecs often generate progressive data streams. For this kind of stream, some encryption schemes have been proposed. Wee et al. (Wee &

*Figure 4. Scalable encryption scheme for MPEG4 FGS video*

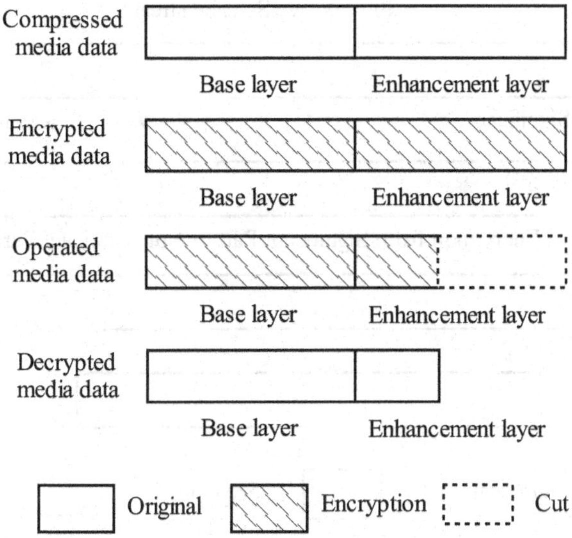

Apostolopoulos, 2001, 2003) proposed the algorithms for secure scalable streaming enabling transcoding without decryption. Lian, Sun, and Wang (2004c) proposed the encryption algorithms for SPIHT and EZW streams, which encrypt the coefficients' signs and permute the coefficient block. Grosbois, Gerbelot, and Ebrahimi (2001) proposed the encryption algorithm for JPEG2000 images, which encrypts the encoded data stream selectively. Lian, Sun, and Wang (2004b) proposed the JPEG2000 image encryption scheme that encrypts the coefficient sign, code pass, and bit-plane in a selective manner. In these algorithms, as shown in Figure 5, the scalable stream is encrypted from the most significant one to the least significant one. To change the bit-rate, some bits at the end of the stream are directly cut off, and the remained bitstream can be decrypted completely.

## THE PROPOSED SECURE MULTIMEDIA TRANSCODING SCHEME

Scalable Video Coding (SVC) provides more refined streams by introducing more scalable parameters. Secure transcoding for SVC streams is more challenging than for partially scalable streams because of the scalable parameters. For example, removing or cutting NAL units are not directly done from the end. They should be controlled by the scalable parameters in order to make the result stream successfully decrypted. Additionally, some means should be taken to assign NAL units subkeys, which synchronize the decryption subkeys with the remained NAL units. To date, there are few encryption schemes for MPEG4 SVC. A straightforward method is to encrypt the video stream NAL unit by NAL unit, as shown in Figure 6. Here, two conditions are satisfied: the NAL is encrypted by a stream cipher, and the NALs are encrypted with the same key. In bit-rate conversion, the encrypted NALs are directly skipped or cut, which does not affect the correct decryption of the remained NALs. Thus, this scheme supports direct bit-rate conversion.

*Figure 5. Scalable video encryption for progressive or scalable stream*

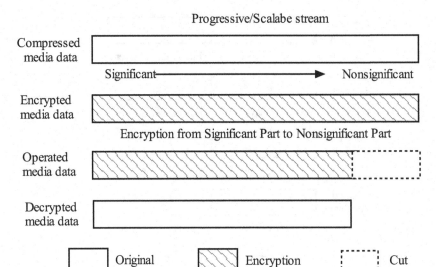

*Figure 6. NAL-based encryption scheme*

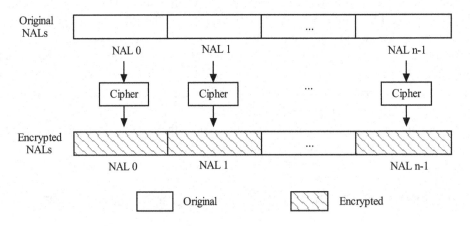

However, there are some disadvantages in this scheme. First, the NALs are encrypted completely, which makes it difficult to get the synchronization information because of changing the file format. Second, using a stream cipher to encrypt NALs cannot confirm the security compared with using a block cipher. Third, it is possible to improve the security by encrypting the NALs with different keys. To avoid these disadvantages, a novel encryption scheme is proposed as follows.

## Architecture of the Scalable Encryption Scheme

The scalable encryption scheme adopts partial encryption means to support a different security level, as shown in Figure 7(a). In scalable video coding, the data stream is composed of various data layers partitioned according to spatial, temporal, or SNR property. According to the significance, the data layers can be ordered according to the method shown in Figure 7(b). Here, only two layers in spatial domain, two layers in temporal domain, and two layers in SNR domain are considered. The data layer's ordering information is stored in the SEI. In this scheme, the security level determines the data layers to be encrypted by layer computing. For example, there are N data layers, and the security level is S ($0 \leq S \leq 100$); then, the number of data layers to be encrypted, L($0 \leq L \leq N$), is computed as:

$$L = \left\lceil \frac{S}{100} \right\rceil \cdot N .$$

In this case, the L lowest data layers are encrypted, and the left N-L layers remain unchanged.

## Base Layer Encryption

In MPEG4 SVC, the base layer is encoded with H.264/AVC. The produced data stream is composed of various parameters; that is, synchronization information (sequence-, picture-, slice-syntax), intramac-

*Figure 7. Architecture of the scalable encryption scheme*

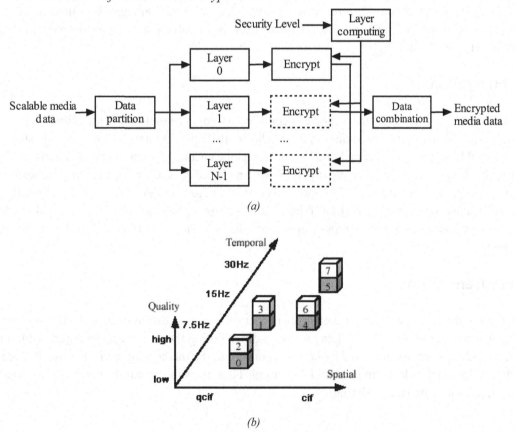

(a)

(b)

*Figure 8. Method of base layer encryption*

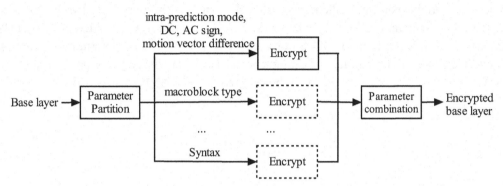

roblock information (macroblock type, coded block pattern, intraprediction mode, and residue data), and intermacroblock information (macroblock type, coded block pattern, interprediction mode, motion vector difference, and residue data). To keep format compliant and time efficient, only some significant parameters in intramacroblock and intermacroblock are encrypted. In the proposed scheme shown in Figure 8, the intraprediction mode, DC coefficient of intramacroblock, AC coefficients' signs of intramacroblock, and motion vector difference are encrypted, and other parameters kept unchanged. Here, the intraprediction mode and DC coefficient can be encrypted with the method proposed in Lian et al., 2005; Lian et al., 2006a).

## FGS Encryption

In MPEG4 SVC, the enhancement layers are encoded with Coarse Granularity Scalability (CGS) or FGS encoding (Li, 2001). In these encoding methods, the coefficients are quantized by variable steps, and the quantized bit-planes are encoded one by one. Bit-plane encoding often generates the data streams with variable length; it is difficult to encrypt them with a block cipher. Considering that the coefficients' number is fixed, only the signs of the quantized coefficients are encrypted. For example, only the first eight coefficients' signs in each 4×4 DCT block are encrypted, as shown in Figure 9. Taking 16×16 Luma intramacroblock, for example, there are in total 16 DCT blocks, and thus, a total of 8×16 bits are encrypted.

## Subkey Generation

In the proposed scheme, a different data layer is encrypted with a different subkey. The subkeys are generated according to the order of data layer encoding. Taking the data layers in Figure 7(b), for example, the subkeys are assigned to data layers according to the method shown in Figure 10. Here, for the i-th (i=0,1,…,7) data layer, the i-th subkey is used. Thus, the subkeys can be computed in a manner synchronized with data layer ordering.

*Figure 9. Method of enhancement layer encryption*

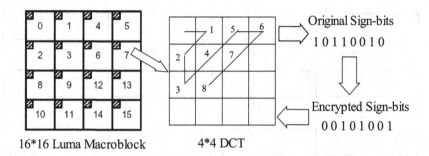

16*16 Luma Macroblock          4*4 DCT

*Figure 10. Method of subkey generation*

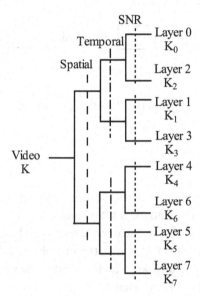

## Decryption of Transcoded Media Data

The encrypted media data's bit rate can be converted by directly skipping or cutting some data layers. For example, in bit-rate conversion shown in Figure 11, the layers ranging from 2 to n-1 are skipped, and part of Layer 1 is directly cut. Then, Layer 0 and the rest of Layer 1 can be decrypted with the suitable subkeys.

## PERFORMANCE EVALUATION

In the proposed scheme, only some sensitive parameters are encrypted, which keep format compliant. Additionally, the parameter encryption operations keep compression ratio unchanged. The security of

*Figure 11. An example of data decryption after bit rate conversion*

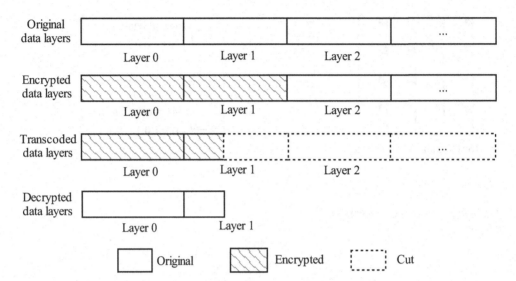

the scheme, which is the most important property, depends on two aspects: cryptographic security and perceptual security.

## Cryptographic Security

Cryptographic security refers to the system's security against cryptographic attack, such as brute-force attack, linear attack, differential attack, statistical attack, and so forth. Generally, it depends on the adopted ciphers. In the proposed cipher, the selected parameters can be encrypted by either such block cipher as DES, IDEA, AES (Richard, 2006), or some stream ciphers. Taking AES, for example, it can resist most of the existing cryptographic attacks, which confirms the multimedia encryption scheme's security. In the following experiments, AES is used.

## Perceptual Security

Perceptual security refers to the intelligibility of the encrypted multimedia content. Generally, the more confused the encrypted multimedia content, the higher the encryption scheme's perceptual security. In the proposed scheme, the base layer prefers to be encrypted, which determines the decoding of enhancement layers. Taking two levels of spatial scalability (CIF/QCIF), three levels of temporal scalability (30, 15, and 7.5 fps), and two levels of SNR scalability (Low-High quality), for example, the perceptual security is tested. First, only the lowest layer (7.5fps-QCIF-low quality) is encrypted; the result is shown in Figure 12. Second, according to the security level, a different number of lowest layers are encrypted, whose quality with Peak Signal-to-Noise Ratio (PSNR) metric is shown in Figure 13. As can be seen, even if encrypting only the lowest layer, the video content is not at all intelligible. Additionally, the encrypted video's quality decreases with the increase of the encrypted layers. Thus, the proposed scheme keeps high perceptual security.

*Figure 12. Result of video encryption*

(a) original          (b) encrypted

## Direct Bit Rate Conversion

In the experiment, the four lowest layers are encrypted. Then, only the lowest two layers are left, and the other layers are cut; finally, the remaining video data are decrypted. The result is shown in Figure 14. As can be seen, after direct bit-rate conversion, the video content can be correctly decrypted.

## Efficiency

The encryption scheme's efficiency is tested by computing the time ratio between encryption/decryption and compression/decompression. As shown in Table 1, the time ratio R is defined as:

$$R = \frac{R_e + R_d}{2}.$$

Here, $R_e$ denotes the time ratio between encryption and compression, and $R_d$ denotes the time ratio between decryption and decompression. In this experiment, the relation between the number of the en-

*Figure 13. Relation between the encrypted layers and perceptual security*

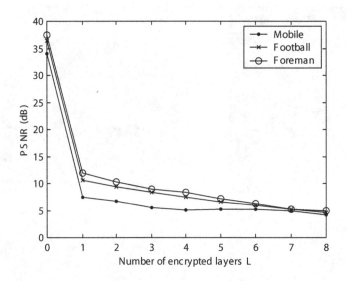

*Figure 14. Video decryption after direct bit-rate conversion*

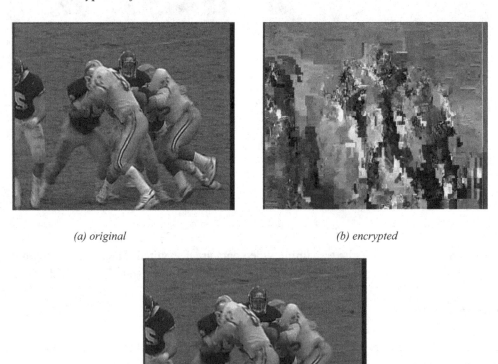

*(a) original*              *(b) encrypted*

*(c) decrypted (after bit rate conversion)*

*Table 1. Time efficiency of the proposed encryption scheme*

| Video | Size | Time ratio R | | | |
|---|---|---|---|---|---|
| | | L=1 | L=2 | L=3 | L=8 |
| Foreman | QCIF | 0.6% | 1.9% | 2.3% | 7.2% |
| Akiyo | QCIF | 0.8% | 1.7% | 2.4% | 6.9% |
| Mother | QCIF | 0.5% | 1.2% | 2.7% | 6.3% |
| Silent | QCIF | 0.7% | 1.6% | 2.2% | 7.8% |
| News | QCIF | 0.6% | 1.1% | 2.8% | 5.7% |
| Salesman | QCIF | 0.4% | 0.9% | 1.7% | 8.0% |
| Mobile | CIF | 0.8% | 1.5% | 2.0% | 9.2% |
| Football | CIF | 1.0% | 1.6% | 3.1% | 9.8% |
| Akiyo | CIF | 0.6% | 0.9% | 1.7% | 9.1% |
| Stephan | CIF | 1.0% | 1.5% | 3.3% | 10.3% |
| Tempete | CIF | 1.0% | 1.4% | 3.0% | 8.4% |
| Foreman | CIF | 0.7% | 1.2% | 2.6% | 7.3% |

crypted layers L and the time ratio R is tested. Seen from the result, the time ratio is generally no bigger than 15%, which keeps the scheme of high time-efficient and suitable for real-time applications.

## CONCLUSION

In this chapter, a secure multimedia transcoding scheme for scalable video coding is presented and analyzed. The proposed scheme satisfies most of the performances required by multimedia encryption, such as security, efficiency, format compliance, compression ratio, direct bit-rate conversion, and so forth. Besides the proposed scheme, some fundamental works related to scalable video coding and multimedia encryption are introduced, the existing encryption schemes supporting multimedia transcoding are reviewed, and some open issues in this research field are presented. The information may provide valuable help to researchers or engineers in secure multimedia transcoding.

## FUTURE RESEARCH DIRECTIONS

The proposed scheme obtains good properties in some aspects, including format compliance, compression ratio, security, efficiency, and direct bit-rate conversion. However, there are still some open issues in scalable video encryption. Additionally, there are some potential research topics.

First, for multimedia encryption, the security against the special attack (Lian et al., 2006a; Said, 2005) that improves multimedia quality by signal processing methods needs to be investigated. In this kind of attack that was recently reported, the unencrypted media content is used to predict the encrypted content. According to this case, most of the existing encryption schemes are expected to be re-evaluated.

Second, subkey generation process needs to be investigated. For scalable video encryption, subkey generation is difficult. In the proposed scheme, the subkeys need to be computed according to the data layer's significance or bit-rate conversion operation. It is expected to generate the subkeys in a random manner while keeping the operated multimedia content recoverable.

Third, in some scenarios, encrypting only enhancement layers is permitted. For example, in secure video preview (Lian, Liu, Ren & Wang, 2007b), the video content is slightly degraded by encrypting the least significant parts, and can be recovered by authorized customers who pay for it. It is expected to design such schemes based on scalable video coding.

Fourth, combining encryption and watermarking for Digital Rights Management (DRM) is now a hot topic (Lian, Liu, Ren & Wang, 2006b; Lian, Liu, Ren & Wang, 2007a). Watermarking technique (Moulin & Koetter, 2005) is often used to verify the ownership of multimedia data. In scalable video coding, the base layer and enhancement layers provide the space for both encryption and watermarking, which protect both multimedia content's confidentiality and copyright.

## REFERENCES

Ahn, J., Shim, H., Jeon, B., & Choi, I. (2004). Digital video scrambling method using intra prediction mode. *PCM2004, Springer, LNCS, 3333*, 386–393.

Ando, K., Watanabe, O., & Kiya, H. (2001). Partial-scrambling of still images based on JPEG2000. *Proceeding of the International Conference on Information, Communications, and Signal Processing*, Singapore.

Ando, K., Watanabe, O., & Kiya, H. (2002). Partial-scrambling of images encoded by JPEG2000. *IEICE Trans., J85-D-11*(2), 282–290.

Chang, Y., Han, R., Li, C., & Smith, J.R. (2004). Secure transcoding of Internet content. *Proceedings of the International Workshop on Intelligent Multimedia Computing and Networking (IMMCN)*, 940–943.

Fukuhara, T., Ando, K., Watanabe, O., & Kiya, H. (2002). Partial-scrambling of JPEG2000 images for security applications. ISO/IEC JTC 1/SC29/WG1, N2439.

Furht, B., & Kirovski, D. (2006). *Multimedia encryption and authentication techniques and applications*. Boca Raton, FL: Auerbach Publications.

Gang, L., Akansu, A.N., Ramkumar, M., & Xie, X. (2001). Online music protection and MP3 compression. *Proceedings of the International Symposium on Intelligent Multimedia, Video and Speech Processing*, 13–16.

Grosbois, R., Gerbelot, P., & Ebrahimi, T. (2001). Authentication and access control in the JPEG 2000 compressed domain. *Proceedings of the SPIE 46th Annual Meeting, Applications of Digital Image Processing XXIV*, San Diego.

ISO/IECFCD15444-1. (2000). Information technology—JPEG2000 image coding system—Part 1: Core coding system.

Kim, G., & Shin, D. (2005). Intellectual property management on MPEG-4 video for hand-held device and mobile video streaming service. *IEEE Transactions on Consumer Electronics, 51*(1), 139–143.

Kunkelmann, T., & Horn, U. (1998). Partial video encryption based on scalable coding. *Proceedings of the 5th International Workshop on Systems, Signals and Image Processing (IWSSIP' 98).*

Li, W. (2001). Overview of fine granularity scalability in MPEG-4 video standard. *IEEE Transactions on Circuits and Systems for Video Technology, 11*(3), 301–317.

Lian, S., Liu, Z., & Ren, Z. (2005). Selective video encryption based on advanced video coding. *Proceedings of the 2005 Pacific-Rim Conference on Multimedia (PCM2005), Part II, LNCS 3768,* 281–290.

Lian, S., Liu, Z., Ren, Z., & Wang, H. (2006a). Secure advanced video coding based on selective encryption algorithms. *IEEE Transactions on Consumer Electronics, 52*(2), 621–629.

Lian, S., Liu, Z., Ren, Z., & Wang, H. (2006b). Commutative watermarking and encryption for media data. *International Journal of Optical Engineering, 45*(8), 0805101-0805103.

Lian, S., Liu, Z., Ren, Z., & Wang, H. (2007a). Commutative encryption and watermarking in compressed video data. *IEEE Circuits and Systems for Video Technology, 17*(6), 774–778.

Lian, S., Liu, Z., Ren, Z., & Wang, Z. (2007b). Multimedia data encryption in block based codecs. *International Journal of Computers and Applications, 29*(1).

Lian, S., Sun, J., & Wang, Z. (2004a). A novel image encryption scheme based on JPEG encoding. *Proceedings of the International Conference on Information Visualization (IV 2004),* 217–220.

Lian, S., Sun, J., & Wang, Z. (2004b). Perceptual cryptography on JPEG2000 compressed images or videos. *Proceedings of the International Conference on Computer and Information Technology (CIT2004),* Wuhan, China, 78–83.

Lian, S., Sun, J., & Wang, Z. (2004c). Perceptual cryptography on SPIHT compressed images or videos. *Proceedings of the IEEE International Conference on Multimedia and Expro (I) (ICME2004),* Taiwan, 3, 2195–2198.

Lian, S., Sun, J., Zhang, D., & Wang, Z. (2004d). A selective image encryption scheme based on JPEG2000 codec. Proceedings of the Pacific-Rim Conference on Multimedia (PCM2004), 3332, 65–72.

Lian, S., Wang, Z., & Sun, J. (2004e). A fast video encryption scheme suitable for network applications. *Proceedings of the International Conference on Communications, Circuits and Systems,* 1, 566–570.

Liu X., & Eskicioglu, A.M. (2003). Selective encryption of multimedia content in distribution networks: Challenges and new directions. *Proceedings of the IASTED International Conference on Communications, Internet and Information Technology (CIIT 2003),* Scottsdale, Arizona.

Moulin, P., & Koetter, R. (2005). Data-hiding codes. *IEEE Proceedings, 93*(12), 2083–2126.

MPEG2 ISO/IEC IS 13818 (1994).

MPEG-4 Video Verification Model version 18.0, ISO/IEC JTC1/SC29/WG11 N3908, Pisa, (2001).

Norcen, R., & Uhl, A. (2003). Selective encryption of the JPEG2000 bitstream. IFIP International Federation for Information Processing, LNCS 2828, 194–204.

Pfarrhofer, R., & Uhl, A. (2005). Selective image encryption using JBIG.IFIP TC-6 TC-11. *Proceedings of the International Conference on Communications and Multimedia Security (CMS 2005)*, Salzburg, 98–107.

Podesser, M., Schmidt, H.-P., & Uhl, A. (2002). Selective bitplane encryption for secure transmission of image data in mobile environments. *Proceedings of the 5th IEEE Nordic Signal Processing Symposium (NORSIG 2002)*.

Pommer, A., & Uhl, A. (2003). Selective encryption of wavelet-packet encoded image data: Efficiency and security. *Communications and Multimedia Security*, 194–204.

Qiao, L., & Nahrstedt, K. (1998). Comparison of MPEG encryption algorithm. *International Journal on Computers and Graphics, 22*(4), 437–448.

Reichel, J., Hanke, K., & Popescu, B. (2004a). Scalable Video model V1.0. ISO/IEC JTC1/SC29/WG11, N6372.

Reichel, J., Wien, M., & Schwarz, H. (2004b). Scalable video model 3. ISO/IEC JTC1/SC29/WG11, N6716.

Richard, A. (2006). *Mollin. An introduction to cryptography*. CRC Press.

Ridge, J., Bao, Y., Karczewicz, M., & Wang, X. (2005). Cyclical block coding for FGS. ISO/IEC JTC1/SC29/WG11, M11509.

Said, A. (1996). A new fast and efficient image codec based on set partitioning in hierarchical trees. *IEEE Transactions on Circuits and Systems for Video Technology, 6*, 243–250.

Said, A. (2005). Measuring the strength of partial encryption schemes. *Proceedings of the IEEE International Conference on Image Processing (ICIP 2005)*, 2, 1126–1129.

Scopigno, R.M., & Belfiore, S. (2004). Image decomposition for selective encryption and flexible network services. IEEE Globecom 2004, Dallas.

Servetti, A., & Martin, J.C. (2002a). Perception-based partial encryption of compressed speech. *IEEE Transactions on Speech and Audio Processing, 10*(8), 637–643.

Servetti, A., & Martin, J.C. (2002b). Perception-based selective encryption of G. 729 speech. *Proceedings of the IEEE ICASSP*. Orlando, Florida, 1, 621–624.

Servetti, A., Testa, C., Carlos, J., & Martin, D. (2003). *Frequency-selective partial encryption of compressed audio*. Paper presented at the International Conference on Audio, Speech and Signal Processing, Hong Kong.

Shapiro, J.M. (1992). Embedded image coding using zerotrees of wavelet coefficients. *IEEE Transactions on Signal Processing, 41*, 657–660.

Shi, C., & Bhargava, B. (1998a). A fast MPEG video encryption algorithm. *Proceedings of the 6th ACM International Multimedia Conference*, Bristol, UK, 81–88.

Shi, C., & Bhargava, B. (1998b). An efficient MPEG video encryption algorithm. *Proceedings of the 6th ACM International Multimedia Conference*. Bristol, UK, 381–386.

Sridharan, S., Dawson, E., & Goldburg, B. (1991). Fast Fourier transform based speech encryption system. *IEE Proceedings of Communications, Speech and Vision, 138*(3), 215–223.

Tang, L. (1996). Methods for encrypting and decrypting MPEG video data efficiently. *Proceedings of the Fourth ACM International Multimedia Conference (ACM Multimedia'96).* Boston, Massachusetts, 219–230.

Taubman, D. (2000). High performance scalable image compression with EBCOT. *IEEE Transactions on Image Processing, 9,* 1158–1170.

Taubman, D., Ordentlich, E., Weinberger, M., & Seroussi, G. (2001). Embedded block coding in JPEG2000. Hewlett-Packard Company Publication.

Tosun, A.S., & Feng, W.-C. (2000). Efficient multi-layer coding and encryption of MPEG video streams. *Proceedings of the IEEE International Conference on Multimedia and Expo., 1,* 119–122.

Tosun, A.S., & Feng, W.C. (2001). Lightweight security mechanisms for wireless video transmission. *Proceedings of the International Conference on Information Technology: Coding and Computing,* Las Vegas, Nevada, 157–161.

Wee, S.J., & Apostolopoulos, J.G. (2001). Secure scalable video streaming for wireless networks. *Proceedings of the IEEE International Conference on Acoustics, Speech, and Signal Processing.* Salt Lake City, Utah, 4, 2049–2052.

Wee, S.J., & Apostolopoulos, J.G. (2003). Secure scalable streaming and secure transcoding with JPEG-2000. *IEEE Int. Image Processing, 1,* I-205–208.

Wen, J.T., Severa, M., Zeng, W.J., Luttrell, M., & Jin, W. (2002). A format-compliant configurable encryption framework for access control of video. *IEEE Transactions on Circuits and Systems for Video Technology, 12*(6), 545–557.

Wu, C., & Kuo, C.C. (2000). Fast encryption methods for audiovisual data confidentiality. *Proceedings of the SPIE International Symposia on Information Technologies 2000,* Boston, Massachusetts, 4209, 284–295.

Wu, C., & Kuo, C.C. (2001). Efficient multimedia encryption via entropy codec design. *Proceedings of the SPIE International Symposium on Electronic Imaging 2001,* San Jose, California, 4314, 128–138.

Yu, H.H., & Yu, X.L. (2003). Progressive and scalable encryption for multimedia content access control. *Proceedings of the IEEE International Conference on Communications, 1,* 547–551.

Yuan, C., Zhu, B., Wang, Y., Li, S., & Zhong, Y. (2003). Efficient and fully scalable encryption for MPEG-4 FGS. *Proceedings of the IEEE International Symposium on Circuits and Systems.*

Zhu, B., Yuan, C., Wang, Y., & Li, S. (2005). Scalable protection for MPEG-4 fine granularity scalability. *IEEE Trans Multimedia, 7*(2), 222–233.

## ADDITIONAL READING

Aggelos, K., & Moti, Y. (2003). Breaking and repairing asymmetric public-key traitor tracing. ACM Digital Rights Management. Berlin: Springer-Verlag, 32–50.

Agi, I., & Gong, L. (1996). An empirical study of MPEG video transmissions. *Proceedings of the Internet Society Symposium on Network and Distributed System Security*. San Diego, California, 137–144.

Anderson, R., & Manifavas, C. (1997). Chameleon—A new kind of stream cipher. Lecture Notes in Computer Science, Fast Software Encryption, Springer-Verlag, 107–113.

Bloom, J. (2003). Security and rights management in digital cinema. *Proceedings of the IEEE International Conference on Acoustic, Speech and Signal Processing*, 4, 712–715.

Bloom, J.A., Cox, I.J., Kalker, T., Linnartz, J.P., Miller, M.L., & Traw, C.B. (1999). Copy protection for digital video. *Proceedings of IEEE, Special Issue on Identification and Protection of Multimedia Information, 87*(7), 1267–1276.

Boneh, D., & Franklin, M. (1999). An efficient public kev traitor tracing scheme. Proc CRYPTO'99, Berlin: Springer-Verlag, 338–353.

Boneh, D., & Shaw, J. (1998). Collusion-secure fingerprinting for digital data. *IEEE Trans. Inform. Theory, 44*, 1897–1905.

Brown, I., Perkins, C., & Crowcroft, J. (1999). Watercasting: Distributed watermarking of multicast media. *Proceedings of the International Workshop on Networked Group Communication,* 1736.

Dachselt, F., & Wolfgang, S. (2001). Chaos and cryptography. *IEEE Trans. Circuits Syst. I, 48*(12), 1498–1509.

Fridrich, J. (1997). Secure image ciphering based on chaos. Final Technical Report RL-TR-97-155. New York: Rome Laboratory.

Fu, M.S., & Au, A.C. (2004). Joint visual cryptography and watermarking. *Proceedings of the International Conference on Multimedia and Expro (ICME2004)*, 975–978.

Fukuhara, T., Ando, K., Watanabe, O., & Kiya, H. (2002). Partial-scrambling of JPEG2000 images for security applications. ISO/IEC JTC 1/SC29/WG1, N2430.

Furht, B. (1999). *Handbook of Internet and multimedia systems and applications*. CRC Press.

Kundur, D., & Karthik, K. (2004). Video fingerprinting and encryption principles for digital rights management. *Proceedings of the IEEE, 92*(6), 918–932.

Kunkelmann, T., & Reineman, R. (1997). A scalable security architecture for multimedia communication standards. *Proceedings of the 4th IEEE International Conference on Multimedia Computing and Systems*. Darmstadt, Germany, 660–663.

Macq, B.M., & Quisquater, J.J. (1995). Cryptology for digital TV broadcasting. *Proceedings of the IEEE, 83*(6), 944–957.

Mao, Y.B., Chen, G.R., & Lian, S.G. (2004). A novel fast image encryption scheme based on the 3D chaotic baker map. *International Journal of Bifurcation and Chaos, 14*(10), 3613–3624.

Matias, Y., & Shamir, A. (1987). A video scrambling technique based on space filling curves. *Proceedings of Advances in Cryptology-CRYPTO'87*, 293, 398–417.

Nakajima, N., & Yamaguchi, Y. (2004). Enhancing registration tolerance of extended visual cryptography for natural images. *Journal of Electronics Imaging, 13*(3), 654–662.

Naor, M., & Shamir, A. (1994). Visual cryptography. In A. De Santis Ed., Advances in Cryptology-Eurocrypt '94, Lecture Notes in Computer Science, Springer-Verlag, Berlin, 950, 1–12.

Romeo, A., Romdotti, G., Mattavelli, M., & Mlynek, D. (1999). Cryptosystem architectures for very high throughput multimedia encryption: The RPK solution. *Proceedings of the 6th IEEE International Conference on Electronics, Circuits and Systems*, 1, 5–8.

Torrubia, A., & Mora, F. (2002). Perceptual cryptography on MPEG layer III bit-streams. *IEEE Transactions on Consumer Electronics, 48*(4), 1046–1050.

Torrubia, A., & Mora, F. (2003). Perceptual cryptography of JPEG compressed images on the JFIF bit-stream domain. *Proceedings of the IEEE International Symposium on Consumer Electronics, ISCE*, 58–59.

Ye, Y., Yang, Q., & Wang, Y. (2003). Magic cube encryption for digital image using chaotic sequence. *Journal of Zhejiang University of Technology, 31*(2), 173–176.

Yen, J.C., & Guo, J.I. (1999). A new MPEG encryption system and its VLSI architecture. *Proceedings of the IEEE Workshop on Signal Processing Systems*, Taipei, 430–437.

Chapter XV
# Multimedia Transcoding in Wireless and Mobile Networks:
## Keyless Self–Encrypting/ Decrypting Scheme for Multimedia Transporting Systems

**Shadi R. Masadeh**
*The Arab Academy for Banking and Financial Sciences, Jordan*

**Walid A. Salameh**
*Princess Sumayya University for Technology, Jordan*

## ABSTRACT

*This chapter presents a keyless self-encrypting/decrypting system to be used in various communications systems. In the world of vast communications systems, data flow through various kinds of media, including free air. Thus the information transmitted is free to anyone who can peer it, which means that there should be a guarding mechanism so the information is transmitted securely over the medium from the sender to the intended receiver, who is supposed to get it in the first place and deter the others from getting the information sent. Many encryption systems have been devised for this purpose, but most of them are built around Public Key Infrastructure (PKI) wherein public key cryptography, a public and private key, is created simultaneously using the same algorithm (a popular one is known as RSA) by a certificate authority (CA). The private key is given only to the requesting party, and the public key is made publicly available (as part of a digital certificate) in a directory that all parties can access. The private key is never shared with anyone or sent across the medium. All of the commonly used encryption systems exchange keys that need to be generated using complex mathematical operations that take noticeable time, which is sometimes done once, and exchanged openly over unsecured medium. We are proposing an expandable keyless self-encrypting/decrypting system, which does not require the use of keys in order o minimize the chances of breaching data exchange security and enhance the data security of everyday communications devices that are otherwise insecured.*

## INTRODUCTION

The advent of communications systems and computing technology has merged the two technologies in multimedia technology, where data are delivered in multiformat containing both textual, video, and audio data, all in the same frame.

The wide use of the Internet has led to the broader use of information sources and imposed a necessity for information security measures to be used in delivering electronic contents from the sender to the intended receiver.

Since old times and out of pure necessity, people have invented encryption to hide the real meaning of the information they intended to send so the information will be delivered only to the person who is meant to decipher it and understand its contents.

Many schemes were developed throughout the ages, and mathematicians started working on the subject to create a scheme that is unbreakable under any attacks so the information will be secured no matter what the others (code breakers) will do to get the information the encrypted data hides.

Throughout the study of previous encryption systems techniques, people learned about the internals of the different standards used in encryption systems such as DES, Triple DES, RC4, RC5, RC6, and AES (Schneier, 1994).

This chapter presents briefly as excerpts from references the underlying techniques in those encryption systems and their points of weakness and strength.

## TERMINOLOGY

Before we discuss encryption and decryption processes, we should get familiar with the terminologies used by cryptographers. Most of the terminology material has been adopted from *Applied Cryptography* by Bruce Schneier.

**Sender and Receiver.** Suppose a sender wants to send a message to a receiver. Moreover, this sender wants to send the message securely to make sure an eavesdropper cannot read the message.

**Messages and Encryption.** Any message is regarded as a plain text (sometimes called clear text). The process of disguising a message in such a way as to hide its substance is encryption. An encrypted message is cipher text. The process of turning cipher text back into plain text is decryption. If you want to follow the ISO 7498-2 standard, use the terms "encipher" and "decipher." It seems that some cultures find the terms "encrypt" and "decrypt" offensive, as they may refer to dead bodies.

The art and science of keeping messages secure is cryptography, which is practiced by cryptographers. Cryptanalysts are practitioners of cryptanalysis, the art and science of breaking cipher text; that is, seeing through the disguise. The branch of mathematics encompassing both cryptography and cryptanalysis is cryptology; its practitioners are cryptologists. Modern cryptologists are generally trained in theoretical mathematics—they have to be.

Plain text is denoted by $M$, for message, or $P$, for plain text. It can be a stream of bits, a text file, a bitmap, a stream of digitized voice, a digital video image, and so forth. As far as a computer is concerned, $M$ is simply binary data. The plain text can be intended for either transmission or storage; in any case, $M$

is the message to be encrypted. Cipher text is denoted by *C*. It is also binary data, sometimes the same size as *M*, sometimes larger. (By combining encryption with compression, *C* may be smaller than *M*. However, encryption does not accomplish this).

The encryption function *E* operates on *M* to produce *C*. Or, in mathematical notation according to Equation 1:

$$E\ (M) = C \tag{1}$$

In the reverse process, the decryption function *D* operates on *C* to produce *M as follows as in* Equation 2:

$$D(C) = M \tag{2}$$

Since the whole point of encrypting and then decrypting a message is to recover the original plain text, the following identity must hold true according to Equation 3:

$$D\ (E\ (M)) = M \tag{3}$$

**Authentication, Integrity, and Nonrepudiation.** In addition to providing confidentiality, cryptography is often asked to do other jobs:

**Authentication.** It should be possible for the receiver of a message to ascertain its origin; an intruder should not be able to masquerade as someone else.

**Integrity.** It should be possible for the receiver of a message to verify that it has not been modified in transit; an intruder should not be able to substitute a false message for a legitimate one.

**Nonrepudiation.** A sender should not be able to falsely deny later that he sent a message.

These are vital requirements for social interaction on computers and are analogous to face-to-face interactions. That someone is who he says he is, that someone's credentials—a driver's license, a medical degree, or a passport—are valid, that a document purporting to come from a person actually came from that person. These are the things that authentication, integrity, and nonrepudiation provide.

## Algorithms and Keys

A cryptographic algorithm, also called a cipher, is the mathematical function used for encryption and decryption. (Generally, there are two related functions: one for encryption and the other for decryption.) If the security of an algorithm is based on keeping the way that algorithm works a secret, then it is a restricted algorithm. Restricted algorithms have historical interest but are woefully inadequate by today's standards. A large or changing group of users cannot use them, because every time a user leaves the group, everyone else must switch to a different algorithm. If someone accidentally reveals the secret, everyone must change their algorithms.

Even more damning, restricted algorithms allow no quality control or standardization. Every group of users must have their own unique algorithm. Such a group can't use off-the-shelf hardware or software products; an eavesdropper can buy the same product and learn the algorithm. They have to write their own algorithms and implementations. If no one in the group is a good cryptographer, then they won't know if they have a secure algorithm, despite these major drawbacks; restricted algorithms are enormously popular for low-security applications. Users either don't realize or don't care about the security problems inherent in their system.

Modern cryptography solves this problem with a key, denoted by $K$. This key might be any one of a large number of values. The range of possible values of the key is called the key space. Both the encryption and decryption operations use this key (i.e., they are dependent on the key and this fact is denoted by the k subscript), so the functions now become according to Equation 4 and Equation 5:

$$E_K(M) = C \tag{4}$$

$$D_K(C) = M \tag{5}$$

Those functions have the property that shows in Equation 6:

$$D_K(E_K(M)) = M \tag{6}$$

Some algorithms use a different encryption key and decryption key.

The encryption key, $K1$, is different from the corresponding decryption key, $K2$. In this case:

$$E_{K1}(M) = C \tag{7}$$

$$D_{K2}(C) = M \tag{8}$$

$$D_{K2}(E_{K1}(M)) = M \tag{9}$$

All of the security in these algorithms is based in the key (or keys); none is based in the details of the algorithm. This means that the algorithm can be published and analyzed. Products using the algorithm can be mass-produced. It doesn't matter if an eavesdropper knows your algorithm; if he or she doesn't know your particular key, she can't read your messages. A cryptosystem is an algorithm, plus all possible plain texts, cipher texts, and keys.

## Symmetric Algorithms

There are two general types of key-based algorithms: symmetric and public-key. Symmetric algorithms, sometimes called conventional algorithms are algorithms where the encryption key can be calculated from the decryption key and vice versa. In most symmetric algorithms, the encryption key and the decryption key are the same. These algorithms, also called secret-key algorithms, single-key algorithms, or one-key algorithms, require that the sender and receiver agree on a key before they can communicate securely. The security of a symmetric algorithm rests in the key; divulging the key means that anyone could encrypt and decrypt messages. As long as the communication needs to remain secret, the key must remain secret, encryption and decryption with a symmetric algorithm as an Equation 4 and Equation 5 as mentioned previously.

Symmetric algorithms can be divided into two categories. Some operate on plain text, a single bit (or sometimes byte) at a time; these are called stream algorithms or stream ciphers. Others operate on the plain text in groups of bits. The groups of bits are called blocks, and the algorithms are called block algorithms or block ciphers. For modern computer algorithms, a typical block size is 64 bits—large enough to preclude analysis and small enough to be workable. (Before computers, algorithms generally operated on plain text one character at a time. You can think of this as a stream algorithm operating on a stream of characters.)

## Public-Key Algorithms

Public-key algorithms (also called asymmetric algorithms) are designed so that the key used for encryption is different from the key used for decryption. Furthermore, the decryption key cannot (at least in any reasonable amount of time) be calculated from the encryption key. The algorithms are called "public-key" because the encryption key can be made public. A complete stranger can use the encryption key to encrypt a message, but only a specific person with the corresponding decryption key can decrypt the message. In these systems, the encryption key is often called the public key, and the decryption key is often called the private key. The private key is sometimes also called the secret key, but to avoid confusion with symmetric algorithms, that tag won't be used here.

Encryption using public key $K$ is denoted by Equation 4 as mentioned previously. Even though the public key and private key are different, decryption with the corresponding private key is denoted by Equation 5, as mentioned earlier. Sometimes messages will be encrypted with the private key and decrypted with the public key; this is used in digital signatures despite the possible confusion, these operations are denoted as in Equation 4 and Equation 5.

## Cryptanalysis

The whole point of cryptography is to keep the plain text (or the key, or both) secret from eavesdroppers. Eavesdroppers are assumed to have complete access to the communications between the sender and receiver. Cryptanalysis is the science of recovering the plain text of a message without access to the key. Successful cryptanalysis may recover the plain text or the key. It also may find weaknesses in a cryptosystem that eventually leads to the previous results.

An attempted cryptanalysis is called an attack. A fundamental assumption in cryptanalysis, first enunciated by the Dutchman A. Kerckhoffs in the 19th century, is that the secrecy must reside entirely in the key (Kahn, 1967).

There are four general types out of seven types of cryptanalytic attacks. Of course, each of them assumes that the cryptanalyst has complete knowledge of the encryption algorithm used.

1.  **Cipher text-only attack.** The cryptanalyst has the cipher text of several messages, all of which have been encrypted using the same encryption algorithm. The cryptanalyst's job is to recover the plain text of as many messages as possible, or better yet, to deduce the key (or keys) used to encrypt the messages in order to decrypt other messages encrypted with the same keys.

Given: C1 = Ek (P1), C2 = Ek (P2)...Ci = Ek (Pi)
Deduce: Either P1, P2...Pi; k; or an algorithm to infer Pi+1 from
Ci+1 = Ek (Pi+1).

2. **Known-plain text attack.** The cryptanalyst has access not only to the cipher text of several messages but also to the plain text of those messages. His or her job is to deduce the key (or keys) used to encrypt the messages or an algorithm to decrypt any new messages encrypted with the same key (or keys).

Given: P1, C1 = Ek (P1), P2, C2 = Ek (P2)...Pi, Ci = Ek (Pi)
Deduce: Either k, or an algorithm to infer Pi+1 from Ci+1 = Ek (Pi+1)

3. **Chosen plain text attack.** The cryptanalyst not only has access to the cipher text and associated plain text for several messages but also chooses the plain text that gets encrypted. This is more powerful than a known-plain text attack because the cryptanalyst can choose specific plain text blocks to encrypt, ones that might yield more information about the key. His job is to deduce the key (or keys) used to encrypt the messages or an algorithm to decrypt any new messages encrypted with the same key (or keys).

Given: P1, C1 = Ek (P1), P2, C2 = Ek (P2)...Pi, Ci = Ek (Pi), where
the cryptanalyst gets to choose P1, P2...Pi
Deduce: Either k, or an algorithm to infer Pi+1 from Ci

4. **Adaptive chosen plain text attack.** This is a special case of a chosen plain text attack. Not only can the cryptanalyst choose the plain text that is encrypted, but he or she can also modify his or her choice based on the results of previous encryption. In a chosen plain text attack, a cryptanalyst might be able to choose only one large block of plain text to be encrypted; in an adaptive chosen plain text attack, a cryptanalyst can choose a smaller block of plain text and then choose another based on the results of the first, and so forth.

5. **Chosen cipher text attack.** The cryptanalyst can choose different cipher texts to be decrypted and has access to the decrypted plain text.
   For example, the cryptanalyst has access to a tamper-proof box that does automatic decryption. His or her job is to deduce the key.

Given: $C1, P1 = Dk (C1), C2, P2 = Dk (C2)...Ci, Pi = Dk (Ci)$
Deduce: $k$

This attack is primarily applicable to public key algorithms. A chosen cipher text attack is sometimes effective against a symmetric algorithm as well. (Sometimes a chosen plain text attack and a chosen cipher text attack are together known as a chosen text attack.)

6. **Chosen key attack.** This attack doesn't mean that the cryptanalyst can choose the key; it means that the cryptanalyst has some knowledge about the relationship between different keys. It's strange and obscure, not very practical.

7. **Rubber hose cryptanalysis.** The cryptanalyst threatens, blackmails, or tortures someone until they give him the key. Bribery is sometimes referred to as a purchase key attack. These are all very powerful attacks and often the best way to break an algorithm.

Known plain text attacks and chosen plain text attacks are more common than you might think. It is not unheard of for a cryptanalyst to get a plain text message that has been encrypted or to bribe someone to encrypt a chosen message. You may not even have to bribe someone; if you give a message to an ambassador, you will probably find that it gets encrypted and sent back to his or her country for consideration. Many messages have standard beginnings and endings that might be known to the cryptanalyst. Encrypted source code is especially vulnerable because of the regular appearance of keywords: # defines, struct, else, return. Encrypted executable code has the same kinds of problems: functions, loop structures, and so forth. Known plain text attacks (and even chosen plain text attacks) were successfully used against both the Germans and the Japanese during World War II (Kahn, 1983, 1991).

The best algorithms we have are the ones that have been made public, have been attacked by the world's best cryptographers for years, and are still unbreakable.

Cryptanalysts don't always have access to the algorithms, as when the United States broke the Japanese diplomatic code PURPLE during World War II (Kahn, 1967), but they often do. If the algorithm is being used in a commercial security program, it is simply a matter of time and money to disassemble the program and recover the algorithm. If the algorithm is being used in a military communications system, it is simply a matter of time and money to buy (or steal) the equipment and reverse-engineer the algorithm.

## SECURITY OF ALGORITHMS

Different algorithms offer different degrees of security; it depends on how hard they are to break. If the cost required to break an algorithm is greater than the value of the encrypted data, then you're probably safe. If the time required to break an algorithm is longer than the time the encrypted data must remain secret, then you're probably safe. If the amount of data encrypted with a single key is less than the amount of data necessary to break the algorithm, then you're probably safe.

I say "probably" because there is always a chance of new breakthroughs in cryptanalysis. On the other hand, the value of most data decreases over time. It is important that the value of the data always remains less than the cost to break the security protecting it.

Lars Knudsen classified these different categories of breaking an algorithm in decreasing order of severity (Knudsen, 1994):

1. **Total break.** A cryptanalyst finds the key, $K$, such that $DK(C) = P$.
2. **Global deduction.** A cryptanalyst finds an alternate algorithm, $A$, equivalent to $DK(C)$, without knowing $K$.
3. **Instance (or local) deduction.** A cryptanalyst finds the plain text of an intercepted cipher text.
4. **Information deduction.** A cryptanalyst gains some information about the key or plain text. This information could be a few bits of the key, some information about the form of the plain text, and so forth. An algorithm is unconditionally secure if, no matter how much cipher text a cryptanalyst has, there is not enough information to recover the plain text.

In point of fact, only a one-time pad is unbreakable given infinite resources. All other cryptosystems are breakable in a cipher text only attack, simply by trying every possible key one by one and checking whether the resulting plain text is meaningful.

Cryptography is more concerned with cryptosystems that are computationally infeasible to break. An algorithm is considered computationally secure (sometimes called strong) if it cannot be broken with available resources, either current or future. Exactly what constitutes "available resources" is open to interpretation; you can measure the complexity of an attack in different ways:

1. **Data complexity.** The amount of data needed as input to the attack.
2. **Processing complexity.** The time needed to perform the attack. This is often called the work factor.
3. **Storage requirements.** The amount of memory needed to do the attack. As a rule of thumb, the complexity of an attack is taken to be the minimum of these three factors. Some attacks involve trading off the three complexities: A faster attack might be possible at the expense of a greater storage requirement. Complexities are expressed as orders of magnitude. If an algorithm has a processing complexity of 2,128, then 2,128 operations are required to break the algorithm. (These operations may be complex and time-consuming.) Still, if you assume that you have enough computing speed to perform a million operations every second and you set a million parallel processors against the task, it will still take more than 1,019 years to recover the key; that's a billion times the age of the universe.

While the complexity of an attack is constant (until some cryptanalyst finds a better attack, of course), computing power is anything but. There have been phenomenal advances in computing power during the last half-century, and there is no reason to think this trend won't continue. Many cryptanalytic attacks are perfect for parallel machines.

The task can be broken down into billions of tiny pieces, and none of the processors need to interact with each other. Pronouncing an algorithm secure simply because it is infeasible to break, given current technology, is dicey at best. Good cryptosystems are designed to be infeasible to break with the computing power that is expected to evolve many years in the future.

## Substitution Ciphers

Before computers, cryptography consisted of character-based algorithms. Different cryptographic algorithms either substituted characters for one another or transposed characters with one another. The better algorithms did both, many times each. Things are more complex these days, but the philosophy remains the same: the primary change is that algorithms work on bits instead of characters. This is actually just a change in the alphabet size: from 26 elements to two elements. Most good cryptographic algorithms still combine elements of substitution and transposition.

## Substitution Ciphers

A substitution cipher is one in which each character in the plain text is substituted for another character in the cipher text. The receiver inverts the substitution on the cipher text to recover the plain text in classical cryptography; there are four types of substitution ciphers:

1. **Simple substitution cipher**, or **monoalphabetic cipher**, is one in which each character of the plain text is replaced with a corresponding character of cipher text. The cryptograms in newspapers are simple substitution ciphers.
2. **Homophonic substitution cipher** is like a simple substitution cryptosystem, except a single character of plain text can map to one of several characters of cipher text. For example, "A" could correspond to either 5, 13, 25, or 56; "B" could correspond to either 7, 19, 31, or 42; and so forth.
3. **PolyGram substitution cipher** is one in which blocks of characters are encrypted in groups. For example, "ABA" could correspond to "RTQ"; "ABB" could correspond to "SLL"; and so forth.
4. **Polyalphabetic substitution cipher** is made up of multiple simple substitution ciphers. For example, there might be five different simple substitution ciphers used; the particular one used changes with the position of each character of the plain text.

The famous Caesar Cipher, in which each plain text character is replaced by the character three to the right modulo 26 ("A" is replaced by "D," "B" is replaced by "E,"..., "W" is replaced by "Z," "X" is replaced by "A," "Y" is replaced by "B," and "Z" is replaced by "C") is a simple substitution cipher.

Simple substitution ciphers can be easily broken because the cipher does not hide the underlying frequencies of the different letters of the plain text. All it takes is about 25 English characters before a good cryptanalyst can reconstruct the plain text. An algorithm for solving these sorts of ciphers can be found in Friedman (1976), Ball (1960), and Konheim (1981).

A good computer algorithm can be found in Hart (1994). Homophonic substitution ciphers were used as early as 1401 by the Duchy of Mantua; details are in Kahn (1967).

They are much more complicated to break than simple substitution ciphers but still do not obscure all of the statistical properties of the plain text language. With a known plain text attack, the ciphers are trivial to break. A cipher text-only attack is harder but only takes a few seconds on a computer (Peleg & Rosenfield, 1979).

PolyGram substitution ciphers are ciphers in which groups of letters are encrypted together. The Playfair cipher, invented in 1854, was used by the British during World War I; it encrypts pairs of letters together. Its cryptanalysis is discussed in Sinkov (1966) and Ball (1960). The Hill cipher is another example of a PolyGram substitution cipher; details are in Hill (1929). Sometimes you see Huffman coding used as a cipher; this is an insecure PolyGram substitution cipher.

Polyalphabetic substitution ciphers were invented by Leon Battista in 1568 (Kahn, 1967). They were used by the Union Army during the American Civil War, despite the fact that they can be broken easily; details are in Friedman (1920) and Ball (1960).

Many commercial computer security products use ciphers of this form, discussed in Schneier (1993, 1994) and Stevens (1990). (Details on how to break this encryption scheme, as used in WordPerfect, can be found in Bennett (1987) and Bergen and Caelli (1991).

## Rotor Machines

In the 1920s, various mechanical encryption devices were invented to automate the process of encryption. Most were based on the concept of a rotor; a mechanical wheel wired to perform a general substitution, a rotor machine has a keyboard and a series of rotors and implements a version of the Vigenère cipher. Each rotor is an arbitrary permutation of the alphabet, has 26 positions, and performs a simple substitution. For example, a rotor might be wired to substitute "F" for "A," "U" for "B," "L" for "C," and so forth. The output pins of one rotor are connected to the input pins of the next.

For example, in a four-rotor machine, the first rotor might substitute "F" for "A," the second might substitute "Y" for "F," the third might substitute "E" for "Y," and the fourth might substitute "C" for "E"; "C" would be the output cipher text. Then some of the rotors shift, so next time the substitutions will be different; it is the combination of several rotors and the gears moving them that makes the machine secure. Because the rotors all move at different rates, the period for an n-rotor machine is $26n$. Some rotor machines can also have a different number of positions on each rotor, further frustrating cryptanalysis.

The best-known rotor device is the Enigma. The Enigma was used by the Germans during World War II. The idea was invented by Arthur Scherbius and Arvid Gerhard Damm in Europe. It was patented in the United States by Arthur Scherbius (1928). The Germans beefed up the basic design considerably for wartime use; the German Enigma had three rotors chosen from a set of five, a plug board that slightly permuted the plain text, and a reflecting rotor that caused each rotor to operate on each plain text letter twice. As complicated as the Enigma was, it was broken during World War II. First, a team of Polish cryptographers broke the German Enigma and explained their attack to the British. The Germans modified their Enigma as the war progressed, and the British continued to cryptanalyze the new versions. For explanations of how rotor ciphers work and how they were broken, see Kahn (1967). Two fascinating accounts of how the Enigma was broken are in Hodges (1983) and Kahn (1991).

## Further Reading

This is not a chapter about classical cryptography, so I will not dwell further on these subjects. Two excellent precomputer cryptology books are Sinkov (1966) and Deavours and Kruh (1985), which present some modern cryptanalysis of cipher machines. Denning (1982) discusses many of these ciphers, and Ball (1960) has some fairly complex mathematical analysis of the same ciphers. Another older cryptography text, which discusses analog cryptography, is Beker and Piper (1980). An article that presents a good overview of the subject is Friedman (1967). Kahn's (1983, 1991) historical cryptography books are also excellent.

## Simple XOR

XOR is exclusive-or operation: '^' in C or • in mathematical notation. It's a standard operation on bits.

*Table 1. Mathematical operation of simple XOR*

$$0 \cdot 0 = 0$$
$$0 \cdot 1 = 1$$
$$1 \cdot 0 = 1$$
$$1 \cdot 1 = 0$$

*Figure 1. Simple-XOR algorithm (Schneier, 1993)*

```
/* Usage:  crypto key input_file output_file */

void main (int argc, char *argv[])

{
       FILE *fi, *fo;
       char *cp;
       int c;

       if ((cp = argv[1]) && *cp!='\0')  {
           if ((fi = fopen(argv[2], "rb")) != NULL)  {
               if ((fo = fopen(argv[3], "wb")) != NULL)  {
                   while ((c = getc(fi)) != EOF)  {
                       if (!*cp) cp = argv[1];
                       c ^= *(cp++);
                       putc(c,fo);
                   }
                   fclose(fo);
               }
               fclose(fi);
           }
       }
}
```

The simple-XOR algorithm as in Figure 1 is really an embarrassment; it's nothing more than a Vigenère polyalphabetic cipher. It's here only because of its prevalence in commercial software packages, at least those in the MS-DOS and Macintosh worlds; unfortunately, if a software security program proclaims that it has a "proprietary" encryption algorithm—significantly faster than DES—the odds are that it is some variant (Schneier, 1993).

This is a symmetric algorithm. The plain text is being XORed with a keyword to generate the cipher text. Since XORing the same value twice restores the original, encryption and decryption use exactly the same program:

$$P \bullet K = C \tag{10}$$

$$C \bullet K = P \tag{11}$$

There's no real security here. This kind of encryption is trivial to break, even without computers (Sinkov, 1966). It will only take a few seconds with a computer. Assume the plain text is English. Furthermore, assume the key length is any small number of bytes. Here's how to break it:

1. Discover the length of the key by a procedure known as counting coincidences (Friedman, 1987). XOR the cipher text against itself shifted various numbers of bytes, and count those bytes that are equal. If the displacement is a multiple of the key length, then something over 6% of the bytes will be equal. If it is not, then less than 0.4% will be equal (assuming a random key encrypting normal ASCII text; other plain text will have different numbers). This is called the index of coincidence. The smallest displacement that indicates a multiple of the key length is the length of the key.

2.   Shift the cipher text by that length and XOR it with itself. This removes the key and leaves you with plain text XORed with the plain text shifted the length of the key. Since English has 1.3 bits of real information per byte, there is plenty of redundancy for determining a unique decryption; despite this, the list of software vendors that tout this toy algorithm as being "almost as secure as DES" is staggering (Schneier, 1993). It is the algorithm (with a 160-bit repeated "key") that the NSA finally allowed the U.S. digital cellular phone industry to use for voice privacy. An XOR might keep your kid sister from reading your files, but it won't stop a cryptanalyst for more than a few minutes.

## One-Time Pads

**One-time pad** is a perfect encryption scheme that was invented in 1917 by Major Joseph Mauborgne and AT&T's Gilbert Vernam (Kahn, 1967). Actually, a one-time pad is a special case of a threshold scheme; classically, a one-time pad is nothing more than a large nonrepeating set of truly random key letters written on sheets of paper and glued together in a pad. In its original form, it was a one-time tape for teletypewriters; the sender uses each key letter on the pad to encrypt exactly one plain text character. Encryption is the addition modulo 26 of the plain text character and the one-time pad key character.

Each key letter is used exactly once for only one message; the sender encrypts the message and then destroys the used pages of the pad or used section of the tape. The receiver has an identical pad and uses each key on the pad, in turn, to decrypt each letter of the cipher text. The receiver destroys the same pad pages or tape section after decrypting the message. New message—new key letters. As example of one-time pad, refer to Figure 2.

Assuming an eavesdropper can't get access to the one-time pad used to encrypt the message, this scheme is perfectly secure. A given cipher text message is equally likely to correspond to any possible plain text message of equal size since every key sequence is equally likely (remember, the key letters are generated randomly); an adversary has no information with which to cryptanalyze the cipher text. The key sequence could just as likely be:

This point bears repeating: Since every plain text message is equally possible, there is no way for the cryptanalyst to determine which plain text message is the correct one. A random key sequence added

*Figure 2. One-time pads scheme (Kahn, 1967)*

ONETIMEPAD
and the key sequence from the
pad is
TBFRGFARFM
then the cipher text is
IPKLPSFHGQ
Because
O + T mod 26 = I
N + B mod 26 = P
E + F mod 26 = K
Etc.

*Figure 3. Key sequence one-time-pads (Kahn, 1967)*

> POYYAEAAZX
> which would decrypt to:
> SALMONEGGS
> or
> BXFGBMTMXM
> Which would decrypt to:
> GREENFLUID

to a nonrandom plain text message produces a completely random cipher text message, and no amount of computing power can change that.

The other important point is that you can never use the key sequence again, ever. Even if you use a multiple-gigabyte pad, if a cryptanalyst has multiple cipher texts whose keys overlap, he or she can reconstruct the plain text. The cryptanalyst slides each pair of cipher texts against each other and counts the number of matches at each position. If they are aligned right, the proportion of matches jumps suddenly—the exact percentages depend on the plain text language. From this point, cryptanalysis is easy. It's like the index of coincidence, but with just two "periods" to compare (Kullback, 1976). Don't do it.

The idea of a one-time pad can be easily extended to binary data. Instead of a one-time pad consisting of letters, use a one-time pad of bits. Instead of adding the plain text to the one-time pad, use an XOR; to decrypt, XOR the cipher text with the same one-time pad. Everything else remains the same, and the security is just as perfect.

This all sounds good, but there are a few problems. Since the key bits must be random and can never be used again, the length of the key sequence must be equal to the length of the message. A one-time pad might be suitable for a few short messages, but it will never work for a 1.544Mbps communications channel. You can store 650 megabytes worth of random bits on a CD-ROM, but there are problems. First, you want exactly two copies of the random bits, but CD-ROMs are economical only for large quantities. And second, you want to be able to destroy the bits already used. CD-ROM has no erase facilities except for physically destroying the entire disk. Digital tape is a much better medium for this sort of thing.

Even if you solve the key distribution and storage problem, you have to make sure the sender and receiver are perfectly synchronized. If the receiver is off by a bit (or if some bits are dropped during the transmission), the message won't make any sense. On the other hand, if some bits are altered during transmission (without any bits being added or removed—something far more likely to happen due to random noise), only those bits will be decrypted incorrectly. But on the other hand, a one-time pad provides no authenticity.

## Computer Algorithms

There are many cryptographic algorithms. These are three of the most common:

- **DES (Data Encryption Standard).** The most popular computer encryption algorithm. DES is a U.S. and international standard. It is a symmetric algorithm; the same key is used for encryption and decryption.

*Table 2. Large numbers (Dyson, 1979)*

**Large Numbers**

| Physical Analogue | Number |
|---|---|
| Odds of being killed by lightning (per day) | 1 in 9 billion ($2^{33}$) |
| Odds of winning the top prize in a U.S. state lottery | 1 in 4,000,000 ($2^{22}$) |
| Odds of winning the top prize in a U.S. state lottery and being killed by lightning in the same day | 1 in $2^{55}$ |
| Odds of drowning (in the U.S. per year) | 1 in 59,000 ($2^{16}$) |
| Odds of being killed in an automobile accident(in the U.S. in 1993) | 1 in 6100 ($2^{13}$) |
| Odds of being killed in an automobile accident(in the U.S. per lifetime) | 1 in 88 ($2^{7}$) |
| Time until the next ice age | 14,000 ($2^{14}$) years |
| Time until the sun goes nova | $10^9$ ($2^{30}$) years |
| Age of the planet | $10^9$ ($2^{30}$) years |
| Age of the Universe | $10^{10}$ ($2^{34}$) years |
| Number of atoms in the planet | $10^{51}$ ($2^{170}$) |
| Number of atoms in the sun | $10^{57}$ ($2^{190}$) |
| Number of atoms in the galaxy | $10^{67}$ ($2^{223}$) |
| Number of atoms in the Universe (dark matter excluded) | $10^{77}$ ($2^{265}$) |
| Volume of the Universe | $10^{84}$ ($2^{280}$) cm³ |
| | |
| **If the Universe is Closed:** | |
| Total lifetime of the Universe | $10^{11}$ ($2^{37}$) years |
| | $10^{18}$ ($2^{61}$) seconds |
| **If the Universe is Open:** | |
| Time until low-mass stars cool off | $10^{14}$ ($2^{47}$) years |
| Time until planets detach from stars | $10^{15}$ ($2^{50}$) years |
| Time until stars detach from galaxies | $10^{19}$ ($2^{64}$) years |
| Time until orbits decay by gravitational radiation | $10^{20}$ ($2^{67}$) years |
| Time until black holes decay by the Hawking process | $10^{64}$ ($2^{213}$) years |
| Time until all matter is liquid at zero temperature | $10^{65}$ ($2^{216}$) years |
| Time until all matter decays to iron | $10^{10^{26}}$ years |
| Time until all matter collapses to black holes | $10^{10^{76}}$ years |

- **RSA (named for its creators—Rivest, Shamir, and Adleman).** The most popular public-key algorithm. It can be used for both encryption and digital signatures.
- **DSA (Digital Signature Algorithm, used as part of the Digital Signature Standard).** Another public-key algorithm. It cannot be used for encryption, but only for digital signatures.

## Large Numbers

We use various large numbers to describe different things in cryptography. Because it is so easy to lose sight of these numbers and what they signify, Table 2 gives physical analogues for some of them; these numbers are order-of-magnitude estimates and have been culled from a variety of sources. Many of the astrophysics numbers are explained in Freeman.

## BREAKING THE CODE

There is a saying that states, "A code created by a human can be broken by a human." Hence, many of the coding systems that seemed unbreakable by the time they were created are becoming breakable nowadays using personal and super computers, so how does the code get broken?

We will show an example of breaking the DES, but first what is the DES?

The DES is a block cipher where the data are a 64-bit block and a 56-bit key. The algorithm is nothing more than a combination of two basic techniques devised by Shannon, which are confusion and diffusion. The fundamental building block of the DES is round in which a single combination of the two techniques (confusion and diffusion) applied as a substitution followed by permutation on the plain text based on the key chosen. The DES uses 16 rounds to encrypt the plain text.

The algorithm used in the DES uses only standard arithmetic and logical operations on 64-bit numbers, so it was easily implemented in the late 1970s hardware technology.

How does the DES encrypt the plain text?

## DECRYPTION

DES decryption consists of the encryption algorithm with the same key but reversed key schedule, using in order K16; K15; : : : ;K1. This works as follows (refer to Figure 7.9). The effect of IP−1 is cancelled by IP in decryption, leaving (R16; L16); consider applying round 1 to this input. The operation on the left half yields, rather than $0\_f$ (R0;K1), now R16_f(L16;K16), which, since L16 = R15 and R16 =

*Figure 4. The algorithm of DES (Menezes, 1996)*

INPUT: plaintext $m_1 \ldots m_{64}$; 64-bit key $K = k_1 \ldots k_{64}$ (includes 8 parity bits).
OUTPUT: 64-bit ciphertext block $C = c_1 \ldots c_{64}$. (For decryption, see Note 7.84.)

1. (key schedule) Compute sixteen 48-bit round keys $K_i$ from $K$ using Algorithm 7.83.
2. $(L_0, R_0) \leftarrow \text{IP}(m_1 m_2 \ldots m_{64})$. (Use IP from Table 7.2 to permute bits; split the result into left and right 32-bit halves $L_0 = m_{58}m_{50}\ldots m_8$, $R_0 = m_{57}m_{49}\ldots m_7$.)
3. (16 rounds) for $i$ from 1 to 16, compute $L_i$ and $R_i$ using Equations (7.4) and (7.5) above, computing $f(R_{i-1},\ K_i) = P(S(E(R_{i-1}) \oplus K_i))$ as follows:

   (a) Expand $R_{i-1} = r_1 r_2 \ldots r_{32}$ from 32 to 48 bits using $E$ per Table 7.3:
   $T \leftarrow E(R_{i-1})$. (Thus $T = r_{32}r_1r_2\ldots r_{32}r_1$.)

   (b) $T' \leftarrow T \oplus K_i$. Represent $T'$ as eight 6-bit character strings: $(B_1, \ldots, B_8) = T'$.

   (c) $T'' \leftarrow (S_1(B_1), S_2(B_2), \ldots S_8(B_8))$. (Here $S_i(B_i)$ maps $B_i = b_1 b_2 \ldots b_6$ to the 4-bit entry in row $r$ and column $c$ of $S_i$ in Table 7.8, page 260 where $r = 2 \cdot b_1 + b_6$, and $b_2 b_3 b_4 b_5$ is the radix-2 representation of $0 \leq c \leq 15$. Thus $S_1(011011)$ yields $r = 1$, $c = 13$, and output 5, i.e., binary 0101.)

   (d) $T''' \leftarrow P(T'')$. (Use $P$ per Table 7.3 to permute the 32 bits of $T'' = t_1 t_2 \ldots t_{32}$, yielding $t_{16}t_7 \ldots t_{25}$.)

4. $b_1 b_2 \ldots b_{64} \leftarrow (R_{16}, L_{16})$. (Exchange final blocks $L_{16}, R_{16}$.)
5. $C \leftarrow \text{IP}^{-1}(b_1 b_2 \ldots b_{64})$. (Transpose using $\text{IP}^{-1}$ from Table 7.2; $C = b_{40}b_8 \ldots b_{25}$.)

*Table 3. DES initial permutation and inverse (IP and IP⁻¹) (Menezes, 1996)*

| IP | | | | | | | | | IP⁻¹ | | | | | | | |
|----|----|----|----|----|----|----|----|---|----|---|----|----|----|----|----|----|
| 58 | 50 | 42 | 34 | 26 | 18 | 10 | 2 | | 40 | 8 | 48 | 16 | 56 | 24 | 64 | 32 |
| 60 | 52 | 44 | 36 | 28 | 20 | 12 | 4 | | 39 | 7 | 47 | 15 | 55 | 23 | 63 | 31 |
| 62 | 54 | 46 | 38 | 30 | 22 | 14 | 6 | | 38 | 6 | 46 | 14 | 54 | 22 | 62 | 30 |
| 64 | 56 | 48 | 40 | 32 | 24 | 16 | 8 | | 37 | 5 | 45 | 13 | 53 | 21 | 61 | 29 |
| 57 | 49 | 41 | 33 | 25 | 17 | 9 | 1 | | 36 | 4 | 44 | 12 | 52 | 20 | 60 | 28 |
| 59 | 51 | 43 | 35 | 27 | 19 | 11 | 3 | | 35 | 3 | 43 | 11 | 51 | 19 | 59 | 27 |
| 61 | 53 | 45 | 37 | 29 | 21 | 13 | 5 | | 34 | 2 | 42 | 10 | 50 | 18 | 58 | 26 |
| 63 | 55 | 47 | 39 | 31 | 23 | 15 | 7 | | 33 | 1 | 41 | 9 | 49 | 17 | 57 | 25 |

*Table 4. DES per-round functions: Expansion E and permutation P (Menezes, 1996)*

| E | | | | | | | P | | | |
|----|----|----|----|----|----|---|----|----|----|----|
| 32 | 1 | 2 | 3 | 4 | 5 | | 16 | 7 | 20 | 21 |
| 4 | 5 | 6 | 7 | 8 | 9 | | 29 | 12 | 28 | 17 |
| 8 | 9 | 10 | 11 | 12 | 13 | | 1 | 15 | 23 | 26 |
| 12 | 13 | 14 | 15 | 16 | 17 | | 5 | 18 | 31 | 10 |
| 16 | 17 | 18 | 19 | 20 | 21 | | 2 | 8 | 24 | 14 |
| 20 | 21 | 22 | 23 | 24 | 25 | | 32 | 27 | 3 | 9 |
| 24 | 25 | 26 | 27 | 28 | 29 | | 19 | 13 | 30 | 6 |
| 28 | 29 | 30 | 31 | 32 | 1 | | 22 | 11 | 4 | 25 |

*Figure 5. DES computation path (Menezes, 1996)*

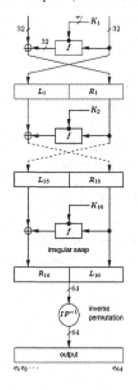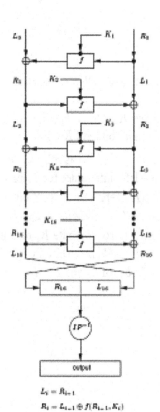

$$L_i = R_{i-1}$$
$$R_i = L_{i-1} \oplus f(R_{i-1}, K_i)$$

*Figure 6. DES inner function F (Menezes, 1996)*

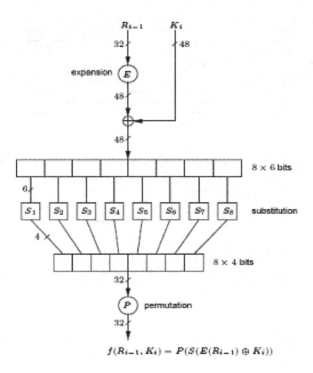

$$f(R_{i-1}, K_i) = P(S(E(R_{i-1}) \oplus K_i))$$

*Figure 7. DES key schedule algorithm (Menezes, 1996)*

INPUT: 64-bit key $K = k_1 \ldots k_{64}$ (including 8 odd-parity bits).
OUTPUT: sixteen 48-bit keys $K_i$, $1 \leq i \leq 16$.

1. Define $v_i$, $1 \leq i \leq 16$ as follows: $v_i = 1$ for $i \in \{1, 2, 9, 16\}$; $v_i = 2$ otherwise. (These are left-shift values for 28-bit circular rotations below.)

2. $T \leftarrow \text{PC1}(K)$; represent $T$ as 28-bit halves $(C_0, D_0)$. (Use PC1 in Table 7.4 to select bits from $K$: $C_0 = k_{57}k_{49} \ldots k_{36}$, $D_0 = k_{63}k_{55} \ldots k_4$.)

3. For $i$ from 1 to 16, compute $K_i$ as follows: $C_i \leftarrow (C_{i-1} \hookleftarrow v_i)$, $D_i \leftarrow (D_{i-1} \hookleftarrow v_i)$, $K_i \leftarrow \text{PC2}(C_i, D_i)$. (Use PC2 in Table 7.4 to select 48 bits from the concatenation $b_1b_2 \ldots b_{56}$ of $C_i$ and $D_i$: $K_i = b_{14}b_{17} \ldots b_{32}$. '$\hookleftarrow$' denotes left circular shift.)

*Table 5. DES key schedule bit selections (PC1 and PC2) (Menezes, 1996)*

| PC1 | | | | | | |
|----|----|----|----|----|----|----|
| 57 | 49 | 41 | 33 | 25 | 17 | 9 |
| 1 | 58 | 50 | 42 | 34 | 26 | 18 |
| 10 | 2 | 59 | 51 | 43 | 35 | 27 |
| 19 | 11 | 3 | 60 | 52 | 44 | 36 |
| above for $C_i$; below for $D_i$ | | | | | | |
| 63 | 55 | 47 | 39 | 31 | 23 | 15 |
| 7 | 62 | 54 | 46 | 38 | 30 | 22 |
| 14 | 6 | 61 | 53 | 45 | 37 | 29 |
| 21 | 13 | 5 | 28 | 20 | 12 | 4 |

| PC2 | | | | | |
|----|----|----|----|----|----|
| 14 | 17 | 11 | 24 | 1 | 5 |
| 3 | 28 | 15 | 6 | 21 | 10 |
| 23 | 19 | 12 | 4 | 26 | 8 |
| 16 | 7 | 27 | 20 | 13 | 2 |
| 41 | 52 | 31 | 37 | 47 | 55 |
| 30 | 40 | 51 | 45 | 33 | 48 |
| 44 | 49 | 39 | 56 | 34 | 53 |
| 46 | 42 | 50 | 36 | 29 | 32 |

L15_f(R15;K16), is equal to L15_f(R15;K16)_f(R15;K16) = L15. Thus, round 1 decryption yields (R15; L15) (i.e., inverting round 16).

After seeing all that and how complex the operation is, how could someone break the code? The answer is … Brute Force.

## What is Brute Force?

Since the algorithm is known and the cipher text is known, then it is a matter of finding the key; as mentioned before, since the key is a 56-bit, then a simple iteration program could start generating sequential keys and test the generated keys on the cipher text until it makes sense. Many attempts have been made to crack the DES and its variants, and nowadays it has become possible to crack even triple DES in about 56 hours, and using advanced hardware, it could be cracked in less than 24 hours. As reported by Matthew Nelson on the CNN Web site on January 21, 1999:

*Cracking the 56-bit DES encryption algorithm no longer takes a number of years to achieve; it can now be done in one day, as was demonstrated by a hacking group participating in RSA Data Security's yearly DES Challenge contest.*

A message, encrypted using the 56-bit DES algorithm was released, with a purse of $1,000 available to whoever could break it in the least amount of time, the algorithm was cracked in record time by the Electronic Frontier Foundation using "Deep Crack," a specially designed supercomputer, and Distributed.Net, a worldwide coalition of computer enthusiasts. The previous record for the amount of time taken to break the code was 56 hours; response from industry observers was mostly in agreement: 56-bit DES is no longer secure.

The breaking of the code should also send a message to government officials who claim that 56-bit encryption using DES is secure for communications, according to analysts, "It's more evidence that the U.S. government claim about being unable to break 56-bit DES is nonsense," said Jim Balderston, an industry analyst at Zona Research, in Redwood City, Calif. "They can crack it and they can apply a lot more computer power than a cobbled together machine."

On the other hand, two professors from Germany—Professor C. Paar (Ruhr University of Bochum) and Professor M. Schimmler (Christian-Albrechts University Kiel)—invented a low-cost $10,000 can-do

*Figure 8. COPACOBANA machine*

brute force attacks on AES, DES, RC4, A5, mD5, SHA, and SHA-1 with secure key lengths of 112 to 256 bits for symmetrical crypto systems and secure key lengths of more than 2,048 bit for asymmetrical crypto systems such as RSA, ECC, and DL. This simple device can achieve the work of 22,865 Pentium 4, 3GHz personal computers, which would cost 3.6 million Euros as compared to a mere 9000 Euros for the COPACOBANA machine illustrated next.

## WHERE DO WE STAND?

We devised an algorithm to encrypt data using a product cipher system that will do both shifting and tans positioning of the data in a simple and fast way without using a key to encrypt/decrypt the information. This we call a keyless encryption/decryption system, which requires very little computing resources in both the time and space domains of the computer and could be modified easily to suit a customer's need. The whole system could be implemented on a System on a Chip (SOC) or microcontroller, or even on a single chip with 8K of memory.

Our system is built about the Automata theorem, which states that if there exists a finite set of characters representing a language L, closed over a character set ($\Sigma$), which in our case is the ASCII code set, so that $\Sigma=\{W|$ all characters of the ASCII character set* $\}$.

This is read as the set of all words (W) such that whatever is said about W to the right of the vertical bar is right. This includes all the words that could be assembled by all legal characters in the language's alphabet in any order with any number of repetitions.

Since (L) is closed of the ASCII character set, then there exists a function such that if applied over the members of (L), the generated output would still be a subset of (L).

If we define a function S to scramble or encrypt the element of (L) such that

$$S(L) = \sum_{m=0}^{n-1} \{W \mid P[m] >> 4 \mid P[n-m] << 4\} \tag{12}$$

*Figure 9. 32-bit encryption process*

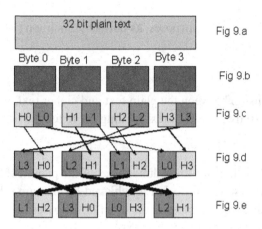

where $\Sigma$ is the character set of all the ASCII codes, (n) is the number of bytes in a given string or block, (m) is a loop iterater to access individual alphabets in the given subset (string), (S) is the scrambled information (cipher text), and P is the plain text information.

The (S) function applies both a logical right shift to the upper side of a byte and logically left shifted lower part of another byte over the field of legal alphabets of the language (L).

S(L) is a scrambling function applied over a subset of alphabet (P) presenting the plain text information of a message, since S(L) and P(L) are both closed over (L), then by induction we can deduce that the function P(L) is the reverse of S(L), so by applying the function S(L) over the scrambled text will produce the original plain text of the original message.

The system achieves two purposes, one of which is to hide the real message of the plain text, and the second is to make it harder to detect the relationship between the plain text and the scrambled (encrypted) text.

In many formal languages, certain letters of the alphabet appear more frequently than others; in English, the letter "e" is likely the most common letter in any sample of text; similarly, the digraph "th" is the most likely pair of letters, and so forth.

In mathematics, physics, and signal processing, frequency analysis is a method to decompose a function, wave, or signal into its frequency components so it is possible to have the frequency spectrum.

In cryptanalysis, frequency analysis is the study of the frequency of letters or groups of letters in a cipher text (encrypted text). This method is used as an aid to break classical ciphers such as transposition ciphers and substitution ciphers, but more complex algorithms can be formed by mixing substitution and transposition to form a product cipher such as the system we are proposing.

Figure 9 resembles the encryption process, and Figures 9a through 9e describe it in further detail.

The data in this scheme are read serially from an input stream or file as a block of 32 bits (Figure 9a) or 4 bytes numbered from 0 to 3, as shown in Figure 9b; then the bytes are separated into constituent nibbles where each byte yields two nibbles that represent the lower and upper halves of the byte, as shown in Figure 9c. Each of the byte nibbles are shifted in a symmetrical way, as shown in Figure 9d;

the nibbles are changed in order so the lower nibbles are shifted into the upper portion, and the higher nibbles are shifted into the lower portion. The nibbles are then exchanged between the bytes, as shown in Figure 9e. The bytes are then changed in order according to our proprietary algorithm to constitute the encrypted text (cipher text).

In this way, our algorithm achieves two purposes, as noted by Shannon (Schneier, 1996).

## Definitions

**Confusion**. Obscures the relationship between the plain text and cipher text, which makes it harder to break and frustrates attempts to study the cipher text looking for redundancies and statistical patterns (substitution).

**Diffusion.** On the other hand, distributes the redundancies of the plain text by spreading it over the cipher text (transposition). In our system, confusion is achieved by changing the nibbles (half byte: 4 bits) of bytes, and diffusion is achieved by changing the order of the bytes in the final pass, which kills the relationship between the plain text and the cipher text.

## THE DECRYPTION PROCESS

Since the encryption process splits the bytes into halves and rearranges the bytes according to our algorithm, and looking back at the encryption formula we used in the encryption process, we can deduce that the decryption process is the same as the encryption process, but the input is the cipher text, and the output is plain text.

*Figure 10. 32-bit decryption process*

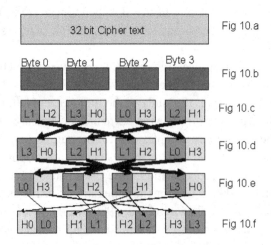

298

Figure 10 resembles the decryption process, and Figures 10a through 10f describe it in further detail.

As shown in Figure 10a, the data are read as a stream of 32-bit or 4 bytes (Figure 10a, Figure 10b). The bytes are then divided into nibbles (Figure 10c), and the nibbles are shifted as in the encryption process, which repositions the nibbles in their original places; and the bytes are changed in locations, which gives original plain text as shown in Figure 10c.

The data arranged in bytes are already scrambled and are read in the same order they are received, as shown in Figure 10d. After the nibble shifting, the data will be as shown in Figure 10e. After rearranging the bytes, we get the original plain text, as shown in Figure 10f.

From that, we find that the decryption process is the same as the encryption process, and the only difference is the type of data read in both cases, which proved that the process is a closed function over the language L, and both P[L] and S[L] are true subsets of the language L, as mentioned earlier and proved to be true by our program.

The differences between this system and other systems (DES. RCx, ....etc) are:

1.  In the other systems, the input is usually a text file, and there is a need to generate a large set of encryption keys. In this system, the file could be any digital data, and there are no keys that reveal the hidden data within the encrypted information. There is also no need to generate the encryption keys.
2.  In the other systems, reapplying the encryption process more than once might increase the complexity of both the encryption and decryption processes, but in this system, applying the encryption process more than once does not increase the complexity, but in fact it decrypts the encrypted data as demonstrated by our program.
3.  There are no complicated mathematical operations associated with our system, which are found in the other systems in order to decrypt the encrypted text.
4.  Other systems require a complicated set of subroutines to achieve their functions, but our system uses a very simple programming approach, as can be seen from the source code listing.

## MULTIMEDIA SECURITY

Our method of multimedia security is based on a proprietary keyless self-encrypting/decrypting scheme, where the multimedia content is transformed from its original format into a special kind of format that can only be understood by our decrypting scheme.

When encryption is used in this context, it converts the original multimedia data into a form that cannot be interpreted without correctly decrypting it, therefore enforcing confidentiality, although it can be used to enforce nonrepudiation when public key encryption is used. Checksums or hash-functions can be used to ensure the integrity of the multimedia data, specifically when the data are transmitted over a network.

A practical example could be using an external module that plugs into the connection port of a cellular GSM phone and diverts the data from the output port to the external module, which encrypts the data and sends them back to the phone to be sent over the air to someone who has the same module on the other side of the link.

In this way, both parties can send each other all kinds of media, including sound and video, encrypted in a way that no others can detect it or can have access to it. All this can be done in real time without the overhead and complexity of generating special keys and using very complex key distribution schemes.

*Keyless Self-Encrypting Algorithm*

- Open file in for reading plain text as binary
- Make sure to read until the end of file
- Form=0 to 3   number of bytes in 32 bit
- P[m]=fgetc(ch,in) reading the input form in
- Till end of loop
- For m=0 to 3
- S[m]=p[m]>>4 | p[3-m]<<4 encryption
- If (m>1)
- S[m]=p[(m+m-1)mod 4]
- Else
- S[m]=p[abs(2m-2)]
- For m=0 to 3
- Output s[m] to output file if there are no larger blocks
- Else make a larger block and wait for the other larger blocks to become available
- When all larger bocks are available, shuffle them as in the algorithm
- If there are no more larger blocks, then write the blocks to the output file

*Keyless Self-Decrypting Algorithm*

- Read all blocks from input file
- Shuffle the blocks
- Break the blocks into smaller ones
- Shuffle the small blocks
- Wait till all large blocks are reassembled
- Shuffled large blocks
- Reassemble the plain text
- Output the plain text to output file
- For m=0 to 3
- Fgetc(s[m],in) read in the ciphered text
- For m=0 to 3
- If (m >1)
- T[m]=s[(m+m-1)mod 4];
- Else
- T[m]=s[abs(2m-2)];
- For m=0 to 3
- P[m]=t[m]<<4 | t[3-m]>>4

- Fputc(p[m],out)*
- *If there are no larger blocks

## CONCLUSION

After thorough testing, we found that our system can do 133K/sec consistently using a PI 100 MHz CPU, which we believe will do well in many kinds of applications requiring this kind of service, clear from results that our algorithm out performs the algorithms in many aspects; most importantly, it fits best for real-time application and multimedia application.

## Further Research Directions

Our keyless self-encrypting/decrypting system is built around a 32-bit encryptor/decryptor and might be further expanded to cover 128 to reach up to 512 bits and more, and will still be efficient in both speed and size, which could be implemented into a hardware solution using a microcontroller and a small-sized memory. Higher order of encryption/decryption systems (512, 2048, etc.) will be presented as an algorithm, and we will elaborate on it as time allows.

## REFERENCES

Ball, R. (1960). *Mathematical recreations and essays*. New York: MacMillan.

Beker, H., & Piper, F. (1982). *Cipher systems: The protection of communications*. London: Northwood Books.

Bennett, J. (1987). Analysis of the encryption algorithm used in WordPerfect word processing program. *Cryptologia, 11*(4), 206–210.

Bergen, H.A., & Caelli, W.J. (1991). File security in WordPerfect 5.0. Cryptologia, 15(1), 57–66.

Deavours, C.A., & Kruh, L. (1985). *Machine cryptography and modern cryptanalysis*. Norwood, MA: Artech House.

Denning, D.E. (1982). *Cryptography and data security*. Addison–Wesley.

Dyson. (1979). Time without end: Physics and biology in an open universe. *Reviews of Modern Physics, 52*(3), 447–460.

Friedman, W.F. (1967). Cryptology. *Encyclopedia Britannica*, vol. 6 (pp. 844–851).

Hart, G.W. (1994). To decode short cryptograms. *Communications of the ACM, 37*(9), 102–108.

Hill, L.S. (1929). Cryptography in an algebraic alphabet. *American Mathematical Monthly, 36*, 306–312.

Hodges, A. (1983). *Alan Turing: The enigma of intelligence*. Simon and Schuster.

Friedman, W.F. (1976). *Elements of cryptanalysis*. Laguna Hills, CA: Aegean Park Press.

Friedman, W.F. (1987). The index of coincidence and its applications in cryptography. Riverbank Publication No. 22, Riverbank Labs, 1920. Reprinted by Aegean Park Press.

Kahn, D. (1967). The codebreakers: The story of secret writing. New York: Macmillan Publishing Co.

Kahn, D. (1983). Kahn on codes. New York: Macmillan Publishing Co.

Kahn, D. (1994). Seizing the enigma. Boston: Houghton Mifflin Co.

Knudsen, L.R. (1994). *Block ciphers—Analysis, design, applications* [doctoral dissertation]. Aarhus University.

Konheim, A.G. (1981). *Cryptography: A primer*. New York: John Wiley & Sons.

Kullback, S. (1976). Statistical methods in cryptanalysis. First printed by U.S. Government Printing Office (1935). Aegean Park Press.

Peleg, S., & Rosenfield, A. (1979). Breaking substitution ciphers using a relaxation algorithm. *Communications of the ACM, 22*(11), 598–605.

Scherbius, A. (1928). Ciphering machine, U.S. Patent #1,657,411.

Schneier, B. (1993). Data guardians. *MacWorld, 10*(2), 145–151.

Schneier, B. (1994). *Protect your Macintosh*. Peachpit Press.

Sinkov, A. (1966). *Elementary cryptanalysis*. Mathematical Association of America.

Stevens, A. (1990). Hacks, spooks, and data encryption. *Dr. Dobb's Journal, 15*(9), 127–134, 147–149.

Williams, E.A. (1959). *An invitation to cryptograms*. New York: Simon and Schuster.

## ADDITIONAL READING

Bellovin, S.M. (1996). Problem areas for the IP security protocols. *Proceedings of the USENIX UNIX Security Symposium.*

Bleichenbacker, D. (1998). Chosen ciphertext attacks against protocols based on RSA PKCS#1. Advances in Cryptology, CRYPTO 98.

Feistel, H., Notz, W.A., & Smith, J.L. Some cryptographic techniques for machine to machine data.

Fluhrer, S., Mantin, I., & Shamir. (2001). Weaknesses in the key scheduling algorithm of RC4.

Konheim, A.G. (1981). *Cryptography: A primer*. New York: John Wiley & Sons.

Newsham, T. (2001). Cracking WEP keys. *Proceedings of Blackhat 2001.*

Nichols, M. (2001b). *Teaching for learning*. New Zealand: TrainInc.co.nz.

Peikari, C., & Fogie, S. (2003). Cracking WEP.

Practical exploitation of RC4 weaknesses in WEP environments (2002).

Shannon, C.E. (1951). Predication and entropy in printed English. *Bell System Technical Journal*, 30(1), 50–64.

Shotsberger, P.G., & Vetter, R. (2001). Teaching and learning in the wireless classroom.

# Chapter XVI
# DSP Techniques for Sound Enhancement of Old Recordings

**Paulo A. A. Esquef**
*Nokia Institute of Technology, Brazil*

**Luiz W.P. Biscainho**
*Federal University of Rio de Janeiro, Brazil*

## ABSTRACT

*This chapter addresses digital signal processing techniques for sound restoration and enhancement. The most common sound degradations found in audio recordings, such as thumps, pops, clicks, and hiss are characterized. Moreover, the most popular solutions for sound restoration are described, with emphasis on their practical applicability. Finally, critical views on the performance of currently available restoration algorithms are provided, along with discussions on new tendencies observed in the field.*

## INTRODUCTION

### A Brief History of Recording Technology

The history of recorded sound starts around 1877 when Thomas A. Edison demonstrated a tinfoil cylinder phonograph that was capable of recording and reproducing human voice for the first time. The following decades were marked by continuous attempts to find more accurate ways to record and reproduce sounds. It is possible to divide the sound recording history roughly into three eras. The acoustic era lasted until the mid-20s when means to record and reproduce sound via electro-mechanical transducers were launched. The electric era witnessed the emergence and development of magnetic tape as well as stereophonic recordings. It reigned until about the beginning of the eighties, when digital recordings came about boosted by the finalization of the compact disc standard in 1980, being a direct consequence of the developments of electronic computers, in conjunction with the ability to record data onto magnetic or optical media.

Nowadays, digital audio technology is found in most consumer audio appliances. Its objectives range from improving the quality of modern and old recording/reproduction techniques to achieving an adequate balance between storage space or transmission capacity requirements and sound quality. A comprehensive timeline with descriptions of the most prominent events that marked the recording technology history is provided by Coleman (2004), Morton (2000), and Schoenherr (2005).

## Aims and Processing Chain

The primary purpose of digital audio restoration is to employ digital signal processing to improve the sound quality of old recordings. A conservative goal consists of eliminating only the audible spurious artifacts that either are introduced by recording and playback mechanisms or result from aging and wear of recorded media, while retaining as faithfully as possible the original recorded sound (Godsill & Rayner, 1998a). Less restricted approaches would allow more intrusive sound modifications, such as elimination of the audience noises and correction of performance mistakes. An even more audacious concept could target at overcoming the intrinsic limitations of the recording media in order to obtain a restored sound with better quality than the originally recorded one.

In any case, a typical audio restoration chain starts with capturing the sound from old matrices and transferring it to a digital form. This stage is crucial for a successful restoration job, since it is likely to substantially affect the final sonic quality of the results. Sound transfer can be a tricky task due to the usual lack of standardization associated with obsolete recording and playback systems. The process may involve searching for the original matrices or best sounding copies and choosing the best way to play back a given matrix. Such job includes finding the right reproducing apparatus in good condition, as well as dealing with diverse recording equalization curves, among other issues.

Prior to the digital era it was already common to transfer sound from old medium types to more modern ones, for instance from 78 RPM (revolutions per minute) to LP (long-playing) disks. Also frequently seen during the electric era were attempts to enhance the sound quality of the recordings by analog means, either within the sound transfer process or at the playback stage (Burwen, 1978; Craven & Gerzon, 1975; Kinzie, Jr. & Gravereaux, 1973). The advent of the digital era and the progressive increases in computation power of digital processors made it possible to employ more and more involved signal processing techniques to digitized audio data. As a consequence, nowadays, audio restoration is mostly carried out through customized DSP algorithms meant to suppress and reduce audible undesirable noises or distortions that are still present in the signal after the sound transfer. Still within the digital domain, the de-noised signal can be further processed if necessary, for example, equalized, prior to the final remastering, which concludes the audio restoration chain.

## Typical Degradations

Most of the undesirable noises found in old recordings can be roughly classified, for didactic reasons, between global and localized disturbances (Godsill & Rayner, 1998a). As these names suggest, global disturbances affect the signal as a whole, whereas localized noises corrupt only limited portions of the signal. Typical examples of global degradations are continuous background disturbances or interferences, such as broadband noise (hiss), buzz, and hum. As for localized degradations, the most obvious examples are short-time impulsive noises, such as clicks, crackles, and pops, as well as low-frequency pulses, also known as thumps. Other common types of degradations, which may not fall clearly into the previous two classes, are slow and fast frequency modulations, which are known as wow and flutter, respectively, and nonlinear distortions, such as amplitude clipping and compression.

## From Older to Newer Ideas

In the analog era, restoration was restricted to some simplistic (although not always trivial) procedures. For example, a general way to reduce surface noise was low-pass filtering the recording according to the rule "the noisier the signal, the more radically filtered." Localized disturbances could be literally cut from a magnetic-tape copy, in spite of the resulting timing squeeze. In case of long portions of lost signal, the recording could be patched by copies of similar passages. Besides being time-consuming, this kind of job demanded too many manual skills for sometimes poor final results.

The digital era opened new avenues for audio processing. However, some general principles were retained, such as search-and-cleaning of localized defects in time-based methods, and overall, possibly non-linear, filtering of global distortions in frequency-based methods. Only recently new paradigms have been launched, for instance, sound restoration by resynthesis (see the section on "Future Directions").

In spite of all commercial interest in audio restoration (or perhaps for this very reason), the related literature is scarce. To the authors' knowledge, in 2006 the only book in print dealing exclusively with digital audio restoration is by Godsill and Rayner (1998a). Other books, like the ones by Ó Ruanaidh and Fitzgerald (1996), Vaseghi (2006), and Veldhuis (1990), grew around particular topics on this subject, but developed into more extended contents.

## Chapter Organization

The purpose of this chapter is to review digital signal processing techniques used in audio restoration for treating disturbances such as thumps, clicks, and hiss. The presentation follows the order of precedence in which the problems are usually tackled. Methods and algorithms devised for dealing with other types of degradations can be found elsewhere (Godsill & Rayner, 1998a). In addition to this brief introduction, the section on "Long Pulse Removal" describes techniques for removal of long pulses of low-frequency content from audio signals. The section on "Audio De-Clicking" reviews a common model-based method for impulsive noise detection in audio signals, covering algorithms for signal reconstruction as well. The section on "Audio De-Hissing" addresses reduction of corrupting broadband noise in audio signals. The chapter concludes with a discussion on future directions concerning the digital audio restoration field.

## LONG-PULSE REMOVAL

Large discontinuities on the groove walls of a disk, such as those provoked by deep scratches or breakages on the disk surface, are bound to excite the mechanical parts of the playback mechanism in an abnormal way. As a consequence, the resulting reproduced signal becomes contaminated by additive long pulses of low-frequency content that are heard as thumps.

*Figure 1. Examples of long pulses: (a) Isolated pulse, (b) superimposed pulses*

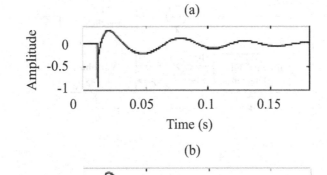

The next sections are devoted to first qualify the degradation and then review three methods of long-pulse removal. The first employs a template matching scheme; the second is based on separation of autoregressive (AR) models; and the third is built upon non-linear filtering techniques.

## Degradation Characterization

A typical long pulse is usually preceded by a short-time impulsive disturbance of high amplitude. The pulse shape after this impulsive transient is related to the impulse response of the stylus-arm set. Therefore, it is acceptable to assume that, ideally and for a given playback equipment, the pulse shape is invariable, only changing in amplitude.

The pulse tail is composed of varying low-frequency components within the range from 5 to 100 Hz, modulated in amplitude by a decaying envelope (Vaseghi, 1988). Moreover, it can be observed that the oscillations become slower as the pulse decays.

In practice, the impulsive-like excitations that drive the stylus-arm mechanism can be far from an ideal impulse, thus implying changes to the shape of the long pulses associated with certain equipment. Moreover, it may happen that the pulses occur in a clustered way, for instance, when there are two or more scratches very close to each other on a disk surface. As a result, new pulses can be generated while the response of the previous one has not yet vanished, yielding the so-called superimposed pulses. The resulting shape of superimposed and isolated pulses can differ substantially from each other. Figure 1 depicts both situations.

*Figure 2. Block diagram of the template matching method for long-pulse removal, (adapted from Vaseghi and Frayling-Cork (1992)*

*Figure 2. Block diagram of the template matching method for long-pulse removal, (adapted from Vaseghi and Frayling-Cork (1992)*

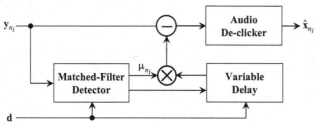

## Template Matching

The template matching method for detecting and suppressing long pulses was introduced by Vaseghi (1988) and Vaseghi and Frayling-Cork (1992) and figures among the first propositions to appear in the literature. A block diagram of the processing stages of the template matching scheme for pulse removal is shown in Figure 2.

The key-point behind the method is the assumption of shape similarity among the pulse occurrences. Thus, if the assumption is valid, each pulse occurrence is considered a version of the template, possibly scaled in amplitude. Provided the availability of a pulse template, the corrupting pulses are detected in the signal by means of cross-correlating the template with the observed noisy signal and looking for values of the cross-correlation coefficient that are close to unity in magnitude. Once detected, a corrupting pulse can be suppressed by subtracting a scaled version of the template from the signal, after proper synchronization.

## Degradation Model

In mathematical terms, a segment of the observed signal corrupted with a long pulse can be modeled as:

$$\mathbf{y}_n = \mathbf{x}_n + \mu \mathbf{d}, \tag{1}$$

where $\mathbf{y}_n = [y_n, y_{n+1}, \ldots, y_{n+N-1}]^{\mathrm{T}}$ is a segment containing the corrupted signal, $\mathbf{x}_n = [x_n, x_{n+1}, \ldots, x_{n+N-1}]^{\mathrm{T}}$ is the corresponding clean version, $\mathbf{d} = [d_0, d_1, \ldots, d_{N-1}]^{\mathrm{T}}$ is the pulse template containing $N$ samples, and $\mu$ is a scaling factor.

### Template Estimation

A pulse template can be obtained from a noise-only excerpt of the signal, if such an occurrence is available. If not, an estimate for the pulse shape has to be obtained from a "noisy" version of the pulse, that is, a pulse that also contains information on the clean signal $\mathbf{x}_n$.

Since the signal of interest is the pulse tail, which contains only low frequencies, the noisy pulse can be passed through a low-pass filter, with cutoff frequency of about 100 Hz, in order to reduce the information associated with the clean signal in the template.

Another possibility consists of using an adaptive template estimation scheme integrated to the pulse detection procedure (Vaseghi, 1988). In this approach the pulse detection algorithm begins with a noisy template. As long as other pulses are being detected, a scheme that averages the detected pulses can be applied to filter out the information associated with the clean audio components. This way, the pulse estimate is progressively refined.

## Pulse Detection

As mentioned before, the samples of the detection signal used in the template matching scheme are the cross-correlation coefficients computed between the template and signal segments contained in a window that slides over the observed signal. This procedure can be realized by filtering the noisy signal through a matched filter whose impulse response is simply formed by a time-reversed version of the template, so that the output of the filter at a given time instant $n$ is computed as:

$$\mathbf{z}_{\mathrm{DET},n} = \mathbf{d}^{\mathrm{T}}\mathbf{y}_n. \tag{2}$$

However, in order to obtain the cross-correlation coefficients it is necessary to divide $\mathbf{z}_{\mathrm{DET},n}$ by $c = (N-1)\sqrt{\sigma_{\mathbf{x}}^2 \sigma_{\mathbf{h}}^2}$, where $\sigma_{\mathbf{x}}^2$ and $\sigma_{\mathbf{h}}^2$ are the variances associated with the input signal segment and the matched filter, respectively. Thus, the cross-correlation coefficient sequence is given by:

$$r_{\mathbf{xh},n} = \frac{\mathbf{z}_{\mathrm{DET},n}}{c}. \tag{3}$$

By property, the values of the cross-correlation coefficients are within the range $-1 \le r_{\mathbf{xh},n} \le 1$. Moreover, values of $|r_{\mathbf{xh},n}|$ close to the unity indicate a strong correlation between the input signal and the template. Thus, pulse detection can be carried out by searching for time instants $n_i$ associated with the local maxima of $|r_{\mathbf{xh},n}|$ whose values are above a user-defined threshold.

## Pulse Suppression

Suppose that a certain pulse is detected and its starting point occurs at instant $n_i$. The pulse suppression is simply realized by subtracting a scaled version of the template from the corrupted signal. Thus, an estimate of the clean signal is computed as:

$$\hat{\mathbf{x}}_{n_i} = \mathbf{y}_{n_i} - \mu_{n_i}\mathbf{d}, \tag{4}$$

where the amplitude scaling factor can be shown to be determined by (Vaseghi, 1988),

$$\mu_{n_i} = \frac{\mathbf{z}_{\mathrm{DET},n}}{\mathbf{d}^{\mathrm{T}}\mathbf{d}}. \tag{5}$$

It should be noticed that the pulse suppression described in equation (5) is only meant to remove the low-frequency part of the pulse. The initial high-amplitude click that drives the pulse remains still to be treated. For this purpose any standard de-clicking method can be applied (see the section on "Audio De-Clicking").

## Performance

Besides its simplicity, another advantage of the template matching method is that it serves to both detect and suppress long pulses. The main drawback of the method is the lack of robustness to deal with pulses whose shape varies over time as well as with superimposed pulses. As regards the former issue, Vaseghi (1988) proposed the use of a database of pulse templates with different shapes, so that the system would search for the best template match the observed pulses. The solution, of course, increases the computational cost of the method. Nonetheless, it leaves unsolved the problem with superimposed pulses, especially when the inter-pulse delay varies over time, as it happens in the case of crossed scratches. The previous shortcomings have motivated the design of more sophisticated algorithms to treat long pulses, as the AR-separation method described in the following section.

## AR Separation

The AR separation method for long-pulse removal was introduced by Godsill (1993). The proposed formulation assumes that both the underlying clean signal and the corrupting pulse are independent stochastic processes governed by AR models (see equation (15) for their definition). As before, each pulse is considered to be an additive disturbance to the audio signal, leading thus to a corrupted signal that can be thought of as a mixture of two AR processes. Provided that the model parameters for both processes can be estimated, signal restoration can be accomplished by separating one of the processes from the mixture.

### Signal and Pulse Models

The mixture of the two AR processes that compose the corrupted signal is given by:

$$\mathbf{y} = \sum_{i=1}^{2} \mathbf{x}_i ,$$

(6)

where, by convention, index $i=1$ will be related to the underlying signal process. Moreover, each of the independent AR processes $\mathbf{x}_i$ is assumed to follow a Gaussian distribution (Godsill & Rayner, 1998a),

$$p_{\mathbf{x}_i}(\mathbf{x}_i) = \frac{1}{(2\pi\sigma_{e_i}^2)^{\frac{N-p_i}{2}}} \exp\left( -\frac{1}{2\sigma_{e_i}^2} \mathbf{x}_i^{\mathrm{T}} \mathbf{A}_i^{\mathrm{T}} \mathbf{A}_i \mathbf{x}_i \right),$$

(7)

where $\sigma_{e_i}^2$ is the variance of the process excitation (which, in this context, consists of white noise), $N$ is the number of samples of the observed process, $p_i$ is the AR-model order, and $\mathbf{A}_i$ is an $(N - p_i) \times N$ matrix of the form:

$$\mathbf{A}_i = \begin{bmatrix} -a_{i_{p_i}} & \cdots & -a_{i_1} & 1 & 0 & \cdots & 0 \\ 0 & -a_{i_{p_i}} & \cdots & -a_{i_1} & 1 & 0 & \cdots \\ \vdots & \ddots & -a_{i_{p_i}} & \cdots & -a_{i_1} & 1 & \vdots \\ 0 & \cdots & 0 & -a_{i_{p_i}} & \cdots & -a_{i_1} & 1 \end{bmatrix},$$

(8)

whose nonzero elements are the AR-model coefficients.

In the AR separation method both the initial click and the low-frequency tail are modeled by the same AR model. However, the variance of the excitation associated with the click part is much higher than that related to the tail. Godsill (1993) then formulates the separation problem in terms of a switched AR model in which the diagonal correlation matrix $\Lambda$ of the excitation noise process has elements defined by:

$$\lambda_k = \sigma_{e_{2,t}}^2 + j_k (\sigma_{e_{2,c}}^2 - \sigma_{e_{2,t}}^2), \tag{9}$$

where $\sigma_{e_{2,t}}^2$ and $\sigma_{e_{2,c}}^2$ are variances of the tail and click parts of the noise process, respectively, whereas $j_k$ is a binary indicator made equal to 1 for those indices $k$ associated with pulse samples that are considered driving clicks.

## Separation Formula

It can be shown that the maximum *a posteriori* (MAP) estimate of the underlying signal process can be computed by (Godsill & Rayner, 1998a):

$$\mathbf{x}_1^{\mathrm{MAP}} = \left( \frac{\mathbf{A}_1^{\mathrm{T}} \mathbf{A}_1}{\sigma_{e_1}^2} + \mathbf{A}_2^{\mathrm{T}} \Lambda^{-1} \mathbf{A}_2 \right)^{-1} \mathbf{A}_2^{\mathrm{T}} \Lambda^{-1} \mathbf{A}_2 \mathbf{y}. \tag{10}$$

The practical problem is then reduced to the estimation of the model parameters and the indicator $j_k$.

An issue that cannot be overlooked is that, even in the ideal case of known model parameters, the separation performance is dependent on excitation variances. Intuitively, high-power processes are more easily separable than low-power ones.

## Parameter Estimation

The estimation of the model parameters associated with the underlying signal can be realized by standard AR model estimators, such as the Yule-Walker and Burg's methods (Hayes, 1996; Kay, 1988; Makhoul, 1977). Models of orders around 50 suffice for the aimed purpose (Godsill & Rayner, 1998a; Janssen, Veldhuis, & Vries, 1986). Since a typical long pulse can last longer than a period within which audio signals can be considered stationary, it is necessary to employ a block-based AR separation scheme. For instance, segments of about 1000 samples can be used, considering signals sampled at 44.1 kHz.

Counting on the assumption of local signal stationarity, Godsill and Tan suggest taking the signal portion that immediately precedes the beginning of the pulse as the source of model estimation for the subsequent block. One can adopt a similar strategy to treat the succeeding blocks, that is, as long as a signal frame is treated it is used as the observation data upon which to estimate the model of the subsequent frame. It should be noticed, however, that such a scheme is prone to propagation errors. Another possibility, devised to reduce the computational costs of the procedure, consists of treating only the signal portion composed of the initial click and the beginning of the pulse tail, leaving the rest of the pulse to be removed by standard high-pass filtering (Godsill, 1993).

When it comes to the estimation of the model parameters associated with the pulse, if a clean pulse is available, the AR model parameters can be estimated from that observation. Of course, this approach counts on the similarity among pulse occurrences. In the lack of a clean pulse, it is possible to use a fixed second order model with coefficients $a_2=2$ and $a_1=-1$ as a reasonable approximation. The variances $\sigma_{e_{2,t}}^2$ and $\sigma_{e_{2,c}}^2$ must be set experimentally. Moreover, it is recommended to decrease $\sigma_{e_{2,t}}^2$ exponentially toward the end of the pulse tail (Godsill & Tan, 1997).

The indicators $j_k$ can be obtained by inverse filtering the corrupted segment through an estimate of its AR model. A similar procedure is used in click detection (see the section on "Click Detection").

## Performance

The AR-separation method has been reported to offer an effective solution for long-pulse removal. Moreover, since no specific shape is assumed for the pulses, it is capable of treating pulses whose form varies over time as well as superimposed pulse occurrences. Another advantage is the joint suppression of the initial click and low-frequency parts of the pulse. The main disadvantage of the AR-separation method lies in its heavy computational load. This issue can be alleviated by employing a separation scheme based on Kalman filtering (Godsill & Tan, 1997).

## Nonlinear Filtering

A more recent proposition for audio de-thumping, which was presented by Esquef, Biscainho, and Väli-mäki (2003), makes use of non-linear filtering techniques for estimating the waveform of long pulses. As with the previous methods, the degradation model is additive, but no hypothesis is made on the pulse shape. It is only assumed that the tail part of the pulse is composed of low-frequency components.

The pulse estimation procedure is divided into two stages: the first is meant to obtain an initial estimate of the pulse shape and is based on a procedure called two-pass split window (TPSW); the second stage employs a polynomial filtering scheme to refine the estimate.

### TPSW Filtering

The two-pass split window was proposed by Struzinski (1984) and Struzinski and Lowe (1984) as a tool to estimate the background noise magnitude in peaky spectra. The key idea consisted of submitting the sampled magnitude spectrum to a couple of linear filters with a non-linear signal modification in between the two filtering steps.

In the first pass a rectangular moving average filter with a center gap, as shown in Figure 3, is employed. Provided that the length of the gap is large enough to encompass the width of observed spectral peaks, the first pass of the procedure produces an average magnitude spectrum in which the influence of the peak values on the average is mitigated at the peak locations. This happens because, at those locations, the peaks and the filter gap coincide. The peaks, however, may still induce on the filtered spectrum an average bias around their locations.

The second pass is meant to correct the aforementioned bias. Prior to it, a sample substitution criterion is applied to the intermediate signal so that, around the peak locations, the original magnitude spectrum is recovered. The output of the second filter, which now can be an ordinary moving average, yields a smooth background magnitude spectrum with little influence of the spectral peaks.

*Figure 3. Example of split window*

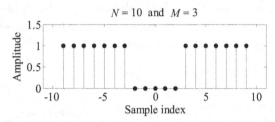

The TPSW filtering procedure can be easily adapted to deal with the problem of long pulse estimation. In this case, the waveform of the pulse tail plays the role of the background spectrum. In mathematical terms, the first pass of the TPSW procedure is realized by a conventional discrete convolution between the noisy signal $\mathbf{y}_n$ and a split window defined by:

$$\mathbf{h}_{SW,n} = \begin{cases} 0, & |n| < M \\ 1, & M \le |n| < N \end{cases} \tag{11}$$

where $N$ and $M$ are odd-valued parameters related to the lengths of the window and its middle gap, respectively. For instance, the split window shown in Figure 3 was generated with parameters $N=10$ and $M=3$. The modification of the intermediate signal prior to the second pass is governed by the following criterion:

$$\mathbf{y}_{M,n} = \begin{cases} \mathbf{y}_{I,n}, & \text{if } |\mathbf{y}_n - \mathbf{y}_{I,n}| > \alpha |\mathbf{y}_{I,n}| \\ \mathbf{y}_n, & \text{otherwise} \end{cases} \tag{12}$$

where, by convention, $\mathbf{y}_{I,n}$ refers to the intermediate signal that results from the first pass and $\alpha \ge 1$ is a parameter that controls the click rejection capability. It should be noticed that no prior information on the location of the pulse clicks is taken into account.

The second pass can be carried out by convolving an ordinary square window with the modified intermediate signal $\mathbf{y}_{M,n}$. This leads to the TPSW-based estimate of the long pulse:

$$\hat{\mathbf{d}}_{TPSW,n} = \frac{1}{2N-1} \sum_{k=-N}^{N} y_{M,n-k}. \tag{13}$$

The effects of the passes are illustrated on subplots (a) and (b) of Figure 4. In the shown examples, the length of the split window was 111 samples with a middle gap of 31 samples, that is, $N=55$ and $M=15$, respectively. The value of $\alpha$ was set experimentally to 8. From subplot (a) it is possible to notice that the pulse clicks are pointing downward and upward at time instants 8 and 20 ms, respectively. Moreover, one can observe how those clicks move the output of the first pass downward and upward, respectively, in their surroundings.

*Figure 4. TPSW results: (a) Input signal (thin solid line) showing an example of the beginning of a superimposed pulse and output of the first pass (bold solid line); (b) intermediate signal (thin solid line) after signal substitution and output of the second pass (bold solid line); (c) input signal (thin solid line) and output of a moving-average filter (bold solid line)*

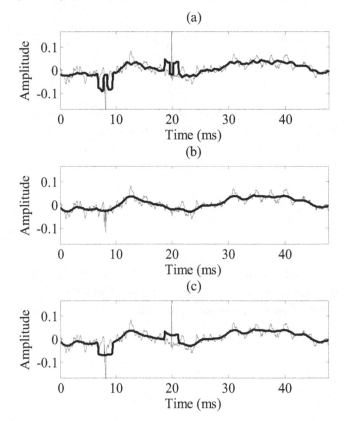

After the second pass, however, the bias is substantially reduced and a signal that approximates the pulse waveform is obtained. Just for comparison purposes, the signal that would result by submitting the noisy signal to a conventional moving-average filter is shown on subplot (c), where the harmful peak influence can be more clearly seen.

Esquef, Biscainho, and Välimäki (2003) show the necessity of adjusting the length of the split windows over time, in order to cope with the frequency variations present in the pulse tail. The adjustment can be done by either changing the effective length of the window over time or using a splicing scheme to merge together three TPSW-based pulse estimates obtained from different split-window sizes.

## Polynomial Fitting

The pulse estimates obtained by the procedures described in the previous section may still contain valuable information on the signal to be restored. This accounts for the need of additional processing

*Figure 5. Illustration of the piece-wise polynomial fitting over segments of a TPSW-based pulse estimate*

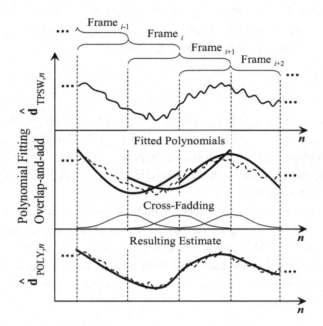

to further refine the pulse estimates. To achieve a suitably smooth pulse estimate, an overlap-and-add polynomial fitting scheme is proposed by Esquef, Biscainho, and Välimäki (2003).

In the presented method, the TPSW-based estimate $\hat{\mathbf{d}}_{\text{TPSW},n}$ is first sub-divided into overlapping short frames. Then a low-order polynomial is fitted to each frame. Finally, the pulse estimate is obtained by adding together the fitted curves. A schematic view of the piece-wise polynomial fitting is depicted in Figure 5.

The level of smoothing attained by the procedure can be controlled by three parameters: the frame overlap percentage, the polynomial order, and the length of the frames. For practical reasons, it is convenient to freeze the overlap factor at 50% or 75% and set the polynomial order to 2. Thus, the user only needs to adjust the length of the frame to control the global smoothness of the pulse estimate. In this case, the longer the frame, the smoother the pulse estimates. Practical values for the frame length range from 50 to 200 samples, considering a sample rate of 44.1 kHz.

In the end, the waveform that results from the polynomial fitting procedure, and which represents final pulse estimate $\hat{\mathbf{d}}_{\text{POLY},n}$, is subtracted from the corrupted signal to yield the de-thumped signal.

## Performance

As with the template matching, the TPSW-based de-thumping method only takes care of suppressing the low-frequency transient of long pulses. The initial pulse click has to be removed later by a de-clicking algorithm (see the section on "Audio De-Clicking"). This should not be considered an extra burden, since de-clicking is usually required as a de-thumping follow up in a typical sound restoration processing chain.

According to Esquef, Biscainho, and Välimäki (2003), the TPSW-based de-thumping method can perform as effectively as the AR-separation method, also when treating superimposed pulses. However, from a computational point of view and for typical values of the processing parameters, the TPSW-based solution can be up to two orders of magnitude less expensive. Comparisons were conducted be means of a set of objective measures and confirmed by informal listening tests.

## Discussion

Among the three de-thumping methods presented, the template matching is the only one that offers a solution for long pulse detection. The AR-separation and the TPSW-based schemes assume the location of the pulses as well as those of the driving initial clicks as *a priori* known information. The template matching is perhaps the most adequate solution when the shape similarity among the corrupting pulses can be accepted as a valid hypothesis.

For more general situations of pulse suppression, including superimposed pulses, the user can opt for either the AR-separation method or the TPSW-based scheme. If keeping the computational costs low is an issue of concern, the most suitable choice would be the TPSW-based solution. Finally, it is important to emphasize that all methods described in this section require a certain degree of interaction with the user, which is needed to choose the values of some processing parameters. Therefore, full automatism cannot be claimed for any of them.

## AUDIO DE-CLICKING

Discontinuities of very short duration present in audio signal are usually heard as clicks. More often, those discontinuities are produced during playback by superficial scratches, accumulated dust or particles, and intrinsic irregularities on a disk surface (Wilson, 1965).

A general model for impulsive noise corruption assumes an additive type of degradation of the form:

$$y_n = x_n + j_n d_n, \tag{14}$$

where $y_n$ is the corrupted signal, $x_n$ is the wanted clean signal, and $j_n d_n$ is the noise component, with $j_n$ being a binary indicator of corrupted samples, that is, $j_{n_i} = 1$ if the sample $y_{n_i}$ is found to be corrupted.

Digital audio de-clickers operate in general between two processing stages: click detection and signal reconstruction. The following sections are meant to describe those stages in more detail.

### Click Detection

One of the most obvious ways to perform click detection is to explore the contrast in frequency content between typical audio signals and clicks. Short-time discontinuities such as clicks contain strong energy on high frequencies as opposed to audio signals, whose energy is more concentrated on low frequencies. Therefore, a straightforward means to produce a detection signal for click location consists of high-pass filtering the signal.

*Figure 6. Click detection via high-pass filtering: (a) Corrupted signal and (b) magnitude of its high-pass filtered version*

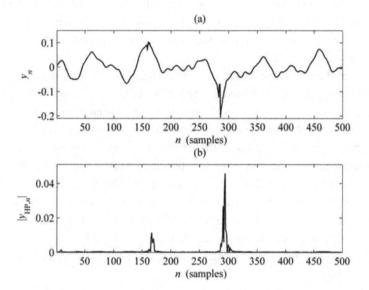

Figure 6 exemplifies the effect of high-pass filtering an audio signal contaminated by clicks. In this case, the audio signal, sampled at 44.1 kHz, was submitted to a 15th-order FIR half-band high-pass filter. It can be noticed that, on the original waveform, it is harder to detect all clicks by amplitude discrimination, especially those with small amplitudes. On the contrary, click occurrences are enhanced in the high-pass filtered version of the signal, $y_{HP,n}$, due to the energy attenuation on the frequency range more associated with the wanted audio content. This reduction on the signal-to-noise ratio (SNR) allows the use of threshold-based amplitude discrimination criteria to locate clicks in the corrupted signal.

## Model-Based Approach

Another option to ease click detection through amplitude criteria is to employ a model-based scheme. A common approach in this direction is to assume that the underlying signal follows an autoregressive (AR) model. High values of the modeling error in relation to the observed data indicate the presence of clicks.

In mathematical terms, the desired clean signal is modeled as:

$$x_n = \sum_{k=1}^{p} a_k x_{n-k} + e_n,$$  (15)

where $a_k$, with $a_0 = 1$, are the coefficients of the $p^{th}$ order AR model and $e_n$ is the modeling error at time instant $n$. An alternative interpretation takes $e_n$ as the excitation signal at the input of an all-pole filter that generates $x_n$ at its output.

In practice, the observed signal must be segmented into short-time frames of $N$ samples in order to render more plausible the hypothesis of local stationarity of audio signals. As a rule of thumb, it suffices to choose a value of $N$ that corresponds to a duration ranging from 20 to 50 ms. Moreover, the available noisy data are used as the observation upon which the estimation of the AR coefficients are carried out. For this purpose any well-known AR model estimator can be employed, such as the autocorrelation or the covariance methods (Hayes, 1996).

Now, assuming that the model is known, a detection signal can be obtained via inverse filtering the observed corrupted data $y_n$ through the model. In other words, $y_n$ is passed through an FIR filter whose coefficients are $(1, -a_1, -a_2, ..., -a_p)$, yielding the signal $e_n$. The initial $p$ samples of $e_n$ are affected by the filter's transient; hence, they should be discarded for click detection purposes.

As with the high-pass filtering approach, the inverse filtering scheme aims at reducing the SNR of the observed data as a means to increase the amplitude contrast between corrupted and clean signal samples. However, the filtering procedure inevitably smears the clicks in time (Vaseghi, 1988), thus hindering their precise location. The higher the filter order, the more prominent the spread of clicks in the detection signal. Therefore, it is recommended to adopt low-order filters, for example, within the range between 10 and 40. It should be noticed that even if those low orders are insufficient to fully model the underlying signal, this is not to worry about, since the primary goal here is click detection, not strict signal modeling.

A suitable click detection criterion is to consider as clicks samples of the corrupted signal that correspond to samples of a detection signal whose magnitude exceed the value of a given threshold. Consider, for instance, a segment of $N$ samples of the detection signal $y_{DS,n}$ associated with of the signal $y_n$. The click indicator can be obtained as:

$$j_n = \begin{cases} 1, & |y_{DS,n}| \geq T \\ 0, & \text{otherwise} \end{cases}, \text{ for } n_i \leq n \leq n_i + N - 1, \tag{16}$$

where $T$ is an adaptive threshold that can be computed as:

$$T = K \text{ median}(|y_{DS,n_i}|, |y_{DS,n_i+1}|, ..., |y_{DS,n_i+N-1}|), \tag{17}$$

with $K$ being a scalar parameter to be adjusted by the user.

The detection signal $y_{DS,n}$ can be either the high-pass filtered version $y_{HP,n}$ of the noisy signal or the modeling error sequence $e_n$. The value of the threshold $T$ varies over time according to the variance of the background component of $y_{DS,n}$. That variance can be estimated in a robust way, for example, via the median operator (Donoho, 1992). The value of $K$, which should be chosen experimentally, controls the balance between missed and false click detections in the signal.

Figure 7 illustrates the effect of inverse filtering on an audio sequence corrupted by impulsive noise. In this case, a 20th order AR model was estimated from the noisy data using Burg's method (Hayes, 1996). It is possible to verify that the magnitude of the detection signal obtained via inverse filtering, $|e_n|$, is composed by a small-magnitude background signal, associated with the stochastic component of $x_n$, and by bursts of high-valued magnitude associated with the corrupting clicks. As with the high-pass filtering case, it seems easier to detect click occurrences by a threshold-based amplitude criterion.

*Figure 7. AR-based inverse filtering for click detection: (a) Corrupted signal and (b) its model error (in solid line) compared with a threshold T, with K=5 (in dashed line)*

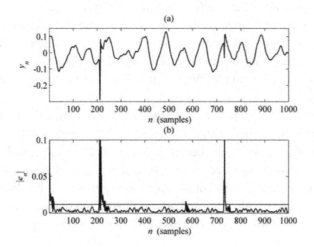

*Figure 8. Processing stages of an AR-based audio de-clicker, (Adapted from Vaseghi & Frayling-Cork, 1992)*

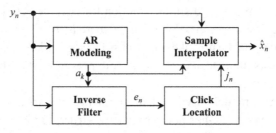

A block diagram showing the typical processing stages of an AR-based audio de-clicker is depicted in Figure 8.

## Performance Improvements

Several means to improve the performance of model-based click detectors have been proposed in the literature. For example, the use of a two-sided linear prediction was suggested by Vaseghi and Rayner (1990). Frequency-warped linear prediction applied to click detection was investigated by Esquef, Karjalainen, and Välimäki (2002). A further improvement on the click detection capability, especially of low-amplitude clicks, is to submit the detection signal to a matched filter, in which the template signal consists of a time-reversed version of the inverse filter coefficients (Vaseghi, 1988). The main drawback of such resource is that it contributes an additional spread to the click occurrences, which may be critical when dealing with clicks well clustered in time.

An example of the effect of passing the detection signal of Figure 7 through a matched filter can be seen in Figure 9. It can be noticed that, for example, the detection of the small-amplitude one-sample click that occurs around sample 570 is greatly facilitated by the matched filter. The costs for that detection gain are the longer filter's transient and the substantial spread that afflicts the clicks in the detection signal.

The threshold-based criterion of equation (15) may fail to provide the precise location and extension of a click. Apart from the signal spread, which, by delaying the end of a click, tends to cause the overestimation of its duration, there is the possibility of intermediate samples of the detection signal associated with a click occurrence having a magnitude that lies below the threshold value (see, for instance, the click occurrence around sample 250 in Figure 9). As a result, a given click can be undesirably split into several parts.

Solutions for the previous problems were proposed by Esquef, Biscainho, Diniz, and Freeland (2000). In the described double-threshold scheme, a higher threshold is used for click detection, whereas a lower threshold is set as a reference for defining the duration of a given detected click. Moreover, a heuristic criterion is adopted to merge into a single occurrence clicks that appear close to each other. An alternative for a more precise click location consists of locating the beginning of the clicks using the original detection signal, obtained via inverse filtering, and estimating the end of the clicks in a similar fashion, but this time inverse filtering the time-reversed version of the corrupted signal (Esquef et al., 2002; Godsill & Rayner, 1998a).

## Performance

Model-based detectors offer a suitable and simple solution for click detection in audio signals. There are, however, limitations in a few situations. For example, there is the risk that genuine impulsive-like events present in the recorded signal be mistaken by clicks. Thus, it is likely that percussive events, such as whip sounds and drum kicks, be detected as clicks. Attempts to restore those sounds may smooth out their original sharp transients.

Another difficult situation for model-based click detection happens when dealing with audio signals that possess a strong harmonic or quasi-harmonic frequency structure (Vaseghi, 1988). In such cases, the low-order models employed within the inverse filtering stage are insufficient to destroy the long-term correlations of samples in the detection signal. As a result, those correlations show up as periodical bursts of high-magnitude values, thus, being susceptible to be taken as click occurrences.

## Advanced Methods

Besides model-based methods there exist other means to detect and locate clicks in audio signals. One of those methods is based on wavelet decomposition of the corrupted signal (Montresor, Valiere, Allard, & Baudry, 1991). As a multiscale transform, the discrete wavelet transform (Mallat, 1999) offers a natural signal decomposition for click detection, since impulsive-like events are bound to appear clearly on the finest scales, thus facilitating their detection.

More advanced techniques employ statistical modeling of both the underlying signal and the noise components. In that direction, powerful tools that employ statistical data detection, inference, and classification based on Bayesian methods have been proposed in the literature (Godsill & Rayner, 1998a).

*Figure 9. Detection signal given by the magnitude of the matched-filter's output (in solid line) compared against a fixed threshold T=0.5 (in dashed line)*

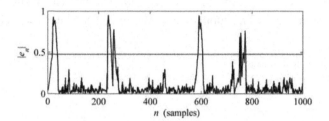

## Signal Recovery

In de-clicking techniques, once the corrupting clicks are located in time, there arises the problem of reconstruction of the audio material in the damaged portions. A variety of DSP solutions for signal recovery exists in the literature. Among the available techniques it is relevant to mention band-limited recovery (Ferreira, 2001; Papoulis, 1975), interpolators based on sinusoidal modeling (George & Smith, 1992; Godsill & Rayner, 1998a; Maher, 1994; Quatieri & McAulay, 1998), waveform substitution schemes (Goodman, Lockhart, Waen, & Wong, 1986; Niedzwiecki & Cisowski, 2001), sub-band methods (Chen & Chen, 1995; Cocchi & Uncini, 2001; Montresor, Valiere, Allard, & Baudry, 1991), and interpolators based on autoregressive models (Godsill & Rayner, 1992, 1998b; Janssen, Veldhuis, & Vries, 1986; Vaseghi, 1988). A comprehensive coverage on interpolators for audio signals can be found in the works of Godsill and Rayner (1998a) and Veldhuis (1990).

Autoregressive processes have been demonstrated to be well suited to model short-time portions of general audio signals. It is no surprise that AR-based interpolators figure among the most adequate techniques for signal reconstruction over short-time portions of audio signals. Therefore, in the next sections, the attention will be focused on AR-based interpolators. First, an interpolator devised to perform a joint signal reconstruction across several distinct gaps of missing samples within a frame of audio signal is described. Its inclusion here is justified by its effective performance and simplicity of formulation. Then, a solution for signal reconstruction over long gaps of missing samples is outlined. It involves the use of AR-based signal extrapolators and signal decomposition into sub-bands.

### Least Squares AR Interpolator

The least squares AR (LSAR) interpolator was introduced by Janssen, Veldhuis and Vries, (1986) and Vaseghi (1988) and attempts to recover the audio information in damaged or missing portions of a signal frame by minimizing the modeling error with respect to signal samples to be restored. In matrix notation, the $p^{\text{th}}$ order AR model stated in equation (15) can be reformulated as:

$$\mathbf{e} = \mathbf{Ax}, \tag{18}$$

where $\mathbf{x} = [x_0, x_1, \ldots, x_{N-1}]^{\text{T}}$ and $\mathbf{A}$ is the $(N-p) \times N$ matrix previously defined in equation (8). Moreover, it is convenient to split the observation vector $\mathbf{x}$ into two parts: one vector containing the known or clean samples $\mathbf{x}_k$ and another with those to be recovered $\mathbf{x}_u$. Thus, it is possible to re-write equation (18) as:

$$\mathbf{e} = \mathbf{A}_u \mathbf{x}_u + \mathbf{A}_k \mathbf{x}_k, \tag{19}$$

where $\mathbf{A}_u$ and $\mathbf{A}_k$ are, respectively, column-wise partitions of matrix $\mathbf{A}$ with direct correspondence to the partition performed on $\mathbf{x}$. By minimizing the cost function $C = \mathbf{e}^T \mathbf{e}$ with respect to the vector of unknown samples $\mathbf{x}_u$ one obtains the LS interpolator solution, which can be shown (Godsill & Rayner, 1998a) to be given by:

$$\hat{\mathbf{x}}_u = -\left(\mathbf{A}_u^T \mathbf{A}_u\right)^{-1} \mathbf{A}_u^T \mathbf{A}_k \mathbf{x}_k. \tag{20}$$

## Performance

The LSAR interpolator is known to perform suitably when filling in short portions of missing samples, say, up to 2 ms. From a practical point of view, it is expected that a given signal block to be treated contains many more known than unknown samples. That helps to assure a less biased and statistically more significant modeling of the underlying signal. Besides, the lower the number of samples to be recovered, the less taxing computationally the interpolation becomes.

When it comes to the choice of the AR model order, it should be taken into account that the objective is to fill in very short gaps in the signal, and not to fit the best model to the signal. Thus, adopting model orders within the range from 40 to 80 usually suffice. Figure 10 demonstrates the performance of the LSAR interpolator over an excerpt of audio signal that contains three artificial gaps of lengths 50, 100, and 200. In this simulation $p=40$ was adopted.

There are some drawbacks associated with running the LSAR interpolator with low-order models. The first occurs when dealing with signals that possess strong harmonic content. In those cases, interpolation of long excerpts may be too smooth or decay in energy toward the middle of the gap. Means to improve the interpolation performance in the previous situations include the use of a pitch-based extended AR model (Vaseghi & Rayner, 1990) and an AR-based interpolator appended with a sinusoidal basis representation (Godsill & Rayner, 1998a).

Another issue associated with AR-based interpolation, especially when treating long gaps, is its inability to reconstruct stochastic components present in the underlying signal. This limitation is directly

*Figure 10. Performance of the LSAR interpolator. The original signal is depicted in dashed line, whereas the interpolated is shown in solid line. Gap locations are delimited by vertical dotted lines.*

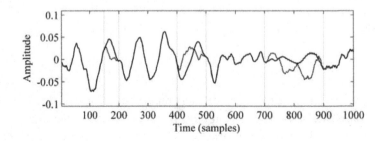

linked to the minimization of the modeling error, as part of the estimation of the unknown samples. As the stochastic components of the signal appear in the modeling error, the resulting recovered signal tends to be smoother than the surrounding portions. Among possible ways to overcome this problem, one finds solutions such as the use of random sampling techniques (Ó Ruanaidh & Fitzgerald, 1994) and sample estimation procedures that impose a lower bound to the minimization of the modeling error (Rayner & Godsill, 1991; Niedzwiecki, 1993).

## Interpolation Across Long Gaps

As mentioned in the previous section, reconstructing long portions of missing audio data can be a difficult job for the LSAR interpolator. When referring to long gaps, one should keep in mind that the non-stationary nature of audio signals in general imposes an upper limit to the extent of signal excerpts that can be meaningfully recovered. Considering that local stationarity can only be assumed within short blocks up to approximately 50 ms, recovering fragments of such duration is already an extreme situation for the AR-based method described.

Perhaps, the most trivial way of improving the performance of AR-based interpolators when dealing with long gaps consists of increasing the model order. However, the number of observation samples needs to be at least equal to, but preferably greater than, the chosen model order. Therefore, depending on the length of the gap to fill in, there may not be many samples left within a stationary frame centered on a given gap, available for model estimation.

Moreover, the time-frequency characteristics of the passage that immediately antecedes a long gap may differ from those of the succeeding excerpt. This fact has motivated the proposition of interpolators that use two different AR models: one for the segment that precedes the gap and another for the ensuing portion. In a work by Etter (1996) an LS solution for a dual AR model interpolation is introduced. In the same direction, an interpolator that merges forward- and backward-extrapolated signals based upon two distinct AR models is presented by Kauppinen, Kauppinen, and Saarinen (2001) and Kauppinen and Roth (2002b). These interpolators are able to fill in long gaps of missing samples better than the LSAR solution, but at the cost of employing high model orders. Of course, the higher the adopted model order, the higher the computational complexity required by the interpolator.

### Multirate AR-Based Interpolator

As an attempt to find a better balance between qualitative performance and computational load, Esquef and Biscainho (2006) proposed an AR-based multirate interpolation scheme. The proposed method is composed of two stages: a fullband interpolation, in which a slightly modified version of the interpolator presented by Kauppinen, Kauppinen, & Saarinen. (2001), Kauppinen and Kauppinen (2002), and Kauppinen and Roth (2002b) is used; then follows the multirate stage, where the interpolator of Kauppinen and Kauppinen (2002) is applied to the signals of the lowest sub-bands.

The original proposition of Kauppinen and Kauppinen (2002) carries out pure signal extrapolation to accomplish audio reconstruction. Taking the forward extrapolation as an example, that means that a high-order AR model is estimated for a fragment of the signal that precedes a gap. Then, appropriate initial states for the AR synthesis filter are obtained and the truncated unforced response of this filter is taken as the forward-extrapolated signal. The same formulation is applied to produce a backward-extrapolated fragment, which is seamlessly merged with the forward-extrapolated one via a cross-fading scheme. The modified scheme of Esquef and Biscainho (2006) uses the same AR synthesis filter and initial states, but excites the filter with the modeling error sequence reversed in time. All other processing steps are identical.

That simple change allows adopting low-order models and yet obtaining non-decaying extrapolated signals, which account for a better signal reconstruction in terms of energy preservation across the gap, at a substantially lower cost. Nonetheless, low-frequency artifacts can be perceived in the restored signals. Here it comes into place the multirate stage, which is meant to reduce the audibility of those disturbances.

The multirate stage decomposes the output of the first stage into six octave sub-bands via a maximally decimated filterbank. Then, the interpolator of Kauppinen and Kauppinen (2002) is applied to the signals of the two lowest sub-bands prior to resynthesis. In those sub-bands, the already filled gap regions and surrounding segments are squeezed in length by the decimation factor of 32. Therefore, re-interpolation of those signals can be performed using low-order AR models, thus easing the interpolation task. Further details on implementation issues and choice of processing parameters can be found in the work by Esquef and Biscainho (2006).

## Performance

The multirate AR-based interpolator described by Esquef and Biscainho (2006) has been confronted against the formulation presented by Kauppinen and Kauppinen (2002), for a case study in which a gap of 1800 samples, at 44.1 sample rate, was to be concealed. Results from formal listening tests revealed that, on average, the multirate scheme can perform comparably to the original method. However, while the latter required AR models with orders of about 1000 to satisfactorily accomplish the task, the former demanded interpolators with orders as low as 50, thus accounting for a reduction of one order of magnitude in computational cost.

*Figure 11. Performance comparisons among the interpolator of Kauppinen and Kauppinen (2002), with model orders 100 and 1000, and that of Esquef and Biscainho (2006) with order 50*

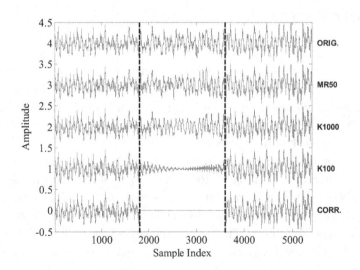

Figure 11 offers comparative results between the two interpolators, for the task of filling in a gap of 1800 samples within an excerpt of rich orchestral music. The corrupted signal, which is labeled as **CORR.**, appears on the bottom of the image. Kauppinen's interpolator with order 100 produced the segment denoted by **K100**. Increasing the order to 1000 yields the recovered signal **K1000**. The interpolation task, as realized by the multirate scheme with interpolators of order 50, generated the signal **MR50**. The original signal, marked as **ORIG.**, is depicted on the top of the figure as a reference. The plots have been shifted in amplitude for clarity.

The computational cost to obtain the signals **K100** and **MR50** is approximately the same. However, it can be observed that, for the length of the gap in question and with order 100, the interpolator of Kauppinen and Kauppinen (2002) suffers from the problem of energy decay toward the middle of the gap. To remedy this problem one can increase the model order to 1000, at the cost of a ten-fold increase in the computational load. Alternatively, the multirate scheme offers similar results at a much lower cost. Additional comparisons among the multirate scheme and competing AR-based interpolators can be found in a work by Esquef and Biscainho (2006).

## AUDIO DE-HISSING

Audio contamination by additive broadband noise, which is perceived as hiss, is a rather common type of signal degradation associated usually with measurement noise. Among the many sources of hiss it is possible to mention thermal noise associated with the transducers and electric amplification circuitry, electro-magnetic interferences, quantization errors in analog to digital conversion, and intrinsic characteristics of the recording media. In the latter matter, magnetic tape and 78 RPM recordings are notable for suffering from hiss contamination.

Compared to the removal of localized disturbances, hiss reduction is a much more taxing problem to solve effectively. Apart from the fact that almost all samples of the signal are affected by the degradation, there is the commonly unavoidable overlap between the audio and noise spectra. And separation of the noise and audio spectra is a key point in well-known de-hissing methods.

The following sections will tackle the fundamentals of two methods for audio de-hissing, namely, the short-time spectral attenuation (STSA) and the wavelet shrinkage.

### Short-Time Spectral Attenuation

#### Formulation

Short-time spectral attenuation is the most popular class of methods for audio de-hissing and originates in noise removal from speech signals (Boll, 1979a, 1979b; Lim, 1978, 1986; Lim & Oppenheim, 1978). The main assumption behind STSA is that the corrupted signal can be modeled as:

$$y_n = x_n + d_n, \tag{21}$$

where $x_n$ is an ergodic stationary process corresponding to the clean signal and $d_n$ is an additive zero-mean process uncorrelated with $x_n$. It is trivial to demonstrate that the power spectral density (PSD) of the corrupted signal is given by:

$$S_{y,\omega} = S_{x,\omega} + S_{d,\omega}, \tag{22}$$

where $S_{x,\omega}$ and $S_{d,\omega}$ are the PSD associated with the underlying clean signal and the noise process, respectively, with $\omega$ denoting frequency. Thus, a direct estimate of the PSD of the clean signal can be attained as:

$$\hat{S}_{x,\omega} = S_{y,\omega} - S_{d,\omega}. \tag{23}$$

If $d_n$ can be considered white noise, then $S_{d,\omega}$ is constant over frequency and proportional to the variance $\sigma_d^2$ of the noise process.

In practice, audio signals can only be considered stationary within frames of short duration. Therefore, a block-based overlap-and-add signal analysis procedure must be employed (Cappé & Laroche, 1995; Godsill, Rayner, & Cappé, 1998). For convenience, it is recommended to adopt window types and overlap factors that guarantee that the windows sum up to a constant value. For instance, Hanning windows, overlapped at 50% and 75% sum up to one and two, respectively. Otherwise, amplitude compensation must be applied to the synthesized signal (Godsill & Rayner 1998a).

Moreover, considering a block of $N$ samples of the noisy signal $y_n$, its PSD can be approximated by the sampled power spectrum of the observed data, computed via the discrete Fourier transform (DFT) (Hayes, 1996):

$$\hat{S}_{y,\omega_k} \approx \frac{\left|\text{DFT}_k\left\{y_n\right\}\right|^2}{N} \equiv |Y_k|^2, \tag{24}$$

with $k$ standing for frequency bin index. As the same approximation holds true for the noise component, the estimated PSD of the clean signal can be approximated by:

$$\left|\hat{X}_k\right|^2 = \begin{cases} |Y_k|^2 - \alpha|D_k|^2, & |Y_k|^2 > \alpha|D_k|^2, \\ 0, & \text{otherwise} \end{cases} \tag{25}$$

where $\alpha$ is a gain factor. The component $|D_k|^2$ can be estimated *a priori* from noise-only portions of the signal. In case of white noise, one can count on the expected spectral flatness of $|D_k|^2$ and replace it with an average level for all $k$. Alternatively, an estimate of this level can be obtained, for instance, by averaging the upper-quarter part of the observed power spectrum $|Y_k|^2$, where it is plausible to assume that the energy of noise component is dominant over that of the signal.

Once an estimate for the magnitude spectrum of the clean signal is obtained, the corresponding estimate of the clean signal itself is produced by taking the inverse DFT of the complex signal, which is formed by $\left|\hat{X}_k\right|e^{j\angle Y_k}$, where $j = \sqrt{-1}$ is the imaginary unity and the symbol $\angle$ stands for phase. Figure 12 summarizes in a functional diagram the processing stages of a standard STSA scheme.

The suppression rule given in equation (25) is the so-called power spectrum subtraction. In general, it is possible to formulate the most common suppression rules as:

$$\left|\hat{X}_k\right| = H_k|Y_k|, \tag{26}$$

*Figure 12. Block diagram of a typical STSA procedure, (Adapted from Wolfe and Godsill (2003)*

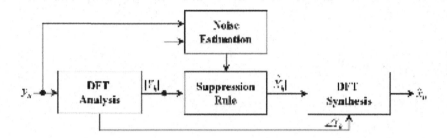

*Figure 13. Comparison among the level of spectral attenuation produced by the power spectrum subtraction, spectral subtraction, and Wiener suppression rules as a function of the signal-to-noise ratio.*

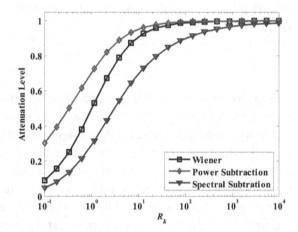

where $H_k$ can be considered a time-varying filter that appropriately attenuates the magnitude spectrum of the noisy signal based upon an estimate of the local SNR measured at each frequency bin $k$. Moreover, the attenuation factor can assume the general form (Lorber & Hoeldrich, 1997):

$$H_k = H_{b,k} = \begin{cases} \left( \left( 1 - \left( \alpha \, \frac{|D_k|}{|Y_k|} \right)^b \right)^{\frac{1}{b}} \right), & |Y_k|^2 > \alpha |D_k|^2, \\ 0, & \text{otherwise} \end{cases} \qquad (27)$$

where $b$ is a selection factor that defines the type of selection rule. For example, adopting $b=1$ yields the so-called spectral subtraction rule, whereas setting $b=2$ leads to the previously seen power spectrum subtraction rule. The well-known Wiener estimator, which minimizes the mean square error between the noisy and clean signals, is just given by $H_k = H_{2,k}^2$.

In order to gain more insight on the effect of suppression rules, it is convenient to set $\alpha=1$ and re-write $H_{b,k}$ as a function of the signal-to-noise ratio, defined as $R_k \equiv |X_k|^2 / |D_k|^2$. This leads to:

$$H_{b,k} = \begin{cases} \left[ 1 - \left( \dfrac{1}{R_k+1} \right)^{\frac{b}{2}} \right]^{\frac{1}{b}}, & R_k > 0 \\ 0, & \text{otherwise} \end{cases} \tag{28}$$

from where one can infer that, as intuitively expected, $H_{b,k}$ decreases with $R_k$. Figure 13 compares the attenuation levels associated with the suppression rules $H_{2,k}$ (power spectrum subtraction), $H_{1,k}$ (spectral subtraction), and $H_{2,k}^2$ (Wiener) as a function of $R_k$.

From Figure 13 it is possible to verify that the power spectrum subtraction rule offers the least intense magnitude spectrum attenuation, whereas the spectral subtraction rule provides the most severe. The Wiener rule rests in between the previous two curves.

## Performance

The conventional implementation of an STSA-based de-hisser can produce notable reduction of the audible background noise. However, the attained results can be marred by two main distortions: the inevitable suppression of valuable high-frequency content from the underlying signal and the annoying audibility of a random tonal noise associated with the remaining components of the noise process left in the signal after restoration. The latter phenomenon, which is also known as musical noise, has its roots on the fragile assumption on the flatness of $|D_k|^2$ over frequency. In reality, in a given frame, the value of $|D_k|^2$ varies around a certain constant average level. Therefore, $R_k$ will be underestimated for an arbitrary set of frequency bins, which varies from frame to frame. As a consequence, at those frequencies, which are randomly distributed along the spectrum, the noise component is less attenuated than it ideally should be and becomes audible for a brief period of time, especially on the high-frequency range.

There have been proposed several means to reduce the musical noise in de-hissed audio signals. Perhaps the simplest solution consists of overestimating the level of the noise power (Berouti, Schwartz, & Makhoul, 1979; Boll, 1979a, 1979b; Lorber & Hoeldrich, 1997; Vaseghi, 1988; Vaseghi & Rayner, 1988). This can be easily carried out by setting $\alpha>1$ in equation (27). The side effect of this option is an even greater loss of valuable components of the recorded signal, especially on the high-frequency range, rendering the restored sound too muffled.

Other straightforward ways of reducing the audibility of musical noise repose on the use of spectral averaging within the computation of the suppression rules (Boll, 1979b), on the adoption of a minimum attenuation level for $H_{b,k}$ (Berouti, Schwartz, & Makhoul, 1979; Lorber & Hoeldrich, 1997), and on the application of heuristic rules over the values of $H_{b,k}$, measured during a set of consecutive processed frames (Vaseghi & Frayling-Cork, 1992). All those options attempt to set a suitable balance among the audibility of a residual noise floor, that of the musical noise, and a faithful preservation of the recorded content on the restored signal.

A more sophisticated solution for decreasing the audibility of musical noise was proposed by Ephraim and Malah (1983, 1984, 1985), and it is known as the Ephraim and Malah suppression rule (EMSR).

The EMSR figures as the optimal, in the minimum mean square error sense, amplitude estimator of a short-time sinusoid marred in additive white noise. Its formulation requires the knowledge of both the *a priori* and the *a posteriori* SNRs associated with a given frequency bin. In a practical implementation, the *a posteriori* SNR refers to $R_k$ measured from the signal frame being processed as before. In its turn, the *a priori* SNR is guessed from a non-linear decision-directed scheme involving previously processed frames.

The EMSR has been demonstrated to be an effective de-hissing method in terms of attaining significant levels of noise reduction without being much afflicted by the presence of musical noise (Cappé, 1994). As regards variants of the EMSR, simpler alternatives to the EMSR were proposed by Wolfe and Godsill (2001b, 2003). Moreover, the incorporation of psychoacoustic criteria within suppression rules used in STSA-based de-hissing methods has been also registered in the literature (Kauppinen & Roth, 2002a; Lorber & Hoeldrich, 1997; Tsoukalas, Mourjopoulos, & Kokkinakis, 1997; Tsoukalas, Paraskevas, & Mourjopoulos, 1993; Wolfe & Godsill, 2000, 2001a) as providing suitable results.

As with de-clicking algorithms, STSA-based de-hissing schemes are unable to discern between spurious noises and genuine noise-like occurrences in audio signals, such as unvoiced speech, drum brushing, and blowing noise in wind instrument sounds. Those events are likely to be mistaken by corrupting noise, thus being subject to either unwanted suppression or severe distortions by the restoration procedure.

## Wavelet Shrinkage

Besides the use of the short-time DFT for signal de-noising, another non-parametric signal analysis tool that has gained substantial attention in the field is the Discrete Wavelet Transform (DWT) (Burrus, Gopinath, & Guo, 1997; Daubechies, 1992; Mallat, 1999). As opposed to the DFT, the DWT projects a given input signal into an orthogonal basis composed of functions that are localized in both time and frequency—all of them scaled and delayed versions of the same "mother-wavelet." This property allows a parsimonious multi-resolution representation for a variety of signals, in that the most relevant signal information is captured by few large-valued DWT coefficients, whereas less important information is mapped into a large number of small-valued coefficients. It must be noted that this capability depends strongly on the choice of the DWT-basis: the more the wavelet resembles the signal to be decomposed, the more compact a faithful representation can be. The DWT has been successfully employed in tasks such as signal compression and de-noising, where its ability to reduce the data space dimension while preserving important details and edges of the signal is much praised.

Theoretical fundamentals and implementation of the DWT can be readily found from the vast available literature and DSP simulation softwares. Thus, without going through its strict formulations and properties, simply consider that $W_{j,k}$ is the set of DWT coefficients associated with a signal frame of $N = 2^J$ samples, contaminated with zero-mean Gaussian white noise with variance $\sigma^2$, uncorrelated with the underlying signal. In this context $J$ refers to the maximum number of scales of the DWT, being $j = 0, \ldots, J-1$ the scale index and $k = 0, \ldots, 2^j - 1$ the coefficient index within a given scale. Index $j = 0$ refers to the coarsest scale level, whereas $j = J-1$ relates to the finest one.

Due to the orthogonality of the transformation, the DWT of a white noise process yields also a set of white noise coefficients with the same variance. Thus, the DWT of a signal corrupted with white noise results in a set of DWT coefficients where the energy of the noise component spreads equally across the scales. On the other hand, the energy associated with a wide range of real-world smooth signals decays approximately exponentially toward the finest scale (Cheng, 1997). By exploring this contrast, Donoho and Johnstone (1994) proposed two threshold-based coefficient shrinkage schemes for signal denoising (Berger, Coifman, & Goldberg, 1994; Donoho, 1995; Donoho & Johnstone, 1994; Teolis & Benedetto, 1994; Whitmal, Rutledge, & Cohen, 1995).

In one of those schemes, called hard-thresholding, the DWT coefficients are either kept or discarded according to the following criterion:

$$\hat{W}_{j,k}^{\text{hard}} = \begin{cases} W_{j,k}, & |W_{j,k}| > \lambda \\ 0, & \text{otherwise} \end{cases}, \tag{29}$$

where $\lambda$ is an adequately chosen threshold value. The other possibility consists of employing a soft-thresholding scheme in which the DWT coefficients values are either modified or discarded based on the rule:

$$\hat{W}_{j,k}^{\text{soft}} = \begin{cases} \text{sign}(W_{j,k}) \, (|W_{j,k}| - \lambda), & |W_{j,k}| > \lambda \\ 0, & \text{otherwise.} \end{cases} \tag{30}$$

After the application of the thresholding criterion over the DWT coefficients, the last step of the wavelet shrinkage is to re-synthesize the signal from $W_{j,k}^{\text{hard}}$ or $W_{j,k}^{\text{soft}}$ via the inverse DWT (IDWT) correspondent to the DWT used in the analysis stage.

The threshold choice has been extensively discussed, leading to different criteria. A simple solution (Donoho & Johnstone, 1994) that attains a bounded deviation from the minimax mean square error is $\lambda = \hat{\sigma}\sqrt{2\log(N)}$, with $\hat{\sigma}$ being an estimate of the noise standard deviation. In practice, $\hat{\sigma}$ can be determined from noise-only excerpts of the input signal or from the coefficients of the finest scale, where the noise components tend to be stronger than the desired signal information.

De-noising by soft-thresholding shrinkage has been demonstrated to almost achieve the minimax mean square error and provide a restored signal at least as smooth as the original clean signal (Donoho, 1995). Apart from the simple aforementioned thresholding rules, DWT coefficient shrinkage can be approached from several other more involved means, for example, Bayesian statistics methods (Abramovich, Sapatinas, & Silverman, 1998; Vidakovic, 1998). For a comprehensive coverage on the most common DWT coefficient shrinkage techniques see the work by Nason (1995).

## Performance

From a computational point of view, wavelet shrinkage is a rather appealing de-noising method, since fast algorithms exist for computing both the DWT and its inverse. These algorithms, which are based on maximally decimated octave-band filterbanks, demand only $O(N)$ floating-point multiplications (Mallat, 1999) to realize either a DWT or an IDWT.

As opposed to STSA methods, which are known for strongly attenuating high-frequency components of the signals and distorting its sharp transients, wavelet shrinkage is capable of preserving fast transients in the restored signal, provided that they overpower the noise level. However, as with STSA methods, wavelet-based de-noising also suffers from the audibility of artifacts derived from the residual noise left in the signal and from non-canceled aliasing components that arise as the result of processing the DWT coefficients prior to signal resynthesis. Moreover, the method cannot discern between originally recorded noise-like broadband sounds and spurious noises.

## Other Methods

Besides non-parametric solutions to audio de-hissing, such as the STSA and Wavelet shrinkage methods, a number of alternatives to tackle the problem have been proposed. For example, autoregressive-based noise reduction of speech sounds was presented by Lim and Oppenheim (1978), and joint treatment of impulsive and broadband noises using AR and ARMA models was demonstrated by Godsill (1993), Godsill and Rayner (1996), Niedzwiecki (1994), and Niedzwiecki and Cisowski (1996).

An adaptive filtering scheme for broadband noise elimination when two copies of the recorded sound source are available was described by Vaseghi (1988) and Vaseghi and Frayling-Cork (1992). Adaptive strategies for audio de-noising that employ Kalman filter techniques were reported by Bari, Canazza, De Poli, and Mian (1999) and Niedzwiecki and Cisowski (1996). Last but not least, hybrid approaches figure in the literature among available solutions for audio de-hissing. For example, a technique that combines sub-band processing with STSA was presented by Jebara, Benazza-Benyahia, and Khelifa (2000), Moorer and Berger (1986), and Ramarapu and Maher (1998), and the use of AR modeling within STSA was covered by Kauppinen and Roth (2002b).

## FUTURE DIRECTIONS

The audio de-noising techniques described in this chapter can attain a certain level of automatism in carrying out the tasks at hand, provided a judicious choice of the processing parameters. As far as the judgment of restored signals go, it is up to a skilled audio restorer to determine whether the sonic quality of the final results have reached an acceptable quality standard. As this process involves subjective assessment of the restored signals, it is dependent among other issues on how well informed the restorer is regarding the contents of the audio program being processed.

It seems reasonable to speculate that in the future audio restoration algorithms can benefit from the incorporation of high-level information about the content of the signal under processing. On a lower layer, knowledge of important facets related to the signal content, such as music genre, sound sources present in the mixture, and recording ambience can be used for guidance of the type of algorithm to employ as well as of a suitable choice of a set of processing parameters. On a more advanced layer, audio content could be embedded as *a priori* information within model-based techniques for signal restoration.

A more audacious and challenging goal would consist of realizing sound restoration by resynthesis. Putting aside issues associated with the artistic fidelity of the results, from a technical point of view such strategy would be multidisciplinary, involving among others audio content analysis; computational auditory scene analysis within a structured-audio framework (Bregman, 1990; Dixon, 2004; Ellis, 1996; Rosenthal & Okuno, 1998; Scheirer, 1999; Vercoe, Gardner, & Scheirer, 1998); sound source modeling and synthesis of musical instrument, speech, and singing voice sounds (Cook, 2002; Miranda, 2002; Serra, 1997; Smith, 1991; Tolonen, 2000; Välimäki, Pakarinen, Erkut, & Karjalainen, 2006); psychoacoustics (Järveläinen, 2003; Zwicker & Fastl, 1999); and auditory modeling (Beerends, 1998). Although in an embrionary stage, restoration by resynthesis has already given signs of practical usability in restricted scenarios (Berger & Nichols, 1994; Esquef, 2004), thus cementing its way as a promising and stimulating long-term research area.

## REFERENCES

Abramovich, F., Sapatinas, T., & Silverman, B. W. (1998). Wavelet thresholding via a Bayesian approach. *Journal of the Royal Statistic Society, Series B, 60*, 725-749.

Bari, A., Canazza, S., De Poli, G., & Mian, G. A. (1999). Some key points on restoration of audio documents by the extended Kalman filter. In *Proceedings of the Diderot Forum on Mathematics and Music* (pp. 37-47). Vienna, Austria.

Beerends, J. G. (1998). Audio quality determination based on perceptual measurement techniques. In M. Kahrs & K. Brandenburg (Eds.), *Applications of digital signal processing to audio and acoustics* (pp. 1-38). Norwell, MA: Kluwer.

Berger, J., Coifman, R. R., & Goldberg, M. J. (1994). Removing noise from music using local trigonometric bases and wavelet packets. *Journal of the Audio Engineering Society, 42*(10), 808-818.

Berger, J., & Nichols, C. (1994). Brahms at the piano: An analysis of data from the Brahms cylinder. *Leonardo Music Journal, 4*, 23-30.

Berouti, M., Schwartz, R., & Makhoul, J. (1979). Enhancement of speech corrupted by acoustic noise. In *Proceedings of the IEEE International Conference of Acoustics, Speech, and Signal Processing* (vol. 4, pp. 208-211), Washington DC: IEEE.

Boll, S. F. (1979a). A spectral subtraction algorithm for suppression of acoustic noise in speech. In *Proceedings of the IEEE International Conference of Acoustics, Speech, and Signal Processing* (vol. 4, pp. 200-203). Washingtond DC: IEEE.

Boll, S. F. (1979b). Suppression of acoustic noise in speech using spectral subtraction. *IEEE Transactions on Acoustics, Speech, and Signal Processing, ASSP-27*(2), 113-120.

Bregman, A. S. (1990). *Auditory scene analysis*. Cambridge, MA: MIT.

Burrus, C. S., Gopinath, R. A., & Guo, H. (1997). *Wavelets and wavelet transform—A primer*. Upper Saddle River, NJ: Prentice-Hall.

Burwen, R. S. (1978). *Suppression of low level impulsive noise*. Presented at the 61st Convention of the AES, New York. AES Preprint 1388.

Cappé, O. (1994). Elimination of the musical noise phenomenon with the Ephraim and Malah noise suppressor. *IEEE Transactions on Speech and Audio Processing, 2*(2), 345-349.

Cappé, O., & Laroche, J. (1995). Evaluation of short-time spectral attenuation techniques for the restoration of musical recordings. *IEEE Transactions on Speech and Audio Processing, 3*(1), 84-93.

Chen, B.-S., & Chen, Y.-L. (1995). Multirate modeling of AR/ARMA stocastic signals and its application to the combined estimation-interpolation problem. *IEEE Transactions on Signal Processing, 43*(10), 2302-2312.

Cheng, C. (1997). High frequency compensation of low sample-rate audio files: A wavelet-based excitation algorithm. In *Proceedings of the International Computer Music Conference* (pp. 458-461). Thessaloniki, Greece.

Cocchi, G., & Uncini, A. (2001). Subbands audio signal recovering using neural nonlinear prediction. In *Proceedings of the IEEE International Conference of Acoustics, Speech, and Signal Processing*, (vol. 2, pp. 1289-1292). Salt Lake City, UT.

Coleman, M. (2004). *Playback: From Victrola to MP3, 100 years of music, machines, and money.* Cambridge, MA: Da Capo.

Cook, P. R. (2002). *Real sound synthesis for interactive applications.* Wellesley, MA: A K Peters.

Craven, P. G., & Gerzon, M. A. (1975). *The elimination of scratch noise from 78 RPM records.* Presented at the 50th Convention of the AES. AES Preprint L-37.

Czyzewski, A. (1997). Learning algorithms for audio signal enhancement, Part I: Neural network implementation for the removal of impulsive distortions. *Journal of the Audio Engineering Society, 45*(10), 815-831.

Daubechies, I. (1992). *Ten lectures on wavelets.* Philadelphia: SIAM.

Dixon, S. (2004). Analysis of musical content in digital audio. In J. DiMarco (Ed.), *Computer graphics and multimedia: Applications, problems, and solutions* (pp. 214-235). Hershey, PA: Idea Group.

Donoho, D. (1992). Wavelet shrinkage and W.V.D: A 10 minute tour. In Y. Meyer & S. Roques (Eds.), *Progress in wavelet analysis and applications* (pp. 109-128). Gig-sur-Yvette, France: Frontières.

Donoho, D., & Johnstone, I. (1994). Ideal spatial adaptation by wavelet shrinkage. *Biometrika, 81*(3), 425-455.

Donoho, D. L. (1995). De-noising by soft-thresholding. *IEEE Transactions on Information Theory, 41*(3), 613-627.

Ellis, D. (1996). *Prediction-driven computational auditory scene analysis.* Unpublished doctoral dissertation, MIT, Department of Electrical Engineering and Computer Science, Cambridge, MA.

Ephraim, Y., & Malah, D. (1983). Speech enhancement using optimal non-linear spectral amplitude estimation. In *Proceedings of the IEEE International Conference of Acoustics, Speech, and Signal Processing*, (vol. 8, pp. 1118-1121) Boston MA.

Ephraim, Y., & Malah, D. (1984). Speech enhancement using a minimum mean-square error short-time spectral amplitude estimator. *IEEE Transactions on Acoustics, Speech, and Signal Processing, 32*(6), 1109-1121.

Ephraim, Y., & Malah, D. (1985). Speech enhancement using a minimum mean-square error log-spectral amplitude estimator. *IEEE Transactions on Acoustics, Speech, and Signal Processing, 33*(2), 443-445.

Esquef, P. A. A. (2004). *Model-based analysis of noisy musical recordings with application to audio restoration*. Unpublished doctoral dissertation, Lab of Acoustics and Audio Signal Processing, Helsinki University of Technology, Espoo, Finland. Retrieved June 30,2006 from http://lib.hut.fi/Diss/2004/isbn9512269503/.

Esquef, P. A. A., & Biscainho, L. W. P. (2006). An efficient method for reconstruction of audio signals across long gaps. *IEEE Transactions on Speech and Audio Processing, 14*(4), 1391-1400.

Esquef, P. A. A., Biscainho, L. W. P., Diniz, P. S. R., & Freeland, F. P. (2000). A double-threshold-based approach to impulsive noise detection in audio signals. In *Proceedings of the X European Signal Processing Conf.* (vol. 4, pp. 2041-2044). Tampere, Finland.

Esquef, P. A. A., Biscainho, L. W. P., & Välimäki, V. (2003). An efficient algorithm for the restoration of audio signals corrupted with low-frequency pulses. *Journal of the Audio Engineering Society, 51*(6), 502-517.

Esquef, P. A. A., Karjalainen, M., & Välimäki, V. (2002), Detection of clicks in audio signals using warped linear prediction. In *Proceedings of the 14th IEEE International Conference of on Digital Signal Processing (DSP2002)* (vol. 2, pp. 1085-1088). Santorini, Greece.

Etter, W. (1996). Restoration of a discrete-time signal segment by interpolation based on the left-sided and right-sided autoregressive parameters. *IEEE Transactions on Signal Processing, 44*(5), 1124-1135.

Ferreira, P. J. S. G. (2001). Iterative and noniterative recovery of missing samples for 1-D band-limited signals. In F. Marvasti (Ed.), *Nonuniform sampling—Theory and practice* (pp. 235-281). New York: Kluwer/Plenum.

George, E. B., & Smith, M. J. T. (1992). Analysis-by-synthesis/overlap-add sinusoidal modeling applied to the analysis and synthesis of musical tones. *Journal of the Audio Engineering Society, 40*(6), 497-516.

Godsill, S. J. (1993). *The restoration of degraded audio signals*. Unpublished doctoral dissertation, Engineering Department, Cambridge University, Cambridge, England. Retrieved June 30, 2006 from http://www-sigproc.eng.cam.ac.uk/»sjg/thesis/

Godsill, S. J., & Rayner, P. J. W. (1992). A Bayesian approach to the detection and correction of error bursts in audio signals. In *Proceedings of the IEEE International Conference of Acoustics, Speech, and Signal Processing* (vol. 2, pp. 261-264). San Fransisco, CA.

Godsill, S. J., & Rayner, P. J. W. (1996). Robust noise reduction for speech and audio signals. In *Proceedings of the IEEE International Conference of Acoustics, Speech, and Signal Processing* (vol. 2, pp. 625-628). Atlanta, GA.

Godsill, S. J., & Rayner, P. J. W. (1998a). *Digital audio restoration—A statistical model based approach*. Berlin, Germany: Springer-Verlag.

Godsill, S. J., & Rayner, P. J. W. (1998b). Statistical reconstruction and analysis of autoregressive signals in impulsive noise using the Gibbs sampler. *IEEE Transactions on Speech and Audio Processing, 6*(4), 352-372.

Godsill, S. J., Rayner, P. J. W., & Cappé, O. (1998). Digital audio restoration. In M. Kahrs & K. Brandenburg (Eds.), *Applications of digital signal processing to audio and acoustics* (pp. 133-194). Boston: Kluwer.

Godsill, S. J., & Tan, C. H. (1997). Removal of low frequency transient noise from old recordings using model-based signal separation techniques. In *Proceedings of the IEEE ASSP Workshop on Applications of Signal Processing to Audio and Acoustics*. New Paltz, NY.

Goodman, D. J., Lockhart, G. B., Waen, O. J., & Wong, W. C. (1986). Waveform substitution techniques for recovering missing speech segments in packet voice communications. *IEEE Transactions on Acoustics, Speech, and Signal Processing, ASSP-34*(6), 1440-1448.

Hayes, M. H. (1996). *Statistical signal processing and modeling.* West Sussex, England: John Wiley.

Jaffe, D., & Smith, J. O. (1983). Extension of the Karplus-Strong plucked string algorithm. *Computer Music Journal, 7*(2), 56-69.

Janssen, A. J. E. M., Veldhuis, R. N. J., & Vries, L. B. (1986). Adaptive interpolation of discrete-time signals that can be modeled as autoregressive processes. *IEEE Transactions on Acoustics, Speech, Signal Processing, ASSP-34*(2), 317-330.

Järveläinen, H. (2003). *Perception of attributes in real and synthetic string instrument sounds.* Unpublished doctoral dissertation, Helsinki University of Technology—Lab of Acoustics and Audio Signal Processing, Espoo, Finland. Retrieved June 30, 2006 from http://lib.hut.fi/Diss/2003/isbn9512263149/

Jebara, S. B., Benazza-Benyahia, A., & Khelifa, A. B. (2000). Reduction of musical noise generated by spectral subtraction by combining wavelet packet transform and Wiener filtering. In *Proceedings of the X European Signal Processing Conference* (vol. 2, pp. 749-752). Tampere, Finland.

Kauppinen, I., & Kauppinen, J. (2002). Reconstruction method for missing or damaged long portions in audio signal. *Journal of the Audio Engineering Society, 50*(7/8), 594-602.

Kauppinen, I., Kauppinen, J., & Saarinen, P. (2001). A method for long extrapolation of audio signals. *Journal of the Audio Engineering Society, 49*(12), 1167-1180.

Kauppinen, I., & Roth, K. (2002a). Adaptive psychoacoustic filter for broadband noise reduction in audio signals. In *Proceedings of the 14th International Conference of Digital Signal Processing* (vol. 2, pp. 962-966). Santorini, Greece.

Kauppinen, I., & Roth, K. (2002b). Audio signal extrapolation—Theory and applications. In *Proceedings of the Fifth IInternational Conference on Digital Audio Effects* (pp. 105-110). Hamburg, Germany. Retrieved June 30, 2006 from http://www.unibw-hamburg.de/EWEB/ANT/dafx2002/papers.html

Kay, S. M. (1988). *Modern spectral estimation.* Upper Saddle River, NJ: Prentice-Hall.

Kinzie, Jr., G. R., & Gravereaux, D. W. (1973). Automatic detection of impulsive noise. *Journal of the Audio Engineering Society, 21*(3), 331-336.

Lim, J. (1978). Evaluation of a correlation subtraction method for enhancing speech degraded by additive white noise. *IEEE Transactions on Acoustics, Speech, and Signal Processing, 26*(5), 471-472.

Lim, J. (1986). Speech enhancement. In *Proceedings of the IEEE International Conference of Acoustics, Speech, and Signal Processing* (vol. 11, pp. 3135-3142). Tokyo, Japan.

Lim, J., & Oppenheim, A. V. (1978). All-pole modeling of degraded speech. *IEEE Transactions on Acoustics, Speech, and Signal Processing, 26*(3), 197-210.

Lorber, M., & Hoeldrich, R. (1997). A combined approach for broadband noise reduction. In *Proceedings of the IEEE ASSP Workshop on Applications of Signal Processing to Audio and Acoustics.* New Paltz, NY.

Maher, R. C. (1994). A method for extrapolation of missing digital audio data. *Journal of the Audio Engineering Society, 42*(5), 350-357.

Makhoul, J. (1977). Stable and efficient lattice methods for linear prediction. *IEEE Transactions on Acoustics, Speech, and Signal Processing, ASSP-25*(5), 423-428.

Mallat, S. (1999). *A wavelet tour of signal processing.* San Diego, CA: Academic Press.

Miranda, E. R. (2002). *Computer sound design: Synthesis techniques and programming.* Oxford, UK: Focal Press.

Montresor, S., Valiere, J. C., Allard, J. F., & Baudry, M. (1991). *Evaluation of two interpolation methods applied to old recordings restoration.* Presented at the 90th Convention of the AES, Paris, France. AES Preprint 3022.

Moorer, J. A., & Berger, M. (1986). Linear-phase bandsplitting: Theory and applications. *Journal of the Audio Engineering Society, 34*(3), 143-152.

Morton, D. (2000). *The technology and culture of sound recording in America.* Piscataway, NJ: Rutgers University Press.

Nason, G. P. (1995). Choice of threshold parameter in wavelet function estimation. In A. Antoniadis & G. Oppenheim (Eds.), *Lecture Notes in statistics* (Vol 103, pp. 261-280). New York: Springer-Verlag.

Niedzwiecki, M. (1993). Statistical reconstruction of multivariate time series. *IEEE Transactions on Signal Processing, 41*(1), 451-457.

Niedzwiecki, M. (1994). Recursive algorithms for elimination of measurement noise and impulsive disturbances from ARMA signals. In *Signal Processing VII: Theories and Applications* (pp. 1289-1292). Edinburgh, UK.

Niedzwiecki, M., & Cisowski, K. (1996). Adaptive scheme for elimination of broadband noise and impulsive disturbances from AR and ARMA signals. *IEEE Transactions on Signal Processing, 44*(3), 528-537.

Niedzwiecki, M., & Cisowski, K. (2001). Smart copying—A new approach to reconstruction of audio signals. *IEEE Transactions on Signal Processing, 49*(10), 2272-2282.

Ó Ruanaidh, J. J., & Fitzgerald, W. J. (1994). Interpolation of missing samples for audio restoration. *Electronics Letters, 30*(8), 622-623.

Ó Ruanaidh, J. J., & Fitzgerald, W. J. (1996). *Numerical Bayesian methods applied to signal processing.* Berlin, Germany: Springer-Verlag.

Papoulis, A. (1975). A new algorithm in spectral analysis and band-limited extrapolation. *IEEE Transactions on Circuits Syst., 22*(9), 735-742.

Quatieri, T. F., & McAulay, R. J. (1998). Audio signal processing based on sinusoidal analysis and synthesis. In M. Kahrs & K. Brandenburg (Eds.), *Applications of digital signal processing to audio and acoustics* (pp. 314-416). Boston: Kluwer.

Ramarapu, P. K., & Maher, R. C. (1998). Methods for reducing audible artifacts in a wavelet-based broadband de-noising system. *Journal of the Audio Engineering Society, 46*(3), 178-190.

Rayner, P. J. W., & Godsill, S. J. (1991). The detection and correction of artifacts in degraded gramophone recordings. In *Proceedings of the IEEE ASSP Workshop on Applications of Signal Processing to Audio and Acoustics* (pp. 151-152). New Paltz, NY.

Rosenthal, D., & Okuno, H. G. (Eds.). (1998). *Computational auditory scene analysis.* Mahwah, NJ: Lawrence Erlbaum.

Scheirer, E. D. (1999). Structured audio and effects processing in the MPEG-4 multimedia standard. *Multimedia Systems, 7*(1), 11-22.

Schoenherr, S. (2005). *Recording technology history.* Retrieved July 6, 2005, from http://history.acusd.edu/gen/recording/notes.html

Serra, X. (1997). Musical sound modeling with sinusoids plus noise. In C. Roads, S. Pope, A. Picialli, & G. De Poli (Eds.), *Musical signal processing* (pp. 91-122). Lisse, Netherlands: Swets & Zeitlinger.

Smith, J. O. (1991). Viewpoints on the history of digital synthesis. In *Proceedings of the International Computer Music Conference* (pp. 1-10). Montreal, Canada.

Struzinski, W. A. (1984). A new normalization algorithm for detection systems. *Journal of the Acoustical Society of America, Supplement, 75*(S1), S43.

Struzinski, W. A., & Lowe, E. D. (1984). A performance comparison of four noise background normalization schemes proposed for signal detection systems. *Journal of the Acoustical Society of America, 76*(6), 1738-1742.

Teolis, A., & Benedetto, J. J. (1994). Noise suppression using a wavelet model. In *Proceedings of the IEEE International Conference of Acoustics, Speech, and Signal Processing* (vol. 1, pp. 17-20).

Tolonen, T. (2000). *Object-based sound source modeling.* Unpublished doctoral dissertation, Helsinki University of Technology, Espoo, Finland. Retrieved June 30, 2006 from http://lib.hut.fi/Diss/2000/isbn9512251965/

Tsoukalas, D., Mourjopoulos, J., & Kokkinakis, G. (1997). Perceptual filters for audio signal enhancement. *Journal of the Audio Engineering Society, 45*(1/2), 22-36.

Tsoukalas, D., Paraskevas, M., & Mourjopoulos, J. (1993). Speech enhancement using psychoacoustic criteria. In *Proceedings of the IEEE International Conference of Acoustics, Speech, and Signal Processing* (vol. 2, pp. 359-362).

Välimäki, V., Pakarinen, J., Erkut, C., & Karjalainen, M. (2006). Discrete-time modeling of musical instruments. *Reports on Progress in Physics, 69*(1), 1-78.

Vaseghi, S. V. (1988). *Algorithms for restoration of archived gramophone recordings.* Unpublished doctoral dissertation, Engineering Department, Cambridge University, Cambridge, England.

Vaseghi, S. V. (2006). *Advanced digital signal processing and noise reduction* (3rd ed.). West Sussex, England: John Wiley.

Vaseghi, S. V., & Frayling-Cork, R. (1992). Restoration of old gramophone recordings. *Journal of the Audio Engineering Society, 40*(10), 791-801.

Vaseghi, S. V., & Rayner, P. J.W. (1988). A new application of adaptive filters for restoration of archived gramophone recordings. In *Proceedings of the IEEE International Conference of Acoustics, Speech, and Signal Processing* (vol. 5, pp. 2548-2551). New York: IEEE.

Vaseghi, S. V., & Rayner, P. J. W. (1990). Detection and suppression of impulsive noise in speech communication systems. *IEEE Proceedings, 137*(1), 38-46.

Veldhuis, R. (1990). *Restoration of lost samples in digital signals.* Upper Saddle River, NJ: Prentice-Hall.

Vercoe, B. L., Gardner, W. G., & Scheirer, E. D. (1998). Structured audio: Creation, transmission, and rendering of parametric sound representations. *Proc. IEEE, 86*(5), 922-940.

Vidakovic, B. (1998). Non-linear wavelet shrinkage with Bayes rules and Bayes factors. *Journal of the American Statistical Association, 93*(441), 173-179.

Whitmal, N. A., Rutledge, J. C., & Cohen, J. (1995). Wavelet-based noise reduction. In *Proceedings of the IEEE International Conference of Acoustics, Speech, and Signal Processing* (vol. 5, pp. 3003-3006). Detroit, MI.

Wilson, P. (1965). Record contamination: Causes and cure. *J. of the Audio Eng. Society, 13*(2), 166-176.

Wolfe, P. J., & Godsill, S. J. (2000). Towards a perceptually optimal spectral amplitude estimator for audio signal enhancement. In *Proceedings of the IEEE International Conference of Acoustics, Speech, and Signal Processing* (vol. 2, pp. 821-824). Istanbul.

Wolfe, P. J., & Godsill, S. J. (2001a). Perceptually motivated approaches to music restoration. *Journal of New Music Research—Special Issue: Music and Mathematics, 30*(1), 83-92.

Wolfe, P. J., & Godsill, S. J. (2001b). Simple alternatives to the Ephraim and Malah suppression rule for speech enhancement. In *Proceedings of the 11th IEEE Signal Processing Workshop on Statistical Signal Processing* (pp. 496-499). Singapore.

Wolfe, P. J., & Godsill, S. J. (2003). Efficient alternatives to the Ephraim and Malah suppression rule for audio signal enhancement. *EURASIP Journal on Applied Signal Processing—Special Issue on Digital Audio for Multimedia Communications, 2003*(10), 1043-1051.

Zwicker, E., & Fastl, H. (1999). *Psychoacoustics: Facts and models* (2nd ed.). Berlin: Springer-Verlag.

*This work was previously published in Advances in Audio and Speech Signal Processing: Technologies and Applications, edited by H. Perez-Meana, pp. 93-130, copyright 2007 by IGI Publishing, formerly known as Idea Group Publishing (an imprint of IGI Global).*

# Chapter XVII
# Digital Watermarking for Multimedia Transaction Tracking

**Dan Yu**
*Nanyang Technological University, Singapore*

**Farook Sattar**
*Nanyang Technological University, Singapore*

## ABSTRACT

*This chapter focuses on the issue of transaction tracking in multimedia distribution applications through digital watermarking terminology. The existing watermarking schemes are summarized and their assumptions as well as the limitations for tracking are analyzed. In particular, an Independent Component Analysis (ICA)-based watermarking scheme is proposed, which can overcome the problems of the existing watermarking schemes. Multiple watermarking technique is exploited—one watermark to identify the rightful owner of the work and the other one to identify the legal user of a copy of the work. In the absence of original data, watermark, embedding locations and strengths, the ICA-based watermarking scheme is introduced for efficient watermark extraction with some side information. The robustness of the proposed scheme against some common signal-processing attacks as well as the related future work are also presented. Finally, some challenging issues in multimedia transaction tracking through digital watermarking are discussed.*

## INTRODUCTION

We are now in a digital information age. Digital information technology has changed our society as well as our lives. The information revolution takes place in the following two forms

- Data/information retrieval/representation
- Data/information dissemination/communication

Digital presentation of data allows information recorded in a digital format, and thus, it brings easy access to generate and replicate the information. It is such an easy access that provides the novelty in the current phase of the information revolution. Digital technology allows primarily use with the new physical communications media, such as satellite and fiber-optic transmission. Therefore, PCs, e-mail, MPCs, LANs, WANs, MANs, intranets, and the Internet have been evolving rapidly since the 1980s. The Internet has a worldwide broadcasting capability, a mechanism for information distribution, and a medium for collaboration and interaction between individuals and their computers regardless of geographic location. This allows researchers and professionals to share relevant data and information with each other.

As image, audio, video, and other works become available in digital form, perfect copies can be easily made. The widespread use of computer networks and the global reach of the World Wide Web have added substantially an astonishing abundance of information in digital form, as well as offering unprecedented ease of access to it. Creating, publishing, distributing, using, and reusing information have become many times easier and faster in the past decade. The good news is the enrichment that this explosive growth in information brings to society as a whole. The bad news is that it can also bring to those who take advantage of the properties of digital information and the Web to copy, distribute, and use information illegally. The Web is an information resource of extraordinary size and depth, yet it is also an information reproduction and dissemination facility of great demand and capability. Therefore, there is currently a significant amount of research in intellectual property protection issues involving multimedia content distribution via the Internet.

Thus the objective of this chapter is to present multimedia transaction tracking through digital watermarking terminology. The Independent Component Analysis (ICA) technique is employed efficiently for watermark extraction in order to verify the recipient of the distributed content, and hence, to trace illegal transaction of the work to be protected.

## MULTIMEDIA DISTRIBUTION FRAMEWORK THROUGH DIGITAL WATERMARKING

The rapid growth of networked multimedia systems has increased the need for the protection and enforcement of intellectual property (IP) rights of digital media. IP protection is becoming increasingly important nowadays. The tasks to achieve IP protection for multimedia distribution on the Internet can be classified as follows:

- **Ownership identification:** The owner of the original work must be able to provide the trustful proof that he/she is the rightful owner of the content.
- **Transaction tracking:** The owner must be able to track the distributions of the work, so that he/she is able to find the person who is responsible for the illegal replication and redistribution.
- **Content authentication:** The owner should be able to detect any illegal attempts to alter the work.

This chapter concentrates on the task of transaction tracking for multimedia distribution applications. Let us consider the scenario when an owner wants to sell or distribute the work to registered users only. To enforce IP rights, two primary problems have to be solved. First of all, the owner must be able to

*Figure 1. A multimedia distribution system where the digital content could be illegally redistributed to an illegal user*

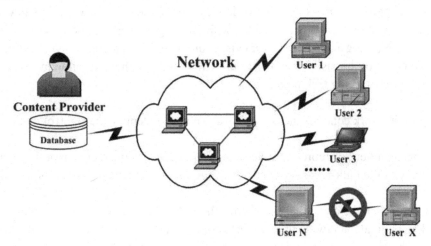

prove that he/she is the legal owner of the distributed content. Second, if the data have been subsequently copied and redistributed illegally, the owner must be able to find the person who is responsible for the illegal copying and redistribution of the data (see Figure 1).

The first technology adopted to enforce protection of IP rights is cryptography. Cryptographic technology (Schneier, 1995) provides an effective tool to secure the distribution process and control the legal uses of the contents that have been received by a user. The contents to be delivered over the Internet are encrypted, and only legal users who hold the decryption key are able to use the encrypted data, whereas the data stream would be useless to a pirate without the appropriate decryption key. However, for an error-free transmission through a network, the contents after the decryption in the cryptography will be exactly the same as the original data. The data contents can be replicated perfectly many times and the user can also manipulate the contents.

Researchers and scientists are then turned to search for other technologies to counter copyright piracy on global networks that are not solvable by cryptography. In this context, recently digital watermarking technology (Cox, Miller, & Bloom, 2002) has drawn much attention. In digital watermarking, the information is transparently embedded into the work, rather than a specific media format, such as the header of a file that could be lost during transmission or file format transformation. Digital watermarking technique thus provides an efficient means for transaction tracking of illegal copying as well as redistribution of multimedia information. For a typical transaction-tracking application, the watermark identifies the first legal recipient of the work. If it is subsequently found that the work has been illegally redistributed, the watermark can then help to identify the person who is responsible for it.

Figure 2 presents a multimedia distribution framework to enforce IP rights through a technique of multiple watermarking. Multiple watermarking (Lu & Mark, 2001; Mintzer & Braudaway, 1999; Sheppard, Safavi-Naini, & Ogunbona, 2001), as suggested by the name, refers to embedding different types of watermarks into single multimedia content to accomplish different goals. For example, one of the watermarks could be used to verify ownership, the second one is to identify the recipient, and the third one is to authenticate content integrity.

For the Internet distribution application, the users first send a request to the content provider whenever they are interested for the multimedia contents. The owner can then distribute the work by signing a watermark to a registered user to uniquely identify the recipient of the work, as shown in Figure 2. All data sent to a registered user are embedded with an assigned watermark as well as the owner's watermark, while maintaining a good perceptual visual quality of the marked content. In this presented framework, the IP rights of the distributed works are enforced from the two following aspects by employing a multiple watermarking technique:

- Every copy of the work contains the owner's watermark to identify the rightful ownership of the work.
- The owner or an authorized representative can uniquely identify the recipient or the legal user of a particular copy of the multimedia content according to the embedded user's unique watermark.

Consider the case when the owner needs to prove the rightful ownership of the content. The owner can present his/her original data (without any marks) of the work as well as his/her watermark as evidence. The two embedded watermarks, including one owner's watermark and one user's watermark, are therefore able to extract by a simple subtraction method (Cox, Miller, & Bloom, 2002; Cox, Leighton, & Shamoon, 1997). One extracted watermark, that is, the owner's watermark, is matched with the previously presented owner's watermark. The rightful ownership of the content is thus verified. It is an essential prerequisite for IP protection to embed the owner's watermark into every copy of the work to be distributed over the Internet. The more difficult and challenging task, as discussed in this chapter, is to

*Figure 2. The multimedia distribution framework by inserting an owner's watermark to identify the ownership of the work and a unique user's watermark to identify each unique legal user*

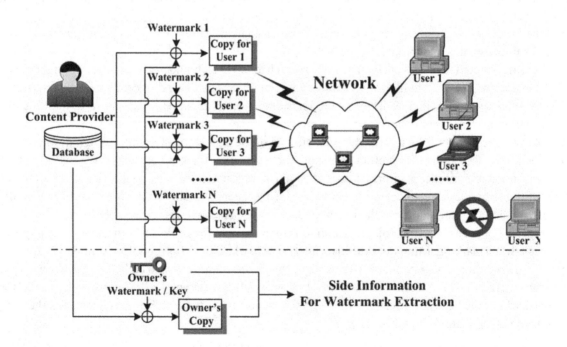

identify the legal users efficiently in the absence of the original data, and hence to trace the transactions of a particular copy of the multimedia content. For the purpose of security in multimedia, the original data are always kept in secret and should not be known to the public during watermark extraction. In some real applications, the owner needs the authorized representatives or service providers to perform the transaction-tracking tasks. For security reasons, the owner also cannot provide the original data to those representatives. Therefore, there arises a challenging issue how to extract the user's watermark in the absence of the original data. This is the main problem in transaction tracking through digital watermarking, which has been discussed in this chapter.

## THE LIMITATIONS OF THE CURRENT WATERMARKING SCHEMES AND SOLUTIONS

A wide range of watermarking algorithms has been proposed. In terms of various applications, the watermarking techniques can be classified into two categories:

1.  **Robust copyright marking:** to provide evidence for proving the rightful ownership of the protected digital media
2.  **Authenticate marking:** to authenticate any possible alteration in the protected digital media

Robust marks can verify the ownership of the digital data, whereas the authenticate marks are used to prove whether an object has been "touched" or manipulated. This chapter focuses on robust watermarking. Robust watermarking, as opposed to authentication marking, requires the embedded watermark to be robust against all types of attacks so that it should be able to survive against attacks before the quality of the watermarked image is drastically degraded.

The major research studies on current robust watermarking techniques include the following key technical points (Barni, Bartolini, Cappellini, & Piva, 1998; Cox et al., 1997; Delaigle, Vleeschouwer, & Macq, 1998; Hartung & Kutter, 1999; Katzenbeisser & Petitcolas, 2000; Nikolaidis, & Pitas, 1998; Parhi & Nishitani, 1999):

*   The choice of a work space to perform the hiding operation, mainly a spatial domain (Nikolaidis & Pitas, 1998), or a transform domain such as full-frame Discrete Cosine Transform (full DCT) (Barni et al., 1998; Cox et al., 1997; Piva, Barni, Bartoloni, & Cappellini, 1997), block DCT (Benham, Memon, Yeo, & Yeung, 1997; Hartung & Girod, 1996; Koch & Zhao, 1995; Langelaar, Lubbe, & Lagendijk, 1997; Podilchuk & Zeng, 1997; Xia, Boncelet, & Arce, 1997), Fourier Transform (FT) (Ruanaidh, Dowling, & Boland, 1996), Mellin-Fourier (Ruanaidh & Pun, 1997, 1998), or wavelet (Dugad, Ratakonda, & Ahuja, 1998; Inoue, Miyazaki, Yamamoto, & Katsura, 1998; Kundur & Hatzinakos, 1998; Wang, Su, & Kuo, 1998; Xie & Arce, 1998)
*   The study of optimal watermark embedding locations based on the human visual system (Delaigle et al., 1998; Kankanhalli, Rajmohan, & Ramakrishnan, 1998; Liu, Kong, Kong, & Liu, 2001; Voloshynovskiy, Herrigel, Baumgaertner, & Pun, 1999)
*   The signal embedding techniques by addition, signal-adaptive addition, or modulation methods (Cox et al., 1997; Piva et al., 1997)

- The watermark detection and extraction algorithms either in blind (Piva et al., 1997) or nonblind manner (Cox et al., 1997)

Watermark recovery is usually more robust if its original, unwatermarked data are available. For example, a simple subtraction method (Cox et al., 1997) is used for watermark extraction at the locations where watermark is embedded. The presence of the watermark is determined by cross-correlation of the original and the recovered watermark. In Piva, Barni, Bartolini, and Cappellini's method (1997), the selected DCT coefficients, where the watermark is embedded, are directly matched with all the possible watermarks stored in the database. As a result, the original data are not required for watermark detection. However, a predefined threshold is still needed to determine the presence of the watermark.

From the viewpoint of the presence of a given watermark at the extraction or verification stage, there are two different types of watermarking systems found in the literature (Katzenbeisser & Petitcolas, 2000). The first type is to embed a specific watermark or information. Most watermarking techniques for copyright protection belong to this watermarking category, where it is assumed that the embedded watermark is previously known. The objective of this type of watermarking scheme is to verify the existence of the previously known watermark with or without the help of this watermark. The second type refers to embedding arbitrary information, which is, for example, useful for tracking the unique receipt of a copy of the distributed data. In such scenario, the watermark embedded in an image copy is previously unknown, therefore, no prior information regarding embedded watermark is available for watermark extraction. It makes the transaction tracking more difficult.

Assumptions as well as limitations for most of the existing watermarking schemes that can cause difficulties and ineffectiveness to apply in multimedia transaction tracking are summarized in the following:

(a)  In some watermarking algorithms, watermark detection and extraction requires the presence of the original content. This is not desirable since the original data should always be kept secret and should not be shown to the public, or sometimes the original data are even not available immediately. Therefore, blind watermarking techniques are of great interest and concern nowadays.

(b)  Most of the existing watermarking schemes (Cox et al., 1997; Cox et al., 2002; Katzenbeisser & Petitcolas, 2000) are based on some assumptions about watermark detection and extraction, such as the previous knowledge of watermark locations, strengths, or some threshold. However, in order to ensure the robustness and invisibility of the watermark, the optimum embedding locations as well as the embedding strengths are generally different for different images. For a large image database, it could be a disadvantage if it requires watermark locations and strengths information for detection and extraction of the watermark. As a result, a large amount of side information needs to be stored.

(c)  As explained previously, Figure 2 shows a framework to prevent illegal redistribution of the data by a legal user. In such scenario, the current watermark detection and extraction algorithms requiring information of the watermark locations and strengths, or even the original watermark, could fail because no one knows which watermark exists in the received copy of the work.

(d)  Moreover, the general watermark detection algorithm is based on a match filter finding the maximum correlation of the recovered watermark with the stored watermarks in the database containing the watermarks used to identify all possible users. It is a rather time-consuming and inefficient process, especially when a large database is needed for distribution among a large number of users.

*Figure 3. Second-level wavelet decomposition of the Lena image*

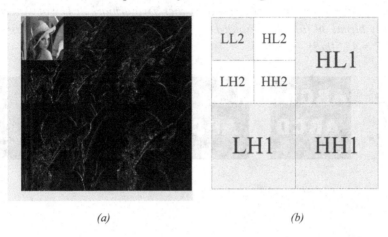

(a)                                    (b)

In this chapter, an Independent Component Analysis (ICA)-based technique is proposed for watermark extraction (Yu, Sattar, & Ma, 2002). The proposed ICA-based blind watermarking scheme (Yu & Sattar, 2003) can overcome the problems of the current watermarking scheme for multimedia tracking as mentioned above. No a priori knowledge of watermark locations, strengths, threshold setting, or the original watermark is required for watermark extraction. This watermarking algorithm is found to be very effective in the application of legal data tracking compared to other watermarking algorithms. Therefore, by adopting this ICA-based watermarking approach, an efficient multimedia distribution framework for copyright protection can be accomplished.

## A NEW ICA-BASED WATERMARKING SCHEME FOR MULTIMEDIA TRANSACTION TRACKING

This section presents an ICA-based wavelet-domain watermarking scheme. Two watermarks are to be embedded into two selected wavelet subbands of the original image. One is the owner's watermark (or the key of the watermarking system), and the other is a unique watermark assigned to a unique legal user. The ICA technique is applied for extraction of the user's watermark with the help of side information. The proposed scheme is described in the context of watermarking in grayscale images, but this technique can be extended to color images and other digital media such as audio and video.

### Proposed Watermark Embedding Scheme

Figure 3 shows a second-level wavelet decomposition of the Lena image into four bands—low-frequency band (LL), high-frequency band (HH), low-high frequency band (LH), and high-low frequency band (HL). Subbands LL and HH are not suitable for watermark embedding among these four subbands. The image quality can be degraded if the watermark is embedding in LL subband since it contains the most

*Figure 4. (a) An NVF masking function, (b) a text signature (64×64 pixels), (c) the modified text water-mark based on the visual mask shown in (a), (d) an owner's watermark or key of watermarking system, (e) the modified key based on (a), (f) original Lena image (256×256 pixels), and (g) a watermarked Lena image (PSNR = 45.50dB)*

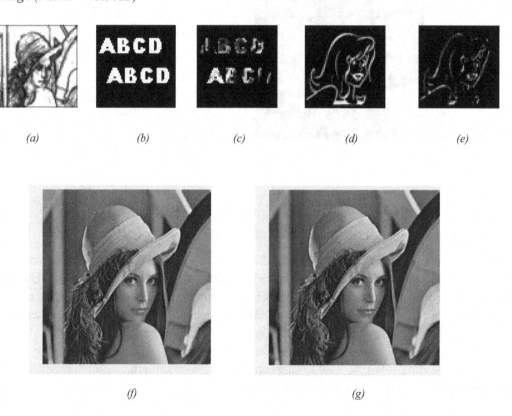

(a)           (b)           (c)           (d)           (e)

(f)                              (g)

important information of an image. Subband HH is insignificant compared to LH and HL subbands, and watermark embedding in such subband find it difficult to survive attacks, such as lossy JPEG compression. Watermark embedding in the two subbands (e.g., LH2 and HL2 of the second-level wavelet decomposition) consisting the middle-frequency pair is to be demonstrated.

Some digital signature/pattern or company logo (**S**), for example, a text image in Figure 4(b), can be used to generate the watermark (**W**) to be embedded. This type of recognizable image pattern is more intuitive and unique than the random sequence to identify the ownership of the work. By using grayscale watermark, our method is found to be more robust against various attacks because the grayscale images can always preserve a certain level of structural information, which are meaningful and recognizable and also can be much more easily verified by human eyes rather than some objective similarity measurements. A masking function—Noise Visibility Function (NVF) (Voloshynovskiy et al., 1999)—is applied to characterize the local image properties, identifying the textured and edge regions where the information can be more strongly embedded. Such high-activity regions are generally highly insensi-

*Figure 5. The proposed watermark embedding algorithm (for second-level wavelet decomposition)*

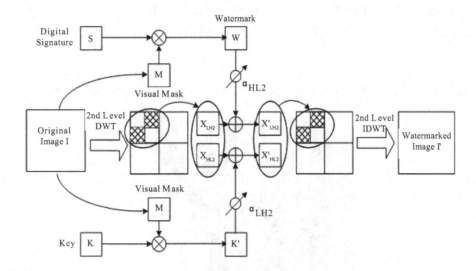

tive to distortion. With the visual mask, the watermark strength can be reasonably increased without visually degrading the image quality.

In the next section, the watermark generation and the detailed embedding algorithm are demonstrated, followed by the generation of side information for watermark extraction.

## Watermark Embedding Algorithm

Figure 5 illustrates the watermark embedding procedure using second-level decomposed middle-frequency pair (LH2 and HL2):

**Step 1:** Perform the second-level discrete wavelet decomposition of the original image **I**. Subbands LH2 and HL2 are selected for the watermark insertion.

**Step 2:** The NVF masking function (Voloshynovskiy et al., 1999), **M**, of the original image is generated. Figure 4(a) shows an NVF mask for the Lena image. For the homogeneous region, NVF approaches 1 (white color), and the strength of the embedded watermark approaches 0. The watermark should be embedded in highly textured regions containing edges instead of homogeneous regions. The original signature image, **S**, is modified according to the generated NVF masking function to ensure the imperceptibility of the watermark embedded. The final watermark is quantized into 0–7 gray levels. The expression for watermark generation is given as

$$W = Q_8 [ ( 1 - M ) . S ], \tag{1}$$

where $\mathbf{Q}_8$ denotes the quantization operator with 8 gray levels. Figure 4(c) shows a text watermark generated using the NVF masking function shown in Figure 4(a).

*Table 1. PSNR (in dB) of the watermarked image with respect to αX*

| α x | 0.01 0 | .05 | 0.10 0 | .15 | 0.20 0 | .25 | 0.30 |
|---|---|---|---|---|---|---|---|
| PSNR (dB) | 67.50 | 53.52 | 47.50 | 43.98 | 41.48 | 39.54 | 37.96 |

*Figure 6. The owner's copy of the Lena image (256×256 pixels and PSNR = 46.72dB)*

**Step 3:** The key **K,** which is also the owner's watermark, is preprocessed by multiplying the same visual mask **M** as

$$K' = Q_8 [ ( 1 - M ) . K ],\qquad(2)$$

where $Q_8$ denotes the quantization operator with 8 gray levels. Figure 4(d) gives a key image for ownership authentication. Figure 4(e) shows the modified key after preprocessing by using the NVF masking function in Figure 4(a).

**Step 4:** The watermark **W** and the modified key **K'** are inserted into the LH2 and HL2 subband, respectively, in the following way:

$$X'_{LH2} = X_{LH2} + \alpha_{LH2} \cdot W = X_{LH2} + \alpha_x \cdot \mu ( | X_{LH2} | ) \cdot W;$$
$$X'_{HL2} = X_{HL2} + \alpha_{HL2} \cdot K2 = X_{HL2} + \alpha_x \cdot \mu ( | X_{HL2} | ) \cdot K',\qquad(3)$$

where **X** and **X'** are the wavelet transform coefficients of the original and the watermarked image, respectively. In Equation 3, $\alpha_{LH2}$ and $\alpha_{HL2}$ denote the weighting coefficients of the watermark embedding in subbands LH2 and HL2, respectively, while $\mu ( | \ | )$ denotes the mean of the absolute value. A common control parameter $\alpha_x$ in Equation 3 is used to adjust the watermark embedding strength to preserve a satisfactory quality of the final watermarked image (Peter, 2001).

**Step 5:** The watermarked image $\mathbf{I}'$ is obtained by the inverse discrete wavelet transform.

**Step 6:** Steps 4 and 5 are repeated until the quality of the final watermarked image is satisfactory, for instance, the PSNR (peak signal-to-noise ratio) measure is within the range of 40–50dB. Particularly the parameter $\alpha_x$ is tuned to adjust the watermark strength to obtain the desired embedding result. Decreasing the magnitude of $\alpha_x$ results in a better quality of the final marked image and vice versa. Figure 4(e) shows a watermarked Lena image with PSNR 45.50dB. Table 1 shows the quality of watermarked image (in dB) with respect to the control parameter $\alpha_x$.

## Side Information for Watermark Extraction

As discussed earlier, the original data may be unavailable in many real applications for security purposes. In order to identify legal users, some side information is necessary to extract the users' watermarks in the absence of the original data. The proposed method allows the owner to create a copy of the data set by embedding only the owner's watermark following the same procedure shown in Figure 5. The owner's watermark is, in fact, the key of the watermarking system that is used for watermark extraction. Using only the owner's copy $\mathbf{I}'_0$ and the key $\mathbf{K}$, the owner is able to identify the recipient of any distributed image by ICA methods. This will be elaborated in the next subsection.

Figure 6 illustrates an owner's copy of the Lena image, embedded with the owner's watermark shown in Figure 4(d). The owner's copy is then obtained by embedding the modified key $\mathbf{K}'$ in the wavelet domain as follows:

$$\mathbf{X}'_{0LH2} = \mathbf{X}_{LH2} + \alpha_{LH2} \cdot \mathbf{K}' = \mathbf{X}_{LH2} + \alpha_{X0} \cdot \mu\left(|\mathbf{X}_{0LH2}|\right) \cdot \mathbf{K}';$$
$$\mathbf{X}'_{0HL2} = \mathbf{X}_{HL2} + \alpha_{HL2} \cdot \mathbf{K}' = \mathbf{X}_{HL2} + \alpha_{X0} \cdot \mu\left(|\mathbf{X}_{0HL2}|\right) \cdot \mathbf{K}', \tag{4}$$

where $\mathbf{X}_0$ and $\mathbf{X}'_0$ are respectively the wavelet transform coefficients of the original image and the watermarked channel, and $\alpha_{X0}$ is a control parameter for the visual quality of the watermarked image $\mathbf{I}'_0$.

Suppose an owner wants to authorize a third party, called appointed representative, to do the tracing task. In such case, the owner should also assign a unique watermark to the appointed representative. This representative's watermark would then replace the owner's watermark embedded in the HL2 wavelet subband. It would also be used as the key during watermark extraction. However, at the same time, for ownership verification, the owner's watermark still needs to be embedded in the wavelet subband selected other than the LH2 and HL2 subbands.

## Proposed Watermark Extraction Scheme Using the ICA Method

In this section, the concept of ICA is briefly introduced. Then a blind watermark extraction scheme is proposed. The ICA technique is employed for watermark extraction successfully, without knowing the original image and any prior information on the embedded watermark, embedding locations, and strengths.

## Independent Component Analysis (ICA)

Independent Component Analysis (ICA) is one of the most widely used methods for performing blind source separation (BSS). It is a very general-purpose statistical technique to recover the independent sources given only sensor observations that are linear mixtures of independent source signals (Hyvärinen, 1999b; Hyvärinen & Oja, 1999; Lee, 1998). ICA has been widely applied in many areas such as audio processing, biomedical signal processing, and telecommunications. In this paper, ICA is further applied in watermarking for blind watermark extraction.

The ICA model consists of two parts: the mixing process and unmixing process. In the mixing process (Hyvärinen, 1999b; Hyvärinen & Oja, 1999; Lee, 1998), the observed linear mixtures $x_1, ..., x_m$ of $n$ number of independent components are defined as

$$x_j = a_{j1}s_1 + a_{j2}s_2 + ... + a_{jn}s_n; \ 1 \leq j \leq m, \tag{5}$$

where $\{s_k, k = 1, ..., n\}$ denote the source variables, that is, the independent components, and $\{a_{jk}, j = 1, ..., m; k = 1, ..., n\}$ are the mixing coefficients. In vector-matrix form, the above mixing model can be expressed as

$$\mathbf{x} = \mathbf{As}, \tag{6}$$

where

$$\mathbf{A} = \begin{pmatrix} a_{11} & a_{12} & \cdots & a_{1n} \\ a_{21} & a_{22} & \cdots & a_{2n} \\ \vdots & \vdots & \ddots & \vdots \\ a_{m1} & a_{m2} & \cdots & a_{mn} \end{pmatrix}$$

is the mixing matrix (Hyvärinen, 1999b; Hyvärinen & Oja, 1999; Lee, 1998), $\mathbf{x} = [x_1 \ x_2 \ ... \ x_m]^T$, $\mathbf{s} = [s_1 \ s_2 \ ... \ s_n]^T$, and $T$ is the transpose operator. For the unmixing process (Hyvärinen, 1999b; Hyvärinen & Oja, 1999; Lee, 1998), after estimating the matrix $\mathbf{A}$, one can compute its inverse—the unmixing matrix $\mathbf{B}$ and the independent components are obtained as

$$\mathbf{s} = \mathbf{Bx}. \tag{7}$$

To ensure the identifiability of the ICA model, the following fundamental restrictions are imposed (Hyvärinen, 1999b; Hyvärinen & Oja, 1999):

- The source signals in the mixing process should be principally statistically independent.
- All independent components $s_k$, with the possible exception of one component, must be non-Gaussian.

- The number of observed linear mixtures $m$ must be at least as large as the number of independent components $n$, that is, $m \geq n$.
- The matrix $\mathbf{A}$ must be of full column rank.

There are many ICA algorithms that have been proposed recently. Some popular ICA methods include Bell and Sejnowski's Infomax (1995), Hyvärinen and Oja's FastICA (1999), Cichocki and Barros' RICA (Robust batch ICA) (1999), Cardoso's JADE (Joint Approximate Diagonalization of Eigen-matrices) (1999), and so on. From the stability standpoint, it is more appropriate to choose RICA or JADE algorithms than Infomax and FastICA algorithms for our watermark extraction process. Both Infomax algorithm and FastICA algorithm require that the values of the mixing coefficients for the sources not be very close (Bell & Sejnowski, 1995; Hyvärinen, 1999a). However, both the watermark and the key are embedded by multiplication with small weighting coefficients to make them invisible. Therefore, the extraction of such weak watermark signals could fail by using Infomax or FastICA algorithm. The extraction results using FastICA algorithm also very much depend on the initial guess of the weighting coefficients (Hyvärinen, 1999a).

Cichocki and Barro's RICA algorithm is an effective blind source separation approach particularly for the temporally correlated sources, since it models the signal as an autoregressive (AR) process (Cichocki & Barros, 1999). The RICA algorithm thus can achieve the best extraction results when both the embedding and extraction are performed in the spatial domain. This is because, generally speaking, the natural images are spatially correlated and can be effectively modeled as temporally correlated sequences. However, for the proposed watermarking scheme described in this chapter, the watermark is embedded in the wavelet domain instead of the spatial domain. The experimental results show that the JADE algorithm (Cardoso, 1999) outperforms the other ICA algorithms for watermark extraction in our proposed watermarking scheme. This could be due to the use of higher-order statistical parameters in the JADE algorithm, such as fourth-order cumulant, which can model the statistical behavior of the wavelet coefficients more effectively. Therefore, the JADE algorithm is employed to elaborate the watermark extraction process in our proposed watermarking scheme, which will be described next.

## Proposed Blind Watermark Extraction Scheme

This section proposes the ICA-based blind watermark extraction scheme. Instead of using the original image, only an owner's copy of the original image is required for watermark extraction. The new useful feature of the proposed scheme is that the proposed method does not require previous knowledge of the original watermark, embedding locations, and watermark strengths for extraction. The main idea is to consider two subbands $(\mathbf{X}'_{\mathbf{R}})$ of the watermarked image to have a mixture image of the wavelet transformed image $(\mathbf{X}_{\mathbf{R}})$ of the original image $(\mathbf{I})$, the watermark image $(\mathbf{W})$, and the modified key $(\mathbf{K}')$. Figure 7 shows the proposed blind watermark extraction scheme. Let us denote the received watermarked image as '. The symbol ($\sim$) is to indicate that the received data may or may not be the same as its original watermarked data due to transmission errors or possibly pirate attacks. This symbol ($\sim$) is removed in the following for simplicity.

**Step 1:** Perform the second-level discrete wavelet decomposition of the watermarked image $\mathbf{I}'$ in order to obtain the wavelet coefficients $\mathbf{X}'_{LH2}$ and $\mathbf{X}'_{HL2}$ for the two selected subbands of LH2 and HL2.

*Figure 7. Proposed blind watermark extraction scheme (using the second-level decomposition)*

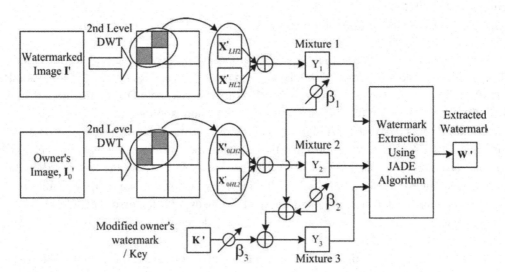

**Step 2:** The first mixture signal $\mathbf{Y}_1$ is obtained by

$$\mathbf{Y}_1 = \mathbf{X}'_{LH2} + \mathbf{X}'_{HL2}. \tag{8}$$

From Equation 3, $\mathbf{X}'_{\mathbf{R}}$ ($\mathbf{R} \in [LH2, HL2]$) are the mixture observations of the wavelet transform of the original image ($\mathbf{X}_{\mathbf{R}}$), the watermark ($\mathbf{W}$), and the modified key ($\mathbf{K}'$), therefore, Equation 8 can be rewritten as

$$\mathbf{Y}_1 = \mathbf{X} + \alpha_1 \mathbf{W} + \alpha_2 \mathbf{K}', \tag{9}$$

where $\mathbf{X} = \mathbf{X}_{LH2} + \mathbf{X}_{HL2}$, $\alpha_1 = \alpha_{\mathbf{x}} \cdot \mu(|\mathbf{X}_{LH2}|)$ and $\alpha_2 = \alpha_{\mathbf{x}} \cdot \mu(|\mathbf{X}_{HL2}|)$. It is found that the first mixture signal is a linear mixture of the three independent sources, that is, $\mathbf{X}$, $\mathbf{W}$ and $\mathbf{K}'$.

**Step 3:** Repeat the procedure in Steps 1 and 2 for the owner's image $\mathbf{I}'_0$. The second mixture $\mathbf{Y}_2$ is obtained by

$$\mathbf{Y}_2 = \mathbf{X}'_{0LH2} + \mathbf{X}'_{0HL2}. \tag{10}$$

Similarly $\mathbf{Y}_2$ is also a linear mixture of the wavelet transform of the original image ($\mathbf{X}_{\mathbf{R}}$, $\mathbf{R} \in [LH2, HL2]$) and the key/owner's watermark ($\mathbf{K}$). It can be written as

$$\mathbf{Y}_2 = \mathbf{X} + \alpha_3 \mathbf{K}', \tag{11}$$

*Figure 8. The extraction result for the user's watermark image (normalized correlation coefficient, r = 0.9790), using JADE ICA method*

where $\alpha_3 = \alpha_{x0} \cdot [\, \mu(|\mathbf{X}_{0LH2}|) + \mu(|\mathbf{X}_{0HL2}|)\,]$.

**Step 4:** From Equations 8 and 10, two mixture images can be obtained containing three sources or independent components in the observations—$\mathbf{X}$, the modified key $\mathbf{K}'$, and the watermark $\mathbf{W}$. As was pointed out earlier, to exploit ICA methods for watermark extraction, it is required that the number of observed linear mixture inputs is at least equal to or larger than the number of independent sources in order to ensure the identifiability of the ICA model (Hyvärinen, 1999b; Hyvärinen & Oja, 1999; Lee, 1998). Therefore, another linear mixture of the three independent sources is needed. The third mixture $\mathbf{Y}_3$ can then be generated by linear superposition of $\mathbf{Y}_1$, $\mathbf{Y}_2$ and $\mathbf{K}'$:

$$\mathbf{Y}_3 = \beta_1 \mathbf{Y}_1 + \beta_2 \mathbf{Y}_2 + \beta_3 \mathbf{K}', \tag{12}$$

where $\beta_1$ and $\beta_2$ are arbitrary real numbers, and $b_3$ is a nonzero arbitrary real number. Either $\beta_1$ or $\beta_2$ can be set to zero to efficiently reduce the computational load of ICA. Note that the modified key $\mathbf{K}'$ can be easily obtained by regenerating the NVF visual mask and multiplying it to the original owner's watermark $\mathbf{K}$.

**Step 5:** The three mixtures input into the JADE ICA algorithm (Cardoso, 1999) and the watermark image $\mathbf{W}'$ is extracted. The user of any image copy can be uniquely identified from the signature of the extracted watermark. Figure 8 shows the extracted watermark from the watermarked image shown in Figure 4(g).

## PERFORMANCE EVALUATION

The robustness results of the proposed watermarking scheme are shown in this section using the Lena image of size 256×256 when the simulations are performed in the MATLAB 6.5 software environment. A watermarked image (PSNR = 45.50 dB) in Figure 4(g) is generated by setting the watermark strength control parameter $\alpha_x$ as 0.15. In the experiments of watermark extraction, the parameters $\beta_1$, $\beta_2$, and $\beta_3$ are set as 0, 1, 1, respectively, to simplify the computational load of the ICA processing, and

Daubechies-1 (Haar) orthogonal filters are employed for wavelet decomposition. In order to investigate the robustness of the watermark, the watermarked image is manipulated by various signal processing techniques, such as JPEG compression and JPEG2000 compression, quantization, cropping, and geometric distortions. The watermark extraction is performed for the distorted watermarked image and the extracted watermark is compared to the original.

## The Performance Index

The performance of the blind watermark extraction result is evaluated in terms of normalized correlation coefficient, $r$, of the extracted watermark $\mathbf{W'}$ and the original watermark $\mathbf{W}$ as

$$r = \frac{\mathbf{W} \cdot \mathbf{W'}}{\sqrt{\mathbf{W}^2 \cdot \mathbf{W'}^2}}. \tag{13}$$

The magnitude range of $r$ is [-1, 1], and the unity holds if the matching between the extracted image and the original image is perfect.

## Robustness Against Compression and Quantization Attacks

In the following, the robustness of the proposed watermarking scheme is compared with some other blind wavelet-domain watermarking schemes (Peter, 2001) in terms of normalized correlation coefficient $r$ as shown in Equation 13. These techniques include Wang, Su, and Kuo's algorithm (1998), Inoue, Miyazaki, Yamamoto, and Katsura's blind algorithm (based on manipulating insignificant coefficients) (1998), Dugad, Ratakonda, and Ahuja's algorithm (1998), Kundur and Hatzinakos' algorithm (1998), and Xie and Arce's algorithm (1998).

Wang et al. (1998) have proposed an adaptive watermarking method to embed watermarks into selected significant subband wavelet coefficients. A blind watermark retrieval technique has been proposed by truncating selected significant coefficients to some specific value. Inoue et al. (1998) have classified insignificant and significant wavelet coefficients using the embedded zerotree wavelet (EZW) algorithm. Thereby, two types of embedding algorithms have been developed in respect to the locations of significant or insignificant coefficients. Information data are detected using the position of the zerotree's root and the threshold value after decomposition of the watermarked image. Dugad et al. (1998) have added the watermark in selected coefficients having significant energy in the transform domain to ensure noneras-ability of the watermark. During watermark detection, all the high-pass coefficients above the threshold are chosen and are correlated with the original copy of the watermark. Kundur and Hatzinakos (1998) have presented a novel technique for the digital watermarking of still images based on the concept of multiresolution wavelet fusion, which is robust to a variety of signal distortions. Xie and Arce (1998) have developed a blind watermarking digital signature for the purpose of authentication. The signature algorithm is first implemented in the wavelet-transform domain and is coupled within the SPIHT (Set Partitioning in Hierarchical Trees) compression algorithm.

Figure 9 shows the comparison results in terms of performance index against the JPEG compression. For the proposed scheme, the extracted watermark's correlation decreases gradually with the compression

*Figure 9. Comparison of results against JPEG compression attacks*

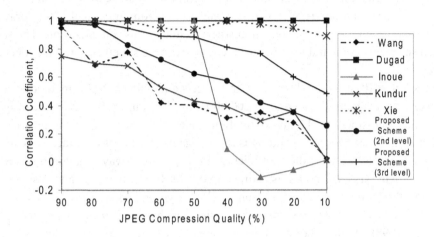

*Figure 10. Comparison of results against JPEG2000 compression attacks*

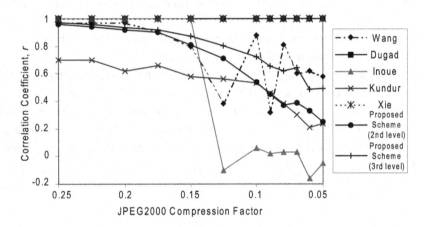

quality factor. The image quality (in PSNR) has degraded significantly to 27 dB when the compression quality becomes quite low to 10%. In such a difficult case, the watermark can still be extracted with the value of $r$ equal to 0.2553 for watermark embedding in second-level wavelet decomposition. According to Figure 9, the presented method can perform better than the Wang et al.'s and the Kundur and Hatzinakos' methods, while performing much better than the Inoue et al.'s method in terms of robustness against JPEG compression attack at a very low compression quality factor.

Figure 10 is the extraction comparison against the JPEG2000 compression attacks. The robustness of the proposed scheme is demonstrated up to the compression factor 0.05 or compression rate 0.4 bpp (bit per pixel). The proposed scheme gives better performance than Kundur and Hatzinakos' method, and comparable performance to the Wang et al.'s method. The extraction performance of the Inoue et al.'s method drops sharply when the JPEG2000 compression factor decreases to 0.125. Embedding in the subbands of higher wavelet decomposition level (see curves for third-level decomposition in Figures 9 and 10) can improve significantly the robustness of the proposed scheme against compression attacks.

Figure 11 shows the extraction results against quantization from gray level 256 to gray level 4 per pixel. The proposed scheme has very good robustness result against quantization. The performance of the proposed scheme is comparable to that of the Xie and Arce's method, and much better than the other methods.

From Figures 9 and 10, it is found that Xie and Arce's and Dugad et al.'s methods have excellent robustness performance against JPEG and JPEG2000 compression. In Xie and Arce's algorithm, the watermark is embedded solely in the approximation image (LL subband) of the host image (Xie & Arce, 1998). Although LL subband embedding is robust against compression attacks, the image quality could be degraded visually because the coefficients of this portion always contain the most important information of an image (Peter, 2001). It is claimed that the robustness of Xie and Arce's method very much depends on the number of decomposition levels. Very good robustness result can be obtained by employing a five-level wavelet decomposition using Daubechies-7/9 bi-orthogonal filters (Peter, 2001; Xie & Arce, 1998). On the other hand, in the Dugad et al.'s method, the watermark is embedded in the significant coefficients of all detail subbands (Dugad et al., 1998); therefore, it is more resistant to compression. During the watermark detection using Dugad et al.'s method, the original watermark is required to compute the correlation for the high-pass coefficients with the values above a threshold (Dugad et al., 1998). The presence of the watermark is determined by comparing this correlation with a threshold setting. It is not as general as our proposed scheme where the original watermark and the threshold are not required for watermark extraction.

The experimental results show that the proposed scheme has good robustness against the most prominent attacks such as JPEG and JPEG2000 compression, quantization, and can be comparable to existing blind wavelet-domain watermarking schemes. Experimental results also show that unlike the Xie and Arce's method (Peter, 2001; Xie & Arce, 1998), the choice of the wavelet transform is not critical concerning the robustness issue of the proposed watermarking method (the corresponding results are not included here).

*Figure 11. Comparison of results against quantization*

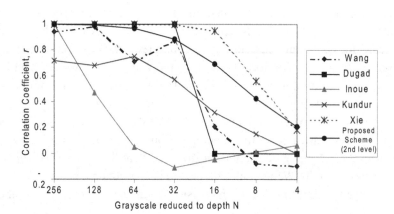

## Robustness Against Cropping and Geometric Distortions

Many watermarking techniques cannot survive geometric transformations such as rotation, scaling, and translation (RST) and sometimes cropping attack as well due to the loss of the synchronization of the watermark detector. A solution to such geometric attacks is to apply a resynchronization process (blind or nonblind) before performing the watermark extraction. Nonblind solution requires the presence of the original data, or at least some knowledge of the image features (Dugelay & Petitcolas, 2000). Davoine, Bas, Hébert, and Chassery (1999) have proposed a nonblind solution by splitting the original image into a set of triangular patches. This mesh serves as a reference mesh and is kept in the memory for synchronization preprocessing. This proposed method, however, is only efficient in the case of involving minor deformations. Johnson, Duric, and Jajodia (1999) have proposed a method to invert affine transformations by estimating the difference in the least square sense between the salient image feature points in the original and transformed images. Kutter (1998) has proposed alternative methods to retrieve the watermark from geometrically distorted image without using the original data. The first method is to preset a part of the watermark to some known values and to use them for spatial resynchronization. This approach decreases the hiding capacity of the useful information, and is also computationally very expensive. The second method proposed by Kutter (1998) is to use self-reference systems that embed the watermark several times at the shifted locations.

Generally speaking, the tuning process can be easier, more accurate and requires less computational load when the original data or reference feature points are available, although it may need extra memory to store the reference data. In our proposed watermarking scheme, original data are not available during the extraction process; however, an owner's or a representative's copy of the data is available. This image copy would be very similar to the original data, thus it is convenient to use it directly as a reference for synchronization of geometric distorted or cropped data. By simple comparisons, the tampered data can be adjusted back to original size and position rapidly and accurately. In the following, the watermark extraction results against attacks of cropping and RST are shown. The effectiveness of employing synchronization preprocessing is demonstrated by showing the significant improvements of extraction results with and without the synchronization.

As shown in Figure 12(a), the face portion of a marked Lena image is cropped. By comparison with the owner's Lena image copy, it can be easily detected that the pixels within a square area, with row index from 121 to 180 and column index from 121 to 180, are corrupted. The absence of the watermark information in this corrupted region (by considering both rows and columns from 31 ($\lceil 121/4 \rceil$) to 45 ($\lceil 180/4 \rceil$) results in an undesired overbrightness effect for the extracted watermark due to its high values in the corrupted region. This makes both the subjective and the objective verification measurements quite poor (see Figure 12(b)). One simple solution is to discard the corresponding undesired high-valued pixels from the extracted watermark and replace them with zero-valued pixels. In this way, according to Figure 12(c), the extracted watermark can be recovered mostly with some information loss in the corrupted region. Therefore, the normalized correlation coefficient $r$ is found to increase from 0.2706 to 0.9036, showing the recovery of the low-contrast watermark (compare Figures 12(b) and 12(c)).

The watermark extraction of the geometrically distorted image may fail due to the loss of synchronization. A resynchronization preprocessing of the received data is necessary to tune it back to the right positions or sizes before input in the watermark decoder. However, the side information in the proposed watermarking scheme—the owner's or the representative's copy of the original image—provides a good reference to assist the synchronization process, and the watermark extraction performance is conse-

*Figure 12. (a) A cropped Lena image, (b) the extracted watermark (r = 0.2706), and (c) the extracted watermark after improving the contrast of (b) (r = 0.9036)*

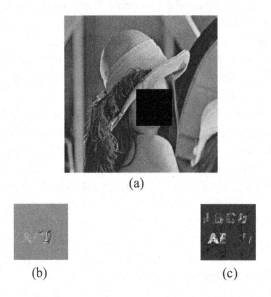

(a)

(b)                                    (c)

quently improved. Figures 13(b), 13(d), and 13(f) show the extraction results under attacks of rotation, scaling, and translation (RST), respectively, after the synchronization process. The watermark extraction results are satisfactory in terms of both the subjective visualization and the objective similarity measurement.

## Discussions

### Watermarking versus Fingerprinting

To enforce IP rights for multimedia distribution over the Internet, it requires not only verification of the legal recipient, but also proof of the rightful ownership of the original work. The term *fingerprinting* (Katzenbeisser & Petitcolas, 2000; Arnold et al., 2003; Trappe, Wu, Wang, & Liu, 2003) is closely related to watermarking in the context of traitor tracking problem. Fingerprinting technique involves the embedding of different watermarks into each distributed copy of the work. The purpose of fingerprinting is to identify the legal recipient rather than the source of digital data. Thus, using the fingerprinting technique alone is not sufficient to enforce IP rights protection in multimedia distribution systems, as the owner cannot provide trustful evidence for proving the ownership. This chapter presents a multiple digital watermarking framework that can achieve the above two demands, that is, identifying the owner and the recipient of the distributed content.

Moreover, fingerprinting has another distinct interpretation, which does not involve the concept of digital watermarking at all. It refers to the extraction of unique features, such as semantically relevant or characteristic features from multimedia signals, in order to distinguish itself from other similar objects (Katzenbeisser & Petitcolas, 2000; Arnold et al., 2003). The extracted features are normally stored

*Figure 13. (a) Lena image rotated by 10°, and (b) the corresponding extracted watermark (r = 0.5847); (c) Lena image downsized by reducing the number of rows and columns by 1/4, and (d) the corresponding extracted watermark (r = 0.4970); (e) Lena image translated to the left and downward by 10 and 36 lines, respectively, and (f) the corresponding extracted watermark (r = 0.5356)*

(a)    (c)    (e)

(b)    (d)    (f)

separately as signatures for authentication of the content rather than inserting them into the content as watermarks. This concept falls out of scope of this chapter.

## Summary and Future Work of the Proposed Watermarking Scheme

The proposed ICA-based watermarking scheme shows its main advantage in terms of generality. Unlike other methods, no a priori information about the original watermark, embedding locations, strengths, as well as the threshold is needed for our blind watermark extraction scheme. Therefore, it is possible to extract the watermark from any copy of the watermarked image, where the embedded watermark is previously unknown. The other advantage of the proposed ICA-based method is that without using a pre-defined threshold, the extracted watermark could simply be verified from visual inspection instead of using the correlation-based matching technique with a threshold setting. This is possible because the embedded watermark used in our scheme is a readable digital signature image or a logo image. The generality of the proposed scheme implicates this method to be a quite useful tool for the transaction tracking in the application of Internet distribution. The only disadvantage to achieving the generality using ICA-based technique could be the complexity of the ICA itself. In this chapter, this has been compromised by the use of JADE algorithm, which is simple and computationally efficient. Furthermore, there are only three mixing sources (i.e., the original data, the key, and the watermark) involved in the presented watermarking scheme, which enables our ICA-based extraction processing to be fast.

In the future, more experiments need to be carried out in order to evaluate the resilience of this scheme against other types of attacks. For example, the collusion attacks and the possible counterattacks for multimedia distribution systems are to be investigated to improve the present scheme. The issue on the generation of a better perceptual mask as used to simulate the human visual system should also be studied to improve the visual quality of the watermarked data.

## CONCLUDING REMARKS AND FUTURE TRENDS

This chapter investigates the multimedia transaction tracking issue by means of digital watermarking. One feasible solution of using an ICA-based watermarking technique is presented to perform ownership verification and traitor tracking for multimedia distribution through public networks. Two watermarks consisting of an owner's watermark for ownership identification and a user's watermark for unique recipient identification are embedded. Watermark is obtained by modification of the signature image with a visual mask in order to prevent the perceptual quality degradation of the watermarked image. The watermarks are inserted in the two middle frequency subband pair at the higher wavelet decomposition level (say second/third decomposition level) of the original image. Without requiring any information such as original watermark, embedding locations, and strengths, our proposed scheme can extract the user's watermark with the help of an owner's copy of the image and the owner's watermark/key. Experimental results show that the proposed watermarking scheme can provide good resistance to attacks of image compression, quantization, cropping, and geometric transformations.

It has been elaborated in this chapter that the ICA-based watermarking scheme can be employed as an efficient tool to trace the recipient of the distributed content. From the general perspective, the challenging issues of digital watermarking in the applications of transaction tracking for the Internet distribution include the following criteria:

- The original data are not available during extraction of the recipient's watermark. Thus the watermarking technique should be blind.
- No prior information about the embedded watermark and the corresponding locations is available for watermark extraction.
- In order to present as trustful evidence in the court to litigate the pirate, a highly robust watermarking scheme against common signal possessing attacks as well as collusion attacks is needed.
- For some applications, for example, searching for the pirated watermarked image using Web crawlers, it is required that the watermarking scheme is able to extract the watermark easily and with low complexity.

There is no doubt that transaction tracking is a more difficult task than copyright protection by means of digital watermarking. More general watermarking techniques are desired such that no original data and prior watermark information is needed for extraction, while providing the methods to be reliable, robust, and computationally efficient.

Another requirement to enforce the IP rights of the distributed work could be such that the owner should be able to detect any illegal attempts manipulating the content. Fragile watermark should be inserted as well in order to protect the integrity of the content. The authentication watermark should be then very sensitive to various attacks and, therefore, able to locate possible modifications. In such scenario, three watermarks would be hidden in the work in order to verify the owner, to identify the user, and to authenticate the content. Since the information-hiding capacity of the cover media is limited, we have further challenges to investigate, for example, how to compromise the three demands including the information-hiding capacity and the imperceptibility and robustness of the hidden watermark.

There has been no rush yet to embrace any of the current watermarking schemes for IP rights protection in multimedia distribution application. In fact, time is still needed for thorough inspection and appraisal to find solutions for better digital watermarking schemes. Before that, scientists and researchers have to fully understand the practical requirements associated with the real problems. In the meantime, the main challenge for researchers is to develop even more transparent and decodable schemes for robust or fragile watermarking, or perhaps to meet more demands required for a practical multimedia distribution system.

## ACKNOWLEDGMENT

The authors would like to thank Professor N.G. Kingsbury for his valuable suggestions and comments that helped to improve the proposed watermarking scheme for transaction tracking in multimedia distribution applications. They are also thankful to Professor K.-K. Ma for contributing useful discussion regarding the use of ICA in image watermarking.

## REFERENCES

Arnold, M., Schmucker, M., & Wolthusen, S.D. (2003). *Techniques and applications of digital watermarking and content protection*. Boston: Artech House.

Barni, M., Bartolini, F., Cappellini, V., & Piva, A. (1998). A DCT-domain system for robust image watermarking. *Signal Processing, 66*, 357–372.

Barni, M., Bartolini, F., Cappellini, V., Piva, A., & Rigacci, F. (1998). A M.A.P. identification criterion for DCT-based watermarking. *Proc. Europ. Signal Processing Conf. (EUSIPCO'98)*, Rhodes, Greece.

Bell, A., & Sejnowski, T. (1995). An information-maximization approach to blind separation and blind deconvolution. *Neural Compt., 7*, 1129–1159.

Benham, D., Memon, N., Yeo, B.-L., & Yeung, M. (1997). Fast watermarking of DCT-based compressed images. *Proc. Int. Conf. Image Science, System, and Technology (CISST'97)*, Las Vegas, NV.

Cardoso, J.-F. (1999). High-order contrasts for independent component analysis. *Neural Computer, 11*, 157–192.

Cichocki, A., & Barros, A.K. (1999). Robust batch algorithm for sequential blind extraction of noisy biomedical signals. *Proc. ISSPA'99, 1*, 363–366.

Cox, I.J., Leighton, F.T., & Shamoon, T. (1997). Secure spread spectrum watermarking for multimedia. *IEEE Trans. on Image Processing, 6*, 1673–1687.

Cox, I.J., Miller, M.L., & Bloom, J.A. (2002). *Digital watermarking*. Morgan Kaufmann.

Davoine, F., Bas, P., Hébert, P.-A., & Chassery, J.-M. (1999). Watermarking et résistance aux déformations géométriques. *Cinquièmes journées d'études et d'échanges sur la compression et la représentation des signaux audiovisuels (CORESA'99)*, Sophia-Antiplis, France.

Delaigle, J.F., Vleeschouwer, C.D., & Macq, B. (1998). Watermarking algorithm based on a human visual model. *Signal Processing, 66*, 319–335.

Dugad, R., Ratakonda, K., & Ahuja, N. (1998). A new wavelet-based scheme for watermarking images. *Proc. Int. Conf. Image Processing (ICIP)*.

Dugelay, J.-L., & Petitcolas, F.A.P. (2000). Possible counter-attacks against random geometric distortions. *Proc. SPIE Security and Watermarking of Multimedia Contents II*, CA.

Hartung, F., & Girod, B. (1996). Digital watermarking of raw and compressed video. *Proc. SPIE digital compression technologies and systems for video commun., 2952*, 205–213.

Hartung, F., & Kutter, M. (1999). Multimedia watermarking technique. *Proc. IEEE, 8*(7), 1079–1106.

Hyvärinen, A. (1999a). Fast and robust fixed-point algorithms for independent component analysis. *IEEE Trans. Neural Networks, 10*, 626–634.

Hyvärinen, A. (1999b). Survey on independent component analysis. *Neural Computing Surveys, 2*, 94–128.

Hyvärinen, A., & Oja, E. (1999). Independent component analysis: a tutorial. Retrieved from *www.cis. hut.fi/projects/ica/*

Inoue, H., Miyazaki, A., Yamamoto, A., & Katsura, T. (1998). A digital watermark based on the wavelet transform and its robustness on image compression. *Proc. Int. Conf. Image Processing (ICIP)*.

Johnson, N.F., Duric, Z., & Jajodia, S. (1999). Recovery of watermarks from distorted images. *Preliminary Proc. of the Third Int. Information Hiding Workshop*, 361–375.

Kankanhalli, M.S., Rajmohan, & Ramakrishnan, K.R. (1998). Content based watermarking of images. *Proc. of the Sixth ACM International Multimedia Conference.*

Katzenbeisser, S., & Petitcolas, F.A.P. (2000). *Information hiding techniques for steganography and digital watermarking.* Boston: Artech House.

Koch, E., & Zhao, J. (1995). Towards robust and hidden image copyright labeling. *Proc. Workshop Nonlinear Signal and Image Processing.*

Kundur, D., & Hatzinakos, D. (1998). Digital watermarking using multiresolution wavelet decomposition. *Proc. of the Int. Conference on Acoustics, Speech, and Signal Processing, 5*, 2969–2972.

Kutter, M. (1998). Watermarking resisting to translation, rotation and scaling. *Proc. of SPIE Int. Symposium on Voice, Video, and Data Communications—Multimedia Systems and Applications, 3528*, 423–431.

Langelaar, C., Lubbe, J.C.A., & Lagendijk, R.L. (1997). Robust labeling methods for copy protection of images. *Proc. Electronic Imaging, 3022*, 298–309.

Lee, T.-W. (1998). *Independent component analysis: Theory and applications*. Kluwer Academic.

Liu, H., Kong, X.-W., Kong, X.-D., & Liu, Y. (2001). Content based color image adaptive watermarking scheme. *Proc. of IEEE International Symposium on Circuits and Systems, 2*, 41–44.

Lu, C.-S., & Mark, Liao H.-Y. (2001). Multipurpose watermarking for image authentication and protection. *IEEE Transaction on Image Processing, 10*.

Mintzer, F., & Braudaway, G. (1999). If one watermark is good, are more better? *Proc. of the International Conference on Acoustics, Speech, and Signal Processing, 4*.

Nikolaidis, N., & Pitas, I. (1998). Robust image watermarking in the spatial domain. *Signal Processing, 66*, 385–403.

Parhi, K.K., & Nishitani, T. (1999). *Digital signal processing for multimedia systems*. New York: Marcel Dekker.

Peter, P. (2001). *Digital image watermarking in the wavelet transform domain*. Unpublished master's thesis.

Piva, A., Barni, M., Bartoloni, E., & Cappellini, V. (1997). DCT-based watermark recovering without resorting to the uncorrupted original image. *Proc. IEEE Int. Conf. Image Processing (ICIP), 1*.

Podilchuk, C., & Zeng, W. (1997). Watermarking of the JPEG bitstream. *Proc. Int. Conf. Imaging Science, Systems, and Applications (CISST'97)*, 253–260.

Ruanaidh, J.J.K.Ó, & Pun, T. (1997). Rotation, scale and translation invariant digital watermarking. *Proc. IEEE Int. Conf. Image Processing (ICIP'97), 1*, 536–539.

Ruanaidh, J.J.K.Ó, & Pun, T. (1998). Rotation, scale and translation invariant digital watermarking. *Signal Processing, 66*(3), 303–318.

Ruanaidh, J.J.K.Ó, Dowling, W.J., & Boland, F.M. (1996). Phase watermarking of digital images. *Proc. Int. Conf. Image Processing (ICIP'96), 3*, 239–242.

Schneier, B. (1995). *Applied cryptography* (2nd ed.). John Wiley and Sons.

Sheppard, N.P., Safavi-Naini, R., & Ogunbona, P. (2001). On multiple watermarking. *Proc. of ACM Multimedia 2001*.

Trappe, W., Wu, M., Wang, J., & Liu, K.J.R. (2003). Anti-collusion fingerprinting for multimedia. *IEEE Trans. on Signal Processing, 51*(4), 1069–1087.

Voloshynovskiy, S., Herrigel, A., Baumgaertner, N., & Pun, T. (1999). A stochastic approach to content adaptive digital image watermarking. *Proc. of Int. Workshop on Information Hiding*.

Wang, H.-J.M., Su, P.-C., & Kuo, C.-C.J. (1998). Wavelet-based digital image watermarking. *Optics Express, 3*(12), 491–496.

Xia, X., Boncelet, C., & Arce, G. (1997). A multiresolution watermark for digital images. *Proc. Int. Conf. Image Processing (ICIP'97), 1*, 548–551.

Xie, L., & Arce, G.R. (1998). Joint wavelet compression and authentication watermarking. *Proc. Int. Conf. Image Processing (ICIP'98)*.

Yu, D., & Sattar, F. (2003). A new blind image watermarking technique based on independent component analysis. *Springer-Verlag Lecture Notes in Computer Science, 2613*, 51–63.

Yu, D., Sattar, F., & Ma, K.-K. (2002). Watermark detection and extraction using independent component analysis method. *EURASIP Journal on Applied Signal Processing—Special Issue on Nonlinear Signal and Image Processing (Part II)*.

*This work was previously published in Digital Watermarking for Digital Media, edited by J. Seitz, pp. 52-86, copyright 2005 by Information Science Publishing (an imprint of IGI Global).*

# Chapter XVIII
# Image Watermarking Algorithms Based on the Discrete Wavelet Transform

**Ali Al-Haj**
*The University of Jordan, Jordan*

## ABSTRACT

*In the last decade, many digital image watermarking algorithms have been proposed and implemented; however, algorithms based on the discrete wavelet transform (DWT) have been widely recognized to be more prevalent than the others. This is due to the wavelets' excellent spatial localization, frequency spread, and multiresolution characteristics, which are similar to the theoretical models of the human visual system. In this chapter, we describe three DWT-based digital image watermarking algorithms. The first algorithm watermarks a given image in the DWT domain, while the second and third algorithms improve the basic algorithm by combining DWT with two powerful transforms. The second algorithm is a hybrid algorithm in which DWT and the discrete cosine transform (DCT) are combined. The third algorithm is also a hybrid algorithm in which DWT and the singular value decomposition transform (SVD) are combined. Performance evaluation results show that combining DWT with DCT or SVD improved the imperceptibility and robustness performance of the basic DWT-based digital watermarking algorithm. Finally, the ideas described in the chapter can be easily extended to watermarking multimedia objects that include audio and video data contents.*

## INTRODUCTION

Advancements in digital image processing and computer networks have considerably facilitated the acquisition, representation, storage, and distribution of images in digital format. These advancements, however, made the unauthorized manipulation and reproduction of original digital images an easy process. Consequently, the design and development of effective digital image copyright protection methods have become necessary. Traditional image security methods include encryption, authentication, and time stamping (Furht & Kirovski, 2006). However, the emerging digital watermarking technology has been recently advocated as the best solution to the multimedia copyright protection problem (Cox, Miller & Bloom, 2002; Katzenbeisser & Petitcolas, 2000; Langelaar, Setyawan & Lagendijk, 2000; Potdar, Han & Chang, 2005). It is expected that digital watermarking will have a wide-span of practical applications such as digital cameras, digital libraries, medical imaging, image databases, surveillance imaging, and video-on-demand systems, among many others (Arnold, Schumucker & Wolthusen, 2003).

Digital image watermarking has been proposed to prevent illegal and malicious copying and distribution of digital images by embedding unnoticeable information (called a watermark) into the image content. The watermark is usually a random number sequence, copyright messages, ownership identifier, or control signal identifying the ownership information. In order for a digital watermark to be effective, it should be robust to common image manipulations like compression, filtering, rotation, scaling cropping, collusion attacks, among many other digital signal processing operations. The watermark should also be imperceptible, which means that the addition of the watermark should not degrade the perceptual quality of the host image. In general, it is not difficult to achieve imperceptibility. Robustness is usually the kernel that decides the success of watermarking algorithms.

Current digital image watermarking techniques can be grouped into two major classes: spatial-domain watermarking techniques and watermarking frequency-domain techniques (Cox et al., 2002). Spatial-domain techniques embed a watermark in a host image by directly modifying its pixels (Chan & Cheng, 2004; Sebe, Domingo-Ferrer & Herrera, 2000). These techniques are easy to implement and require few computational resources; however, they are sensitive to alterations and are not robust against common digital signal processing operations such compression. On the other hand, transform-domain watermarking techniques modify the coefficients of the transformed image according to a predetermined embedding scheme. The scheme disperses the watermark in the spatial domain of the image, hence making it very difficult to remove the embedded watermark. Compared to spatial domain techniques, frequency-domain watermarking techniques proved to be more effective with respect to achieving the imperceptibility and robustness requirements of digital watermarking algorithms (Cox et al., 2002). Commonly used frequency-domain transforms include the Discrete Wavelet Transform (DWT) (Mallat, 1989), the Discrete Cosine Transform (DCT) (Rao & Yip, 1990), and the Discrete Fourier Transform (DFT) (Mitra, 1998).

DWT has been used in digital watermarking more frequently than other transforms. This is due to its excellent spatial localization, frequency spread, and multiresolution characteristics, which are similar to the theoretical models of the human visual system (Vetterli & Kovačević, 1995). By virtue of these properties, an efficient relationship between the transform and coefficients and visual masking properties of the human visual system has been constructed (Wolfang, Podilchuk & Delp, 1999). Effective utilization of this relationship facilitated the development of many imperceptible and robust DWT-based watermarking algorithms. Further performance improvements in DWT-based digital image watermarking algorithms could be obtained by combining DWT with other frequency transforms such as the DCT, or linear algebraic transforms such as the SVD transform (Deprettere, 1988). The idea of applying more than one transform is based on the fact that combining two transforms could compensate for the drawbacks of each other, resulting in effective watermarking techniques.

In this chapter, we will describe three DWT-based digital image watermarking algorithms. The first is the DWT-only basic algorithm in which watermarking is done by altering the coefficients of selected DWT subbands. Improvement on the basic algorithm is described in the second DWT-DCT algorithm in which DCT is applied on the same selected DWT subbands. The third DWT-SVD algorithm is also a hybrid algorithm in which the selected DWT subbands are further transformed using the powerful SVD linear algebra matrix transform. The remainder of the chapter is organized as follows. A brief introduction of the DWT, DCT, and SVD transforms and their relevance to the watermarking problem is given in the next section. This is followed by two core sections in which we describe the algorithms in detail and present their performance results. Finally, some concluding remarks regarding the effectiveness of DWT-based digital image watermarking are given, followed by our thoughts on possible future research directions.

## TRANSFORM DOMAIN WATERMARKING

Frequency-domain transforms such the DCT and the DWT, and linear algebraic transforms such as the SVD have been used extensively in many digital signal processing applications. In this section, we briefly introduce the three transforms and outline their relevance to the problem of digital watermarking.

### The Discrete Wavelet Transform

Wavelets are special functions that, in a form analogous to sines and cosines in Fourier analysis, are used as basal functions for representing signals (Strang & Nguyen, 1996). For 2-D images, applying DWT corresponds to processing the image by 2-D filters in each dimension. The filters divide the input image into four nonoverlapping multiresolution subbands: $LL_1$, $LH_1$, $HL_1$, and $HH_1$. The $LL_1$ subband represents the coarse-scale DWT coefficients while the $LH_1$, $HL_1$, and $HH_1$ subbands represent the fine-scale DWT coefficients. To obtain the next coarser scale of wavelet coefficients, the $LL_1$ subband is further processed until some final scale $N$ is reached. When $N$ is reached, we will have $3N + 1$ subbands consisting of the multiresolution subbands $LL_N$ and $LH_x$, $HL_x$ and $HH_x$ where $x$ ranges from $1$ until $N$. Figure 1 shows the wavelet decomposition when the scale $N$ equals to $3$.

Due to its excellent spatio-frequency localization properties, the DWT is very suitable to identify areas in the host image where a watermark can be embedded effectively. In particular, this property allows the exploitation of the masking effect of the human visual system such that if a DWT coefficient is modified, only the region corresponding to that coefficient will be modified. In general, most of the image energy is concentrated at the lower frequency subbands $LL_x$, and therefore, embedding watermarks in these subbands may degrade the image significantly. Embedding in the low frequency subbands, however, could increase robustness significantly. On the other hand, the high frequency subbands $HH_x$ include the edges and textures of the image, for which the human eye is not generally sensitive to changes in such subbands. This allows the watermark to be embedded without being perceived by the human eye. The compromise adopted by many DWT-based watermarking algorithms is to embed the watermark in the middle frequency subbands $LH_x$ and $HL_x$ where acceptable performance of imperceptibility and robustness could be achieved (Guo & Georganas, 2002; Guzman, Miyatake & Meana, 2004; Hsu & Wu, 1998; Huang & Yang, 2004; Jung et al., 2003; Niu, Lu & Sun, 2000; Reddy & Chatterji, 2005; Safabakhsh, Zaboli & Tabibiazar, 2004; Tay & Havlicek, 2002; Wang, Doherty & Van Dyke, 2002).

*Figure 1. Three-level DWT decomposition*

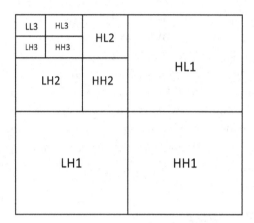

## The Discrete Cosine Transform

The Discrete Cosine Transform (DCT) is a popular technique used for converting a signal into its elementary frequency components. It represents an input image as a sum of sinusoids of varying magnitudes and frequencies (Furht, 1990). The popular block-based DCT transform segments an image nonoverlapping blocks and applies DCT to each block. This results in giving three frequency subbands: low frequency subband $F_L$, mid-frequency subband $F_M$, and high frequency subband $F_H$, as shown in Figure 2.

DCT-based watermarking is based on two facts. The first fact is that much of the signal energy lies at low frequency subband $F_L$, which contains the most important visual parts of the image. The second fact is that high frequency components of the image in the $F_H$ subband are usually removed through compression and noise attacks. The watermark is therefore embedded by modifying the coefficients of the middle frequency subband $F_M$ so that the visibility of the image will not be affected, and the watermark will not be removed by compression (Chu, 2003; Deng & Wang, 2003; Lin & Chin, 2000; Wu & Hsieh, 2000).

## The Singular Value Decomposition Transform

The DCT and DWT transforms attempt to decompose an image in terms of a standard basis set. This need not necessarily be the optimal representation for a given image. On the other hand, singular value decomposition (SVD) is a numerical technique for diagonalizing matrices in which the transformed domain consists of basis states that are optimal in some sense (Andrews & Patterson, 1976). The SVD of an $N \times N$ matrix $A$ is defined by the operation $A = U S V^T$, as shown in Figure 3.

The SVD of a given image gives the matrices $S$, $U$, and $V^T$. The diagonal entries of $S$ specify the luminance of the image, while the corresponding pair of singular vectors $U$ and $V^T$ specify the geometry of the image. In SVD-based watermarking, slight variations in the elements of matrix $S$ do not affect visual perception of the quality of the cover image. Therefore, SVD-based watermarking algorithms add the watermark information to the singular values of the diagonal matrix S in such a way to meet

*Figure 2. DCT multiresolution frequency bands*

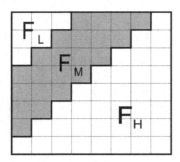

the imperceptibility and robustness requirements of effective digital image watermarking algorithms (Chang Tsai & Lin, 2005; Zhang & Li, 2005).

## DWT-BASED WATERMARKING ALGORITHMS

In this section, we will describe three DWT-based watermarking algorithms: the basic DWT-only algorithm, the hybrid DWT-DCT algorithm, and the hybrid DWT-SVD algorithm.

### The DWT-Only Algorithm

The watermark embedding procedure is depicted in Figure 4 and described in detail in the following steps.

**Step 1.** Apply DWT to the original host image in order to decompose it into four nonoverlapping multiresolution subbands: $LL_1$, $HL_1$, $LH_1$, and $HH_1$.

**Step 2.** Apply DWT again to the $HL_1$ subband to get four smaller subbands, and choose the $HL_2$ subband, as shown in Figure 5(a). Or apply DWT to the $HH_1$ subband to get four smaller subbands, and choose the $HH_2$ subband, as shown in Figure 5(b)

**Step 3.** Reformulate the grey-scale watermark image into a vector of zeros and ones.

**Step 4.** Generate a uniformly distributed, highly uncorrelated, zero-mean, two-dimensional pseudo-random sequence (*PN*) using a secret seed value. The *PN* sequence is used to embed the zero watermark bit in the host image.

**Step 5.** Embed the pseudorandom sequence *PN* in the selected DWT subband with a gain factor $\alpha$. Number of elements in the selected subband and the pseudorandom sequence *PN* must be equal for embedding to take place. If we donate *X* as coefficients matrix of the selected subband, then embedding is done according to Equations 1 and 2 as follows:

*Figure 3. The SVD operation SVD (A) = U S V^T*

$$\begin{bmatrix} \sigma_{11} & 0 & 0. & 0 \\ 0 & \sigma_{22} & 0 & 0 \\ . & . & . & . \\ 0 & 0 & 0 & \sigma_{nn} \end{bmatrix} \begin{bmatrix} U_{1,1} & . & . & U_{1,n} \\ U_{2,1} & . & . & U_{2,n} \\ . & . & . & . \\ U_{n,1} & . & . & U_{n,n} \end{bmatrix} \quad SVD(A) = \begin{bmatrix} V_{1,1} & . & . & V_{1,n} \\ V_{2,1} & . & . & V_{2,n} \\ . & . & . & . \\ V_{n,1} & . & . & V_{n,n} \end{bmatrix}^T$$

*Figure 4. DWT-only watermark embedding procedure*

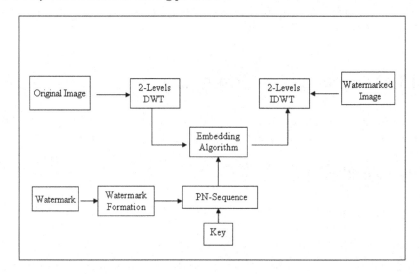

If the watermark bit is *0* then

$$X' = X + \alpha * PN \tag{1}$$

otherwise, if the watermark bit is *1* then,

$$X' = X \tag{2}$$

**Step 6.** Apply the inverse DWT (IDWT) on the DWT transformed image, including the modified subband, to produce the watermarked host image.

The watermark extraction procedure is depicted in Figure 6 and described in detail in the following steps. Since the DWT-only algorithm is a blind watermarking algorithm, the original host image is not required in the watermark extraction procedure.

*Figure 5. Multiresolution DWT subbands of the original image*

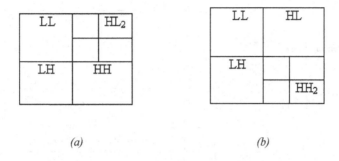

(a)　　　　　　　　　　　　　　(b)

**Step 1.** Apply DWT to decompose the watermarked image into four nonoverlapping multiresolution subbands: $LL_1$, $HL_1$, $LH_1$, and $HH_1$.

**Step 2.** Apply DWT to the $HL_1$ subband to get four smaller subbands, and choose the subband $HL_2$. Or apply DWT to the $HH_1$ subband to get four smaller subbands, and choose the subband $HH_2$.

**Step 3.** Regenerate the pseudorandom sequence (PN sequence) using the same seed used in the watermark embedding procedure described previously.

**Step 4**. Calculate the correlation between the watermarked subband $HL_2$ (or $HH_2$) and the generated pseudorandom sequence (PN sequence). This step is repeated *m* times, where *m* is number of bit elements in the watermark vector.

**Step 5.** Compare each correlation value with the mean correlation value. If the calculated value is greater than the mean, then the extracted watermark bit will be taken as a 0; otherwise, it is taken as a 1. A mean correlation value of 0.75 is used.

**Step 6.** Reconstruct the watermark image using the extracted watermark bits, and compute the similarity between the original and extracted watermarks.

## The Hybrid DWT-DCT Watermarking Algorithm

The watermark embedding procedure is depicted in Figure 7 followed by a detailed explanation.

**Step 1.** Apply DWT to decompose the cover host image into four nonoverlapping multiresolution subbands: $LL_1$, $HL_1$, $LH_1$, and $HH_1$.

**Step 2.** Apply DWT to the $HL_1$ subband to get four smaller subbands and choose the subband $HL_2$, as shown in Figure 5(a). Or apply DWT to the $HH_1$ subband to get four smaller subbands, and choose the subband $HH_2$, as shown in Figure 5(b)

*Figure 6. DWT-only watermark extraction procedure*

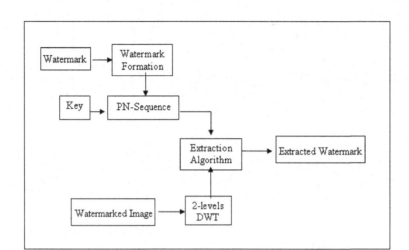

*Figure 7. Hybrid DWT-DCT watermark embedding procedure*

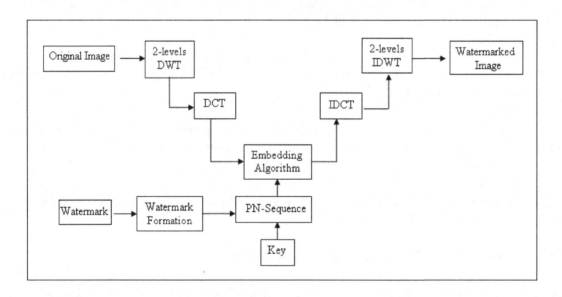

**Step 3.** Divide the subband $HL_2$ (or $HH_2$) into *4 x 4* blocks.

**Step 4.** Apply DCT to each block in the chosen subband ($HL_2$ or $HH_2$).

**Step 5.** Reformulate the grey-scale watermark image into a vector of zeros and ones.

**Step 6.** Generate two uncorrelated pseudorandom sequences. One sequence is used to embed the watermark bit 0 (PN_0), and the other sequence is used to embed the watermark bit 1 (PN_1). The number of elements in each of the two pseudorandom sequences must be equal to the number of mid-band elements of the DCT-transformed DWT subbands.

**Step 7.** Embed the two pseudorandom sequences, PN_0 and PN_1, with a gain factor $\alpha$, in the DCT transformed *4x4* blocks of the selected DWT subbands of the host image. Embedding is not applied to all coefficients of the DCT block, but only to the mid-band DCT coefficients. If we donate $X$ as the matrix of the mid-band coefficients of the DCT transformed block, then embedding is done as follows:

If the watermark bit is *0* then

$$X' = X + \alpha * PN\_0 \tag{3}$$

otherwise, if the watermark bit is *1* then,

$$X' = X + \alpha * PN\_1 \tag{4}$$

**Step 8.** Apply inverse DCT (IDCT) to each block after its mid-band coefficients have been modified to embed the watermark bits, as described in the previous step.

**Step 9.** Apply the inverse DWT (IDWT) on the DWT transformed image, including the modified subband, to produce the watermarked host image.

The watermark extraction procedure is depicted in Figure 8 and described in detail in the following steps. The DWT-DCT algorithm is a blind watermarking algorithm, and thus, the original host image is not required to extract the watermark.

**Step 1.** Apply DWT to decompose the watermarked image into four nonoverlapping multiresolution subbands: $LL_1$, $HL_1$, $LH_1$, and $HH_1$.

**Step 2.** Apply DWT to $HL_1$ to get four smaller subbands, and choose the $HL_2$ subband, as shown in Figure 5(a). Or apply DWT to the $HH_1$ subband to get four smaller subbands, and choose the $HH_2$ subband, as shown in Figure 5(b).

**Step 3.** Divide the subband $HL_2$ (or $HH_2$) into *4 x 4* blocks.

**Step 4.** Apply DCT to each block in the chosen subband ($HL_2$ or $HH_2$) and extract the mid-band coefficients of each DCT transformed block.

**Step 5.** Regenerate the two pseudorandom sequences (PN_0 and PN_1) using the same seed used in the watermark embedding procedure.

*Figure 8. Hybrid DWT-DCT watermark extraction procedure*

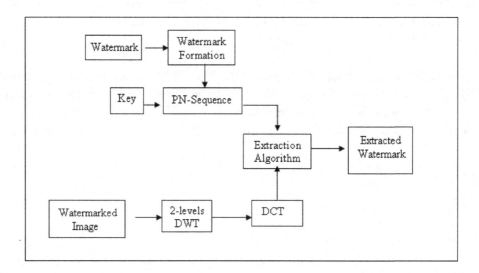

*Figure 9. Hybrid DWT-SVD watermark embedding procedure*

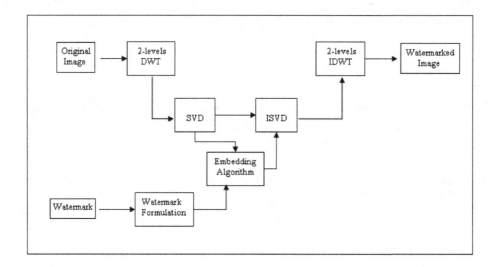

**Step 6.** For each block in the subband $HL_2$ (or $HH_2$) calculate the correlation between the mid-band coefficients and the two generated pseudorandom sequences (PN_0 and PN_1). If the correlation with the PN_0 was higher than the correlation with PN_1, then the extracted watermark bit is considered 0; otherwise, the extracted watermark is considered 1.

**Step 7.** Reconstruct the watermark using the extracted watermark bits, and compute the similarity between the original and extracted watermarks.

## The Hybrid DWT-SVD Algorithm

The watermark embedding procedure is depicted in Figure 9 and described in detail in the following steps.

**Step 1.** Apply DWT to decompose the cover host image into four nonoverlapping multiresolution subbands: $LL_1$, $HL_1$, $LH_1$, and $HH_1$.

**Step 2.** Apply DWT to the $HL_1$ subband to get four smaller subbands, and choose the subband $HL_2$, as shown in Figure 5(a). Or apply DWT to the $HH_1$ subband to get four smaller subbands, and choose the subband $HH_2$, as shown in Figure 5(b).

**Step 3.** Divide the subband $HL_2$ (or $HH_2$) into *4 x 4* blocks.

**Step 4.** Apply SVD to each block in $HL_2$ (or $HH_2$) according to Equation 5, where the *A* matrix in the equation refers to any block in the chosen subband.

$$A = U S V^T \tag{5}$$

**Step 5.** Reformulate the grey-scale watermark image into a vector of zeros and ones.

**Step 6.** Modify the singular values matrix *S* of each block according to the value of the watermark bit. If the watermark bit is 0, *S* is modified according to the watermark embedding formula given in Equation 6, where $\alpha$ is a scaling factor that has a value in the range $1 \geq \alpha \geq 0$.

$$S' = S(1 + \alpha) \tag{6}$$

otherwise, if the watermark bit is 1, *S* remains unchanged, as given in Equation 7.

$$S' = S \tag{7}$$

**Step 7.** Apply inverse SVD (ISVD) by multiplying the orthogonal matrices *U* and $V^T$ with the modified matrix *S'*, as given in Equation 8.

$$A = U S' V^T \tag{8}$$

**Step 8.** Apply the inverse DWT (IDWT) on the DWT transformed image, including the modified subband, to produce the watermarked host image.

The watermark extraction procedure is depicted in Figure 10 and described in detail in the following steps.

*Figure 10. Hybrid DWT-SVD watermark extraction procedure*

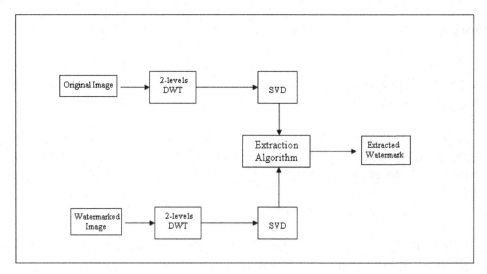

**Step 1.** Decompose the watermarked image using DWT into four nonoverlapping multiresolution subbands: $LL_1$, $HL_1$, $LH_1$, and $HH_1$. Again, we apply DWT to the $HL_1$ subband to get subband $HL_2$, or to the $HH_1$ subband to get subband $HH_2$, as shown in Figure 5.

**Step 2.** This algorithms is a nonblind watermarking algorithm and thus requires the original image in the extraction process. Therefore, we also decompose the original image using DWT into four nonoverlapping multiresolution subbands: $LL_1$, $HL_1$, $LH_1$, and $HH_1$. Again, we apply DWT to the $HL_1$ subband to get subband $HL_2$, or to the $HH_1$ subband to get subband $HH_2$, as shown in Figure 5.

**Step 3.** Divide subband $HL_2$ (or $HH_2$) of the original and watermarked images into *4 x 4* blocks.

**Step 4.** Apply SVD to each block in the chosen subband of the watermarked image and extract the singular values matrix using equation 5, and name it $S_1$. Similarly, apply SVD to each block in the subband of the original image and extract the singular values matrix using equation 5, and name it $S_2$.

**Step 5.** Find the difference between all singular values $S_1$ and $S_2$. If the difference exceeds a threshold value of 0.75, take the extracted watermark bit as 0. Otherwise, if the difference is less than this threshold value, then take the extracted bit as 1.

**Step 6.** Reconstruct the watermark using the extracted watermark bits and compute the similarity between the original and extracted watermarks.

*Figure 11. "Lina" host image*

*Figure 12. Original watermark*

Copyright

## PERFORMANCE EVALUATION

We evaluated the performance of the three DWT-based image watermarking algorithms using a 512x512 "Lena" as the original cover host image, and a 256x256 grey-scale image of the expression "copyright" as the watermark image. The two images are shown in Figures 11 and 12, respectively.

### Performance Evaluation Metrics

Watermarking algorithms are usually evaluated with respect to two metrics: imperceptibility and robustness (Cox et al., 2002; Ejima & Myazaki, 2001). The two metrics are described next.

**Imperceptibility.** Imperceptibility means that the perceived quality of the host image should not be distorted by the presence of the watermark. As a measure of the quality of a watermarked image, the peak signal to noise ratio (PSNR) is typically used. PSNR in decibels (dB) is represented as follows:

$$PSNR_{dB} = 10 \cdot \log_{10}\left(\frac{MAX^2_I}{MSE}\right) = 20 \cdot \log_{10}\left(\frac{MAX_I}{\sqrt{MSE}}\right) \dots\dots\dots\dots\dots \quad (9)$$

where *MSE* is the mean square error between the original image and the watermarked image, and $MAX_I$ is the maximum pixel value of the image which is equal to 255 in our implementations since pixels were represented using 8 bits per sample.

**Robustness.** Robustness is a measure of the immunity of the watermark against attempts to remove or degrade it, intentionally or unintentionally, by different types of digital signal processing attacks (Voloshynovskiy, Pereira & Pun, 2001). In this chapter, we will report on robustness results we obtained for three major digital signal processing operations (attacks): Gaussian noise, image compression, and image cropping. The three attacks are a few; however, they are good representatives of the more general attacks. That is, the Gaussian noise is a watermark degrading attack, JPEG compression is a watermark removal attack, and cropping is a watermark dispositioning geometrical attack. We measured the similarity between the original watermark and the watermark extracted from the attacked image using the correlation factor $\rho$ using Equation 10.

$$\rho(w, \hat{w}) = \frac{\sum_{i=1}^{N} w_i \hat{w}_i}{\sqrt{\sum_{i=1}^{N} w_i^2} \sqrt{\sum_{i=1}^{N} \hat{w}_i^2}} \dots\dots\dots\dots \tag{10}$$

where $N$ is the number of pixels in a watermark, and $w$ and $\hat{w}$ are the original and extracted watermarks, respectively. The correlation factor $\rho$ may take values between 0 (random relationship) and 1 (perfect linear relationship). In general, a correlation coefficient of about 0.75 or above is considered acceptable.

## Performance Results of the DWT-Only Watermarking Algorithm

We carried out the watermark embedding algorithm described in the previous section. First, the one-level DWT of the "Lina" image produced four 256x256 subbands: $LL_1$, $LH_1$, $HL_1$, and $HH_1$. Then the watermark was embedded in subbands $LL_1$, $LH_1$, and $HH_1$ in order to study the effect of DWT subbands on the performance. Evaluation results with respect to imperceptibility and robustness are presented next.

**Imperceptibility.** The PSNR values obtained for the $LL_1$, $LH_1$, and $HH_1$ subbands were 63.873, 74.227, and 71.251, respectively. These values and their corresponding watermarked images are shown in Table 1. It is clear that the $LL_1$ subband produced the least PSNR, and therefore, it was decided that it is unsuitable for embedding watermark information. This is expected since $LL_1$ contains the lower frequency components of the image, and modifying such components can be easily noticed by the human visual system due to its sensitivity to variations in the low-frequency regions.

To study the effect of subband selection further, we embedded the watermark in $LL_2$, $HL_2$, and $HH_2$, which are the DWT subbands of the second DWT level. The results, shown in Table 2, reinforce the previous finding regarding the inappropriateness of the $LL_x$ subbands for embedding watermark information. The results also show that a second level of DWT improved PSNR when the watermark was embedded in the $LH_2$ and $HH_2$ subbands. The PSNR obtained for the $HL_2$ and $HH_2$ were 80.190, and 77.098, respectively. The PSNR difference is modest between the two subbands; however, the main finding is that the second-level DWT gave better results than the first-level DWT. This suggests that improvement in imperceptibility is achievable by applying DWT beyond the first level.

*Table 1. The "Lina" host image watermarked at different one-DWT subbands*

*Table 2. The "Lina" host image watermarked at different two-DWT subbands*

**Robustness.** As we have already concluded that embedding a watermark in the low subbands $LL_x$ degrades the original image and gives relatively low PSNR values compared with those obtained for the $LH_2$ and $HH_2$ subbands, we decided to exclude the $LL_x$ subbands from our experiments on robustness. Table 3 shows the correlation between the original watermark and the watermarks extracted from the $HL_2$ (or $HH_2$) subband after being subjected to different attacks.

The results given in Table 3 show that embedding in $HH_2$ gives slightly better robustness than $HL_2$ with respect to the cropping attack. This result is illustrated in Figure 13, which shows the watermarked image cropped at different ratios; and Figure 14, which shows the extracted watermarks from their corresponding watermarked images.

The results in Table 3 also show that embedding in $HL_2$ gives better robustness than $HH_2$ with respect to the JPEG compression attack. This result is illustrated in Figures 15 and 16, which show the watermarked image compressed at different ratios and the corresponding extracted watermarks, respectively.

*Table 3. Correlation values due to three different attacks*

| Subband | Correlation Factor | | | | | | | | |
|---|---|---|---|---|---|---|---|---|---|
| | Gaussian Noise (Mean) | | | Compression (Quality) | | | Cropping (Block Size) | | |
| | 0 | 0.4 | 0.8 | 0 | 40 | 80 | 8 | 152 | 200 |
| LH2 | 0.726 | 0.652 | 0.467 | 0.447 | 0.698 | 0.726 | 0.723 | 0.643 | 0.574 |
| HH2 | 0.989 | 0.868 | 0.546 | 0.023 | 0.065 | 0.314 | 0.723 | 0.704 | 0.643 |

*Figure 13. HH2-watermarked images cropped at different ratios*

*Figure 14. Extracted watermarks from the cropped watermarked images shown in Figure 13*

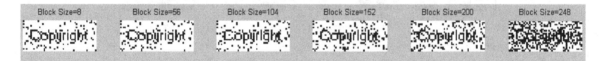

## Performance of the Cascaded DWT-DCT Watermarking Algorithm

We carried out the watermark embedding algorithm described in the previous section. Applying the one-level DWT of the "Lina" image produced four 256x256 subbands: $LL_1$, $LH_1$, $HL_1$, and $HH_1$. Since we concluded earlier that embedding the watermark beyond the first DWT level is more effective, we decided to embed the watermark in $HL_2$ (or $HH_2$). The selected 128x128 subband was divided into 4x4 blocks, giving a total of 1,024 blocks. The DCT transform was then applied to each block in the chosen subband, after which the watermark was embedded according to Equations 3 and 4 in the previous section.

**Imperceptibility.** We evaluated imperceptibility of the hybrid DWT-DCT algorithm by measuring PSNR for the $HL_2$ and $HH_2$ subbands. $HL_2$ gave a PSNR value of 97.072, while $HH_2$ gave 97.083. The difference is small between the two PSNR values, indicating comparable performance of the two subbands. In contrast, and as shown in Table 4, the difference between the PSNR values of the DWT-Only

*Figure 15. HL2-based watermarked images compressed at different quality rates*

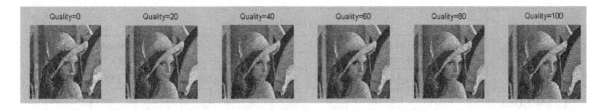

*Figure 16. Extracted watermarks from the compressed watermarked images shown in Figure 15*

and the hybrid DWT-DCT algorithms is relatively large. This indicates that an improvement in imperceptibility can be achieved by applying DCT on a DWT transformed $HL_2$ (or $HH_2$) subband.

**Robustness.** Table 5 shows the correlation values between the original watermark and the watermarks extracted from the $HL_2$ and $HH_2$ subbands after being subjected to different attacks independently.

The correlation values given in Table 5 show clearly that the hybrid DWT-DCT watermarking algorithm outperforms the conventional DWT-Only algorithm with respect to robustness against the Gaussian noise and cropping attacks. The results are better regardless of whether the watermark was embedded

*Table 4. The "Lina" host image watermarked at different two-DWT subbands*

| Original Image | Watermarked Image | | | |
|---|---|---|---|---|
| | DWT-Only (HL2) | DWT-DCT (HL2) | DWT-Only (HH2) | DWT-DCT (HH2) |
| | PSNR =80.190 | PSNR=97.072 | PSNR=77.098 | PSNR=97.083 |

*Table 5. Correlation values due to three different attacks*

| Algorithm | Correlation Factor | | | | | | | | |
|---|---|---|---|---|---|---|---|---|---|
| | Gaussian Noise (Mean) | | | Compression (Quality) | | | Cropping (Block Size) | | |
| | 0 | 0.4 | 0.8 | 0 | 40 | 80 | 8 | 152 | 200 |
| DWT-Only (HL2) | 0.736 | 0.660 | 0.445 | 0.478 | 0.733 | 0.741 | 0.746 | 0.623 | 0.550 |
| DWT-DCT (HL2) | 0.9738 | 0.8359 | 0.5029 | 0.012 | 0.604 | 0.958 | 0.968 | 0.778 | 0.549 |
| DWT-Only (HH2) | 0.726 | 0.652 | 0.467 | 0.447 | 0.698 | 0.726 | 0.723 | 0.643 | 0.574 |
| DWT-DCT (HH2) | 0.989 | 0.868 | 0.546 | 0.023 | 0.065 | 0.314 | 0.989 | 0.884 | 0.696 |

*Figure 17. Extracted watermarks from the cropped HH2-watermarked image using DWT-Only*

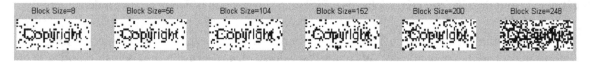

*Figure 18. Extracted watermarks from the cropped HH2-watermarked image using DWT and DCT*

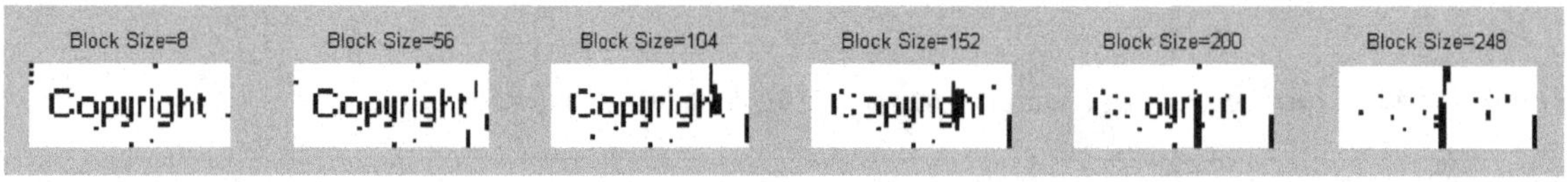

in $HL_2$ or $HH_2$; however, $HH_2$ gave better robustness against cropping compared with $HL_2$. Figure 17 shows the extracted watermarks from $HH_2$ when DWT-Only was used. In contrast, the better DWT-DCT results are shown in Figure 18, which shows the extracted watermarks from the $HH_2$ subband.

As given in Table 5 and illustrated in Figures 19 and 20, the robustness of the DWT-Only algorithm against the JPEG compression attack is better than that of the DWT-DCT algorithm. This is due to the fact that the DCT is the core component of the JPEG compression, and therefore applying DCT at an already DCT-transformed image degraded the quality of the embedded watermark greatly.

*Figure 19. Extracted watermarks from the compressed HL2-watermarked image using DWT only*

*Figure 20. Extracted watermarks from the compressed HL2-watermarked image using DWT and DCT*

## Performance of the Hybrid DWT-SVD Watermarking Algorithm

Similar to the DWT-DCT algorithm described in the previous section, we applied a two-level DWT on the "Lina" image producing four multiresolution subbands: $LL_2$, $LH_2$, $HL_2$, and $HH_2$. Since we concluded earlier that embedding the watermark beyond the first DWT level is more effective, we decided to embed the watermark in the $HL_2$ (or $HH_2$) subband. The 128x128 chosen subband was divided into 4x4 blocks, giving a total of 1,024 blocks. The SVD transform was then applied to each block in the chosen subband, after which the watermark was embedded according to Equations 6 and 7 in the previous section.

**Imperceptibility.** We evaluated imperceptibility for the hybrid DWT-SVD algorithm by measuring PSNR for the $HL_2$ and $HH_2$ subbands. $HL_2$ gave a PSNR value of 101.780, while $HH_2$ gave a value of 103.064. The difference is small between the two PSNR values, indicating comparable performance of the two subbands. In contrast, and as shown in Table 6, the difference between the PSNR values for the DWT-Only and the hybrid DWT-SVD algorithms is relatively large. This result indicates that an improvement in imperceptibility can be achieved by applying SVD on the DWT-transformed $HL_2$ (or $HH_2$) subband.

**Robustness.** Table 7 shows the correlation values between the original watermark and the watermark extracted from watermarked $HL_2$ and $HH_2$ subbands after being subjected to different attacks.

The correlation values given in Table 7 show clearly that the hybrid DWT-SVD watermarking algorithm outperforms the conventional DWT-Only algorithm with respect to robustness. The DWT-SVD results are better regardless of whether the watermark was embedded in $HL_2$ or $HH_2$. However, $HH_2$ gave much better robustness against cropping compared with $HL_2$. Figure 21 shows the extracted watermarks from the same $HH_2$ when DWT-Only was used. In contrast, the better DWT-SVD result is shown in Figure 22, which shows the extracted watermarks from $HH_2$.

Also, the $HH_2$ subband gave better robustness against compression compared with $HL_2$. The better robustness performance of $HH_2$ against the JPEG compression attack is illustrated in Figures 23 and 24. Figure 23 shows the extracted watermarks when DWT-Only was used. In contrast, the better DWT-SVD result is shown in Figure 24, which shows the extracted watermarks from the same $HH_2$ subband.

*Table 6. The "Lina" host image watermarked at different two-DWT subbands*

| Original Image | Watermarked Image | | | |
|---|---|---|---|---|
| | DWT-Only (HL$_2$) | DWT-SVD (HL$_2$) | DWT-Only (HH$_2$) | DWT-SVD (HH$_2$) |
| | PSNR = 80.190 | PSNR = 101.780 | PSNR=77.098 | PSNR=103.064 |

*Table 7. Correlation values due to three different attacks*

| Algorithm | Correlation Factor | | | | | | | | |
|---|---|---|---|---|---|---|---|---|---|
| | Gaussian Noise (Mean) | | | Compression (Quality) | | | Cropping (Block Size) | | |
| | 0 | 0.4 | 0.8 | 0 | 40 | 80 | 8 | 152 | 200 |
| DWT (HL2) | 0.736 | 0.660 | 0.445 | 0.478 | 0.733 | 0.741 | 0.746 | 0.623 | 0.550 |
| DWT-SVD (HL2) | 0.984 | 0.984 | 0.984 | 0.984 | 0.979 | 0.979 | 0.994 | 0.818 | 0.759 |
| DWT (HH2) | 0.726 | 0.652 | 0.467 | 0.447 | 0.698 | 0.726 | 0.723 | 0.643 | 0.574 |
| DWT-SVD (HH2) | 1 | 1 | 1 | 1 | 1 | 1 | 1 | 0.984 | 0.974 |

*Figure 21. Extracted watermarks from the cropped HH2-watermarked image using DWT-Only*

*Figure 22. Extracted watermarks from the cropped HH2-watermarked image using DWT and SVD*

*Figure 23. Extracted watermarks from the compressed HH2-watermarked image using DWT-Only*

*Figure 24. Extracted watermarks from the compressed HH2-watermarked image using DWT and SVD*

## Discussion

We described the implementations of three DWT-based watermarking algorithms. The first algorithm was the basic DWT-Only algorithm in which we embedded the watermark in the first- and second-level DWT subbands of the host image. The results we obtained indicated a better imperceptibility performance when the watermark was embedded in the $HL_2$ or $HH_2$ subbands. The robustness performance, however, was not acceptable. To improve performance, we combined DWT with another equally powerful transform: the DCT. The hybrid DWT-DCT watermarking algorithm's imperceptibility performance was better than the performance of the DWT-Only algorithm. Similarly, the improvement in robustness brought by the hybrid DWT-DCT algorithm was considerably high. Finally, we combined DWT with SVD; a well-known matrix decomposition technique that has been applied successfully in many image processing applications. The results we obtained using the hybrid DWT-SVD were even better than the hybrid DWT-DCT with respect to both imperceptibility and robustness. A comparison between the performances of the three DWT-based watermarking algorithms is summarized next.

**Imperceptibility.** Table 8 shows the PSNR values obtained for the three DWT-based methods. It is clear that the hybrid DWT-DCT and DWT-SVD algorithms improved the performance of the DWT-Only algorithm considerably, with the DWT-SVD giving slightly better results.

*Table 8. The "Lina" host image watermarked using different watermarking algorithms*

**Watermarked Image**

| Original Image | DWT-Only | DWT-DCT | DWT-SVD |
|:---:|:---:|:---:|:---:|
| | (HL₂) | (HH₂) | (HH₂) |

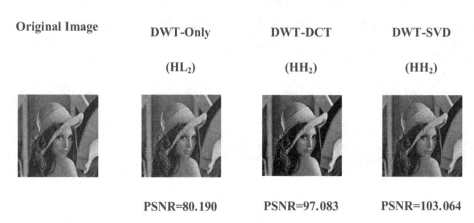

| | PSNR=80.190 | PSNR=97.083 | PSNR=103.064 |

*Table 9. Correlation values due to three different attacks*

| Algorithm | Correlation | | | | | | | | |
|:---:|:---:|:---:|:---:|:---:|:---:|:---:|:---:|:---:|:---:|
| | Gaussian Noise (Mean) | | | Compression (Quality) | | | Cropping (Block Size) | | |
| | 0 | 0.4 | 0.8 | 0 | 40 | 80 | 8 | 152 | 200 |
| DWT-Only (HL2) | 0.736 | 0.660 | 0.445 | 0.478 | 0.733 | 0.741 | 0.723 | 0.643 | 0.574 |
| DWT–DCT (HH2) | 0.989 | 0.868 | 0.546 | 0.023 | 0.065 | 0.314 | 0.989 | 0.884 | 0.696 |
| DWT–SVD (HH2) | 1 | 1 | 1 | 1 | 1 | 1 | 1 | 0.984 | 0.974 |

**Robustness.** We next compare the robustness of the three DWT-based watermarking algorithms against the Gaussian noise, image compression, and image cropping attacks. As said earlier, the three attacks are representative attacks such that Gaussian noise is a watermark degrading attack, JPEG compression is a watermark removal attack, and cropping is a watermark dispositioning geometrical attack. The correlation values between the original watermark and the extracted watermark are shown in Table 9. Again, it is clear that the hybrid DWT-DCT and DWT-SVD algorithms improved robustness of the DWT-Only algorithm considerably, with the DWT-SVD giving slightly better results.

*Figure 25. Main page of the graphical user interface (GUI)*

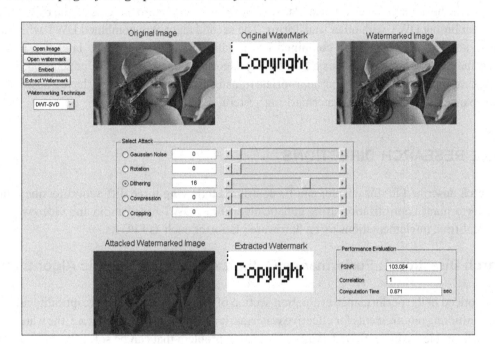

## Graphical User Interface

We developed a user-friendly graphical user interface (GUI) to facilitate evaluating the performance of the three watermarking algorithms under different settings. The GUI includes a set of buttons that are clearly marked to do specific operations such as load host image, load a watermark, embed the watermark into the chosen original image, and extract the watermark. The main page of the GUI, shown in Figure 25, enables users to choose different watermarking algorithm (DWT-Only, DWT-DCT, or DWT-SVD), different host images, different watermarks, and different attacks (Gaussian noise, rotation, dithering, compression, and cropping). There is also a slider for each attack to adjust the level of the attack. After running the selected algorithm, the GUI displays the results, which include the watermarked image, the attacked watermarked image, the extracted watermark, and the PSNR and correlation values. Computation time is also displayed to compare the computational complexity of the different algorithms.

## CONCLUSION

The discrete wavelet transform DWT is a core signal analysis tool in modern digital signal processing. It has been applied successfully in many image processing applications in the last decade. Recently, it has also been gaining momentum as a valuable tool in digital multimedia watermarking. In this chapter, we described three DWT-based digital image watermarking algorithms. The first algorithm was the basic DWT-Only algorithm in which we embedded the watermark in the first- and second-level DWT subbands of the host image. The second and third algorithms were improvements on the basic algorithm made by combining DWT with other transforms. The second algorithm combined DWT with the DCT transform, and the third algorithm combined DWT with SVD transform. The later two algorithms improved the performance of the basic DWT-Only algorithm considerably. In conclusion, in digital watermarking applications, combining appropriate transforms with the DWT may have a positive impact on performance of the underlying watermarking system.

## FUTURE RESEARCH DIRECTIONS

The research described in this chapter can be continued following three different directions stated as follows: performance optimization using genetic algorithms, DWT-based audio and video watermarking, and real-time implementations using hardware platforms such as FPGAs.

### Research Direction 1: Performance Optimization Using Genetic Algorithms

We have noticed in the performance evaluation section of this chapter that imperceptibility and robustness are conflicting requirements for effective watermarking performance. Therefore, the watermarking performance problem can be viewed as an optimization problem that can be solved with respect to imperceptibility and robustness using genetic algorithms. We anticipate that using genetic algorithms can optimize the image quality after watermark embedding while maintaining robustness of the watermark against various image manipulations and signal processing attacks. The main idea with genetic-DWT-based watermarking is not to embed the watermark information by modifying all DWT coefficients of the selected subband, but rather to utilize genetic algorithms to modify a small subset of coefficients that will result in an optimized robust and imperceptible watermarked image.

### Research Direction 2: DWT-Based Video and Audio Watermarking

The ideas and algorithms described in this chapter can be easily extended to implement DWT-based video watermarking since a video is a sequence of frames or still images. However, video watermarking has several unique issues of its own that must be investigated, such as watermark embedding locations within the frames of the host video, properties of the video watermark, and type of special attacks the host video is expected to survive. Research on DWT-based audio watermarking can also be carried out; however, audio watermarking will need a different treatment than video watermarking. This is due to the fact that audio signals are one-dimensional and the level of tolerable degradation a watermarked audio signal can handle is very low. A challenging research theme would be to watermark audiovisual clips in real time using the DWT-based video and audio watermarking algorithms.

### Research Direction 3: Real-Time Implementations Using FPGAs

An attractive research direction that is highly relevant to the subject of this chapter is to develop efficient hardware implementations of the DWT-based watermarking algorithms described in this chapter. A potential hardware platform is programmable logic devices such as FPGAs. Indeed, an FPGA-based implementation would allow for single-chip, real-time watermarking, which is required in digital home appliances, including MP3 music players, DVD players and recorders, digital TVs, digital still cameras, wireless appliances. In fact, any device capable of displaying or capturing multimedia content may need to have a built-in FPGA-based hardware watermarking module.

# REFERENCES

Andrews, H., & Patterson, C. (1976). Singular value decompositions and digital image Processing. *IEEE Transactions on Acoustics, Speech, and Signal Processing, 24*(1), 26–53.

Arnold, M., Schumucker, M., & Wolthusen, S. (2003). *Techniques and applications of digital watermarking and content protection*. Boston, MA: Artech House.

Chan, C., & Cheng, L. (2004). Hiding data in images by simple LSB substitution. *Pattern Recognition, 37*(3), 469–474.

Chang, C., Tsai, P., & Lin, C. (2005). SVD-based digital image watermarking scheme. *Pattern Recognition Letters, 26*(10), 1577–1586.

Chu, W. (2003). DCT-based image watermarking using subsampling. *IEEE Transactions on Multimedia, 5*(1), 34–38.

Cox, I., Miller, M., & Bloom, J. (2002). *Digital watermarking*. CA: Academic Press.

Deng, F., & Wang, B. (2003). A novel technique for robust image watermarking in the DCT domain. *Proceedings of the International IEEE Conference on Neural Networks and Signal Processing*.

Deprettere, E. (1988). *Singular value decomposition and signal processing*. Holland: Elsevier.

Ejima, M., & Myazaki, A. (2001). On the evaluation of performance of digital watermarking in the frequency domain. *Proceedings of the IEEE International Conference on Image Processing*, Thessaloniki, Greece.

Furht, B., & Kirovski, D. (2006). *Encryption and authentications: Techniques and Applications*. Auerbach Publications.

Guo, H., & Georganas, N. (2002). Multi-resolution image watermarking scheme in the spectrum domain. *Proceedings of the IEEE Canadian Conference on Electrical and Computer Engineering*, Canada.

Guzman, V., Miyatake, M., & Meana, H. (2004). *Analysis of wavelet-based watermarking algorithm*. Paper presented at the 14th International IEEE Conference on Electronics, Communications and Computers, Veracruz, Mexico.

Hsu, C., & Wu, J. (1998). Multiresolution watermarking for digital images. *IEEE Transactions on Circuits and Systems-II, 45*(8), 1097–1101.

Huang, J., & Yang, C. (2004). *Image digital watermarking algorithm using multiresolution wavelet transform*. Paper presented at the International IEEE Conference on Systems, Man, and Cybernetics, The Hague, The Netherlands.

Jung, H., et al. (2003). *Image watermarking based on wavelet transform using threshold selection*. Paper presented at the International IEEE SICE Conference.

Katzenbeisser, S., & Petitcolas, F. (2000). *Information hiding: Techniques for steganography and digital watermarking*. Boston, MA: Artech House.

Langelaar, G., Setyawan, I., & Lagendijk, R. (2000). Watermarking digital image and video data: A state-of-art overview. *IEEE Signal Processing Magazine, 17*(5), 20–46.

Lin, S., & Chin, C. (2000). A robust DCT-based watermarking for copyright protection. *IEEE Transactions on Consumer Electronics, 46*(3), 415–421.

Mallat, S. (1989). A theory for multi-resolution signal decomposition: The wavelet representation. *IEEE Transactions on Pattern Analysis And Machine Intelligence, 11*(7), 674–693.

Mitra, S. (1998). *Digital signal processing*. Columbus, OH: McGraw-Hill.

Mukherjee, D., Maitra, S., & Acton, S. (2004). Spatial domain digital watermarking of multimedia objects for buyer authentication. *IEEE Transactions on Multimedia, 6*(1), 1–15.

Niu, X., Lu, Z., & Sun, S. (2000). Digital image watermarking based on multi-resolution decomposition. *IEEE Electronics Letters, 36*(13), 1108–1110.

Piva, A., Barni, M., & Bartolini, F. (1998). *Copyright protection of digital images by means of frequency domain watermarking*. Paper presented at the SPIE Conference on Mathematics of Data/Image Coding, Compression, and Encryption, USA.

Potdar, V., Han, S., & Chang, E. (2005). *A survey of digital image watermarking Techniques*. Paper presented at the 3rd International IEEE Conference on Industrial Informatics, Perth, Australia.

Rao, K., & Yip, P. (1990). *Discrete cosine transform: Algorithms, advantages, applications*. Academic Press.

Reddy, A., & Chatterji, B. (2005). A new wavelet based logo-watermarking scheme. *Pattern Recognition Letters, 26*(7), 1019–1027.

Safabakhsh, R., Zaboli, S., & Tabibiazar, A. (2004). Digital watermarking on still images using wavelet transform. *Proceedings of the International IEEE Conference on Information Technology: Coding and Computing*, Las Vegas, Nevada.

Sebe, F., Domingo-Ferrer, J., & Herrera, J. (2000). *Spatial domain image watermarking robust against compression, filtering, cropping, and scaling*. Paper presented at the 3rd International Workshop on Information Security, Wollongong, Australia.

Strang, G., & Nguyen, T. (1996). *Wavelets and filter banks*. Wellesley, MA: Wellesley-Cambridge Press.

Tay, P., & Havlicek, J. (2002). Image watermarking using wavelets. *Proceedings of the IEEE Midwest Symposium on Circuits and Systems*, Tulsa, Oklahoma.

Vetterli, M., & Kovačević, J. (1995). *Wavelets and subband coding*. Prentice Hall.

Voloshynovskiy, S., Pereira, S., & Pun, T. (2001). Attacks on digital watermarks: Classification, estimation-based attacks, and benchmarks. *Communications Magazine, 39*(8), 118–126.

Wang, C., Doherty, J., & Van Dyke, R. (2002). A wavelet-based watermarking algorithm for ownership verification of digital images. *IEEE Transactions on Image Processing, 11*(2), 77–78.

Wolfgang, R., Podilchuk, C., & Delp, E. (1999). Perceptual watermarks for digital images and video. *Proceedings of the IEEE, 87*(7), 1108–1126.

Wu, C., & Hsieh, W. (2000). Digital watermarking using zerotree of DCT. *IEEE Transactions on Consumer Electronics, 46*(1), 87–94.

Zhang, X., & Li, K. (2005). Comments on "An SVD-based watermarking scheme for protecting rightful ownership." *IEEE Transactions on Multimedia, 7*(2), 593–594.

## ADDITIONAL READING

Chu, W. (2003). DCT-based image watermarking using subsampling. *IEEE Transactions on Multimedia, 5*(1), 34–38.

Fung, W., & Kunisa, A. (2005). *Rotation, scaling, and translation-invariant multi-bit watermarking based on log-polar mapping and discrete Fourier transform*. Paper presented at the International Conference on Multimedia and Expo, Amsterdam, The Netherlands.

Ganic, E., & Eskicioglu, A. (2004). *Robust DWT-SVD domain image watermarking: Embedding data in all frequencies*. Paper presented in the ACM Workshop on Multimedia and Security, Germany.

Hartung, F., & Kutter, M. (1999). Multimedia watermarking techniques. *Proceedings of the IEEE, 87*(7), 1079–1107.

Hernandez, J., Amado, M., & Perez-Gonzalez, F. (2000). DCT-domain watermarking techniques for still images: Detector performance analysis and a new structure. *IEEE Transactions on Image Processing, 9*(1), 55–68.

Hernandez, M., Miyatake, M., & Meana, H. (2005). *Analysis of a DFT-based watermarking algorithm*. Paper presented at the 2nd International IEEE Conference on Electrical and Electronics Engineering, Mexico City, Mexico.

Hsieh, M., Tseng, D., & Huang, Y. (2001). Hiding digital watermarks using multiresolution wavelet transform. *IEEE Transactions on Industrial Electronics, 48*(5), 875–882.

Hu, J., Huang, J., Huand, D., & Shi, Y. (2002). Image fragile watermarking based on fusion of multi-resolution tamper detection. *Electronics Letters, 38*(24), 1512–1513.

Huang, F., & Guan, Z. (2004). A hybrid SVD-DCT watermarking method based on LPSNR. *Pattern Recognition Letters, 25*(15), 1769–1775.

Langellar, L., & Lagendijk, R. (2001). Optimal differential energy watermarking of DCT encoded images and video. *IEEE Transactions on Image Processing, 10*(1), 148–158.

Lu, C. (2004). *Multimedia security.* Hershey, PA: Idea Group Publishing.

Ma, L., Li, C., & Song, S. (2006). *Digital watermarking of spectral images using DWT-SVD.* Paper presented at the International IEEE Conference on Communications, Circuits and Systems, Guilin, China.

Mukherjee, D., Maitra, S., & Acton, S. (2004). Spatial domain digital watermarking of multimedia objects for buyer authentication. *IEEE Transactions on Multimedia, 6*(1), 1–15.

Nikolaidis, A., & Pitas, I. (2003). Asymptotically optimal detection for additive watermarking in the DCT and DWT domains. *IEEE Transactions on Image Processing, 2*(10), 563–571.

Piva, A., Barni, M., & Bartolini, F. (1998). *Copyright protection of digital images by means of frequency domain watermarking.* Paper presented at the SPIE Conference on Mathematics of Data/Image Coding, Compression, and Encryption, USA.

Qiang, L., Zhong, C., & Zhuo, Y. (2007). *Adaptive DWT-SVD domain image watermarking using human visual model.* Paper presented in the 9th International IEEE Conference on Advanced Communication Technology, Korea.

Shah, R., Argawal, A., & Ganesan, S. (2005). *Frequency domain real time digital watermarking.* Paper presented at the 3rd International IEEE Conference on Electronic Information Technology, Hsinchu, Taiwan.

Shieh, C., Huang, H., Wang, F., & Pan, J. (2004). Genetic watermarking based on transform-domain techniques. *Pattern Recognition, 37*(3), 555–565.

Solachidis, V., & Pitas, I. (2001). Circularly symmetric watermark embedding in 2-D DFT domain. *IEEE Transactions on Image Processing, 10*(11), 1741–1753.

Suhail, M., & Obaidat, M. (2003). Digital watermarking-based DCT and JPEG model. *IEEE Transactions on Instrumentation and Measurement, 52*(5), 1640–1647.

Tripathi, S., Jian, R., & Gayatri, V. (2006). Novel DCT and DWT based watermarking techniques for digital images. *Proceedings of the International IEEE Conference on Pattern Recognition.* Hong Kong, China.

Tsai, M., & Hung, H. (2005). *DCT and DWT-based image watermarking using subsampling.* Paper presented at the Fourth International IEEE Conference on Machine Learning and Cybernetics, China.

Wang, R., Lin, C., & Lin, J. (2001). Image hiding by optimal LSB substitution and genetic algorithm. *Pattern Recognition, 34*(3), 671–683.

Wang, S., & Lin, Y. (2004). Wavelet tree quantization for copyright protection watermarking. *IEEE Transactions on Image Processing, 13*(2), 154–164.

Yang, S. (2003). Filter evaluation for DWT-domain image watermarking. *Electronics Letters, 39*(24), 1723–1725.

# Compilation of References

A.A.VV. Scalable extension of H.264/AVC. Retrieved May 31, 2007, from http://ip.hhi.de/imagecom_G1/savce/index.htm

Aad, I., & Castelluccia, C. (2001). Differentiation mechanisms for IEEE 802.11. *Proceedings of the IEEE Infocom*, Anchorage, Alaska, 209–218.

Abraham, S., Feder, P.M., Recchione, M.C., & Zhang, H. (2007). The capacity of VoIP over 802.11. *Bell Labs Technical Journal, 11*, 253–271.

Abramovich, F., Sapatinas, T., & Silverman, B. W. (1998). Wavelet thresholding via a Bayesian approach. *Journal of the Royal Statistic Society, Series B, 60*, 725-749.

Adam, N.R., Atluri, V., Adiwijaya, I., & Banerjee, S. (2001). A dynamic manifestation approach for providing universal access to digital library objects. *IEEE Transactions on Knowledge and Data Engineering, 13*(4), 705–716.

Adams, W. H. et al. (2003). Semantic indexing of multimedia content using visual, audio and text cues. *EURASIP Journal on Applied Signal Processing, 2*, 170–185.

Adler, D. (1996). Virtual audio—Three-dimensional audio in virtual environments. *Internal Report ISRN SICS-T--96/03-SE*. Swedish Institute of Computer Science (SICS).

Adomavicious, G., & Tuzhilin, A. (1999). User profiling in personalization applications through rule discovery and validation. *Proceedings of the ACM Fifth International Conference on Data Mining and Knowledge Discovery (KDD'99)* (pp. 377-381).

Agboma, F., & Liotta, A. (2007).. Addressing user expectations in mobile content delivery. *Mobile Information Systems Journal 3(3-4)*, 153-164..

Ahmed, K., Kooij, R., & Brunnström, K. (2006). Perceived quality of channel zapping. In *ITU-T Workshop on QoE/QoS 2006*.

Ahn, J., Shim, H., Jeon, B., & Choi, I. (2004). Digital video scrambling method using intra prediction mode. *PCM2004, Springer, LNCS, 3333*, 386–393.

Akutsu, M., Hamada, A., & Tonomura, Y. (1998). Video handling with music and speech detection. *IEEE Multimedia, 5*(3), 17–25.

Albanese, A., Blomer, J., Edmonds, J., Luby, M., & Sudan, M. (1996). Priority encoding transmission. *IEEE Transactions on Information Theory, 42*(6), 1737–1744.

Aldrich, S. E., Marks, R. T., Lewis, J. M., & Seybold, P. B. (2000). *What kind of the total customer experience does your e-business deliver?* Patricia Seybold Group.

Allen, J. F. (1983). Maintaining knowledge about temporal intervals. *Communications of the ACM, 26*(11), 832–843.

Almeida, J., Eager, D., & Vernon, M. (2001). A hybrid caching strategy for streaming media files. *Proceedings of the SPIE/ACM Conference on Multimedia Computing and Networking, 4312*, 200–212.

Ando, K., Watanabe, O., & Kiya, H. (2001). Partial-scrambling of still images based on JPEG2000. *Proceeding of the International Conference on Information, Communications, and Signal Processing*, Singapore.

Ando, K., Watanabe, O., & Kiya, H. (2002). Partial-scrambling of images encoded by JPEG2000. *IEICE Trans., J85-D-11*(2), 282–290.

Andrews, H., & Patterson, C. (1976). Singular value decompositions and digital image Processing. *IEEE Transactions on Acoustics, Speech, and Signal Processing, 24*(1), 26–53.

Ankrum, D. R. (1996). Viewing distance at computer workstations. *Work Place Ergonomics,* 10-12.

Apostolopoulos, J.G. (2001). Reliable video communication over lossy packet networks using multiple state encoding and path diversity. *Proceedings of the SPIE, Visual Communications and Image Processing, VCIP 2001,* 392–409.

Apteker, R. T., Fisher, A. A., Kisimov, V. S., & Neishlos, H. (1994). Distributed multimedia: User perception and dynamic QoS. In *Proceedings of SPIE* (pp. 226-234).

Apteker, R.T., Fisher, J.A., Kisimov, V.S., & Neishlos, H. (1995). Video acceptability and frame rate. *IEEE Transaction Multimedia, 3*(3), 32–40.

Archambault, D., & Burger, D. (2001). From multimodality to multimodalities: The need for independent models. *Proceedings of Universal Access in Human-Computer Interaction Conference*, New Orleans, Louisiana, 227–231.

Arean, R., Kovacevic, J., & Goyal, V.K. (2000). Multiple description perceptual audio coding with correlating transforms. *IEEE Transactions on Speech Audio Processing, 8*(2), 140–145.

Arnold, M., Schmucker, M., & Wolthusen, S.D. (2003). *Techniques and applications of digital watermarking and content protection.* Boston: Artech House.

Arnold, M., Schumucker, M., & Wolthusen, S. (2003). *Techniques and applications of digital watermarking and content protection.* Boston, MA: Artech House.

Asadi, M.K., & Dufourd, J.-C. (2004). Multimedia adaptation by transmoding in MPEG-21. *Proceedings of the International Workshop on Image Analysis for Multimedia Interactive Services*, Lisbon, Portugal.

Assuncao, P., & Ghanbari, M. (1997). Congestion control of video traffic with transcoders. *Proceedings of the IEEE International Conference on Communications, ICC'97*, Montreal, Canada, 523–527.

Assuncao, P., & Ghanbari, M. (1998). A frequency-domain video transcoder for dynamic bit-rate reduction of MPEG-2 bit streams. *IEEE Transactions on Circuits and Systems for Video Technology, 8*(8).

Assuncao, P.A.A., & Ghanbari, M. (1997). Transcoding of single-layer MPEG video into lower rates. *IEE Proceedings of Vision, Image and Signal Processing, 144*(6), 377–383.

Assunçno, P., & Ghanbari, M., (1996). Post-processing of MPEG-2 coded video for transmission at lower bit-rates. *Proceedings of the IEEE International Conference on Acoustics, Speech and Signal Processing*, Atlanta, Georgia.

Ayersman, D. J., & Reed, W. M. (1998). Relationships among hypermedia-based mental models and hypermedia knowledge. *Journal of Research on Computing in Education, 30*(3), 222-238.

Balasubramanian, V., & Venkatasubramanian, N. (2003). *Server transcoding of multimedia information for cross disability access. Proceedings of the ACM/SPIE Conference on Multimedia Computing and Networking*, Santa Clara, California, 45–56.

Ball, R. (1960). *Mathematical recreations and essays.* New York: MacMillan.

Balsree, R., Thawani, A., Gopalan, S., & Sridhar, V. (2005). Inter-frame similarity based video transcoding. *Proceedings of the Seventh IEEE International Symposium on Multimedia.*

Bandelloni, R., Berti, S., & Paternò, F. (2004). Mixed-initiative, trans-modal interface migration. *Proceedings of the Mobile HCI 2004 (MHCI04)*, Glasgow, UK, 216–227.

Barber, P. J., & Laws, J. V. (1994). Image quality and video communication. In R. Damper, W. Hall, & J. Richards (Eds.), *Proceedings of IEEE International Symposium on Multimedia Technologies & their Future Applications* (pp. 163-178). London, UK: Pentech Press.

Bari, A., Canazza, S., De Poli, G., & Mian, G. A. (1999). Some key points on restoration of audio documents by the extended Kalman filter. In *Proceedings of the Diderot Forum on Mathematics and Music* (pp. 37-47). Vienna, Austria.

Barnard, K., & Forsyth, D. A. (2001). Learning the semantics of words and pictures. In *Proceedings of the International Conference on Computer Vision*, Vancouver, Canada.

Barni, M., Bartolini, F., & Bianco, P. (2000). On the performance of syntax-based error detection in H.263 video coding: A quantitative analysis. *Proceedings of Image and Video Communication, SPIE*, 3974, 949–956.

Barni, M., Bartolini, F., Cappellini, V., & Piva, A. (1998). A DCT-domain system for robust image watermarking. *Signal Processing, 66,* 357–372.

Barni, M., Bartolini, F., Cappellini, V., Piva, A., & Rigacci, F. (1998). A M.A.P. identification criterion for DCT-based watermarking. *Proc. Europ. Signal Processing Conf. (EUSIPCO'98)*, Rhodes, Greece.

Beerends, J. G. (1998). Audio quality determination based on perceptual measurement techniques. In M. Kahrs & K. Brandenburg (Eds.), *Applications of digital signal processing to audio and acoustics* (pp. 1-38). Norwell, MA: Kluwer.

Beerends, J. G., & De Caluwe, F. E. (1999). The influence of video quality on perceived audio quality and vice versa. *Journal of the Audio Engineering Society, 47,* 355-362.

Beker, H., & Piper, F. (1982). *Cipher systems: The protection of communications*. London: Northwood Books.

Bell, A., & Sejnowski, T. (1995). An information-maximization approach to blind separation and blind deconvolution. *Neural Compt., 7,* 1129–1159.

Benham, D., Memon, N., Yeo, B.-L., & Yeung, M. (1997). Fast watermarking of DCT-based compressed images.

*Proc. Int. Conf. Image Science, System, and Technology (CISST'97)*, Las Vegas, NV.

Benitez, A. (2005). *Multimedia knowledge: Discovery, classification, browsing, and retrieval* [doctoral thesis]. New York: Columbia University.

Benitez, A. B. et al. (2002). Semantics of multimedia in MPEG-7. In *Proceedings of the IEEE International Conference on Image Processing, Rochester*, NY.

Benitez, A. B., & Chang, S. F. (2002). Multimedia knowledge integration, summarization and evaluation. In *Proceedings of the International Workshop on Multimedia Data Mining in conjunction with the International Conference on Knowledge Discovery & Data Mining*, Alberta, Canada.

Bennett, J. (1987). Analysis of the encryption algorithm used in WordPerfect word processing program. *Cryptologia, 11*(4), 206–210.

Bergen, H.A., & Caelli, W.J. (1991). File security in WordPerfect 5.0. Cryptologia, 15(1), 57–66.

Berger, J., & Nichols, C. (1994). Brahms at the piano: An analysis of data from the Brahms cylinder. *Leonardo Music Journal, 4,* 23-30.

Berger, J., Coifman, R. R., & Goldberg, M. J. (1994). Removing noise from music using local trigonometric bases and wavelet packets. *Journal of the Audio Engineering Society, 42*(10), 808-818.

Berouti, M., Schwartz, R., & Makhoul, J. (1979). Enhancement of speech corrupted by acoustic noise. In *Proceedings of the IEEE International Conference of Acoustics, Speech, and Signal Processing* (vol. 4, pp. 208-211), Washington DC: IEEE.

Bhargava, B. (1996). Adaptable software for communications in video conferencing. *Proceedings of the IETE International Conference on Multi-media Information Systems (MULTIMEDIA 96)*, New Delhi, India.

Bhargava, B. (2002). Guest editorial: Quality of service in multimedia networks. *Mutimedia Tools and Applications an International Journal.*

Biberman, L. M. (1973). *Perception of displayed information*. Plenum Press.

Bjontegaard, G., & Lillevold, K. (2002). Context-adaptive VLC (CVLC) coding of coefficients. *Proceedings of the JVT-C028 Joint Video Team Meeting*, Fairfax, Virginia.

Bjork, N., & Christopoulos, C. (1998). Transcoder architectures for video coding. *Proceedings of the IEEE International Conference on Acoustics, Speech and Signal Processing*, Seattle, Washington, 2813–2816.

Blattner, M.M. (1996). Multimedia interface: Designing for diversity. *Multimedia Tools and Application, 3*, 87–122.

Blei, D., & Jordan, M. (2003). Modeling annotated data. In *Proceedings of the ACM SIGIR Conference on Research and Development in Information Retrieval*, Toronto, Canada.

Bodnar, A., Corbett, R., & Nekrasovski, D. (2004). AROMA: Ambient awareness through olfaction in a messaging application. *Proceedings of the ICMI'04*, ACM.

Boll, S. F. (1979a). A spectral subtraction algorithm for suppression of acoustic noise in speech. In *Proceedings of the IEEE International Conference of Acoustics, Speech, and Signal Processing* (vol. 4, pp. 200-203). Washingtond DC: IEEE.

Boll, S. F. (1979b). Suppression of acoustic noise in speech using spectral subtraction. *IEEE Transactions on Acoustics, Speech, and Signal Processing, ASSP-27*(2), 113-120.

Boll, S., Klas, W., & Wandel, J. (1999). A cross-media adaptation strategy for multimedia presentations. *Proceedings of the ACM Multimedia'99*, Orlando, Florida, 37–46.

Bovik, A. (Ed.). (2000). *Handbook of image and video processing*. San Diego: Academic Press.

Bregman, A. S. (1990). *Auditory scene analysis*. Cambridge, MA: MIT.

Brewster, S.A. (2002). Overcoming the lack of screen space on mobile computers. *Personal and Ubiquitous Computing, 6*(3), 188–205.

Brunelli, R., Mich, O., & Modena, C. M. (1999). A survey on the automatic indexing of video data. *Journal of Visual Communication and Image Representation, 10*(2), 78–112.

Brusilovsky, P. (1996). Adaptive hypermedia: An attempt to analyze and generalize. In P. Brusilovsky, P. Kommers, & Streitz (Eds.), *Multimedia, hypermedia, and virtual reality* (pp. 288-304). Berlin: Springer-Verlag.

Brusilovsky, P. (1996). Methods and techniques of adaptive hypermedia. *User Modeling and User Adapted Interaction, 6*(2-3), 87-129.

Brusilovsky, P. (2001). Adaptive hypermedia. *User Modeling and User-Adapted Interaction, 11*, 87-110.

Brusilovsky, P., & Maybury, M. T. (2002). From adaptive hypermedia to the adaptive Web. In P. Brusilovsky & M. T. Maybury (Eds.), *Communications of the ACM, 45*(5), *Special Issue on the Adaptive Web*, 31-33.

Burdea, G., & Coiffet, P. (2003). *Virtual reality technology*. (Second edition). New York: John Wiley and Sons.

Burrus, C. S., Gopinath, R. A., & Guo, H. (1997). *Wavelets and wavelet transform—A primer*. Upper Saddle River, NJ: Prentice-Hall.

Burwen, R. S. (1978). *Suppression of low level impulsive noise*. Presented at the 61st Convention of the AES, New York. AES Preprint 1388.

Cai, C., Chen, J., Ma, K.K., & Mitra, S.K. (2007). Multiple description wavelet coding with dual decomposition and cross packetization. *Signal, Image and Video Processing, 1*(1), 53–61.

Callet, L.P., Viard-Gaudin, C., & Péchard, S. (2006). No reference and reduced reference video quality metrics for end to end QoS monitoring. *IEICE Transactions on Communications, 89*(3), 289–296.

CAP Gemini Ernst & Young. (2004). Online availability of public services: How is Europe progressing? *European Commission DG Information Society.*

Cappé, O. (1994). Elimination of the musical noise phenomenon with the Ephraim and Malah noise suppressor. *IEEE Transactions on Speech and Audio Processing, 2*(2), 345-349.

Cappé, O., & Laroche, J. (1995). Evaluation of short-time spectral attenuation techniques for the restoration of musical recordings. *IEEE Transactions on Speech and Audio Processing, 3*(1), 84-93.

Cardoso, J.-F. (1999). High-order contrasts for independent component analysis. *Neural Computer, 11*, 157–192.

Carlsson, C., & Hagsand., D. (1993). DIVE—Multi-user virtual reality system. *Proceedings of the VRAIS '93, IEEE Virtual Reality Annual International Symposium.*

Carneiro, G., & Vasconcelos, N. (2005). Formulating semantic image annotation as a supervised learning problem. In *Proceedings of the IEEE Conference on Computer Vision and Pattern Recognition*, San Diego, CA.

Castelli, V., & Bergman, L.D. (Ed.). ( 2002). *Image databases: Searches and retrieval of digital imagery.* New York: Wiley.

Cervantes Medina, L.A., & Garcia Ruiz, M.A. (2004). Development of a collaborative virtual reality environment for the medical diagnosis of bone trauma (in Spanish). *Proceedings of the Encuentro Internacional de Ciencias de la Computación, Taller de Computación Clínica e Informática Médica*, University of Colima, Mexico.

Chakareski, J., Han, S., & Girod, B. (2005). Layered coding vs. multiple descriptions for video streaming over multiple paths. *Springer Multimedia Systems, 10*, 275–285.

Chan, C., & Cheng, L. (2004). Hiding data in images by simple LSB substitution. *Pattern Recognition, 37*(3), 469–474.

Chan, C.-L., Su, T.-C., Huang, S.-Y., & Wang, J.-S. (2005). Optimal chaining scheme for video-on-demand applications on collaborative networks. *IEEE Transactions on Multimedia, 7*(5), 972–980.

Chang, C., Tsai, P., & Lin, C. (2005). SVD-based digital image watermarking scheme. *Pattern Recognition Letters, 26*(10), 1577–1586.

Chang, H.S., Sull, S., & Lee, S.U. (1999). Efficient video indexing scheme for content-based retrieval. *IEEE Trans. Circ. Syst. Video Technol., 9*(8), 1269–1279.

Chang, S.F., & Messerschmidt, D.G. (1995). Manipulation and compositing of MC-DCT compressed video. *IEEE J. Select. Areas Commun., 13*, 1–11.

Chang, S.-F., & Vetro, A. (2005). Video adaptation: Concepts, technologies, and open issues. *Proceedings of the IEEE, 93*(1), 148–158.

Chang, Y., Han, R., Li, C., & Smith, J.R. (2004). Secure transcoding of Internet content. *Proceedings of the International Workshop on Intelligent Multimedia Computing and Networking (IMMCN)*, 940–943.

Chen, B.-S., & Chen, Y.-L. (1995). Multirate modeling of AR/ARMA stocastic signals and its application to the combined estimation-interpolation problem. *IEEE Transactions on Signal Processing, 43*(10), 2302-2312.

Chen, M., He, Y., & Lagendijk, R.L. (2005). A fragile watermark error detection scheme for wireless video communications. *IEEE Transaction on Multimedia, 7*(2), 201–211.

Cheng, C. (1997). High frequency compensation of low sample-rate audio files: A wavelet-based excitation algorithm. In *Proceedings of the International Computer Music Conference* (pp. 458-461). Thessaloniki, Greece.

Chistel, M., Smith, M., Taylor, C., & Winkler, D. (2004). Evolving video skims into useful multimedia abstractions. In *Proceedings of CHI '98* ACM Press.

Choi, S., & Shin, K.G. (2000). A unified wireless LAN architecture for real-time and non-real-time communication services. *IEEE/ACM Transaction on Network*, 44–59.

Chorianopoulos, K. (2004). *Virtual television channels conceptual model, user interface design and affective usability evaluation.* Unpublished doctoral thesis, Greece: Athens University of Economics and Business.

Chu, W. (2003). DCT-based image watermarking using subsampling. *IEEE Transactions on Multimedia, 5*(1), 34–38.

Cichocki, A., & Barros, A.K. (1999). Robust batch algorithm for sequential blind extraction of noisy biomedical signals. *Proc. ISSPA'99, 1*, 363–366.

Cingil, I., Dogac, A., & Azgin, A. (2000). A broader approach to personalization. *Communications of the ACM, 43*(8), 136-141.

Claypool, M., &Tanner, J. (1999). The effects of jitter on the perceptual quality of video. *Proceedings of the ACM Multimedia*, 115–118.

Cocchi, G., & Uncini, A. (2001). Subbands audio signal recovering using neural nonlinear prediction. In *Proceedings of the IEEE International Conference of Acoustics, Speech, and Signal Processing*, (vol. 2, pp. 1289-1292). Salt Lake City, UT.

Coleman, M. (2004). *Playback: From Victrola to MP3, 100 years of music, machines, and money.* Cambridge, MA: Da Capo.

comScore. (2007). comScore study reveals that mobile TV currently most popular among males and younger age segments [press release].

Conci, N., & De Natale, F.G.B. (2007). Multiple description video coding using coefficient ordering and interpolation. *Signal Processing, Image Communication. Special Issue on Mobile Video, 22*, 252–265.

Conci, N., & De Natale, F.G.B. (2007). Real-time multiple description intra-coding by sorting and interpolation of coefficients. *Signal Image and Video Processing, 1*(1), 1–10.

Conci, N., Berlanda Scorza, G., & Sacchi, C. (2005). A cross-layer approach for efficient MPEG-4 video streaming using multicarrier spread-spectrum transmission and unequal error protection. *Proceedings of the IEEE International Conference on Image Processing, ICIP 2005, 1*, 201–204.

Cook, P. R. (2002). *Real sound synthesis for interactive applications.* Wellesley, MA: A K Peters.

Correia, P., Faria, S.M., & Assuncao, P.A. (2001). Matching MPEG-1/2 coded video to mobile applications. *Proceedings of the 4th International Symposium on Wireless Personal Multimedia Communications*, Aalborg, Denmark, 2, 699–704.

Costa, C.E., Eisenberg, Y., Zhai, F., & Katsaggelos, A.K. (2004). Energy efficient transmission of fine granular scalable video. *Proceedings of the IEEE International Conference on Communications, ICC '04, 5*, 3096–3100.

Cox, I., Miller, M., & Bloom, J. (2002). *Digital watermarking.* CA: Academic Press.

Cox, I.J., Leighton, F.T., & Shamoon, T. (1997). Secure spread spectrum watermarking for multimedia. *IEEE Trans. on Image Processing, 6*, 1673–1687.

Cox, I.J., Miller, M.L., & Bloom, J.A. (2002). *Digital watermarking.* Morgan Kaufmann.

Craven, P. G., & Gerzon, M. A. (1975). *The elimination of scratch noise from 78 RPM records.* Presented at the 50th Convention of the AES. AES Preprint L-37.

Cucchiara, R., Grana, C., & Prati, A. (2003). Semantic video transcoding using classes of relevance. *International Journal of Image and Graphics, 3*(1), 145–169.

Czyzewski, A. (1997). Learning algorithms for audio signal enhancement, Part I: Neural network implementation for the removal of impulsive distortions. *Journal of the Audio Engineering Society, 45*(10), 815-831.

Dal Lago, G. (2006). *Microdisplay emotions.* Retrieved from http://www.srlabs.it/articoli_uk/ics.htm

Dan, A., Dias, D.M., Mukherjee, R., Sitaram, D., & Tewari, R. (1995). Buffering and caching in large-scale video servers. *Proceedings of the IEEE International Computer Conference*, 217–225.

Dan, A., Shahabuddin, P., Sitaram, D., & Towsley, D. (1995). Channel allocation under batching and VCR control in movie-on-demand servers. *Journal of Parallel and Distributed Computing, 30*(2), 168–179.

Dan, A., Sitaram, D., & Shahabuddin, P. (1994). Scheduling policies for an on-demand video server with batching. *Proceedings of the ACM Conference on Multimedia*, 391–398.

Daubechies, I. (1992). *Ten lectures on wavelets*. Philadelphia: SIAM.

David, S., Man, L., & Renaud, C. (Eds.). (2006). *QoS and QoE management in UMTS cellular Systems*. Wiley.

Davoine, F., Bas, P., Hébert, P.-A., & Chassery, J.-M. (1999). Watermarking et résistance aux déformations géométriques. *Cinquièmes journées d'études et d'échanges sur la compression et la représentation des signaux audiovisuels (CORESA'99)*, Sophia-Antiplis, France.

De Bra, P., & Nejdl, W. (2004). Adaptive hypermedia and adaptive Web-based systems. *Proceedings of the Third International Conference (AH 2004)*, Springer Lecture Notes in Computer Science, 3137.

De Bra, P., Aroyo, L., & Chepegin, V. (2004). The next big thing: Adaptive Web-based systems. *Journal of Digital Information, 5*(1), Article no. 247.

De Bra, P., Brusilovsky, P., & Houben, G. (1999). Adaptive hypermedia: From systems to framework. *ACM Computing Surveys, 31*(4es), 12.

De Paepe, T., et al. (1998). A virtual environment for learning Chinese. *VR in the Schools, 1*(4).

De Vries, E. (2006). *Renowned Philips picture enhancement techniques will enable mobile devices to display high-quality TV images*. Retrieved from http://www.research.philips.com/technologies/display/picenhance/index.html

Deavours, C.A., & Kruh, L. (1985). *Machine cryptography and modern cryptanalysis*. Norwood, MA: Artech House.

Dede, C., Salzman, M., Loftin, R.B., & Ash, K. (1997). *Using virtual reality technology to convey abstract scientific concepts*. Hillsdale, NJ: Lawrence Erlbaum.

Deerwester, S., Dumais, S. T., Furnas, G. W., Landauer, T. K., & Harshman, R. (1990). Indexing by latent semantic analysis. *Journal of the American Society for Information Science, 41*(6), 391–407.

Delaigle, J.F., Vleeschouwer, C.D., & Macq, B. (1998). Watermarking algorithm based on a human visual model. *Signal Processing, 66*, 319–335.

Deng, F., & Wang, B. (2003). A novel technique for robust image watermarking in the DCT domain. Pro*ceedings of the International IEEE Conference on Neural Networks and Signal Processing*.

Deng, J., & Chang, R.S. (1999). A priority scheme for IEEE 802.11 DCF access method. *IEICE Transactions in Communications*, 96–102.

Denning, D.E. (1982). *Cryptography and data security*. Addison–Wesley.

Deprettere, E. (1988). *Singular value decomposition and signal processing*. Holland: Elsevier.

Ding, G., Ghafoor, H., & Bhargava B. (2003). Error resilient video transmission over wireless networks. *Proceedings of the IEEE Workshop on Software Technologies for Future Embedded Systems*, Hokkaido, Japan, 31–34.

Dinh, H.Q., Walker, N., Song, C., Kobayashi, A., & Hodges, L.F. (1999). Evaluating the importance of multisensory input on memory and the sense of presence in virtual environments. *Proceedings of the IEEE Virtual Reality '99*, 222–228.

Dixon, S. (2004). Analysis of musical content in digital audio. In J. DiMarco (Ed.), *Computer graphics and multimedia: Applications, problems, and solutions* (pp. 214-235). Hershey, PA: Idea Group.

Dlaska, A. (2002). Sites of construction: Language learning, multimedia, and the international engineer. *Computers and Education, 39*.

Donoho, D. (1992). Wavelet shrinkage and W.V.D: A 10 minute tour. In Y. Meyer & S. Roques (Eds.), *Progress in wavelet analysis and applications* (pp. 109-128). Gig-sur-Yvette, France: Frontières.

Donoho, D. L. (1995). De-noising by soft-thresholding. *IEEE Transactions on Information Theory, 41*(3), 613-627.

Donoho, D., & Johnstone, I. (1994). Ideal spatial adaptation by wavelet shrinkage. *Biometrika, 81*(3), 425-455.

Doshi, B.T., Eggenschwiler, D., Rao, A., Samadi, B., Wang, Y.T., & Wolfson, J. (2007). VoIP network architectures and QoS strategy. *Bell Labs Technical Journal, 7*, 41–59.

Drucker, P., Glatzer, A., De Mar, S., & Wong, C. (2004). SmartSkip: Consumer level browsing and skipping of digital video content. In *Proceedings of the SIGCHI conference on Human factors in computing systems: Changing our world, changing ourselves* (pp. 219-226). New York: ACM Press.

Dugad, R., & Ahuja, N. (2001). A fast scheme for image size change in the compressed domain. *IEEE Transactions on Circuit and Systems for Video Technology, 11*(4), 461–474.

Dugad, R., Ratakonda, K., & Ahuja, N. (1998). A new wavelet-based scheme for watermarking images. *Proc. Int. Conf. Image Processing (ICIP)*.

Dugelay, J.-L., & Petitcolas, F.A.P. (2000). Possible counter-attacks against random geometric distortions. *Proc. SPIE Security and Watermarking of Multimedia Contents II*, CA.

Dumas, J.S., & Redish, J.C. (1999). *A practical guide to usability testing*. Exeter, England: Intellect.

Duygulu, P., Barnard, K., de Freitas, N., & Forsyth, D. (2002). Object recognition as machine translation: Learning a lexicon for a fixed image vocabulary. In *Proceedings of the European Conference on Computer Vision*, Copenhagen, Denmark.

Dyson. (1979). Time without end: Physics and biology in an open universe. *Reviews of Modern Physics, 52*(3), 447–460.

EBU. (2003). BPN 056:SAMVIQ—Subjective assessment methodology for video quality.

Edwards, A. (2007). Unpublished manuscript.

Ejima, M., & Myazaki, A. (2001). On the evaluation of performance of digital watermarking in the frequency domain. *Proceedings of the IEEE International Conference on Image Processing*, Thessaloniki, Greece.

Ekin, A., Tekalp, A. M., & Mehrotra, R. (2003). Automatic video analysis and summarization. *IEEE Transactions on Image Processing, 12*(7), 796–807.

Eklund, J., & Sinclair, K. (2000). An empirical appraisal of the effectiveness of adaptive interfaces of instructional systems. *Educational Technology and Society, 3*(4), 165-177.

Eleftheriadis, A., & Anastassiou, D. (1995). Constrained and general dynamic rate shaping of compressed digital video. *Proceedings of the IEEE International Conference on Image Processing*, Washington, DC.

Elias, P. (1975). Universal codeword sets and representations of the integers. *IEEE Transaction on Information Theory, 21*(2).

Ellis, D. (1996). *Prediction-driven computational auditory scene analysis*. Unpublished doctoral dissertation, MIT, Department of Electrical Engineering and Computer Science, Cambridge, MA.

Elting, C., Zwickel, J., & Malaka, R. (2002). Device-dependent modality selection for user-interfaces—An empirical study. *Proceedings of the International Conference on Intelligent User-Interfaces*, San Francisco, California, 55–62.

Empririx. (2003). *Assuring QoE on next generation networks* [white paper].

Ephraim, Y., & Malah, D. (1983). Speech enhancement using optimal non-linear spectral amplitude estimation. In *Proceedings of the IEEE International Conference of Acoustics, Speech, and Signal Processing*, (vol. 8, pp. 1118-1121) Boston MA.

Ephraim, Y., & Malah, D. (1984). Speech enhancement using a minimum mean-square error short-time spectral amplitude estimator. *IEEE Transactions on Acoustics, Speech, and Signal Processing, 32*(6), 1109-1121.

Ephraim, Y., & Malah, D. (1985). Speech enhancement using a minimum mean-square error log-spectral amplitude estimator. *IEEE Transactions on Acoustics, Speech, and Signal Processing, 33*(2), 443-445.

Eronen, L., & Vuorimaa, P. (2000). User interfaces for digital television: A navigator case study. In *Proceedings of the Working Conference on Advanced Visual Interfaces AVI 2000* (pp. 276-279). New York: ACM Press.

Esquef, P. A. A. (2004). *Model-based analysis of noisy musical recordings with application to audio restoration.* Unpublished doctoral dissertation, Lab of Acoustics and Audio Signal Processing, Helsinki University of Technology, Espoo, Finland. Retrieved June 30, 2006 from http://lib.hut.fi/Diss/2004/isbn9512269503/.

Esquef, P. A. A., & Biscainho, L. W. P. (2006). An efficient method for reconstruction of audio signals across long gaps. *IEEE Transactions on Speech and Audio Processing, 14*(4), 1391-1400.

Esquef, P. A. A., Biscainho, L. W. P., & Välimäki, V. (2003). An efficient algorithm for the restoration of audio signals corrupted with low-frequency pulses. *Journal of the Audio Engineering Society, 51*(6), 502-517.

Esquef, P. A. A., Biscainho, L. W. P., Diniz, P. S. R., & Freeland, F. P. (2000). A double-threshold-based approach to impulsive noise detection in audio signals. In *Proceedings of the X European Signal Processing Conf.* (vol. 4, pp. 2041-2044). Tampere, Finland.

Esquef, P. A. A., Karjalainen, M., & Välimäki, V. (2002), Detection of clicks in audio signals using warped linear prediction. In *Proceedings of the 14th IEEE International Conference of on Digital Signal Processing (DSP2002)* (vol. 2, pp. 1085-1088). Santorini, Greece.

Etter, W. (1996). Restoration of a discrete-time signal segment by interpolation based on the left-sided and right-sided autoregressive parameters. *IEEE Transactions on Signal Processing, 44*(5), 1124-1135.

Europe's Information Society. (2004). *User interaction.* Retrieved from http://europa.eu.int/information_society/activities/egovernment_research/focus/user_interaction/index_en.htm

Fechner, G.T. (1966). *Elements of psychophysics.* Holt Rinehart & Winston.

Feng, S. L., Lavrenko, V., & Manmatha, R. (2004). Multiple Bernoulli relevance models for image and video annotation. In *Proceedings of the IEEE Conference on Computer Vision and Pattern Recognition*, Cambridge, UK.

Ferreira, P. J. S. G. (2001). Iterative and noniterative recovery of missing samples for 1-D band-limited signals. In F. Marvasti (Ed.), *Nonuniform sampling—Theory and practice* (pp. 235-281). New York: Kluwer/Plenum.

Fitzmaurice, G.W., Zhai, S., & Chignell, M.H. (1993). Virtual reality for palmtop computers. *ACM Transactions on Information Systems, 11*(3). 197–218.

Forney, G.D. (1973). The Viterbi algorithm. *Proceedings of the IEEE, 61*(3), 268–278.

Forsyth, D., & Ponce, J. (2003). *Computer vision: A modern approach.* Prentice Hall.

Fowler, D. (1999). The next Internet. *NetWorker, 3*(3), 20–29.

Franchi, N., Fumagalli, M., Lancini, R., & Tubaro, S. (2003). Multiple description video coding for scalable and robust transmission over IP. *IEEE Transactions on Circuits and Systems for Video Technology, 15*(3), 321–334.

Frecon, E., Smith, G., Steed, A., Stenius, M., & Stahl, O. (2001). An overview of the COVEN platform. *Presence, 10*(1).

Friedman, W.F. (1967). Cryptology. *Encyclopedia Britannica*, vol. 6 (pp. 844–851).

Friedman, W.F. (1976). *Elements of cryptanalysis.* Laguna Hills, CA: Aegean Park Press.

Friedman, W.F. (1987). The index of coincidence and its applications in cryptography. Riverbank Publication

No. 22, Riverbank Labs, 1920. Reprinted by Aegean Park Press.

Frossard, P., & Verscheure, O. (2002). Batched patch caching for streaming media. *IEEE Communication Letter, 6*(4), 159–161.

Fukuhara, T., Ando, K., Watanabe, O., & Kiya, H. (2002). Partial-scrambling of JPEG2000 images for security applications. ISO/IEC JTC 1/SC29/WG1, N2439.

Fung, K.-T., Chan, Y.-L., & Siu, W.-C. (2002). New architecture for dynamic frame-skipping transcoder. *IEEE Transactions on Image Processing, 11*(8), 886–900.

Furht, B., & Kirovski, D. (2006). *Encryption and authentications: Techniques and Applications.* Auerbach Publications.

Furht, B., & Kirovski, D. (2006). *Multimedia encryption and authentication techniques and applications.* Boca Raton, FL: Auerbach Publications.

Gan, T., Gan, L., & Ma, K-K. (2006). Reducing video-quality fluctuations for streaming scalable video using unequal error protection, retransmission, and interleaving. *IEEE Transactions on Image Processing, 15*(4), 819–832.

Gang, L., Akansu, A.N., Ramkumar, M., & Xie, X. (2001). Online music protection and MP3 compression. *Proceedings of the International Symposium on Intelligent Multimedia, Video and Speech Processing,* 13–16.

Ganz, A., & Phonphoem, A. (2001). Robust SuperPoll with chaining protocol for IEEE 802.11 wireless LANs in support of multimedia applications. *Wireless Networks, 7,* 65–73.

Garcia-Ruiz, M.A., & Alvarez-Cardenas, O. (2005). Application of virtual reality in collaborative work of small and medium enterprises. *Proceedings of the Sixth International Congress of Computer Science,* Colima, Mexico.

Gauntlett, D., & Hill, A. (1999). *TV living: Television, culture and everyday life.* Routledge.

Geography of Cyberspace Directory. http://www.cyber-geography.org/

George, E. B., & Smith, M. J. T. (1992). Analysis-by-synthesis/overlap-add sinusoidal modeling applied to the analysis and synthesis of musical tones. *Journal of the Audio Engineering Society, 40*(6), 497-516.

Germanakos, P., Samaras, G., & Christodoulou, E. (200510-12). Multi-channel delivery of services—the road from e-government to m-government: Further technological challenges and implications. *Proceedings of the 1st European Conference on Mobile Government (Euro mGov 2005),* Brighton (pp. 210-220).

Ghinea, G., & Thomas, J.P. (1998). QoS impact on user perception and understanding of multimedia clips. *Proceedings of the ACM Multimedia,* Bristol, UK, 98, 49–54.

Ghinea, G., Thomas, J.P., & Fish, R.S. (1999). Multimedia, network protocols and users—Bridging the Gap. *Proceedings of the ACM Multimedia, 1,* 473–476.

Gilliam, D. (2006). The appeal of mobile video: Reading between the lines. Retrieved from http://www.tdgresearch.com/tdg_opinions_the_appeal_of_mobile_video.htm

Girod, B., Aaron, A.M., Rane, S., & Rebollo-Monedero, D. (2005). Distributed video coding. *Proceedings of the IEEE, 93*(1), 71–83.

Godsill, S. J. (1993). *The restoration of degraded audio signals.* Unpublished doctoral dissertation, Engineering Department, Cambridge University, Cambridge, England. Retrieved June 30, 2006 from http://www-sigproc.eng.cam.ac.uk/»sjg/thesis/

Godsill, S. J., & Rayner, P. J. W. (1992). A Bayesian approach to the detection and correction of error bursts in audio signals. In *Proceedings of the IEEE International Conference of Acoustics, Speech, and Signal Processing* (vol. 2, pp. 261-264). San Fransisco, CA.

Godsill, S. J., & Rayner, P. J. W. (1996). Robust noise reduction for speech and audio signals. In *Proceedings of the IEEE International Conference of Acoustics, Speech, and Signal Processing* (vol. 2, pp. 625-628). Atlanta, GA.

Godsill, S. J., & Rayner, P. J. W. (1998). *Digital audio restoration—A statistical model based approach*. Berlin, Germany: Springer-Verlag.

Godsill, S. J., & Rayner, P. J. W. (1998). Statistical reconstruction and analysis of autoregressive signals in impulsive noise using the Gibbs sampler. *IEEE Transactions on Speech and Audio Processing, 6*(4), 352-372.

Godsill, S. J., & Tan, C. H. (1997). Removal of low frequency transient noise from old recordings using model-based signal separation techniques. In *Proceedings of the IEEE ASSP Workshop on Applications of Signal Processing to Audio and Acoustics*. New Paltz, NY.

Godsill, S. J., Rayner, P. J. W., & Cappé, O. (1998). Digital audio restoration. In M. Kahrs & K. Brandenburg (Eds.), *Applications of digital signal processing to audio and acoustics* (pp. 133-194). Boston: Kluwer.

Golomb, S.W. (1996). Run-length encodings. *IEEE Transaction on Information Theory, 12*, 399–401.

Gonzalez, R.C., & Woods, R.E. (2002). *Digital image processing* (2nd ed.). Upper Saddle River, NJ: Prentice Hall.

Goodman, D. J., Lockhart, G. B., Waen, O. J., & Wong, W. C. (1986). Waveform substitution techniques for recovering missing speech segments in packet voice communications. *IEEE Transactions on Acoustics, Speech, and Signal Processing, ASSP-34*(6), 1440-1448.

Gou, K.H., Hofmann, M.A., Ng, E., Paul, S., & Zhang, H. (2002). High quality streaming multimedia. *US PATENT 6,377,972 B1*.

Goyal, V.K. (2001). Multiple description coding: Compression meets the network. *IEEE Signal Processing Magazine, 18*(5), 74–93.

Grimstead, I.J., Avis, N.J., & Walker, D.W. (2005). Visualization across the pond: How a wireless PDA can collaborate with million-polygon datasets via 9,000km of cable. *Proceedings of the Tenth International Conference on 3D Web Technology*, Bangor, United Kingdom, 47–56.

Grosbois, R., Gerbelot, P., & Ebrahimi, T. (2001). Authentication and access control in the JPEG 2000 compressed domain. *Proceedings of the SPIE 46th Annual Meeting, Applications of Digital Image Processing XXIV*, San Diego.

Gulliver, R.S., & Ghinea, G. (2006). Defining user perception of distributed multimedia quality. *ACM Transactions on Multimedia Computing, Communications, and Applications, 2*, 241–257.

Guo, H., & Georganas, N. (2002). Multi-resolution image watermarking scheme in the spectrum domain. *Proceedings of the IEEE Canadian Conference on Electrical and Computer Engineering*, Canada.

Guzman, V., Miyatake, M., & Meana, H. (2004). *Analysis of wavelet-based watermarking algorithm*. Paper presented at the 14th International IEEE Conference on Electronics, Communications and Computers, Veracruz, Mexico.

Gwinn, E., & Hughlett, M. (2005, October 10). Mobile TV for your cell phone. *Chicago Tribune*. Retrieved from http://home.hamptonroads.com/stories/story.cfm?story=93423&ran=38197

H.264/AVC ITU-T Recommendation H.264 and ISO/IEC 11496-10 (MPEG-4). (2005). AVC: Advanced video coding for generic audiovisual services, version 3.

Han, J., & Kim, H. (2006). Optimization of requantization codebook for vector quantization. *IEEE Transactions on Image Processing, 15*(5).

Han, R., Bhagwat, P., LaMaire, R., Mummert, T., Perret, V., & Rubas, J. (1998). Dynamic adaptation in an image transcoding proxy for mobile Web browsing. *IEEE Personal Communications*, 8–17.

Hands, D. (2004). A basic multimedia quality model. *IEEE Transaction on Multimedia, 6*(6), 806–816.

Hands, D.P. QoS for mobile multimedia, BTexact Technologies. Retrieved from http://www.iee.org/oncomms/pn/visualinformation/%20P-Qos_For_Mobile_Multimedia.pdf

Harabagiu, S., et al. (2000). Falcon: Boosting knowledge for answer engines. In *Proceedings of the Text Retrieval Conference*, Gaithersburg, MD.

Hart, G.W. (1994). To decode short cryptograms. *Communications of the ACM, 37*(9), 102–108.

Hartley, R., & Zisserman, A. (2004). *Multiple view geometry in computer vision* (2nd ed.). Cambridge University Press.

Hartung, F., & Girod, B. (1996). Digital watermarking of raw and compressed video. *Proc. SPIE digital compression technologies and systems for video commun., 2952*, 205–213.

Hartung, F., & Kutter, M. (1999). Multimedia watermarking technique. *Proc. IEEE, 8*(7), 1079–1106.

Hastie, T., Tibshirani, R., & Friedman, J. (2001). *The elements of statistical learning: Data mining, inference and prediction*. Springer.

Hayes, M. H. (1996). *Statistical signal processing and modeling*. West Sussex, England: John Wiley.

He, X., Zemel, R. S., & Carreira-Perpiñán, M. Á. (2004). Multiscale conditional random fields for image labeling. In *Proceedings of the IEEE International Conference on Computer Vision and Pattern Recognition*, Cambridge, UK.

Hellström, G. (1997). Quality measurement on video communication for sign language. In *Proceedings of 16th International Symposium on Human Factor in Telecommunications* (pp. 217-224).

Hernández Díaz, M., & Yánez García, K. (2007). *Technical aspects of the implementation of a haptic device for its use in an educational virtual environment* [unpublished telematics engineering thesis]. School of Telematics, University of Colima, Mexico.

Hill, L.S. (1929). Cryptography in an algebraic alphabet. *American Mathematical Monthly, 36*, 306–312.

Hodges, A. (1983). *Alan Turing: The enigma of intelligence*. Simon and Schuster.

Hofmann, T., & Puzicha, J. (1998). *Statistical models for co-occurrence data* (No. 1635 A. I. Memo). Massachusetts Institute of Technology.

Holmstrom, D. (2003). *Content based pre-encoding video filter for mobile TV*. Unpublished thesis, Umea University, Sweden. Retrieved from http://exjob.interaktion.nu/files/id_examensarbete_5.pdf

Holzinger, A., Nischelwitzer, A., & Meisenberger, M. (2005). Lifelong-learning support by m-learning: Example scenarios. *eLearn, 11*.

Horn, D. B. (2002). The effects of spatial and temporal video distortion on lie detection performance. In *Proceedings of CHI'02*.

Hsu, C., & Wu, J. (1998). Multiresolution watermarking for digital images. *IEEE Transactions on Circuits and Systems-II, 45*(8), 1097–1101.

Hua, K.A., Cai, Y., & Sheu. S. (1998). Multicast technique for true video-on-demand services. *ACM Multimedia*, 191–200.

Huang, J., & Yang, C. (2004). *Image digital watermarking algorithm using multiresolution wavelet transform*. Paper presented at the International IEEE Conference on Systems, Man, and Cybernetics, The Hague, The Netherlands.

Huang, Y., & Hui, L. (2003). An adaptive spatial filter for additive Gaussian and impulse noise reduction in video signals. *Proceedings of the ICICS PCM 2003*, 402–406.

Hudson, J.M., & Bruckman, A. (2002). Disinhibition in a CSCL environment. *Proceedings of Computer Support for Collaborative Learning (CSCL)*, Boulder, Colorado, 629–630.

Hyvärinen, A. (1999a). Fast and robust fixed-point algorithms for independent component analysis. *IEEE Trans. Neural Networks, 10*, 626–634.

Hyvärinen, A. (1999b). Survey on independent component analysis. *Neural Computing Surveys, 2*, 94–128.

Hyvärinen, A., & Oja, E. (1999). Independent component analysis: a tutorial. Retrieved from *www.cis.hut.fi/projects/ica/*

IBM. (2002). *Functions of mobile multimedia QOS control.* Retrieved from http://www.trl.ibm.com/projects/mmqos/system_e.htm

IETF RFC 3828. (2004). The lightweight user datagram protocol (UDP-Lite).

Inoue, H., Miyazaki, A., Yamamoto, A., & Katsura, T. (1998). A digital watermark based on the wavelet transform and its robustness on image compression. *Proc. Int. Conf. Image Processing (ICIP).*

Interchange of Data between Administrations. (2004). *Multi-channel delivery of e-government services.* Retrieved from http://europa.eu.int/idabc/

ISO 9241-11. (1998). Ergonomic requirements for office work with visual display terminals (VDTs)—Part 11: Guidance on usability.

ISO/IEC 11 172. (1993). Information technology—Coding of moving pictures and associated audio for digital storage media at up to about 1.5 Mbit/s. .

ISO/IEC 13 818. (1995). Information technology—Generic coding of moving pictures and associated audio information.

ISO/IEC 21000. (2003). *Information technology—Multimedia framework.* International Standard, Parts 1–7.

ISO/IEC. (1995). Generic coding of moving pictures and associated audio (MPEG-2). ISO/IEC 13818-2 standard.

ISO/IEC. (2003). IS 15938-5:2001: Information Technology—Multimedia Content Description Interface—Multimedia Description Schemes.

ISO/IEC. (2004). IS 21000-7:2004 Information Technology—Multimedia Framework—Part 7: DIA.

ISO/IEC. (2006). IS 21000-7:2006 FPDAM/1: Conversions and permissions.

ISO/IECFCD15444-1. (2000). Information technology—JPEG2000 image coding system—Part 1: Core coding system.

ITU. (1999). ITU-T recommendation P.910: Subjective video quality assessment methods for multimedia applications.

ITU. (2002). ITU-R recommendation BT.500-11: Methodology for the subjective assessment of the quality of television pictures.

ITU-R. (1997). Recommendation BS.1116. Methods for the subjective assessment of small impairments in audio systems including multichannel sound systems.

ITU-R. (2002). Recommendation BT500, methodology for the subjective assessment of the quality of television pictures.

ITU-R. (2004). BT 1683, objective perceptual video quality measurement techniques for standard definition digital broadcast television in the presence of a full reference.

ITU-T Rec. H.324. (1998). Terminal for low bit-rate multimedia communication.

ITU-T Recommendation. P.930. (1996). Principles of a reference impairment system for video.

ITU-T. (1996). Recommedation P.800, methods for subjective determination of transmission quality.

ITU-T. (1999). Recommedation P.910, subjective video quality assessment methods for multimedia applications.

ITU-T. (2004). J.144, objective perceptual video quality measurement techniques for digital cable television in the presence of a full reference.

Iwata, H., Yano, H. Uemura, T., & Moriya, T. (2004). Food simulator: A haptic interface for biting. *Proceedings of the IEEE Virtual Reality Conference* VR'04.

Jackson, R.L., Taylor, W., & Winn, W. (1999). Peer collaboration and virtual environments: A preliminary investigation of multi-participant virtual reality applied in science education. *Proceedings of the ACM 1999 Symposium on Applied Computing*, San Antonio, Texas, 121–125.

Jaffe, D., & Smith, J. O. (1983). Extension of the Karplus-Strong plucked string algorithm. *Computer Music Journal, 7*(2), 56-69.

Jain, R. (2004). Quality of experience. *IEEE Multimedia, 11,* 95-96.

Jannach, D., & Leopold, K. (2005). A multimedia adaptation framework based on semantic Web technology. *Proceedings of the 2nd European Semantic Web Conference*, Heraklion, Greece, 61–68.

Janssen, A. J. E. M., Veldhuis, R. N. J., & Vries, L. B. (1986). Adaptive interpolation of discrete-time signals that can be modeled as autoregressive processes. *IEEE Transactions on Acoustics, Speech, Signal Processing, ASSP-34*(2), 317-330.

Järveläinen, H. (2003). *Perception of attributes in real and synthetic string instrument sounds*. Unpublished doctoral dissertation, Helsinki University of Technology—Lab of Acoustics and Audio Signal Processing, Espoo, Finland. Retrieved June 30, 2006 from http://lib.hut.fi/Diss/2003/isbn9512263149/

Jebara, S. B., Benazza-Benyahia, A., & Khelifa, A. B. (2000). Reduction of musical noise generated by spectral subtraction by combining wavelet packet transform and Wiener filtering. In *Proceedings of the X European Signal Processing Conference* (vol. 2, pp. 749-752). Tampere, Finland.

Jeffay, K., & Zhang H. (2002), *Readings in multimedia computing and networking*. San Francisco: Morgan Kaufman.

Jeon, J., Lavrenko, V., & Manmatha, R. (2003). Automatic image annotation and retrieval using cross-media relevance models. In *Proceedings of the ACM SIGIR Conference on Research and Development in Information Retrieval*, Toronto, Canada.

Jha, S.K., & Hassan, M. (2002). *Engineering Internet Qos*. Norwood, MA: Artech House Inc.

Jiangchuan, L., Chu, X., & Xu, J. (2003). Proxy cache management for grained scalable video streaming [technical report]. Chinese University of Hong Kong.

JM H.264/AVC Software Coordination, Joint Model Software, ver. 10.2. (2005). http://iphome.hhi.de/suehring/tml/

Johnson, D.W., & Johnson, R.T. (1994). Learning together. In S. Sharan (Ed.), *Handbook of cooperative learning methods*. Westport, CT: Greenwood Press.

Johnson, N.F., Duric, Z., & Jajodia, S. (1999). Recovery of watermarks from distorted images. *Preliminary Proc. of the Third Int. Information Hiding Workshop*, 361–375.

Johnson, W.L., et al. (2004). Tactical language training system: An interim report. *Proceedings of the 7th International Conference on Intelligent Tutoring Systems*, Maceio, Brazil.

Joly, A., Nathalie,M., & Marcel, B. (2001). Audio-visual quality and interactions between television audio and video. *Proceedings of the International Symposium on Signal Processing and its Applications*, Malaysia.

Jumisko-Pyykkö, S., & Häkkinen, J. (2006). "I would like see the face and at least hear the voice": Effects of screen size and audio-video bitrate ratio on perception of quality in mobile television. In G. Doukidis, K. Chorianopoulos, & G. Lekakos (Eds.), *Proceedings of EuroITV '06* (pp. 339-348). Athens: University of Economics and Business.

Jumisko-Pyykkö, S., Vadakital,V., Liinasuo, M., & Hannuksela, M.M. (2006). Acceptance of audiovisual quality in erroneous television sequences over a DVB-H channel. *Proceedings of the Workshop in Video Processing and Quality Metrics for Consumer Electronics*, 1–5.

Jumisko-Pyykkö, S., Vinod Kumar, M. V., Liinasuo, M., & Hannuksela, M. (2006). Acceptance of audiovisual quality in erroneous television sequences over a DVB-H channel. In *Proceedings of the Second International Workshop in Video Processing and Quality Metrics for Consumer Electronics*.

Jung, H., et al. (2003). *Image watermarking based on wavelet transform using threshold selection*. Paper presented at the International IEEE SICE Conference.

Kahn, D. (1967). The codebreakers: The story of secret writing. New York: Macmillan Publishing Co.

Kahn, D. (1983). Kahn on codes. New York: Macmillan Publishing Co.

Kahn, D. (1994). Seizing the enigma. Boston: Houghton Mifflin Co.

Kalva, H., Petljanski, B., & Furht, B. (2005). Complexity reduction tools for MPEG-2 to H.264 video transcoding. *WSEAS Transactions on Information Science & Applications, 2*, 295–300.

Kankanhalli, M.S., Rajmohan, & Ramakrishnan, K.R. (1998). Content based watermarking of images. *Proc. of the Sixth ACM International Multimedia Conference.*

Katzenbeisser, S., & Petitcolas, F. (2000). *Information hiding: Techniques for steganography and digital watermarking*. Boston, MA: Artech House.

Katzenbeisser, S., & Petitcolas, F.A.P. (2000). *Information hiding techniques for steganography and digital watermarking*. Boston: Artech House.

Kaup, A. (2002). Video analysis for universal multimedia messaging. *Proceedings of the 5th IEEE Southwest Symp. Image Analysis and Interpretation*, Santa Fe, New Mexico, 211–215.

Kauppinen, I., & Kauppinen, J. (2002). Reconstruction method for missing or damaged long portions in audio signal. *Journal of the Audio Engineering Society, 50*(7/8), 594-602.

Kauppinen, I., & Roth, K. (2002a). Adaptive psychoacoustic filter for broadband noise reduction in audio signals. In *Proceedings of the 14th International Conference of Digital Signal Processing* (vol. 2, pp. 962-966). Santorini, Greece.

Kauppinen, I., & Roth, K. (2002b). Audio signal extrapolation—Theory and applications. In *Proceedings of the Fifth IInternational Conference on Digital Audio Effects*

(pp. 105-110). Hamburg, Germany. Retrieved June 30, 2006 from http://www.unibw-hamburg.de/EWEB/ANT/dafx2002/papers.html

Kauppinen, I., Kauppinen, J., & Saarinen, P. (2001). A method for long extrapolation of audio signals. *Journal of the Audio Engineering Society, 49*(12), 1167-1180.

Kay, S. M. (1988). *Modern spectral estimation*. Upper Saddle River, NJ: Prentice-Hall.

Kaye, J. (2004). Making scents: Aromatic output for HCI. *Interactions.*

Keesman, G., Hellinghuizen, R., Hoekesma, F., & Heidman, G. (1996). Transcoding of MPEG bitstreams. *Signal Process. Image Comm., 8*, 481–500.

Keesman, G., Hellinghuizen, R., Hoeksema, F., & Heideman, G. (1996). Transcoding of MPEG bitstreams. *Signal Processing Image Communication, 8.*

Ketola, P., & Röykkee, M. (2001). The three facets of usability in mobile handsets. *Proceedings of the CHI Workshop, Mobile Communications: Understanding Users, Adoption & Design*. Seattle, Washington.

Khan, J., & Patel, D. (2003). Extreme rate transcoding for dynamic video rate adaptation. *Proceedings of the 4th International Conference on Wireless and Optical Communication.*

Khan, J., & Yang, S. (2003). Delay and jitter minimization in high performance Internet computing. *Proceedings of the International Conference on High Performance Computing*, Hyderabad, India.

Kies, J. K., Williges, R. C., & Rosson, M. B. (1996). *Controlled laboratory experimentation and field study evaluation of video conference for distance learning applications* (Rep. No. HCIL 96-02). Blacksburg: Virginia Tech.

Kim, G., & Shin, D. (2005). Intellectual property management on MPEG-4 video for hand-held device and mobile video streaming service. *IEEE Transactions on Consumer Electronics, 51*(1), 139–143.

Kim, J.-G., Wang, Y., & Chang, S.-F. (2003). Content-adaptive utility based video adaptation. *Proceedings of the International Conference on Multimedia & Expo*, Baltimore, Maryland, 281–284.

Kim, M.B., Nam, J., Baek, W., Son, J., & Hong, J. (2003). The adaptation of 3D stereoscopic video in MPEG-21 DIA. *Signal Processing: Image Communication, 18*(8), 685–697.

Kim, N.W., Kim, T.Y., & Choi, J.S. (2002). Motion analysis using the normalization of motion vectors on MPEG compressed domain. *Proceedings of the ITC-CSCC2002*, 1408–1411.

Kim, S.E. (2006). *Efficient and QoS guaranteed data transport in heterogeneous wireless mobile networks* [doctoral dissertation]. Georgia Institute of Technology.

Kim, W. (2002). Personalization: Definition, status, and challenges ahead. *JOT, 1*(1), 29-40.

Kinzie, Jr., G. R., & Gravereaux, D. W. (1973). Automatic detection of impulsive noise. *Journal of the Audio Engineering Society, 21*(3), 331-336.

Knoche, H. (2005). *FirstYear report.* Unpublished thesis, University College London.

Knoche, H., & McCarthy, J. (2004). Mobile users' needs and expectations of future multimedia services. In *Proceedings of the WWRF12.*

Knoche, H., & Sasse, M. A. (2006). Breaking the news on mobile TV: User requirements of a popular mobile content. In *Proceedings of IS&T/SPIE Symposium on Electronic Imaging.*

Knoche, H., De Meer, H., & Kirsh, D. (2005). Compensating for low frame rates. In *CHI'05 extended abstracts on Human factors in computing systems* (pp. 1553-1556).

Knoche, H., McCarthy, J., & Sasse, M. A. (2005). Can small be beautiful? Assessing image resolution requirements for Mobile TV. In *ACM Multimedia* ACM.

Knoche, H., McCarthy, J., & Sasse, M. A. (2006). A close-up on mobile TV: The effect of low resolutions on shot types. In G. Doukidis, K. Chorianopoulos, & G. Lekakos (Eds.), *Proceedings of EuroITV '06* (pp. 359-367). Greece: Athens University of Economics and Business.

Knoche, H., McCarthy, J., & Sasse, M.A. (2005). Can small be beautiful? Assessing image resolution requirements for mobile TV. *Proceedings of the ACM Multimedia*, 829–838.

Knoche, H., McCarthy, J., & Sasse, M.A. (2008). How low can you go? The effect of low resolutions on shot types in mobile TV. *Personalized and Mobile Digital TV Applications in Springer Multimedia Tools and Applications Series, 36(1-2),* 145-166.

Knudsen, L.R. (1994). *Block ciphers—Analysis, design, applications* [doctoral dissertation]. Aarhus University.

Koch, E., & Zhao, J. (1995). Towards robust and hidden image copyright labeling. *Proc. Workshop Nonlinear Signal and Image Processing.*

Konheim, A.G. (1981). *Cryptography: A primer.* New York: John Wiley & Sons.

Koucheryavy, Y., Moltchanov, D., & Harju, J. (2003). Performance evaluation of live video streaming service in 802.11b WLAN environment under different load conditions. *Proceedings of the MIPS*, Italy, 30–41.

KPMG. (2006). Consumers and convergence challenges and opportunities in meeting next generation customer needs.

Krishnan, D.R.P., & Shavitt, Y. (2000). Caching location problem. *IEEE/ACM Transactions Networking, 8*(5), 795–825.

Krithivasan, S., & Iyer, S. (2006). Strategies for efficient streaming in delay-tolerant multimedia applications. *Proceedings of the IEEE ISM 2006*, 419–426.

Kullback, S. (1976). Statistical methods in cryptanalysis. First printed by U.S. Government Printing Office (1935). Aegean Park Press.

Kumar, S., & Herbert, M. (2003a). Discriminative random fields: A discriminative framework for contextual interaction in classification. In *Proceedings of the IEEE International Conference on Computer Vision*, Nice, France.

Kumar, S., & Herbert, M. (2003b). Man-made structure detection in natural images using causal multiscale random field. In *Proceedings of the IEEE International Conference on Computer Vision and Pattern Recognition*, Madison, WI.

Kundur, D., & Hatzinakos, D. (1998). Digital watermarking using multiresolution wavelet decomposition. *Proc. of the Int. Conference on Acoustics, Speech, and Signal Processing, 5*, 2969–2972.

Kunert, T., & Krömker, H. (2006). Proven interaction design solutions for accessing and viewing interactive TV content items. In G. Doukidis, K. Chorianopoulos, & G. Lekakos (Eds.), *Proceedings of EuroITV 2006* (pp. 242-250). Greece: Athens University of Economics and Business.

Kunkelmann, T., & Horn, U. (1998). Partial video encryption based on scalable coding. *Proceedings of the 5th International Workshop on Systems, Signals and Image Processing (IWSSIP' 98)*.

Kutter, M. (1998). Watermarking resisting to translation, rotation and scaling. *Proc. of SPIE Int. Symposium on Voice, Video, and Data Communications—Multimedia Systems and Applications, 3528*, 423–431.

Lafferty, J., McCallum, A., & Pereira, F. (2001). Conditional random fields: Probabilistic models for segmenting and labeling sequence data. In *Proceedings of the International Conference on Machine Learning*, San Francisco.

Lagkas, T.D., Papadimitriou, G.I., & Pomportsis, A.S. (2006). QAP: A QoS supportive adaptive polling protocol for wireless LANs. *Computer Communications*, 618–633.

LAN MAN Standards Committee of the IEEE Computer Society. (1999). *IEEE standard 802.11-1999 wireless LAN medium access control (MAC) and physical layer (PHY) specifications*. IEEE Press.

LAN MAN Standards Committee of the IEEE Computer Society. (2003). *IEEE 802.11e/D6.0, draft supplement to part 11: Wireless medium access control and physical layer (PHY) specifications: Medium access control (MAC) enhancements for quality of service (QoS)*. IEEE.

Langelaar, C., Lubbe, J.C.A., & Lagendijk, R.L. (1997). Robust labeling methods for copy protection of images. *Proc. Electronic Imaging, 3022*, 298–309.

Langelaar, G., Setyawan, I., & Lagendijk, R. (2000). Watermarking digital image and video data: A state-of-art overview. *IEEE Signal Processing Magazine, 17*(5), 20–46.

Lankhorst, M. M., Kranenburg, Salden, A., & Peddemors A. J. H. (2002). Enabling technology for personalizing mobile services. *Proceedings of the 35th Annual Hawaii International Conference on System Sciences (HICSS-35'02): Vol. 3*(3) (p. 87).

Larsen-Freeman, D. (2000). *Technique and principles in language teaching*. Oxford, UK: Oxford University Press.

Lavrenko, V., Manmatha, R., & Jeon, J. (2003). A model for learning the semantics of pictures. In *Proceedings of the Neural Information Processing System Conference*, Vancouver, Canada.

Law, K.L.E., & So, S. (2005). Real-time perceptual QoS satisfactions of multimedia information. *Proceedings of the 2nd ACM International Workshop on Performance Evaluation of Wireless Ad Hoc, Sensor, and Ubiquitous Networks*, Canada, 277–278.

Le, J., & Kim, J.-W. (2004). Differentiation mechanisms over IEEE 802.11 wireless LAN for network-adaptive video transmission. *Lecture Notes in Computer Science, 3090*, 553–562.

Lee, C., Lehoczky, J., Siewiorek, D., Rajkumar, R., & Hansen, J. (1999). A scalable solution to the multi-resource QoS problem. *Proceedings of the 20th IEEE Real-Time Systems Symposium*, Phoenix, Arizona, 315–326.

Lee, H.-C., & Kim, S.-D. (2003). Iterative key frame selection in the rate-constraint environment. *Signal Processing: Image Communication, 18*(1), 1–15.

Lee, M., McGowan, W.J., & Recchione, C.M. (2007). Enabling wireless VoIP. *Bell Labs Technical Journal, 11*, 201–215.

Lee, T.-W. (1998). *Independent component analysis: Theory and applications*. Kluwer Academic.

Lee, Y.-C., Kim, J., Altunbasak, Y., & Mersereau, R.M. (2003). Layered coding vs. multiple description coded video over error-prone networks. *Signal Processing: Image Communication, 18*(5), 337–356.

Lei, Z., & Georganas, N. (2002). H.263 video transcoding for spatial resolution downscaling. *Proceedings of the International Conference on Information Technology*.

Lemay-Yates Associates Inc. (2005). *Mobile TV technology discussion*. Lemay-Yates Associates Inc.

Lengwehasatit, K., & Ortega, A. (2000). Rate-complexity-distortion optimization for quadtree-based DCT coding. *Proceedings of the Conference on Image Processing*, Vancouver, Canada, 821–824.

Leonardi, R., Migliotari, P., & Prandini, M. (2004). Semantic indexing of soccer audio-visual sequences: A multimodal approach based on controlled Markov chains. *IEEE Transactions on Circuits Systems and Video Technology, 14*(5), 634–643.

Levine, W.M., & Shefner, J.M. (2000). *Fundamentals of sensation and perception* (3rd ed.). Oxford University Press.

Lewis, R., & Luciana, J. (2005). *Digital media: An Introduction*. Pearson Prentice Hall.

Li, B., & Battiti, R. (2007). Achieving optimal performance in IEEE 802.11 wireless LANs with the combination of link adaptation and adaptive backoff. *International Journal of Computer and Telecommunications Networking*, 1574–1600.

Li, B., & Sezan, I. (2003). Semantic sports video analysis: Approaches and new applications. In *Proceedings of the IEEE International Conference on Image Processing*, Barcelona, Spain.

Li, J., & Wang, J. Z. (2003). Automatic linguistic indexing of pictures by a statistical modeling approach. *IEEE Transactions on Pattern Analysis and Machine Intelligence, 25*(9), 1075–1088.

Li, W. (2001). Overview of fine granularity scalability in MPEG-4 video standard. *IEEE Transactions on Circuit and Systems for Video Technology, 11*(3), 301–317.

Li, Z.-N., & Drew, M.S. (2004). *Fundamentals of multimedia*. Pearson Prentice Hall.

Lian, S., Liu, Z., & Ren, Z. (2005). Selective video encryption based on advanced video coding. *Proceedings of the 2005 Pacific-Rim Conference on Multimedia (PCM2005), Part II, LNCS 3768*, 281–290.

Lian, S., Liu, Z., Ren, Z., & Wang, H. (2006a). Secure advanced video coding based on selective encryption algorithms. *IEEE Transactions on Consumer Electronics, 52*(2), 621–629.

Lian, S., Liu, Z., Ren, Z., & Wang, H. (2006b). Commutative watermarking and encryption for media data. *International Journal of Optical Engineering, 45*(8), 0805101-0805103.

Lian, S., Liu, Z., Ren, Z., & Wang, H. (2007a). Commutative encryption and watermarking in compressed video data. *IEEE Circuits and Systems for Video Technology, 17*(6), 774–778.

Lian, S., Liu, Z., Ren, Z., & Wang, Z. (2007b). Multimedia data encryption in block based codecs. *International Journal of Computers and Applications, 29*(1).

Lian, S., Sun, J., & Wang, Z. (2004a). A novel image encryption scheme based on JPEG encoding. *Proceedings of the International Conference on Information Visualization (IV 2004)*, 217–220.

Lian, S., Sun, J., & Wang, Z. (2004b). Perceptual cryptography on JPEG2000 compressed images or videos. *Proceedings of the International Conference on Computer and Information Technology (CIT2004)*, Wuhan, China, 78–83.

Lian, S., Sun, J., & Wang, Z. (2004c). Perceptual cryptography on SPIHT compressed images or videos. *Proceedings of the IEEE International Conference on Multimedia and Expro (I) (ICME2004)*, Taiwan, 3, 2195–2198.

Lian, S., Sun, J., Zhang, D., & Wang, Z. (2004d). A selective image encryption scheme based on JPEG2000 codec. Proceedings of the Pacific-Rim Conference on Multimedia (PCM2004), 3332, 65–72.

Lian, S., Wang, Z., & Sun, J. (2004e). A fast video encryption scheme suitable for network applications. *Proceedings of the International Conference on Communications, Circuits and Systems, 1*, 566–570.

Lienhart, R. (2003). Video OCR: A survey and practitioner's guide. In A. Rosenfeld, D. Doermann, & D. DeMenthon (Eds.), *Video mining* (pp. 155–184), Kluwer Academic Publisher.

Lim, J. (1978). Evaluation of a correlation subtraction method for enhancing speech degraded by additive white noise. *IEEE Transactions on Acoustics, Speech, and Signal Processing, 26*(5), 471-472.

Lim, J. (1986). Speech enhancement. In *Proceedings of the IEEE International Conference of Acoustics, Speech, and Signal Processing* (vol. 11, pp. 3135-3142). Tokyo, Japan.

Lim, J., & Oppenheim, A. V. (1978). All-pole modeling of degraded speech. *IEEE Transactions on Acoustics, Speech, and Signal Processing, 26*(3), 197-210.

Lin, S., & Chin, C. (2000). A robust DCT-based watermarking for copyright protection. *IEEE Transactions on Consumer Electronics, 46*(3), 415–421.

Lindberg, D. (1996). The H.324 multimedia communication standard. *IEEE Communication Magazine, 34*, 46–51.

Liu X., & Eskicioglu, A.M. (2003). Selective encryption of multimedia content in distribution networks: Challenges and new directions. *Proceedings of the IASTED International Conference on Communications, Internet and Information Technology (CIIT 2003)*, Scottsdale, Arizona.

Liu, H., Kong, X.-W., Kong, X.-D., & Liu, Y. (2001). Content based color image adaptive watermarking scheme. *Proc. of IEEE International Symposium on Circuits and Systems, 2*, 41–44.

Lloyd, E., Maclean,R., & Stirling, A. (2006). Mobile TV—Results from the BT Movio DAB-IP pilot in London. *EBU Technical Review*. Retrieved from http://www.ebu.ch/en/technical/trev/trev_frameset-index.html

Lombard, M., Grabe, M. E., Reich, R. D., Campanella, C., & Ditton, T. B. (1996). Screen size and viewer responses to television: A review of research. In *Annual Conference of the Association for Education in Journalism and Mass Communication*.

Lorber, M., & Hoeldrich, R. (1997). A combined approach for broadband noise reduction. In *Proceedings of the IEEE ASSP Workshop on Applications of Signal Processing to Audio and Acoustics*. New Paltz, NY.

Lowe, D. (1999). Object recognition from local scale-invariant features. In *Proceedings of the International Conference on Computer Vision*, Kerkyra, Corfu, Greece.

Lowe, D., & Hall, W. (1999). *Hypermedia and the Web: An engineering approach*. New York: Wiley.

Lu, C.-S., & Mark, Liao H.-Y. (2001). Multipurpose watermarking for image authentication and protection. *IEEE Transaction on Image Processing, 10*.

Lu, L., Zhang, H-J., & Jiang, H. (2002). Content analysis for audio classification and segmentation. *IEEE Transactions on Speech and Audio Processing, 10*(7), 293–302.

Lucy, S., & Sara, K. (2006). *Usability guidelines for mobile TV design*. Serco.

Lum, W.Y., & Lau, F.C.M. (2002). A QoS-sensitive content adaptation system for mobile computing. *Proceedings of the Computer Software and Applications Conference*, Oxford, UK, 680–685.

Luo, Y., & Hwang, J. N. (2003). Video sequence modeling by dynamic Bayesian networks: A systematic approach from coarse-to-fine grains. In *Proceedings of the IEEE International Conference on Image Processing*, Barcelona, Spain.

Luther, A. C. (1996). *Principles of digital audio and video*. Boston, London: Artech House Publishers.

Macedonia, M.R., Zyda, M.J., Pratt, D.R., & Barnham, P.T. (1994). NPSNET: A network software architecture for large-scale virtual environments. *Presence; Teleoperators and Virtual Environments, 3*(4).

MacIntyre, P., & Gardner, R. (1991). Methods and results in the study of foreign language anxiety: A review of the literature. *Language Learning, 41*, 25–57.

Maher, R. C. (1994). A method for extrapolation of missing digital audio data. *Journal of the Audio Engineering Society, 42*(5), 350-357.

Makhoul, J. (1977). Stable and efficient lattice methods for linear prediction. *IEEE Transactions on Acoustics, Speech, and Signal Processing, ASSP-25*(5), 423-428.

Mäki, J. (2005). *Finnish mobile TV pilot.* Research International Finland.

Mallat, S. (1989). A theory for multi-resolution signal decomposition: The wavelet representation. *IEEE Transactions on Pattern Analysis And Machine Intelligence, 11*(7), 674–693.

Mallat, S. (1999). *A wavelet tour of signal processing.* San Diego, CA: Academic Press.

Marpe, D., Wiegand, T., & Sullivan, G.J. (2006). The H.264 / MPEG4 advanced video coding standard and its applications. *IEEE Communications Magazine, 44*(8), 134–144.

Marr, D. (1983). *Vision.* San Francisco: W.H. Freeman.

Matlis, J. (2006). Internet2. *Computerworld.*

Matty, K.R., & Kondi, L.P. (2005). Balanced multiple description video coding using optimal partitioning of the DCT coefficients. *IEEE Transactions on Circuits and Systems for Video Technology, 15*(7), 928–935.

McCarthy, J., & Wright, P. (2004). *Technology as experience.* Cambridge, MA: MIT Press.

McCarthy, J., Sasse, M.A., & Miras, D. (2004). Sharp or smooth? Comparing the effects of quantization vs. frame rate for streamed video. *Proceedings of the SIGCHI*, 535–542.

McManus, M.M. (1997). Computer supported collaborative learning. *SIGGROUP Bull, 18*(1), 7–9.

Miano, J. (1999). *Compressed image file formats: JPEG, PNG, GIF, XBM, BMP.* Reading, MA: Addison-Wesley.

Miguel, A.C., Mohr, A.E., & Riskin, E.A. (1999). SPIHT for generalized multiple description coding. *Proceedings of the International Conference on Image Processing, ICIP '99, 1*, 842–846.

Miller, G. A. (1995). Wordnet: A lexical database for English. *Communications of the ACM, 38*(11), 39–41.

Mintzer, F., & Braudaway, G. (1999). If one watermark is good, are more better? *Proc. of the International Conference on Acoustics, Speech, and Signal Processing, 4.*

Miranda, E. R. (2002). *Computer sound design: Synthesis techniques and programming.* Oxford, UK: Focal Press.

Mishra, S., & Sharma, R.C. (2005). *Interactive multimedia in education and training.* Hershey, PA: Idea Group.

Mitra, S. (1998). *Digital signal processing.* Columbus, OH: McGraw-Hill.

Mobasher, B., Dai, H., Luo, T., Nakagawa, M., & Wiltshire, J. (2002). Discovery of aggregate usage profiles for Web personalization. *Data Mining and Knowledge Discovery, 6*(1), 61- 82.

Mohan, R., Smith, J. R., & Li, C.-S. (1999). Adapting multimedia Internet content for universal access. *IEEE Trans. Multimedia, 1*(1), 104–114.

Montresor, S., Valiere, J. C., Allard, J. F., & Baudry, M. (1991). *Evaluation of two interpolation methods applied to old recordings restoration.* Presented at the 90th Convention of the AES, Paris, France. AES Preprint 3022.

Moody, L., & Schmidt, G. (2004). Going wireless: The emergence of wireless networks in education. *J. Comput. Small Coll, 19*(4), 151–158.

Moon, Y.-S., Lee, S.-H., Whang, K.-Y., & Song, W.-S. (2003). Dynamic buffer allocation in video-on-demand systems. *IEEE Transactions on Knowledge and Data Engineering, 15*(6), 1535–1551.

Moorer, J. A., & Berger, M. (1986). Linear-phase band-splitting: Theory and applications. *Journal of the Audio Engineering Society, 34*(3), 143-152.

Mori, Y., Takahashi, H., & Oka, R. (1999). Image-to-word transformation based on dividing and vector quantizing images with words. In *Proceedings of the First International Workshop on Multimedia Intelligent Storage and Retrieval Management*, Orlando, FL.

Morrison, D.G., Nilsson, M.E., & Ghanbari, M. (1994). Reduction of the bit-rate of compressed video while in its coded form. *Proceedings of the Sixth International Workshop Packet Video*, Portland, Oregon.

Morton, D. (2000). *The technology and culture of sound recording in America*. Piscataway, NJ: Rutgers University Press.

Moulin, P., & Koetter, R. (2005). Data-hiding codes. *IEEE Proceedings, 93*(12), 2083–2126.

MPEG2 ISO/IEC IS 13818 (1994).

MPEG-4 Video Verification Model version 18.0, ISO/IEC JTC1/SC29/WG11 N3908, Pisa, (2001).

Mukherjee, D., Delfosse, E., Kim, J.-G., & Wang, Y. (2005). Optimal adaptation decision-taking for terminal and network quality-of-service. *IEEE Trans. Multimedia, 7*(3), 454–462.

Mukherjee, D., Maitra, S., & Acton, S. (2004). Spatial domain digital watermarking of multimedia objects for buyer authentication. *IEEE Transactions on Multimedia, 6*(1), 1–15.

Mukherjee, J., & Mitra, S.K. (2002). Image resizing in the compressed domain using subband DCT. *IEEE Transactions on Circuit and Systems for Video Technology, 12*(7), 620–627.

Mulvenna, M. D., Anand, S. S., & Buchner, A. G. (2000). Personalization on the net using Web mining. *Communications of the ACM, 43*(8), 123-125.

Murphy, S., Searles, M., Rambeau, C., & Murphy, L. (2004). Evaluating the impact of network performance on video streaming quality for categorised video content. *Proceedings of the Packet Video Workshop*.

Nagao, K., Shirai, Y., & Squire, K. (2001). Semantic annotation and transcoding: Making Web content more accessible. *IEEE Multimedia, 8*(2), 69–81.

Nakaizumi, F., Yanagida, Y., Noma, H., & Hosaka, K. (2006). SpotScents: A novel method of natural scent delivery using multiple scent projectors. *Proceedings of IEEE Virtual Reality 2006*, Alexandria, Virginia.

Naphade, M. R., & Huang, T. S. (2000). *Stochastic modeling of soundtrack for efficient segmentation and indexing of video*. In *Proceedings of the Conference on SPIE, Storage and Retrieval for Media Databases*, San Jose, CA.

Naphade, M. R., & Huang, T. S. (2001). A probabilistic framework for semantic video indexing filtering and retrieval. *IEEE Transactions on Multimedia, 3*(1), 141–151.

Naphade, M., & Smith, J. (2003). Learning visual models of semantic concepts. In *Proceedings of the IEEE International Conference on Image Processing*, Barcelona, Spain.

Naphade, M., et al. (1998). A high performance shot boundary detection algorithm using multiple cues. In *Proceedings of the IEEE International Conference on Image Processing*, Chicago.

Nason, G. P. (1995). Choice of threshold parameter in wavelet function estimation. In A. Antoniadis & G. Oppenheim (Eds.), *Lecture Notes in statistics* (Vol 103, pp. 261-280). New York: Springer-Verlag.

Natsev, A., Naphade, M., & Smith, J. (2003). Exploring semantic dependencies for scalable concept detection. In *Proceedings of the IEEE International Conference on Image Processing*, Barcelona, Spain.

Nemethova, O., Canadas, J., & Rupp, M. (2005). Improved detection for H.264 encoded video sequences over mobile networks. *Proceedings of the International*

*Symposium on Communication Theory and Application*, Ambleside, UK.

Nemethova, O., Zahumensky, M., & Rupp, M. (2004). Preprocessing of ball game video-sequences for robust transmission over mobile networks. In *Proceedings of the CIC 2004 The 9th CDMA International Conference*.

Neumann, W. R., Crigler, A. N., & Bove, V. M. (1991). Television sound and viewer perceptions. In *Proceedings of the Joint IEEE/Audio Eng. Soc. Meetings* (pp. 101-104).

Ni, Q., Romdhani, L., & Turletti, T. (2004). A survey of QoS enhancements for IEEE 802.11 wireless LAN. *Journal of Wireless Communications and Mobile Computing, 4*(5), 547–566.

Niedzwiecki, M. (1993). Statistical reconstruction of multivariate time series. *IEEE Transactions on Signal Processing, 41*(1), 451-457.

Niedzwiecki, M. (1994). Recursive algorithms for elimination of measurement noise and impulsive disturbances from ARMA signals. In *Signal Processing VII: Theories and Applications* (pp. 1289-1292). Edinburgh, UK.

Niedzwiecki, M., & Cisowski, K. (1996). Adaptive scheme for elimination of broadband noise and impulsive disturbances from AR and ARMA signals. *IEEE Transactions on Signal Processing, 44*(3), 528-537.

Niedzwiecki, M., & Cisowski, K. (2001). Smart copying—A new approach to reconstruction of audio signals. *IEEE Transactions on Signal Processing, 49*(10), 2272-2282.

Nielsen, J. (1995). *Multimedia and hypertext: The Internet and beyond*. San Diego: AP Professional.

Nikolaidis, N., & Pitas, I. (1998). Robust image watermarking in the spatial domain. *Signal Processing, 66*, 385–403.

Niu, X., Lu, Z., & Sun, S. (2000). Digital image watermarking based on multi-resolution decomposition. *IEEE Electronics Letters, 36*(13), 1108–1110.

Nokia. (2004). *Quality of experience (QoE) of mobile services: Can it be measured and improved?* White Paper No. 11212-1004. Finland.

Nokia. (2005). Finnish mobile TV: Pilot results. Retrieved from http://www.mobiletv.nokia.com/download_counter.php?file=/onAir/finland/files/RIPress.pdf

Norcen, R., & Uhl, A. (2003). Selective encryption of the JPEG2000 bitstream. IFIP International Federation for Information Processing, LNCS 2828, 194–204.

Ó Ruanaidh, J. J., & Fitzgerald, W. J. (1994). Interpolation of missing samples for audio restoration. *Electronics Letters, 30*(8), 622-623.

Ó Ruanaidh, J. J., & Fitzgerald, W. J. (1996). *Numerical Bayesian methods applied to signal processing*. Berlin, Germany: Springer-Verlag.

O'Reilly, T. (2005). What is Web2.0: Design patterns and business models for the next generation of software. Retrieved from http://www.oreillynet.com/pub/a/oreilly/tim/news/2005/09/30/what-is-web-20.html

Ohm, J.-R. (2005). Advances in scalable video coding. *Proceedings of the IEEE, 93*(1), 42–56.

Olista. (2007). Live trials by Olista with European mobile operators demonstrate common barriers for mobile data services [press release 120207-1].

Orchard, M.T., Wang, Y., Vaishampayan, V., & Reibman, A.R. (2001). Multiple description coding using pairwise correlating transforms. *IEEE Transactions On Image Processing, 10*(3), 351–366.

Ortega, A., & Ramchandran, K. (1998). Rate-distortion methods for image and video compression. *IEEE Signal Processing Magazine, 15*(6), 23–50.

Ortega, A., Ramchandran, K., & Vetterli, M. (1994). Optimal trellis-based buffered compression and fast approximations. *IEEE Trans. Image Processing, 3*(1), 26–40.

Ostermann, J., et al. (2004). Video coding with H.264/AVC: Tools, performance and complexity. *IEEE Circuit and Systems Magazine, 4*(1), 7–28.

Owens, D. A., & Wolfe-Kelly, K. (1987). Near work, visual fatigue, and variations of oculomotor tonus. *Investigative Ophthalmology and Visual Science, 28,* 743-749.

Pack, P., & Choi, Y. (2004). Fast handoff scheme based on mobility prediction in public wireless LAN systems. *IEE Proceedings Communications, 151*(5), 489–495.

Pallis, G., & Vakali, A. (2006). Insight and perspectives for content delivery networks. *Communications of the ACM, 49*(1), 101–106.

Panayiotou, C., & Samaras, G. (2004). mPersona: Personalized portals for the wireless user: An agent approach. *Journal of ACM/ Baltzer Mobile Networking and Applications (MONET), Special Issue on Mobile and Pervasive Commerce, 9*(6), 663-677.

Panis, G., et al. (2003). Bitstream syntax description: A tool for multimedia resource adaptation within MPEG-21. *Signal Processing: Image Communication, 18*(8), 721–747.

Papanikolaou, K.A., Grigoriadou, M., Kornilakis, H., & Magoulas, G.D. (2002). INSPIRE: An intelligent system for personalized instruction in a remote environment. In S. Reich, M. M. Tzagarakis, & P. M. E. De Bra (Eds.), *OHS/SC/AH 2001, LNCS 2266* (pp. 215-225). Springer-Verlag.

Papoulis, A. (1975). A new algorithm in spectral analysis and band-limited extrapolation. *IEEE Transactions on Circuits Syst., 22*(9), 735-742.

Pappas, T., & Hinds, R. (1995). On video and audio integration for conferencing. In *Proceedings of SPIE—The International Society for Optical Engineering.*

Parhi, K.K., & Nishitani, T. (1999). *Digital signal processing for multimedia systems.* New York: Marcel Dekker.

Patil, V., Kumar, R., & Mukherjee, J. (2006). A fast arbitrary factor video resizing algorithm. *IEEE Transactions on Circuit and Systems for Video Technology, 16*(9), 1164–1170.

Pazzani, J. M. (1999). A framework for collaborative, content-based, and demographic filtering. *Artificial Intelligence Review, 13*(5-6), 393-408.

Pearl, J. (1988). *Probabilistic reasoning in intelligent systems: Networks of plausible inference.* Los Angeles: Morgan Kaufmann Publishers.

Peleg, S., & Rosenfield, A. (1979). Breaking substitution ciphers using a relaxation algorithm. *Communications of the ACM, 22*(11), 598–605.

Pereira, F., & Burnett, I. (2003). Universal multimedia experiences for tomorrow. *IEEE Signal Processing Magazine, 20*(2), 63–73.

Pereira, F., & Ebrahimi, T. (2002). *MPEG-4 book.* Upper Saddle River, NJ: Prentice-Hall.

Peter, P. (2001). *Digital image watermarking in the wavelet transform domain.* Unpublished master's thesis.

Pfarrhofer, R., & Uhl, A. (2005). Selective image encryption using JBIG.IFIP TC-6 TC-11. *Proceedings of the International Conference on Communications and Multimedia Security (CMS 2005),* Salzburg, 98–107.

Piva, A., Barni, M., & Bartolini, F. (1998). *Copyright protection of digital images by means of frequency domain watermarking.* Paper presented at the SPIE Conference on Mathematics of Data/Image Coding, Compression, and Encryption, USA.

Piva, A., Barni, M., Bartoloni, E., & Cappellini, V. (1997). DCT-based watermark recovering without resorting to the uncorrupted original image. *Proc. IEEE Int. Conf. Image Processing (ICIP), 1.*

Podesser, M., Schmidt, H.-P., & Uhl, A. (2002). Selective bitplane encryption for secure transmission of image data in mobile environments. *Proceedings of the 5th IEEE Nordic Signal Processing Symposium (NORSIG 2002).*

Podilchuk, C., & Zeng, W. (1997). Watermarking of the JPEG bitstream. *Proc. Int. Conf. Imaging Science, Systems, and Applications (CISST'97),* 253–260.

Pohlmann, K.C. (2000). *Principles of digital audio* (4th Ed.). New York: McGraw-Hill.

Pommer, A., & Uhl, A. (2003). Selective encryption of wavelet-packet encoded image data: Efficiency and security. *Communications and Multimedia Security,* 194–204.

Postel, J. (1980). User datagram protocol. *IETF Request for Comments (RFC) 768.*

Potdar, V., Han, S., & Chang, E. (2005). *A survey of digital image watermarking Techniques.* Paper presented at the 3rd International IEEE Conference on Industrial Informatics, Perth, Australia.

Prangl, M., Szkaliczki, T., & Hellwagner, H. (2007). A framework for utility-based multimedia adaptation. *IEEE Trans. Circ. Syst. Video Technol., 17*(6), 719–728.

Preece, J., Rogers, Y., & Sharp, H. (2002). Interaction design: Beyond human computer interaction. New York: John Wiley and Sons.

Preece, J., Rogers, Y., Sharp, H., Benyon, D., Holland, S., & Carey, T. (1994). *Human-computer interaction.* Wokingham, UK: Addison-Wesley.

Puri, A., & Eleftheriadis, A. (1998). MPEG-4: An object-based multimedia coding standard supporting mobile applications. *Mobile Networks and Applications, 3*(1).

Qian Zhang, W.Z., & Zhang, Y.-Q. (2001). Resource allocation for multimedia streaming over the Internet. *IEEE Transaction on Multimedia, 3*(3), 339–355.

Qiao, L., & Nahrstedt, K. (1998). Comparison of MPEG encryption algorithm. *International Journal on Computers and Graphics, 22*(4), 437–448.

Quatieri, T. F., & McAulay, R. J. (1998). Audio signal processing based on sinusoidal analysis and synthesis. In M. Kahrs & K. Brandenburg (Eds.), *Applications of digital signal processing to audio and acoustics* (pp. 314-416). Boston: Kluwer.

Quattoni, A., Collins, M., & Darrell, T. (2004). Conditional random fields for object recognition. In *Proceedings of the Neural Information Processing Systems Conference*, Vancouver, Canada.

Rabiner, L. R. (1989). A tutorial on hidden Markov models and selected applications in speech recognition. *Proceedings of IEEE, 77*(2), 257–286.

Radha, H., Van der Schaar, M., & Chen, Y. (2001). The MPEG-4 fine-grained scalable video coding method for multimedia streaming over IP. *IEEE Transactions on Multimedia, 3*(1), 53–68.

Raghavan, S.V, & Tripathi, S.K. (1998). *Network multimedia, concept, architecture and design, system.* Prentice Hall.

Ramani, I., & Savage S. (2005). SyncScan: Practical fast handoff for 802.11 infrastructure networks. *Proceedings of the IEEE Infocom Conference*, Miami, Florida.

Ramarapu, P. K., & Maher, R. C. (1998). Methods for reducing audible artifacts in a wavelet-based broadband de-noising system. *Journal of the Audio Engineering Society, 46*(3), 178-190.

Rao, K., & Yip, P. (1990). *Discrete cosine transform: Algorithms, advantages, applications.* Academic Press.

Rayner, P. J. W., & Godsill, S. J. (1991). The detection and correction of artifacts in degraded gramophone recordings. In *Proceedings of the IEEE ASSP Workshop on Applications of Signal Processing to Audio and Acoustics* (pp. 151-152). New Paltz, NY.

Razzak, Md.A., & Zeng, B. (2001). Multiple description image transmission for diversity systems using block-based DC separation. *IEEE International Symposium on Circuits and Systems, 5*, 93–96.

Reddy, A., & Chatterji, B. (2005). A new wavelet based logo-watermarking scheme. *Pattern Recognition Letters, 26*(7), 1019–1027.

Reeves, B., & Nass, C. (1998). *The media equation: How people treat computers, television, and new media like real people and places.* University of Chicago Press.

Reeves, B., Lang, A., Kim, E., & Tartar, D. (1999). The effects of screen size and message content on attention and arousal. *Media Psychology, 1*, 49-68.

Reibman, A., Jafarkhani, H., Wang, Y., & Orchard, M.T. (2001). Multiple description video using rate-distortion splitting. *Proceedings of the International Conference on Image Processing, ICIP 2001, 1*, 978–981.

Reibman, A.R., Jafarkhani, H., Wang, Y., Orchard, M., & Puri, R. (2002). Multiple-description video coding using motion compensated temporal prediction. *IEEE Transactions on Circuits and Systems for Video Technology, 12*(3), 193–204.

Reichel, J., Hanke, K., & Popescu, B. (2004a). Scalable Video model V1.0. ISO/IEC JTC1/SC29/WG11, N6372.

Reichel, J., Wien, M., & Schwarz, H. (2004b). Scalable video model 3. ISO/IEC JTC1/SC29/WG11, N6716.

Rejaie, R., Handley, M., & Estrin, D. (2000). Layered quality adaptation for Internet video streaming. *IEEE International Journal on Selected Areas in Communications, 18*(12), 2530–2543.

Richard, A. (2006). *Mollin. An introduction to cryptography.* CRC Press.

Richardson, I.E.G. (2003). *H.264 and MPEG-4 video compression: Video coding for next generation multimedia.* Wiley.

Ridge, J., Bao, Y., Karczewicz, M., & Wang, X. (2005). Cyclical block coding for FGS. ISO/IEC JTC1/SC29/WG11, M11509.

Robert, E.M. (1986). On judging quality by price: Price dependent expectations, not price dependent preferences. *Southern Economic Journal, 52*(3), 665–672.

Romantic drama in China soap opera only for mobile phones. (2005, June 28). *Guardian Newspapers Limited.* Retrieved from http://www.buzzle.com/editorials/6-28-2005-72274.asp

Rose, H., & Billinghurst, M. (1996). Zengo sayu: An immersive educational environment for learning Japanese [technical report]. Human-Interface Technology Laboratory, University of Washington.

Rosenthal, D., & Okuno, H. G. (Eds.). (1998). *Computational auditory scene analysis.* Mahwah, NJ: Lawrence Erlbaum.

Rossi, G., Schwade, D., & Guimaraes, M. R. (2001). Designing personalized Web applications. *ACM Proceedings of the 10th International Conference on World Wide Web* (pp. 275-284).

Ruanaidh, J.J.K.Ó., & Pun, T. (1997). Rotation, scale and translation invariant digital watermarking. *Proc. IEEE Int. Conf. Image Processing (ICIP'97), 1,* 536–539.

Ruanaidh, J.J.K.Ó, & Pun, T. (1998). Rotation, scale and translation invariant digital watermarking. *Signal Processing, 66*(3), 303–318.

Ruanaidh, J.J.K.Ó, Dowling, W.J., & Boland, F.M. (1996). Phase watermarking of digital images. *Proc. Int. Conf. Image Processing (ICIP'96), 3,* 239–242.

Rubin, A. M. (1981). An examination of television viewing motivations. *Communication Research, 9,* 141-165.

Ruiz, M.P., & García, E. (2002). Adaptive multimedia applications to improve user-perceived QoS in multihop wireless ad hoc networks. *Proceedings of the IEEE International Conference on Wireless LANs and Home Networks*, Atlanta, Georgia, 673–684.

Safabakhsh, R., Zaboli, S., & Tabibiazar, A. (2004). Digital watermarking on still images using wavelet transform. *Proceedings of the International IEEE Conference on Information Technology: Coding and Computing*, Las Vegas, Nevada.

Safranek, R.J., Kalmanek, C., & Garg, R. (1995). Methods for matching compressed video to ATM networks. *Proceedings of the International Conference on Image*, Washington, DC.

Said, A. (1996). A new fast and efficient image codec based on set partitioning in hierarchical trees. *IEEE Transactions on Circuits and Systems for Video Technology, 6,* 243–250.

Said, A. (2005). Measuring the strength of partial encryption schemes. *Proceedings of the IEEE International Conference on Image Processing (ICIP 2005), 2,* 1126–1129.

Salkintzis, K.A. (2004). Interworking techniques and architectures for WLAN/3G integration toward 4G mobile data networks. *IEEE Wireless Commun.*, 50–61.

Sambe, Y., Watanabe, S., Yu, D., Nakamura, T., & Wakamiya, N. (2005). High-speed distributed video transcoding for multiple rates and formats. *IEICE Transactions on Information and Systems, E88-D*(8).

Sayood, K. (2000). *Introduction to data compression* (2nd Ed.). San Francisco: Morgan Kaufmann.

Scheirer, E. D. (1999). Structured audio and effects processing in the MPEG-4 multimedia standard. *Multimedia Systems, 7*(1), 11-22.

Scherbius, A. (1928). Ciphering machine, U.S. Patent #1,657,411.

Schneier, B. (1993). Data guardians. *MacWorld, 10*(2), 145–151.

Schneier, B. (1994). *Protect your Macintosh*. Peachpit Press.

Schneier, B. (1995). *Applied cryptography* (2nd ed.). John Wiley and Sons.

Schneier, B. (1996). *Applied cryptography* (2nd edition). John Wiley & Sons.

Schoenherr, S. (2005). *Recording technology history*. Retrieved July 6, 2005, from http://history.acusd.edu/gen/recording/notes.html

Schulzrinne, H., Casner, S., Frederick, R., & Jacobson, V. (2003). RTP: A transport protocol for real time applications. *IETF Request for Comments (RFC) 3550*.

Schulzrinne, H., Rao, A., & Lanphier, R. (1998). Real time streaming protocol. *IETF Request for Comments (RFC) 2326*.

Schwarz, H., Marpe, D., & Wiegand, T. (2004). SNR-scalable extension of H.264/AVC. *Proceedings of the IEEE International Conference on Image Processing, ICIP '04, 5*, 3113–3116.

Schwarz, H., Marpe, D., & Wiegand, T. (2007), Overview of the scalable video coding extension of the H.264 / AVC standard. *IEEE Transactions on Circuits and Systems for Video Technology, 17*(9), 1103–1120.

Scopigno, R.M., & Belfiore, S. (2004). Image decomposition for selective encryption and flexible network services. IEEE Globecom 2004, Dallas.

Sebe, F., Domingo-Ferrer, J., & Herrera, J. (2000). *Spatial domain image watermarking robust against compression, filtering, cropping, and scaling*. Paper presented at the 3rd International Workshop on Information Security, Wollongong, Australia.

Selier, C., & Chuberre, N. (2005). Satellite digital multimedia broadcasting (SDMB) system presentation. In *Proceedings of 14th IST Mobile & Wireless Communications Summit*.

Sen, J.R.S., & Towsley, D. (1999). Proxy prefix caching for multimedia streams. *IEEE Transaction on Multimedia*, 1310–1318).

Sen, S., Rexford, J., & Towsley, D. (1999). Proxy prefix caching for multimedia streams. *Proceedings of the Eighteenth Annual Joint Conference of the IEEE Computer and Communications Societies, 3*(3), 310–1319.

Serco. (2006). *Usability guidelines for Mobile TV design*. Retrieved from http://www.serco.com/Images/Mobile%20TV%20guidelines_tcm3-13804.pdf

Serra, X. (1997). Musical sound modeling with sinusoids plus noise. In C. Roads, S. Pope, A. Picialli, & G. De Poli (Eds.), *Musical signal processing* (pp. 91-122). Lisse, Netherlands: Swets & Zeitlinger.

Servetti, A., & Martin, J.C. (2002a). Perception-based partial encryption of compressed speech. *IEEE Transactions on Speech and Audio Processing, 10*(8), 637–643.

Servetti, A., & Martin, J.C. (2002b). Perception-based selective encryption of G. 729 speech. *Proceedings of the IEEE ICASSP*. Orlando, Florida, 1, 621–624.

Servetti, A., Testa, C., Carlos, J., & Martin, D. (2003). *Frequency-selective partial encryption of compressed audio*. Paper presented at the International Conference on Audio, Speech and Signal Processing, Hong Kong.

Servetto, S.D., Ramchandran, K., Vaishampayan, V.A., & Nahrstedt, K. (2000). Multiple description wavelet based image coding. *IEEE Transactions on Image Processing, 9*(5), 813–826.

Seyler, A. J., & Budrikis, Z. L. (1964). Detail perception after scene changes in television image presentations. *IEEE Transactions on Information Theory, 11,* 31-42.

Shanableh, T., & Ghanabari, M. (2005). Multilayer transcoding with format portability for multicasting single-layered video. *IEEE Transactions on Multimedia, 7*(1), 1–15.

Shanableh, T., & Ghanbari, M. (2000). Heterogeneous video transcoding to lower spatio-temporal resolutions and different encoding formats. *IEEE Transactions on Multimedia, 2*(2), 101–110.

Shapiro, J.M. (1992). Embedded image coding using zerotrees of wavelet coefficients. *IEEE Transactions on Signal Processing, 41*, 657–660.

Shapiro, L.G., & Stockman, G.C. (2001). *Computer vision.* Upper Saddle River, NJ: Prentice Hall.

Shen, B. (2006). Optimal requantization-based rate adaptation for H.264. *Proceedings of the IEEE ICME*, 317–320.

Shen, B., Lee, S-J., & Basu, S. (2000). Caching strategies in transcoding-enabled proxy systems for streaming media distribution networks. *IEEE Transaction on Multimedia, 6*(2), 375–386.

Sheppard, N.P., Safavi-Naini, R., & Ogunbona, P. (2001). On multiple watermarking. *Proc. of ACM Multimedia 2001.*

Sherman, W.R., & Craig, A.B. (2003). *Understanding virtual reality.* San Francisco, CA: Morgan Kauffman.

Shi, C., & Bhargava, B. (1998a). A fast MPEG video encryption algorithm. *Proceedings of the 6th ACM International Multimedia Conference*, Bristol, UK, 81–88.

Shi, C., & Bhargava, B. (1998b). An efficient MPEG video encryption algorithm. *Proceedings of the 6th ACM International Multimedia Conference.* Bristol, UK, 381–386.

Shi, J., & Malik, J. (2000). Normalized cuts and image segmentation. *IEEE Transactions on Pattern Analysis and Machine Intelligence, 22*(8), 888–905.

Shirmohammadi, S., El Saddik, A., Georganas, N.D., & Steinmetz, R. (2001). Web-based multimedia tools for sharing educational resources. *J. Educ. Resour. Comput, 1*(1es), 9.

Shu, H., & Chau, L. (2006). The realization of arbitrary downsizing video transcoding. *IEEE Transactions on Circuits and Systems for Video Technology, 16*(4).

Shu, H., & Chau, L.-P. (2004). Frame-skipping transcoding with motion change consideration. *Proceedings of the IEEE International Symposium Circuits Systems, ISCAS '04, 3*, 773–776.

Shu, H., & Chau, L.-P. (2006). The realization of arbitrary downsizing video transcoding. *IEEE Transactions on Circuit and Systems for Video Technology, 16*(4), 540–546.

Siller, M. (2006). *An agent-based platform to map quality of service to experience in active and conventional networks* [doctoral thesis]. Colchester, England: University of Essex.

Siller, M., & Woods, J.C. (2003). QoS arbitration for improving the QoE in multimedia transmission. *Proceedings of IEE Visual Information Engineering*, 238–241.

Sinkov, A. (1966). *Elementary cryptanalysis.* Mathematical Association of America.

Sivasubramanian, S., Szymaniak, M., Pierre, G., & Steen, M. (2004). Replication for Web hosting systems. *ACM Computing Surveys, 36*(3), 291–334.

Sling Media. (2006). *SlingPlayer mobile.* Retrieved from http://www.slingmedia.com

Smeulders, A. W. M., Worring, M., Santini, S., Gupta, A., & Jain, R. (2000). Content-based image retrieval at the end of the early years. *IEEE Transactions on Pattern Analysis and Machine Intelligence, 22*(12), 1349–1380.

Smith, J. O. (1991). Viewpoints on the history of digital synthesis. In *Proceedings of the International Computer Music Conference* (pp. 1-10). Montreal, Canada.

Snoek, C. G. M., & Worring, M. (2005). Multimedia event based video indexing using time intervals. *IEEE Transactions on Multimedia, 7*(4), 638-647.

Snoek, C. G. M., & Worring, M. (2005). Multimodal video indexing: A review of the state-of-the-art. *Multimedia Tools and Applications, 25*(1), 5–35.

Sobrinho, J.L., & Krishnakumar, A.S. (1996). Real-time traffic over the IEEE 802.11 medium access control layer. *Bell Labs Technical Journal, 172–187.*

Sodergard, C. (2003). Mobile television—Technology and user experiences report on the mobile-TV project. VTT Information Technology.

Södergård, C. (2003). *Mobile television—Technology and user experiences. Report on the Mobile-TV project* (Rep. No. P506). VTT Information Technology.

Song, S., Won, Y., & Song, I. (2004). Empirical study of user perception behavior for mobile streaming. In *Proceedings of the tenth ACM international conference on Multimedia* (pp. 327-330). New York: ACM Press.

Souvannavong, F., Merialdo, B., & Huet, B. (2003). Latent semantic indexing for video content modeling and analysis. In *Proceedings of the TREC Video Retrieval Evaluation Workshop*, Gaithersburg, MD.

Sridharan, S., Dawson, E., & Goldburg, B. (1991). Fast Fourier transform based speech encryption system. *IEE Proceedings of Communications, Speech and Vision, 138*(3), 215–223.

Srikanth, M., Varner, J., Bowden, M., & Moldovan, D. (2005). Exploiting ontologies for automatic image annotation. In *Proceedings of the ACM SIGIR Conference on Research and Development in Information Retrieval*, Salvador, Brazil.

Stamou, G., & Kollias, S. (Ed.). (2005). *Multimedia content and the semantic Web, methods, standards, and tools.* John Wiley & Sons, Ltd.

Steinmetz, R. (1996). Human perception of jitter and media synchronization. *IEEE Journal on Selected Areas in Communications, 14,* 61-72.

Steinmetz, R., & Nahhrsteddt, K. (1995). *Multimedi: Computing, communications & applications.* Upper Saddle River, NJ: Prentice Hall PTR.

Stevens, A. (1990). Hacks, spooks, and data encryption. *Dr. Dobb's Journal, 15*(9), 127–134, 147–149.

Stockbridge, L. (2006). Mobile TV: Experience of the UK Vodafone and Sky service. Retrieved from http://www. serco.com/Images/EuroITV%20mobile%20TV%20pre sentation_tcm3-13849.pdf

Strang, G., & Nguyen, T. (1996). *Wavelets and filter banks.* Wellesley, MA: Wellesley-Cambridge Press.

Struzinski, W. A. (1984). A new normalization algorithm for detection systems. *Journal of the Acoustical Society of America, Supplement, 75*(S1), S43.

Struzinski, W. A., & Lowe, E. D. (1984). A performance comparison of four noise background normalization schemes proposed for signal detection systems. *Journal of the Acoustical Society of America, 76*(6), 1738-1742.

Su, G-M., & Wu, M. (2005). Efficient bandwidth resource allocation for low-delay multi-user video streaming. *IEEE Transaction for Circuits and Systems for Video Technology, 15*(9), 1124–1137.

Sun, H., Kwok, W., & Zdepski, J.W. (1996). Architecture for MPEG compressed bitstream scaling. *IEEE Trans. Circuits Syst. Video Technol., 6,* 191–199.

Sun, H., Kwok, W., & Zdepski, J.W. (1996). Architectures for MPEG compressed bitstream scaling. *IEEE Transactions on Circuits and Systems for Video Technology, 6*(2), 191–199.

Sun, H., Vetro, A., Bao, J., & Poon, T. (1997). A new approach for memory-efficient ATV decoding. *IEEE Trans. Consumer Electron., 43,* 517–525.

Sun, W., & Zdepski, J. (1996). Architecture for MPEG compressed bitstream scaling. *IEEE Transactions on Circuit Systems Video Technology, 6*(2).

Survey of Content Delivery Networks/. http://cgi.di.uoa. gr/~grad0377/cdnsurvey.pdf

Tan, Y-P., Saur, D. D., Kulkarni, S. R., & Ramadge, P. J. (2000). Rapid estimation of camera motion from compressed video with application to video annotation. *IEEE Transactions on Circuits and Systems for Video Technology, 10*(1), 133–146.

Tang, L. (1996). Methods for encrypting and decrypting MPEG video data efficiently. *Proceedings of the Fourth ACM International Multimedia Conference (ACM Multimedia'96).* Boston, Massachusetts, 219–230.

Tansley, R. (2000). *The multimedia thesaurus: Adding a semantic layer to multimedia information* [doctoral thesis]. University of Southampton, UK.

Taubman, D. (2000). High performance scalable image compression with EBCOT. *IEEE Transactions on Image Processing, 9*, 1158–1170.

Taubman, D., Ordentlich, E., Weinberger, M., & Seroussi, G. (2001). Embedded block coding in JPEG2000. Hewlett-Packard Company Publication.

Taubman, D.S., & Marcellin, M.W. (2002). *JPEG2000: Image compression fundamentals, standards and practices*. Norwell, MA: Kluwer Academic Publishers.

Taubman, D.S., & Marcellin, M.W. (2002). JPEG2000: *Image compression fundamentals, standards, and practice*. Norwell, MA: Kluwer Academics Publisher.

Tay, P., & Havlicek, J. (2002). Image watermarking using wavelets. *Proceedings of the IEEE Midwest Symposium on Circuits and Systems*, Tulsa, Oklahoma.

Taylor, A., & Harper, R. (2002). Switching on to switch off: An analysis of routine TV watching habits and their implications for electronic programme guide design. *usableiTV, 1*, 7-13.

Teolis, A., & Benedetto, J. J. (1994). Noise suppression using a wavelet model. In *Proceedings of the IEEE International Conference of Acoustics, Speech, and Signal Processing* (vol. 1, pp. 17-20).

Teyeb, O., Sørensen, T,B., Mogensen, P., & Wigard, J. (2006). Evaluation of packet service performance in UMTS and heterogeneous networks. *Proceedings of the ACM Workshop on Quality of Service & Security for Wireless and Mobile Networks*, 95–102.

Thang, T.C., Jung, Y.J., & Ro, Y.M. (2005a). Modality conversion for QoS management in universal multimedia access. *IEE Proc. Vision, Image & Signal Processing, 152*(3), 374–384.

Thang, T.C., Jung, Y.J., & Ro, Y.M. (2005b). Effective adaptation of multimedia documents with modality conversion. *Signal Processing: Image Communication, 20*(5), 413–434.

Thang, T.C., Jung, Y.J., & Ro, Y.M. (2005c). Semantic quality for content-aware video adaptation. *Proceedings of the IEEE MMSP2005*, Shanghai, China.

Thang, T.C., Jung, Y.J., Lee, J.W., & Ro, Y.M. (2004). Modality conversion for universal multimedia services. *Proceedings of the International Workshop on Image Analysis for Multimedia Interactive Services*, Lisbon, Portugal.

Thang, T.C., Kim, Y.S., Kim, C.S., & Ro, Y.M. (2006). Quality models for audiovisual streaming. *Proceedings of the SPIE Electronic Imaging*, San Jose, California.

Thang, T.C., Yang, S., Ro, Y.M., & Wong, K.E. (2007). Media accessibility for low vision users in the MPEG-21 multimedia framework. *IEICE Trans. Information and Systems. E90-D*(8), 1271–1278.

Thompson, R. (1998). *Grammar of the shot*. Elsevier Focal Press.

Tolonen, T. (2000). *Object-based sound source modeling*. Unpublished doctoral dissertation, Helsinki University of Technology, Espoo, Finland. Retrieved June 30, 2006 from http://lib.hut.fi/Diss/2000/isbn9512251965/

Top of the Web (2003). Survey on quality and usage of public e-services. Top of the Web. Retrieved from http://www.idt.unisg.ch/org/idt/ceegov.nsf/0/1ae4025175a16a90c1256df6002a0fef/$FILE/Final_report_2003_quality_and_usage.pdf

Tosun, A.S., & Feng, W.-C. (2000). Efficient multilayer coding and encryption of MPEG video streams. *Proceedings of the IEEE International Conference on Multimedia and Expo., 1*, 119–122.

Tosun, A.S., & Feng, W.C. (2001). Lightweight security mechanisms for wireless video transmission. *Proceedings of the International Conference on Information Technology: Coding and Computing*, Las Vegas, Nevada, 157–161.

Trappe, W., Wu, M., Wang, J., & Liu, K.J.R. (2003). Anticollusion fingerprinting for multimedia. *IEEE Trans. on Signal Processing, 51*(4), 1069–1087.

TRECVID. (2004). *TREC video retrieval evaluation.* Retrieved November 2005, from http://www-nlpir.nist. gov/projects/trecvid/

TS 26.234 3rd Generation Partnership Project, Technical Specification Group Services and System Aspects. (2005).Transparent end-to-end packet-switched streaming service (PSS); Protocol and codecs, ver. 5.7.0. http:// www.3gpp.org/

TS 26.235 3rd Generation Partnership Project, Technical Specification Group Services and System Aspects. (2005). Packet switched conversational multimedia applications; Default codecs (Release 6), ver. 6.4.0. http://www.3gpp.org/

Tse, T., Vegh, S., Marchionini, G., & Shneiderman, B. (1999). An exploratory study of video browsing user interface designs and research methodologies: Effectiveness in information seeking tasks. In *Proceedings of the 62nd ASIS Annual Meeting* (pp. 681-692).

Tseng, B. L., Lin, C-Y., Naphade, M., Natsev, A., & Smith, J. (2003). Normalised classifier fusion for semantic visual concept detection. In *Proceedings of the IEEE International Conference on Image Processing*, Barcelona, Spain.

Tsoukalas, D., Mourjopoulos, J., & Kokkinakis, G. (1997). Perceptual filters for audio signal enhancement. *Journal of the Audio Engineering Society, 45*(1/2), 22-36.

Tsoukalas, D., Paraskevas, M., & Mourjopoulos, J. (1993). Speech enhancement using psychoacoustic criteria. In *Proceedings of the IEEE International Conference of Acoustics, Speech, and Signal Processing* (vol. 2, pp. 359-362).

Tudor, P.N. (1995). MPEG-2 video compression. *Electronics and Communication Engineering Journal, 7*(6), 257–264.

Tudor, P.N., & Werner, O.H. (1997). Real-time transcoding of MPEG-2 video bit streams. *Proceedings of the International Broadcasting Convention*, Amsterdam, The Netherlands, 286–301.

Tzanetakis, G., & Cook, P. (2002). Musical genre classification of audio signals. *IEEE Transactions on Speech and Audio Processing, 10*(5), 293–302.

Vaidya, N.H., Bahl, P., & Gupa, S. (2000). Distributed fair scheduling in a wireless LAN. *Proceedings of the Sixth Annual International Conference on Mobile Computing and Networking (Mobicom 2000)*, Boston, Massachusetts, 167–178.

Vailaya, A., Figueiredo, M., Jain, A. K., & Zhang, H. J. (2001). Image classification for content-based indexing. *IEEE Transactions on Image Processing, 10*(1), 117–130.

Vailaya, A., Figueiredo, M., Jain, A., & Zhang, H. (1999). A Bayesian framework for semantic classification of outdoor vacation images. In *Proceedings of the SPIE: Storage and Retrieval for Image and Video Databases VII*, San Jose, CA.

Vaishampayan, V.A. (1993). Design of multiple description scalar quantizers. *IEEE Transactions on Information Theory, 39*(3), 821–834.

Välimäki, V., Pakarinen, J., Erkut, C., & Karjalainen, M. (2006). Discrete-time modeling of musical instruments. *Reports on Progress in Physics, 69*(1), 1-78.

van Beek, P., Smith, J.R., Ebrahimi, T., Suzuki, T., & Askelof, J. (2003). Metadata-driven multimedia access. *IEEE Signal Processing Magazine, 20*(2), 40–52.

Van der Schaar, M., & Radha, H. (2001a). Unequal packet loss resilience for fine-granular-scalability video. *IEEE Transactions on Multimedia, 3*(4), 381–394.

Van der Schaar, M., Boland, L.G., & Li, Q. (2001b). Novel applications of fine-granular-scalability: Internet & wireless video, scalable storage, personalized TV, universal media coding. *SCI2001/ISAS2001.*

Vasconcelos, N., & Lippman, A. (1998). A Bayesian framework for semantic content characterization. In *Proceedings of the IEEE Conference on Computer Vision and Pattern Recognition*, Santa Barbara, CA.

Vasconcelos, N., & Lippman, A. (2000). A probabilistic architecture for content-based image retrieval. In

*Proceedings of the IEEE Computer Vision and Pattern Recognition, Hilton Head*, SC.

Vaseghi, S. V. (1988). *Algorithms for restoration of archived gramophone recordings*. Unpublished doctoral dissertation, Engineering Department, Cambridge University, Cambridge, England.

Vaseghi, S. V. (2006). *Advanced digital signal processing and noise reduction* (3rd ed.). West Sussex, England: John Wiley.

Vaseghi, S. V., & Frayling-Cork, R. (1992). Restoration of old gramophone recordings. *Journal of the Audio Engineering Society, 40*(10), 791-801.

Vaseghi, S. V., & Rayner, P. J. W. (1990). Detection and suppression of impulsive noise in speech communication systems. *IEEE Proceedings, 137*(1), 38-46.

Vaseghi, S. V., & Rayner, P. J.W. (1988). A new application of adaptive filters for restoration of archived gramophone recordings. In *Proceedings of the IEEE International Conference of Acoustics, Speech, and Signal Processing* (vol. 5, pp. 2548-2551). New York: IEEE.

Vatakis, A., & Spence, C. (in press). Evaluating the influence of frame rate on the temporal aspects of audiovisual speech perception. *Neuroscience Letters*.

Vaughan, T. (2004). *Multimedia: Making it work* (6th Ed.). McGraw Hill.

Veldhuis, R. (1990). *Restoration of lost samples in digital signals*. Upper Saddle River, NJ: Prentice-Hall.

Vercoe, B. L., Gardner, W. G., & Scheirer, E. D. (1998). Structured audio: Creation, transmission, and rendering of parametric sound representations. *Proc. IEEE, 86*(5), 922-940.

Veres, A., Campbell, A.T., Barry, M., & Sun, L.H. (2001). Supporting service differentiation in wireless packet networks using distributed control. *IEEE Journal of Selected Areas in Communications (JSAC), Special Issue on Mobility and Resource Management in Next-Generation Wireless Systems*, 2094–2104.

Vetro, A. (2004). MPEG-21 digital item adaptation: Enabling universal multimedia access. *IEEE Multimedia, 11*(1), 84–87.

Vetro, A., Christopoulos, C., & Sun, H. (2003). Video transcoding architectures and techniques: An overview. *IEEE Signal Processing Magazine, 20*(2), 18–29.

Vetro, A., Sun, H., & Wang, Y. (2001). Object-based transcoding for adaptable video content delivery. *IEEE Transaction on Circuits and Systems for Video Technology, 11*(3).

Vetter, R., Ward, C., & Shapiro, S. (1995). Using color and text in multimedia projections. *IEEE Multimedia, 2*(4), 46–54.

Vetterli, M., & Kovačević, J. (1995). *Wavelets and subband coding*. Prentice Hall.

Vidakovic, B. (1998). Non-linear wavelet shrinkage with Bayes rules and Bayes factors. *Journal of the American Statistical Association, 93*(441), 173-179.

Video Technology Magazine. Retrieved September 28, 2007, from http://www.videotechnology.com/0904/formats.html

Vince, J. (2004). Introduction to virtual reality. London, UK: Springer.

Voelcker, R., Hands, D., Davis, A., Bourret, A., & Bayart, D. (2003). Video quality measurement—Predicting subjective quality using perceptual models. *Journal of the Communications Network, 1*(3).

Voldhaug, J. E., Johansen, S., & Perkis, A. (2005). Automatic football video highlights extraction. In *Proceedings of NORSIG-05*.

Volokh, E. (2000). Personalization and privacy. *The Communications of the Association for Computing Machinery, 43*(8), 84.

Voloshynovskiy, S., Herrigel, A., Baumgaertner, N., & Pun, T. (1999). A stochastic approach to content adaptive digital image watermarking. *Proc. of Int. Workshop on Information Hiding*.

Voloshynovskiy, S., Pereira, S., & Pun, T. (2001). Attacks on digital watermarks: Classification, estimation-based attacks, and benchmarks. *Communications Magazine, 39*(8), 118–126.

VQEG. (2007). VQEG multimedia test plan. Retrieved from http://www.vqeg.org

Wagner, D. (2005). Enabling mobile learning. *Educause Review, 40*(3), 41–52.

Wang, C., Doherty, J., & Van Dyke, R. (2002). A wavelet-based watermarking algorithm for ownership verification of digital images. *IEEE Transactions on Image Processing, 11*(2), 77–78.

Wang, D., Speranza, F., Vincent, A., Martin, T., & Blanchfield, P. (2003). Towards optimal rate control: A study of the impact of spatial resolution, frame rate and quantization on subjective quality and bitrate. In T. Ebrahimi & T. Sikora (Eds.), *Visual communications and image processing* (pp. 198-209).

Wang, H.-J.M., Su, P.-C., & Kuo, C.-C.J. (1998). Wavelet-based digital image watermarking. *Optics Express, 3*(12), 491–496.

Wang, J., & Lin, J. (2002). Are personalization systems really personal? Effects of conformity in reducing information overload. *Proceedings of the 36th Hawaii International Conference on Systems Sciences (HICSS'03).* 0-7695-1874-5/03.

Wang, Y., Liu, Z., & Huang, J-C. (2000). Multimedia content analysis using both audio and visual clues. *IEEE Signal Processing, 17*(6), 12–36.

Wang, Y., Ostermann, J., & Zhang, Y.Q. (2002). *Video processing and communication.* Upper Saddle River, NJ: Prentice Hall.

Wang, Y., Reibman, A.R., & Lin, S. (2005). Multiple description coding for video delivery. *Proceedings of the IEEE, 93*(1), 57–70.

Warabino, T., Ota, S., Morikawa, D., & Ohashi, M. (2000). Video transcoding proxy for 3G wireless mobile Internet access. *IEEE Communications Magazine*, 66–71.

Watson, A. & Sasse, M.A. (1998). Measuring perceived quality of speech and video in multimedia conferencing applications. *Proceedings of the ACM Multimedia98*, Bristol, UK, 55–60.

Watson, A.B., Hu, J., & McGowan III,,J.F. (2001). DVQ: A digital video quality metric based on human vision. *Journal of Electronic Imaging, 10*(1), 20–29.

Webster, A.A., Jones, C.T., & Pinson, M.H. (1993). An objective video quality assessments system based on human perception. *Proceedings of the SPIE, 1913*, 15–26.

Wee, S.J., & Apostolopoulos, J.G. (2001). Secure scalable video streaming for wireless networks. *Proceedings of the IEEE International Conference on Acoustics, Speech, and Signal Processing.* Salt Lake City, Utah, 4, 2049–2052.

Wee, S.J., & Apostolopoulos, J.G. (2003). Secure scalable streaming and secure transcoding with JPEG-2000. *IEEE Int. Image Processing, 1*, I-205–208.

Wee, S.J., & Apostolopoulus, J. (2001). Secure scalable streaming enabling transcoding without decryption. *Proceedings of the International Conference on Image Processing, ICIP '01, 1*, 437–440.

Weidmann, C., & Nemethova, O. (2006). Improved sequential decoding of H.264 video with VLC resynchronization. *Proceedings of the IST Mobile Summit 2006*, Myconos, Greece.

Wen, J.T., Severa, M., Zeng, W.J., Luttrell, M., & Jin, W. (2002). A format-compliant configurable encryption framework for access control of video. *IEEE Transactions on Circuits and Systems for Video Technology, 12*(6), 545–557.

Wenger, S. (2003). H.264/AVC over IP. *IEEE Transactions on Circuits and Systems for Video Technology, 13*(7), 645–656.

Wenger, S., Wang, Y.-K., & Hannuksela, M.M. (2006). RTP payload format for H.264/SVC scalable video coding. *Journal of Zhejiang University of Science A, 7*(5), 657–667.

Werner, O. (1999). Requantization for transcoding of MPEG-2 intraframes. *IEEE Transactions on Image Processing, 8*(2), 179–191.

Westerink, J. H., & Roufs, J. A. (1989). Subjective image quality as a function of viewing distance, resolution, and picture size. *SMPTE Journal.*

Westerveld, T., & de Vries, A. P. (2003). Experimental result analysis for a generative probabilistic image retrieval model. In *Proceedings of the ACM SIGIR Conference on Research and Development in Information Retrieval,* Toronto, Canada.

Westerveld, T., de Vries, A. P., Ianeva, T., Boldareva, L., & Hiemstra, D. (2003). Combining information sources for video retrieval. In *Proceedings of the TREC Video Retrieval Evaluation Workshop,* Gaithersburg, MD.

Whitmal, N. A., Rutledge, J. C., & Cohen, J. (1995). Wavelet-based noise reduction. In *Proceedings of the IEEE International Conference of Acoustics, Speech, and Signal Processing* (vol. 5, pp. 3003-3006). Detroit, MI.

Wiegand, T., Sullivan, G.J., Bjontegaard, G., & Luthra, A. (2003). Overview of the H.264/AVC video coding standard. *IEEE Transactions on Circuits and Systems for Video Technology, 13*(7), 560–576.

Williams, E.A. (1959). *An invitation to cryptograms.* New York: Simon and Schuster.

Wilson, P. (1965). Record contamination: Causes and cure. *J. of the Audio Eng. Society, 13*(2), 166-176.

Winkler, S. (2005). *Digital video quality: Vision models and metrics.* John Wiley & Sons, Ltd.

Winkler, S., & Campos, R. (2003). Video quality evaluation for Internet streaming applications. *Proceedings of the SPIE: Human Vision and Electronic Imaging, 5007,* 104–115.

Winkler, S., & Dufaux, F. (2003). Video quality evaluation for mobile applications. *Proceedings of the SPIE: Visual Communications and Image Processing, 5150,* 593–603.

Winkler, S., & Faller, C. (2005). Maximizing audiovisual quality at low bitrates. In *Proceedings of Workshop on Video Processing and Quality Metrics.*

Winkler, S., & Faller, C. (2005). Maximizing audiovisual quality at low bitrates. *Proceedings of the Workshop on Video Processing and Quality Metrics.*

Witsenhausen, H.S., & Wyner, A.D. (1981). Source coding for multiple descriptions II: A binary source. *Bell Systems Technologies Journal, 60*(10), 2281–2292.

Wolf, J.K., Wyner, A.D., & Ziv, J. (1980). Source coding for multiple descriptions. *Bell Systems Technologies Journal, 59*(8), 1417–1426.

Wolf, S., & Pinson, M.H. (2005). Low bandwidth reduced reference video quality monitoring system. *Proceedings of the Workshop on Video Processing and Quality Metrics for Consumer Electronics.*

Wolfe, P. J., & Godsill, S. J. (2000). Towards a perceptually optimal spectral amplitude estimator for audio signal enhancement. In *Proceedings of the IEEE International Conference of Acoustics, Speech, and Signal Processing* (vol. 2, pp. 821-824). Istanbul.

Wolfe, P. J., & Godsill, S. J. (2001a). Perceptually motivated approaches to music restoration. *Journal of New Music Research—Special Issue: Music and Mathematics, 30*(1), 83-92.

Wolfe, P. J., & Godsill, S. J. (2001b). Simple alternatives to the Ephraim and Malah suppression rule for speech enhancement. In *Proceedings of the 11th IEEE Signal Processing Workshop on Statistical Signal Processing* (pp. 496-499). Singapore.

Wolfe, P. J., & Godsill, S. J. (2003). Efficient alternatives to the Ephraim and Malah suppression rule for audio signal enhancement. *EURASIP Journal on Applied Signal Processing—Special Issue on Digital Audio for Multimedia Communications, 2003*(10), 1043-1051.

Wolfgang, R., Podilchuk, C., & Delp, E. (1999). Perceptual watermarks for digital images and video. *Proceedings of the IEEE, 87*(7), 1108–1126.

Wu, C., & Hsieh, W. (2000). Digital watermarking using zerotree of DCT. *IEEE Transactions on Consumer Electronics, 46*(1), 87–94.

Wu, C., & Kuo, C.C. (2000). Fast encryption methods for audiovisual data confidentiality. *Proceedings of the SPIE International Symposia on Information Technologies 2000*, Boston, Massachusetts, 4209, 284–295.

Wu, C., & Kuo, C.C. (2001). Efficient multimedia encryption via entropy codec design. *Proceedings of the SPIE International Symposium on Electronic Imaging 2001*, San Jose, California, 4314, 128–138.

Wu, C.-H., & Chen, J.-H. (1997). Speech activated telephony email reader (SATER) based on speaker verification and text-to-speech conversion. *IEEE Trans. Consumer Electronics, 43*, 707–716.

Wu, D., Hou, Y.-T., Zhu, W., Zhang, Y.-Q., & Peha, J.-M. (2001). Streaming approach over Internet—Approaches and directions. *IEEE Transaction on Circuits and Systems for Video Technology, 11*(3), 282–300.

Wu, S.-L., Fan-Jiang, S., & Chou, Z.-T. (2006). An efficient quality-of-service MAC protocol for infrastructure WLANs. *Journal of Network and Computer Applications*, 235–261.

Xia, X., Boncelet, C., & Arce, G. (1997). A multiresolution watermark for digital images. *Proc. Int. Conf. Image Processing (ICIP'97), 1*, 548–551.

Xie, L., & Arce, G.R. (1998). Joint wavelet compression and authentication watermarking. *Proc. Int. Conf. Image Processing (ICIP'98)*.

Xin, J., Lin, C., & Sun, M. (2005). Digital video transcoding. *Proceedings of the IEEE, 93*(1).

Xin, J., Lin, C-W., & Sun, M.-T. (2005). Digital video transcoding. *Proceedings of the IEEE, 93*(1), 84–97.

Xu, J., Li, B., & Lee, D.L. (2002). Placement problem for transparent data replication proxy services. *IEEE Journal on Selected Areas in Communications, 20*(7), 1383–1398.

Yang, F., Wan, S., Chang, Y., & Wu, H.R. (2005). A novel objective no-reference metric for digital video quality assessment. *IEEE Signal Processing Letters, 12*(10), 685–688.

Yavlinsky, A., Schofield, E., & Rüger, S. (2005). Automated image annotation using global features and robust nonparametric density estimation. In *Proceedings of the International Conference on Image and Video Retrieval*, Singapore.

Yee, Y.C., Choong, K.N., Low, L.Y.A., Tan, S.W., & Chien, S.F. (2007). A conservative approach to adaptive call admission control for QoS provisioning in multimedia wireless networks. *Computer Communications*, 249–260.

Yeh, J.-Y., & Chen, C. (2002). Support of multimedia services with the IEEE 802.11 MAC protocol. *Proceedings of the IEEE ICC*, New York, 600–604.

Youn, J., & Sun M.-T. (1998). Motion estimation for high performance transcoding. *Proceedings of the IEEE International Conference on Consumer Electronics*, Los Angeles, California.

Youn, J., & Sun, M. (2000). Video transcoding with H.263 bit-streams. *Journal of Visual Communication and Image Representation, 11*(4).

Youn, J., & Sun, M.-T. (2000). Video transcoding with H.263 bit-streams. *Journal of Visual Communication and Image Representation, 11*.

Youn, J., Sun, M.-T., & Lin, C.-W. (1999). Motion vector refinement for high-performance transcoding. *IEEE Transactions on Multimedia, 1*(1), 30–41.

Yu, D., & Sattar, F. (2003). A new blind image watermarking technique based on independent component analysis. *Springer-Verlag Lecture Notes in Computer Science, 2613*, 51–63.

Yu, D., Sattar, F., & Ma, K.-K. (2002). Watermark detection and extraction using independent component analysis method. *EURASIP Journal on Applied Signal Processing—Special Issue on Nonlinear Signal and Image Processing (Part II)*.

Yu, H.H., & Yu, X.L. (2003). Progressive and scalable encryption for multimedia content access control.

*Proceedings of the IEEE International Conference on Communications, 1,* 547–551.

Yuan, C., Zhu, B., Wang, Y., Li, S., & Zhong, Y. (2003). Efficient and fully scalable encryption for MPEG-4 FGS. *Proceedings of the IEEE International Symposium on Circuits and Systems.*

Yuliang, L., & Dean, G. (1999). Cognitive styles and distance education. *Online Journal of Distance Learning Administration, 2*(3), Article 005.

Zapater, M.N., & Bressan,G. (2007). A proposed approach for quality of experience assurance for IPTV. *Proceedings of the IEEE Digital Society.*

Zhang, X., & Li, K. (2005). Comments on "An SVD-based watermarking scheme for protecting rightful ownership." *IEEE Transactions on Multimedia, 7*(2), 593–594.

Zhu, B., Yuan, C., Wang, Y., & Li, S. (2005). Scalable protection for MPEG-4 fine granularity scalability. *IEEE Trans Multimedia, 7*(2), 222–233.

Zhu, R., & Yang, Y. (2006). Adaptive scheduler to improve QoS in IEEE 802.11e wireless LANs. *Proceedings of the First International Conference on Innovative Computing, Information and Control*, China, 1, 377–380.

Zillman, D. (1988). Mood management: Using entertainment to full advantage. In L. Donohew, H. E. Sypher, & E. T. Higgins (Eds.), *Communication, social cognition, and affect* (pp. 147-172). Hillsdale, NJ: Erlbaum.

Zohrab, P. (1996). Virtual language and culture reality (VLCR). *VR in the Schools, 3*(4).

Zurita, G., & Nussbaum, M. (2004). Computer supported collaborative learning using wirelessly interconnected handheld computers. *Computers in Education, 42.*

Zurita, G., & Nussbaum, M. (2004). mCSCL: Mobile computer supported collaborative learning. *Computers & Education, 42*(3), 289–314.

Zwicker, E., & Fastl, H. (1999). *Psychoacoustics: Facts and models* (2$^{nd}$ ed.). Berlin: Springer-Verlag.

# About the Contributors

**Ashraf Ahmad** obtained his PhD degree in computer science and engineering from National Chiao Tung University (NCTU) in Taiwan. He obtained his BSc degree from Princess Sumya University for technology (PSUT) in Jordan. Ahmad is currently an assistant professor in the Department of Computer Science at PSUT, Jordan. His interest areas includes multimedia semantic features extraction, analysis, multimedia retrieval, and multimedia communication. Ahmad has authored more than 40 scientific publications, including journal papers, conference papers, and book chapters. In addition, Ahmad has several US and international patents in his field of expertise. He serves on the program committees for several international conferences. He is also a reviewer and referee for several conferences and journals. His work has been published and presented at various international conferences. Ahmad was listed in *Who's Who in the World* in 2006 and *Who's Who in Asia* in 2007. In addition, he was elected as one of the 2000 Outstanding Intellectuals of the 21st Century for 2006 for his outstanding contribution in the field of video processing and communications. Ahmad was chosen as one of the recipients of the Leading Scientist award in 2006.

\* \* \*

**Florence Agboma** is a PhD candidate in the Department of Computing and Electronic Systems at the University of Essex, UK. Her research interests include quality of experience of mobile services, multimedia applications, quality of service management, and peer-to-peer streaming. Agboma received an MSc degree in computer information and networks from the University of Essex and a BSc degree in electronic communication systems from the University of Plymouth, UK. She is a student member of the IEEE and IET societies.

**Bashar Ahmad** is a PhD student in the Department of Telekooperation, Johannes Kepler University Linz. He received his MSc degree in computer science and information engineering from National Chio Tung University, Hisnchu, Taiwan, in 2004; and his BSc degree in computer science from Princess Sumaya University for Technology, Amman, Jordan, in 2002. Ahmad is currently doing research in the field of wireless LAN, QoS, mobility, and MAC-layer enhancement. He worked as a software engineer in the wireless LAN industry for three years; his duties involved embedded systems design and development, wireless technology integration, and enhancements.

**Ali Al-Haj** received a BSc degree in electrical engineering from Yarmouk University, Jordan, in 1985; an MSc degree in electronics engineering from Tottori University, Japan, in 1988; and a PhD degree in electronics engineering from Osaka University, Japan, in 1993. He then worked as a research associate at ATR Advanced Telecommunications Research Laboratories in Kyoto, Japan, until 1995. He joined Princess Sumaya University, Jordan, in October 1995, where he is now an associate professor. Al-Haj has published conference and journal papers in dataflow computing, parallel information retrieval, VLSI digital signal processing, neural networks, and digital watermarking. He is currently on sabbatical from Princess Sumaya University, Jordan, Department of Computer Engineering.

**Raul Aquino-Santos** holds a PhD from the Department of Electrical and Electronic Engineering of the University of Sheffield, England. His current research interests include wireless and sensor networks and the implementation of quality of service for online educational applications.

**Nicola Conci** received bachelor's and master's degrees in telecommunications engineering in 2002 and 2004, respectively, from the University of Trento, Italy. In 2007, he obtained a PhD from the International ICT Doctorate School at the University of Trento. Conci's scientific interests are related to image and video processing, focusing on scalable and multiple description coding. He received the Best Student Paper Award at the International Conference MOBIMEDIA 2006 (ACM, Alghero, Italy) with the paper titled *Multiple Description Video Coding Using Coefficient Ordering and Interpolation*. In 2007, he was a visiting student at the Image Processing Lab (Prof. S.K. Mitra) at the University of California Santa Barbara.

**Francesco G.B. De Natale,** MSc electronic engineering, 1990; PhD telecommunications, 1994, University of Genoa, Italy, is professor of telecommunications at the University of Trento, Italy, where he is the head of the Department of Information and Communication Technologies (DIT) and responsible for the Multimedia Signal Processing and Understanding Lab. His research interests are focused mainly on multimedia data compression, processing, and transmission. He was general co-chair of Packet Video 2000 and technical program co-chair of the IEEE International Conference on Image Processing (ICIP) 2005. In 1998, he was co-recipient of the IEEE Chester-Sall Best Paper Award. De Natale is a senior member of IEEE.

**Arthur Edwards** is senior professor/researcher at the College of Telematics of the University of Colima, where his primary interest is computer assisted language learning, multimedia applications, collaborative learning environments, educational information systems, virtual reality applications, and wireless and mobile learning systems.

**Samir Abou El-Seoud** received his BSc degree in physics, electronics, and mathematics in 1967, his higher diploma in computing from the Technical University of Darmstadt (TUD)/Germany in 1975, and his doctor of science from TUD in 1979. El-Seoud held various academic positions at TUD Germany and abroad, the latest being full-professor in 1987. His main research is focused on numerical parallel algorithms, scientific computations, and computational fluid mechanics. Currently, he is interested in e-learning and computer aided learning. El-Seoud joined PSUT in 2004.

**Aboul Ella Hassanien** received his BSc with honors in 1986 and an MSc degree in 1993, both from Ain Shams University, Faculty of Science, Pure Mathematics and Computer Science Department, Cairo, Egypt. In September 1998, he received his doctoral degree from the Department of Computer

Science, Graduate School of Science & Engineering, Tokyo Institute of Technology, Japan. He is an associate Professor at Cairo University, Faculty of Computer and Information, IT Department. Currently, he is a visiting professor at Kuwait University, College of Business Administration, Quantitative and Information System Department. He has authored/co-authored more than 80 research publications in peer-reviewed reputed journals and conference proceedings. He has served as the program committee member of various international conferences and reviewer for various international journals. Since 2004, he has been actively involved on the technical committee in the International Association of Science and Technology for Development (IASTED) for Image Processing and Signal Processing. He has received the Excellence Younger Researcher Award from Kuwait University for the academic year 2003-2004. He has guest edited many special issues for international scientific journals. He has directed many funded research projects. Hassanien was a member of the Interim Advisory Board committee of the International Rough Set Society. He is the editor and co-editor for more than six books in the area of rough computing, computational intelligence, and e-commerce. His research interests include rough set theory, wavelet theory, X-ray mammogram analysis, medical image analysis, fuzzy image processing, and multimedia data mining.

**Sridhar Iyer** is an associate professor in the Department of Computer Science and Engineering at IIT Bombay. Prior to this, he was a faculty member in the Department of Computer Science and Engineering at IIT Guwahati. His research interests include networking protocols and multimedia tools for distance education, wireless networking, mobile computing frameworks, and some areas in program/protocol verification. Iyer received his BTech, MTech, and PhD from the Department of Computer Science and Engineering at IIT Bombay.

**Javed I. Khan** is currently a professor at Kent State University, Ohio. He received his PhD from the University of Hawaii and a BSc from Bangladesh University of Engineering & Technology (BUET). His research interests include extreme networking, cross-layer optimization, complex system, and digital divide. His research has been funded by the US Defense Advanced Research Project Agency and National Science Foundation. He has also worked at NASA for the Space Communication Team. As a Fulbright senior specialist, he also studies the issues for high performance higher education networking. He is a member of ACM, IEEE, and Internet Society. More information about Khan's research can be found at medianet.kent.edu.

**Baha Khasawneh**. received his PhD degree in computer science from The George Washington University in 2000. He is currently an assistant professor and chairman of the Department of Computer Graphics and Animation at Princess Sumaya University for Technology. His research is focused on multimedia systems mainly in image processing, multimedia, transmission, and protection. He also has a research interest in e-learning and the delivery of multimedia content in an e-learning environment. Khasawneh has published a number of papers in these areas of interest. Khasawneh has been a member of the Jordanian Engineering Association since 1985 and a reviewer for several conferences and journals.

**Gabriele Kotsis** received her master's degree in 1991 (honored with the Award of the Austrian Computer Society), her PhD in 1995 (honored with the Heinz-Zemanek Preis), and the venia docendi in 2000 (computer science, from the University of Vienna). She worked as a researcher and teacher at the University of Vienna from 1991 to 2001, at the Vienna University for Economics and Business Administration in 2001, and at the Copenhagen Business School in 2002. Since December 2002, she has held a full professor position at the Telecooperation Department at the Johannes Kepler University Linz. Her research interests include performance management of computer systems and networks, workgroup computing, mobile and Internet computing, telemedia, and telecooperation. She has experience in national and international research projects in those areas, including, for example, the EU-funded international BISANTE project on network traffic modeling and simulation, where she was technical leader; and the EMMUS project on multimedia usability where she was project coordinator. Kotsis is the author of numerous publications in international conferences and journals and is co-editor of several books. She is a member of the IEEE and ACM and acting president of the Austrian Computer Society. She is actively participating in the organization of international conferences.

**Saraswathi Krithivasan** is a doctoral student in the Department of Computer Science and Engineering at IIT Bombay, conducting her research in the area of multimedia dissemination over heterogeneous networks. She holds an MS in computer science and an MBA with specialization in international business, both from the University of Massachusetts. She managed the Distance Education Program at IIT Bombay from 2000 to 2005.

**Shiguo Lian,** member of IEEE, SPIE, EURASIP, and Chinese Association of Images & Graphics, got his PhD degree in multimedia security from Nanjing University of Science & Technology in 2005. He was a research assistant at City University of Hong Kong in 2004. He has being with France Telecom R&D Beijing since 2005, focusing on multimedia content protection, including digital rights management, multimedia encryption, watermarking, and authentication. He got the nomination prize of the 2006 Innovation Prize in France Telecom. He is author or co-author of three books, 50 international journal or conference papers, eight book chapters, and six patents.

**Antonio Liotta** is a senior lecturer in computer networks and service management. He has published more than 60 papers and two patents in the area of telecommunication services, distributed computing, and advanced networking. Liotta is a registered practitioner of the UK Higher Education Academy, a member of the Peer Review College of EPSRC (UK Engineering and Physical Sciences Research Council), and a member of the Board of Editors of the *Journal of Network and System Management*. He has served on the technical program committees of more than 60 international conferences.

**Shadi Masadeh** earned his BSc degree in the field of computer science technology from Philadelphia University, Amman, Jordan, in 2000; and a master's degree from Al-Neelein University of Sudan in 2003 in the field of information technology, with a thesis titled *Mathematical Approach for Ciphering/Deciphering Techniques*. He worked as an instructor at Al-Isra University of Amman, Jordan, for one academic year. He is currently working at Jordan Ministry of Education as a network engineer. Masadeh is a certified CCNA and MCAD.NET and a member of the Jordan Association of Engineers. Currently, he is pursuing a PhD degree in computer information technology at the Arab Academy for Banking and Financial Sciences.

**Olivia Nemethova** received BS and MS degrees from Slovak University of Technology in Bratislava in 1999 and 2001, respectively, both in informatics and telecommunications. She received a PhD in electrical engineering from Vienna University of Technology in 2007. From 2001 until 2003, she was with Siemens as a system engineer. She worked on UMTS standardization within 3GPP TSG RAN2 as a Siemens delegate. In parallel, she worked within an international property rights management team responsible for evaluation of IPRs regarding radio access networks. In 2003, she joined the Institute of Communications and Radio-Frequency Engineering at Vienna University of Technology as a research and teaching assistant. Her current research interests include error resilient transmission of multimedia over wireless networks, video processing, and mobile communications.

**Annanda Thavymony Rath** is currently a lecturer and researcher in the Computer Science Department at the Institute of Technology of Cambodia (ITC). He graduated with an engineering degree in computer science from ITC in 2004 and a master's degree in 2006 from the Indian Institute of Technology (IIT), Bombay.

**Yong Man Ro** received a BS from the Department of EE at Yonsei University, Seoul, Korea, in 1985; and MS and PhD degrees from the Department of EE in KAIST in 1987 and 1992, respectively. He is currently a professor of multimedia group and the director of IVY Lab. He received the Young Investigator finalist award of ISMRM in 1992 and This Year's Scientist award (Korea) in 2003. He participated in international standardizations, including MPEG-7, MPEG-21, and JVT, where he contributed several standardizations, including texture descriptor, modality conversion for QoS, multiple ROI coding, and so forth. He was a co-program chair of IWDW 2004 and has been working as TPC member for many international conferences. His current research interests include multimedia adaptation/modality conversion, multimedia information retrieval, and multimedia security.

**Miguel Angel Garcia-Ruiz** graduated in computer systems engineering and obtained an MSc in computer science from the University of Colima, Mexico. He received his PhD in computer science and artificial intelligence from Sussex University, England. He currently does research on virtual reality in education and human-computer interaction.

**Markus Rupp** received a Dipl-Ing degree in 1988 from the University of Saarbruecken, Germany, and a Dr-Ing degree in 1993 from the Technische Universitaet Darmstadt, Germany, where he worked with Eberhardt Haensler on designing new algorithms for acoustical and electrical echo compensation. From November 1993 until July 1995, he had a postdoctoral position at the University of Santa Barbara, California, with Sanjit Mitra, where he worked with Ali H. Sayed on a robustness description of adaptive filters with impact on neural networks and active noise control. From October 1995 until August 2001, he was a member of the technical staff in the Wireless Technology Research Department of Bell-Labs at Crawford Hill, New Jersey, where he worked on various topics related to adaptive equalization and rapid implementation for IS-136, 802.11, and UMTS. He is presently a full professor for digital signal processing in mobile communications at the Technical University of Vienna. He was associate editor of IEEE Transactions on Signal Processing from 2002 to 2005; he is currently associate editor of *JASP EURASIP Journal of Applied Signal Processing*, *JES EURASIP Journal on Embedded Systems*, *Research Letters in Signal Processing*, *Research Letters in Communications*, and is elected AdCom member of EURASIP. He has authored and co-authored more than 250 papers and patents on adaptive filtering, wireless communications, and rapid prototyping, as well as automatic design methods.

**Walid A. Salameh** is a professor of computer science. Currently, he is the dean of the King Hussein School for Information Technology. He received his PhD in computer engineering from METU in 1991 and his MSc from the same university in 1987. His research interests are wireless networks and e-learning.

**Luca Superiori** received BS and MS degrees in electronic engineering in 2002 and 2005, respectively, both from the University of Cagliari, Italy. His diploma thesis was titled *Fractal Coding Algorithm for Colour Image using Earth Mover's Distance as Distortion Metric.* Currently, he is working at the Institute of Communications and Radio-Frequency Engineering at Vienna University of Technology as research assistant. His current research interests include low-resolution video processing, video encoding, and multimedia streaming over wireless networks.

**David Taniar** holds bachelor's (honors), master's, and PhD degrees in computer science/information technology, with a particular specialty in databases. His research now expands to data mining, mobile information systems, and Web technology. He publishes extensively every year. He is currently a senior lecturer at the Faculty of Information Technology, Monash University, Australia. He first joined Monash University in 1997 as a lecturer in the Gippsland School of Computing and Information Technology. After a short stay at the Department of Computer Science, RMIT University in 1999-2000, he joined the School of Business Systems at Clayton in the beginning of 2001 as a senior lecturer. He also had previously taught computing at Swinburne from 1991 to 1996. Taniar has also held a number of technical positions in industry, where he was involved in building applications for banks (ANZ and NAB) and major industrial companies (Telecom, SECV, DEET Canberra, Caltex NZ, Gas and Fuel Brisbane). He is a founding editor-in-chief of a number of international journals, including the *International Journal of Data Warehousing and Mining*; the *International Journal of Business Intelligence and Data Mining, Mobile Information Systems*; the *Journal of Mobile Multimedia*; the *International Journal of Web Information Systems*; and the *International Journal of Web and Grid Services*. He is also an editorial board member of numerous international journals. He is elected as a Fellow of the Royal Society of Arts, Manufactures and Commerce (FRSA); and Fellow of the Institute for Management Information Systems (FIMIS). He is also listed in *Who's Who in the World* and *Who's Who in Science and Engineering.*

**Truong Cong Thang** received BE and ME degrees from Hanoi University of Technology, Vietnam, in 1997 and 2000; and a PhD degree from Information and Communication University (ICU), Korea, in 2006. From 1997 to 2000, he worked as an engineer in Vietnam Post and Telecom (VNPT). He was a research assistant from 2001 to 2005 and then a post-doc in 2006 in the Image and Video System Lab of ICU. Since 2007, he has been a researcher for the Korea Electronics and Telecommunications Research Institute (ETRI), Korea. His research interests include image/video processing, content adaptation, scalable video coding, and MPEG/ITU-T standards.

**Seung S. Yang** was born in Seoul, Republic of Korea. He received a PhD in computer science from Kent State University, Ohio, in 2004. He received a master's of engineering and a bachelor's of engineering in computer science from Soongsil University, Seoul, Korea, in 1995. He worked as a research engineer in the Telecommunication Research Center for Samsung Electronics for four years. At the center, he researched and developed a large-scale ATM switching system. He currently is an assistant professor in the Department of Computer Information Systems at Virginia State University, Virginia. His major research areas are distributed adaptive networks, sensor networks, high-performance computation and communication networks, and multimedia transmission and visualization systems.

# Index